ONLY

GREAT WORLD TRIALS

CONTRIBUTORS

John S. Bowman

Michela Bowman

Rodney Carlisle

Samuel Willard Crompton

Colin Evans

Michael Golay

Bernard Ryan, Jr

Tom Smith

Eva Weber

Janet Bond Wood

NEW ENGLAND
PUBLISHING
ASSOCIATES

Edited and prepared for publication by
New England Publishing Associates, Inc.

PRINCIPALS
Elizabeth Frost Knappman &
Edward W. Knappman

STAFF
Editorial Administration:
Rebecca Berardy & Ron Formica

PICTURE RESEARCH EDITOR
Victoria Harlow

COPY EDITORS
Barbara Jean DiMauro
Dorothy Anderson

INDEXER
Miccinello Associates

GREAT
WORLD
TRIALS

EDWARD W. KNAPPMAN,

EDITOR

A New England Publishing Associates Book

GALE

Detroit   New York   Toronto   London

Gale Research staff:

Allison McNeill, *Developmental Editor*; Lawrence W. Baker, *Managing Editor*; Leah Knight, *Aquisitions Editor*

Mary Beth Trimper, *Production Director*; Evi Seoud, *Assistant Production Manager*; Shanna P. Heilveil, *Production Assistant*

Cynthia Baldwin, *Product Design Manager*; Mary Krzewinski, *Art Director*; Barbara J. Yarrow, *Graphic Services Manager*; Randy Bassett, *Image Database Supervisor*; Mikal Ansari and Robert Duncan, *Imaging Specialists*; Pamela Hayes, *Photography Coordinator*

Front cover photo: Wang Hongwen at the Jiang Qing and Gang of Four Trial (1980): AP/Wide World Photos. Back cover photos: Karla Homolka (1995): AP/Wide World Photos; Oscar Wilde (1895): Library of Congress.

Highlights

Great World Trials provides an abundance of information on 100 of the most significant and celebrated trials in world history, from ancient times to the present. Included are brief and accurate summaries of trials known for their historic significance, political significance, or public notoriety. *Great World Trials* covers a broad scope of international trials, including:

- Jesus of Nazareth Trial (A.D. 33)
- Joan of Arc Trial (1431)
- Mary, Queen of Scots Trial (1586)
- Galileo Galilei Trial (1633)
- *Bounty* Mutineers Court-Martial (1792)
- Oscar Wilde Trial (1895)
- Archduke Franz Ferdinand's Assassins Trial (1914)
- The Nuremberg Trial (1945–46)
- Nelson Mandela Trial (1963–64)
- Guildford Four Trial (1975)
- Klaus Barbie Trial (1987)
- Beirut Hijacking Trial (1988–89)
- Tiananmen Square Dissidents Trial (1991)
- Rosemary West Trial (1995)
- Yigal Amir Trial (1996)

Each trial begins with the facts—setting up key players, the charges, and the site of the trial, followed by a narrative that explains the circumstances that led to the trial, pre-trial maneuvers, the trial itself, the judgement, appeals (if any), and any subsequent implications of the trial.

Special features:

- Four tables of contents—chronological, alphabetical, by subject, and by country—provide easy access to any specific trial
- Entries end with suggestions for further reading, enabling users to easily continue research on a particular trial
- Over 90 subject-specific photographs and drawings
- Comprehensive index lists key figures, subjects, and areas of law

CONTENTS

In Chronological Order
(by date of trial)

GREAT

WORLD

TRIALS

CONTENTS

In Alphabetical Order
(by name of trial)

CONTENTS

In Subject Order
(by the crime[s] charged)

CONTENTS

In Order by Country
(by name of trial)

**Greece,
Ancient**

Hungary

India

Ireland

Israel

PREFACE

Great World Trials brings together the stories of 100 of the most significant and celebrated trials in world history. Trials held in the United States have been excluded, as they were exhaustively covered in the companion volume **Great American Trials** (Gale Research/Visible Ink Press, 1994).

Spanning 25 centuries of history and encompassing the legal philosophies and judicial systems of more than 30 countries, **Great World Trials** of necessity uses a very broad working definition of the word *trial*. (Indeed, many of the legal terms American readers are familiar with may have little meaning or even contrary meanings in the context of other systems of jurisprudence.) The very concept of what constitutes a trial—much less a fair trial—differs radically from one society to another. For example, trials in contemporary China, such as those of the Tiananmen Square dissidents or of Jiang Qing and the Gang of Four, seem to most Westerners less a process to determine guilt or innocence than a species of ideological theater, in which the testimony, the verdicts, and the sentences have all been pre-scripted to indoctrinate the public. Even in a single nation, over the course of its history, the concept and the purpose of a trial changes radically. The treason trial and subsequent beheading of Mary, Queen of Scots in 1586, for instance, bears more resemblance to one of Stalin's purge trials in the 1930s than it does to any modern-day British trial.

Yet there is a common denominator among all the trials in these pages, indeed among all trials in all times and places. Each trial, however rigged, venal, or tyrannical, was intended to provide a cloak of legitimacy for the punishment of a real or imagined infraction of the rules of the contemporary social order.

As with any encyclopedic undertaking, the selection process was a complex one and inevitably involved some subjectivity, given space limitations. Thousands of trials had some historic, political, or legal significance or had attracted wide public attention for one reason or another. From these, I have attempted to select the 100 I judged best met the following criteria:

Political Significance: Many trials in this volume were chosen because of their political implications. Either the crime challenged the dominant political classes or the defendants were perceived as martyrs persecuted by the authorities. And, in some cases, the defendants were themselves politicians perceived as villains. Particularly in earlier periods, when ecclesiastical and secular powers were closely allied, if not one and the same, many of the trials were designed to protect the established religion. Indeed, of the 15 trials I have included from before the 18th century, religious beliefs were central to no fewer than 11, including those of Alcibiades, Socrates, Jesus of Nazareth, Sir Thomas More, and Galileo Galilei.

Historical Significance: In more recent centuries, secular political trials have been at the forefront of public attention and have had the greatest impact on history. Among those found in *Great World Trials* are trials sparked by the French Revolution (Louis XVI and Marie Antoinette, and Charlotte Corday), Irish nationalism (Daniel O'Connell, Roger Casement, and the Guildford Four), ideological battles (Rosa Luxemburg's assassins, the Moscow purge, and the Red Brigades), wars (Nuremberg, Vidkun Quisling, and Adolf Eichmann), and decolonization (Mohandas Gandhi, Jomo Kenyatta, and Nelson Mandela).

Public Attention: Since the age of mass media began in the mid-19th century, many trials with little political or historical impact have captured public attention for a variety of reasons—the lurid details of the crime; the fame of the victim, the accused, or the lawyers; an apparent perversion of justice; or because the issues raised by the trial amplified deepseated public fears and anxieties. I have selected a representative cross section of the most celebrated of these trials, including those of Oscar Wilde, Adelaide Bartlett, Henriette Caillaux, Steven Truscott, and Robert Thompson and Jon Venables.

In my selection process, I have intentionally applied these criteria more leniently to recent trials than to those from the distant past. This was done to serve the needs of readers, who, I suspect, are far more likely to need or desire information on recent trials.

Although my goal was to achieve wide geographic representation among the cases in this volume, nearly two-thirds of the trials occurred in European countries. This was inevitable for several reasons. First, the legal systems that most of the world now follow had their origins in Europe. Second, prior to the 20th century, the record of trials conducted outside of Europe or European colonies is very sparse indeed. Third, the needs and interests of North American readers and researchers, the primary intended audience for this book, guided my selection.

Another editor might have included some trials that I did not or might have omitted some that I included, but the vast majority of trials would make any editor's list of the most important trials in world history. Several precautions were taken to avoid oversights and omissions: After I had sifted through reference books and national histories to compile a list of 200 prospective trials for inclusion, the editorial staff at Gale Research and members of a specially selected panel of advisers carefully evaluated my list, added suggestions, and finally winnowed the list down to the 100 trials included in this volume. Although this assistance has been very helpful, the responsibility for any omissions is mine.

Each entry begins with a set of basic facts about the trial. This is followed by a narrative explaining the circumstances that led to the trial, pretrial maneuvers, the trial itself, the judgment, and any subsequent appeals. Although the writers tried to provide the maximum amount of accurate information in the space available, they also sought to entertain as well as to inform.

The extent of sources consulted varies considerably with the trial. Some trials produced shelves of well-researched histories. Others are barely mentioned in secondary sources. Contributors to this book dug as deep into the sources as necessary to establish the essential facts of each trial. However, for some trials prior to the mid-19th century, the surviving records are spotty, failing even to note the full names of judges or lawyers.

Every entry ends with suggestions for further reading. Contributors were asked to include in these suggestions the most readily and widely available sources of additional information. As the intended audience for this book consists of general readers rather than legal researchers, legal citations have been excluded.

The trials are presented in chronological order. This was chosen as the most logical sequence for two reasons. First, many trials are emblematic of a particular historical period and are directly or indirectly linked, such as the trials of Luther, More, Servatus, Bruno, and Galileo during the periods of the Reformation and Counter-Reformation. Second, there is simply no preferable alternative. Without a generally accepted convention for naming trials, an alphabetical arrangement would be of little benefit to readers. *Great World Trials* contains four tables of contents—chronological, alphabetical, by subject, and by country—plus a comprehensive index; readers should have little difficulty in locating any specific trial.

Many people made vital contributions to the planning, writing, editing, and production of *Great World Trials*:

Chris Nasso and Leah Knight of Gale Research, and Becky Nelson of Visible Ink Press helped launch this project and offered many useful suggestions when this book was in its formative stages. Allison McNeill of Gale consistently provided sound advice as well as courteous and prompt help as the book progressed from the planning stage through the editorial and production processes. For their roles on the advisory panel I thank Joseph T. Meda, Virginia M. Dorwaldt, Joyce Valenza, Mark Levine, and Dean Hentz.

The writers who contributed to *Great World Trials*—John Bowman, Michela Bowman, Rodney Carlisle, Samuel Willard Crompton, Colin Evans, Michael Golay, Bernie Ryan, Tom Smith, Eva Weber, and Janet Bond Wood—often did research above and beyond what I asked of them and consistently produced readable and informative entries under their tight deadlines. Barbara Jean DiMauro and Dorothy Anderson copyedited this book with exceptional care and professional skill. Victoria Harlow's picture research, as always, was both creative and efficient, and Angie Miccinello did a first-rate job of proofreading and indexing.

Finally, my wife and partner, Elizabeth Frost Knappman, and my daughter, Amanda, deserve special thanks for their patience, affection, and support throughout the past two years.

—*Edward W. Knappman*
September 1996

Alcibiades Trial: 415 B.C.

Defendant: Alcibiades **Crime Charged:** Blasphemy **Judges:** The Assembly of Athens **Place:** Athens, Greece **Date of Trial:** 415 B.C. **Verdict:** Guilty **Sentence:** Death, confiscation of all property, publicly cursed by the priesthood

SIGNIFICANCE
In the history of ancient Greece, no figure was more irresponsible, more unpredictable, or a greater genius than Alcibiades, who was tried and condemned to death in absentia, restored to honor, and again rejected by the populace.

The Greek city-state civilization was flourishing when Alcibiades was born in Athens in 450 B.C. His father had been a distinguished politician and an Athenian general in the Persian wars. Athens headed the Delian League, a confederation of 200 cities in the Aegean Islands and along the coasts of Asia Minor, the Hellespont, and Thrace. Athens's vast navy was vital to its security, for Athens imported its food and depended on trade for its prosperity.

In the decades before and after Alcibiades's birth, Athens's democratic political system, dynamic economy, flourishing culture, and powerful fleet enabled it to establish hegemony over a wide area of the Eastern Mediterranean. Sparta was just the opposite: a conservative landlocked power built on an agrarian economy and governed by an oligarchy. War between the two city-states was inevitable, but in 445 they signed the Peace of Thirty Years, which recognized the maritime empire of Athens and guaranteed Sparta its domination of the land.

A Dissolute Generation

Perhaps also inevitable in the hedonistic atmosphere of Athens was the evolution of a dissolute younger generation. One of the most popular members was Alcibiades, a strikingly handsome young man who probably had a genius IQ and seldom took anyone's advice.

By the time he was 35, Alcibiades was the most popular man in Athens—an irrepressible womanizer and an elegant orator who could charm the multitudes despite his reputation for debauchery and extravagance. He flaunted his wealth by building a magnificent mansion that those multitudes, who lived in a city of rather small homes, resented.

War Is Declared

In 416, word reached Athens that Syracuse was planning to subjugate Sicily. Alcibiades addressed the Assembly. The Athenian empire must grow or disintegrate, he said. The Sicilian Greeks were weak, and it would be easy to take the entire island. The Assembly declared war on Syracuse, authorized construction of a giant fleet, and voted Alcibiades and his longtime political opponent Nicias (who had argued against the war) as cogenerals in command of the expedition.

By June 7, 415 B.C., the armada was ready to sail. That morning, Athens awoke to find that throughout the city statues of Hermes, god of travelers and symbol of fertility, had been vandalized. Noses, ears, and phalli of the statues had been knocked off.

Athens was hysterical. The Council and the Assembly launched an investigation. Back came a report, admittedly from unreliable aliens and slaves, that a group of drunken men led by Alcibiades had done the damage.

Alcibiades denied the charge and demanded an immediate trial. Meanwhile, during an Assembly session at the docks at Piraeus, with the fleet flagship standing at its moorings offshore, a second charge was made: Alcibiades had participated in blasphemous parodies of the Eleusinian mysteries.

The Assembly debated. An immediate trial, it knew, was likely to bring an acquittal, for the Assembly dared not risk alienating the Athenian sailors and soldiers of the Sicilian expedition, who, to a man, backed Alcibiades. It would be easier (as Greek historian Thucydides later wrote) "to bring some more serious accusations against him . . . when he was away, and thus to bring him back to stand his trial."

Alcibiades sailed with the fleet on July 1.

Ordered Home

Within days, an informer named Teucrus appeared before the Council with lists of those who had vandalized the statues and those who had blasphemed the mysteries. Several had already been named as Alcibiades's accomplices. Some immediately fled; others were arrested and executed.

A second informer, Diocleides, named 42 conspirators, including Alcibiades, who had defamed the statues. All were well-to-do citizens known as respectable conservatives, and all were arrested and imprisoned, except the absent Alcibiades. A testimonial banquet gave thanks to Diocleides.

But one of those imprisoned, Andocides, sent word to the authorities that Teucrus, the first informer, had told the truth and that Diocleides had fabricated his list of 42. Recalled by the Council, Diocleides admitted that, though he had claimed he recognized the conspirators by the light of the full moon. There had been no moon on the night of the vandalism. All prisoners except Andocides were released, and Diocleides was executed.

More witnesses came forward. A well-born woman, Agariste, charged Alcibiades with performing a mockery of the mysteries in the home of Andocides's cousin Charmides. A slave named Lydus asserted that, in his master's house, he had seen the mysteries blasphemed by Alcibiades. And finally, still from prison, Andocides provided information that directly implicated Alcibiades in the Eleusinian blasphemy.

The formal indictment was made in the Assembly by Thessalus, whose father was the prominent statesman Cimon: "Alcibiades has committed a crime against the goddesses Ceres and Proserpine, by representing in derision the holy mysteries and showing them to his companions in his own house. Where, being habited in such robes as are used by the chief priest when he shows the holy things, he named himself the chief priest . . . and saluted the rest of his company as Initiates and Novices. All of which was done contrary to the laws and institutions of the Eumolpidae, and the heralds and priests of the temple at Eleusis."

The Assembly dispatched a high-speed state galley to fetch home the cogeneral of the Sicilian expedition.

Alcibiades boarded the galley without resistance, but when the ship put in at Thurii in southern Italy, he escaped. There, someone asked him if he did not trust his native country. "In everything else, yes," he replied. "But in a matter that touches my life, I would not trust even my own mother, lest she might by mistake throw in the black ball instead of the white." He then found his way to Argos.

The enraged Assembly deliberated. It pronounced judgment on the accused in absentia and condemned him to death, ordering confiscation of all his property and commanding the priesthood to curse his name publicly.

An embittered Alcibiades turned up in Sparta. There he urged the Spartan Assembly to send a fleet to help Syracuse retain Sicily and an army to take command of all Attica except Athens, thus depriving that city of the tribute paid by its subject cities. The Spartans acted on his advice.

Now a Spartan

Alcibiades adopted the Spartan way of life, going shoeless and wearing rough tunics. Yet old habits persisted. In 413, he advised Sparta's King Agis to lead an extended army invasion of Attica. Agis returned after the long absence to find that his queen had taken the handsome Alcibiades as her lover and borne him a son. By then Alcibiades had gained a Spartan army commission and was heading a squadron en route to Asia. The king ordered him assassinated. Alcibiades escaped to Sardis, in Asia Minor. From there, he supported an oligarchic faction in Athens, the Council of Four Hundred, that seized the government in 411. A counterrevolution shortly blocked the Four Hundred's plans to let the Spartan army into Athens, then collapsed as the Athenian navy took charge and restored the democracy. The democratic Assembly then offered amnesty to Alcibiades, who came home to universal acclaim in 407—severely defeating Spartan fleets along the way.

But Athens had not provided pay for his crews, so Alcibiades went to Caria to raise funds. In his absence, a Spartan fleet demolished the Athenian flotilla. Relieved of command by the Athenians, and knowing that his assassination had been ordered by the Spartans, Alcibiades fled to Phrygia, where a Persian general provided him a castle complete with a courtesan. There, two assassins set fire to the building and, when Alcibiades emerged to demand his right to fight for his life, slew him with arrows and javelins. He was 46.

—Bernard Ryan, Jr.

Suggestions for Further Reading

Benson, E. F. *The Life of Alcibiades*. New York: Appleton, 1929.

Durant, Will. *The Life of Greece*. Vol. 2 of *The Story of Civilization*. New York: Simon & Schuster, 1939.

Forrest, W. G. *The Emergence of Greek Democracy: 800–400 B.C.* New York: McGraw-Hill, 1966.

Grant, Michael. *The Classical Greeks*. New York: Scribner's, 1989.

———. *Readings in the Classical Historians*. New York: Scribner's, 1992.

Green, Peter. *Armada from Athens*. Garden City, N.Y.: Doubleday, 1970.

Kitto, Humphrey David Findlay. *The Greeks*. Baltimore: Penguin, 1957.

McFarland, John W., and Pleasant and Audrey Graves. *Lives from Plutarch*. New York: Random House, 1966.

Plutarch. *Lives*. Edited by Charles W. Eliot. The Harvard Classics. New York: Collier, 1909.

Socrates Trial: 399 B.C.

Defendant: Socrates   **Crimes Charged:** Disbelief in orthodox religion,
introduction of strange new divinities, corruption of the youth
Chief Defense Lawyer: Socrates   **Chief Prosecutors:** Anytus, Meletus,
Lycon   **Judge:** The king-archon of Athens   **Place:** Athens, Greece
Date of Trial: 399 B.C.   **Verdict:** Guilty   **Sentence:** Execution

SIGNIFICANCE

The trial of Socrates provides one of the earliest examples in all history of the fact
that those who are dismayed by the destruction of their country are ready to
blame any likely scapegoat. It also offers a powerful example of a brilliant mind's
determination to stick to its philosophy of duty, even in the face of death.

In 399 B.C., the Greek philosopher Socrates was 70 years old. He had served as a warrior on bloody battlefields and as presiding courtroom judge in controversial cases. In heat or cold, he went shoeless and lightly clothed; his bald head, squat figure, and awkward gait were known throughout Athens. For 30 years or more, he had often entertained and sometimes irritated strollers in the marketplace by quizzing them about their souls and their ideals. But he was best known and most beloved among the young, to whose education he had devoted his life. Probably the strongest influence on his philosophical development had come from the Sophists—paid teachers of philosophy and rhetoric who were skilled in the practice of clever and subtle reasoning. His critical mind rejected pretense, and his behavior strictly followed whatever path of logic his mind developed. Above all else, he believed in moral goodness. He could not understand how anyone could see what was right but not do what was right.

Five years earlier, in 406 B.C., Socrates had defied the current government, an oligarchy of extremists known as "the Thirty Tyrants," who had ordered him and four others to go to Salamis and bring back an Athenian who had emigrated there to avoid the government's brutality and rapacity. Socrates alone had refused to comply with the order, saying he would no longer participate in public affairs. His reason, he said, was the warning messages that were coming to him from an internal voice, a divine counselor of whom he had spoken often in public. In fact, he insisted, the deity was calling on him to lead a revival of moral fervor and to establish a scientific base for it.

By 403 B.C., the Thirty had been overthrown. Full democracy and freedom were restored in Athens. But the atmosphere that followed was one of bitterness and despair. The city, said many citizens, had been ruined by the teachings of men like Socrates, who did too much thinking and had produced the attitude of immorality expressed by the Thirty. A growing movement to make Socrates a scapegoat was well under way.

Socrates was accused and convicted of charges of impiety and corruption of youth in 399 BC. He was sentenced to die and Athenian officials ordered Socrates to kill himself by drinking hemlock.

Socrates Accused

The movement to blame Socrates peaked in 399 B.C., when three Athenians brought a formal accusation against the philosopher. They were led by Anytus, a wealthy leather dealer who had helped restore democracy to Athens but was not pleased with the denunciations of the city's statesmen and politicians that Socrates freely dispensed. Another accuser was Meletus, a young poet who resented the aged philosopher's ability to demonstrate that the current crop of poets were ignorant of their art. The third was Lycon, an orator, who felt personally insulted by what Socrates had to say about orators.

Under Athenian due process, an indictment was taken to the city's civil governor, known as the king-archon. He called a preliminary hearing to determine whether the case was serious enough to warrant a trial. The indictment, prepared and presented by Meletus, brought three charges: "Socrates is guilty of crime, first, for not worshipping the gods the city worships, and [second] for introducing new divinities of his own; next [third], for corrupting the youth. The penalty due is death."

Athenian Law

Athenian law permitted a variety of different procedures in criminal trials. In a case such as this—a trial for impiety—the accuser was allowed to conclude his indictment with a proposed penalty. Another rule applied the laws against perjury only to false testimony given by witnesses. Defendant and prosecutors were required to swear they were telling the truth at the preliminary hearing, but during the trial itself, neither was required to take an oath to tell only the truth.

The king-archon found sufficient cause for a trial to be held before a *dikastery*, or law court of citizen judges. This panel was like a modern-day jury but considerably larger, varying in size from case to case. For the trial of Socrates, reports differ on the size of the panel, ranging from 500 to 567, but the majority of historians say it was 501—the odd number to prevent a tie in the final vote.

Jury duty was voluntary. Some 6,000 of the jury pool in Athens were chosen by lot to serve for a year, with large groups then assigned to the city's complex variety of courts.

Socrates on Trial

Little would be known today about the trial of Socrates were it not for one young poet who loved him dearly—an aristocrat named Plato, some 40 years the philospher's junior. He attended the trial and, after the execution of Socrates, felt compelled to protect his memory. Plato wrote his recollection of the series of speeches that Socrates had made in his own defense during the trial, a defense for which the elderly philosopher had refused to prepare beforehand. Plato's report on the trial became known as the *Apology*.

Socrates began his defense by describing the "call" he felt to convince his fellows of their ignorance in order, ultimately, to help them. His mission from his god, he said, was to rouse the intellectually lazy "like a gadfly that settles on a sluggish horse." He assured the jury that if he were found not guilty of the charges, he would continue his practices and added that he viewed the sentence of death with absolute indifference.

To the jury, such a defense seemed presumptuous. It violated the ethical and religious foundations that the restored democracy was eager to reestablish in the Athenian state. A narrow majority of the jury—some historians say 3; some, 30; some, as many as 61 votes—found Socrates guilty on all three charges.

Next came debate on the sentence. Under the law, prosecutors and defendant each had to propose the penalty. Anytus and Meletus proposed the sentence of death. Socrates began by declaring that he would not acknowledge guilt by setting forth any opinion on his punishment. Rather, he said, as a benefactor of the state, he should be rewarded with free meals at the Prytaneum, or town hall, for the rest of his life. The joke was not well received. He then offered to pay a fine of 30 minæ, a substantial sum. Instead, some 80 additional jurymen joined the previous majority in voting for the death penalty.

Prison and Execution

Usually, execution was immediate, but in this case it was delayed for a month because of a rule that said no one could be put to death while the state galley (the official ship of Athens) was on its periodic sacred mission to Delos. Each morning, Socrates met in his cell with his wife, his three sons, and his friends, conversing as he always had. Friends proposed various plans of escape. Socrates refused all such proposals, telling them his duty as a citizen was to obey the laws, even if they were not well administered.

On his last day, the condemned philosopher's friends stayed with him until, at dusk, his jailer said the time had come and handed him a cup of hemlock poison. Taking it, Socrates said, "What do you say about making a libation out of this cup to any god? May I, or not?"

The jailer answered, "We only prepare, Socrates, just so much as we deem enough."

"I understand," said Socrates. He then drank the cup down. As his friends wept, he strolled about the cell for a few minutes, then lay down, covered himself with his cloak, and expired.

"Thus died the man," Plato later wrote, "who of all with whom we are acquainted was in death the noblest, in life the wisest and most just."

—Bernard Ryan, Jr.

Suggestions for Further Reading

Brickhouse, Thomas C., and Nicholas D. Smith. *Socrates on Trial*. Princeton, N.J.: Princeton University Press, 1989.

Plato. *The Last Days of Socrates*. Translated by Hugh Tredennick. New York: Penguin, 1954.

Stone, I. F. *The Trial of Socrates*. Boston: Little, Brown, 1988.

Vlastos, Gregory. *Socrates*. Ithaca, N.Y.: Cornell University Press, 1991.

Wilson, Pearl Cleveland. *The Living Socrates*. Owings Mills, Md.: Stemmer House, 1975.

Gaius Verres Trial: 70 B.C.

Defendant: Gaius Verres   **Crimes Charged:** Misconduct as governor of
Sicily (extortion, theft, bribery, and other crimes)
Chief Defense Lawyer: Quintus Hortensius   **Chief Prosecutor:** Marcus
Tullius Cicero   **Judges:** M. Acilius Glabrio, 24 Roman senators
Place: Rome (present-day Italy)   **Dates of Trial:** August 5–14, 70 B.C.
Verdict: Guilty   **Sentence:** A substantial fine (of unknown sum), lifetime
banishment from Italy

SIGNIFICANCE

Scholars continue to debate whether this trial was a routine instance of the corruption pervasive in late republican Rome or a stirring instance of the conflict between the status quo and reformist elements in Roman society. They also dispute whether Cicero conducted his prosecution motivated by the highest ideals of exposing corruption or whether he was essentially trying to advance his political career. But in all instances, it remains one of the most dramatic, most revealing, and best-recorded trials in the ancient world because of the survival of Cicero's eloquent speeches.

As Rome entered the first century B.C., as a city, state, and empire, it was in almost constant turmoil. At the bottom of it all was the relentless struggle for power and profit. Supposedly, Rome had a republican government, but in practice, the mass of people had little or no say in anything that occurred. The elite minority who ruled Rome jockeyed for power with a mixture of anarchy and autocracy, using any means they could to enrich themselves. Nowhere was the corruption more blatant than in the far-flung possessions that Rome had conquered over the years—Sicily, for instance, the island off the southwestern tip of the mainland. To be appointed governor of one of these provinces was virtually a license to rob and cheat anyone and everyone.

In 73 B.C., the new governor of Sicily was Gaius Verres, a low-born man who, through his evidently clever and cunning ways, had manipulated and maneuvered his way to the higher reaches of Roman government. He had a reputation for a luxurious lifestyle, for his ability to profit in any way he could from Rome's troubles, and for exploiting influential friends in Rome. The normal term of office for a governor was only one year, but events in Rome kept

Verres in office for three. The longer he stayed, the more his rapacious nature was emboldened to commit a series of crimes against not only the Sicilians but also his fellow Romans. When he finally went back to Rome late in 71 B.C., the Sicilians decided they would seek to have him prosecuted in Rome and also try to obtain restitution for some of the money and property he had stolen. They turned to a rising young lawyer in Rome, Marcus Tullius Cicero, to argue their case.

An artist's rendering of Cicero. Cicero prosecuted Gaius Verres, in August, 70 B.C., when he was brought to trial facing charges of misconduct as the governor of Sicily.

Cicero the Prosecutor

Cicero was of upper-middle-class descent, from the countryside. He had been brought to Rome as a boy, and through his intelligence, diligence, and oratorical talents was making a name for himself as a lawyer. But he had still higher ambitions—a career in public service that would culminate in the highest elective office Rome had to offer, a consulship. Because the courts and legal procedures in Rome were inextricably entwined with the politics of the day, a brilliant lawyer such as Cicero could also advance his prospects as a politician. He had already begun his climb up the "slippery pole" by holding the first in a series of ever more important public posts, that of finance commissioner (*quaestor*) in Sicily in 76–75 B.C. In this post, Cicero had gained the respect of all concerned, and on leaving, he had invited the Sicilians to call on him for help in Rome if the occasion ever arose.

So it was that when Verres was to be brought to trial, Cicero agreed to take on the role of prosecutor. Verres had enlisted as his defense lawyer Quintus Hortensius, regarded as one of the most able lawyers in Rome. Moreover, Verres sought to use his influence to have one of his former assistants, Quintus Caecilius, appointed prosecutor, thereby virtually guaranteeing a finding of innocence. In the preliminary proceeding (known as a *divination*), Cicero exposed this collusion and had himself appointed prosecutor. Whether he was motivated by idealism—a desire to put an end to such corruption, a duty to help the Sicilians—or by his ambition to advance his political reputation, he was taking on a controversial and potentially ruinous task. Verres was aligned with many powerful individuals in Rome. If he were to be found guilty, it might reflect on many of these men and might limit their own chances of profiting from the commonly accepted types of corruption.

The Trial

Before the trial began, Cicero obtained permission to collect testimony and evidence in Sicily, and he spent almost two months there doing just that during the late winter of 70 B.C. Then came the elections in July for many of the major offices, including the two new consuls: One of those elected was none other than Verres' defense lawyer, Hortensius. Moreover, a new judge was chosen to preside over the court that would hear cases like the one against Verres beginning the following year. Verres and his supporters calculated that if the trial could be postponed until then, this judge would favor Verres. This and other plots on his part failed, and the trial opened in the Roman Forum on August 5. The judge, M. Acilius Glabrio, if hardly a bold reformer, was at least regarded as a judge willing to conduct a fair trial. About 24 Roman senators formed something between a panel of judges and a jury.

The usual procedure called for the prosecutor to deliver a long speech reviewing the case to be presented. Such speeches often took up several days, but Cicero knew there was to be a major public holiday in 10 days. If the court recessed, the trial might very well be put off until after the biased judge took over. Cicero thus surprised everyone by opening with a brief speech. He only summarized the bribery and other crimes Verres had engaged in. He then charged that Hortensius, after having been elected consul, had promised Verres that he would be acquitted if they could postpone the trial to the following year. He also claimed that the Senate itself was on trial, for if Verres was acquitted, the public would see that as proof of senatorial corruption. Cicero all but evoked the threat of some sort of popular uprising: "The people will no longer be thinking of looking for other men better qualified from the Senate but for another class of men altogether to man their courts."

Cicero immediately began to examine the witnesses he had lined up for the prosecution. The speed with which he moved disconcerted Hortensius, and the defense never caught up. But Cicero's case was based on far more than clever tactics. One by one, the witnesses testified to the excesses and crimes that surpassed the routine corruption, which had become a way of life for provincial governors. (Because there is no record of the actual testimony of the witnesses, we must rely solely on Cicero's own speeches in which he refers to the testimony.)

Even allowing for some exaggeration on Cicero's part, Verres's crimes were serious. He had dragged the heirs of well-off, deceased Sicilians into court and frightened them into paying a bribe for one alleged offense or another. Verres had traveled about Sicily and stayed with wealthy Sicilians. Relying on the power of his position, he had deprived them of many of their finest possessions—statues, vases, valuable works in metal—by begging, by forceful requests, or through outright robbery. He had not hesitated to steal works from public monuments and sacred temples. He had stolen so many works that he had a ship built (at taxpayers' expense) especially to carry his plunder back to Rome.

Verres had used several methods to enrich himself from the grain that was both donated and sold by Sicilians to Rome. He had cheated on customs duties and extorted payments for every office and privilege granted to Sicilians. He had exacted vengeance against anyone he perceived as opposed to him, punishing and executing with the cruelest of methods, even crucifying one man who had tried to escape from prison. And when a large pirate ship had been captured, Verres had helped himself to its plunder and allowed many of the pirates to go free.

Although Cicero claimed to have valid testimony and evidence of all these crimes, he undoubtedly charged Verres with some crimes based on little more than hearsay and anecdotal evidence. Cicero claimed, for instance, that while serving in Asia, Verres had a father and son executed because they had foiled his plans to rape the family's daughter. Cicero also alleged that Verres had boasted that after three years of ruling Sicily, he had enough loot to hire the best lawyers, bribe all the best judges, and live out his life in luxury. "In this man," Cicero concluded, "I find all wickedness combined. There is no lust, no iniquity, no shamelessness of which his life does not supply us with ample evidence." Some of the testimony revealed Verres to have been so greedy and cruel that the spectators became aroused and the court had to call for a recess to avoid a riot.

The witnesses' damning testimony and Cicero's brilliant rhetoric continued for nine days, but well before it ended, Verres and his lawyer realized that he would have no chance. Hortensius effectively gave up and advised Verres to plead guilty. Rather than face the sentence that would follow, Verres fled from Italy before his trial ended. On August 14, the jury returned its verdict of guilty and called for a large fine (of a sum unknown) as well as permanent banishment from Italy. Had Verres not already gone into voluntary exile (he spent it in what is now Marseilles, France), he might well have been given more severe punishment.

The Aftermath

In his haste to complete the trial, Cicero had had time to deliver only two speeches—one at the hearing when he had himself appointed prosecutor; the other, his introductory speech on the first day of the trial. Soon after the trial ended, he prepared five more speeches in which he set forth in great detail, greater rhetoric, and probably still greater exaggeration his arguments against Verres. All seven speeches, now known as "The Verrines," were quickly published and circulated. They probably helped Cicero to be elected consul in 64 B.C., and they have since contributed to his reputation as one of the great orator-lawyers of all time. In his own day, however, they did not help to save his life. In 43 B.C., Cicero was assassinated by agents of the new rulers of Rome, Mark Antony and Octavian Augustus. As part of the same cruel purge of some 2,000 prominent Romans, Verres was also assassinated—allegedly because Antony coveted his vast collection of largely stolen art.

—John S. Bowman

Suggestions for Further Reading

Alexander, Michael. *Trials in the Late Roman Republic, 149 B.C. to 50 B.C.* Toronto: University of Toronto Press, 1990.

Cicero, Marcus Tullius. *The Verrine Orations.* Translated by L. H. G. Greenwood. Loeb Classical Library. Cambridge: Harvard University Press, 1967.

Cowles, Frank H. *Gaius Verres: An Historical Study.* Ithaca, N.Y.: Cornell University, 1916.

Greenidge, A. H. J. *The Legal Procedure of Cicero's Time.* New York: Oxford University Clarendon Press, 1901.

Haskell, H. J. *This Was Cicero: Modern Politics in a Roman Toga.* New York: Alfred Knopf, 1942.

Mitchell, Thomas. *Cicero: The Ascending Years.* New Haven, Conn.: Yale University Press, 1979.

Wilkin, Robert. *Eternal Lawyer: A Legal Biography of Cicero.* New York: Macmillan, 1947.

Jesus of Nazareth Trial: A.D. 33

Defendant: Jesus of Nazareth   **Crimes Charged:** Blasphemy (that he presented himself as the Messiah, the Son of God); high treason (that he defied the authority of Rome)   **Chief Defense Lawyer:** None
Chief Prosecutors: The high priests   **Judges:** Caiaphas, high priest; Pilate, Roman procurator (governor) of Judea; and in one account, Herod Antipas, tetrarch (ruler) of Galilee   **Place:** Jerusalem, Judea   **Date of Trial:** Probably just before the Passover festival, A.D. 33 (converted by modern scholars to the year 26 of the Christian Era)   **Verdict:** Innocent of any crimes against the Roman state but guilty of blasphemy   **Sentence:** Flogging, crucifixion

SIGNIFICANCE

The trial of Jesus has had great significance for both the spiritual and the secular worlds. For Christians, the death of Jesus and his subsequent resurrection is a sign of God's covenant of love and forgiveness of sins. And to the extent that Christianity has been the dominant religion of the Western world and many of its outposts, the trial and execution of Jesus of Nazareth has been featured in many areas of secular civilization, provoking historical debates and inspiring creative works.

For several years, the young man named Jesus had been traveling throughout Judea and Galilee preaching his message of a new Kingdom of God and performing his "miracles." This greatly disturbed the leaders of the Jewish religious establishment, and they were further unsettled when Jesus made what was virtually a triumphal entry into Jerusalem on the Sunday before Passover. The final blow came when Jesus went to the Great Temple and, charging that the money changers and sellers of animals had made of the temple "a den of robbers," threw over the tables and chairs and drove away those involved in commercial activity in the Temple precincts. With this defiant act, Jesus infuriated the Sadducees, high priests of the Jewish aristocracy who controlled the Temple in Jerusalem. The activities that Jesus interrupted were perfectly legitimate within the Jewish tradition and regulated by rabbinic law: Money changers were changing the coins of the Roman government (didrachms and denarii) into shekels with which Jews could pay their Temple tax and also buy doves and other sacrificial animals during the upcoming Passover festival. Their concern for the effect Jesus had on a spellbound crowd, attending to his every word at the Temple, kept the high priests from having him stoned immediately, but the Sadducees would not forgive this latest act of defiance by Jesus.

Throughout his ministry, Jesus had maintained an independent, even hostile, attitude toward much of organized Judaism. His apparent intent was to bring a new message about God's relationship to the world on the strength of his own personal authority. From the perspective of the established priesthood, here was a mere carpenter's son from Galilee not only challenging the high priests but also scorning the laws of worship that rested on a thousand years of Jewish tradition. This was especially galling to the Pharisees, highly devout Jews who studied the traditional Jewish laws to determine what additional rules were needed to ensure that the spirit of God's law was maintained. From very early in his ministry, Jesus had antagonized the Pharisees, whose laws regulated posture at meals, washing hands, fasting, working on the Sabbath—virtually every aspect of secular and spiritual life. Even before the incident at the Temple, Jesus regularly broke the laws that governed the Jewish culture: He healed the sick on the Sabbath, and he did not wash before meals. More seriously, he forgave people their sins, something that the Pharisees said only God could do. It was even said that he claimed to have raised the dead back to life. Above all, there were rumors he called himself the Messiah. Something needed to be done. So, following the Temple incident and after much discussion, the supreme court of chief priests and elders (the Sanhedrin), who enforced Jewish law in Jerusalem, decided Jesus had to be arrested and tried.

To accomplish this, the priests paid Judas, one of Jesus' disciples, 30 pieces of silver to lead them to Jesus so they could arrest him. On a night before the festival of Passover, after Jesus had finished praying in the garden of Gethsemane, Judas, in the company of a several high priests, elders, and Pharisees—but no Roman soldiers—approached Jesus and kissed him. Immediately, Jesus was arrested and taken to the house of Caiaphas, the high priest. Under Jewish law, the Sanhedrin were not supposed to conduct their trials at night nor in a private home nor during Passover. Nonetheless, Jesus was tried that night. He was accused of boasting that he would destroy the Temple and then rebuild it and of other various blasphemies. Unfortunately for Caiaphas, the priests could find no witnesses to testify truthfully to Jesus' alleged acts.

Then Caiaphas questioned Jesus, asking, "I put you under oath before the living God; tell us if you are the Messiah, the Son of God."

Jesus responded, "You have said so. But I tell you, from now on you will see the Son of Man seated at the right hand of Power and coming on the clouds of heaven."

Caiaphas, very excited, said, "He has blasphemed! Why do we still need witnesses? You have now heard his blasphemy. What is your verdict?"

The chief priests and elders in attendance said, "He deserves death." In the morning, the Sanhedrin again convened to conduct a legal trial. Some authorities say the Sanhedrin was not empowered to carry out a death sentence because of Roman rule; others say the Sanhedrin could put a Jew to death by stoning but could not reach consensus on Jesus' guilt. Whatever the reason, Jesus was taken the next morning to Pilate, the Roman governor of Judea.

The chief priests told Pilate, "We found this man perverting our nation, forbidding us to pay taxes to the emperor and saying that he himself is the Messiah, a king."

This sixth-century mosaic (in basilica of Sant' Apollinare Nouvo, Ravenna, Italy) portrays Jesus of Nazareth as he appears before Pilate with a riotous crowd gathered around them.

Pilate asked Jesus, "Are you the King of the Jews?"

"You say so," was again Jesus' only response. He would not respond to the charges of the chief priests and elders that Pilate asked about. This persistent boldness in the face of his authority as the representative of the Roman emperor amazed, perhaps unnerved, Pilate.

Pilate told the crowd that he had found no basis for prosecuting Jesus under Roman law, but this was met by an insistent protest from the chief priests: "He stirs up the people by teaching throughout Judea and Galilee, where he came from originally."

Evidently seeking to avoid a decision, when Pilate heard Jesus was a Galilean, he sent him to be examined by Herod Antipas, the ruler of Galilee, who also happened to be in Jerusalem.

Herod had heard of Jesus and was excited to meet him, hoping to be entertained by having the accused perform some miracles—as though they were mere "magic tricks." Jesus, however, refused to answer any of Herod's questions and, after being mocked by Herod and his guards, was returned to Pilate.

With Jesus again in his jurisdiction, Pilate rendered his judgment: "You brought me this man as one who was perverting the people, and here I have examined him in your presence and have not found this man guilty of any of your charges against him. Neither has Herod, for he sent him back to us. Indeed, he has done nothing to deserve death. I will therefore have him flogged and release him."

However, the chief priests, the elders, and the scribes would not accept such lenient treatment of a man they regarded as a serious threat to their established religious traditions and beliefs.

It was the custom of Rome to release a prisoner during the Passover festival, so Pilate asked the crowd gathered outside the Praetorium, "Whom do you want me to release for you—Barabbas or Jesus of Nazareth?" (Barabbas had been found guilty of sedition and murder.)

The chief priests and elders had convinced the crowd that they should ask for Barabbas, and they did. Pilate asked, "Then what should I do with Jesus?" and the crowd responded, "Let him be crucified!"

Although Pilate, it appears, had concluded Jesus was not guilty of any crime against Rome, he was less concerned about justice than preserving the peace in Jerusalem. Fearing that the crowd might grow riotous if he did not crucify Jesus, Pilote acquiesced. Taking some water in a bowl, he washed his hands before the crowd, saying, "I am innocent of this man's blood; see to it yourselves."

Pilate had Jesus flogged, as was the tradition before a death sentence was carried out, and turned Jesus over to Roman soldiers to carry out the crucifixion at the place called Golgotha (Calvary in the Latin version of the Gospels). On his cross was written "This is Jesus, King of the Jews." The Roman soldiers gambled for the garments of Jesus, then left his body to be taken away by some of his followers.

The trial of Jesus went unnoticed in the official records of the time, but it was set down in the four Gospels—the books of Matthew, Mark, Luke, and John that recount the life of Jesus. Although they differ in many details, these accounts tell essentially the same story, the one that has engaged and inspired so many people across the centuries.

—Janet Bond Wood

Suggestions for Further Reading

Brown, Raymond E. *The Death of the Messiah*. Vols. I and II, *The Anchor Bible Reference Library*, New York: Doubleday, 1994.

The HarperCollins Study Bible. London: HarperCollins Publishers, 1993.

Jesus and His Times. Pleasantville, N.Y.: The Reader's Digest Association, Inc., 1987.

Sherwin-White, A. N. *Roman Society and Roman Law in the New Testament.* Oxford: Clarendon Press, 1963.

Watson, Alan. *The Trial of Jesus.* Athens: The University of Georgia Press, 1995.

Joan of Arc Trial: 1431

Defendant: Joan of Arc   **Crimes Charged:** Heresy, male dress
Chief Defense Lawyers: None   **Chief Prosecutor:** Pierre Cauchon, bishop
of Beauvais   **Judge:** Pierre Cauchon and his tribunal   **Place:** Rouen, France
Dates of Trial: January 9–March 17, 1431   **Verdict:** Guilty
Sentence: Death by burning at the stake

SIGNIFICANCE

Joan's trial and martyrdom made her a figure of universal dimension, a timeless
image of purity and heroism. In life and in death, she helped create the modern
French nation.

She heard voices for the first time at age 13. From out of a dazzling light came this command: "Joan, be a good and dutiful child; go often to church." She obeyed the voice. But even before she heard the voice, Joan had been a devout girl, meek and submissive, and skilled in the art of spinning. Near the end of her life, a peasant testified that she had nursed the sick and given alms to the poor. "I know it for certain," he said. "I was a child then, and she took care of me."

Born in 1412 or 1413 in the village of Domrémy in Lorraine, in northeastern France, Joan was the third daughter of Jacques Darc (or d'Arc), a peasant, and his wife, Isabelle Romee. This corner of France had been much fought over. Domrémy had been victimized more than once during the long dynastic struggle known as the Hundred Years' War. In the summer of Joan's 16th year, the Darcs fled before the advance of an unfriendly army. They returned to find the village ransacked, the church burned, storehouses looted, livestock carried off, crops trampled in the fields.

The Hundred Years' War had begun in 1337, when the English king Edward III claimed the throne of France. His successors pressed the claim. Henry V, the victor over the French in the decisive battle of Agincourt in 1415, named his heir, Henry VI, the future king of France and England. The French pretender was the dauphin Charles VII, whose sister was Henry VI's mother. By 1429, the English and their Burgundian allies held much of northern France, and English forces were besieging Orléans on the Loire, the key to Charles's possessions to the south.

"The Maid of Orléans"

The voices spoke again: Saint Catherine, Saint Margaret, the archangel Michael (the emblem of French resistance to the English). "Joan, go thou to the assistance of the king of France, and thou shalt restore his kingdom to him," one told her. She had found her vocation. A virgin peasant girl, 18 years old, the image of purity (she did not menstruate nor would she ever), Joan would become a soldier, expel the English from France, and see Charles anointed.

She journeyed to the fortified town of Vaucouleurs in February 1429 and persuaded the local strongman, Robert de Baudricourt, to provide her an escort to Charles's court at Chinon. She arrived there dressed in men's clothes and in the company of a half dozen men-at-arms. The dauphin's council debated two days before allowing her to see him. Some of the councilors suspected her of sorcery. A panel of theologians examined her and asked for proof of the authenticity of her visions in the form of a sign or a miracle. "My sign will be to raise the siege of Orléans," she answered. "Give me the men-at-arms and I shall go." She then told Charles it was his destiny to be crowned king of France in the cathedral at Reims.

Convicted as a heretic and executed in 1431, Joan of Arc was proclaimed a Saint by Pope Benedict XV in 1920.

Encased in white armor, astride a black charger, so the legend goes, Joan set out for Orléans. The English had been progressively weakened over the winter. They were so undermanned that, in purely military terms, the lifting of the siege would not have needed a miracle. Still, Joan's inspired leadership had everything to do with the outcome. By May 8, the siege had been broken, the English driven off, and Joan had earned the sobriquet "the Maid of Orléans." Charles reached Reims on July 15. On July 17, a Sunday, he was anointed as Joan had foretold.

The English regrouped and made arrangements to crown their own claimant, Henry VI. Meanwhile, Joan had commanded a failed assault on Paris, and her relations with Charles had begun to cool. In any case, he preferred negotiation to fighting. In what amounted to a freelance operation, Joan led a party to the defense of Compiègne. She was captured in battle there on May 23, 1430, and handed over to the English, who determined to put her on trial as a sorceress. Their aim: to show that a witch had led Charles VII to his coronation.

The Trial

The trial—a confused, tortuous Inquisition-style affair in which the accused could only guess at the specific charges against her—opened at Rouen on January 9, 1431. Pierre Cauchon, the bishop of Beauvais, presided, a vicar of the Inquisition at his side. From the start, Cauchon seemed to recognize that a charge of witchcraft could not be sustained. It was quietly changed to heresy. As the trial progressed, it became clear that the chief issues were the voices Joan had heard and her male dress.

A long file of ecclesiastics and lawyers, sometimes as many as 70 learned men at a session, interrogated Joan. She consistently maintained the truthfulness and divine origin of the voices; she refused to give up her man's shirt, breeches, doublet, and hose. At one point, the examiners questioned her closely on her virginity, insinuating that she had been little more than a camp follower and had lived with soldiers. There were claims that she could "produce thunder and other marvels if she liked." The judges asked, too, whether she had used charms or amulets to protect herself in battle. And they accused her of inverting nature by wearing men's clothes—an anathema, according to ancient Church law.

If the English burned to expose Charles as a usurper, the ecclesiastics were driven to punish Joan's evident defiance of the Church hierarchy. Throughout the trial, she insisted on setting the promptings of her own conscience above the authority of the Church. Those things that had been revealed to her were true, despite anything the Church might say. In a radiant moment in one of the early public sessions, she challenged Cauchon: "You tell me you are my judge; ponder with great care over what you mean to do, for in very truth I was sent of God, and you are putting yourself in great jeopardy."

The examiners continued to belabor the point. The Church hierarchy had not certified the voices and the visions, and therefore, they were not authentic. Joan must submit to this judgment. She responded: "I came to the king of France sent by God, by the Virgin, by the saints and the Church *victorious* above; to *that* Church do I submit myself, my works, all I have done, all I have still to do."

"And the Church *militant?*" the judges persisted.

"I shall answer nothing further at this time."

At times, a touch of asperity tinged her answers. The examiners were curious. Was Saint Michael, when he appeared to her, naked or dressed?

"Do you think," she answered, "our Lord did not have the wherewithal to clothe him?"

On another occasion, they wanted to know whether God hated the English.

"Whether He loves them or hates them and what He proposes to do with their souls, I know not; but this I know for certain, that all of them will be thrown out of France, except those who perish there."

After several sessions, the interrogations were shifted from the public rooms at Rouen Castle to Joan's cell, where secret sessions were held before a smaller number of judges. The final cross-examination took place on March 17. Pierre Cauchon and the Inquisition's man might have believed they had revealed Joan as a heretic, but they had failed to persuade the Rouen legal experts. Early in the case, one of them, Master John Lohier, had drawn up a long list of legal errors that in his view invalidated the entire proceedings. "This is a trial to impugn the honor of the prince whose cause this girl is supporting; you should frankly say so, and you should have a counsel appointed for her," he had advised. But precisely because this was in part a political trial, Cauchon knew he could ignore the lawyers.

In a scene from the Vigils of Charles VII, Joan forces out camp followers.

The Verdict

The tribunal convicted Joan of heresy and of wearing men's clothes. There followed a series of admonitions—harangues intended to force her to recant, for the English insisted on the recantation as a means of discrediting Charles. "Abjure, or you shall burn," she was told. The judges threatened torture; there was evidence that the English guards attempted to rape the prisoner in her cell. Joan agreed to sign an abjuration. In return, she was assured, by a person she believed to be in authority, that she would be removed from the hated English and delivered up to the Church.

In fact, the sentence turned out to be life in an English prison, "on the bread of sorrow and the water of affliction, there to mourn for your sins." Within a few days, Joan retracted her recantation, resuming male dress and announcing that the saints had again spoken to her. The retraction permitted the tribunal to convict her as a relapsed heretic—and burn her at the stake.

On May 30, 1431, dressed now for her last moments modestly in a woman's long shift, she was taken in a cart to the Old Market Place in Rouen. An enormous pyre had been built there, and Joan's jailers escorted her to the top of it. The executioner lit the fire. A witness known to history only as the Bourgeois de Paris left this account:

> She was soon dead and her clothes all burned. Then the fire was raked back, and her naked body shown to all the people and all the secrets that could or should belong to a woman, to take away any doubts from the people's minds. When they had stared long enough at her dead body bound to the stake, the executioner got a big fire going again round her poor carcass, which was soon burned, both flesh and bone reduced to ashes.

Someone claimed, just before the end, to have seen a dove fly out of Joan's mouth. When the embers cooled, the ashes were scattered in the Seine. The heresy charge failed to stick. Only 25 years after her execution, a papal decree confirmed her rehabilitation. In 1920, Pope Benedict XV proclaimed Joan of Arc a saint.

—Michael Golay

Suggestions for Further Reading

Anonymous. *A Parisian Journal, 1405–99.* Translated by J. Shirley. Oxford: Oxford University Press, 1968.

Anonymous. *The Trial of Jeanne d'Arc.* Translated by W. P. Barrett. New York: Gotham House, 1932.

Gies, Frances. *Joan of Arc: The Legend and the Reality.* New York: Harper & Row, 1981.

Michelet, Jules. *Joan of Arc.* Translated by Albert Guerard. Ann Arbor: University of Michigan Press, 1957.

Sackville-West, Vita. *Saint Joan of Arc.* Garden City, N.Y.: Doubleday, 1936.

Shaw, George Bernard. *Saint Joan.* New York: Dodd, Mead, 1946.

Warner, Marina. *Joan of Arc: The Image of Female Heroism.* New York: Alfred A. Knopf, 1981.

Martin Luther Trial: 1521

Defendant: Martin Luther **Crime Charged:** Heresy
Chief Defense Lawyer: Jerome Schurf **Chief Prosecutor:** The Archbishop of Trier **Judge:** Holy Roman Emperor Charles V **Place:** Worms, Germany
Dates of Trial: April 17–18, 1521 **Verdict:** Guilty
Sentence: Excommunication and ban of Empire

SIGNIFICANCE

With broad support from the Germans, Luther deflected the papal campaign against him and his teachings. Luther's brilliant theological work, his charisma as a preacher, and his successful defiance of papal authority immeasurably advanced the cause of the Protestant Reformation.

By the early 16th century, the sale of indulgences had long been an accepted fund-raising practice of the Roman Catholic Church. For a certain sum, a soul could be freed from purgatory. This common form of clerical mediation gnawed at the conscience of the Augustinian friar Martin Luther, a preacher and scriptural scholar at the university in the Saxon town of Wittenberg. In 1517, when German representatives of papal authority began selling indulgences to finance the rebuilding of St. Peter's in Rome, he rebelled.

Working furiously, Luther drew up his 95 theses, attacking indulgences and other forms of corruption and challenging the priesthood's right of absolution. "Doesn't it disturb you," he wrote a friend, "that Christ's unfortunate people are tormented and fooled by indulgences?" On October 31, Luther nailed his diatribe to the door of the Schlosskirche in Wittenberg.

Challenges to church corruption were fairly common during the first decades of the 16th century. "These pastors given to us are shepherds only in name," the bishop of Liège complained. "They care for nothing, but fleece and batten on the sins of the people." Luther found many allies in his own chapter of Augustinians. Yet it was one thing to attack venal officials, quite another to confront the larger question of church practice or the supreme authority of the pope.

The Response

Rome did not take Luther's outburst seriously at first. By the summer of 1518, though, complaints had begun to reach Pope Leo X (Giovanni de Medici of Florence) from beyond the Alps. The dispute over indulgences formed part of a larger struggle: prophetic Christians against Catholic Church timeservers, spiritualists against humanists, the poor against the rich, Germany against Rome. The Holy Father moved to the attack, raising a formal charge of suspicion of heresy against Luther and directing a member of the Curia, Sylvester Prierias, to prepare a rebuttal of the 95 theses.

Prierias's screed exalted the pope as "the oracle of God." It asserted that the authority of the church overrode that of the scriptures. It attacked Luther directly, calling him "a leper and a loathsome fellow," as well as "a false libeler and calumniator," not to mention "a dog and the son of a bitch, born to snap and bite at the sky with his canine mouth." Luther had, Prierias finished, "a brain of brass and a nose of iron."

Luther received the attack, together with a summons to Rome, at Wittenberg on August 7, 1518. Turning to his powerful supporters in Saxony, he asked to have his case tried in Germany. Rome agreed to this change of venue and ordered him to Augsburg for a hearing before the cardinal legate, Thomas de Vio Cajetan.

Cajetan, a reformer himself, sympathized with much of Luther's argument in the 95 theses. All the same, church authority would be upheld above all. Cajetan tried to reason Luther out of his rebellion. He made it clear that Luther had been summoned to Augsburg for a recantation, not a discussion of the case on its merits. They met three times in mid-October.

"He [Cajetan] promises to handle everything leniently and in a fatherly way," Luther wrote a supporter. "He continually repeated one thing: recant, acknowledge that you are wrong; that is the way the Pope wants it and not otherwise whether you like it or not."

But Luther's thought had carried him well beyond the point of no return. He denied the necessity of priestly mediation between man and God. In faith alone, not faith with good works, he believed, lay salvation. Luther escalated his assault on the pontiff's authority. In a 1519 disputation, he publicly denied the supremacy of the pope.

Wary of alienating the Germans, Rome acted cautiously and quietly. Cajetan continued to hope the Saxons would move against Luther. "Take counsel of your conscience and either send Brother Martin to Rome or exile him from your country," Cajetan wrote the Saxon authorities. The Saxon elector, Frederick III, backed Luther and refused to surrender him to Rome. There matters stood for more than a year.

The Message Travels

Luther published widely in 1519, and his influence grew exponentially. New editions of his work appeared. A Swiss editor wrote in his introduction to one of these editions: "Here you have the theological works of the Reverend Martin Luther, whom many consider a Daniel sent at length in mercy by Christ to correct abuses and restore a theology based on the Gospel and Paul."

Inspired, even possessed, Luther worked himself into a state of near exhaustion. "God is pushing me—he drives me on, rather than leading," he wrote his mentor, the Augustinian vicar general Johann Staupitz. "I cannot control my own life. I long to be quiet but am driven to the middle of the storm."

He continued to develop his doctrine of justification by faith alone, and he refined his argument that nothing in the scriptures established papal primacy. Nor, he added, was it the obligation of all Christians to obey the pope: The Greeks and the Russians, for example, declined to recognize Rome's authority.

"Confidentially," Luther wrote in March 1520, "I do not know whether the Pope is the Antichrist himself or whether he is his apostle, so miserably is Christ corrupted and crucified by the Pope."

The Vatican had reopened the case against Luther in January 1520. Matters came to a crisis that year with Luther's publication of three fresh polemics. One invited the German princes, including Luther's protector, the elector Frederick, to take church reform into their own hands. A second attacked aspects of the Mass and the doctrine

Martin Luther, the German reformer, was found guilty of heresy in Worms, Germany on April 18, 1521.

of transubstantiation. The third proclaimed that faith freed Christians from the obligation of good works.

On June 1, the cardinals formally approved a papal bull declaring Luther a heretic. "Exsurge, Domine" censured 41 of the 95 theses and gave Luther 60 days from the date it came into his hands to recant or be excommunicated.

On September 6, Luther petitioned the pope for a hearing, though in anything but the tone of a penitent. "I have never thought ill of you personally," he assured Pope Leo X. "I have truly despised your See, the Roman Curia, which, however, neither you nor anyone else can deny is more corrupt than any Babylon or Sodom ever was." In late September, papal authorities posted the bull in public places in all the German towns. In many places, Luther's supporters tore it down and burned it.

Luther himself treated it with contempt. "This Bull seems to have had its miserable conception at some all-night carousal of a horde of prostitutes," he commented. Alternatively, the enervating heat of a Roman summer might explain it. "Maybe," Luther said, "it was jumbled together in the raging dog days."

On December 10, 1520, having failed to recant, Luther, then 36 years old, was declared a heretic. In Cologne and Louvain, obedient conservatives made bonfires of his books. But in many towns, Luther's partisans burned papal books.

The Trial

Luther continued to enjoy the protection of Frederick. The elector told the pope's emissaries that Luther should be allowed to appear before an independent tribunal, as he had offered to do, and that Rome should demonstrate, using the Scriptures, precisely where he had erred.

Early in 1521, the temporal authority, the Holy Roman Emperor Charles V, summoned Luther to appear before the diet (formal assembly) of German electors meeting that year at Worms. Luther reached the crowded little capital after a long journey, much of it on foot, on April 16. There, an order awaited him to appear before the emperor, the archbishop of Trier, and other high officials at 4 P.M. the following day. Luther trimmed his tonsure and slipped into the habit of an Augustinian friar. A Wittenberg lawyer, Jerome Schurf, accompanied him to the imperial chambers.

Luther opened by saying he stood ready to be shown where his doctrines were wrong. Motioning toward a stack of books, one of the archbishop's men asked Luther whether he had written them and, if so, whether he was prepared to disavow them. Luther turned for a brief word with Schurf, then asked for 24 hours to consider the question. Charles granted his request, with the stipulation that he answer directly.

The hearing resumed the next day, April 18, in a hot, overcrowded palace chamber. Luther, who had been ill, broke out in a soaking sweat, but his nerves and voice were steady. He apologized for any offense he may have given inadvertently. Yes, he admitted, he had written the books in question, which he acknowledged could be taken, collectively, as an attack "against some private and (as they say) distinguished individuals—those, namely, who strive to preserve the Roman tyranny and to destroy the godliness which I teach."

The archbishop's chancellor, Johann von Eck, laid out the church's unanswerable case against heresy.

"What the doctors have discussed as doctrine, the church has defined as its judgment, the faith in which our fathers and ancestors confidently died and as a legacy have transmitted to us," Von Eck reminded the court. "We are forbidden to argue about this faith by the law of both pontiff and emperor. Both are going to judge those who with headlong rashness refuse to submit to the decisions of the Church."

Luther replied plainly, as he had promised to do the day before. His answer, as he put it, was "neither horned nor toothed": "Unless I am convinced by the testimony of the scriptures or by clear reason, I am bound by the scriptures I have quoted and my conscience is captive to the word of God. I cannot and I will not retract anything. Here I stand, may God help me, Amen."

The Outcome

The emperor retired to prepare a statement for delivery to the diet the next day, April 19. "I am determined to proceed against him as a notorious heretic," Charles announced, and he directed the diet to do its duty and get on with the punishment. Charles V put Luther under the ban of Empire. The electors, avoiding a direct clash with their young emperor, reluctantly approved the Edict of Worms that formally condemned Luther.

There was, it turned out, no punishment to speak of. Luther had become too powerful; no German would surrender him to Rome. Leaving Worms, he connived in his own kidnapping, in which his friends waylaid him in the Thuringian Forest and spirited him off for safekeeping in semiseclusion in the remote Wartburg Castle. There he continued to flaunt authority.

"I thought his Imperial Majesty would have got together one or fifty scholars and overcome this monk in a straightforward manner," he wrote. "But all that happened was this: Are these your books? Yes. Do you want to renounce them or not? No. Then go away!"

Luther went on with his work. In Wartburg, he began his translation of the Bible into German. Back in Wittenberg early in 1522, he continued his assault on traditional Church practices. He discarded his monk's habit in 1524. In the following year, he married.

His doctrines spread rapidly through Germany and beyond. By the close of the 16th century, 50 years after Luther's death, two-thirds of the German population had embraced Lutheranism. To the north, in the Scandinavian countries, the structure that had been built on the great heretic's works had become the official state religion.

—*Michael Golay*

Suggestions for Further Reading

Erikson, Erik H. *Young Man Luther*. London: Faber & Faber, 1958.

Fife, R. H. *The Revolt of Martin Luther*. New York: Columbia University Press, 1957.

Friedenthal, Richard. *Luther*. Translated by John Nowell. London: Weidenfeld and Nicholson, 1967.

Todd, John M. *Luther: A Life*. New York: Crossroad Publishing, 1982.

Thomas More Trial: 1535

Defendant: Sir Thomas More   **Crime Charged:** Treason
Chief Defense Lawyer: Sir Thomas More   **Chief Prosecutor:** Richard Riche
Judges: Thomas Cromwell, 17 others   **Place:** London, England
Date of Trial: July 1, 1535   **Verdict:** Guilty   **Sentence:** Death

SIGNIFICANCE

Writer, politician, ascetic, lawyer: Sir Thomas More truly was a "man for all seasons." But as his trial for treason made plain, above all, he was a man of infinite courage.

As Lord Chancellor, Sir Thomas More (1478–1535) was one of the most powerful men in England, but by 1532, declining health and mounting doubts about King Henry VIII had led him to relinquish the seals of office and retire from public life. From a distance, this most devout of Catholics could only watch in dismay as Henry embarked on a collision course with the papacy. Weary of his wife, Catherine, and infuriated by Rome's refusal to annul their marriage, Henry passed a statute naming himself head of the Church of England. At a stroke, Catholic domination of the English monarchy was consigned to history. On May 23, 1533, Archbishop Thomas Cranmer dutifully granted what Pope Clement VII had not, and nine days later Anne Boleyn, heavily pregnant with the future Elizabeth I, was crowned queen of England. (She had already married Henry in a secret ceremony some four months earlier.)

Conspicuous by his absence from, and bitterly vocal in his opposition to, Anne's coronation, More knew he was navigating treacherous waters. His sternest test came when he was summoned to appear before royal commissioners to assent under oath to the Act of Succession (1534), which declared Henry's marriage to Catherine void and that with Anne valid. Although prepared to acknowledge that Anne was the anointed queen, More refused the oath as then administered because it entailed a repudiation of papal supremacy. For this act of defiance, he was thrown into the Tower of London. His evasiveness while being interrogated on May 7, 1535, about the Act of Supremacy (1534), which also declared Henry to be the "supreme head" of the established Church of England, led to his being charged with various counts of treason.

Seven weeks later, on July 1, 1535, More was ferried up the Thames to Westminster Hall, where a panel of 18 judges headed by the king's secretary,

Thomas Cromwell, would decide his fate. Scanning the faces of the other commissioners must have removed any doubt in More's mind about what lay in store for him: Among those sitting in judgment were Thomas and George Boleyn, father and brother, respectively, of the recently crowned queen.

The judges saw a man weakened by his harsh incarceration, dirty and unkempt, yet still able to cross swords with the sharpest intellect. As the practice of the time required, the judges acted as both prosecutors and advisers to the accused, but More eschewed their counsel, aware that his own knowledge of the law was second to none.

Thomas More, a devoted Catholic, was executed in 1535 after he refused to take an oath of Supremacy to Henry VIII as head of the church. (Archive Photo)

Multiple Treasons

In effect, More faced four counts of treason: 1) that, when interrogated on May 7, he had refused to accept royal supremacy over the Church of England; 2) that he had engaged in treasonable correspondence with Bishop John Fisher (executed for treason on June 22, 1535) while both were prisoners in the Tower; 3) that he allegedly referred to the Act of Supremacy as a two-edged sword, so that by accepting it one saved the body and killed the soul and that by rejecting it one saved the soul but killed the body; and 4) that he "falsely, traitorously, and maliciously" spoke against the Supremacy Act during a conversation with one of Cromwell's cronies, the solicitor general Richard Riche.

More dealt with each charge in turn. He reminded the court that during the May 7 interrogation he had been silent and, under English common law, silence was regarded as acquiescence. In no way, he argued, could this silence be interpreted as opposition. Concerning the eight letters he had exchanged with Fisher: Since they had been burned and since nothing Fisher had said about their contents could be construed as treasonable, they could not be held against him. As for the "two-edged sword," More claimed that this was merely hypothetical rhetoric, hardly the stuff of sedition.

There was enough substance in More's argument to convince the commission that these charges should, indeed, be dropped, which left the government's case resting entirely on his June 12 conversation with Riche in the Tower of London. Sadly, no account exists of Riche's actual testimony, but we do know that at its conclusion More issued a ringing rebuttal, flatly charging the witness with perjury:

If this oath of yours, Master Riche, be true, then pray I that I never see God in the face, which I would not say, were it otherwise, to win the whole world!

Although More's piety is a matter of record, it should be remembered that he was also a hardened politician, well used to the rough-and-tumble of court intrigue, and a master of finely honed invective, as he now demonstrated with a scathing attack on his accuser's credibility. Reminding the commissioners that he and Riche had once lived in the same parish, where the latter's reputation for duplicity was notorious, More asked incredulously, "Can it therefore seem likely . . . that I would, in so weighty a cause, so unadvisedly overshoot myself as to trust Master Riche?"

More devoted the remainder of his defense to cataloging his long and loyal service to the king, without any hope that it would affect the outcome. Convicted of treason, he waited until Lord Chancellor Thomas Audley arose to pass sentence, then interrupted, "My Lord, when I was toward the law, the manner in such a case was to ask the prisoner before judgment, why judgment should not be given against him."

A Final Gambit

Granted further permission to speak, More now began to argue that sentence should not be passed because the statute by which he had been judged was invalid. To his way of thinking, the Act of Supremacy contradicted a higher ordinance, the law of the Catholic Church, the law of God, and in such a conflict the will of Parliament must yield. Such reasoning tested the patience of those chosen to judge him, principally the Duke of Norfolk, who snarled, "Now, More, you show the plain, obstinate malice of your soul."

But More would not be deflected. Invoking memories of the Magna Carta, he denounced the recent statute as contrary to that great bulwark of English law. It was a theme that obviously impressed many of his accusers; several of the judges began to exchange anxious glances, leading Lord Chief Justice Sir John Fitz-James to exclaim, "I must needs confess that if the act of Parliament be not unlawful, then is not the indictment in my conscience insufficient?" But the commissioners' trepidation was short-lived, and Audley duly passed sentence.

With his final speech, More scaled the heights of eloquence:

More have I not to say, my lords, but like as the blessed apostle Saint Paul . . . was present and consented to the death of Saint Stephen, and kept their clothes that stoned him to death, and yet be they now both twain holy saints in heaven, and shall continue there friends forever, so I verily trust, and shall therefore right heartily pray, that though your lordships have now here in earth been judges to my condemnation, we may yet hereafter in heaven merrily all meet together, to our everlasting salvation.

Condemned at first to the traitor's death of hanging, drawing, and quartering, More had his sentence commuted to beheading, and on July 6, 1535, he walked steadfastly to the block on Tower Hill. Right to the last, Henry VIII feared More's oratory and had that morning sent an emissary to his cell. Sir Thomas Pope announced, "The king's pleasure is . . . that at your execution you shall not use many words." Mindful of the peril that might befall his family were he to ignore such entreaties, More agreed. He met his death quietly and well.

Although More's conviction has been attacked on grounds that it was obtained through the testimony of a single witness, there can be no doubt that, as the law then stood, it was a legitimate decision. Sentiment in England was growing that two witnesses should be necessary to condemn a man in a capital case, but that requirement was not legally enacted until 1547, and common law had always been willing to accept just one witness if that person was deemed to be of good character. Often, it was impossible to do otherwise, as More himself had wryly noted earlier in his career when discussing the difficulty of finding credible witnesses to crimes such as heresy and treason. People guilty of those offenses do not customarily bring notaries with them to record the deed.

Four centuries after his death, on May 19, 1935, Thomas More was canonized as a saint of the Roman Catholic Church.

—Colin Evans

Suggestions for Further Reading

Marius, Richard. *Thomas More.* New York: Alfred Knopf, 1984.

Reynolds, E. E. *The Field Is Won.* Tunbridge Wells, England: Burns & Oates, 1968.

Rupp, G. *Thomas More.* London: Collins, 1978.

Michael Servetus Trial: 1553

Defendant: Michael Servetus **Crime Charged:** Heresy **Accuser:** Nicolaus de la Fontaine **Judges:** Geneva's Council of 25 **Place:** Geneva, Switzerland **Date of Trial:** October 25, 1553 **Verdict:** Guilty **Sentence:** Death by burning at the stake

SIGNIFICANCE

Michael Servetus was tried and executed for publishing works arguing for a unitarian view of God. His trial and execution in Geneva, when John Calvin was emerging as the religious and temporal leader of that city-state, has often been taken to demonstrate the rigidity of Calvin's views. This point has been contested by those who argue that such executions were common over a 200-year period and as late as 1612 in Britain.

Michael Servetus (Miguel Serveto) was a Spanish physician, trained in Paris, who studied the circulation of blood and wrote on that subject long before William Harvey received credit for the discovery of pulmonary circulation.

In 1531, at the age of 20, Servetus published *De Trinitatas erroribus libri septem* (*On the Errors of the Trinity in Seven Books*), a work that was widely condemned as heretical by both Protestants and Catholics. When his identity as the author became widely known, he went into hiding under an assumed name. He called himself Michael Villanovanus, basing the name on the village of his birth in Spain. He was able to conceal his identity for more than 20 years. He lived at first in Paris, where he studied medicine and gave lectures as a member of the faculty of the University of Paris. In 1538, Servetus published a work on astrology for which he was brought to trial in Paris on charges of heresy. He made a brilliant defense at this trial and was acquitted by the Inquisition, but the University of Paris ordered him to cease lecturing.

He moved to Avignon and later to Charliue in France, then settled in a small town near Lyons, where he continued his medical practice, his editing work, and his theological studies. During this period, he produced several works, including a translation of the Bible, complete with marginal notes, which helped later scholars interpret his evolving theological ideas.

Calvin Denounces Servetus as Heretic

In 1545, Servetus began work on another theological treatise and opened correspondence with John Calvin. However, Calvin continued to regard Servetus's views as extreme heresy and warned Servetus that should he ever visit Geneva, he would not leave alive. Servetus published another theological work, *Christianismi Restitutio* (*Restitution of Christianity*) in 1553, this time under his own name, and sent a copy to Calvin, who promptly denounced Servetus to the Inquisition at Lyons. The work reflected extensive scholarship and knowledge of Greek and Hebrew and argued that of the Trinity, only God is eternal. By June, Servetus was arrested and tried for heresy by Roman Catholic authorities in Vienne, France.

He was condemned and taken prisoner in the archbishop's palace, where he was lured by being told that his medical services were required to treat other prisoners. On April 7, 1553, he escaped through a clever ruse, concealing a set of clothing under his nightdress and receiving permission to walk in the garden of the palace at four in the morning. He leaped from the terraced garden to the roof of a building below and then made for a bridge across the Rhone river. Although the city gates were locked and a thorough search made, Servetus vanished, presumably taking refuge with friends and grateful former patients. On June 17, the inquisitor read a brief describing all the theological errors in *Restitutio* and then ordered that 500 copies of the book and an effigy of Servetus be burned.

In August, Servetus passed through Geneva on the way to Italy. In Geneva, attendance at church on Sunday was compulsory, and Servetus attended a sermon by Calvin. Recognized in the congregation, he was arrested on Calvin's orders. Servetus was held in a filthy dungeon for more than two months, then brought to trial before the governing council of the city, the Geneva Council of 25.

The Perrinists, a political-religious faction in Geneva opposed to Calvin and his imposition of rules of behavior on the townspeople, assumed that the trial of Servetus would discredit Calvin by suggesting that his reputation had attracted heretics to the community. Calvin, unlike Martin Luther and John Huss, had argued that the turning over of heretics to the secular authority for trial was proper, as did the Catholic Church at the time. So, rather than objecting to the trial by the council, Calvin encouraged its actions.

Burned at the Stake

At the trial of Servetus, John Calvin served not as a prosecutor or an accuser, but more as a technical expert and "friend of the court." Calvin, however, apparently provided the formal accuser, Nicolaus de la Fontaine, his secretary, with detailed charges and evidence. The letters and manuscripts that Servetus had sent Calvin were introduced as evidence. The council consulted with authorities in the nearby cities of Berne, Zurich, Schaffhausen, and Basel. The council decided on October 25, 1553, that Servetus be taken outside the gates of the city to Champel and be burned alive. Calvin later noted that he had argued that Servetus should indeed be executed but by the more humane method of beheading. There is no independent record that the council considered this advice.

Servetus was read his sentence and then put to the stake on October 27, 1553. Servetus died with the book and manuscript that he had sent to Calvin strapped to him. His last words reflected his unitarian belief: "Jesus, thou son of the eternal God, have pity on me." The remark was taken to mean that he regarded God as eternal, but not Jesus. A sympathetic biographer observed that had Servetus simply altered his wording to say, "Eternal Jesus, have pity on me," he might have been spared the sentence at the last moment.

The Historical Debate

The decision of the Geneva Council of 25 in this case was supported not only by the nearby Swiss jurisdictions but also by a number of reform theologians, including Martin Bucer, as well as by Roman Catholic authorities. Cardinal Robert Bellarmine later referred to the acceptance of the Geneva Council's jurisdiction by Calvin in the Servetus case as proof that even heretics (Calvin, from Bellarmine's viewpoint) accepted that heresy should be tried by civil authority.

Defenders of Calvin against later criticism for the execution of Servetus have developed several arguments: that the trial was not under Calvin's control, that his view of the severity of heresy was typical of the era, that Servetus had already been convicted by a Roman Catholic inquisition, and that Calvin and his fellow conservative reformers, such as Luther and Bucer, had to dissociate themselves from the more radical reformers like Jakob Hutter and Servetus. Calvin and his followers regarded themselves as reformers of the Church, but they never believed that reform should foster what more modern observers would think of as religious freedom or civil tolerance for a wide variety of views. In fact, Servetus himself did not accept any such concept of religious toleration, arguing that his views were correct and that those of others were heretical. Indeed, Servetus may have provoked Calvin's denunciation because he several times had accused Calvin of heresy.

Examined closely, the views of Servetus did challenge many central tenets of Christianity held by both Protestants and Catholics in his era. One scholar has defined Servetus as a "total heretic." Among other beliefs, Servetus explicitly rejected contemporary views of the Trinity, moved in the direction of historical and philological interpretation of the Bible, and appeared to accept a Gnostic view of the Antichrist as a nearly eternal being. At his trial in Geneva, Servetus was accused of such "heresies," along with Judaizing Christianity; some suspected that he had falsely converted to Christianity, a common practice among the persecuted Jews of Spain.

Servetus is regarded as one of the theological founders of modern Unitarianism, and his religious treatises were reprinted by Unitarians and antiquarian publishers in Germany and Britain and, later, by scholarly presses. Over the four centuries since Servetus's trial, a polemical literature regarding Servetus and Calvin has steadily grown, with defenders and critics on both sides.

—Rodney Carlisle

Suggestions for Further Reading

Bainton, Roland. *Hunted Heretic: The Life and Death of Michael Servetus, 1511–1553*. Boston: Beacon Press, 1953.

Fulton, John F. *Michael Servetus: Humanist and Martyr*. New York: Herbert Reichner, 1953.

Wilbur, Earl M. *A History of Unitarianism: Socinianism and Its Antecedents*. Cambridge, Mass.: Harvard University Press, 1946.

Zweig, Stefan. *Erasmus and the Right to Heresy*. Reprint. London: Souvenir Press, 1979.

Martin Guerre Trials: 1560

Defendant: Martin Guerre (Arnaud du Tilh) **Crimes Charged:** Defrauding the Guerre family and others, abusing Bertrande Guerre
Chief Defense Lawyer: None **Chief Prosecutors:** King's attorneys
Judges: Firmin Vayssiere (according to Natalie Davis) (first trial); Jean Coras and about 11 others (second trial) **Places:** Rieux, France, (first trial); Toulouse, France (second trial) **Dates of Trials:** January–April 1560 (first trial), May–September 12, 1560 (second trial) **Verdicts:** Guilty (both trials)
Sentences: Beheading and quartering (first trial), hanging and burning (second trial)

SIGNIFICANCE

On one level, this is simply a titillating and curious case that allows everyone to speculate about human conduct and motives, especially those of the wife of Martin Guerre. For historians, however, it presents a unique opportunity to examine how otherwise anonymous people of centuries past behaved and thought in the apparently limited spheres of action available to village folk.

Viewed from a distance, the lives of villagers in the 16th century had a routine, predictable quality—a dull sameness. Examined close-up, the lives of many individuals were far more varied, dynamic, and even extraordinary. Sanxi Daguerre was a Basque, people of ancient origin who lived in the region that straddled the French-Spanish border. For reasons unknown, in 1527 this villager chose to take his wife, his young son, Martin, and his brother, Pierre, and move from the Atlantic coast some 275 kilometers (170 miles) to the east and settle in the French village of Artigat. The two brothers acquired land, established a tile works, and prospered. In order to blend in with their new neighbors, they changed their name to Guerre and adopted their neighbors' language. In evidence of their acceptance, young Martin married Bertrande de Rols, the daughter of one of the better-off families in the region, in 1538.

Martin was only 13 years old, and Bertrande was even younger; marriages of this kind were clearly arranged for the convenience of the families and involved transfers of property, not romance. Not surprisingly, young Martin was impotent for the first eight years of their marriage, but in 1547, Bertrande gave birth to a son. During those years, Bertrande had matured into a "beautiful" young woman, according to the judge who later presided at the trial. Martin, meanwhile, seemed to be a rather feckless young man, most interested in engaging in swordplay and acrobatics with the other village youth. It seems that he was also feeling too much pressure from his family responsibilities, or possibly he was just desirous of seeing more of the world. In any case, after an incident in 1548 in which he was accused of stealing some grain from his father, Martin left his wife, his son, his property, and his village and totally vanished.

As year followed year, Bertrande proved to be a strong-willed young woman, even though she was financially dependent on her two families. It must have been difficult, since the law in those days considered her to be a married woman unless she could prove Martin's death. When Martin's parents died, the father's brother, Pierre, was appointed administrator of the estate that would have otherwise passed to Martin and his heirs. What Bertrande's personal feelings and ambitions were cannot be known, but in 1556, her life took a surprising turn. Her husband, Martin Guerre, returned.

The New Martin Guerre

At least he was a man who claimed to be Martin Guerre. He said that he had spent the past years living in Spain and serving in the army of the king of France. He appeared somewhat shorter and stockier than the man who had vanished some eight years before, and he did not speak any Basque. Both these discrepancies were explained away as simply due to the passage of years. Furthermore, he seemed to recognize his family and his neighbors and to know all kinds of details about their shared pasts. His sisters were the first to accept him. And most important of all, Bertrande took him back into her home and bed as her husband.

Within a few years, Bertrande and Martin appeared to have reestablished a normal life in Artigat; Bertrande gave birth to two children (one died in infancy). Martin advanced their economic situation by leasing, buying, and selling land. Not content with this, however, in 1559, he chose to bring a lawsuit against his uncle, Pierre, claiming that Pierre, as administrator of the family's finances, had cheated him and Bertrande out of certain monies. Although the financial suit was

Shown is the first page of *Arrest Memorable*, a book written on the case of Martin Guerre by Jean de Coras in 1561.

settled, Pierre became so angry that he began to go about Artigat making a scandalous charge: This Martin Guerre was an impostor!

Pierre was able to persuade some in the village to take up his charge, but just as many continued to accept this Martin Guerre as the true one. As for the most important witness, Bertrande was reported as saying: "He is Martin Guerre my husband or else some devil in his skin. I know him well. Whoever is so mad as to say the contrary, I'll have him killed."

Then sometime in the fall of 1559, a French soldier passed through Artigat and said that this Martin Guerre was an impostor—and that he knew that the real Martin Guerre had lost a leg in a battle two years earlier. Excited by this news, Pierre set about to investigate actively just who the alleged impostor was.

Very soon Pierre was able to find several men in the area who confirmed his suspicions: The impostor was one Arnaud du Tilh from the village of Sajas, some 240 kilometers (150 miles) northwest of Artigat. (In those days, in rural France, this was distant enough to be practically in a different country.). Eventually, it would come out that Arnaud had been regarded as a "dissolute" youth, "absorbed in every vice"—presumably because he swore, drank, gambled, and frequented prostitutes. His main talents had been a glibness in speech and an excellent memory—the skills of an actor, as it happened. After some trouble with the law, young Arnaud had gone off to join the king's army.

Although Arnaud would later deny this, it is possible that he had met the real Martin Guerre during their military service in the mid-1550s and saw there was some resemblance. Arnaud insisted, rather, that he had never met Martin but had adopted the idea of posing as him only when friends of the real Martin mistook Arnaud for Guerre. In any case, after informing himself on as many details as possible about the real Martin Guerre and his wife and family and village, he went to Artigat and commenced his new life. His motives for such a risky action can never be known for sure, but it would appear that it had to be more than just some simple economic decision, even more than some attraction to the lovely young Bertrande. Something about this must have appealed to the adventurous spirit of the frustrated, young Arnaud.

The First Trial

Armed with his newfound knowledge about the alleged impostor, Pierre Guerre personally arrested him in January 1560 and took him to the nearby town of Rieux, the location of the district court. What then followed was not a trial in the modern sense; it was more what we would call a judicial hearing, with no jury and no defense lawyer for the accused. First, the judge, an attorney for the king and the court, and agents took written testimony from a long list of witnesses provided by both sides. (It has been suggested that, although Bertrande acceded to Pierre's demands that she join him in charging this Martin to be an impostor, she nominated witnesses who supported her in claiming the opposite.) Then the hearing in Rieux began with the judge questioning Martin Guerre, Bertrande, and those witnesses who supported Pierre's charges.

Martin Guerre's own cross-examination of the witnesses so intrigued the judge that he allowed the proceedings to continue, and more people were called to Rieux. Eventually, some 150 witnesses testified in person at the trial; about 40 insisted that the prisoner was the real Martin Guerre, about 50 said he was Arnaud du Tilh or some other impostor, and the remaining said they could not be sure. The most ambivalent testimony was that of Bertrande, for in some respects she was also on trial: If this man was an impostor, why had she gone along with him all these years? When the defendant faced her and said he would accept a death sentence if she would swear under oath that he was not the true Martin Guerre, she said nothing. The defendant, meanwhile, showed an amazing knowledge of the details of the life of Martin Guerre before his disappearance.

In the end, though, the judge declared the defendant guilty of fraud and also of abusing Bertrande. Still technically a plaintiff, Bertrande asked that he only pay a fine and legal fees as well as ask her pardon in a public ceremony. The judge, however, sentenced the defendant to be beheaded and his body quartered (that is, cut up and displayed in public). Arnaud du Tilh immediately appealed the decision, and by April 30, he was being held in chains in a prison in Toulouse, the largest city in the region and the seat of the superior courts.

The Second Trial

The new trial was before an appeals court made up of about 12 judges, but one of their number had to be appointed "reporter"—effectively, the judge responsible for personally pursuing the case and for recommending a sentence. Jean Coras, a distinguished jurist in his day, was so appointed. (It is his account of the case that serves as the principal source for all later versions.) The trial began before the full court with the defendant cross-examining Bertrande and Pierre; so convincing was he that the judges decided that "the prisoner was the true husband and that the imposture came from the side of the wife and the uncle"—and they, too, were placed in prison.

In the weeks that followed, some 25 to 30 witnesses were called, many of them to confront the defendants. Through all this, Jean Coras devoted his full legal intelligence and conscience to all he was hearing and seeing. He was determined to come to a conclusion based on an objective analysis of the testimony and evidence, and the more he studied them, the less certain he was that the case against the alleged impostor was proved beyond doubt. Gradually, he became convinced that Bertrande had been forced by her uncle, Pierre, to turn against her husband; he also decided that Pierre was the villain in all this—that he was trying to get even with his nephew for demanding a proper accounting of the family's finances. As for the claims that the defendant was Arnaud du Tilh, the very testimony that Arnaud was a man "given over to every kind of wickedness" proved that this upstanding man who appeared before the court could not be that man. Above all, considering that this marriage involved children, Coras decided, "it was better to leave unpunished a guilty person than to condemn an innocent one."

The Real Martin Guerre

By late July, following Jean Coras's recommendations, the court seemed ready to find the defendant, Martin Guerre, innocent and to charge Pierre Guerre with various crimes. Then out of nowhere appeared a man with a wooden leg, claiming to be the real Martin Guerre. He said that he had gone to Spain after leaving Artigat, gained employment as a servant in a prominent Spanish family, went to fight with the Spanish army in Flanders, lost his leg during the famous battle at Saint-Quentin in 1557, and returned to Spain, where he was rewarded with a position in a military order. It is not clear why he chose to return to France at that time, but return he had.

Jean Coras and the other judges began a new round of hearings, and at first they were left uncertain when the new Martin Guerre seemed less clear about certain details of his past in Artigat than did the alleged impostor. In the end, though, they were convinced when they saw how the members of the Guerre family instantly accepted the newcomer as the true Martin. The final blow came when Bertrande was brought from her cell and, upon seeing the newcomer, broke down, embraced him, and asked for his forgiveness. The real Martin Guerre was not, however, quite so willing to forgive, and he scolded Bertrande for her behavior.

For Jean Coras and the other judges, the case was over. They had only to decide on the punishments for all involved. Bertrande was excused for the

The first visual representation of Martin Guerre's case was done by Jacob Cats, Allen de Werken (Amsterdam, 1568).

weakness of the female sex, and her children by Arnaud were declared legitimate. Whatever wrongs he had done along the way, Pierre was excused because he had been proved right in the end. Martin Guerre himself was reproved for having deserted his family and country but was excused for having suffered enough.

As for the impostor, Arnaud du Tilh, he was sentenced to be hanged on a gallows erected before the house of Martin and Bertrande Guerre and then to have his corpse burned. Arnaud's final words were to urge Martin to be kind to Bertrande, who, Arnaud said, had been truly deceived. Nothing more is recorded of Martin and Bertrande's situation except that they had two more children. And in the centuries since, despite all the attention expended on this case, no one has ever been able to prove exactly what Bertrande's true role or thoughts were.

Recent motion pictures based on the case of Martin Guerre include 1983's *The Return of Martin Guerre*, and *Sommersby*, released in 1993.

—*John S. Bowman*

Suggestions for Further Reading

Coras, Jean de. *Arrest Memorable du Parlement de Tolose...* Lyons, France: Antoine Vincent, 1561.

Davis, Natalie Zemon. *The Return of Martin Guerre*. Cambridge, Mass.: Harvard University Press, 1983.

Le Sueur, Guillaume. *Histoire Admirable d'un Faux et Suppose Mary*. Paris: Vincent Sertenas, 1561.

Lewis, Janet. *The Wife of Martin Guerre*. San Francisco: Colt, 1941.

Praviel, Armand. *L'Incroyable Odyssee de Martin Guerre*. Paris: Librairie Gallimard, 1933.

Mary, Queen of Scots Trial: 1586

Defendant: Mary Stuart **Crime Charged:** Treason **Chief Prosecutors:** Sir Thomas Bromley, Sir Francis Walsingham, Robert Cecil **Judges:** The king's commissioners **Place:** Fotheringay, England **Dates of Trial:** October 15–16, 1586 **Verdict:** Guilty **Sentence:** Death

SIGNIFICANCE
Trials for treason were nothing new in England, but never before had the defendant been someone of such exalted rank.

Following the death of her first husband, Francis II of France, Mary Stuart returned to Scotland, the country of her birth, in 1561, but it was far from a happy homecoming. Scottish nobility at that time was racked with turmoil and was increasingly Protestant; few trusted such an avowed Catholic. Even so, had Mary restricted herself to domestic matters, some dignity might have been restored to the Scottish crown, but always her eyes turned south to the throne of England, then in the far from secure hands of her cousin Elizabeth I. An additional drawback to Mary's standing was her ardent nature. A fleeting marriage to Lord Darnley, followed by an even briefer union with one of Darnley's assassins, the earl of Bothwell, served only to harden local sentiment against the beautiful Queen of Scots.

In 1568, fearing for her life, she sought refuge in England, where a cautious Elizabeth had her incarcerated. Mary's imprisonment was to last 19 years. Throughout, she remained the object of plot and counterplot, as Catholic supporters conspired fruitlessly to secure her freedom. Courtiers who had Elizabeth's ear urged decisive action to rid England of this perennial thorn in its side, but the queen had little stomach for such a drastic measure.

In the early part of 1586, Sir Francis Walsingham, a leading secretary of state and a staunch Puritan, decided to take matters into his own hands. Forerunner of the modern spymasters, Walsingham maintained a nationwide network of agents who fed him information about every aspect of public life. Like other intelligence chiefs since, he was not above a little covert dabbling in the affairs of state, an attitude that he shared with his close ally, Robert Cecil, chief treasurer and habitual intriguer. Together, they resolved to amass enough evidence to convince Elizabeth that permitting Mary to live was not only unwise but also unthinkable.

Through one of his agents—Gilbert Gifford, who acted as a letter carrier for Mary—Walsingham got wind of yet another Catholic plot to free the beleaguered queen. A northern squire, Sir Anthony Babington, had gathered around him half a dozen like-minded zealots and had hatched a plan designed to topple Elizabeth and place Mary on the throne. When Babington wrote to Mary of the conspiracy's existence, she foolishly wrote back, unaware that every letter was passing through Walsingham's hands. With his confidence inflated to dangerous levels, Babington disclosed his intention to kill Elizabeth. Assisted by her secretaries, Claude Nau and Gilbert Curle, Mary drafted an enciphered response that did not specifically overrule this course of action. This suggested to the conspirators, as it did to Walsingham, that such an omission amounted to tacit approval of the scheme. Damning though that communication was, Walsingham wanted more. Accordingly, he forged a postscript to one of Mary's letters, requesting first the names of the conspirators, then asking to be kept informed of developments.

Conspirators Captured

Babington received the amended letter at the end of July. On August 3, he wrote back to the Scottish queen, acknowledging its receipt. Then Walsingham gave orders for the conspirators to be rounded up. Under interrogation, Babington admitted all and was forced to reconstruct his deadly letter. On August 11, an emissary from Elizabeth went to Chartley Hall in Staffordshire, where Mary was being held, and told her that her treachery was known. At the same time, Nau and Curle were taken into custody. Mary felt betrayed by her secretaries, but that is to judge them too harshly. Facing the very real possibility of their own demise, they merely attested to the content of the letters, although the possibility exists that Nau was yet another of Walsingham's agents. (He was spirited to France and freedom after a few months, whereas Curle remained under close imprisonment for a year.)

Under the stewardship of Cecil and Walsingham, a commission of knights and barons was appointed to adjudicate the question of Mary's guilt. Despite pleas from the French ambassador that Mary be permitted the assistance of a

Mary Stuart, tried and convicted of treason, was publicly beheaded in October 1586. (Archive Photo)

lawyer, Elizabeth refused, thus maintaining the ancient tradition of refusing counsel to any defendant charged with treason.

Mary's examination began on Wednesday, October 15, 1586. She hobbled into the Great Hall at Fotheringay with painful slowness, almost crippled by rheumatism. After scanning the faces of the commissioners, she remarked to her attendant, Sir James Melville, "Ah! Here are many counselors, but not one for me." She was visibly irked that she was not seated on the throne that had been positioned there but on a smaller chair, a humiliation carefully orchestrated by Cecil. "I am a Queen by right of birth and my place should be there under the dais!" she announced archly. It was her only show of annoyance. Throughout the remainder of the trial her composure was magnificent and, to at least a few of the commission members, more than a little unsettling.

The first speech from the lord chancellor, Sir Thomas Bromley, declared how Elizabeth, upon learning that the Queen of Scots had conspired to usurp her, had had no choice but to convoke this public assembly in order to examine the accusation. The accused, he stated, would be given every opportunity to respond to the charges. In reply, Mary said, "I came into this kingdom [England] under promise of assistance, and aid, against my enemies and not as a subject . . . instead of which I have been detained and imprisoned."

She listened to evidence concerning the capture of Babington and his coconspirators, together with details of the written confessions and depositions extracted from Nau and Curle. Quite justifiably, she protested against the secondhand nature of this testimony, refusing to admit anything on such indirect proofs, saying, "I do not deny that I have earnestly wished for liberty and done my utmost to procure it for myself. In this I acted from a very natural wish." Later she added, "Can I be responsible for the criminal projects of a few desperate men, which they planned without my knowledge or participation?"

As evidence of her current lack of ambition, the 44-year-old queen made reference to her enfeebled physical state: "My advancing age and bodily weakness both prevent me from wishing to resume the reins of government. I have perhaps only two or three years to live in this world, and I do not aspire to any public position. . . ."

Cecil Intervenes

Such an assertion did not sit well with Cecil, the self-appointed chief inquisitor, as he harped on Mary's refusal to ratify the Treaty of Edinburgh (1560), in which her claims to the English throne were formally abandoned. Mary stoutly denied accusations that she had always coveted Elizabeth's throne, stating her position in the clearest and most unequivocal of terms. Although harboring no desire to depose Elizabeth, she declared herself to have "no scruple of conscience in desiring the second rank as being the legitimate and nearest heir."

As the evidence unfolded, it was apparent that time had ameliorated her earlier bitterness toward Nau and Curle. Although appalled at the manner in which their evidence was introduced, she said, "For my part, I do not wish to accuse my secretaries, but I see plainly that what they have said is from fear of torture and death. Under promise of their lives and in order to save themselves, they have excused themselves at my expense."

Unfortunately, the trial could not maintain such levels of magnanimity and soon descended into a morass of noisy charges from the commissioners. Alone, and speaking in a language that she had acquired only late in life, Mary defended herself admirably, but by the end of the first day she was exhausted. Such an ordeal would tax the strongest spirit: Mary had spent half her life in custody, with strictly rationed exercise; even so, she had sufficient clarity of thought to recognize that the evidence of Nau and Curle was critical to the prosecution's case, leading her to proclaim just before the proceedings closed for the day, "If they were in my presence now they would clear me on the spot."

The next morning, visibly more pale, Mary entered the chamber slowly, but for some reason, the entire mood of the court seemed to have changed overnight. Gone were the rough exchanges of the previous day; in their place were reasoned, if not altogether truthful, speeches. Once, when Cecil uttered a piece of spectacularly imaginative fiction that he tried to palm off as evidence, Mary burst out, "You are indeed my adversary!" The scheming courtier smoothly replied, "I am the adversary to the adversaries of Queen Elizabeth." That, clearly, included Mary, Queen of Scots.

Around the court, there was no slackening of the determination that Mary should pay with her head. Many of her closest servants regarded a death sentence as a fait accompli. Ominously, as the commission had gathered that morning, Mary's entourage had not been able to help noticing that, almost without exception, every court member was attired in riding dress and boots, a clear indication that the proceedings were not expected to last the day. Mary herself was under no illusions. Leaving the court that day, she drew shy, almost embarrassed laughter from the commissioners when she observed wryly, "May God keep me from having to do with you all again."

Treachery Confirmed

Her wish was granted. On October 25, the commissioners reconvened at the Star Chamber Court in London to hear evidence from Nau and Curle. Both reaffirmed their testimony on oath and stated they had given it "frankly and voluntarily." The commission accordingly found Mary guilty of "compassing and imagining since June 1st matters tending to the death and destruction of the Queen of England." Upon receipt of the verdict, both houses of Parliament urged Elizabeth to pass sentence of death immediately.

For weeks, then months, Elizabeth procrastinated, despite a barrage of ministerial advice. "As long as life is in her [Mary], there is hope," said one. "So long as they [Catholics] live in hope, we live in fear." Finally, on February 1, 1587, Elizabeth yielded to the relentless pressure and signed the death warrant. One week later, on the morning of February 8, Mary was beheaded in the Great

Hall at Fotheringay. It was a gruesome affair. Twice the headsman botched his task. Only after the third blow was he able to grab a handful of Mary's red hair and yank the severed head aloft with a cry of "God Save the Queen!" Suddenly the moment was frozen—a close-cropped gray head slid from the luxuriant auburn tresses and thudded to the ground, leaving the executioner clutching a red wig. Only in death had Mary's legendary beauty deserted her. Later that day, her body was buried within the precincts of the castle, at a spot that remains unknown.

Surprisingly enough, death on the axeman's block held no terrors for Mary. For years, she had feared assassination in some murky dungeon. When Mary received the news that she would be publicly beheaded, her physician reported, "Her heart beat faster and she was more cheerful and she was in better health than ever before." If, by her death, Mary hoped to advance the cause of Catholicism, she was mistaken. Her most enduring legacy was one of diminished regard for royalty, making it that much easier for her grandson, Charles I, to suffer the same fate as she.

—Colin Evans

Suggestions for Further Reading

Angus, Duke of Hamilton. *Maria R.* Edinburgh: Mainstream, 1991.

Cannon, John, and Ralph Griffiths. *The Oxford History of the British Monarchy.* Oxford: Oxford University Press, 1988.

Fraser, Antonia. *Mary, Queen of Scots.* New York: Delacorte Press, 1969.

Thomson, George M. *Crime of Mary Stuart.* New York: Dutton, 1967.

Wormald, Jenny. *Mary, Queen of Scots.* London: Collins & Brown, 1991.

Giordano Bruno Trials: 1592 and 1600

Defendant: Giordano Bruno   **Crime Charged:** Heresy
Chief Defense Lawyer: None   **Chief Prosecutor:** The Holy Office of the Inquisition   **Judges:** The Cardinal General Inquisitors   **Places:** Venice and Rome   **Dates of Trials:** May 26, 1592; February 8, 1600   **Verdict:** Guilty
Sentence: Burning at the stake

SIGNIFICANCE

Revived with the spread of the Protestant Reformation in the mid-16th century, the Inquisition vigorously sought out suspected heretics. Dissident thinkers who fell into the inquisitors' hands were forced to recant or were punished. With the long, painstaking prosecution of Bruno, the Holy Office showed late Renaissance Italy it would ruthlessly defend the official faith.

An itinerant scholar, an "academician with no academy," Giordano Bruno baffled and irritated the orthodox, Catholic and Protestant alike, wherever his wanderings led him. His restless, speculative mind brought him at the last into fatal conflict with the Counter-Reformation inquisitors of the Holy Office in Rome.

From a later perspective, Bruno is an appealing figure. His system of thought, all-embracing and poetic, influenced the 17th-century philosophers Spinoza and Leibniz. The modernist James Joyce, in many ways a temperamental heir of Bruno's, celebrated him in a famous essay as "The Nolan" (suggesting, perhaps unintentionally, an obscure chieftain out of Irish mythology) and in *Finnegans Wake* as "Mr. Brown," a member of the firm of "Brown and Nolan." To his contemporaries, though, and especially to those in authority, Bruno was insufferable—and dangerous too.

Bruno was born in Nola, near Naples, in 1548 and was pushed into the Dominican order as an adolescent; he became a priest in 1572. Four years later, he deserted the Dominicans, fleeing Italy just ahead of a prosecution for heresy. Religion, he concluded, might be useful in governing the ignorant; philosophers should be exempt from such restraints. He landed first in Geneva and joined the Calvinists. But they had scant tolerance for his skepticism, and he soon moved on, first to Paris, where he encountered what he called the "three-headed hellhound of Aristotle, Ptolemy and dogma," then to England.

Homeward Bound

In England, Bruno found congenial company in the circle of the soldier-courtier-poet Sir Philip Sidney. These were productive years, in which in lectures and in books, Bruno developed the notion, suggested by Copernicus, that the world of man did not necessarily lie at the center of the universe. He also pursued his interests in magic and in the development of memory systems that he believed could give the mind quasi-magical powers.

Conflict with the powerful and anti-Copernican Oxford philosophers drove Bruno out of England in 1585. He returned to Paris before continuing on to Germany, where he lived for brief spells in several German towns, including Martin Luther's Wittenberg. He actually became a Lutheran for a time. But he had no more use for Luther's doctrine than for the pope's. Nor could the Lutherans accept Bruno's developing pantheistic philosophy. Just as the Calvinists had done in Geneva, they drove him out of their communion.

"I dislike unanimity and I hate commonality," Bruno wrote in an attempt to explain why he found himself unable to stay out of trouble. "I am suspicious of majorities. It is the One which wins my love; the One that gives me freedom in my bondage, peace in my torment, wealth in my poverty, life in my death."

The offer of a tutor's post took Bruno over the Alps to Venice in mid-1591. The Venetian Holy Office maintained a stubborn independence from Rome, and Bruno doubtless thought he would be safe there. For reasons that remain obscure, he soon had a falling out with his host and chief pupil, one Zuane Mocenigo. Possibly, Mocenigo expected more from Bruno's system of memory training than the master could deliver. In any case, with prompting from "the constraints of his conscience and by the order of his confessor," Mocenigo denounced Bruno to the Inquisition as a lapsed priest and a heretic.

So Bruno, 44 years old, began an ordeal of nearly eight years of imprisonment, interrogation, trial, and deprivation.

Because of his atheistic religious beliefs, Giordano Bruno was arrested in 1592 on charges of heresy. Found guilty on February 8, 1600, he was burned at the stake 11 days later.

The Trials

The hearings opened on May 26, 1592, with depositions from two booksellers who had known Bruno in Germany and elsewhere. The first testified that his contacts in the publishing center of Frankfurt reported Bruno to be "a man of no religion." The second had attended Bruno's lectures, and he said he had never heard him deliver any opinion contrary to the teachings of the Mother Church.

A third witness, Jacob Britano, said he had known Bruno in Frankfurt, Zurich, and Venice. Britano went on: "The Prior of the Convent in Frankfurt told me that Bruno was mainly occupied in writing and devising foolishness and astrology and seeking new things. The Prior said he had a fine talent as a man of letters, was a 'universal' man. The Prior believed that he had no religion, for he said Giordano declares that he knows more than the Apostles knew and that he would have dared, had he so desired, to bring about that the whole world should be of one religion."

The inquisitors cross-examined Bruno on every aspect of his life and thought, with particular emphasis on the Three Persons of the Trinity. Bruno admitted he did not consider the Second and Third Persons as entirely distinct from the First. "But in fact," he insisted, "I never wrote or taught this, but merely doubted." In any case, he said, the passages in his work that might be regarded as heretical had not been meant as challenges to religious orthodoxy but as philosophical expressions—the testing and weighing of ideas, the exercise of a probing mind.

Fighting hard for an acquittal, Bruno admitted he had neglected to observe fast or abstinence days, and he acknowledged his mistake in praising the English queen Elizabeth, herself a notorious heretic. And he offered the Holy Office an all-purpose confession: "All the errors which I have committed until today, and all heresies which I have believed, and the doubts I have entertained concerning the Catholic Faith and in matters determined by the Holy Church, I now abhor and detest them all and I repent having done, held, said, believed or doubted concerning anything non-Catholic."

Left to themselves, the easygoing, lenient Venetians might have accepted Bruno's apology and permitted the matter to rest. But the papal authorities had taken an interest in the case. In September, the Vatican summoned Bruno to stand trial in Rome. The Venetians delayed at first but eventually agreed to hand him over. On February 27, 1593, the jailers of the Holy Office led him into the dungeons of the Castello Sant'Angelo in Rome.

Year after year, remorselessly, the inquisitors pursued their investigation, alternating periods of intense examination with long months of malign neglect. Bruno complained of the cold, of inadequate food, of lack of books. All the same, he worked on his written defense, consulting his well-stocked mind and such published materials as his captors allowed him. On January 14, 1599, the judges at last revealed the core of their case: eight allegedly heretical propositions extracted from Bruno's published works. They demanded a recantation, point by point.

The Verdict

Bruno put up a stout defense. He tried to show that Copernicanism and Catholicism could be compatible. Whereas he had written that the universe is infinite, Catholic dogma held that God alone is infinite. Responded Bruno: "It would not be worthy of God to manifest himself in less than an infinite universe." The judges remained unpersuaded. Finally, on December 21, 1599, all his arguments exhausted, Bruno declared he had nothing to retract. On February 8, 1600, seven years and four months after his arrest, the Cardinals General reached a verdict: "We hereby publish, announce, pronounce, sentence and declare thee the aforesaid Brother Giordano Bruno to be an impenitent and pertinacious heretic, and therefore to have incurred all the ecclesiastical censures and pains of the Holy Canon, the laws and the constitutions, both general and particular, imposed on such confessed impenitent pertinacious and obstinate heretics."

The judges gave him eight days to recant or be burned at the stake. "You are more afraid of this than I am," Bruno, still defiant, told them. On February 19, three days after the deadline, the jailers led him out to the Campo di Fiori, stripped him naked, tied him to the stake, and forced a wedge into his mouth to keep him from blaspheming. A group of priests gathered around the pyre, chanting and waving crucifixes. A German witness, one Gaspar Schopp, observed the condemned man closely. "When the image of our Saviour was shown to him before his death he angrily rejected it with averted face," Schopp reported.

—Michael Golay

Suggestions for Further Reading

Hale, J. R., ed. *A Concise Encyclopedia of the Italian Renaissance.* New York: Oxford University Press, 1981.

de Santillana, Giorgio. *The Age of Adventure: The Renaissance Philosophers.* New York: George Braziller, 1957.

Singer, Dorothy W. *Giordano Bruno: His Life and Thought.* New York: Henry Schuman, 1950.

Yates, Frances. *Lull & Bruno.* Boston: K. Paul, 1982.

Walter Raleigh Trials: 1603 and 1618

Defendant: Sir Walter Raleigh   **Crimes Charged:** Conspiracy, treason
Chief Defense Lawyer: None (Raleigh was his own advocate at both trials)
Chief Prosecutors: Edward Coke (first trial); Sir Henry Yelverton, Sir Thomas
Coventry (second trial)   **Judges:** Panel of 11 commissioners led by Lord
Chief Justice John Popham (first trial); panel of commissioners led by Lord
Chief Justice Henry Montague (second trial)   **Places:** Winchester, England
(first trial); London, England (second trial)   **Dates of Trials:** November 17,
1603; October 22, 1618   **Verdicts:** Guilty   **Sentences:** Death (commuted
by King James I after first trial)

SIGNIFICANCE

For centuries, history has viewed Sir Walter Raleigh's fate as a miscarriage of
justice. But did history get it wrong?

As the man who had planned the colonization of Virginia and Carolina, introduced the potato and tobacco to Britain, and led his ship against the Spanish Armada, Sir Walter Raleigh enjoyed almost unprecedented levels of patronage from his monarch, Queen Elizabeth I. But in 1592 came his first inkling of just how ephemeral royal indulgence could be. News that he had seduced and secretly married one of the queen's ladies-in-waiting led to his being thrown into the Tower of London. Although released soon after, Raleigh never regained his former glories. With the accession of James I in 1603, his star declined further still. The new king loathed him and ordered the seizure of his assets. Soon there came vague rumors of a Spanish plot to usurp the throne, with whispers of Raleigh's involvement. Within months, the disgraced hero found himself facing charges of treason.

Because an outbreak of plague in London was claiming 2,000 lives a week, his trial was transferred to Winchester, some 60 miles to the southwest. The journey betrayed what was to come, with angry mobs lining the route to hurl stones and tobacco pipes at Raleigh as he passed. On November 17, 1603, a panel of 11 commissioners convened to hear charges of treason levied by Attorney General Edward Coke. As his own advocate, Raleigh craved the court's indulgence: "Sickness hath of later weakened me and my memory was always bad. The points of the indictment be many, and in the evidence perhaps more will be urged. I beseech you, my lords, let me answer every point severally, for I shall not carry all to the end.''

Coke spat back, ''The king's evidence ought not to be broken or dismembered, whereby it might lose much of its grace and vigor.'' Whatever reputation Coke later gained as a jurist owed little to his conduct of this trial, as he snarled at the accused, ''I will prove you to be the most notorious traitor that ever came to the bar!''

Raleigh replied in the breezy manner he would maintain throughout: ''Your words cannot condemn me. My innocency is my defense. Prove against me any one thing of the many that you have broke, and I will confess all the indictment, and that I am the most horrible traitor that ever lived, and worthy to be crucified with a thousand torments.''

''Nay, I will prove all. Thou art a monster!'' hissed Coke. ''Thou hast an English face but a Spanish heart!''

Raleigh continued to taunt Coke. ''Master Attorney, I am no traitor. Whether I live or die, I shall stand as true a subject as ever the king hath. You may call me a traitor at your pleasure, yet it becomes not a man of quality and virtue to do so, for I do not yet hear you charge me with treason.''

The one-sidedness of these exchanges led an observer to comment that Raleigh ''behaved himself so worthily, so wisely, so temperately, that in half a

This Victorian engraving shows Sir Walter Raleigh's birthplace, Hayes Barton, located near East Budlleigh in Devon.

day the mind of all the company was changed from the extremest hate to the greatest pity."

Raleigh's Legal Blunder

Skillfully and with mounting confidence, Raleigh navigated the sea of contradictory dates and half-remembered secondhand conversations. Then came a tactical blunder. His claim that "by the law and statutes of this realm in cases of treason, a man ought to be convicted by the testimony of two witnesses if they be living" prompted Lord Chief Justice John Popham to remind him that recent amendments to the treason laws had sealed this loophole. When Raleigh grumbled that he was being tried by inequitable means, Popham replied, "Equity is from the king; you can only have justice from us."

A portrait of English explorer, Sir Walter Raleigh.

Still Raleigh wouldn't let go: "I know not, my lord, how you conceive the law."

In reply, Popham uttered the single statement that history remembers him for: "We do not conceive the law. We *know* the law."

The only witness to actually adduce evidence of Raleigh's alleged treason was a hitherto unknown sailor named Dyer. "Being at Lisbon," he said, "there came to be a Portugal gentleman who asked me how the king of England did, and whether he was crowned. I answered him that I hoped our noble king was well and crowned by this. . . . 'Nay,' said he, 'your king shall never be crowned for Don Cobham [Lord Henry Brooke Cobham, a confidant of Raleigh's, who attempted to save his own skin by betraying his erstwhile friend.] and Don Raleigh will cut his throat before he come to be crowned.'"

When Raleigh queried the admissibility of such distant hearsay, Coke retorted, "It shows that your treason had wings." To which Raleigh protested that three times he had risked his life fighting the Spaniards: Were these the actions of a man allegedly in receipt of Spanish gold? Coke was ready for him. Triumphantly he produced a letter written by Cobham in which he claimed that, but for Raleigh's goading, he would never have contacted agents of Spain. In the face of such an admission, Raleigh was helpless and was sentenced to death.

Just days before his intended execution, he watched from his cell window at Winchester Castle as a macabre vignette unfolded in the courtyard below. At half-hour intervals, Cobham and two others were led to the block and told to prepare for the end. After 30 minutes spent teetering on the brink of oblivion, each knelt to face the ax, only to then be reprieved. Such sadism—typical of James I; the pardons had been signed three days earlier—mattered little to Raleigh, who immediately dashed off a letter begging for similar mercy.

Reprieved

Gleefully, the new king acceded, but only after ensuring that Raleigh's groveling plea was broadcast in every quarter, so that, in a time when honor was often more highly prized than life itself, the once heroic explorer became a figure of contempt. Although he spent the next 12 years of his life at the Tower of London, he was confined more than incarcerated. His wife visited him regularly, and he fathered a son; in a small garden, he grew the plants and herbs from which he concocted medicines; and he wrote voluminously, producing his monumental *History of the World*, the work that cemented his literary reputation.

Throughout, he petitioned for his freedom, endeavoring to persuade James that gold mines in Guiana, run by the Spaniards, were ripe for plunder. In 1616, the request was granted, and 15 troublesome months later, he set sail on his final voyage. It was a catastrophe. The promised gold failed to materialize, and he lost 250 men in combat with the Spanish. Why Raleigh chose to return to England is a mystery; better than most he knew the penalties for failure at court, but return he did. And in August 1618, he was dispatched to the Bloody Tower for the third and last time in his life.

On October 22, 1618, he faced yet another panel of judges, where the attorney general, Sir Henry Yelverton, recited the litany of charges against him, dividing them into "faults before going on this last voyage . . . faults committed in his voyage . . . [and] faults committed since." Much of the evidence was a rehash of his earlier trial, and once again, Raleigh heard himself sentenced to death or, more correctly, heard the original sentence reaffirmed. On October 28, he made his final representations at the Palace of Westminster, only for Lord Chief Justice Henry Montague to tell him that, in law, he had been a dead man for the past 15 years "and might at any minute be cut off." The next morning, Sir Walter Raleigh was beheaded in Old Palace Yard, next to Westminster Hall.

Was Raleigh an Innocent Man or a Traitor?

The unjustness of Raleigh's conviction has long been one of the staples of British history, but dramatic new evidence uncovered at Oxford's Bodleian Library and made public in November 1995 has turned that concept on its head. While examining documents untouched for 250 years, researchers accidentally stumbled across the first complete account of the prosecution case against Raleigh, including statements in the defendant's own hand that reveal that he did indeed speak of wanting Spain to invade England and had even offered his services as a spy in return for £1,500 ($6,000) a year.

From these disclosures, it would appear as though Raleigh's reputation as innocent victim derives primarily from the courtroom conduct of Edward Coke, whose ill-judged belligerence toward the defendant was so poorly received that Raleigh underwent instant conversion from admitted traitor to hallowed martyr.

—*Colin Evans*

Suggestions for Further Reading

Cannon, John, and Ralph Griffiths. *The Oxford History of the British Monarchy*. Oxford: Oxford University Press, 1988.

Feiling, Sir Keith. *A History of England*. New York: Macmillan, 1959.

Lacey, Robert. *Sir Walter Ralegh* [sic]. New York: Atheneum, 1973.

Magnus, Philip. *Sir Walter Raleigh*. New York: Macmillan, 1956.

Gunpowder Plot Trial: 1606

Defendants: Thomas Bates, Sir Everard Digby, Guy Fawkes, John Grant, Robert Keyes, Ambrose Rookwood, Robert Winter, Thomas Winter
Crime Charged: Treason   **Chief Defense Lawyer:** None
Chief Prosecutor: Sir Edward Coke   **Judges:** Panel of five judges headed by Sir John Popham   **Place:** London, England
Date of Trial: January 27, 1606   **Verdict:** Guilty   **Sentence:** Death

SIGNIFICANCE

Following the Act of Supremacy (1534), which proclaimed Henry VIII, and not the pope, as head of the Church in England, the country had been racked by religious turmoil. As Protestants moved from target to tormentor, the Catholic backlash was formidable. By far, the most potent expression of this dissent was the conspiracy that became known as the Gunpowder Plot.

As the 16th century drew to a close, England's Catholic community was in danger of extinction. Under Queen Elizabeth I, there had been a systematic attempt to annihilate every aspect of perceived Roman influence: Laws made it a crime punishable by death to attempt to convert anyone to Catholicism, and taxes and other hardships made the simple act of Catholic worship an expensive and often perilous undertaking. Catholic hopes that intolerance would ease on the accession of James I in 1603 were short-lived. Urged on by his chief adviser, Sir Robert Cecil, James gave full rein to the punitive statutes.

One person who despaired of any worthwhile improvement for his fellow Catholics was Robert Catesby, a wealthy midlands landowner. Toward the end of 1603, he approached John Wright, Thomas Percy, and Thomas Winter, three men of similar position and inclination as he, and they began to discuss ways of easing their distress. According to a confession later extracted from Winter, it was Catesby who first mooted the idea of slaying the twin demons James I and Robert Cecil. Next to join the conspiracy was Guy Fawkes, a shadowy figure about whom little is known but whose name remains synonymous with the Gunpowder Plot.

In December 1604, the plotters—who by this time had added Robert Keyes, another prominent Catholic, to their number—rented a property adjacent to the houses of Parliament and began tunneling between the two buildings. After Christmas, they began ferrying barrels of gunpowder across the River Thames to the tunnel. Their intention was to detonate the explosives on the day that James I opened Parliament, killing not just the monarch and his son, the Prince of Wales, but Cecil and most of the Privy Council as well, thereby leaving the country without a central government.

It was around this time that Catesby, during confession, discussed with a Jesuit priest named Father Henry Garnet the ethical considerations of killing unsuspecting Catholic parliamentarians, pondering whether such sacrifice was ever justified, even if it advanced the Catholic cause. Garnet later insisted that Catesby's inquiry had been couched in the vaguest of terms and included no reference to the Gunpowder Plot. Upon learning of the plot's existence, he counseled against it but was bound by the terms of the confessional to say nothing, a vow that would later cost him dearly.

Gradually, the conspiracy widened. Sir Everard Digby, Ambrose Rookwood, and John Grant, all wealthy committed Catholics, were initiated into the plot; so, too, were Thomas Bates and Thomas Winter's brother, Robert. An important addition to the cabal at this time was Francis Tresham, later suspected of betraying the plot to the government.

Gun Powder Treaſon.

In this contemporary drawing, the illustrator portrays God keeping an eye on the Gunpowder Plot conspirators.

Betrayal?

Although Tresham's true allegiance is shrouded in mystery, it is virtually certain that Robert Cecil, one of the plotters' prime targets and the best-informed politician in England at that time, was aware of the tunnel's existence throughout every inch of its construction. Fanatical in his opposition to Catholics—especially Jesuits—Cecil knew exactly what the plotters had in mind but did nothing to hinder their progress, preferring to wait until he could extract the maximum political advantage from their perfidy. Such deviousness would explain how the tunnelers managed to dispose of all the earth from the tunnel and obtain so much gunpowder, which at that time in England was strictly rationed. Cecil waited until the final moment before striking.

At around midnight on November 4, 1605, with James I due to open Parliament the very next day, Guy Fawkes was arrested in the cellars of the houses of Parliament while standing guard over three dozen barrels of gunpowder, enough to cause a massive explosion. News of Fawkes's arrest threw the other plotters into disarray. Many fled north. On November 8, Catesby and Percy were killed by a sheriff's posse; after a brief fight, the remaining conspiracy members were rounded up and dispatched to the Tower of London for interrogation.

Fawkes already knew just how harrowing such an experience could be. Two days on the rack had broken everything except his spirit. The tower's lieutenant, Sir William Waad—no neophyte in matters of coaxing information from reluctant prisoners—marveled at Fawkes's resilience. Even so, he promised Cecil, "I am confident, notwithstanding his resolute mind, in the end he will be more open." And so it proved, though by the time of Fawkes's final statement, given on November 17, he did not have strength enough to sign it.

Cecil seethed over Fawkes's "confession": Nowhere did it contain any mention of Jesuit culpability. That would come, after days of torture, from Thomas Bates; and yet, mysteriously, this confession vanished, leaving doubt that it ever existed, except in Cecil's fertile imagination. More curiosity surrounded the news on December 23 that Tresham had suddenly died in custody, the hastiness of his burial fueling speculation that he had been murdered to guarantee his silence.

Show Trial

Seventeenth-century trials of prominent figures were not really trials in the accepted sense of the word. Invariably, guilt—actual or otherwise—had already been established to the government's satisfaction; the court process was merely a rubber stamp for public consumption. So it was, before a panel of five judges headed by Lord Chief Justice Sir John Popham, that the trial opened at Westminster Hall in London on January 27, 1606. First to speak for the Crown was the master of the rolls, Sir Edward Phillips. He briefly outlined the nature of the crimes before yielding to Sir Edward Coke, the attorney general, who had achieved notoriety for his prosecutions of the Earl of Essex and Sir Walter Raleigh.

Renowned for his savage invective, Coke began in, what was for him, fairly subdued fashion. The defendants were, he said, men of substance "most perniciously seduced, abused, [and] corrupted." Soon, though, the bullying advocate was at his inflammatory worst, excoriating "the greatest treasons that ever were plotted in England and concerning the greatest king that ever was in England." When it came to the Jesuits and their alleged complicity, Coke toppled over the brink of reason: "I never yet knew a treason without a Romish priest," he thundered, "[these] men that use the reverence of Religion . . . to cover their impiety, blasphemy, treason, and rebellion and all manner of wickedness," all of which prefaced a vituperative attack on the absent Father Garnet and his alleged part in the conspiracy.

Rumors abounded that an interested observer of this diatribe was King James himself, who, together with members of his family, followed the proceedings from a private room overlooking the court.

The defense consisted of depositions made earlier by the accused. All were humble, even penitent in tone. Thomas Winter caught the general mood: "Not out of hope to obtain pardon . . . I must say the fault is greater than can be forgiven . . . since I see such courses to Almighty God, and that all or most material parts have already been confessed." How much credence can be attached to this "confession" is debatable, since not only was it obtained under duress, it was also signed "Winter," a curious anomaly considering that the defendant always spelled his surname Wintour."

Then it was Coke's turn again, this time to bait the defendants with details of the agonies that awaited them:

> For which cause also shall he be strangled, being hanged up by the neck between heaven and earth, as deemed unworthy of both or either. Then he is to be cut down alive and to have his privy parts cut off and burned before his face as being unworthily begotten and unfit to leave any generation after him. His bowels and inlaid parts taken out and burned, who inwardly hath conceived and harbored in his heart such horrible treason. After, to have his head cut off, which had imagined the mischief. And lastly his body to be quartered.

At the conclusion of Coke's harangue, the jury adjourned to a nearby room. A few minutes later the jury returned with the inevitable verdict.

Asked why sentence should not be passed upon them, Thomas Winter appealed for mercy on his brother's behalf, but his pleas fell on deaf ears, and Robert Winter, like the others, was condemned to death by Lord Chief Justice Popham. Afterward, Digby, who alone among the conspirators had pleaded not guilty, was tried separately and similarly sentenced. After the trial, all the defendants were marched by torchlight back to the Tower of London, where they spent their final days in solitude.

The executions were every bit as horrific as Coke had demanded. On January 30, 1606, Digby, Grant, Bates, and Thomas Winter were drawn upon hurdles to their place of execution at Saint Paul's. The next day, the remainder were similarly dealt with at Old Palace Yard, Westminster, within view of the very building they had sought to destroy. Contrition played no part in their final utterances from the scaffold; indeed, Rookwood's dying wish was that God would "make the King a Catholic." Fawkes, broken by torture and sickness, quite literally crawled to his death. That same day, the man whom Cecil had misguidedly judged to be one of the major conspirators, Father Henry Garnet, was taken into custody. He, too, was later executed.

Although the work of just a handful of extremists, the Gunpowder Plot dealt a dreadful blow to English Catholicism. The already draconian laws were further toughened, forbidding Catholics to live in or near London, denying them access to the professions of law and medicine, and browbeating wealthy Catholics into attending Protestant churches on pain of having two-thirds of their property confiscated. A rather less onerous outcome of the Gunpowder Plot was the day of thanksgiving that James I inaugurated, which became known as Guy Fawkes Day. To this day in Britain, every November 5 bonfires are lit and "guys"—effigies of Guy Fawkes—are burned, usually accompanied by a fireworks display.

—Colin Evans

Suggestions for Further Reading

Cannon, John, and Ralph Griffiths. *The Oxford History of the British Monarchy.* Oxford: Oxford University Press, 1988.

Haynes, Alan. *The Gunpowder Plot.* Dover, England: Alan Sutton, 1994.

Winstock, Lewis. *Gunpowder, Treason and Plot.* New York: Putnam, 1973.

Galileo Galilei Trial: 1633

Defendant: Galileo Galilei   **Crime Charged:** Vehement suspicion of heresy
Chief Defense Lawyer: None   **Chief Prosecutor:** Vincenzo Maculano,
Commissary General of the Congregation of the Holy Office
Judges: Vincenzo Maculano and the Holy Office   **Place:** Rome, Italy
Dates: April 12–June 22, 1633   **Verdict:** Guilty   **Sentence:** Abjuration

SIGNIFICANCE
The trial of Galileo Galilei raised fundamental questions, still not entirely settled, about the relationship between religion and scientific inquiry. In the short term, it confirmed absolute papal authority over such matters.

Controversial, quick-witted, sarcastic, contemptuous of timid thinking, Galileo Galilei pushed the limits of scientific inquiry, a compulsion that often led him into trouble. Take, for example, the telescope, a 1608 invention that Galileo redesigned and dramatically improved. He used the perfected instrument to make a number of critical astronomical discoveries, some of them tending to confirm what he already believed: that Copernicus had been correct in 1543 when he theorized that the Earth did not stand still but revolved around the sun.

Galileo was born in Pisa, Italy, in 1564. He studied mathematics and astronomy and eventually taught at the university there. His work on the laws of motion contradicted accepted Aristotelian thought and drew such hostility from the conservative Pisan faculty that he resigned in 1591 to seek the freer air of Florence. His work at the University of Padua (1592–1610) enhanced his reputation as a scientist of seminal importance. Students came from all over Europe to hear his lectures.

The 1616 Inquiry

Galileo in 1613 published a vigorous defense of Copernican theory that attracted the unfavorable attention of the Roman Catholic Church. In 1616, he answered a summons to appear in Rome before the Congregation of the Holy Office, successor to the medieval Inquisition. The initial investigation cleared Galileo, but the inquisitors instructed him to abandon Copernicus's heretical views of Earth's motion. Copernican theory, taken absolutely, could neither be accepted nor defended, they told him.

Persistent rumor held that the Holy Office had condemned Galileo for heresy and had forced him to abjure. To counter the slander, Galileo asked a sympathetic Vatican functionary, Cardinal Robert Bellarmine, to attest by letter that he had not been tried, still less convicted. Wrote Bellarmine on May 26, 1616:

Galileo has not abjured in our hands, or in the hands of others here in Rome, or anywhere else that we know, any opinion or doctrine of his; nor has he received any penances, salutary or otherwise. On the contrary, he has only been notified of the declaration made by the Holy Father and published by the Sacred Congregation of the Index, whose content is that the doctrine attributed to Copernicus (that the earth moves around the sun and the sun stands at the center of the world without moving from east to west) is contrary to Holy Scripture and therefore cannot be defended or held.

The Church of Santa Maria Sopra Minerva in Rome. The adjacent building, the headquarters of the Inquisition, was the location of Galileo's trial.

Galileo evidently promised the Inquisition he would drop his advocacy of condemned doctrines, and for some years he occupied himself with other scientific matters. Then, in 1632, he returned to Copernican themes, publishing his *Dialogue Concerning the Two Chief World Systems*. A forceful defense of Copernicus, it was without question an attack on accepted scientific authority.

The Summons

The *Dialogue* appeared at an awkward moment for Pope Urban VII. Other books of doubtful orthodoxy had been published recently, and Galileo's seemed yet another challenge to papal authority. Besides, someone had told Pope Urban that the book caricatured him as an ignoramus. The pope had larger problems as well. The great Catholic-Protestant conflict of the Thirty Years' War ground on, with no end in view. Pope Urban's Habsburg allies were dissatisfied with his leadership of the Counter-Reformation; they had spoken openly of stripping him of his office. Galileo may have been a victim of the pope's need to assert his power. In the autumn of 1632, the Congregation of the Holy Office ordered Galileo to Rome to answer for the *Dialogue*.

Pleading advanced years and ill health, the difficulty of winter travel, and an outbreak of plague in Florence, Galileo begged to be excused from the journey. The inquisitors were insistent. Carried on a stretcher, Galileo arrived in Rome in February 1633, on the first Sunday of Lent. The Holy Office ignored him, a psychological torture that continued for several weeks. At least Galileo enjoyed a degree of physical comfort. Awaiting trial, he lodged in the Villa Medici, the Rome embassy of his patron, the Grand Duke of Tuscany.

The Trial

The proceedings opened April 12, 1633, before the Dominican commissary general of the Holy Office, Vincenzo Maculano. As was usual, the inquisitors did not allow the accused to have counsel, nor, at first, did they inform Galileo of the specifics of the case against him.

The Holy Office put the scientific issue plainly: Did Earth stand still or revolve around the sun? The inquisitors were curious, too, about several related questions. Must physical truth be observable, or can something be true even though only its effects can be detected? Were artificial instruments, such as the telescope, legitimate for use in the search for truth? Finally, there were, for the Holy Office, the overarching issues of the scientific authority of the Bible and the temporal authority of the pope.

Maculano and his assistant, Carlo Sinceri, prosecutor of the Holy Office, began by asking Galileo whether he knew or could guess why he had been summoned.

"I imagine," Galileo answered, "it is to account for my recently printed book." He went on to identify a copy as his work, to describe its contents in a general way, and to say he had written it in Florence over a period of seven or eight years.

Maculano asked about the 1616 inquiry. Galileo answered forthrightly, acknowledging that Cardinal Bellarmine and others had warned him off Copernicus's doctrine. He then produced a copy of the "certificate" Bellarmine had written for him.

The inquisitors pressed the matter. Had Galileo been given any sort of injunction? He said he could recall no such thing. They then produced an injunction, said to have been read to Galileo in front of witnesses. It stated that he must not "hold, teach or defend in any way whatsoever, verbally or in writing," Copernican views about Earth's motion. Galileo repeated that he could not recall the words.

Finally, Maculano questioned him about publication of the *Dialogue*. How and from whom had he obtained permission to print it?

Galileo replied that the master of the Sacred Palace, an organ of the church bureaucracy in Rome, had reviewed the manuscript and had licensed it for publication.

Had he told the master anything about his encounter with the Inquisition in 1616?

At this point, Galileo denied the evidence of his own work. "I did not judge it necessary to tell [the master], having no scruples since with the said book I had neither held nor defended the opinion of the earth's motion and the sun's stability; on the contrary, in the said book I show the contrary of Copernicus's opinion and show that Copernicus's reasons are invalid and inconclusive."

With this, Maculano dismissed the accused and put him under house arrest in a room of the Palace of the Holy Office. So far as Galileo knew, there matters stood for a full two weeks. But in the interval, the inquisitors had received a set of reports from a special commission established to review the *Dialogue*. One of the commissioners, the Jesuit Melchior Inchofer, wrote in his April 17 report,

> I am of the opinion that Galileo not only teaches and defends the immobility or rest of the sun or center of the universe, around which both the planets and the earth revolve with their own motions, but also that he is vehemently suspected of firmly adhering to this opinion, and indeed that he holds it.

During the last week in April, Maculano went privately to Galileo and advised him to avoid a long trial and a lot of trouble—solitary confinement for a long stretch, certainly, and torture, probably—by confessing. When Galileo appeared for the second hearing on April 30, he went prepared to admit his mistake in return for what he believed would be a token sentence.

Galileo claimed he had been carried away by the glitter of his own arguments to make too strong a case for Copernicus. "My error has been—and I confess it—one of vainglorious ambition," he said.

Maculano dismissed the accused but allowed him to return a little later to add to his statement. Now Galileo offered to revise the *Dialogue* to reflect authorized scientific opinion:

> I promise to resume the arguments already brought in favor of the said opinion, which is false and has been condemned, and to confute them in such most effectual manner as by the blessing of God may be supplied to me. I pray, therefore, this holy Tribunal to aid me in this good resolution and enable me to put it in effect.

The third session convened on May 10. On that day, Galileo presented his entire defense. He said again that he could not recall the injunction of 1616.

Again, he offered to revise the book. Galileo concluded with a plea for leniency. The shadowy, unreal, and unbearably intense atmosphere of the Inquisition had broken down the last of the old man's defenses:

> Lastly, it remains for me to beg you to take into consideration my pitiable state of bodily indisposition to which, at the age of seventy years, I have been reduced by ten months of constant mental anxiety and the fatigue of a long and toilsome journey at the most inclement season. I am persuaded and encouraged to do so by the faith I have in the clemency and goodness of my most Eminent Lords, my judges; with the hope that they may be pleased, in answer to my prayer, to remit what may appear to their entire justice the rightful addition that is still lacking to such sufferings to make an adequate punishment for my crimes, out of consideration for my declining age, which, too, humbly commends itself to them.

Pictured is Galileo's villa at Arcetri, just outside of Florence. He was released from prison in December 1633, and it was here that Galileo spent the last nine years of his life in exile.

This, however, did not end the matter. The pope had not yet been satisfied. Possibly, a rumor that Galileo had practiced the proscribed art of astrology and had used it to predict the date of the pope's death further influenced Pope Urban against him. On June 16, the Holy Office met to pass sentence. At Pope Urban's insistence, there would be a further interrogation, "even under the threat of torture." Galileo would be forced to abjure; he would be condemned to imprisonment at the pleasure of the Holy Office; he could no longer "treat further, in whatever manner, either in words or in writing, of the mobility of the Earth and the stability of the Sun." The *Dialogue* would be prohibited. Finally, the inquisitor in Florence would "read the sentence in full assembly and in the presence of most of those who profess the mathematical art." Galileo would thus be forced to abase himself in front of his scientific peers.

The inquisitors did not carry out the threat of torture. In the final interrogation on June 21, Galileo fell in with all the Holy Office's demands: "I do not hold this opinion of Copernicus," he said, "and I have not held it after being ordered by injunction to abandon it. For the rest, I am here in your hands; do as you please."

Dressed in the white robe of a penitent, Galileo made his way the next day to the hall of the Dominican convent of Santa Maria sopra Minerva and knelt to hear the sentence read. The harshness of it surprised even Maculano. Then Galileo recanted:

> With sincere heart and unfeigned faith I abjure, curse and detest the above-mentioned errors and heresies, and in general every other error, heresy and sect contrary to the Holy Church; and I swear that in the future I will never again say or assert, orally or in writing, anything which might cause a similar suspicion about me; on the contrary, if I should come to know any heretic or anyone suspected of heresy, I will denounce him to this Holy Office.

Many years afterward, the tale circulated that Galileo had ended his abjuration with a *sotto voce* but defiant *Eppur su muove*—"But it still moves." This is apocryphal. Galileo turned to new fields of inquiry and never dealt in Copernican theory again. In 1638, four years before his death, he published *Two New Sciences*, a treatise that became a foundation of modern physics and engineering. His *Dialogue* remained on the Vatican's Index of banned books until 1835.

—Michael Golay

Suggestions for Further Reading

Brecht, Bertolt. *Galileo*. Edited by Eric Bentley. New York: Grove Press, 1966.

Drake, Stillman. *Galileo*. New York: Hill and Wang, 1980.

Finocchiaro, Maurice A., ed. *The Galileo Affair: A Documentary History*. Berkeley: University of California Press, 1989.

Galilei, Galileo. *Dialogue Concerning the Two Chief World Systems*. Translated by Drake Stillman. Berkeley: University of California Press, 1967.

Koestler, Arthur. *The Sleepwalkers: A History of Man's Changing Vision of the Universe*. New York: Macmillan, 1959.

Langford, Jerome J. *Galileo, Science and the Church*. Ann Arbor: University of Michigan Press, 1966.

Ronan, Colin A. *Galileo*. New York: G. P. Putnam's Sons, 1974.

Charles I Trial: 1649

Defendant: Charles Stuart **Crime Charged:** Treason
Chief Defense Lawyer: None **Chief Prosecutor:** John Cook **Judge:** John Bradshaw **Place:** London, England **Dates of Trial:** January 20–27, 1649
Verdict: Guilty **Sentence:** Death

SIGNIFICANCE
Until the mid-17th century, intentional dislocations in the British royal lineage were usually clandestine affairs—a prime example being the murder of Edward II in 1327—but all that changed with the trial of Charles I. For the first time a reigning British monarch found himself subject to an ordinance passed by commoners. Although the constitutionality of that ordinance might have been questionable, its effects are being felt to the present day.

Upon his accession to the throne in 1625, Charles I was valued for his wide-ranging appreciation of the arts and a shy, almost diffident manner in complete contrast to that of his coarse and boorish father, James I. Unfortunately, all these qualities paled into insignificance when set against the new king's insatiable appetite for expensive international conflict. Ill-starred ventures in France and Spain made impossible demands on the Royal Exchequer and kept Charles constantly at odds with Parliament. Their long-running feud reached a bitter climax on January 4, 1642, when Charles forced his way into the House of Commons in a foolish and vain bid to arrest five recalcitrant members. By year's end, the country was engulfed in a civil war between supporters of Parliament and those loyal to the king.

It was a bloody dispute. In February 1647, aware that his position had become untenable, Charles surrendered and was placed in parliamentary custody. From his writings, it is clear that the worst he feared was forced abdication; this fear was reflected in his efforts to guarantee the succession of his son, Charles II, the Prince of Wales. The first few months of leisurely captivity seemed to bear out this belief, but from his confines at Hampton Court, Charles soon sensed a hardening of the mood against him. He began to hatch plots and once succeeded in escaping briefly to Carisbrooke Castle on the Isle of Wight, but any lingering hopes of a Royalist revival were dashed by Oliver Cromwell's crushing victory at Preston in 1648. Cromwell, by now the most powerful man in England, decided that the time had come to deal with the troublesome monarch.

On January 1, 1649, an ordinance passed the House of Commons demanding that the king be tried for treason on grounds that he had waged war against Parliament and the country. However, when it was sent to the House of Lords for approval, the motion was rejected out of hand. Determined to assert its authority, the Commons retaliated by passing the bill a second time, together with an ordinance establishing a High Court of Justice of 135 commissioners, made up of Parliamentarians and soldiers. The net around England's king was beginning to tighten.

Reluctant Commission

On January 19, 1649, a coach and six brought Charles from Windsor Castle to London. The next day, he faced a commission headed by the chief justice of Chester, John Bradshaw, a relatively minor figure in matters of law, but someone who had distinguished himself by being just about the only judge in England prepared to chair such contentious proceedings. This air of general reluctance was to plague the tribunal throughout its brief existence, as Cromwell toiled sometimes frantically to maintain a quorum. Of the original 135 commissioners summoned, barely half were in attendance when proceedings got under way in the lofty splendor of Westminster Hall; excuses ranged from illness to pressing concerns elsewhere in the country. Self-preservation was clearly a factor; feelings were running high in the capital, and it was not beyond the realm of possibility that a cadre of Charles's supporters might attempt to free their king by any means possible. Confirmation of the personal peril that many commissioners felt was evidenced by Bradshaw's decision to have his hat reinforced with metal plates.

John Glover's engraving of the House of Commons (circa 1648)

Charles experienced no such trepidation. He entered the hall clad entirely in black, except for his collar and cuffs. Deliberately, he made his way to the dock that had been specially prepared for him, out of public view, and listened as Solicitor General John Cook dictated the charge: "I do in the name and on the behalf of the people of England exhibit and bring into this court a charge of high treason and other high crimes whereof I do accuse Charles Stuart, King of England—"

"By your favor, hold!" Charles interrupted, but he was ordered to silence, and the charge continued.

"—[of having conspired] to overthrow the rights and liberties of the people . . . [and had] trayterously and maliciously levyed war against the present Parliament and the people therein represented." To substantiate the accusation, Cook recounted a litany of battles from the civil war and drew attention to the attempted use of foreign troops to further Royalist aims.

At the charge's conclusion, Charles openly laughed in the face of his accusers, demanding to know by what authority he had been brought there. "I am your King. I have a trust committed to me by God, by old and lawful descent. I will not betray that trust to a new unlawful authority." These were themes he returned to repeatedly—the illegality of the hearing and that he was being tried by a rump of an outdated and unrepresentative House of Commons that had been elected more than eight years earlier.

"I stand more for the liberty of my people than any here that sitteth to be my judge," declared the king, an assertion that brought a furious retort from Bradshaw: "You, instead of answering, interrogate this court, which doth not become you in this condition."

Charles replied breezily, "Well, let me tell you, to say that you have legal authority will satisfy no reasonable man."

At this point, the hearing was adjourned for the Sabbath. As Charles was escorted back to his quarters, crowds jeered and cheered him in equal measure. There was no such division among his guards: To a man, they hated him. All weekend they subjected their prisoner to a barrage of insults and indignities, such as blowing tobacco smoke—which he detested—into his face whenever he tried to rest, all designed to wear him down and make him less resilient when court resumed on Monday morning.

At that time, Bradshaw took up where he had left off on Saturday. "The court expects that you apply yourself to the charge not to lose any more time, but to give a positive answer thereto."

Charles remained intransigent. "I would know by what power I am called hither—I mean lawful, there are many unlawful authorities in the world, there are robbers and highwaymen." Told he was being tried by the authority of the people of England, he snapped, "If power without law may make laws, I do not know what subject he is in England that can be sure of his life."

Bradshaw's fury rose. "Confess or deny the charge!"

"By what authority do you sit?"

"Take him away!" roared Bradshaw.

"I do require that I may give my reasons."

"'Tis not for a prisoner to *require*!"

"I am not an ordinary prisoner—"

At this, one of the commissioners, Colonel John Hewson, rushed forward, cried out "Justice!" and spat in the king's face.

"Well, sir," remarked Charles, wiping his face, "God hath justice in store for both you and me."

The next day, Bradshaw again attempted to get Charles to respond to the charge. When the defendant launched into yet another round of delaying tactics, Bradshaw instructed Cook to read the charge one final time. At its conclusion, Charles still refused to acknowledge the tribunal's legitimacy.

Ordered from Court

Bradshaw's patience finally cracked. "Sir!" he bellowed, "this is the third time you have publicly disowned this court and put an affront against it." Brushing aside Charles's protests, Bradshaw continued: "How far you have preserved the fundamental laws and freedom of the subject, your actions have spoken it. For truly, sir, men's intentions are used to being shown by their actions. You have written your meaning in bloody characters throughout the whole kingdom. Clerk, record the default! And, gentlemen, you that brought the prisoner, take him back again." Nonplussed at being dismissed in so peremptory a fashion, Charles began to shout out a response, but it was lost in the uproar as he was dragged away.

For the remainder of that week, the commission heard evidence in the Painted Chamber adjoining Westminster Hall, while Charles remained under guard at Cotton House. This was the period during which Cromwell turned the screws. Although the most powerful commissioner in attendance, he had taken little verbal part in the trial, but his was always the hand at the tiller. By Friday, he had steered the court into agreeing that the next day sentence would be passed.

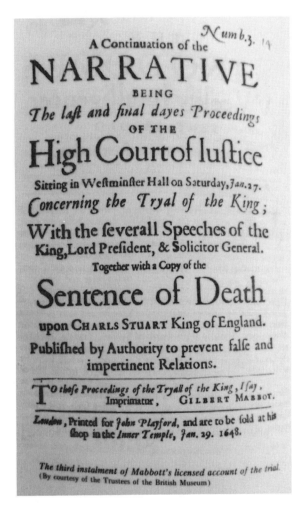

A Continuation of the *Numb.3.*

NARRATIVE

BEING

The last and final dayes Proceedings

OF THE

High Court of Iustice

Sitting in Westminster Hall on Saturday, Jan. 27.

Concerning the Tryal of the King;

With the severall Speeches of the King, Lord President, & Solicitor General.

Together with a Copy of the

Sentence of Death

upon CHARLS STUART King of England.

Published by Authority to prevent false and impertinent Relations.

To those Proceedings of the Tryall of the King, I say, Imprimatur, GILBERT MABBOT.

London, Printed for *John Playford*, and are to be sold at his shop in the *Inner Temple*, *Jan. 29.* 1648.

The third instalment of Mabbott's licensed account of the trial.
(By courtesy of the Trustees of the British Museum)

Pictured is a portion of the third installment of Mabbott's licensed account of Charles I's trial, published on January 29, 1648.

On January 27, Charles was brought back into Westminster Hall to hear his fate. As Bradshaw began to read aloud the verdict of the commissioners, two masked women in the gallery cried out, "It is a lie . . . Oliver Cromwell is a tyrant." One was thought to be Lady Fairfax, wife of one of the absent commissioners, but in the furor, the two dissidents managed to effect their escape, so it was impossible to be certain. When Bradshaw concluded, he allowed Charles one last statement, provided that he did not again impugn the court's integrity. It was time for the king to play his final card. Shrewdly, he requested an opportunity to address the Houses of Lords and Commons, in effect going over the head of this commission and asking directly for what was undeniably his right, according to the constitution.

This fair request caused considerable disquiet to some on the commission. One in particular, John Downes, shrugged off Cromwell's rebukes and demanded a full discussion of this sudden development. Bradshaw hastily adjourned the court. Out of public hearing, Downes gave further voice to his concerns but was impotent in the face of Cromwell's implacable will. Downes had only delayed the inevitable. A short while later, the court reconvened to hear the judgment. "For all which treasons and crimes this Court doth adjudge that the said Charles Stuart, as a tyrant, traytor, murtherer, and publique enimy to the good people of this nation, shall be put to death by the severing of his heade from his body."

Still protesting the illegality of his trial, Charles was hauled away to the Palace at Saint James to await execution. In all, 59 of the original 135 commissioners signed the death warrant, Bradshaw being first, then Lord Grey, then Oliver Cromwell.

Execution

Three days later, Charles stepped from a window at the Banqueting Hall in Westminster onto a specially erected wooden scaffold that had been draped in black. Earlier he had asked his valet to give him an extra shirt. "The season is so sharp as shall probably make me shake, which some observers may imagine proceeds from fear." In the few moments left him, he made a brief speech in which he reiterated his belief in the right of the monarchy. "I must tell you that the liberty and freedom [of the people] consists in having a government, those laws by which their life and their goods may be most their own. It is not for having a share in government, Sir, that is nothing pertaining to them. A subject and a sovereign are clear and different things." He then laid his head on the wooden block. A single blow of the executioner's ax and it was all over.

Britain proved to be a reluctant republic. On Cromwell's death in 1658, his son, Richard, assumed the mantle of lord protector, but lacking the forcefulness of character that so distinguished his father, he survived for barely a year. His departure for the Continent heralded the restoration of Charles II to the throne. A popular monarch, welcomed by most of the country, Charles immediately embarked on the pursuit of his father's inquisitors. Forty-one signatories to the death warrant were still alive. Many fled abroad to escape the royal wrath, but several were captured, and of these, nine were tried and put to death. Remorse did not feature prominently in their testimony. Thomas Harrison, one of the most disdainful of the regicides, proudly proclaimed, "This was not a thing done in a corner."

Even the grave offered no sanctuary from the new monarch's vengeance. In 1658, Cromwell had been buried amidst great pomp in Westminster Abbey.

Now, his body was exhumed and dragged through the streets of London to be hanged publicly at Tyburn. Later, it was reburied in a common pit. For the next two decades, until it was blown down in a gale, Cromwell's severed head stood on a pole outside Westminster Hall.

If history is divided on the merits of Charles I as a monarch and a man, there is less dispute about the consequences of his execution. Never again would a king or queen of England wield the kind of absolute power that previous generations had taken for granted. Quite literally at a stroke, the Divine Right of the monarchy was consigned to the pages of antiquity, and for that reason alone, the trial of Charles I must rank among the most significant in British history.

—Colin Evans

Suggestions for Further Reading

Ashley, Maurice. *The Battle of Naseby and the Fall of King Charles I.* New York: St. Martin's Press, 1992.

Bowle, J. *Charles I.* Boston: Little Brown, 1975.

Cannon, John and Ralph Griffiths. *The Oxford History of the British Monarchy.* Oxford: Oxford University Press, 1988.

Daniels, C. W. and J. Morrill. *Charles I.* Cambridge: Cambridge University Press, 1988.

Gregg, Pauline. *King Charles I.* Berkeley: University of California Press, 1984.

John Byng Court-Martial: 1756–57

Defendant: Admiral John Byng   **Crime Charged:** Dereliction of duty
Chief Defense Lawyer: None (Byng defended himself)
Judge Advocate: Charles Fearne   **Senior Presiding Officer:** Admiral
Thomas Smith   **Place:** Portsmouth, England   **Dates of Trial:** December 28,
1756–January 27, 1757   **Verdict:** Guilty   **Sentence:** Death

SIGNIFICANCE
The most infamous court-martial in British naval history.

By the beginning of 1756, information reaching England made it clear that war with France was inevitable. With the French fleet massing in the Mediterranean, intelligence reports warned that the island of Minorca, then under British control, was in imminent danger of attack. Despite the gravity of the situation, the British government dragged its heels, and not until March did they authorize a response. Admiral John Byng was ordered to the Mediterranean, with a fiat to defend Minorca at all costs.

Unfortunately, the ships put at his disposal were the very worst that the British navy had to offer—sluggish, leaky hulks in desperate need of repair—and only after considerable protest did Byng, aboard the *Ramillies*, lead his 10-ship squadron out into the English Channel on April 6, 1756. Undermanned, ill-equipped, and bedeviled by bad weather, the fleet limped into Gibraltar on May 2 to grim news: two weeks earlier 15,000 French troops had invaded Minorca and laid siege to the British garrison at Fort St. Philippe.

After making some much-needed repairs and taking on a detachment of fusiliers, Byng entered the Mediterranean and headed due northwest. Twelve days later, on May 20, he engaged the French fleet off Minorca. The fighting, fast and ferocious, cruelly exposed British deficiencies, as French warships under the Marquis de la Galissonnière scored at will. Questionable tactics and indifferent seamanship completed the rout. After consulting his fellow officers, Byng withdrew to Gibraltar. He arrived on June 20, by which time news of Galissonnière's triumph had already reached London. Desperate to divert attention from its own lamentable misconduct, the government ordered Byng back to England in disgrace. Upon his arrival, he was arrested for failing to relieve the garrison at Fort St. Philippe and told to prepare for court-martial.

On the morning of December 28, 1756, the court-martial convened aboard the *St. George* in Portsmouth harbor. The choice of venue was ironic: In happier days, Byng had been master of this very ship; now he was to be tried in the quarters he had once occupied. The court-martial, made up of four admirals (the most senior being Thomas Smith) and nine captains, listened closely as Judge Advocate Charles Fearne read out the charge: "that he, the said John Byng, having command of His Majesty's fleet in the Mediterranean . . . on the 20th day of May last, did withdraw, or keep back, and did not do his utmost to take, seize and destroy the ships of the French King . . . and that he . . . did not do his utmost to relieve St. Philip's Castle . . . but acted contrary to and in breach of his instructions." The rest of that day was filled with points of law, and the court adjourned without having heard any testimony.

First Witness

The next morning Vice Admiral Temple West, who had also been recalled to England in disgrace, took the stand. He detailed the battle off Minorca, in particular the willingness or otherwise of some British ships to engage the enemy. Byng drew from West several helpful admissions, including a ship-by-ship account of the British fleet's unpreparedness that so alarmed the court that it ordered the room to be cleared while it discussed the matter.

Next to testify was General William Blakeney, elderly governor of the British garrison on Minorca, who had surrendered Fort St. Philippe to the French on June 20 after a heavy attack. Oddly enough, Blakeney returned to

The trial of British Admiral John Byng occurred on the sailing vessel, *St. George* in 1757. Byng is sitting in a chair, placed in front of the table, and faces witnesses across from him. Other court members view the trial from the far side of the table.

England a hero and was granted a barony. Ever since, he had noisily broadcast the view that if only Byng had landed his forces, Minorca could have been saved from the French, a clearly preposterous assumption, as his subsequent capitulation demonstrated. Under constant harrying from Byng, the old general reluctantly conceded his foolishness, then went on to embarrass both the court and himself with a rambling bout of self-justification that led to his being excused.

Then followed testimony from the various captains under Byng's command. Some, like Augustus Hervey, were wholeheartedly supportive, but others, in particular Captain James Gilchrist, saw a chance to settle old scores. He had been rejected by Byng earlier when a candidate for promotion; now his assertion that "Admiral Byng did not bear down before the wind upon the enemy, nor any of his division" had a clear ring of vindictiveness about it.

Byng had always maintained that the reason for his perceived tardiness had been that another ship, *Intrepid,* had unexpectedly crossed his bow. After *Intrepid*'s commander, Captain Philip Durell, admitted that he had contravened the 24th Article of the Fighting Instructions by going to the assistance of another ship, he was asked by Captain Charles Holmes, a member of the court, "Might not the *Ramillies* in the heat of the battle have been liable to run on board of you?" But before Durell could answer, another jurist intervened: "If you think it will hurt you, don't answer." It was an invitation that Durell accepted gratefully, and he left without further comment.

In many respects, the most impressive witness was not a naval man, but Lord Robert Bertie, commander of the fusiliers, who had joined the fleet at Gibraltar. When Bertie took the stand, the court-martial was floundering under a mountainous burden of disputed battle tactics, contentious wind directions, and varying interpretations of the Fighting Instructions. Bertie brought much-needed clarity to the proceedings with his confirmation that the *Intrepid* had sailed dangerously close under the *Ramillies'* bow.

Eye Inflammation

Byng rose triumphantly to his feet. Throughout the hearing he had labored under a double handicap: First, he was denied counsel, and thus had to defend himself; second, an eye inflammation made it impossible for him to read documents. He now overcame this latter impediment by passing a written series of questions to Admiral Smith, who then put them to Bertie.

"Did you perceive any backwardness in the Admiral during the action, or any mark of fear or confusion, either from his countenance or behavior?"

"He seemed to me to give his orders coolly and distinctly, and I do not apprehend that he was the least wanting in personal courage."

"Did the Admiral appear solicitous to engage the enemy, and to assist His Majesty's ships that were engaged with the enemy?"

"Yes ... I never heard anyone of the *Ramillies* speak the least disrespectfully of the Admiral or ever hint that [he] had not done his duty."

This was the kind of clear, unequivocal testimony that should have brought the indictment to its knees, but, of course, Bertie was a *soldier*, and it is hard to escape the impression that the court-martial accorded less weight to his testimony than it did to supposed naval experts.

One of those "experts" was Captain Henry Ward, master of the *Culloden* and a man whose antipathy toward the defendant was transparent, especially since his own conduct during the battle had been the subject of criticism. Ward's claim to have approached within 100 yards of the enemy failed to explain why only 16 of *Culloden*'s guns had been fired and how his ship had managed to avoid sustaining so much as a scratch. The inconsistencies mounted. Ward's first lieutenant, James Worth, was vague about when the ship's log was compiled— "I can give no . . . account of when it was inserted,"—but emphatically denied suggestions that essential details were changed several days after the battle. This suspicion had arisen when it was found that the *Culloden*'s log was virtually a word-for-word copy of that of the *Intrepid*.

On January 18, 1757, Byng again handed the court a sheaf of papers, which were read aloud by Judge Advocate Fearne. They reiterated Byng's belief that he was being made a scapegoat for political ineptitude: "I never retreated from the island till it was impracticable to make any further attempt; . . . the place was not lost by me . . . but by those who might have sent double the force two months earlier."

Testimony concluded on a peculiar note: Byng had hoped to call several defense witnesses, but for reasons that have never been made public, he was restricted to just two witnesses, neither of whom added anything of any substance.

Plea for Clemency

Now it was up to the court to decide the outcome. Ordinarily, such procedures were quick, but here there were too many factors at work for a speedy outcome. At last, on January 27, 1757, after a week of equivocation, the decision was announced. Byng, confidently expecting acquittal, listened in disbelief to the guilty verdict. Although sentence of death was mandatory, it was significant that every member of the court-martial added a plea for clemency. However, George II, in tandem with his senior ministers, was in no mood for mercy. The fall of Minorca had engulfed Britain in the Seven Years' War, and public outrage demanded a sacrifice.

On March 14, 1757, aboard the *Monarch*, Byng went before a firing squad of scarlet-coated marines. He knelt on a cushion and fastened a handkerchief around his eyes, then took a second handkerchief from his pocket. After a few moments of prayer, he dropped the handkerchief to the deck. It was the signal to the firing squad. Later that day, the master of the *Monarch* recorded in his log: "At 12 Mr. Byng was shot dead. . . ."

The court-martial of Admiral John Byng has long been considered one of the grimmest episodes in British judicial history. He might not have been a great sailor, but his integrity was beyond reproach, and the worst that could be leveled against him were accusations of indecisiveness and perhaps naïveté. He remains the only British admiral to be executed for dereliction of duty.

Admiral Byng was condemned to death at his court-martial. Aboard the HMS *Monarch,* Byng signals to the firing squad that he is ready to die.

An interesting commentary to this case was provided by the great French writer Voltaire. He had followed Byng's tribulations with keen interest, and in *Candide* he used the incident to highlight British hypocrisy. Upon visiting Portsmouth, Candide happens to see someone facing a firing squad onboard ship. Told that the condemned man is a high-ranking naval officer, Candide further learns that "in this country it is thought well to kill an admiral from time to time to encourage the others."

—Colin Evans

Suggestions for Further Reading

Crimes and Punishment. Vol. 2. London: Phoebus, 1974.

Encyclopaedia Britannica, Vol. 2. Chicago: Encyclopedia Britannica, 1993.

Pope, Dudley. *At 12 Mr. Byng Was Shot. . . .* Philadelphia: Lippincott, 1962.

Souden, John. *Byng's Tours.* London: Century, 1991.

Bounty Mutineers Court-Martial: 1792

Defendants: Thomas Burkett, Michael Byrn, Joseph Coleman, Thomas Ellison, Peter Heywood, Thomas McIntosh, John Millward, James Morrison, William Muspratt, Charles Norman **Chief Defense Lawyers:** Stephen Barney, Edward Christian **Crime Charged:** Mutiny **Judge:** Court-martial presided over by Lord Alexander Hood **Place:** Portsmouth, England **Dates of Court-Martial:** September 12–18, 1792 **Verdict:** Burkett, Ellison, Heywood, Millward, Morrison, Muspratt—guilty. However, Heywood and Morrison were pardoned, and Muspratt's conviction was overturned. **Sentence:** Death

SIGNIFICANCE

Much discussed and much filmed, the mutiny on the *Bounty* is one of history's most enduring nautical sagas.

On December 23, 1787, the *Bounty*, a 215-ton merchantman, put out from Spithead on the English south coast, bound for the Pacific, half a world away. Its mission was to collect breadfruit plants from the Society Islands for transportation to the West Indies, where it was hoped they would flourish and provide a cheap, easily cultivated diet for the slaves. Master of the vessel was an ambitious 33-year-old lieutenant named William Bligh. Having fallen behind in the promotion race, Bligh saw this as a prime opportunity to revive his flagging career. He had at his command a 45-strong crew, ranging from seasoned officers to press-ganged civilians, and in a remarkably short period of time he managed to alienate them all. He achieved this through a variety of means, but it was primarily his ungovernable temper that did most to bring about the estrangement. At times of stress—frequent in such cramped confines—Bligh's incoherent, arm-waving furies were a sight to behold. Insults poured from his lips at a prodigious rate, and whenever his tongue ran out of venom, there was always the lash to keep his men in check.

Floggings became an almost daily occurrence. Oddly enough, the crew accepted this as part and parcel of late 18th-century naval life; what the crew could *not* tolerate was the hunger. From the outset, Bligh starved his crew, misappropriating food for himself and blaming any discrepancy on the rabble below decks. Those who complained saw their already meager rations halved.

Throughout 1788, the *Bounty* was a floating powder keg as it plied the Pacific in search of the elusive breadfruit. By the following spring, morale aboard ship had sunk to lethal levels. It bottomed-out on the night of April 27, 1789, when Bligh accused his second-in-command, Fletcher Christian, of stealing coconuts. For Christian, an honorable man, it was the final straw; the next day, he and half a dozen crew members seized control of the ship.

Bligh and 18 others were placed in a small launch and cast adrift in the South Pacific. The remainder, including men who had taken no active part in the mutiny, disappeared in the *Bounty*. Six weeks and more than 3,000 miles later, Bligh's tiny boat and the majority of its crew reached safety on Timor. By any consideration, their survival must be counted among the most heroic of all time, as Bligh glowingly pointed out in his report. Less easy to explain was how a mere handful of men had managed to usurp his authority. In typical fashion, the lieutenant simply upped the number of mutineers to include all but three of those who had remained on the *Bounty*. A ship dispatched to arrest these men eventually located 10 of them living on the island of Tahiti, and they were returned to England to face charges of mutiny. Signally absent from these captives was Fletcher Christian: Neither he nor the *Bounty* was anywhere to be seen.

Captain William Bligh had just completed his triumphant launch voyage in 1790 when this painting was done in London by artist J. Russell.

Best-Seller

Such were the distances and the slowness of communications that the court-martial did not get under way until late 1792, by which time Captain Bligh (he had since been promoted) was once again in the Pacific and so was unable to give evidence. He had made good use of the interim, writing a best-selling account of the mutiny, with himself as hero, and blaming its genesis on the fact that the crew had become besotted with Tahitian women. This was not an issue that troubled the court-martial when it gathered on September 12 aboard H.M.S. *Duke*, moored in Portsmouth Harbor. Headed by Lord Alexander Hood, the panel of naval officers had no interest in discerning the causes of the mutiny, merely the identity of the mutineers.

Because of the navy's long-standing aversion to lawyers, most of the defendants received only oblique legal assistance from land-based advocates. The most visible counsel, and, as it turned out, the most helpful, was Stephen Barney, who aided Muspratt. Also conspicuous was Edward Christian, who held a watching brief for his absent brother.

Testimony from numerous crew members soon made it apparent that there was no case against Charles Norman, Joseph Coleman, and Thomas McIntosh. Bligh himself had said as much in his report, which was before the court, admitting that all three had been detained aboard the *Bounty* against their will. Similar sympathy was felt for Michael Byrn, a half-blind Irish fiddler, whose sole function had been to provide music for the crew. His attempt to board the launch had been thwarted by the same disability that now made it necessary for his statement to be read out for him. It began achingly: "It has pleased the Almighty, amongst the Events of His unsearchable Providence, nearly to deprive me of Sight, which often puts out of my Power to carry out the Intentions of my Mind into Execution." Not even 18th-century courts-martial were immune to such moving submissions; his acquittal was a formality.

Less straightforward was the case against Peter Heywood, charged under the stern law that to do nothing during a mutiny was to aid the mutineers by default.

William Purcell, who had been cast adrift in the boat with Bligh, said he had seen Midshipman Heywood on deck, appearing confused and with one hand idly fingering a cutlass. When Purcell had cried out, "In the name of God, Peter, what do you do with that?" Heywood had immediately relinquished his grip on the cutlass, apparently unaware till then what inference might be drawn from this involuntary gesture.

Lieutenant Thomas Hayward told of seeing Heywood unarmed on deck, and that he "rather supposed" Heywood was on the side of the mutineers; however, this was "only . . . an opinion," as Heywood "was not in the least employed during the active part of it."

The crucial evidence came from Lieutenant John Hallet. He had seen Heywood on deck, not armed, not doing anything, merely "standing still, looking attentively towards Captain Bligh." Then, "Captain Bligh said something to him, but what I did not hear, upon which he [Heywood] laughed, turned round, and walked away. Mr. Bligh was then standing with his arms tied behind his back—Christian holding the cord with one hand and bayonet to his breast with the other." What Hallet neglected to mention was that during this confrontation, Bligh was dressed only in a nightshirt and acting in so demented a fashion that anyone might have found humor in such circumstances. Now it appeared as though a single laugh might put Heywood's neck in a noose. Other witnesses rallied to Heywood's cause, however, canceling out much of Hallet's testimony.

Thomas Burkett, giving evidence on his own behalf, described Hayward and Hallet tearfully pleading with Christian *not* to send them away in the boat with Bligh, an allegation repeated by Thomas Ellison, who added that when the "two gentlemen rec'd the order they weep't bitterly." The case against Ellison, Burkett, and John Millward was so overwhelming as to eliminate any chance of acquittal.

Solo Defense

James Morrison, the boatswain's mate, was the only accused to conduct his own defense without benefit of counsel. As the journal that he kept while on board the *Bounty* reveals, he was an observant, intelligent man, and the thoughtful manner in which he questioned all the witnesses made a very great impression on the court-martial. He, like Heywood, had done nothing, but under maritime law, both were culpable, as was made plain on September 18, 1792, when the minutes were read out: "The Court . . . agreed that the Charges had been proved against the said Peter Heywood, James Morrison, Thomas Ellison, Thomas Burkett, John Millward and William Muspratt, and did adjudge them and each of them to suffer Death by being hanged by the Neck."

However, the minutes went on, "The Court, in Consideration of various Circumstances, did humbly and most earnestly recommend the said Peter Heywood and James Morrison to His Majesty's Royal Mercy." As expected, Norman, Coleman, McIntosh, and Byrn were acquitted.

Muspratt had a final card to play. Under prompting from Stephen Barney, he argued that, because all the prisoners had been tried together and so could not give evidence for each other, he had been unable to call Byrn and Norman, who, he stated, would otherwise have given evidence for him. In this respect, a court-martial differed from a civil trial, and it was, submitted Muspratt, a "difference, my Lord, [that] is dreadful to the Subject and fatal to me."

On October 26, 1792, Heywood and Morrison received the king's pardon, and Muspratt's conviction was overturned on a point of law. For the three remaining mutineers there was no mercy. Boats filled Portsmouth Harbor on the morning of October 29 as the men were hanged from the yardarm aboard H.M.S. *Brunswick*.

The whereabouts of the *Bounty* remained a mystery until 1808, when the American ship *Topaz* put in to Pitcairn Island, a remote atoll in the East Pacific, only to discover English-speaking natives there. One islander, the solitary white man, gave his name as Alexander Smith and claimed to be the last surviving

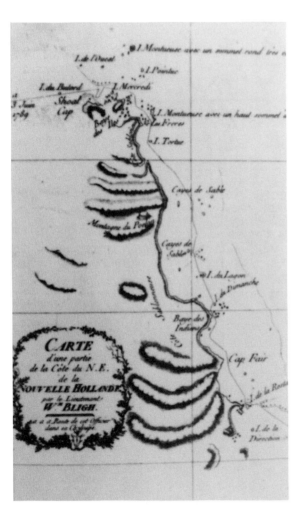

This map, published in 1790, was taken from Captain William Bligh's narrative and shows the path of his trip within the Great Barrier Reef.

member of the *Bounty* mutineers. The rest, he said, had either died of natural causes or had been murdered. In 1957, divers confirmed that a wreck found off Pitcairn Island was, indeed, the *Bounty*.

But the story has one final twist. In 1808, Peter Heywood was walking down Fore Street in Plymouth Dock when he saw a man ahead of him who was the perfect image of his old friend Fletcher Christian. The man, unsettled by Heywood's obvious interest, hastened into a maze of narrow cobbled alleyways, where Heywood lost him. Other reports, too, placed the architect of the mutiny on the *Bounty* back in England in the early 19th century, though there is no evidence to substantiate any of these claims.

—Colin Evans

Suggestions for Further Reading

Crimes and Punishment. Vol. 6. London: Phoebus, 1974.

McKee, Alexander. *H.M.S. Bounty.* New York: William Morrow, 1962.

Rutter, Owen. *The Court-Martial of the* Bounty *Mutineers*. London: Hodge, 1931.

Wilkinson, C. S. *The Wake of the Bounty.* London: Cassell, 1953.

Louis XVI and Marie Antoinette Trials: 1792 and 1793

Defendants: Louis XVI and Marie Antoinette   **Crimes Charged:** Various acts of treason   **Chief Defense Lawyers:** Chrètien de L. de Malesherbes, François-Denis Tronchet, and Romain de Sèze (Louis); Claude Chauveau-Lagarde (Marie)   **Chief Prosecutors:** National Convention (Louis), Revolutionary Tribunal (Marie)   **Judges:** National Convention (Louis), Revolutionary Tribunal (Marie)   **Place:** Paris, France   **Dates of Trials:** December 26, 1792 (Louis); October 14–15, 1793 (Marie)   **Verdict:** Guilty (both)   **Sentence:** Execution by guillotine (both)

SIGNIFICANCE

The trials of Louis XVI and Marie Antoinette brought France's ancien régime to a close. The proceedings, with their political aims and mockery of legal forms, foreshadowed the show trials of the totalitarian era of the 20th century.

For a time, Louis XVI tried to accommodate the French Revolution. Military force, after all, had failed. His calling out of troops in the spring of 1789 touched off insurrectionary outbreaks in Paris, culminating in the storming of the Bastille on July 14. In the aftermath, Louis and his ministers devised various constitutional schemes that they hoped would reconcile republicanism and the monarchy. Nothing seemed to work. In effect under house arrest, he attempted flight: In June 1791, Louis and his consort, Queen Marie Antoinette, reached Varennes near the Belgian frontier before they were intercepted, arrested, and returned to Paris.

War with Austria brought on the monarchy's final collapse. The powerful Girondist faction pushed Louis into the conflict in April 1792, but Parisian opinion blamed the king alone for the initial French setbacks. On August 10, armed crowds attacked Tuileries Palace. The king, Marie Antoinette, and their two children escaped, though there were hundreds of casualties among the Swiss palace guards and the insurrectionists. A day or two later, at the urging of the Commune of Paris, the National Assembly "suspended" the king and jailed the royal family in the medieval keep known as the Temple.

It was a comfortable sort of prison, at least at first. A domestic staff of 13 looked after the family, and Louis's captors allowed him to send out for books. He was forbidden, however, to wear his decorations on his afternoon walk, and the authorities, perhaps suspecting he might try to cheat the guillotine, denied him a razor. Louis protested by refusing to allow himself to be shaved. He and Antoinette spent their mornings tutoring the dauphin, Louis Charles, and his sister, Marie Thèrese.

The Indictment

The National Convention summoned the king on December 11, referring to him, over his protests, as Louis Capet. "It was the surname of one of my ancestors," he tried to explain. Before a full house and packed galleries, the king stood for the reading of the indictment. It accused him, among other acts of treason, of having three times ordered troops to fire on the people (the last time on August 10) and, incidentally, of having cornered the Hamburg coffee and sugar markets.

The convention also charged Louis with attempting to seduce the French with alms. "You distributed money among the populace for the treacherous purpose of acquiring popularity and enslaving the nation," Bertrand Barrère, the convention president, suggested.

"I always took pleasure in relieving the needy," Louis allowed, "but never had any treacherous purpose."

The convention ordered Louis returned to the Temple and held in solitary confinement to await trial. Louis's three defending lawyers had less than two weeks to prepare his case. They advised him to challenge the authority of the National Convention, which sat as both judge and jury. The king decided instead to refute the accusations, arguing that, as the legitimate ruler of France, he had broken no law.

Marie Antoinette, as a young woman, in a painting by Le Maitre.

A number of radical deputies asserted that Louis should not be tried at all, simply sentenced. In any case, argued one of their leaders, Maximilien Robespierre, the trial already had taken place; the armed outbreak of August 10 had settled the question of the king's guilt. "Louis cannot be judged; he has already been judged," said Robespierre. "To suggest putting Louis XVI on trial, in whatever way, is a step backward; it is a counter-revolutionary idea, because it put the Revolution itself in the dock." Nevertheless, the convention chose to observe the forms of law and bring the accused to court.

The Trial of Louis XVI

The trial opened the morning of December 26, 1792. One of the king's lawyers, Romain de Sèze, argued that, far from being a tyrant, Louis had been a victim of circumstances. He ended his opening statement with an appeal to a higher verdict. "I stop before history," he said, "remember that it will pass judgment on your judgment and that its judgment will endure."

Clean-shaven now (his razor had been restored to him), Louis spoke briefly. Observers were struck by his calm, quiet dignity. He alluded to his attempts to reach an accord with the revolutionaries, and he emphatically denied ever having knowingly caused a French death. In one of his longer speeches of his one-day trial, he said,

> I confess that the repeated signs I have given that I love the people and my behavior throughout my reign seem to me abundant proof that I was not afraid to spare any trouble in order to prevent bloodshed, and forever banish such an imputation.

The verdict was a foregone conclusion. When the convention met again on January 15, 1793, all 693 members present voted the king's guilt. The sentence was another matter. In a dramatic roll call that lasted throughout the night of January 16–17, each deputy approached the bar to call out his vote. Some lingered to deliver short speeches. "I do not recognize a humanity that massacres people and pardons despots," said Robespierre, casting his ballot for execution. In a surprisingly close vote, the deputies approved the death sentence; there were several pleas for a reprieve. The American revolutionary Thomas Paine, speaking through an interpreter, proposed deporting Louis to the United States, where he could be rehabilitated in the purer atmosphere of the New World.

The convention confirmed the death sentence on January 20. That evening, the jailers allowed Louis to see his family for the first time since December 11. Marie Antoinette and the children had not been told of the outcome. In a short, painful meeting, he let them know where matters stood.

The Execution

The execution grounds were in what is today the Place de la Concorde. Louis arose early on January 21 and heard mass, and at 8 o'clock the guards came for him. He rode in an enclosed coach, escorted by 1,200 foot soldiers. The entourage made its way from the Temple to the Place de la Concorde at a walking pace, a journey of two hours. At around 10 o'clock, under a gray, murky sky, Louis mounted the steep steps of the scaffold.

A large crowd, 20,000 people or perhaps more, had gathered to watch. The executioner's men removed Louis's coat, tied his hands behind his back, and cut his hair. He launched into a speech. "I die innocent of all the crimes of which I have been charged," he called out; then a roll of drums muffled his last words. The executioner strapped him onto the plank, slid it forward and gave a tug on the cord. The blade fell. One of the men plucked the king's severed head out of the basket into which it had fallen and showed it, dripping blood, to the crowd.

The Trial and Execution of the Widow Capet

Marie Antoinette, the daughter of the Austrian Emperor Francis I and Maria Thèresa, had been a strong-willed, extravagant queen and a conservative, even reactionary, adviser to her husband. The guards came during the night of August 2, 1793, and carried her off to the most squalid of Parisian prisons, the Conciergerie on the Ile de la Cité. She was locked, alone, in an 11-foot by 6-foot room, with two gendarmes assigned to watch over her day and night.

Feelings ran high against the widow Capet. Marie Antoinette's captors referred to her as "the Austrian she-wolf" and as "a monster who needed to slake her thirst on the blood of the French." She was only 37, but prison had aged her. Her hair had gone thin, and she had lost weight; she looked haggard and ill. For some time she had suffered severe, agonizingly painful cramps during her menstrual periods.

The Revolutionary Tribunal sent for the queen on the evening of October 12. In a shadowy room, lit only by two flickering candles, the interrogators set out their case. Marie Antoinette, they stipulated, had been queen. "One cannot reign innocently," the radical journalist and Paris Commune leader Jacques Réné Hébert had written, and so she could be accounted guilty on this charge from the start. The examiners went on to question her about sending money and information to Austria to be used in the war against France, about influencing her husband against liberal ideas, and about instigating the 1791 flight to Varennes.

There were 35 questions altogether, though some were statements really, not queries at all, as in this sweeping charge from the examining magistrate,

In prison, Marie Antoinette bids a sad farewell to her children prior to her execution in October 1793.

Nicolas Hermann: "Never for one moment have you ceased wanting to destroy liberty. You wanted to reign at any price and to reascend the throne over the dead bodies of patriots."

"We had no need to reascend the throne; we were there," Marie Antoinette answered. "But we never wished for anything but France's happiness."

Hermann asked whether Marie Antoinette believed that kings were necessary for the people's well-being.

"An individual cannot decide such matters," she replied.

That night, after the prisoner had been returned to her cell, the prosecutor, Antoine Fouquier-Tinville, drew up an eight-page indictment against her.

The Trial

The tribunal ordered the trial to go forward on October 14, a Monday. Marie Antoinette's counsel asked for a delay, protesting he had not been given sufficient time to study the indictment and prepare a defense. The request was denied, and the proceedings opened on schedule, Hermann presiding. A succession of witnesses testified that the queen had conspired with Austria against France, had organized a counterrevolutionary movement, had engineered the famine of 1789.

These were familiar accusations. Then, shockingly, Hèbert, the radical journalist, charged that she had taught her son to masturbate—and worse. "From what young Capet has confessed," said Hèbert, referring to Louis Charles, the dauphin, "there had been, between mother and son, an act of incest."

Marie Antoinette said nothing at first. Perhaps her voice had failed her. Finally, Hermann asked, "What reply do you make to the witness's deposition?"

"I have no knowledge of the incidents Hèbert speaks of."

She had long been the subject of lurid sexual gossip: couplings with the king's own brother, various ménages, a lesbian love triangle. But she could hardly have been prepared for this. After a short silence, one of the jurors insisted that she respond. "I appeal to all the mothers who are in this room," Marie Antoinette said at last, "is such a crime possible?"

The prosecution continued its assault on the queen's character. On the second day, Tuesday, Fouquier-Tinville returned to the accusation that she had been a faithless and manipulative wife.

"It seems to be proved, despite your denials, that through your influence you made the former king, your husband, do whatever you wished."

"There is a difference between advising that something should be done and having it carried out."

"You made use of his weak character to make him carry out many evil deeds."

"I never knew him to have such a character as you describe."

Late at night, near the end of the proceedings, Marie Antoinette rose to make a final statement. "Yesterday I did not know the witnesses and I did not know what they would testify," she said. "Well, no one has uttered anything positive against me. I conclude by observing that I was only the wife of Louis XVI and I was bound to conform to his will." This plea for mitigation, if that was what it was, had no apparent effect on the jurors. They deliberated for barely an hour before returning a guilty verdict and a sentence of death on two specific counts: aiding Austria with money and information, and plotting to touch off a civil war.

Marie Antoinette awoke at dawn the next day, rose, and changed into a white piqué dress. At 11 o'clock, the executioners came. They tied her hands and cut her hair and led her out to the tumbrel. The queen of France sat facing backward in the open cart, which made its way slowly from the island prison to the Place de la Concorde. "The bitch was audacious and insolent right to the very end," Hèbert wrote. Not so; her strength failed her at the last and she had to be helped out of the tumbrel and onto the scaffold. There, the executioner affixed her to the plank and sent the blade hissing down. She was buried in an unmarked grave.

—Michael Golay

Suggestions for Further Reading

Cronin, Vincent. *Louis and Antoinette*. New York: William Morrow, 1975.

Doyle, William. *The Oxford History of the French Revolution*. Oxford, England: Clarendon Press, 1989.

Jordan, David. *The King's Trial*. Berkeley: University of California Press, 1979.

Schama, Simon. *Citizens: A Chronicle of the French Revolution*. New York: Alfred A. Knopf, 1989.

Walzer, Michael, ed. *Regicide and Revolution*. Cambridge, England: Cambridge University Press, 1974.

Charlotte Corday Trial: 1793

Defendant: Charlotte Corday d'Armont   **Crime Charged:** Murder
Chief Defense Lawyer: Chauveau de la Garde   **Chief Prosecutor:** Antoine
Fouquier-Tinville   **Judge:** Jacques Montané   **Place:** Paris, France
Dates of Trial: July 13–17, 1793   **Verdict:** Guilty
Sentence: Death by guillotine

SIGNIFICANCE

Charlotte Corday's killing of the Jacobin Jean-Paul Marat unleashed a new and
more destructive phase of the Reign of Terror in revolutionary France. To royalists
and moderate opponents of the Jacobins, she became a rallying point: a heroine
and a martyr.

Girondin refugees poured into the Norman town of Caen in the late spring of
1793. The militant Jacobins had driven their moderate rivals from the
Convention in Paris and scattered them. Girondins were filling the prisons and
providing a steady stream of victims for the Reign of Terror of Robespierre,
Danton, and Jean-Paul Marat. In Caen and in other provincial centers, Girondin
leaders hoped to regroup, rally, and recruit a counterrevolutionary army for a
march on Paris.

Girondins had reason to believe the Jacobin ascendancy would be short-
lived. In Lyon, Marseille, and Toulon, moderate factions were in revolt against
Paris and the radicals. Social and economic conditions were becoming desperate:
Unemployment had risen, prices were shooting upward, food and other
necessaries were in short supply. And Jacobin excesses—arrests, extortion, and
the incessant whirring of the great blade of the guillotine—had turned many
ordinary people away from the Revolution.

The Making of an Assassin

In Caen in the summer of 1793, Charlotte Corday d'Armont read, listened,
and decided to act. She was born into a family of minor Norman gentry and was a
distant descendant of the dramatist Pierre Corneille. Corday was convent-
educated, brought up on the works of Plutarch, Voltaire, and Rousseau. Corday
became a champion of the Republic, which she exalted as the agent of the moral

transformation of France. The Jacobins, she believed, were destroying the Revolution.

Lurid stories of the Terror circulated in Caen, a center of Girondin strength in mid-1793. Norman leaders drafted a manifesto denouncing the Convention as a "conspiratorial commune engorged with blood and gold." The Girondin press in Caen identified the chief culprit as Marat, the most notorious and bloodthirsty of all the Jacobins:

> Let Marat's head fall and the Republic is saved. Purge France of this man of blood. Marat sees the Public Safety only in a river of blood; well then his own must flow, for his head must fall to save two hundred thousand others.

So Charlotte Corday, 24 years old, resolved to become a patriotic avenger, a martyr in the Republican cause. "One can die but once," she wrote a friend, "and what consoles me for the horror of our situation is that no one will lose in losing me."

She had a personal motive as well. As her mother lay dying in childbirth in 1782, the curé of the church of Saint-Gilles in Caen, the Abbé Gombault, had given her last rites. Eleven years later, the Jacobins forced him from his church, threatened to deport him, and finally arrested him. On April 5, 1793, the Abbé Gombault became the first of the Caennais to go to the guillotine.

The Killing

Jean-Paul Marat had risen to the height of his powers by the summer of 1793. He had been a scientist-physician before the Revolution, interested in optics, aeronautics, and electrical therapy. Europe's scientific elite had not taken him seriously, regarding him as a bit of a quack. With the upheaval of 1789 he found his true vocation at last—and a means of avenging himself on an ungrateful establishment. He became a Revolutionary journalist, the apocalyptic, confrontational, and scurrilous editor of *L'Ami du Peuple*. Marat's birdlike appearance led his friends to liken him to an eagle. To his enemies, he was a carrion crow.

Corday's Victorian-era biographer, Austin Dobson, sketched Marat as a failed and embittered monster, "half dwarf, half maniac, foiled plagiarist and *savant manqué*, prurient romancer, rancorous libeler, envious, resentful and despised." In July 1793, he was suffering intensely from a recurrent ailment that caused his skin to break out in gross sores and scaly flakes all over his body. He could find relief only in a cool bath, and so he had set up to work from the tub in the tiled bathroom of his apartment in the rue des Cordeliers.

On July 9, Corday boarded a coach in Caen bound for Paris. Reaching the capital two days later, she took lodgings in the rue des Victoires. On the morning of the 13th, a bright, hot Saturday, she set out for the Palais-Royal, stopping at a shop in the galleries there to buy a city hat, a dark one with green ribbons. And at a cutler's shop she bought a knife, a wooden-handled kitchen knife with a 5-inch blade.

She had hoped to kill Marat in the Convention, in front of his accomplices and accessories. Instead, she had to settle for a visit to the rue des Cordeliers. She took a carriage there, arriving around 11:30. A woman turned her away at the door, saying Marat was too ill to receive callers. She wrote him a brief and tantalizing note, saying she brought evidence of conspiracies among the escaped Girondins.

Corday returned at 7 that evening with another note requesting an audience. This time, in the confusion of deliveries of newspapers and bread, she managed to reach the head of the stairs before anyone stopped her. She began to speak in a high voice of treason in Caen, hoping Marat would overhear.

"Let her in," he called out from the bath.

She pulled a chair up next to the tub. For a quarter hour they discussed counterrevolutionary intrigue, and Corday supplied Marat with a list of the Caen plotters. "Good," he told her. "In a few days I will have them all guillotined."

At these words, Corday drew the knife from the top of her dress and struck downward, hard, plunging the blade deep beneath the clavicle on Marat's right side. He sank into the water, tinged red now from the blood gushing from his severed carotid artery. When he called out, an aide rushed in and threw a chair at the assassin. A neighbor who had heard the cry rushed in from across the street and tried to stanch the bleeding. But within a few minutes, Marat was dead.

Charlotte Corday was guillotined on July 17, 1793, for the stabbing death of Jacobin leader, Jean-Paul Marat.

Trial and Execution

Revolutionary justice was swift. Six policemen interrogated Corday in Marat's apartment immediately after the killing. She made no attempt to deny her responsibility.

She had come from Caen for the sole purpose of killing Jean-Paul Marat, she said, and she had acted quite alone.

An angry crowd gathered to shout for Corday's death as the police led her from the house in the rue des Cordeliers to a cell in the Abbaye prison. There, and later in the Conciergerie, she continued to assert that she had not been part of an intrigue, that she had neither required nor sought assistance to carry out her assassin's errand.

All the same, the judges of the Revolutionary Tribunal were certain there was a vast web of conspiracy. "It has been mathematically demonstrated that this monster to whom nature has given the form of a woman is an envoy of . . . all the other conspirators of Caen," the Jacobin Georges Couthon insisted. But Corday would admit only to having read Girondin newspapers.

"Was it from those newspapers that you learned that Marat was an anarchist?" asked Jacques Montané, the tribunal president.

"Yes, I knew that he was perverting France. I have killed one man to save a hundred thousand. I was a republican well before the Revolution and I have never lacked energy."

Montané wondered whether she had practiced before attacking Marat. She flared at the question, then admitted it had been a lucky blow.

"Who were the persons who counseled you to commit this murder?" he went on.

"I would never have committed such an attack on the advice of others," she repeated. "I alone conceived the plan and executed it."

Finally, Montané asked Corday what she thought she had achieved: "Do you think you have killed all the Marats?"

"With this one dead, the others, perhaps, will be afraid."

The tribunal moved swiftly to convict and condemn her. Dressed in the scarlet shirt of an assassin, she composed her last letters in the cell in the Conciergerie. "I beg you to forget me or rather rejoice at my fate," she wrote her father. "The cause is good."

The executioner came for her in the early evening of July 17. She stood upright in the tumbrel, knees braced against the tailgate, all the way to the scaffold. Pierre Notelet stood among the onlookers crowding the rue Saint-Honoré to see her pass. Her image haunted him for a long time.

"Her beautiful face was so calm that one would have said she was a statue," Notelet recalled. "For eight days I was in love with Charlotte Corday."

—*Michael Golay*

Suggestions for Further Reading

Dobson, Austin. *Four Frenchwomen*. Freeport, N.Y.: Books for Libraries Press, 1972 reprint.

Doyle, William. *The Oxford History of the French Revolution*. Oxford: Clarendon Press, 1989.

Schama, Simon. *Citizens: A Chronicle of the French Revolution*. New York: Alfred A. Knopf, 1989.

Wilson, Robert McNair. *Women of the French Revolution*. Port Washington, N.Y.: Kennikat Press, 1970.

Daniel M'Naghten Trial: 1843

Defendant: Daniel M'Naghten   **Crime Charged:** Murder
Chief Defense Lawyer: Sir Alexander Cockburn, Q.C.
Chief Prosecutors: Sir William Follet, Q.C.; Russell Gurney   **Judges:** Lord
Chief Justice Tindal, Mr. Justice Williams, Mr. Justice Coleridge
Place: London, England   **Dates of Trial:** March 3–4, 1843
Verdict: Not guilty

SIGNIFICANCE
This landmark case resulted in the establishment of the guidelines for determining insanity in Anglo-American law.

In the gloom of a January 1843 evening, Edward Drummond, private secretary to Prime Minister Sir Robert Peel, was shot down just yards from his employer's official residence at Downing Street, Whitehall, London. The gunman, who made no attempt to escape, was arrested on the spot. He gave his name as Daniel M'Naghten, and from a statement made at the time, it became clear that he had shot Drummond by mistake, believing him to be the prime minister. M'Naghten, a Scottish artisan who suffered from extreme delusions of persecution, explained to the arresting officers that Peel had been at the forefront of a government conspiracy to destroy him.

Five days after the shooting, Drummond died from his wounds and M'Naghten found himself facing charges of murder. His trial at the Old Bailey became a showpiece event of that year's social calendar, resulting in a packed courtroom on March 3, 1843, when Solicitor General, Sir William Follet, Q.C. (Queen's Counsel), outlined the Crown's case. After describing the events of the shooting, he told the jury, "You will be satisfied that it was the life of Sir Robert Peel that he [M'Naghten] intended to take."

Evidence of premeditation came from a government employee, Edward Howe, who testified: "I know the prisoner before the bar. I first saw him about a fortnight before the 20th January last. He was then standing at the top of the steps of the [Privy] Council Office, which is at the corner of Downing Street. Sir Robert Peel's residence is in Privy Gardens, which is nearly opposite the end of Downing Street. Sir Robert Peel at times walks up Downing Street to his official residence. . . . On the 20th of January, between three and four o'clock, I again observed the prisoner standing at the Council Office steps, when I said, 'You will excuse me taking the liberty, sir, but I belong to the office next door; you are a police officer, are you not?' To which he replied, 'Yes,' and I said, 'I suppose, then, it is all right.'"

Within the hour, M'Naghten had shot Drummond near the spot described by Howe. Some idea of M'Naghten's mental confusion was provided by Inspector John Tierney, who had interviewed the defendant shortly after his arrest: "I suppose you know who the gentleman is you shot at?" Tierney had asked.

M'Naghten had looked at him in bemusement before replying, "It is Sir Robert Peel, is it not?"

The trial of Daniel M'Naghten, accused of trying to murder Sir Robert Peel in 1843. (Hulton-Deutsch Collection)

The prosecution, eager to prove that M'Naghten was mentally competent, produced a succession of witnesses who variously described him as "a man of very sober habits," given to reading extracts from the Bible, and "very reserved in his manners." Joseph Forrester, a hairdresser in M'Naghten's hometown of Glasgow, who had known the defendant for more than a year, also said that he "never saw anything in his manner to lead me to suppose that he was not in his right senses." Under cross-examination, he denied ever having described the defendant as "daft [mad]."

A more menacing tone was injected by longtime acquaintance Robert Gordon, who, while admitting that he had "never noticed anything particular or strange in his manner," did recall a walk he and M'Naghten had taken through

Whitehall, the course of which took them past Peel's house. "That is where Sir Robert Peel lives," M'Naghten had pointed and said vehemently, "Damn and sink him!"

Admits Shooting

In his opening address, chief defense counsel Sir Alexander Cockburn, Q.C., admitted the fatal shooting but said that "the defense of the accused will rest upon his mental condition at the time that the offense was committed." Cockburn explained how, under the laws of England, "insanity absolved from responsibility and from the consequences that would attach to the violation of the law." He then cited various cases, including that of John Bellingham, who, in 1812, had assassinated then Prime Minister Spencer Perceval, a crime for which Bellingham was tried and executed. "The general opinion now," said Cockburn, "seems to be that the verdict had been improperly obtained." Finally, Cockburn promised the jury, "I am bound to show that the prisoner was acting under a delusion, and that the act sprang out of that delusion . . . and when I have done so, I shall be entitled to your verdict."

The first defense witness was the defendant's father, also named Daniel. He told how his son "would frequently pass me in the street and not speak to or notice me."

"What was your opinion with respect to your son's mind?" asked Follet on cross-examination.

"It certainly was my impression that his intellect was impaired."

"Did you consult any medical gentlemen?"

"I did not, because I thought the delusions under which he was laboring would pass away," replied the elder M'Naghten.

Hugh Wilson, a commissioner of police at Glasgow, said that 18 months earlier, M'Naghten had come to him complaining that he was being pursued surreptitiously by Jesuits. Later, he had enlarged this complaint to include the Tories, police officers, and Catholic priests, all of whom had banded together in a monstrous plot to persecute him.

Once the circumstances of M'Naghten's background had been dealt with to the defense's satisfaction, the defense then introduced its expert witnesses. Chief among these was E. T. Monro, a doctor who described himself as having "30 years [experience] on the subject of lunacy." Together with several other medical men, Monro had examined M'Naghten in Newgate Prison. His findings received the closest scrutiny from an openly skeptical chief Crown prosecutor.

"Did you ask him [M'Naghten] if he knew whom he fired at?" asked Follet.

"I am not quite certain. I think I asked the prisoner whom he fired at."

"Did he not say he would not have fired if he had known that it was not Sir Robert Peel?"

"No, I think he did not. On this point he observed that the person at whom he fired gave him as he passed a scowling look. At that moment all the feelings of months and years rushed into his mind, and he thought that he could only obtain peace by shooting him."

Follet was not convinced. "Do you mean to say, Dr. Monro, that you could satisfy yourself as to a person's state of mind by merely going into a cell and putting questions to him?"

"In many instances I can."

"Do you consider a person laboring under a morbid delusion of unsound mind?"

"I do."

"Do you think insanity may exist without any morbid delusions?"

"Yes, a person may be an imbecile . . . [and] a person may be of unsound mind, and yet be able to manage the usual affairs of life."

"May insanity exist with a moral perception of right and wrong?"

"Yes, it is very common."

"A person may have a delusion and know murder to be a crime?"

"If there existed antecedent symptoms, I should consider the murder to be an overt act, the crowning piece of his insanity. But if he had stolen a ten pound note it would not have tallied with his delusions."

Quick as a flash, Follet interjected, "But suppose he had stolen the note from one of his persecutors?" Unfortunately, Dr. Monro's answer went unheard, drowned out by the gales of laughter that reverberated around the oak-paneled courtroom.

Yet another psychiatrist, Dr. W. Hutchinson, also gave his opinion that the defendant was insane. Follet sounded incredulous as he asked, "Do you mean to say that the delusion prevented the prisoner from exercising any control over his actions?"

"The act was the consequence of the delusion, which was irresistible."

"Nothing you have heard during the past two days has altered your mind on the subject?"

Hutchinson was resolute: "My opinion of the prisoner's insanity is the same."

The M'Naghten Rule

Late on the second day of the trial, after two other doctors also expressed the view that M'Naghten's insanity was real not feigned, Lord Chief Justice Tindal told the prosecution that he intended stopping the case. He advised the jury that there was no need for him to review the evidence and invited the jury to return a verdict of "not guilty, on the ground of insanity," which the jury duly did.

The verdict was far from popular, particularly with Queen Victoria. In 1840, she herself had been the target of an assassination attempt when Edward Oxford, a man who had suffered from a long-standing mental deficiency, fired a gun at her. Oxford had appeared unable to comprehend the significance of what he had done, why he had done it, or why he was on trial. During his trial, the jury was instructed that "if this man was the agent of [a] controlling disease which he could not resist, he is entitled to acquittal." The verdict of not guilty by virtue of insanity had infuriated the monarch then, and the M'Naghten verdict did not sit well with her now.

Victoria was not alone in her disapproval. So great was the furor over the M'Naghten verdict that it led to an almost unprecedented procedure. The House of Lords passed a resolution ordering Chief Justice Tindal and his bench colleagues to appear before it to answer specific questions regarding the doctrine of insanity in criminal trials. The outcome was the so-called M'Naghten Rule of insanity: To establish a defense on the ground of insanity, it must be clearly proved that, at the time of the committing of the act, the party was laboring under such a defect of reason, from disease of the mind, as to not know the nature and quality of the act he was doing, or, if he did know it, that he did not know what he was doing was wrong.

Although adhered to throughout most of the next century, the M'Naghten Rule is nowadays largely disregarded in British courts. Increasing awareness of the nature and variety of mental disease has made a mockery of a statute whose parameters are so narrow that Daniel M'Naghten himself would probably have been excluded from its provisions.

—Colin Evans

Suggestions for Further Reading

Cremona, Marise. *Criminal Law*. London: Macmillan, 1989.

Crimes and Punishment. Vols. 1 and 2. London: Phoebus 1974.

Elliott, D. W., and Michael J Allen. *Casebook on Criminal Law*. London: Sweet & Maxwell, 1989.

Lunde, Donald T. *Murder and Madness*. New York: Simon & Schuster, 1976.

Daniel O'Connell Trial: 1844

Defendant: Daniel O'Connell   **Crime Charged:** Seditious conspiracy
Chief Defense Lawyers: Daniel O'Connell, Thomas O'Hagan, Q.C., James O'Hea, Q.C., Richard Sheil, Q.C.   **Chief Prosecutor:** Sir Frederick Pollock, Q.C.   **Judges:** Charles Burton, Philip Crampton, Louis Perrin   **Place:** Dublin, Ireland   **Dates of Trial:** January 15–February 10, 1844   **Verdict:** Guilty
Sentence: One year's imprisonment and £2,000 fine

SIGNIFICANCE

The British government's political agenda, coupled with a biased jury, played a major role in the show trial of this peace-loving Irish nationalist.

In the early 19th-century struggle for Irish independence, no name shone brighter than that of Daniel O'Connell. A lawyer from County Kerry, O'Connell first achieved prominence with his condemnation of the Act of Union (1800), which abolished the Irish Parliament. As a mark of his displeasure, he organized a nationwide series of meetings, the aim of which was to petition for Ireland's separation from Britain. He was first elected to the British House of Commons in 1828 but, being Catholic, was barred from taking his seat. One year later, after passage of the Emancipation Act, he fought an uncontested election that saw him returned to Westminster.

O'Connell soon made his presence felt. In 1835, he helped topple Sir Robert Peel's administration, and in the same year entered into the Lichfield House Compact, promising the Whig Party leaders a period of "perfect calm in Ireland" while the government enacted reform measures. Disillusioned by the pace of Whig reform, O'Connell founded the Repeal Association to dissolve the Anglo-Irish legislative union. His stamina seemed boundless. During 1843, at the age of 68, he traveled in excess of 5,000 miles around Ireland, preaching the doctrine of peaceful separation from Britain.

Most of these rallies were held in open fields and attracted vast audiences; crowds that came to hear both the message and the messenger, for O'Connell was a masterful orator, with a natural gift for striking a chord in the Irish heart. Usually, his addresses were models of diplomacy, but in August of 1843, he was heard to criticize the recent Queen's speech that had opened Parliament. It was the lapse that hard-line British officials had hungered for. In October 1843, just two days after a planned meeting at Clontarf had been abandoned under government pressure, O'Connell, his son John, and seven other prominent Irish nationalists, including two clergymen, were arrested.

Having already lost several comrades to the hangman's rope, O'Connell harbored no illusions about the gravity of his situation. So, there can be no doubting his relief upon learning that the charges levied against him were only those of seditious conspiracy. It might mean a stiff jail sentence, but at least the threat of a death sentence for treason had been removed.

Irish liberator Daniel O'Connell was brought to trial in the winter of 1844 on charges of seditious conspiracy. Pictured is O'Connell's home at Darrynane Abbey.

Few of O'Connell's countrymen doubted that the sole object of this particular legal exercise was to silence Daniel O'Connell once and for all. It was a view shared across the Irish Sea, where politicians were convinced that, without its most eloquent and charismatic spokesman, the repeal movement would suffer a massive, possibly mortal, blow. However, in order to support the charge of conspiracy, it was necessary to arraign the other defendants. Apart from the O'Connells, they were Richard Barrett, Gavin Duffy, John Gray, Thomas Ray, Thomas Steele, Reverend Thomas Tierney, Reverend Peter Tyrrell.

Solemn March

Huge crowds turned out on the morning of January 15, 1844, as, three months later than anticipated, the defendants were escorted by Dublin's Lord

Mayor in full regalia through the city's streets to the Four Courts. The solemnity was short-lived. Inside the court, a carnival atmosphere took hold as the public scrambled for seats and openly wagered on the outcome.

Right from the outset, the government's intentions were brutally obvious: The roll of jurors' names—deliberately out-of-date—reflected a Protestant bias of roughly 15–1 over Catholics. Since it was generally admitted that this trial would be settled along sectarian lines, no one could argue with O'Connell's demand for a more current and representative list of jurors. An amended list did increase Catholic representation to one in four, yet when it came time to actually pick the jury, two sheets of jurors' names—that just happened to contain the names of mainly Catholic jurors—were missing. Such shabby tactics did nothing to allay the commonly held suspicion that the jury was hopelessly stacked against O'Connell and his codefendants even before the trial started.

In his opening address, Attorney General Sir Frederick Pollock claimed that the defendants had "conspired and confederated together to raise and create discontent and disaffection amongst Her Majesty's subjects." It was a catchall charge, depressingly easy to bring, and devilishly difficult to disprove, though that did not prevent the various defense counsel from trying. Motions and countermotions were argued at great length on behalf of each defendant. By the standards of the age this was an extraordinarily long trial—three weeks— with much of the delay being accounted for by the bewildering array of advocates in attendance. At times, the three-member bench, headed by Chief Justice Burton, seemed unable to distinguish between prosecution and defense, hardly surprising since the defense ranks alone numbered ten counsel, including five Queen's Counsels, the highest ranking members of the British bar.

O'Connell Leads His Own Defense

As a trained lawyer, O'Connell donned wig and gown to defend himself, a task he performed with his customary flair. Aware of his own celebrity and determined not to be upstaged, he would wait until all the defendants and counsel were present before stage-managing his grand entrance. Such theatricality played well with the public gallery but failed to impress the bench, which constantly chided O'Connell about his tardiness.

In some respects, O'Connell played right into the prosecution's hands, because such diversions tended to overshadow the skimpiness of its case. The first witness, Charles Ross, a newspaper reporter, told how, on August 28, 1843, he had attended an open-air meeting—just one of the 40 that O'Connell had addressed that year—at which some "45,000 people" were in attendance. According to Ross, this was the meeting at which O'Connell criticized a speech recently made by Queen Victoria and had gone on to openly espouse the breakup of the union between Britain and Ireland. Yet another reporter, John Macnamara, describing a meeting held on July 16, 1843, consulted his shorthand notes. O'Connell, he claimed, had said, "It is with infinite pleasure that I now announce to you the certainty of our carrying the repeal of the Union."

The reporters were succeeded in the witness box by numerous police officers who corroborated the content of the statements. That O'Connell had made these speeches was not in dispute—it could hardly be otherwise with so many in attendance—but did they constitute sedition (incitement of resistance to authority)? Naturally, the chief defendant thought not, and in his main submission to the court, he alluded to the nonviolent principles that had governed his actions for more than 40 years:

Released from Richmond Penitentiary in September 1844, O'Connell was honored in this triumphant parade held in Dublin on May 30, 1845, to celebrate the anniversary of his imprisonment.

From the day when first I entered the arena of politics until the present hour, I have never neglected an opportunity of impressing upon the minds of my fellow-countrymen the fact, that I was an apostle of that political sect who held that liberty was only to be attained under such agencies as were strictly consistent with the law and the constitution—that freedom was to be attained, not by the effusion of human blood, but by the constitutional combination of good and wise men; by perseverance in the courses of tranquillity and good order, and by an utter abhorrence of violence and bloodshed. It is my proudest boast, that throughout a long and eventful life, I have faithfully devoted myself to the promulgation of that principle, and, without vanity, I can assert, that I am the first public man who ever proclaimed it. Other politicians have said—"Win your liberties by peaceable means if you can," but there was *arrière pensée* [ulterior motive] in this admonition, and they always had in contemplation an appeal to physical force, in case other means should prove abortive. I am not one of these. I have preached under every contingency, and I have again and again declared my intention to abandon the cause of repeal if a single drop of human blood were shed by those who advocated the measure.

Although the prosecution could not produce a single witness to deny the veracity of these claims, that seems to have mattered little to the jury. Any verdict other than guilty from such a predominantly Protestant panel was out of the question, and, despite the lack of evidence, on February 10, 1844, O'Connell and his fellow defendants were convicted of most charges.

Once the court announced that it would delay sentence, O'Connell sailed immediately for England. Five days later, he entered the House of Commons to huge roars of acclaim before setting off on a tour of England that saw every town and city cheer him to the echo. On May 30, he and his fellow defendants returned to Dublin to hear sentence passed. In delivering his judgment, Chief Justice Burton made the extraordinary admission that O'Connell "had that design [achieving the repeal of the Union without bloodshed] rooted in his mind, and that it was by the great influence which he possessed as a leader . . . that he kept the country, or part of the country where he resided, from the dreadful operation of civil war and the shedding of human blood." Such an unusual statement was interpreted as an expression of the bench's keenness to distance itself from the verdict. Then Burton passed sentence: one year's imprisonment and a fine of £2,000 ($8,000), considerably less than O'Connell had feared.

O'Connell served his time in Dublin's Richmond Jail under far from arduous conditions, ensconced in the prison governor's own comfortable quarters. Just months later, on September 4, 1844, a panel of judges convened at the House of Lords to hear O'Connell's appeal and those of his fellow defendants. By a 3–2 majority, the earlier verdicts were reversed on grounds that the jury composition had been flawed. Three days later, O'Connell drove through the prison gates at the head of a triumphant procession. But it was a Pyrrhic victory. O'Connell's health was in sharp decline, and leadership of the campaign for Irish independence passed into the hands of younger, more radical men. Worn out by the struggle, the man they called "the Liberator" died in 1847 at the age of 71.

—*Colin Evans*

Suggestions for Further Reading

Edwards, R. D. *Daniel O'Connell and his World*. London: Thames & Hudson, 1975.

Hickey, D. J., and J. E. Doherty. *A Dictionary of Irish History: 1800–1980*. New York: Barnes & Noble, 1981.

Lecky, W.E.H. *Leaders of Public Opinion in Ireland*. New York: De Capo Press, 1973.

MacDonagh, Oliver. *The Emancipist: Daniel O'Connell: 1830–47*. New York: St. Martin's Press, 1989.

William Kirwan Trial: 1852

Defendant: William Kirwan **Crime Charged:** Murder
Chief Defense Lawyers: Isaac Butt, Q.C.; Walter Burke, Q.C.; William W.
Brereton, Q.C.; John A. Curran **Chief Prosecutors:** John G. Smyly, Q.C.;
Edmund Hayes, Q.C.; John Pennefather **Judges:** Hon. Philip C. Crampton,
Right Hon. Richard W. Greene **Place:** Dublin, Ireland
Dates of Trial: December 8–10, 1852 **Verdict:** Guilty
Sentence: Death, later commuted to life imprisonment

SIGNIFICANCE
An early classic of forensic medicine that sought to answer one of criminology's
most baffling questions—how had Maria Kirwan met her death?

Just northeast of Dublin, overlooked by the fishing village of Howth, stands "Ireland's Eye," a chunk of craggy quartzite rising up from the sea about a mile offshore. Originally settled by seventh-century monks, the island had become a bird sanctuary and had long been popular with day-trippers. Two such visitors were William and Maria Kirwan, a Dublin couple married for 11 years, who, on the morning of September 6, 1852, set off in a boat manned by Patrick Nangle and headed for the uninhabited island. Kirwan, an artist, intended to paint while his wife bathed. They landed at a spot known as Martello Tower, and Kirwan gave instructions for Nangle to return that night at 8 o'clock to pick them up. Around noon, Nangle brought a second party of day-trippers to the island. They stayed for a few hours and saw the Kirwans together and individually but did not speak to them. They did notice, though, that when Nangle returned to collect them that afternoon, Maria peered anxiously in their direction, but she declined their offer of passage back to the mainland, and the boat left.

At 7 P.M., with dusk falling fast, a fishing smack passed close to Ireland's Eye. At the helm was Thomas Larkin. Suddenly a loud scream came from the direction of the island, then another, fainter this time, and finally a third, quieter still. All this took place over several minutes. Squinting into the gloom, Larkin saw nothing and sailed on. Helped by the stillness of the night, however, the piercing screams had reached the mainland, where they were verified by four different people. (This was by no means an uncommon occurrence; boisterous visitors to Ireland's Eye could often be heard in Howth.) Later, everyone agreed that the cries were those of a woman in distress.

As arranged, at 8 P.M. Patrick Nangle and his cousin, Michael Nangle, arrived to collect the Kirwans. By now it was totally dark, and, unable to see their intended passengers, they cried out to announce their arrival. From out of the murk stepped William Kirwan, alone. His wife, he explained, had gone bathing at an inlet known as the Long Hole some 90 minutes earlier, and he had not seen her since. When their calls went unheeded, Kirwan and Patrick Nangle set off to search for the missing woman.

At the Long Hole, they found Maria's bruised and bloody body draped across a rock, her bathing dress pulled up to the armpits; although a strong swimmer, she appeared to have drowned. The body was carried back to the mainland, where Kirwan's insistence that it be washed without delay prompted a local nurse to remind him that the police would wish to view the bloodstained corpse. "I don't care a damn for the police," he snarled, "the body must be washed!" Kirwan also attracted adverse attention because his clothing was soaked from the waist down, yet his wife's body had been found above the high-tide mark.

Adultery

At the inquest the next day, Kirwan's vague testimony made no mention of any screams, and a verdict of accidental death was recorded. But the whispers would not go away. Especially when it became known that for years Kirwan had been in the habit of spending four nights a week with his wife, Maria, and the remainder with a Miss Teresa Kenny, also of Dublin, who had borne him no fewer than seven children. Add on the incendiary element of religion—Kirwan was Protestant; his wife, Catholic—and it came as no surprise when authorities ordered an exhumation. On October 6, 31 days after her death, Maria's body was disinterred; the resulting autopsy led to Kirwan's being charged with deliberately drowning his wife.

A packed Dublin courtroom heard opening arguments on December 8, 1852. The prosecution scored early with Margaret Campbell, a Howth landlady who had taken the Kirwans in as summer lodgers. After confirming Kirwan's habit of being absent from the house three nights every week, she described persistent quarrels between the couple. "I heard angry words from Mr. Kirwan to his wife. I heard him say 'I'll finish you!' On the same evening I heard her say to him, 'Let me alone, let me alone!' Next morning I heard her say to him she was black from the usage she had got the previous night—across her thighs." Sounds from the bedroom left Mrs. Campbell in no doubt that Kirwan was beating his wife.

Patrick Nangle, when questioned by defense counsel, William Brereton, Q.C. (Queen's Counsel), dismissed suggestions that Maria's extensive injuries might have been caused either by crabs biting the flesh or by constant pounding against the rocks: First, there were no crabs where the body lay; second, the water had been very calm that night. He also disclosed damaging details about the search at Long Hole for Maria's missing clothes. Apparently Kirwan had ordered him to look "there on the rock," pointing toward a large ledge. Despite his best efforts, Patrick was unable to locate the missing clothes and told Kirwan, who then went to look for himself. He came back carrying a shawl and "something white" and told Patrick to try again. Much to his puzzlement, Patrick then found the clothes in a spot where he had previously looked. This "something white," claimed the prosecution, was the dead woman's chemise, which was never found. Kirwan, they alleged, had soaked it in water, then used it to suffocate Maria, giving the superficial impression of drowning.

In most respects, Michael Nangle's testimony mirrored that of his cousin's but did include the significant addition that when Kirwan and Patrick were searching the far side of the island, he could hear their shouts quite distinctly.

This business of the screams was one that plainly troubled defense counsel Isaac Butt, Q.C. He strove manfully to bring out minor discrepancies in the various witnesses' statements, but could do nothing to undermine the central facts they all agreed upon—that around 7 o'clock at least three screams had been heard coming from Ireland's Eye.

Autopsy Findings

At this point, the trial turned to the testimony of Dr. George Hatchell, who had performed the autopsy. "From the appearances you observed on the body," asked prosecutor John Smyly, Q.C., "are you able, as a medical man, to form an opinion as to the cause of death?"

Hatchell replied, "I am of the opinion that death was caused by asphyxia, or a sudden stopping of respiration. From the . . . engorgement of the lungs, and other circumstances, I should say that in all probability the simple stoppage of respiration must have been combined with pressure of some kind, or constriction, which caused the sudden stoppage. I do not think that simple drowning would produce to the same extent the appearances I saw."

Under cross-examination, Hatchell did admit the possibility that death might have resulted from an epileptic fit but insisted that the amount of blood in the lungs must have been caused by a vigorous struggle for life, whether alone or with another.

One person who might have shed some light on events was Teresa Kenny, but when called by the prosecution to give evidence, she failed to appear. Her excuse? A cut thumb. Curiously, her absence did not arouse censure.

The defense called just two witnesses. The most telling contribution came from a Dr. Adams, who, while conceding that the amount of internal bleeding was the most he had ever encountered in a victim of asphyxia, was quite emphatic when Justice Philip Crampton asked, "Supposing death to have taken place by forcible submersion, or from accidental drowning, would you be able, from the appearances described, to state to which species of death they were attributable?"

"My Lord," said Adams, "in my opinion, no man living could do so."

Closing for the Crown, Edmund Hayes, Q.C., dealt with belated defense claims that Maria Kirwan had drowned during an epileptic seizure. "If there was any evidence that this lady had been previously affected by epilepsy or anything of that kind, there might have been a shadow of ground upon which to found the assertion. As the prisoner has forborne to produce such testimony, it is not too much to infer that there was none to produce; we must take it as proved that the deceased was a perfectly healthy woman." And why did Kirwan say nothing about the screams? Sitting, as he had been, by Martello Tower, between the Long Hole and the mainland, he must have heard them, "and yet this affectionate husband is deaf to these dreadful shrieks." Surely, had she been subject to fits, he would have run to her assistance? Instead, an hour later, he is found calmly waiting for the boat.

These were the thoughts that the jury took with it to its deliberations. Just before midnight on December 9, the jury found Kirwan guilty, and the next morning he was sentenced to death.

Considerable unease greeted the verdict, with several Dublin doctors publishing pamphlets condemning the prosecution's medical evidence. So fervent did this dissent become, that it was decided to commute Kirwan's sentence to life imprisonment. Despite the best efforts of his supporters, William Kirwan spent the next quarter of a century behind bars. Freed in 1879, on condition that he leave the country, he sailed for America and there married Teresa Kenny, the mother of his seven children. He died in obscurity.

Given the weight of circumstantial evidence against Kirwan, it is perhaps surprising that the prosecution relied so heavily on medical testimony, particularly in light of the fact that the coffin had been buried in a waterlogged part of the cemetery, thus greatly hastening decomposition of the body. Because homicide by drowning is very rare, pathologists to this day argue about what really happened that fall evening on Ireland's Eye.

—Colin Evans

Suggestions for Further Reading

Goodman, Jonathan, ed. *The Seaside Murders*. London: Allison & Busby, 1985.

Roughead, William. *Famous Crimes*. London: William Hodge, 1935.

Wilson, Colin, and Patricia Pitman. *Encyclopedia of Murder*. New York: G. P. Putnam, 1961.

Whistler *v.* Ruskin: 1878

Plaintiff: James Whistler   **Defendant:** John Ruskin
Plaintiff's Claim: Damages for libel   **Chief Defense Lawyer:** Sir John Holker, Q.C.   **Chief Lawyer for Plaintiff:** Serjeant John Parry   **Judge:** Sir John Huddlestone   **Place:** London, England   **Dates of Trial:** November 25–26, 1878   **Decision:** Jury found for plaintiff but awarded only 1 farthing—less than 1 cent—in damages

SIGNIFICANCE
What are the permissible limits of criticism in the arts? Here, a jury essentially decided that the courtroom was no place to settle such disputes.

In July 1877, eminent London art critic John Ruskin attended a controversial exhibition at the newly opened Grosvenor Gallery. His review, published in a journal called *Fors Clavigera*, included the following paragraph:

> For Mr. Whistler's own sake, no less than for the protection of the purchaser, Sir Coutts Lindsay ought not to have admitted works into the gallery in which the ill-educated conceit of the artist so nearly approached the aspect of willful imposture. I have seen, and heard, much of Cockney impudence before now, but never expected to hear a coxcomb ask two hundred guineas [approximately $840] for flinging a pot of paint in the public's face.

The recipient of this stinging assault was James Whistler, a 44-year-old Massachusetts-born artist transplanted to Europe in 1855, and someone who had achieved that great rarity for a painter—recognition in his own lifetime. Painting was far from being Whistler's only accomplishment. In the salons of London, the elegant American's devastating wit and ability to turn a neat phrase had afforded him almost legendary status. For such a man to endure such an attack was inconceivable, but lurking beneath the libel suit he filed immediately was an ulterior motive—Whistler was flat broke and saw this as a golden opportunity to replenish his depleted coffers.

Ruskin was no fool. Although sharp-witted with a pen, he lacked such ability in person, certainly when compared with a verbal heavyweight like Whistler, and for this reason he was absent from court—excused on medical grounds—when proceedings commenced on November 25, 1878. As expected, Whistler kept the court constantly amused during the two-day-long trial. Asked by Sir John Holker, Q.C., appearing for Ruskin, to define the subject of the picture that had so upset the critic—*Nocturne in Black and Gold: The Falling Rocket*—Whistler replied, "It is a nightpiece and represents the fireworks at Cremorne Gardens [an amusement park on the banks of the River Thames]."

"Not a view of Cremorne?"

"If I called it a *View of Cremorne* it would certainly bring about nothing but disappointment on the part of the beholders. It is an artistic arrangement. That is why I call it a 'nocturne.'"

"I suppose you are willing to admit that your pictures exhibit some eccentricities. You have been told that over and over again."

"Yes, very often," sighed Whistler, to considerable laughter.

"You sent your pictures to the Grosvenor Gallery to invite the admiration of the public?"

"That would have been such a vast absurdity on my part that I don't think I could have."

Holker was not impressed. "Did it take much time to paint *Nocturne in Black and Gold?* How soon did you knock it off?"

"I beg your pardon?" demanded Whistler.

British art critic, John Ruskin, in an 1882 photograph by Barraud.

"I was using an expression which is rather more applicable to my own profession."

"Thank you for the compliment."

"How long did it take you to knock off one of your pictures?"

"Oh, I 'knock one off' possibly in a couple of days. One day to do the work and another to finish it."

"The labor of two days is that for which you ask two hundred guineas?"

Memorable Riposte

Whistler's reply has been quoted and requoted a million times since: "No, I ask it for a knowledge I have gained in the work of a lifetime."

Such cheering greeted this response that the judge, Sir John Huddlestone, had to gavel the proceedings to silence. "This is not an arena for applause," he thundered. "If this manifestation of feeling is repeated, I shall have to clear the court."

Holker bulled on. "You know that many critics entirely disagree with your views as to these pictures?"

"It would be beyond me to agree with the critics." Again the public gallery rocked with laughter.

"You don't approve of criticism?"

"It is not for me to criticize the critics. I should not disapprove in any way of technical criticism by a man whose life is passed in the practice of the science he criticizes; but for the opinion of a man whose life is not so passed I would have as little respect as you would have if he expressed an opinion on the law. I hold that none but an artist can be a competent critic. It is not only when a criticism is unjust that I object to it, but when it is incompetent."

That lunch hour the jury was taken to a nearby gallery where Whistler's paintings were on display. Afterward, they listened to the art critic W. M. Rossetti being questioned by Whistler's counsel, Serjeant Parry, "Do you, or do you not, consider them works of a conscientious artist desirous of working well in his profession?"

"I do decidedly. I consider Mr. Whistler a sincere and good artist."

Holker stood up. "Is two hundred guineas a stiffish price for a picture like this?" he asked Rossetti.

"I would rather not express an opinion as to the value of a picture, but if pressed I should say two hundred guineas is the full value of it, not a 'stiffish price.'"

"Do you think it is worth that money?"

"Yes."

Albert Moore, a close friend of the plaintiff, agreed. "The pictures produced, in common with all Mr. Whistler's works, have a large aim not often followed . . . no living painter, I believe, could succeed in the same way, in the same qualities. I consider the pictures beautiful works of art; I wish I could paint as well."

James Whistler, working at his printing press in the rue Notre-Dame-des-Champs, Paris, 1893.

Contemptuous Defense

Opening for the defense, Holker heaped scorn on Whistler's ability, sneering, "I do not know when so much amusement has been afforded to the British public as by Mr. Whistler's pictures." He then called Edward Burne-Jones, an accomplished artist, to defend his client. Under direct examination, Burne-Jones endorsed Ruskin's belief in high finish as a vital attribute for a painting, with the degree of labor involved being reflected in the cost. In Burne-Jones's own work, Ruskin's notion of highly detailed, finished pictures reached its zenith: In fact, the article that first caused the libel suit to come to court was written in praise of Burne-Jones. Nonetheless, despite his affinities to Ruskin, Burne-Jones had hesitated before appearing in court. Once on the stand, however, he minimized Whistler's work as "incomplete" and "a sketch in short."

Next came W. P. Frith, an artist known for large, intricate group paintings. Asked whether composition and detail were important elements in a picture, Frith responded, "Very. Without them a picture cannot be called a work of art." Under cross-examination, Frith did admit championing the great British artist John Turner but qualified his praise by saying, "When I say that Turner should be an idol of painters, I refer to his earlier works and not to the period when he was half crazy and produced works about as insane as the people who admire them." It was an observation that again filled the public gallery with laughter.

In his final address to the jury, Parry lamented Ruskin's absence from court. "Mr. Ruskin cared not whether his decree injuriously affected others and loftily declined to discuss his judgment or to justify himself before a jury." He then cited Ruskin's record of indiscriminate abuse directed toward others. "He is a man who exceeds the fair limits of criticism and allows personal feelings to carry him too far. . . . This is the language of a libelous mind, utterly indifferent to others' feelings, but gratifying to its own vanity. Mr. Ruskin might delight in the reflection that he is a smart, a pungent, and a telling writer, but he must not be allowed to trade in libel. The works of Mr. Whistler are open to fair and honest criticism. He had not shrunk from any public investigation, but his detractor has." Parry concluded, "Is he [Whistler] to be expelled from the realm of art by the man who sits there as a despot? I hope the jury will say by its verdict that Mr. Ruskin has no right to drive Mr. Whistler out by defamatory and libelous accusations."

It had been marvelous entertainment, but the jury made plain its opinion of this suit's merit by awarding Whistler just 1 farthing (less than 1 cent) in damages, the lowest amount permissible. Compounding Whistler's misery was the order that both sides should pay their own costs. His great gamble had failed. One year later he was driven into bankruptcy.

—Colin Evans

Suggestions for Further Reading

Anderson, Ronald, and Anne Koval. *James McNeill Whistler*. New York: Carroll & Graf, 1995.

Getscher, Robert H. *James Abbott McNeill Whistler*. New York: George Braziller, 1991.

Gordon, Fleming. *James Abbott McNeill Whistler: A Life*. New York: St. Martin's Press, 1991.

Merrill, Linda. *A Pot of Paint*. Washington, D.C.: Smithsonian Institute, 1992.

Ned Kelly Trial: 1880

Defendant: Edward "Ned" Kelly   **Crime Charged:** Murder
Chief Defense Lawyer: Bindon (first name not recorded)
Chief Prosecutor: C. A. Smyth   **Judge:** Sir Redmond Barry
Place: Melbourne, Australia   **Dates of Trial:** October 28–29, 1880
Verdict: Guilty   **Sentence:** Death

SIGNIFICANCE
Glorified in film and song, Ned Kelly has become an Australian icon. But did this desperado really deserve his heroic reputation?

In the hundred years or so since their disappearance, Australian bushrangers have acquired the kind of romanticized celebrity bestowed upon their outlaw contemporaries of America's Wild West. Most notable among them was Edward "Ned" Kelly, who in the late 1870s led a gang that robbed and rustled its way across northeastern Victoria and into neighboring New South Wales. By 1878, the authorities had decided that enough was enough, and in October of that year, two police parties were dispatched with orders to bring Kelly to justice. They tracked him to a place called Stringybark Creek in the Wombat Ranges, but Kelly, who had been joined by his brother, Dan, and two other renegades, Joe Byrne and Steve Hart, managed to fight off the posse with a fusillade of bullets that left three police officers dead. Then the gang escaped.

As the reward for the capture of the Kelly Gang escalated to a staggering £8,000 (approximately $32,000)—more than 20 times the average annual salary of that time—the gang became ever more resourceful. In 1880, gang members stole some cast iron, from which Kelly forged himself an armored suit that weighed 97 pounds. The outfit covered all of his torso, and with its high cylindrical headpiece and narrow horizontal eye slit gave him an almost Robocop-like appearance.

On June 27, 1880, Ned Kelly led his men into the tiny settlement of Glenrowan, Victoria. Their intention was to rob the Melbourne train, and to this end they ordered some of the villagers to rip up the railroad tracks. Then the villagers—more than 60 in number—were herded at gunpoint into the Glenrowan Inn, where Kelly and his thugs laid siege to the well-stocked bar. In the wild drinking bout that followed, a schoolteacher was able to slip away from under the noses of his captors and flag down the oncoming train. He also alerted the police, who surrounded the hotel.

In the ensuing gun battle, Dan Kelly, Byrne, and Hart were shot to death. Only Ned Kelly survived. According to legend, in the early hours of June 28, clad in his armored suit, he abandoned the hotel and advanced on the police, guns blazing. His sense of invincibility endured only until the police marksmen lowered their aim—Kelly had forgotten about his legs. Unprotected, they were cut to shreds by 23 bullets that left him in a blood-soaked heap.

The reward poster for one of Australia's most notorious criminals, Ned Kelly.

News that the 25-year-old bushranger had been captured spread to every corner of Australia and led to remarkable scenes in Melbourne when his trial began on October 28, 1880. Large numbers of police, armed with revolvers, were needed to keep back the crowds that surged around the supreme court building.

Bloodbath Described

Two years to the day after his three fellow officers had been shot dead, the main prosecution witness, Constable M'Intyre, described the fateful events at Stringybark Creek. He told of a mission gone horribly wrong, one that saw his being captured by the Kelly Gang. At one point, Kelly had approached the hapless M'Intyre and leered, "Mind you don't move, or I'll put a hole through you."

Soon after M'Intyre had been captured, another posse member, Constable Lonergan, arrived. In chilling detail, M'Intyre told how Ned Kelly leveled his rifle at Lonergan and took careful aim. The bullet hit Lonergan full in the chest. He fell to the ground, where he remained motionless for a few moments before groaning, "Oh Christ, I am shot." No other shots were fired, but neither Kelly nor his cronies moved a muscle to help the stricken man, who struggled on the ground for a few more moments, then died.

Seconds later, two other officers, Sergeant Kennedy and Constable Scanlan, were ambushed. In all the confusion and with bullets flying around his head, M'Intyre was able to make his escape. Kennedy and Scanlan fared less well. Both died at the scene. M'Intyre, who made his way back to safety, raised the alarm, but pursuit was fruitless. M'Intyre told the court that he did not see Kelly again until after his arrest at Glenrowan.

Because of his notoriety, Kelly had experienced difficulty finding counsel to represent him. At the last moment, a local man named Bindon took on the thankless task. His cross-examination of M'Intyre was sketchy and unenthusiastic and drew just one minor concession from the witness—an admission that he had not seen an arrest warrant for the Kelly Gang before setting out to pursue them. In light of M'Intyre's other testimony, Bindon's assertion that the Kelly Gang had been pursued illegally sounded risible.

Next came a string of witnesses who testified to various admissions made by the prisoner at Faithfull's Creek Station, a settlement near Euroa that had been attacked by the Kelly Gang. Chief among these was George Stephens, a groom, who claimed to have overheard Kelly bragging that he had shot Lonergan. The impact of Stephens's statement was ameliorated somewhat by his subsequent admission under cross-examination that he was a former police officer who had been dismissed in 1868 for being absent without leave and was actively trying to get his job back.

Someone whose evidence could not be impeached in any way was Henry Dudley. He too had been at Faithfull's Creek Station and testified that, while there, Kelly had flaunted a large gold watch, saying, "That's a good watch, is it not? It belonged to poor Kennedy."

James Gloucester, a draper, and yet another who overheard Kelly's boastful admission, did concede under cross-examination that Kelly had expressed sorrow that Kennedy had chosen to fight and not surrender.

Details of Kelly's last stand at Glenrowan came from one of the arresting officers, Henry Richards. He told how, after Kelly had been taken into custody, the prisoner claimed that he had not really intended to shoot the police officers, only take their weapons. Claims of Kelly's cowardice came from another constable, who alleged that Kelly had begged for his life with the words, "Save me. I saved you."

Cowardly Killer

This seemingly concerted attempt to explode the myth that had already begun to shroud the defendant was a central theme when the chief Crown prosecutor, C. A. Smyth, closed his case. He told the jury that "Kelly was not a hero, he was a mean thief, who picked the pockets of the men he had murdered."

As no witnesses were presented for the defense, Bindon merely addressed the court. He ridiculed M'Intyre's evidence, questioning how, with bullets flying everywhere, he had been able to recount the events in such minute detail. Closing, he urged the jury "not to take away the life of a man on the prejudicial evidence of a single man." The judge, Justice Sir Redmond Barry, reinforced this stance in his summing-up, exhorting the jury not only to view M'Intyre's evidence objectively but also to afford similar consideration to all the police evidence.

On October 29, the jury returned a verdict of guilty. Asked if he wished to make a statement, Kelly initiated a lengthy and curious exchange with the judge, saying, "Well, it is rather late for me to speak now.... I wish I had insisted on being allowed to examine the witnesses myself. If I had examined them, I am confident I would have thrown a different light on the case.... On the evidence that has been given, no juryman could have given any other verdict."

To which Judge Barry replied, "The verdict pronounced by the jury is one which you must have fully expected?"

"Yes, under the circumstances."

"No circumstances that I can conceive could have altered the result of your trial," the judge concluded.

When Barry passed sentence of death, adding the traditional postscript, "May the Lord have mercy on your soul," Kelly, defiant to the end, retorted, "I will go a little further than that, and say that I will see you there where I go."

Despite more than 60,000 signatories to a petition to save his life, Kelly was hanged on the morning of November 11, 1880. When told, an hour before his execution, that all chances of a reprieve had foundered, he merely shrugged, "Such is life." He took this insouciance to the gallows.

Among his countrymen, Ned Kelly has achieved an almost legendary status, a latter-day Robin Hood, coerced into a life of crime by police victimization. Judging from all the available evidence, there is little to substantiate this belief, confirming the suspicion that fables have a way of outliving facts. Several movies based on Ned Kelly's life have been made, most recently in 1970, when Mick Jagger played the title role.

—Colin Evans

Suggestions for Further Reading

Cave, Colin F. *Ned Kelly: Man and Myth*. Melbourne: Cassell, 1967.

Cox, Harry. *The Australians*. Philadelphia: Chilton Books, 1966.

Crimes and Punishment. Vols. 1 and 8. London, Phoebus: 1974.

Alexander II's Assassins Trial: 1881

Defendants: Nikolai Rysakov, Timothy Mikhailov, Gesya Helfmann, Nikolai Kibalchich, Andrei Zhelyabov, Sofia Perovskaya

Crimes Charged: "Tsaricide," membership in a secret society dedicated to overthrowing the government and existing social order

Chief Defense Lawyers: Court-appointed counsel for all defendants, except Zhelyabov, who conducted his own defense. The historical records contain the last name of only one defense lawyer, Gerard, the attorney for Kibalchich.

Chief Prosecutors: Assistant Prosecutor Muravieff. (The historial records do not report his first name.) **Judges:** Senator Fuchs, presiding over a ten-member panel. (The historial records do not report his first name.)

Place: Saint Petersburg, Russia **Dates of Trial:** March 26–29, 1881

Verdict: Guilty on 20 charges of "tsaricide"; not guilty on some of lesser charges **Sentence:** Death

SIGNIFICANCE

The assassination of Alexander II ended governmental social reform in 19th-century Russia. The execution of his killers crippled the revolutionary party known as The People's Will.

A lmost from the moment of his accession in 1855, Tsar Alexander II pulled the Russian empire forward. During his rule, local self-government was introduced. Educational institutions and the armed forces were modernized. Judicial reforms included the introduction of the jury system. Alexander II's greatest act was the emancipation of the serfs, legally ending a system of tithed labor that enslaved more than 20 million peasants.

Yet some Russians felt that the reforms of the "Tsar Liberator" were insufficient. Heavy tax burdens on the peasants remained, and police repression could be brutally arbitrary. With no constitutional body to make reforms or take the blame for inaction, the tsar's ultimate power made him a symbol of tyranny to young activists impatient with the pace of change.

The People's Will Plots Tsar's Death

The most violent revolutionary group of the era called itself The People's Will. Although their ranks were small, members of The People's Will dedicated themselves to producing a social upheaval in which the monarchy would be destroyed and the country's wealth redistributed among the suffering classes. Believing the Tsar's assassination would encourage the peasantry to rise, The People's Will officially condemned Alexander II to death.

Three attempts had been made on Alexander II's life by 1879. Although The People's Will was better organized than earlier would-be assassins, it initially was no more successful. The revolutionaries spent months laying explosives along rail lines to the tsar's Crimean summer home, only to blow up the wrong train. A terrorist posing as a carpenter ignited a bomb in the basement of the Winter Palace, obliterating the royal dining room. Eleven people were killed in the explosion, but Alexander was elsewhere in the palace and was untouched.

In 1881, a plan took shape to kill the tsar during one of his Sunday excursions. A small cheese shop was rented along a route frequently taken by the emperor. The plotters began digging an underground passage to enable them to blow up the tsar when he passed overhead. Four bomb throwers would be stationed in the streets in case the attempt failed.

Suspicious policemen posing as health inspectors examined the cheese shop but failed to find the subterranean tunnel. Yet, Andrei Zhelyabov, the plot's chief organizer, was arrested on February 27, leaving the other conspirators to wonder if their plan was about to collapse.

Alexander Killed

On the afternoon of March 1, the tsar left the Winter Palace to review a weekly parade of his troops. He was returning along the Ekaterinsky Canal when one of Zhelyabov's recruits, Nikolai Rysakov, threw a tin canister at the carriage. The chemical-filled cylinder exploded, injuring the horses and several passersby, but the tsar was unhurt. The emperor got out of his damaged carriage to survey the bomb crater, inquire about the wounded, and berate Rysakov, who was quickly grabbed by a gathering crowd. A second terrorist, named Ignaty Grinivetsky, stood close by, watching.

As Alexander walked past, Grinivetsky detonated a second bomb. Grinivetsky was seriously injured by the blast, which mortally wounded his quarry. "Home to die," mumbled the tsar as his mangled body was eased into a carriage. "It's cold." Within an hour, thousands of Russians kneeling in prayer outside the Winter Palace learned that the tsar was dead.

Grinivetsky died of his wounds that evening, and investigators kept Rysakov talking about his fellow conspirators. Police arrested plotter Gesya Helfmann, but not quickly enough to prevent her roommate, Nikolai Sablin, from committing suicide during the raid. When the third designated bomb-thrower, Timothy Mikhailov, arrived at the Helfmann-Sablin apartment, police arrested him. Rysakov identified Helfmann and Mikhailov as conspirators. The leadership of The People's Will suffered a more serious blow a week later, when police captured Sofia Perovskaya on the street. Perovskaya, Zhelyabov's lover and the well-educated daughter of a former St. Petersburg governor, had coordinated the assassination plot after Zhelyabov's capture.

Arrests continued, but authorities were eager for a quick trial and charged six people for the tsar's murder: Rysakov, Mikhailov, Helfmann, Perovskaya, Zhelyabov, and former engineering student Nikolai Kibalchich, who had overseen the organization's bomb making.

Six Tried for "Tsaricide"

The defendants faced 24 counts, including "tsaricide" and belonging to a secret revolutionary society. The attempt to blow up the royal train and the cheese shop plot were included in the indictment. A 10-member panel drawn from various social classes would decide the case. Skittish authorities subjected press coverage to censorship by the assistant prosecutor.

When court convened on March 26, a guard with a drawn sword stood in the center of the room alongside a table full of captured explosives. A black-draped portrait of the dead tsar stared down as the prosecutor described the assassination. He quoted Alexander II's concern for a mortally wounded young butcher's boy, who lay crying in pain in the street. "I am safe, thank God, but. . . ."

Alexander II, shortly before his assassination.

"Do not thank God yet," Rysakov was alleged to have replied.

The nervous Rysakov denied having said that. Helfmann refused to testify. So did Mikhailov, whom the others insisted had taken no part in the assassination. Kibalchich, the explosives expert, corrected the prosecutor for contending that the cheese shop bomb would have caused massive civilian casualties. The bookish Kibalchich gave a detailed analysis of the hypothetical blast, explaining that only the tsar's carriage would have sustained fatal damage.

Most of the defendants were represented by ineffectual court-appointed lawyers. Only Kibalchich's attorney, Gerard, put up a fight. Kibalchich maintained that he had adopted terrorism only when peaceful change seemed impossible. Gerard forcefully argued that his client's life supported the claim. Kibalchich's career had been destroyed when the act of lending a banned book to a peasant earned him three years' imprisonment without a trial.

Andrei Zhelyabov carried on his struggle in the courtroom, catching witnesses in lies, ridiculing the prosecutor's histrionic speeches, and turning every question into an explanation of his cause. When asked about his religion, Zhelyabov replied:

> I admit the teaching of Christ to be the basis of my moral convictions. I believe in truth and justice. I consider religion without deeds to be of no value. I hold it to be the duty of a sincere Christian to fight on behalf of the weak and oppressed and, if need be, to suffer for them. That is my faith.

After his motion to be tried by a jury was denied, Zhelyabov rejected legal representation. Presenting his own defense gave the articulate revolutionary an opportunity he exploited to the hilt. Ignoring the judge's admonitions to address only the charges, Zhelyabov insisted that his motives for killing the tsar were inextricably bound to his political convictions. Defending himself within this context enabled Zhelyabov to speak eloquently about his views and the aims of The People's Will. He insisted that its members had been driven to violence after peaceful efforts to provoke change had failed. Zhelyabov freely admitted his part in the plots against the tsar.

When the trial ended after three days, Rysakov tried to save himself. Although he had clearly thrown a bomb at the tsar, Rysakov denied ever having approved of terrorism. The court was probably more stunned by Kibalchich's final statement, in which he asked that his plans for a rocket-powered "flying machine" be given to his attorney.

Six Sentenced to Hang

The death penalty had been abolished in Russia more than a century earlier. In this case, the prosecution demanded that an exception be made. Final arguments ended after midnight on March 29. At 3 A.M., the court returned with verdicts. Rysakov, Helfmann, and Mikhailov were acquitted of plotting to mine the cheese shop tunnel. The court declined to rule on whether Mikhailov belonged to a revolutionary group. On 20 remaining counts relating to the tsar's murder, however, all six defendants were found guilty.

An argument over whether minors, like 19-year-old Rysakov, should face capital punishment sent the court behind closed doors again. It was 6:20 A.M. when the judges returned to the dreary courtroom and sentenced all six defendants to death.

Only Mikhailov and Rysakov appealed their sentences to Tsar Alexander III. Both appeals were immediately rejected by the new ruler, who had exerted considerable pressure on the court to ensure that his father's killers would face execution. He also approved the execution of Perovskaya, whose noble parentage required that her sentence be royally confirmed. On the same day that the appeals were denied, Helfmann revealed that she was pregnant. Her death sentence was postponed until her appeal for clemency could be heard.

The other five revolutionaries were removed from their cells on April 2. With signs reading "TSARICIDE" suspended around their necks, they were transported through the streets to a specially erected gallows in Semenovski Square. Eighty thousand people watched a clumsy hangman dispatch the condemned prisoners, one by one. It took three attempts to kill Mikhailov, whose heavy body kept pulling the rope from its mooring. The defiant Zhelyabov struggled with his captors to the end.

Tsar Alexander III granted the pregnant Helfmann's petition for mercy on July 2, 1881. Her sentence was commuted from death to penal servitude for life. She gave birth to a daughter in her cell, but the child was taken from her. Helfmann died in prison in February 1882. The terrorists were not the only ones punished. One general and two police "health inspectors" who had failed to discover the cheese shop tunnel were sentenced to exile in Archangel, near the Arctic Circle.

Arrests continued to empty the ranks of The People's Will. Ivan Emilianov, the fourth bomb thrower assigned to the assassination squad, was eventually arrested and sentenced to life at hard labor. At his trial in 1882, Emilianov recalled watching the fatal bomb explode and instinctively rushing to help the wounded tsar, still carrying his bomb under his arm.

The execution of those who had committed "tsaricide" did not produce the popular revolution they had anticipated. In fact, many peasants resented the revolutionaries for killing the tsar, whom they considered their protector for having abolished serfdom. Future constitutional reforms planned by Alexander II were never implemented. Alexander III answered the hunger for progress with a brutal regime that withered the freedoms his father had promulgated. Nearly 40 years of tsarist repression remained before popular uprisings dreamed of by the revolutionaries of the 19th century would sweep away the Romanov dynasty forever.

—Tom Smith

Suggestions for Further Reading

Engel, Barbara Alpen, and Rosenthal, Clifford N. *Five Sisters: Women Against the Tsar.* New York: Alfred A. Knopf, 1975.

Footman, David. *The Alexander Conspiracy: A Life of A. I. Zhelyabov.* LaSalle, Ill.: Open Court, 1974.

Tarsaïdzé, Alexandre. *Katia: Wife Before God.* New York: Macmillan, 1970.

Tessendorf, K. C. *Kill the Tsar!* New York: Atheneum, 1986.

Westwood, J. N. *Endurance and Endeavor: Russian History 1812–1971.* London: Oxford University Press, 1973.

Adelaide Bartlett Trial: 1886

Defendant: Adelaide Bartlett **Crime Charged:** Murder
Chief Defense Lawyer: Edward Clarke, Q.C. **Chief Prosecutors:** Sir
Charles Russell, Q.C.; Harry Poland, Q.C.; Robert Wright **Judge:** Justice
Alfred Wills **Place:** London, England **Dates of Trial:** April 12–17, 1886
Verdict: Not guilty

SIGNIFICANCE
Of all the classic Victorian poison trials, none has aroused so much controversy as
"The Pimlico Murder."

In 1875, Adelaide Tremoïlle, age 19, from Orléans, France, married a prosperous London grocer named Edwin Bartlett, 29. Beautiful and headstrong, Adelaide was no simpering Victorian maiden. Within a year she had caused mayhem among the Bartlett family, first enjoying a torrid, if brief, affair with her husband's brother, then instigating a feud with her father-in-law that would last a decade. Gradually, an uneasy peace was restored, and in 1881, she became pregnant; after a difficult confinement, she gave birth to a stillborn baby, an experience so traumatic that she vowed never to have another child.

As the marriage continued to crumble, Adelaide became friendly with a young Wesleyan minister, the Reverend George Dyson. Not long afterward, in October 1885, the Bartletts moved to Pimlico, a fashionable London suburb; simultaneously, Edwin's hitherto robust health began to fail. Dr. Alfred Leach, newly qualified and dangerously gullible, diagnosed subacute gastritis and prescribed various medicines, which Adelaide administered. Nothing could arrest Edwin's decline, however, and in the early hours of January 1, 1886, he died.

An autopsy revealed large quantities of the irritant poison chloroform in Edwin's stomach, yet no traces of inflammation could be found in the mouth or throat, kindling speculation as to how it had been administered. When it became known that, at Adelaide's request, Dyson had purchased numerous bottles of chloroform and that a bottle had mysteriously disappeared from Edwin's bedroom at the time of his death, both were charged with murder.

At this juncture something most unusual happened: Adelaide Bartlett engaged the services of Edward Clarke, Q.C. (Queen's Counsel) to conduct her defense. To explain how a woman of relatively modest means was able to afford one of the most expensive members of the bar, we need to return briefly to the circumstances of Adelaide's birth. Although born into a minor aristocratic French family, she was actually illegitimate. Her true father, wrote Edward Clarke many years later, was "an Englishman of good social position," and it was he who funded her defense.

As is customary in English murder trials involving poison, the lead prosecution brief was entrusted to the attorney general, at that time Sir Charles Russell, Q.C., and his first action when court convened on April 12, 1886, caused uproar. Consideration of the evidence convinced him that "there was no case to be submitted to the jury upon which I could properly ask them to convict George Dyson," leaving Justice Alfred Wills no choice but to discharge the hapless clergyman. Wearing an expression of immense relief, Dyson vacated the dock, leaving Adelaide to face the murder charge alone.

During the infamous Pimlico poisoning trial, Mr. Bartlett is cross-examined by Edward Clarke, Q. C. (Hulton-Deutsch Collection)

Turncoat

Dyson promptly turned from defendant to chief accuser, providing the court with intimate details of the Bartletts' marriage. After recounting Edwin's reputedly strange views about matrimony—that men should be allowed two wives, one for companionship, the other for service—and that both should be wives in the "full and complete sense," Dyson dealt with his own unconventional relationship with Adelaide: "I remarked . . . how her husband seemed to throw us together. . . . She told me that his life was not likely to be a long one, and that he knew it. [She told me that Edwin] had confidence in me . . . and that he wished me to be a guardian [and] friend to her when he was gone."

Spurred on by Edwin's apparently terminal illness, Dyson agreed when Adelaide asked him to purchase chloroform to alleviate her husband's chronic insomnia. Dyson visited three different pharmacists, telling each a different story in order to obtain the chloroform. Although he had often seen Adelaide poring over Squire's *Companion to the British Pharmacopoeia*, it had never occurred to him that she might want the poison "for any dangerous or improper use." In that case, asked Clarke, why, immediately after Edwin's death and before its cause was known, had Dyson thrown away three empty chloroform bottles in his possession?

"The thought was in my mind . . . that . . . possibly it was the chloroform I had bought [that] had been the cause of Mr. Bartlett's death. . . . I thought I should be a ruined man if the truth came out."

Dyson was followed into the witness box by Dr. Leach. On one issue the physician would not be shaken—Adelaide had nursed her husband unstintingly. At one point he had said to her, "Now, Mrs. Bartlett, there is no excuse for you not going to bed."

"What is the use of my going to bed, doctor? He will walk around the room like a ghost. He will not sleep unless I sit and hold his toe!"

Leach further tantalized the court with more details from Adelaide's version of life with Edwin: "Marital relations . . . were, in deference to certain peculiar views held by the husband, to be of an entirely platonic nature; sexual intercourse was not to occur. The terms of this compact were adhered to with a solitary exception, when a breach of the terms was permitted in consequence of her fondness for children and her anxiety to become a mother. After her confinement, the former terms . . . were resumed."

Until the last few weeks of his life.

This was when, according to Adelaide, Edwin, having "given me to Mr. Dyson," began to make sexual demands. Repulsed by this sudden and unwanted interest, Adelaide told Leach she had used the chloroform to ward off her husband's advances.

It was quite a story, and one that kept the thrilled observers on the edge of their seats. A more sober tone was interjected by Dr. Thomas Stevenson, a government analyst. After explaining the physiological effects of ingesting chloroform, he said it would not be possible to swallow it without realizing that it was harmful. "It would produce pain and a hot fiery taste. I have swallowed it myself and I have found that it is very hot and very sweet and burning."

Suicide?

Which was exactly what Clarke wanted to hear. Right from the outset he had maintained that Edwin had swallowed the chloroform as an act of suicide and that nowhere had chloroform been used as an agent of murder, since it was virtually impossible to administer without the victim's compliance. Clarke produced no witnesses to support this view: In fact, he produced no witnesses at all. Because English law then did not permit defendants to take the stand and give evidence, Adelaide Bartlett remained a mute spectator to the proceedings that would decide her fate.

For most of the trial, Sir Charles Russell had allowed himself to be distracted by outside political interests, prompting subsequent allegations that he had not applied himself to the prosecution with all possible vigor. But his final speech was a masterpiece of common sense as he ridiculed the stories that Adelaide had fed to the men around her. "One act of coition in order to gratify her desire to have a child!" he jeered. "How did she know that one act of coition would place her in the position to count with certainty or probability on the fruition of her hopes?" And when it came to how Edwin had actually ingested the chloroform, Russell was not short of suggestions: "If the draught had been handed to him in a glass and given to him as if for an ordinary purpose, with drops of chloroform in it, and water or some other thing to drink, then it was conceivable that the dying man would have gulped it down, believing in its innocence and not suspecting that the prisoner had administered something [that] was wrong and injurious."

Clarke leaped to his feet. "My lord, I protest against any such suggestion being put forward, for the first time, at this stage of the case, when it was not even hinted at by the learned counsel for the prosecution in his opening or in the examination of any of the witnesses." His concern was well-founded; Russell's account sounded disturbingly plausible. For the first time a conceivable theory had been adduced of how chloroform might have entered Edwin's stomach.

At the conclusion of Russell's speech, Clarke sought to regain the initiative. He asked if Annie Walker, the nurse who had attended Adelaide in her confinement, might be brought back to the stand. It was a highly unusual departure, but in the absence of any objection from the Crown, Justice Wills agreed.

Clarke: "At the time you nursed Mrs. Bartlett in her confinement, did you become aware from anything she said to you with regard to its having been the result of a single act?"

"Yes, sir," replied Nurse Walker.

Satisfied this provided corroboration of the prisoner's tale of a virtually sexless marriage, Clarke withdrew in triumph, certain he had scored a major point for the defense. However, Justice Wills wanted to hear *all* that had been said regarding the Bartletts' intimate life.

"That it happened only once—on a Sunday afternoon," Walker said.

"She said so?"

"Both of them; that there was always some preventive used."

The judge pounced. "You say you heard that from both of them?"

"Both of them."

Clarke had blundered. This was the clearest evidence yet that, far from being a platonic relationship, as Adelaide had claimed, the couple had engaged in sex regularly. The *once* that Adelaide had mentioned, referred to the single occasion when some form of contraception was not used.

During his summing-up, Justice Wills instructed members of the jury to disregard the theory advanced by Russell in his closing speech and restrict themselves to matters of evidence that had been introduced. About the use of chloroform to treat insomnia, as a fellow sufferer himself, he was sympathetic. "I know the uncommon strength of mind ... it takes to resist that impulse. Fortunately for myself, I soon became aware that one had better undergo any misery than resort to the fatal practice of taking narcotics." About Adelaide, he was less charitable, deploring her interest in a book called *Esoteric Anthropology*, which advanced some radical ideas on contraception and marital relations. He was equally scathing about the fact that, after Edwin's death, a search of his clothes revealed condoms in the pockets. Since he was never known to have consorted with other women, Wills found it impossible to believe they had not been "used at home."

The verdict, when it came from the jury foreman, was delivered with some gratuitous editorializing. "We have well considered the evidence, and, although we think grave suspicion is attached to the prisoner, we do not think there is sufficient evidence to show how or by whom the chloroform was administered."

"Then you say that the prisoner is not guilty?"

"Not guilty."

Upon hearing these words, Clarke, who had never doubted his client's innocence, broke down and wept for the only time in a career that spanned half a century. Adelaide Bartlett, rather more composed, disappeared from the dock and public view without a word. After a tumultuous life, she is believed to have died in Boston, Massachusetts, sometime in the 1930s.

A week after the trial ended, *The Lancet*, Britain's premier medical journal, in discussing the trial, commented, "However strong was that suspicion, there was certainly not sufficient evidence to prove beyond all reasonable doubt that a murder had been committed."

True enough. But an alternative and more commonly held view was said to have been expressed by Sir James Paget, sergeant surgeon to Queen Victoria: "Mrs. Bartlett was no doubt quite properly acquitted, but now it is hoped [that] in the interest of science ... she will tell us how she did it!"

—*Colin Evans*

Suggestions for Further Reading

Bridges, Yseult. *Poison and Adelaide Bartlett*. London: Hutchinson, 1962.

Clarke, Sir Edward. *The Story of My Life*. London: John Murray, 1918.

Clarke, Kate. *The Pimlico Murder*. London: Souvenir Press, 1990.

Hall, Sir John. *Trial of Adelaide Bartlett*. London: William Hodge, 1927.

Florence Maybrick Trial: 1889

Defendant: Florence Chandler Maybrick   **Crime Charged:** Murder
Chief Defense Lawyers: Sir Charles Russell, Arnold Cleaver, Richard Cleaver, William Pickford   **Chief Prosecutors:** John Addison, William McConnell, Thomas Swift   **Judge:** Sir James Fitzjames Stephen   **Place:** Liverpool, England   **Dates of Trial:** July 31–August 7, 1889   **Verdict:** Guilty
Sentence: Death

SIGNIFICANCE

This trial stands as a classic miscarriage of justice, as the jury convicted Florence Maybrick more for adultery than for murder. It was also a watershed in English jurisprudence, for it resulted in two major changes in criminal law.

Florence Chandler was an 18-year-old American traveling alone when she met 42-year-old James Maybrick, an English cotton broker, during a voyage from New York City to Liverpool, England, in 1881. Maybrick spent six months a year in Norfolk, Virginia, buying cotton for English mills. Florence, educated by tutors and governesses, had grown up traveling frequently between the United States and Europe.

Within six months, Florence and James were married. By 1886, they had two children, James and Gladys, and a large Liverpool home, Battlecrease House, with a retinue of servants.

The Maybricks enjoyed a busy social life. Maybrick's brothers, Thomas, Edwin, and Michael, visited frequently. James's business took him often to London, usually for several days at a time.

Five Other Children

Florence learned in 1887 that James had sired five other children—three before their marriage, two since—by a mistress. After that discovery, she no longer slept with her husband.

In December 1888, James invited cotton broker Alfred Brierley to dinner at Battlecrease House. Florence was charmed. The handsome 38-year-old bachelor was soon a frequent dinner guest. And on March 22, 1889, Florence and Alfred met in Flatman's Hotel in London for a weekend together.

A week later, at the Grand National horse race, Florence took Brierley's arm and they strolled off to check the accuracy of a rumor that the Prince of Wales was in the grandstand. When they returned, Maybrick furiously chastised his wife. Afterward, she told a friend, "I will give it to him hot and heavy for speaking to me like that in public."

At home that evening the servants heard violent quarreling. Maybrick said, "Such a scandal will be all over town tomorrow. Florie, I never thought it would come to this." The next morning, Florence had a black eye.

Early in April, complaining of headaches and numbness of a leg and a hand, Maybrick was examined in London by Dr. Charles Fuller, who prescribed a tonic for indigestion.

While James was in London, two of the servants saw flypapers soaking in a basin in Mrs. Maybrick's bedroom. The sight reminded them of a murder case five years earlier in which two sisters, using arsenic soaked from flypapers, poisoned four victims.

On April 27, Maybrick vomited. He complained of chills and numbness. Dr. Richard Humphreys diagnosed chronic dyspepsia. Over several days, as a variety of drugs brought no improvement, more doctors were summoned and nurses were hired.

"My Own Darling"

May 8 found Florence writing to Brierley, who had written her that he feared Maybrick was tracking their London tryst. Busy in the sickroom, she asked nurse Alice Yapp to mail the letter. Yapp let three-year-old Gladys carry it. Gladys, Yapp later testified, dropped it in the mud. Intending to transfer the letter to a clean envelope, Yapp took it out, saw the words "My own darling," and read the letter. She took it to Edwin Maybrick.

That evening, Michael Maybrick read the letter, heard about the flypapers, declared, "The woman is an adulteress," and cautioned Maybrick's doctors and nurses to bar Florence from the sickroom.

Arsenic Here, There, Everywhere

Maybrick died during the evening of May 11. That night, nurse Yapp showed Edwin a package labeled "Arsenic: Poison for Cats" found in Mrs. Maybrick's trunk. Searching Battlecrease House, the brothers found arsenic in hatboxes, basins, packets, and jars and on a handkerchief in Florence's dressing gown. Michael sent a bottle of meat juice she had handled furtively at James's bedside to a laboratory for testing.

Florence was charged with murder. Young James and Gladys were taken to stay with Dr. Fuller. Florence's mother, the Baroness von Roques, arrived from Paris and hired England's foremost barrister, Sir Charles Russell.

When the trial opened on July 31, 1889, countless newspapers had already depicted the American socialite as an adulterous poisoner. Crowds packed St. George's Hall and the streets outside, hissing the closed carriage that brought the prisoner from jail.

Prosecutor John Addison described the rendezvous at Flatman's, the Grand National quarrel and subsequent fight, the onset of Maybrick's illness, and the accused's purchase of flypapers. He described the process of death by arsenic poisoning. He read Florence's letter to Brierley. Then Michael Maybrick testified on the plentiful amounts of arsenic found in Battlecrease House.

Cross-examining, Sir Charles brought out the fact that the meat juice suspected by Michael had proved harmless, that countless suspected vials and boxes contained no arsenic, that Michael had destroyed a letter from Florence about her husband's taking a white powder, and that Maybrick was himself an adulterer.

"A Dangerous Habit"

As each witness testified, Sir Charles's cross-examination established the picture: Maybrick had been a hypochondriac who had "a dangerous habit" of overdosing. He had complained of numbness as early as 1882 and specifically asked his wife to add "some of his white powder" to meat juice prescribed by his doctors.

Cross-examining the chemist who sold the flypapers, Sir Charles established that arsenic was a common ingredient in cosmetics. The servants admitted that the soaking flypapers had not been concealed. Maybrick's doctor agreed that arsenic passed rapidly through the system, yet tests of Maybrick's feces and urine for two days before death had revealed none. He admitted that the idea of foul play had been suggested to him not by symptoms of poison but by Michael Maybrick.

"A Pick-Me-Up"

For the defense, Nicholas Bateson, who had shared Maybrick's bachelor quarters in Norfolk, testified to Maybrick's having taken arsenic for malaria. Mariner Robert Thompson told of having seen Maybrick buy arsenic in Norfolk. A Norfolk waiter described having bought arsenic for Maybrick. A Liverpool chemist testified to Maybrick's 10-year habit of stopping in for an arsenic "pick-me-up." A wholesale druggist said he had employed a Maybrick cousin whom the deceased often visited in the warehouse, where access to arsenic was easy. Finally, Dr. Charles Tidy, examiner of forensic medicine at London Hospital, and Dr. Rawdon MacNamara, professor at the Royal College of Surgeons of Ireland, testified that all the symptoms and post-mortem analyses were consistent with death from gastroenteritis, but not from arsenic. Clearly, Maybrick had succumbed to his longtime habit rather than to acute poisoning by his wife.

Florence Maybrick's Statement

Sir Charles prevailed upon Judge James Fitzjames Stephen to permit his client to make a statement. In tears, she remarked:

> The flypapers were bought with the intention of using [them] as a cosmetic. I have been in the habit of using a face-wash prescribed by Dr. Greggs, of Brooklyn. It consisted of arsenic, tincture of benzoin, elderflower water, and other ingredients. This prescription I mislaid last April, and, as I was suffering from slight eruption of the face, I thought I should make a substitute . . . I now refer to the bottle of meat essence. On Thursday, my husband implored me to give him his powder. I was terribly anxious, and his distress utterly unnerved me. He had told me that the powder would not harm him, and that I could put it in his food . . .

Summing up, Sir Charles stressed "how strongly suspicion had been generated in the minds of the servants in that house" by Florence's brothers-in-law.

Judge Stephen's rambling summary of the evidence took two days. He confused dates, mixed up witnesses, referred to newspaper clippings strewn about his bench, and advised the jury that "there is strong evidence of the prisoner having been actuated by a motive at once strong and disgraceful."

After deliberating for 38 minutes, the jury found Florence Maybrick guilty on August 7. The sentence was execution. Since England had no court of appeal in a criminal case, the hanging was set for Monday morning, August 25.

Within days, a million people had signed petitions in favor of Florence Maybrick. Crowds jammed public halls in London, Liverpool, and Manchester to hear

speakers on her behalf. But only Queen Victoria stood between her and the gallows. Four days before the execution date, the queen commuted the sentence to penal servitude for life.

Within two years, Judge Stephen was committed to an insane asylum. Florence Maybrick served 15 years while, on both sides of the Atlantic, thousands continued to protest. When her Bible was found long after the trial, Dr. Greggs's face-wash prescription was among its pages. From the day of James Maybrick's death, Florence never again saw her children, who had been adopted by Dr. Fuller and his wife. Released in 1904, she was forbidden to write or speak publicly of her case in England. She went immediately to the United States, where she lectured widely and profitably and published a book on her ordeal.

Although Florence Maybrick was sentenced to life imprisonment for murdering her husband, she was released after serving only 15 years. This 1904 photo was taken just after her release from prison.

The Maybrick case produced two major changes in English jurisprudence. In 1898, the rule that an accused person could not give evidence was removed by the passage of England's Criminal Evidence Act. In 1907, the creation of the Court of Criminal Appeal corrected the historic lack of any procedure for a person convicted by a jury to ask for a review of the case.

In 1911, in Rossland, British Columbia, a young mining engineer, James Maybrick Fuller, inadvertently drank potassium cyanide (thinking it was water) at his laboratory bench and died immediately. Gladys Maybrick Fuller lived out a full life in England.

By 1915, Florence Maybrick had disappeared. In October 1941, in tiny Gaylordsville, Connecticut, an elderly recluse named Mrs. Chandler was found dead. Papers in her ramshackle cottage revealed her true identity. Florence Maybrick was buried in the cemetery of the South Kent School, a nearby boys' boarding school whose faculty members and students had befriended the eccentric old lady.

—Bernard Ryan, Jr.

Suggestions for Further Reading

Boswell, Charles, and Lewis Thompson. *The Girl with the Scarlet Brand*. New York: Fawcett, 1954.

Christie, Trevor L. *Etched in Arsenic*. Philadelphia: Lippincott, 1968.

Hodge, James J. *Famous Trials* (3d series). Harmondsworth, England: Penguin, 1950.

Irving, H. B. *Trial of Mrs Maybrick*. Rev. ed. Edinburgh and London: William Hodge, 1922.

Lustgarten, Edgar. *Verdict in Dispute*. New York: Scribner's, 1950.

Maybrick, Florence Elizabeth. *Mrs. Maybrick's Own Story: My Fifteen Lost Years*. New York: Funk and Wagnalls, 1905.

Morland, Nigel. *This Friendless Lady*. London: Frederick Muller, 1957.

Ryan, Bernard. *The Poisoned Life of Mrs. Maybrick*. London: William Kimber, 1977. London: Penguin, 1989.

Shearing, Joseph. *Airing in a Closed Carriage*. New York: Harper, 1943.

O'Shea *v.* Parnell and O'Shea: 1890

Plaintiff: William O'Shea   **Defendants:** Charles Parnell, Katherine O'Shea
Plaintiff's Claim: Divorce on the grounds of adultery
Chief Defense Lawyer: Sir Frank Lockwood, Q.C.
Chief Lawyer for Plaintiff: Sir Edward Clarke, Q.C.   **Judge:** Justice Charles
Butt   **Place:** London, England   **Dates of Trial:** November 15–17, 1890
Decision: Jury found for plaintiff

SIGNIFICANCE
Political scandal, rumors of a duel, salacious tales of locked rooms and frantic
escapes: For Victorian England, these were the ingredients of a notorious divorce
trial; for countless novelists and playwrights since, this saga has taken its place
alongside the great love affairs in history.

By the late 19th century, there was no more divisive issue in British politics
than the campaign for Irish Home Rule. At the forefront of that struggle was
Charles Stewart Parnell, who, within two years of being elected the member of
parliament (MP) for Meath in 1875, had become undisputed leader of the
nationalist cause. A fiery populist, Parnell was a hero in his homeland of Ireland
and a perennial source of consternation to the British government, which jailed
him in late 1881 for dissent. Parnell made the most of what was a leisurely
incarceration, reaping tremendous political capital from his captors' foolishness.
He was released the following spring, and for the remainder of the decade, his
political star soared, his name inextricably linked to home rule. But the clouds
were gathering.

Like Parnell, Captain William O'Shea was a nationalist MP, and it was
largely he who had orchestrated Parnell's release from prison. The irony of this
could not have been lost on either man, since Parnell was already enmeshed in a
passionate and reckless liaison with O'Shea's beautiful wife, Katherine. (Indeed,
before Parnell was imprisoned, O'Shea had challenged him to a duel. The
challenge was declined.)

Out of deference to mutual ambition, the affair was swept under the
carpet, and Parnell went on with the task of uniting the disparate Irish factions.
With that goal seemingly in hand, calamity struck. On December 23, 1889,
O'Shea filed a petition for divorce, citing Parnell as co-respondent. For the bulk

of Parnell's supporters, unaware of just how tangled his personal life had become, the suit was seen as politically motivated, a cynical attempt to wreck home rule.

This was a view that Parnell did nothing to dispel, assuring his colleagues that the allegations were groundless. Yet even as the Irish Parliamentary Party rallied to his side, its leader was offering O'Shea £20,000 ($80,000) to withdraw his petition and allow Katherine to countersue for adultery. Had Parnell been able to raise the funds, in all likelihood the bribe would have succeeded, but such a sum was beyond him, leaving the financially disappointed O'Shea no alternative but to proceed with the suit. Two weeks before the suit was due to be heard, Katherine countersued, alleging 17 instances of infidelity.

Extraordinary Capitulation

Parnell, known publicly as a man of immense integrity, was expected to fight the action vigorously, yet when the court met on November 15, 1890, Sir Frank Lockwood, Q.C (Queen's Counsel), acting for Katherine O'Shea, stunned everyone present by announcing that, after consulting with his client, he did "not intend to cross-examine any witnesses, to call in witnesses, nor to take any part in these proceedings." Parnell, too, thought so little of his chances that he did not even bother to be represented in court. Such a capitulation caught the plaintiff's counsel, Sir Edward Clarke, Q.C, off guard. Writing years later, he said that, as late as the morning of the case, he had expected Captain O'Shea to withdraw his action (probably in anticipation of a successful

Charles Stewart Parnell presents testimony from the witness box during the May 1889 trial.

bribe attempt).

Because Victorian divorce actions were decided by a jury, Clarke was free to make the very most of his case, and this he did with his customary force and cogency. The trial seemed to be meandering toward its predictable conclusion on November 17, with Justice Charles Butt preparing to send the jury out to consider its verdict, when one of the jurors stood up to address him. How, he asked, could all doubts about the countercharges be dispelled if there were no cross-examination of Captain O'Shea himself? "We are asked," he said, "to decide on the question of the petitioner's neglect of his wife, my lord, and I should like particularly to ask some questions as to that charge."

The judge allowed O'Shea to be recalled. Clarke agreed that any member of the jury could ask O'Shea questions, but he himself first put to his client queries about neglect and the separate living arrangements at the O'Shea household. "During the whole time until the actual discovery of your wife's unfaithfulness, had you been living on perfectly friendly and affectionate terms with her?"

"Certainly." As proof, O'Shea cited hundreds of letters between himself and his wife, which had been introduced into court: "Among those letters are a number of telegrams from Mrs. O'Shea about her coming to visit me and dine with me. . . . In none of those letters did Mrs. O'Shea ever complain of the arrangement between us."

When the juror who had first spoken pressed him on the point, O'Shea replied, "No one has ever made the slightest pretense that there was a want of attention on my part. In fact my diaries show clearly that I was a kind husband and a kind father."

Still, the juryman wasn't satisfied. Why then, he asked, having already challenged Parnell to a duel, did O'Shea invite him to dinner in 1881? O'Shea responded rather too quickly: "The dinner you refer to was before that."

"But . . . your evidence shows that you had him to dinner after that?"

Caught in a deliberate lie, O'Shea attempted to bluff: "I did so because it appeared to me at the time that there was no foundation for my suspicions."

This exchange marked the prelude to full public disclosure of the O'Sheas' marital status, their sleeping arrangements at home, the frequency of Parnell's visits, whether Katherine left the house and was away all night. Clarke followed this up with a list of the many addresses at which Parnell and Katherine had been seen together—Brighton, Eastbourne, Regent's Park—calling various witnesses to confirm their presence there and Parnell's penchant for aliases such as Smith, Stewart, and Preston.

Servants at the O'Shea residence testified that Parnell had stayed in the house at night with Katherine when O'Shea had not been there. One said that Parnell "never slept in the house when Captain O'Shea was at home, but he did so frequently when Captain O'Shea was away."

Far and away the most damaging witness was Caroline Pethers, a servant at the O'Sheas' Brighton home. She said that two or three days after Captain and Mrs. O'Shea had taken the house, a gentleman appeared, whom she recognized by his photograph. "He went by the name of Mr. Charles Stewart. Sometimes he called when Captain O'Shea was at home, nearly always when he was away and always came to the house the beach way. . . . Mr. Stewart wore a light cloth cap over his eyes. He drove out at night with Mrs. O'Shea, but never during the day."

Cuckolded Husband Returns

Pethers' next revelation sent reporters into a frenzy. Apparently, Captain O'Shea had come home one day and rung the front doorbell while Parnell and Katherine were locked in the darkened drawing room together. After being admitted by Pethers' husband, O'Shea went upstairs. Ten minutes later, said Pethers, Parnell himself rang the front doorbell and asked to see Captain O'Shea. According to Pethers, the only way he could have accomplished such a feat was by using either of the two rope fire escapes from the drawing room balcony. She said this had happened three or four times. The prospect of the massively dignified Charles Stewart Parnell clambering down from balconies to escape cuckolded husbands conjured up enough farcical images to keep London newspapers in copy for days.

The jury, with witnesses Harriet Wool and Caroline Pethers, listen to evidence presented by Captain O'Shea.

Parnell's fateful decision not to defend the action was a gift to someone with the forensic talents of Sir Edward Clarke. Deploring the fact that Parnell "had not even thought fit to appear . . . [allowing] judgment to go by default," Clarke implied that such an appearance would only have compounded Parnell's problems by adding perjury—lying while under oath—to his list of woes. "For some persons the criminal law has terrors which the moral law has not, and it is perhaps not to be wondered at that Mr. Parnell does not venture to add a criminal offense to that course of faithlessness and falsehood by which during those years he has betrayed the wife of the friend who trusted him."

After this barrage, all that remained was Katherine's rather tepid countersuit of adultery, which had cited her own sister. Anna Steele briefly took the stand to rebut the allegations and left with her head held high and her reputation intact. Again, there was no cross-examination. In light of the unopposed evidence, Justice Butt summed up in the only way possible, and the jury agreed: adultery without connivance. In essence, Parnell was not blamed for seducing Katherine away from her husband.

That night, Parnell and Katherine received a copy of the decree nisi from their lawyers, thus officially terminating the O'Shea's marriage. Both were delighted. Parnell, blinded by love, was convinced that the ordeal had done him no political harm, and the initial response of his countrymen seemed to bear him out. In Britain, however, evangelical opinion was so hostile that the Irish Parliamentary Party was forced to rethink its position. And then there was the Roman Catholic hierarchy in Ireland to consider. It had never trusted the Protestant Parnell and now declared him morally unfit for leadership. Parnell, who must have known his chances of political survival were shrinking by the day, countered with ever more radical appeals that found favor with the young but failed to attract broad-based support. In the end, after a long and acrimonious debate, he was rejected as leader by the Irish Parliamentary Party.

For the man who had refused to give up the woman he loved, the scandal brought personal ruin and the abandonment of all immediate hope for Irish home rule. Parnell accepted his fate philosophically. Six months after the trial, he married his beloved Katie, a time that he described as the happiest of his life. But that happiness was cruelly brief. On October 6, 1891, at the age of 46, Charles Stewart Parnell died from a heart attack.

—Colin Evans

Suggestions for Further Reading

Hickey, D. J., and J. E. Doherty. *A Dictionary of Irish History 1800–1980.* New York: Barnes & Noble, 1981.

Kee, Robert. *The Laurel and the Ivy.* London: Hamish Hamilton, 1993.

Lyons, F.S.L. *Charles Stewart Parnell.* London: Collins, 1977.

O'Shea, K. *Charles Stewart Parnell.* London: Cassell, 1973.

William Gordon-Cumming *v.* Stanley Wilson, Berkeley Levett, and Others: 1891

Plaintiff: Sir William Gordon-Cumming   **Defendants:** Stanley Wilson, Berkeley Levett, others   **Plaintiff Claim:** Slander
Chief Defense Lawyers: Sir Charles Russell, Q.C.; Herbert Asquith, Q.C.
Chief Lawyers for Plaintiff: Sir Edward Clarke, Q.C.; Charles Gill
Judge: Lord Chief Justice John Coleridge   **Place:** London, England
Dates of Trial: June 1–9, 1891   **Decision:** Jury found for defendants

SIGNIFICANCE
For the first time in more than four centuries, the heir to the British throne was called to give testimony in a court of law.

Horse racing has always figured prominently in the British social calendar, and in September 1890, the Prince of Wales traveled north to Doncaster to watch the season's final classic, the St. Leger. For the duration of the three-day meeting, he stayed at Tranby Croft, the home of his friends Mr. and Mrs. Arthur Wilson. After dinner on the first night, the guests played baccarat, a card game that the prince had introduced into England from Europe. Baccarat roughly corresponds to blackjack, except that the intention is to score as close to 9, rather than 21, as possible, and the bank is held by one of the players, not by the house. Apart from those players drawing cards, others watching the action may place bets, in much the same way as at craps.

As was his custom, the prince took the bank. Among those playing was Sir William Gordon-Cumming, lieutenant colonel in the Scots Guards, an experienced gambler and longtime friend of the prince. Owing to the makeshift nature of the gaming table—just three ordinary tables pushed together and covered with a multicolored tablecloth—Gordon-Cumming suggested that, to avoid confusion, everyone place his stakes on a sheet of white paper in front of him. But the idea did not meet with general approval, and he was, in fact, the only player to adopt this method. The heaviest gambler present, Gordon-Cumming was a dashing player and soon attracted attention as his stakes fluctuated between £5 and £25 ($20 and $100).

Next to Gordon-Cumming sat 21-year-old Stanley Wilson, son of the hosts and a newcomer to baccarat. During one particular hand, Wilson was puzzled because Gordon-Cumming had a £5 chip in front of him, yet when it came time for him to be paid, the stake had grown to £15. Some time later, Wilson thought he saw Gordon-Cumming add three chips to his stake after the cards had fallen in his favor. Turning to the person on his other side, Berkeley Levett, Wilson whispered, "This is too hot! The man next to me is cheating."

1891

William Gordon-

Cumming *v.*

Stanley Wilson,

Berkeley Levett,

and Others

"Impossible," replied Levett, a lieutenant in the same regiment as Gordon-Cumming, but after a few hands, he, too, became convinced that his superior officer was cheating. The next night, other houseguests watched Gordon-Cumming and spotted apparent irregularities. They took their suspicions first to General Owen Williams and Lord Coventry, two other guests who knew Gordon-Cumming well, and then to the prince. Anxious to avoid any scandal, the prince jumped at a suggestion that the best way to cover up the incident would be if Gordon-Cumming signed a document swearing never to play cards again.

Only then was Gordon-Cumming made aware of the allegations against him. He received the news with openmouthed incredulity and proclaimed his innocence vehemently, but in the end, to spare his hosts any scandal that might accrue should these charges ever be made public, he reluctantly agreed to sign the document they had prepared.

As Gordon-Cumming feared, the promised silence was not forthcoming. The whispers were insidious and becoming louder as friends puzzled over why this once most enthusiastic gambler now refused every invitation to play. By January 1891, his position had become untenable, and he issued writs for slander against Stanley Wilson, Levett, and three other players.

Famous Advocate

Once it became known that the Prince of Wales was involved in yet another scandal (the heir's private life regularly filled newspaper columns) public interest skyrocketed, especially when it was learned that the solicitor general, Sir Edward Clarke, Q.C. (Queen's Counsel), believed Gordon-Cumming's account of events and had agreed to fight the action on his behalf.

The suit was heard on June 1, 1891, before Lord Chief Justice John Coleridge, whose wife, perched on the bench beside him, was determined not to miss a minute of what promised to be a highlight of the social season. Just to the judge's left, and slightly lower, sat the Prince of Wales. Clarke trod carefully at first, not wanting to ruffle any royal feathers, claiming that his client, in a moment of panic, had signed the document with scarcely a thought to the outcome. This was also Gordon-Cumming's stance when he testified that immense pressure had been put on him to sign the document in order that a scandal might be averted. He also explained his method of staking, the *coup de trois*. If he won a hand for, say, £5, he would leave the initial stake, add the winning £5, then add another £5, making £15 in all for the next hand. This was a recognized staking system, but one which novice baccarat players such as Wilson and Levett might easily mistake for cheating.

Clarke's final questions to his client were as follows:

"Did you cheat at baccarat that night?"

"I did not."

"Is there any truth whatever in the accusation against you?"

"There is none whatsoever."

Gordon-Cumming stood up well to an assault from Sir Charles Russell, Q.C., impressing everyone in court, except, of course, those with a vested interest. These included the Prince of Wales, who now took his place in the witness-box, marking the first occasion upon which an heir to the throne had appeared in court since Prince Henry, the hero of Agincourt, was cited for contempt in 1411.

Both advocates treated the prince with kid gloves. Clarke, especially, was deferential. Russell, rather more forthright, seemed irked by the prince's refusal to actually declare the plaintiff guilty of cheating. What had been a fairly lukewarm affair was made anything but when, just as the prince was leaving the witness-box, a juryman, Goddard Clarke, leaped to his feet and shouted, "Excuse me, Your Royal Highness, I have a question or two to ask you." The court froze. Just about the only person who seemed unaffected was the prince himself. He listened attentively as Clarke asked the question that both counsel had conspicuously avoided. "Are this jury to understand that you, as banker on these two occasions, saw nothing of the alleged malpractices of the plaintiff?"

"No; it is not usual for a banker to see anything in dealing cards," the prince replied, "especially when you are playing among friends in their house. You do not for a moment suspect anything of the sort."

"What was your Royal Highness' opinion at the time as to the charges made against Sir William Gordon-Cumming?"

Although this request for an opinion should have been disallowed, the moment was too highly charged for it to go unanswered, and the prince replied, "They seemed so strongly supported—unanimously so—by those who brought them forward that I felt no other course was open to me but to believe what I was told."

The defendants cut a sorry sight on the stand. Wilson and Levett, in particular, seemed to have only the flimsiest grasp of baccarat and gambling, fostering suspicions that these two young men had been hasty in their actions and were now desperate to conceal such foolhardiness.

Astonishing Charge

Clarke's final speech to the jury was wholly different in tone and manner from his earlier efforts. Much of what he had heard during the trial convinced him that the entire exercise had been designed to protect the reputation of the Prince of Wales, and he lost no opportunity to say so: "If you [the jury] find that

Sir William Gordon-Cumming was not guilty of that which is charged against him, and if, as I trust he may, he goes forth from this Court justified by your verdict, I am bound to say that I think it is impossible that Sir William Gordon-Cumming's name should be removed from the Army List, and that the names of Field Marshall the Prince of Wales and of Major General Owen Williams should remain there."

A gasp ran through the court, with the prince staring impassively at the man who dared advance such a suggestion. The remainder of Clarke's speech, which he always considered among the finest he ever made, cut huge swaths through the credibility of the defendants, and at its conclusion, most felt that Gordon-Cumming would be vindicated.

But they had reckoned without Lord Chief Justice Coleridge. Throughout, he had leaned over backward to accommodate the defendants; now, during his summing-up, he allowed personal prejudice to mar what should have been an impartial précis of the evidence. He made much of the fact that the plaintiff had kept his winnings and asked the members of the jury if, under the circumstances, they would have done similarly; then, referring to the document that Gordon-Cumming had signed, he sniffed, "I cannot understand a man doing as this man did." In the face of such prompting, it came as no surprise when, on June 9, the jury found for the defendants, although loud booing greeted the verdict and the defendants had to be escorted from the court.

Gordon-Cumming was ruined. Dismissal from the army followed hard on the heels of banishment from his clubs, and he adjourned to his Scottish estates, where he lived in bitter isolation until his death in 1930.

It is clear that something happened at Tranby Croft, but what? Following the trial, two entirely contradictory stories gained popular currency. The first concerned Gordon-Cumming's reputation as a blatant seducer of other men's wives and girlfriends and charged that the Prince of Wales had finally settled an old score with the notorious rake. Others believed that the person actually caught cheating was the prince himself and that an elaborate plot had been hatched to protect the future king of England. Unfortunately, no one has been able to produce a single shred of evidence to support either theory.

—Colin Evans

Suggestions for Further Reading

Clarke, Sir Edward. *The Story of My Life*. London: John Murray, 1918.

Crimes and Punishment. Vol. 17. London: Phoebus, 1974.

Havers, Michael, Edward Grayson, and Peter Shankland. *The Royal Baccarat Scandal*. London: Souvenir Press, 1988.

Shore, W. Teignmouth, ed. *The Baccarat Case*. London: William Hodge, 1932.

Thomas Neill Cream Trial: 1892

Defendant: Thomas Neill Cream **Crime Charged:** Murder
Chief Defense Lawyers: Gerald Geoghegan, Clifford Luxmoore Drew, W. Howel Scratton, H. Warburton **Chief Prosecutors:** Sir Charles Russell, Q.C.; Bernard Coleridge, Q.C.; Henry Sutton; Charles Gill **Judge:** Justice Henry Hawkins **Place:** London, England **Dates of Trial:** October 17–21, 1892
Verdict: Guilty **Sentence:** Death

SIGNIFICANCE
It required a remarkable departure from customary legal procedure to convict this most remarkable of killers.

In 1876, Scottish-born Thomas Neill Cream received a medical degree from McGill University in Montreal and shortly thereafter embarked on one of the most extraordinary criminal careers that the world has witnessed. He graduated quickly from insurance fraud and attempted blackmail, to illegal abortions, and it was this latter capacity that forced his flight from Canada in 1879, when a chambermaid died after a botched operation. His arrival in Chicago was soon followed by a prison sentence for murder after one of his patients, Daniel Stott, succumbed to poison. Ironically, it was Cream himself who had alerted the authorities to the advisability of an exhumation, thus displaying for the first time the self-destructive exhibitionism that would plague him.

Released in 1891, Cream sailed for England. That October, a London prostitute, Ellen Donworth, was found dying in the street. With her final breath, she said that "a tall gentleman" had made her drink from a bottle "with white stuff in [it]." An autopsy revealed massive amounts of strychnine. In a letter to the local coroner, "A. O'Brien, detective" offered to reveal the murderer's identity in return for £300,000 ($1.2 million). Another letter to the well-known firm of stationers W. H. Smith named one of their employees as the murderer and offered the "superior" legal services of "H. Bayne, barrister" should the case ever go to trial. Understandably, police dismissed both letters as the work of a crank.

One week later, on October 20, the killer struck again. Matilda Clover was found sprawled across her bed, gasping that "Fred" had made her take some pills. Another prostitute in the house who had glimpsed "Fred" in the dimly lit hallway, described him as a "toff" (dandy), with a heavy mustache, tall, wearing a high silk hat and long cape. The circumstances and description went unheeded. Clover's death was recorded as due to alcoholic poisoning.

More outlandish letters began turning up. One, to a fashionable West End physician and signed "M. Malone," accused the physician of Clover's murder and threatened exposure unless he handed over £2,500 ($10,000). It was the very absurdity of these letters that led police to disregard them; consequently, no order was obtained for the exhumation of Clover's body. Meanwhile, the enigmatic Dr. Cream decided to winter in Canada.

Double Murder

Cream returned to London the following spring. In the early hours of April 12, 1892, Police Constable George Comley was patrolling his beat, not far from where the first murder had taken place, when he noticed a couple in a doorway. He recognized the girl as Emma Shrivell, a prostitute. Her companion, a tall man, wore an expensive silk hat and gold-rimmed spectacles, items not normally seen in that part of London. Less than an hour later, Comley was back to answer an emergency call. Shrivell and another girl, Alice Marsh, were both writhing in agony on the floor of Emma's apartment. Before dying, they described a man named "Fred" whom they had been entertaining at supper. Fred had given them "long, thin pills," which they had obediently swallowed before he left.

It was soon after this that Cream, calling himself "Dr. Neill," approached Scotland Yard, demanding to know why he was suspected of murder and complaining that the constant police surveillance was ruining his practice. Sergeant Patrick McIntyre was baffled—neither he nor anyone else at the Yard had heard of this fellow—but he was intrigued by Neill's inside knowledge of the murders, especially his claim that the killer of Marsh and Shrivell was the son of a Devonshire doctor, Joseph Harper. Neill showed McIntyre a letter he said the girls had received before their deaths. Its contents warned them against "Dr. Harper's son," lest he serve them as he had done Matilda Clover and Lou Harvey. Since no one had hitherto mentioned poison in connection with Clover's death, a hasty exhumation was arranged. Once again strychnine was found. But who was Lou Harvey? The death register revealed nothing, and not until detectives began contacting their underworld informants did they learn that Lou Harvey was not dead at all; in fact, she was alive and well and ready to talk.

Louisa Harris, alias Lou Harvey, said she had met Neill at the Alhambra Theater on the evening of October 26, 1891. After spending the night together at a hotel, they had arranged to meet the next evening near the Thames. Unnerved by Neill's odd demeanor, Louisa asked her boyfriend, Charles Harvey, to keep guard on her in case of any trouble. Under Harvey's watchful eye, Louisa met her client. The stranger wasted no time in producing some pills that he said would improve her complexion. Louisa later said in court that she pretended to swallow the pills, but instead "threw them over the Embankment." The stranger then gave her five shillings and arranged to meet her that night at 11 o'clock, but he never showed up. She described him as wearing "gold-rimmed glasses ... he had a dress suit on ... spoke with a foreign twang. . . . I noticed he was a very hairy man. . . ." Later, she amplified this to include "No beard, he had a mustache ... the top of his head was bald. He was cross-eyed." By chance, Louisa had met Neill again one month later. At first he hadn't recognized her, but once his memory cleared, he stalked off, apparently baffled because his capsules had failed.

In the meantime, police had contacted Dr. Joseph Harper in Devon. He showed them a blackmail demand for £1,500 ($6,000), or else the writer would expose Harper's son as the murderer of Shrivell and Marsh. Comparisons of this letter and the earlier one shown to police by "Dr. Neill" determined the handwriting to be identical. Police now had enough to arrest Cream for blackmail. One month later, during July, the charge was amended to murder.

The November 5, 1892, *Illustrated Police News* portrays Dr. Thomas Neill Cream as a condemned man.

Frail Case

The trial of Thomas Neill Cream should have been a formality, except that the prosecution struck a hitch. At that time, it was customary in England to not charge a defendant with more than one murder at a time. Cumulatively, the weight of circumstantial evidence against Cream was overwhelming; taken in isolation, each case came up short. Unless they could introduce the evidence in total, prosecutors glumly estimated, their chances of conviction were no better than 50-50.

Accordingly, when the trial was called at the Old Bailey on October 17, 1892, Cream faced just one count of murder—that of Matilda Clover. But

Attorney-General Sir Charles Russell, Q.C. (Queen's Counsel), argued strongly that evidence regarding the deaths of Ellen Donworth, Emma Shrivell, and Alice Marsh, and the attempted murder of Louisa Harris, should be introduced because it showed that the prisoner "was in possession of and was dealing with strychnine" and that his actions indicated a "systematic and deliberate mode of procedure."

Predictably, Gerald Geoghegan, chief defense counsel, fought tooth and nail on this point but to no avail. Justice Henry Hawkins ruled that it was "impossible on the present occasion to keep separate and distinct the various cases. . . . It would be the height of absurdity to say that they [the prosecutors] should never in any circumstances allow two crimes to be investigated at the same time." With this decision, the prosecution was home and dry.

Russell built a massive case. First, there was the letter stating that Matilda Clover had died from strychnine, written before her body had been exhumed. Next, came the revelation that seven bottles of strychnine had been found at Cream's lodgings, along with 500 copies of an extraordinary pamphlet that the defendant had ordered in Canada in January 1892. It read:

> To the guests of the Metropole Hotel
> Ladies and Gentlemen,
> I hereby notify you that the person who murdered Ellen Donworth on the
> 13th last October is today in the employ of the Metropole Hotel and that
> your lives are in danger as long as you remain in this Hotel.
> Yours respectfully,
> W. H. Murray
> London, April 1892

As further evidence of Cream's erratic and possibly homicidal behavior, the prosecution called a Canadian salesman, John McCulloch. So anxious was the government to have McCulloch testify that it had offered him first-class passage to England, £50 ($200) a month, and a pound a day subsistence allowance. It was money well spent.

McCulloch described a March 1892 meeting with Cream at Blanchard's Hotel in Quebec, when the accused had produced some "whitish crystals" in a bottle, which he said he put into capsules and "gave to the women to get them out of the family way." Next, he had demonstrated a set of false whiskers used to "prevent identification when operating." McCulloch also spoke of Cream's penchant for obscene photographs and prostitutes. "He told me that he had had lots of fun in London with the women . . . as many as three women on one night, between the hours of 10 P.M. and 3 A.M. . . . had used them, and had paid no more than a shilling to each."

After other witnesses testified to hearing the defendant boast of using strychnine on prostitutes, Emily Sleaper, the daughter of Cream's landlady in London, described how Cream told her that Donworth had been murdered by an English lord, and that Dr. William Harper had killed Marsh and Shrivell. When she told Cream that he must be mad, he reacted angrily, insisting he had received information from a "detective friend" from America.

Insane?

Oddly enough, this was the only reference to Cream's mental state during the five-day trial. Although startlingly abnormal, he was, within the narrow framework of the M'Naghten Rules, competent and culpable; nothing in the Victorian statute book covered his singular kind of madness. Although constrained by the law of the time from testifying on his own behalf, Cream made no secret of his contempt for every aspect of the proceedings. Often he was convulsed in laughter. The defense never called any witnesses for the simple reason that there weren't any. This left only the judge's summing-up. Referring to the entirely circumstantial nature of the evidence, Justice Hawkins reminded the jury that it "was not to be expected in every case that there should be mathematical proof of the commission of the crime," only reasonable certainty. Found guilty, Cream was sentenced to death.

Earlier references to the defendant's indiscriminate personal drug abuse—witnesses had spoken of seeing him stupefied with opium, and he continually complained of headaches that could be alleviated only by massive medication—now manifested themselves in the condemned cell, as Cream spent his final weeks either prostrate from pain or else in a whirling frenzy. Deathwatch guards could only gape in amazement as their charge danced merrily around his cell, singing at the top of his lungs. On November 15, 1892, Cream was hanged.

9. "The execution of Dr. Thomas Neill Cream: Closing scenes in the career of a great criminal," *Illustrated Police News,* 19 November 1892. By permission of the British Library.

From the November 19, 1892, *Illustrated Police News,* the closing scenes on the execution of Dr. Thomas Neill Cream.

Even then, this bizarre saga had one final twist. According to the executioner, as Cream stood bound and hooded on the scaffold, he yelled out, "I am Jack the—" just as the trap door fell. So was Cream really Jack the Ripper? The answer is no. While history's most notorious unknown killer was eviscerating London prostitutes during the fall of 1888, Cream was 4,000 miles away in Joliet State Prison in Illinois, serving time for murder. Setting aside arcane theories of "doubles in crime," one can only conclude that, even as the world collapsed beneath him, Thomas Neill Cream, homicide's arch self-promoter, could not resist one final parting shot.

—Colin Evans

Suggestions for Further Reading

Gaute, J. H., and Robin Odell. *The New Murderers' Who's Who*. New York: Dorset Press, 1991.

McLaren, Angus. *A Prescription for Murder*. Chicago: University of Chicago Press, 1993.

Shore, W. Teignmouth. *Trial of Thomas Neill Cream*. London: Hodge, 1923.

Wilson, Colin, and Patricia Pitman. *Encyclopedia of Murder*. New York: G. P. Putnam, 1961.

Alfred Dreyfus Trials: 1894 and 1899

Defendant: Alfred Dreyfus   **Crime Charged:** Treason
Chief Defense Lawyers: Maitre Edgar Demange, Fernand Labori
Chief Prosecutors: André Brisset, Major Carrière   **Judges:** E. Maurel, A.
Jouaust   **Places:** Paris and Rennes, France   **Dates of Trials:** December
19–22, 1894; August 7–September 9, 1899   **Verdicts:** Guilty
Sentence: Deportation to the Devil's Island penal colony, French Guiana
Final Outcome: Verdicts annulled; Dreyfus declared innocent

SIGNIFICANCE

The Dreyfus case exposed a deep vein of anti-Semitism in late 19th-century
France. To some, the Dreyfus affair foreshadowed the rise of the modern
totalitarian state. Others regard Dreyfus's eventual acquittal as a triumph, however belated, of enduring French ideals. The effects linger today. In August 1995,
after a French army publication cast doubt on Dreyfus's innocence, the army
formally and publicly reaffirmed the official view: that Dreyfus was the victim of a
terrible injustice.

A cover letter, or *bordereau*, listing five restricted military documents turned
up in the Statistical Section of the French War Office in September 1894.
Investigators viewed the letter as evidence that a French traitor had delivered a
packet of secret documents to the German military attaché in Paris.

The investigating officers proceeded on two broad assumptions: (1) the
spy would likely be an artillery officer, and (2) the spy would likely be an officer
assigned to the General Staff as a probationer. Only a few men met both
qualifications. One was Alfred Dreyfus, 35 years old, an artillery captain on staff
duty. "The name of Dreyfus was the only one we could think of," recalled
Colonel Pierre-Elie Fabre. Dreyfus was an Alsatian, the son of a wealthy
manufacturer. He was a Jew in an overwhelmingly Catholic army. And Dreyfus
had made a poor impression on some of his superiors. They found him cool,
standoffish. "A bit too sure of himself," one said. Fabre compared Dreyfus's
handwriting with that of the *bordereau*. There seemed to be a match.

The order came down for Dreyfus's arrest. Major Armand du Paty de
Clam, of the War Office, subjected him to a series of interrogations, night after
night for more than two weeks, in his cell at the Cherche-Midi Prison. At no time

did Du Paty detail the specific charges. The questions bewildered Dreyfus. It was as though he were struggling to awake from a nightmare. Meantime, the Statistical Section began fabricating a dossier that would incriminate him.

Dreyfus seemed baffled, dazed. His jailer studied him closely. He looked, prison commandant Ferdinand Forzinetti thought, like a madman. His eyes were bloodshot. The things in his cell had been thrown about. Intuitively, Forzinetti believed him innocent. "You are off the track," Forzinetti told a senior general. "This officer is not guilty." On December 4, the military judge advocate prepared a bill of particulars accusing Dreyfus of treason and ordering a court-martial.

Most of the evidence amounted to little more than whimsy. Handwriting experts concluded Dreyfus had not penned the *bordereau*. What remained? Dreyfus spoke German. He expressed curiosity about military matters. He questioned his fellow officers about professional issues. He had a habit of lingering in offices. "Wherever he passed," the judge advocate said, "documents disappeared." Most damning, Dreyfus was a Jew. Du Paty, who built the case against Dreyfus, had violently anti-Semitic attitudes. Someone had stolen the documents and sold them to France's enemies. In Du Paty's view, the thief could not possibly have been a true Frenchman.

Here, then, were the origins of "The Affair," as the 12-year ordeal of Dreyfus and of France would come to be called. There were deeper causes and a larger context: the legacy of defeat at Prussia's hands and the loss of the provinces of Alsace and Lorraine in 1870–71, widespread corruption in government, challenges from the left to the conservative, nationalist bulwarks of the army and the church, and spreading anti-Semitism. Alfred Dreyfus was at once the principal victim and the chief symbol of the violent convulsions of late nineteenth-century France.

The First Trial

The court-martial of Dreyfus convened at noon December 19, 1894, in a small room in the Cherche-Midi. The military prosecutor, André Brisset, demanded a closed trial. Dreyfus's lawyer, Edgar Demange, argued for a public proceeding. The president of the court ruled for the prosecution.

Witnesses were heard on December 19, 20, and 21. Du Paty testified that he had become certain of Dreyfus's guilt when he observed how Dreyfus's foot moved imperceptibly as he sat cross-legged during interrogations. Major Hubert Henry, a Statistical Section officer who had forged the incriminating documents, took the stand to say that an informer had identified Dreyfus as the traitor.

"Do you affirm that the treasonous officer was Captain Dreyfus?" the court president asked.

"I swear to it," Henry answered.

Several defense witnesses testified to Dreyfus's honesty, loyalty, and excellent service record. Dreyfus himself had little to say, beyond affirming his innocence: As a French Alsatian, he said, he could not possibly have spied for

French soldier Alfred Dreyfus was accused and convicted of revealing military secrets to the Germans in 1894. In 1895, his degradation became public as Dreyfus was forced to march around the courtyard of the Ecole Militaire in front of the troops.

the German conqueror. On December 22, Demange delivered his long final argument, a three-hour exposé of a prosecution case that should never have come to trial.

"If an order has not been issued to convict him," Demange predicted as the judges retired to chambers, "he will be acquitted this evening."

During the deliberations, Du Paty delivered to the judges a packet of "evidence"—more forgeries—purporting to prove Dreyfus's guilt. At 7:30, the court announced a unanimous verdict of guilty. The sentence: military degradation and deportation to the penal colony at Devil's Island in French Guiana.

A few days later, the authorities rejected Dreyfus's plea for an appeal. On the gray, cold morning of January 5, 1895, he arrived under guard at the courtyard of the Ecole Militaire in the Place Fontenoy for the degradation. Several thousand Parisians milled in the streets beyond the walls. Shouts of "Death to the Jew!" and "Death to Judas!" could be heard above the din. "I shall approach this ordeal, which is worse than death, with my head held high and without embarrassment," Dreyfus told Demange. The clerk of the court-martial read out the verdict. Decorations, symbols of rank, even the red stripes on Dreyfus's trousers were torn off. An officer broke Dreyfus's sword over his knee.

An escort led Dreyfus away to his cell. A journalist who had witnessed the degradation described Dreyfus as "a walking corpse, a zombie on parade." It was an apt phrase. "I would have been happier in my grave," Dreyfus wrote his wife that night.

The Affair

Documents kept disappearing from the War Ministry. In March 1896, Major Georges Picquart, the newly appointed chief of intelligence, discovered a scrap of paper—a *petit bleu*, the message card used to communicate via pneumatic tube—that seemed to point to a new suspect. After several months of investigation, Picquart became convinced of the guilt of a shadowy, intriguing officer named Charles Esterhazy.

This illustration, from the January 13, 1895, edition of *Le Petit Journal, Supplement Illustre,* depicts Dreyfus's humiliation as his sword is broken by a member of the troops.

Picquart learned that Esterhazy had written the *bordereau*, had been in the pay of the German military attaché, and had passed French military secrets to the Germans. In August, Picquart denounced Esterhazy to the chief of the General Staff. Dreyfus's supporters—his brother; his wife, Lucie; friends who believed him a blameless victim of malice—campaigned for a retrial. In October, the army banished the meddlesome Picquart, ordering him to report to a colonial regiment in Algeria. Meanwhile, Major Henry added new forgeries to the Dreyfus dossier.

The high command refused to acknowledge the possibility of error. With Picquart's exposure of Esterhazy, the Dreyfus matter exploded into a national crisis—a case study in mass hysteria, in the words of one student of The Affair. Anti-Dreyfusards accused the condemned man's defenders of conspiring to destroy France. To the Dreyfusards, the conviction represented a towering and shameful injustice. Dreyfus's champions, most notably, the radical politician Georges Clemenceau and the author Émile Zola, continued to advance his cause. Picquart pursued his lonely quest to bring down the real traitor.

Risking destruction of his career, Picquart passed on all he knew of the case to sympathetic politicians. High-level government officials pressured the army to arrest Esterhazy. On January 10, 1898, Esterhazy appeared before a court-martial in Paris. To cries of "Long live the army!" and "Down with the Jews!" the court acquitted him the next day. Zola responded with his celebrated broadside *J'accuse!* A few weeks later, the German foreign minister told the Reichstag there had never been a connection, ever, between Dreyfus and any German agency.

There matters stood for another eight months. In August, in a sensational turn of events, Major Henry admitted he had fabricated evidence used against Dreyfus. "It was for the good of the country and of the Army," he explained in extenuation. Then, taking a razor to his throat, he killed himself. Esterhazy, meantime, had fled France. In September, he admitted publicly that he had written the *bordereau*—on orders from his superior, he claimed, in an effort to entrap the spy.

The Second Trial

The High Court of Appeals heard Dreyfus's plea for a new trial in the spring of 1899. After a two-month review, the court on June 3 rescinded and annulled the 1894 verdict and ordered a new court-martial at Rennes, in Brittany. Six days later, a French warship carried Dreyfus away from Devil's Island.

The second trial opened August 7 in the auditorium of a Rennes school, the judges grouped at a large table on the stage. Colonel Albert Jouaust, the court president, questioned Dreyfus harshly, beginning with the *bordereau*, then moving on to the old charges about gambling, women, his habit of striking up conversations with other officers. Dreyfus's answers were short. At one point, when he began to reply at greater length, Jouaust cut him off. "That is unnecessary talk," he said. "Do you deny it, or don't you?"

Jouaust and the others were sitting in judgment on a near wreck of a man. Devil's Island had ruined Dreyfus's health and had prematurely aged him. His hair had gone white. Missing several teeth, he spoke with a slight whistle. Permitted once again to wear the uniform of a captain of artillery, he had padded the tunic to give the illusion of robustness.

Dreyfus expressed little emotion during the trial. His enemies found him cold and calculating. "What was needed was an actor," one of the Dreyfusards observed, "and he was a soldier." During three days of closed sessions, the court reviewed the secret dossier. On August 12, General Auguste Mercier, the war minister in 1894–95, testified that he remained convinced of Dreyfus's guilt, despite Picquart's investigations, Henry's admission and suicide, and Esterhazy's flight. If there had been the least doubt, Mercier said, he would have admitted error. For once, Dreyfus flared.

"That is what you should do!" Dreyfus shouted, rising to his feet and pointing at Mercier.

Dreyfus sat quietly most of the time, taking in the trial with evident detachment. He refused to play to the judges' sympathies. At one point, a former colonial official described the double shackles in which Dreyfus had been held on Devil's Island. Dreyfus broke in, "I am not here to speak of the atrocious forms of torture inflicted on an innocent man, but to defend my honor."

The defendant paid the strictest attention, though, to the testimony of Picquart, who finally had been dismissed from the service for his role in challenging the initial verdict. "Dreyfus naturally drank in all the witness's words," the Associated Press reported, "and closely scanned the faces of the judges, as though seeking to read their thoughts." Speaking forcefully and defiantly, Picquart left little room for doubt that the defendant had been wrongly accused.

None of this made much impression on the anti-Dreyfusards, who continued to pour invective upon the defendant and his allies. To Maurice Barrès, Dreyfus's supporters reeked of corruption. Demange, Dreyfus's lawyer, asked questions "with the solemnity of a headwaiter passing the turbot," Barrès thought. Dreyfus *was* guilty, he wrote, not of spying (by now even the most benighted bigot could see that, whatever else he was, whatever else he had done, Dreyfus had not sold stolen secrets to the Germans), but of casting "the Army and the Nation into turmoil." In other words, Dreyfus's guilt or innocence was irrelevant.

The lawyers summed up their cases on September 7, 8, and 9. The prosecutor, Carrière, suggested the judges need not worry too much about the question of proof. A belief in Dreyfus's guilt would suffice. "Are you intimately convinced?" he asked. Dreyfus spoke only briefly, whispering yet again, in his weak, whistling voice, that he was innocent.

Deliberations began at 3:15 P.M. on September 9. At 4:45, the judges returned with the verdict: "In the name of the French people, by a majority of five votes to two, yes, the accused is guilty," Jouaust said. "By a majority there are extenuating circumstances." Ten days later, the French government pardoned Dreyfus.

The End of The Affair

So, at last, Dreyfus went free. Still, he and his supporters continued to press for a reversal of the verdict. By 1906, when the High Court of Appeals took up the case again, anti-Semitism had abated and much of the passion had drained out of The Affair. The public prosecutor asked the court to annul the Rennes verdict and declare Dreyfus innocent. After a brief deliberation, the court concurred. Dreyfus, fully rehabilitated, returned to the army in July 1906. He retired a year later. Mobilized at the outbreak of World War I, he fought at Chemin des Dames and Verdun and remained on active service until the armistice.

To the end of his life, Dreyfus refused to accept the larger meaning of his case. With its virulent anti-Semitism, its manipulation of mob opinion, and its exaltation of the corporate power of the state, the conspiracy against Dreyfus was a prelude to fascism, as 20th-century American political scientist Hannah Arendt saw it. To Dreyfus, the army had simply accused the wrong man. "Dreyfus as a symbol of justice is not me," he wrote a supporter. "That Dreyfus was created by you." Rather, as he put it, "I was only an artillery officer whom a tragic error prevented from following his course."

Dreyfus died in Paris on July 12, 1935.

—Michael Golay

Suggestions for Further Reading

Bredin, Jean-Denis. *The Affair: The Case of Alfred Dreyfus.* Translated by Jeffrey Mehlman. New York: George Braziller, 1986.

Chapman, Guy. *The Dreyfus Case: A Reassessment.* Westport, Conn.: Greenwood Press, 1979.

Halasz, Nicholas. *Captain Dreyfus: History of a Mass Hysteria.* New York: Simon & Schuster, 1955.

Hoffman, Robert L. *More Than a Trial: The Struggle over Captain Dreyfus.* New York: Free Press, 1980.

Snyder, Louis L. *The Dreyfus Case: A Documentary History.* New Brunswick, N.J.: Rutgers University Press, 1973.

Oscar Wilde Trials: 1895

Defendant: Oscar Wilde **Crimes Charged:** Sodomy, indecency
Chief Defense Lawyers: Sir Edward Clarke, Q.C.; Charles Mathews; Travers Humphreys **Chief Prosecutors:** Charles Gill, Horace Avory, Arthur Gill (first trial); Sir Frank Lockwood, Q.C.; Charles Gill (second trial) **Judges:** Justice Arthur Charles (first trial), Justice Alfred Wills (second trial) **Place:** London, England **Dates of Trial:** April 26–May 1, 1895; May 22–26, 1895
Verdicts: Mistrial (first trial), guilty (second trial)
Sentence: Two years' hard labor

SIGNIFICANCE
What began with a rash libel suit culminated in the downfall of Britain's finest playwright of the time.

On February 18, 1895, the Marquess of Queensberry, a noted sporting peer and the man who wrote the rules for boxing that still bear his name, called at the Albemarle Club in London. Though clearly in a foul mood, his temper was finely focused as he prepared to deliver what he hoped would be the knockout blow in a long-running feud that had festered for three years. When, as anticipated, his intended quarry proved not to be in attendance, Queensberry left his calling card, upon which he wrote: "To Oscar Wilde posing as a Somdomite [sic]."

The provocation was planned and pernicious. At age 40, Oscar Wilde, dramatist, wit, raconteur, and master of the comic paradox, was at the peak of his celebrity, with two plays, *The Importance of Being Earnest* and *An Ideal Husband*, running on both sides of the Atlantic. He was also very closely acquainted with Queensberry's 22-year-old son, Lord Alfred Douglas. The two had met in 1892, and since then rumors about the exact nature of their friendship had kept London's café society agog. Queensberry watched the liaison, first with anguish, then with fury, trying everything in his power to come between them, even threatening to shoot Wilde if he did not end this "most loathsome and disgusting relationship." When even this failed, he decided to flush Wilde into the open.

In Victorian England, homosexuality was a serious crime, and Queensberry knew that Wilde, after reading the calling card, would have no alternative but to sue for libel. Queensberry's defense would be that what he had stated was true and that the public needed to be protected from such perverts; the ensuing scandal of a trial, he reasoned, would ruin his archenemy. Against the advice of such luminaries as George Bernard Shaw and Frank Harris, and egged on by the malicious Lord Alfred, Wilde took the bait and filed suit.

When the case came to court on April 3, 1895, in London, Wilde eagerly seized the opportunity to exercise his dazzling wit. Some of his responses to cross-examination rank among the finest ever heard, but the unrelieved cleverness began to wear dangerously thin as Edward Carson, Q.C. (Queen's Counsel), counsel for Queensberry, probed ambiguities in Wilde's writings. Total capitulation followed Carson's announcement on day three that he intended producing several young male witnesses who would testify that Wilde had engaged their services for immoral purposes. Immediately, Wilde's counsel, Sir Edward Clarke, Q.C., announced a withdrawal of his client's action.

A young Oscar Wilde published his first volume of poetry in 1881. (Library of Congress)

The Tables Turn

Most expected this to be the end of the matter, but they had not reckoned with Queensberry's vindictiveness. He promptly forwarded copies of witnesses' statements to the director of public prosecutions, and as a consequence, it was now Wilde who stood in the very dock that Queensberry had previously occupied, charged with numerous acts of indecency and sodomy. Accused with him was Alfred Taylor, widely suspected of being a procurer for the flamboyant playwright.

Testimony commenced on April 26, 1895. On this occasion, the witnesses Queensberry had so meticulously rounded up for the aborted libel trial did take the witness stand, and they painted a sordid picture. Charles Parker, a 21-year-old valet, described how Taylor had escorted him and his brother to a restaurant, where they were inspected by Wilde.

Parker went on, "Subsequently Wilde said to me, 'This is the boy for me! Will you go to the Savoy Hotel with me?' I consented, and Wilde drove me in a cab to the hotel. At the Savoy he committed the act of sodomy upon me."

"Did Wilde give you any money on that occasion?" asked chief Crown prosecutor Charles Gill.

"Before I left, Wilde gave me £2 [$8], telling me to call at the Savoy Hotel in a week," Parker affirmed. Later, Wilde visited Parker at his lodgings. "I was asked by Wilde to imagine that I was a woman, and that he was my lover. . . . I had to sit on his knee."

Alfred Wood, an unemployed clerk, claimed he had been introduced to Wilde by Lord Alfred Douglas. Again the assignation took place at a restaurant.

"What happened next?" asked Gill.

"After dinner I went with Mr. Wilde to 16 Tite Street [Wilde's home]. There was no one in the house to my knowledge. Mr. Wilde let himself in with a latchkey. We went up to his bedroom where he had hock and seltzer. Here an act of the grossest indecency occurred. Mr. Wilde used his influence to induce me to consent. He made me nearly drunk."

Further evidence came from a Savoy Hotel chambermaid who claimed that she had seen a youth, 16-year-old Edward Shelley, in Wilde's bed at the hotel.

Upon taking the stand, Wilde resolutely denied every allegation, causing Gill to turn, instead, to correspondence between the defendant and Lord Alfred Douglas, in particular a poem that Douglas had written titled *Two Loves*. Gill requested clarification of a line that read "I am the Love that dare not speak its name." "Is it not clear that the love described relates to natural love and unnatural love?"

"No," said Wilde.

"What is 'the Love that dare not speak its name?'"

Superb Speech

Wilde's response is worth quoting in full:

"The Love that dare not speak its name in this century" is such a great affection of an elder for a younger man as there was between David and Jonathan, such as Plato made the very basis of his philosophy, and such as you might find in the sonnets of Michelangelo and Shakespeare. It is that deep, spiritual affection that is as pure as it is perfect, and dictates and pervades great works of art like those of Shakespeare and Michelangelo, and those two letters of mine such as they are. It is in this century so much misunderstood that it may be described as "the Love that dare not speak its name," and on account of it I am placed where I am now. It is beautiful, it is fine, it is the noblest form of affection. There is nothing unnatural about it. It repeatedly exists between an elder and a younger man, when the elder man has intellect and the younger man has all the joy, hope, and glamour of life before him. That it should be so the world does not understand. The world mocks at it and sometimes puts one in the pillory for it.

Wilde's eloquence brought an ovation from the gallery and obviously sowed seeds of doubt among the jury. On May 1, 1895, the jury declared itself unable to reach a verdict, and Justice Arthur Charles had no choice but to declare a mistrial. Upon leaving the court, Wilde was immediately rearrested and charged with yet another 15 counts of impropriety.

Three weeks later, on May 22, he again stepped into court to face his accusers, this time alone (Alfred Taylor, his codefendant in the previous trial, had been convicted but not sentenced). On this occasion, Gill was relegated to second string as the Crown entrusted its lead brief to the solicitor general, Sir Frank Lockwood, Q.C. For some reason, the string of young male prosecution witnesses failed to make the same impact as before, perhaps because by this time their testimony was well known, but Alfred Wood again revealed the sinister side of his nature.

Soon after the first of Oscar Wilde's trials, the Marquess of Queensberry has a heated argument with his oldest son, Percy, just outside the courthouse.

"You have met Lord Alfred Douglas?" asked Gill.

"Yes . . . he gave me a suit of clothes."

"And you found four letters in one of the pockets?"

"Yes."

"From who?"

"From Mr. Wilde to Lord Alfred."

"What happened to the letters?"

"Allen [a friend] stole them. He kept one of them, saying, 'This one's quite hot enough for me.'"

"You went to Mr. Wilde and asked him for money?"

"Yes. I told him I was tired of life, tired of those big dinners, and tired of mixing with people like Wilde and Douglas and those people."

Blackmail Ring

What happened next had already been described by Wilde at the libel trial. He had paid Wood £15 ($60) for the letter, only to then receive a visit from someone called William Allen. Wilde knew what to expect. "I suppose you have come about my beautiful letter to Lord Alfred Douglas," he said. "I consider it to be a work of art."

Allen had replied, "A very curious construction can be put on that letter."

Wilde sighed, "Art is rarely intelligible to the criminal classes."

To which Allen said, "A man offered me £60 [$240] for it."

Wilde seemed pleased. "If you take my advice you will sell my letter to him for £60. I myself have never received so large a sum for any prose work of that length; but I am glad to find that there is someone in England who considers a letter of mine worth £60." When Allen underwent a change of heart and complained that he was completely broke, Wilde gave him a half sovereign ($2), and he left.

Allen then passed the letter to yet another young man, Robert Clibborn. He, too, showed up at Wilde's doorstep. By this time, having passed through several sets of hands, the letter was quite soiled. Wilde chided Clibborn for such slovenliness, describing it as "quite unpardonable that better care was not taken of this original manuscript of mine. . . . I am afraid you are leading a wonderfully wicked life."

When Clibborn suggested that "there is good and bad in every one of us," Wilde agreed, saying, "this is more than possible." Clibborn, too, left with just a single half sovereign in his pocket. Between them, the trio of blackmailers extracted a paltry £16 ($64) from their victim, hapless in the face of his studied indifference.

But there was no trace of that insouciance now, as defense counsel Sir Edward Clarke noted in his final address. Deploring the decline that had befallen Wilde in just two months, Clarke described him thus: "Broken as he is now, as anyone who saw him at the first trial must see he is, by being kept in prison without bail."

Unlike their counterparts a month earlier, this particular jury had no doubts: Guilty. On May 26, 1895, Wilde wept as he heard Justice Alfred Wills pass sentence—two years' hard labor. It was a savage sentence, the maximum permissible, but Wilde's troubles were not over yet. Still thirsting for revenge, Queensberry decided to pursue his old adversary through the courts for the defense costs he had incurred in the libel trial. Wilde, brought from his cell, manacled and helpless, stood in the dock and heard himself declared bankrupt.

He served his time in full and emerged from prison a shattered man. Aware that there was no place for him in England, he undertook a self-imposed exile in Europe, finally settling in Paris. On November 30, 1900, he died of cerebral meningitis at age 46. Perhaps the last word on this tragically brief life is best left to Wilde himself, with a stanza from *The Ballad of Reading Gaol,* a poem he completed after a failed reunion with Lord Alfred Douglas in Italy:

> And all men kill the thing they love,
> By all let this be heard,
> Some do it with a bitter look,
> Some with a flattering word,
> The coward does it with a kiss,
> The brave man with a sword.

—Colin Evans

Suggestions for Further Reading

Crimes and Punishment. Vol. 16. London: Phoebus, 1974.

Ellmann, Richard. *Oscar Wilde.* New York: Alfred A. Knopf, 1988.

Fido, Martin. *Oscar Wilde.* New York: Viking Press, 1973.

Goodman, Jonathan. *The Oscar Wilde File.* London: W. H. Allen, 1988.

Hyde, H. Montgomery. *Oscar Wilde.* New York: Farrar, Straus and Giroux, 1975.

Jullian, Philippe. *Oscar Wilde.* New York: Viking Press, 1969.

Émile Zola Trial: 1898

Defendant: Émile Zola   **Crime Charged:** Defamation
Chief Defense Lawyers: Fernand Labori, Albert Clemenceau
Chief Prosecutor: Edmond van Cassel   **Judge:** M. Delegorgue
Place: Paris, France   **Dates:** February 7–23, 1898   **Verdict:** Guilty
Sentence: One year in prison; 3,000 franc fine. (Zola went into exile to escape jail; he and others were granted amnesty in 1900.)

SIGNIFICANCE

Zola's famous broadside *J'accuse,* which led to the slander charges against him, helped turn an obscure injustice into a cause célèbre. It emboldened the supporters of Alfred Dreyfus and brought many converts to the Dreyfusard cause.

Émile Zola had scant interest in military matters and no connection with Alfred Dreyfus, the former French army officer who had been convicted of selling secrets to Germany. All the same, the case began to trouble his conscience. In the autumn of 1897, the author of best-selling novels of French life and manners turned from naturalistic fiction to political journalism of the most incendiary kind. And in consequence, Zola converted the Dreyfus case from "an affair" into "The Affair," the decade-long convulsion that rocked turn-of-the century France to its foundations.

Dreyfus, an Alsatian-born Jew, had been accused in 1894 of supplying classified artillery documents to the Germans. To be sure, evidence of treason had existed—a *bordereau,* or cover letter, listing a number of secret papers presumably delivered to the German embassy in Paris. Investigators had no evidence linking Dreyfus to the crime. Still, someone had to be guilty. Alfred Dreyfus had had access to the papers. And he stood a little apart from his general staff colleagues: aloof, a man with few friends, an outsider. Using forged documents and the spurious conclusions of handwriting analysts, a court-martial had convicted Dreyfus of treason in December 1894 and deported him to the penal colony of Devil's Island in French Guiana.

The Novelist Speaks

Toward the end of 1897, Zola began preparing a series of articles on the case, an appeal to public opinion on Dreyfus's behalf. He concluded that anti-Semitism, not the evidence, had convicted Alfred Dreyfus and that the French army and its political allies had conspired to destroy an innocent man.

"France must come to her senses, restore justice and self-respect, put an end to the mockery of justice in the military courts, stop their secret sessions and the withholding of important documents," Zola asserted in his *Lettre á la France* early in January 1898. "What folly to think that one can keep history from being written. It will be written, and those responsible will be duly named and recorded, no matter how small their role."

A few days after Zola's *Lettre á la France* was published, in another secret trial, a court-martial acquitted Major Charles Esterhazy, the officer impartial investigators by then were convinced had been the real author of the incriminating *bordereau*.

On January 13, Zola responded with his incandescent *J'accuse!*

Anticipating Esterhazy's acquittal, Zola had begun writing his famous screed before he learned of the verdict. He addressed it to the president of France, Félix Faure. French statesman Georges Clemenceau provided the title by which it became known to the world: *J'accuse!* It took up the entire front page of a special edition of the news sheet *L'Aurore*. Zola charged high military officials with being involved in a frame-up of an innocent man and then covering up the crime. Within a few hours, more than 200,000 French men and women had read Zola's powerful indictment:

> I accuse General Mercier of having become an accomplice in one of the great iniquities of the century. . . .
>
> I accuse General Billot of having had in his hands the definitive evidence of Dreyfus's innocence and of having stifled it. . . .
>
> I accuse General Boisdeffre and General Gonse of being guilty of the same crime. . . .
>
> Finally, I accuse the [Dreyfus] court-martial of having violated the law in condemning a man on the basis of a document kept secret, and I accuse the [Esterhazy] court-martial of having covered up that illegality on command by committing in turn the juridical crime of knowingly acquitting a guilty man.

In challenging the army, a pillar of traditional France, Zola ran considerable risks. In late middle age (he turned 58 in 1898), he had become the leading figure of the French literary establishment. His works, particularly the 20-novel cycle collectively titled *Les Rougon-Macquart*, published between 1871 and 1893, had brought him wealth and worldwide renown. By reigniting the controversy, he could expect to alienate a substantial part of his audience, the largely anti-Dreyfusard middle class. The gutter press would savage him. The sales of his books would suffer. He could abandon all expectation of entering the L'Académie Française. A friend wrote, "What glory for you in the future! But what nastiness and humiliation for the present."

The Outcry

Reactions were swift and furious. Publication of *J'accuse!* touched off a wave of anti-Semitic demonstrations, and the nationalists moved immediately to the attack. Zola's father's Italian origins were recalled, with sinister implication. "Who exactly is this Monsieur Zola? The man is not French. Émile Zola thinks quite naturally with the thoughts of an uprooted Venetian," the anti-Dreyfusard man of letters Maurice Barrès observed.

On the other side, the partisans of Dreyfus rejoiced. "The party of justice had been born," the Dreyfusard leader Joseph Reinach declared. "Dreyfusism was reinvigorated," wrote the left-wing politician Léon Blum. "We could feel the confidence well up and rise within us."

One week after *J'accuse!* appeared, the Assize Court of the Seine served papers on Zola, charging him with defamation. The charge involved only 15 lines of the broadside—the ones that claimed the Esterhazy court-martial had, on orders, knowingly acquitted a guilty man. Zola, of course, could not possibly prove that the command had come down to absolve Esterhazy, and the narrow scope of the charge would allow the court to limit testimony on Dreyfus during Zola's trial.

French novelist and reformer, Émile Zola, was charged with the crime of libel for his attacks on the Army over the Dreyfus affair. (AP/Wide World)

Zola told the newspaper *Le Temps* that he intended to proclaim his innocence before the court and to clarify his motive in entangling himself in The Affair. He had become convinced, he said, that judicial error in the Dreyfus case and the perverse refusal to put it right threatened the liberties of French men and women everywhere.

"But there is something other than the violations of the law," Zola went on. "There remains the certainty of the innocence of Dreyfus. As far as I am concerned, his innocence is as clear as the sun in the sky."

The Trial

The trial opened on February 7, 1898, in the Palace of Justice on the Ile de la Cité. Crowds packed into the courtroom; some observers were obliged to sit cross-legged on the floor. Gaslight cast a yellow tinge over the scene, and the room grew stiflingly hot. The chief judge, Delegorgue, announced at the outset that he would bar testimony about "the thing previously judged"—the Dreyfus case.

In his complaint, the war minister, General Albert Billot, asserted that Zola's charges were patently false. "Chiefs and subordinates are above such outrages," he said. "The opinion of Parliament, the country and the Army has already placed them beyond reason of attack." By this logic, Zola stood little chance of an acquittal.

The chance narrowed further each time Delegorgue blocked Zola's bid to introduce testimony on the Dreyfus case. The judge refused to let Madame Dreyfus testify. His rulings from the bench consistently favored the prosecution. And, contrary to common practice, he permitted himself the indulgence of interrupting Zola's witnesses before cross-examination had begun.

"I demand to be allowed the same rights accorded to thieves and murderers," Zola finally protested.

His counsel, Fernand Labori, tried a different approach.

"Will you permit me, then, to ask in our common interest, what practical means you see by which we may ascertain the truth?"

"That does not concern me!" Delegorgue replied.

Most of Labori's witnesses, including several officers deeply implicated in the Dreyfus conspiracy, simply refused to testify. One, Raoul de Boisdeffre, the chief of staff, coyly told the jury that the army had secret proof of Dreyfus's guilt but would not make it public for fear of touching off a crisis with a foreign power—Germany.

Colonel Georges Picquart did cooperate, however. His investigation had identified Esterhazy as the author of the *bordereau*. Insofar as Delegorgue allowed him to speak, Picquart confirmed the innocence of Dreyfus and the guilt of Esterhazy.

Esterhazy refused to answer any of Labori's questions. The lawyer insisted that the judge compel Esterhazy to respond. "Oh, come now," Delegorgue said.

"How is it that one cannot speak of justice in a courtroom?" Albert Clemenceau, Labori's assistant, blurted out.

"There is something above that—the honor and safety of the country," the judge answered.

The summing-up began February 21. The prosecutor, Edmond van Cassel, affirmed Dreyfus's guilt and told the jury the Esterhazy proceeding had been "regular, deliberate and legal." Zola, vain, preening, drunk on his own words, had caused the heart of France to bleed, he exhorted.

"No, it is not true that a court-martial has rendered a verdict in obedience to orders," van Cassel said. "It is not true that seven officers have been found to obey anything other than their own free and honest consciences. You must condemn those who have outraged them. France awaits your verdict with confidence."

Zola spoke for himself: "These are abominable political practices, dishonorable to a free nation," he said of all that had gone into the making of *L'Affaire*. "I stand before you of my own free will. I alone have decided that an obscure and monstrous matter should be brought before your jurisdiction. My act has no other object, and my person is nothing; I have sacrificed it, satisfied to have placed in your hands not only the honor of the Army but the threatened honor of the entire nation."

The Verdict

The jury deliberated for only 35 minutes on February 23 before returning a guilty verdict. The courtroom crowd shouted its approval: "Long live the Army! Down with the Jews! Death to Zola!" Turning toward his wife, the novelist muttered, "These people are cannibals." The judges gave Zola the maximum sentence: one year in prison, and a 3,000-franc fine.

Labori contested the Assize Court verdict, and an appeals judge overturned it on a technicality. On July 18, 1898, just before a guilty verdict in the retrial could be announced, Zola slipped out of the courtroom. He boarded the boat train that evening for England and exile.

On June 3, 1899, an appeals court voided the judgment of the Dreyfus court-martial of 1894. Two days later, the fugitive Zola returned to Paris from London. Though another military court found Dreyfus guilty in the retrial, the president of the republic pardoned the long-suffering artillery captain. On December 14, 1900, President Émile Loubet granted amnesty to everyone involved in the Dreyfus affair.

Zola died in 1902, four years before France's High Court of Appeal finally and unequivocally declared Alfred Dreyfus innocent.

—Michael Golay

Suggestions for Further Reading

Bredin, Jean-Denis. *The Affair: The Case of Alfred Dreyfus*. Translated by Jeffrey Mehlman. New York: George Braziller, 1986.

Brown, Frederick. *Zola: A Life*. New York: Farrar, Straus & Giroux, 1995.

Josephson, Matthew. *Zola and His Time*. New York: The Macaulay Company, 1928.

Schom, Alan. *Émile Zola*. New York: Henry Holt, 1987.

Stinie Morrison Trial: 1911

Defendant: Stinie Morrison   **Crime Charged:** Murder
Chief Defense Lawyers: Edward Abinger, Alasdair MacGregor, Roland Oliver
Chief Prosecutors: Sir Richard Muir, Q.C.; William Leycester; Ingleby Oddie
Judge: Justice Charles Darling   **Place:** London, England
Dates of Trial: March 6–15, 1911   **Verdict:** Guilty   **Sentence:** Death

SIGNIFICANCE

Many believe that a calamitous miscalculation by the defense counsel in this, one of England's most celebrated murder trials, resulted in a miscarriage of justice.

On New Year's Day, 1911, a police officer patrolling Clapham Common in South London found the body of a middle-aged man among some bushes. He had been battered and stabbed to death, and something resembling a crude letter *S* had been gouged into each side of his face. He also appeared to have been robbed. When later that day the victim was identified as Leon Beron, a Polish slum landlord, minds cast back to an incident two weeks earlier, when three London police officers had been shot dead by a gang of Eastern European anarchists. Public outrage at the triple murder prompted speculation that Beron's death might be a revenge killing, with claims that the letter *S* stood for *spic*, a derogatory term meaning "informer."

Detectives soon came up with a suspect. Since immigrating to England in 1898, Stinie Morrison, a Russian-born recidivist, had spent no less than 11 years behind bars; more important, during December 1910, he and Beron were often seen together at the kosher Warsaw restaurant in Whitechapel, huddled over lemon tea in deep discussion. Beron was an enigma. His appetite for gold jewelry so far exceeded the income from his real estate investments that many believed him to be dealing in stolen property, which might explain his hushed conversations with a professional thief like Stinie Morrison.

At 11:45 P.M. on New Year's Eve, the two men were seen leaving the Warsaw together. They made a distinctive pair, with Beron nine inches the shorter, and for the next two hours, several witnesses placed them in Whitechapel. Morrison would later claim that at the time of the murder— around 3 A.M.—he was home in bed, a fact attested to by his landlady; but detectives preferred to concentrate on the evidence of a waiter at the Warsaw. According to Joe Mintz, the waiter, before leaving the restaurant Morrison had collected a long, narrow parcel from behind the counter. It was, he said, a flute, but Mintz had doubted this because of the parcel's considerable weight. Police, convinced that the parcel contained the murder weapon and that Morrison had wielded that weapon, focused all their efforts on locating Morrison. They finally tracked him down on the morning of January 8, 1911, when he was arrested at a café near his lodgings.

Press Prejudice

When Morrison stepped into the dock for the start of his nine-day trial on March 6, a vicious anti-Semitic campaign waged by the press had already guaranteed his place as one of the most vilified defendants on record. Neither was he aided by his appointed counsel. Despite a lengthy career, Edward

Waxwork of Stinie Morrison, also known as the Clapham Common Murderer. (Hulton-Deutsch Collection)

Abinger had never risen above the mediocre; he was hardly someone capable of locking horns with the chief prosecutor, Sir Richard Muir, Q.C. (Queen's Counsel), one of the bar's deadliest cross-examiners.

It was the Crown's contention that Morrison had lured Beron to Clapham Common with the intent to rob him and that robbery had turned to murder. At the heart of the Crown's case was the hazy and, at times, downright suspicious evidence of three cabdrivers. The first, Edward Hayman, maintained that he had ferried two men who fit the descriptions of Beron and Morrison to Lavender

Hill (adjacent to Clapham Common) on the night of the murder at around 2 A.M. Abinger was not impressed.

Abinger: "When did you first go to the police station?"

Hayman: "About a week afterwards. I think it was the ninth."

When Abinger asked why he had taken so long, Hayman claimed that he had not seen a reward poster until January 6.

Abinger: "Why did you not go on the day you saw it?"

Hayman shifted uneasily, unable to dispel the view that his belated intervention had been motivated by a desire to claim the modest reward. Abinger reminded him that by the time he definitely identified Morrison—on January 17—pictures of the accused had already been plastered across newspapers for several days beforehand. "I might go a week without looking at a paper," Hayman mumbled.

Plainly troubled by this less than satisfactory response, Justice Charles Darling intervened to quiz the witness himself, whereupon Hayman asserted that he had "no doubt whatever" that his identification was accurate.

A second cabdriver, Alfred Stephens, who claimed to have driven the accused from Clapham to Kennington, also conceded that his identification had come only after he had seen photographs of the accused. The third cabbie, Alfred Castling, recalled driving two men, one of whom resembled Morrison, from Kennington back north of the river Thames to Finsbury Park at 3:30 A.M., but like his colleagues, he, too, had seen photographs of Morrison before identifying him.

Someone who actually knew the defendant was Nellie Deitch, and she claimed to have seen Morrison and Beron touring Whitechapel together after 2 A.M. on the night in question. Such evidence, which was highly favorable to Morrison, should have delighted Abinger, but instead, this erratic and excitable advocate studied the expensively groomed woman in the witness-box and wondered how an artisan's wife could afford such finery. What he did next was catastrophic.

The Criminal Evidence Act (1898) is chiefly memorable as the legislation that, for the first time, allowed defendants to enter the witness-box on their own behalf. A less-remembered feature of that same act ensured that a defendant's background, especially any criminal record, could not be revealed to the jury for fear of influencing the verdict. This was conditional, however, on the defense's not attacking the character of Crown witnesses. If the defense chose to do so, it would lay its client open to similar tactics. Abinger gambled all.

Earlier, he had sailed close to the wind by accusing a prosecution witness of having once attempted suicide—at that time a serious crime. Now he attempted to portray Nellie Deitch as a common brothel keeper, someone not to be trusted. Despite repeated warnings from the bench about the dangers inherent in this line of questioning, Abinger plowed on. But Mrs. Deitch stood firm and emerged unscathed—which is more than can be said for Stinie Morrison.

Whether Abinger advised his client not to take the stand is unknown. Even had he done so, it is unlikely that the confident Russian would have heeded the admonition. Morrison loved to talk, but as the first two questions demonstrated, he was virtually incapable of uttering a truthful word.

Abinger: "How old are you?"

Morrison: "Twenty-nine, between twenty-nine and thirty."

Abinger: "Where were you born?"

Morrison: "Australia."

Why Morrison felt compelled to lie about such an insignificant detail is unfathomable, but it was manna from heaven for the prosecution. Muir began his cross-examination in a subdued fashion, skillfully extracting one blatant lie after another from the defendant; then, in a voice so low as to be almost inaudible, he dropped the bombshell. "When were you first convicted of a felony?"

For the first time Morrison became rattled, stammering, "I cannot say— 1900, or something like that."

"Was it December 17, 1898?"

"That might have been it," admitted Morrison.

This was the price of Abinger's recklessness, a full and merciless account of the defendant's prodigious criminal record. Muir painted his canvas with broad, damning strokes: The defendant was not only a burglar who carried housebreaking tools, he said, but also a frequenter of prostitutes, a moral degenerate. By the time Muir sat down, the jury would probably have believed Morrison capable of anything, even murder.

Amazing Scenes

Abinger's tribulations were not over yet. In the midst of his closing address to the jury, he was interrupted when the dead man's elderly brother, Solomon Beron, crept unnoticed into the well of the court and began throwing a series of ill-directed punches at him. Beron was dragged from the court, bellowing, "He's going to get him off! He's going to get him off!"

One observer inclined to that view was Justice Darling. Although privately he held no doubts about Morrison's guilt, his summing-up leaned heavily toward acquittal, suggesting to the jury that the evidence was "not sufficiently cast-iron to act as the basis of proof in a criminal charge." He was also skeptical of the cabdrivers' evidence. "They gave a description. Let us assume they gave it to the best of their ability, let us assume they were honest . . . are you so certain that they really took notice enough . . . to be able some days afterwards to swear with certainty to the man they had driven?"

Whatever doubts the judge entertained were not shared by the jury; they took just 35 minutes to find Morrison guilty. One final moment of drama came as Darling concluded passing sentence of death with the traditional "May God have mercy on your soul." From across the court, the prisoner roared, "I decline such mercy. I do not believe there is a God in Heaven either!"

Paradoxically, the very press that had done so much to prejudice popular opinion against Morrison now began to question the fairness of his trial. In response to the campaign, Home Secretary Winston Churchill, clearly perturbed by several aspects of the case, commuted the sentence to life imprisonment. It was a shabby compromise. The official view seemed to be that though there wasn't sufficient evidence to hang Morrison, neither was there the slightest intention of letting him go. In jail, Morrison began a succession of well-publicized hunger strikes that drew thousands to his cause, but his every petition was denied. Weakened by the repeated deprivations, his heart gave out on January 24, 1921; he was 41 years old.

So did Stinie Morrison kill Leon Beron? One thing is certain: Had he refrained from entering the witness-box, it would have put a much greater burden of proof on the Crown's confused, often contradictory case. But all that was negated by his absurd and pointless perjury. Exposed liars—even if they are innocent—never look good.

—Colin Evans

Suggestions for Further Reading

Lewis, Roy Harley. *Edwardian Murders*. North Pomfret, Vt.: David & Charles, 1989.

Linklater, Eric. *The Corpse on Clapham Common*. London: Macmillan, 1971.

Moulton, H. Fletcher. *The Trial of Steinie* [sic] *Morrison*. London: William Hodge, 1922.

Rose, Andrew. *Stinie: Murder on the Common*. London: Penguin, 1989.

Titanic Inquiry: 1912

Chief Lawyers: Sir Rufus Isaacs, K.C.; Sir John Simon, K.C.
Judge: Lord John Mersey   **Place:** London, England
Dates of Inquiry: May 2–July 3, 1912

SIGNIFICANCE
Whitewash or thorough investigation? Doubts about the British *Titanic* inquiry have never been resolved.

At 46,328 tons and 882 feet in length, with 8 decks, the top rising to the height of an 11-story building, the *Titanic* was not only the largest ship afloat in 1912, but the grandest as well. And it was safe too. Beneath the baroque splendor of the public rooms and cabins, engineers had fashioned such an artful arrangement of watertight bulkheads over the double-bottomed hull that one euphoric English journalist had described the ship as "practically unsinkable." But on her maiden voyage to New York, on the night of April 14, in good visibility and riding a calm sea off Newfoundland, the unsinkable yielded to the unthinkable.

The iceberg was spotted at 11:40 P.M. The collision came seconds later. Dwarfing its suddenly diminutive adversary, the huge wall of ice ripped a 300-foot gash along the *Titanic*'s starboard hull, just above the double bottom. It was a mortal blow. Freezing water tore through the helpless bulkheads, and two and a half hours later the pride of the White Star Line slid quietly beneath the North Atlantic. The loss of life was colossal—1,522 passengers and crew dead, just 705 saved in 20 half-empty lifeboats and rafts. Why there were so few lifeboats and how they came to be occupied by a disproportionate number of first-class passengers were just two of the questions that would prompt inquiries on both sides of the Atlantic, but uppermost in every mind was a solitary thought: How could it have happened?

To adjudicate this matter, the British Board of Trade, under Section 477 of the Merchant Shipping Act, 1894, took the unusual step of appointing a wreck commissioner, entrusting this temporary position to Lord John Mersey. Assisting him in his task were five assessors, all men with long nautical experience: Professor John Biles, Rear Admiral Somerset Gough-Calthorpe, Commander F. Lyon, Captain Arthur Wellesley Clarke, and Edward Chaston.

The *Titanic* lifeboat, number 14, hauling a collapsible "D" to the *Carpathia* on the morning of April 15, 1912. Officer Lowe is standing at the back of the lifeboat. (Prints & Photographs Division, Library of Congress)

Goaded into action rather earlier than it would have wished (by an American inquiry, chaired by Senator William Alden Smith, already in progress), the commission met at the hastily converted London Scottish Drill Hall on May 2, 1912. Long curtains had been draped over bare brickwork, and dominating one wall was a large-scale model of the *Titanic* and a chart of the North Atlantic.

Facing Lord Mersey was an intimidating array of lawyers. Besides the two premier barristers—Attorney General Sir Rufus Isaacs, K.C. (King's Counsel), and Solicitor General Sir John Simon, K.C.—Sir Robert Finlay, K.C., appeared for the White Star Line, and W. D. Harbinson, K.C., protected the interests of the third-class passengers. Thomas Scanlan spoke for the national Sailors' and Firemen's Union. Among the half dozen other counsel was Henry Duke, K.C., representing Sir Cosmo and Lady Duff Gordon, wealthy passengers who allegedly had attempted to bribe oarsmen in their lifeboat not to go back to pick up more passengers.

Survival of the Richest?

One of those oarsmen, Charles Hendrickson, testified that "there was plenty of room for another dozen in the boat," but that the coxswain had been prevented from going back.

Harbinson took up this theme. "You say that . . . this was due to the protests of the Duff Gordons?"

"Yes," said Hendrickson.

"You say you heard cries?"

"Yes."

"Agonizing cries?"

"Yes, terrible cries."

"At what distance?"

"About two hundred yards."

In response, Duff Gordon silkily explained that he had offered the seamen "a fiver [£5] each to start new kit" after learning that, thenceforth, they would not be receiving any wages. His wife, too, heatedly refuted any suggestion that she had obstructed efforts to return.

Tragically, the person who could have done most to enlighten the proceedings was not present: Captain Edward Smith, master of the *Titanic*, had gone down with his ship. This meant that every eye was turned on J. Bruce Ismay, president of the White Star Line, a survivor in one of the last lifeboats and the man who had, allegedly, ordered Smith to proceed at near maximum speed despite warnings of icebergs in the vicinity.

Under questioning from Isaacs, Ismay admitted having received a telegraphed warning. Isaacs was puzzled: "If you were approaching ice in the night, it would be desirable, would it not, to slow down?"

"I am not a navigator," replied Ismay.

"Answer the question," insisted Lord Mersey.

"I say no. I am not a navigator."

Isaacs continued to harry Ismay, until the latter feebly said, "I say he [Smith] was justified in going fast to get out of it if the conditions were suitable and right and the weather clear."

"I think we understand," said Isaacs pointedly, before turning to the lack of lifeboats.

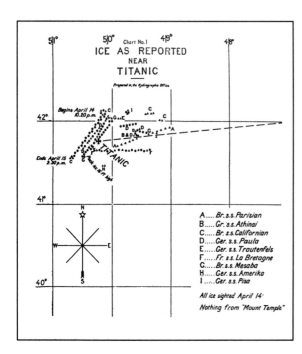

A U.S. Senate document shows a map drawn after the sinking of the *Titanic*. The sketch, done by the U.S. Navy Hydrographic Office, clearly shows an immense field of ice in the path of the *Titanic*.

Again, Ismay was unconvincing. The *Titanic* had carried the minimum number of lifeboats prescribed by the Board of Trade, he said, because the ship was thought to be virtually unsinkable and was thus a gigantic lifeboat itself. Such arrogance explained why it was decided to reduce the number of lifeboats to one per davit, even though the davits were designed to carry four lifeboats each. This was done so there might be more deck space for passengers.

Next, the inquiry dealt with one of the more mysterious aspects of the tragedy. Officers from the *Titanic* told of seeing another ship, some five or six miles distant, that failed to respond to either the eight distress rockets fired from the *Titanic*'s decks or to repeated Morse signal messages. Most believed that ship to have been the *Californian*, a 6,000-tonner under the command of Captain Walter Lord and bound for Boston. Called to testify, Lord gave a very poor account of himself. From day one his statements were riddled with contradictions and blatant falsehoods, discrepancies that the American inquiry, held April 19 to May 18 in New York and Washington, D.C., had been quick to highlight. Lord admitted that, yes, he had seen a ship at around 11 P.M., that various officers aboard the *Californian* had reported seeing eight distress rockets, and that a ship had been visible for much of the time between 11:45 P.M. and 2:20 A.M., but he refused to be budged from his assertion that this ship was *not* the *Titanic*. "You can never mistake those ships," he told Isaacs, "by the blaze of light."

Radio Officer Asleep

When asked by Thomas Scanlan why he had not summoned the assistance of his radio officer, Lord exploded: "At one o'clock in the morning?" A product of the old school, Lord seemed deeply mistrustful of new technology.

Isaacs steadily tightened the screws. "You have already told us that you were not satisfied that was a company's signal." (At that time, ships identified themselves to other vessels at night by means of rockets much smaller and less intense than distress flares.)

"I asked the officer, 'Was it a company signal?' "

"And he did not know?" interrupted Mersey.

"He did not know," agreed Lord.

"That did not satisfy you?" asked Isaacs again.

"It did not satisfy me."

Next came, perhaps, the most telling question of the entire inquiry. "Then, if it was not that, it might have been a distress signal?"

"It might have been," Lord squirmed. With those four words, his culpability was exposed for all the world to see.

Lord Mersey certainly thought so. In his report, delivered on July 30, 1912, he wrote, "These circumstances convince me that the ship seen by the *Californian* was the *Titanic* and if so, according to Captain Lord, the two vessels were about five miles apart at the time of the disaster. . . . When she first saw the rockets, the *Californian* could have pushed through the ice . . . and . . . come to the assistance of the *Titanic*. Had she done so she might have saved many if not all of the lives that were lost."

Otherwise, Mersey found little to criticize. Captain Smith had been merely following orders, the White Star Line met every Board of Trade guideline, there was no truth to allegations of favoritism in the lifeboats, and charges of bribery against the Duff Gordons were "unfounded," although Mersey added, "I think that if he had encouraged the men to return . . . they would probably have made an effort to do so and could have saved some lives." Ismay, too, was absolved of all blame. In conclusion, Mersey recommended "more watertight compartments in ocean-going ships, the provision of lifeboats for all onboard, and a better lookout."

Such blandness inevitably prompted charges of a whitewash, and certainly the American inquiry dealt far more harshly with all concerned. Senator Smith's report, issued May 30, two months before the British report, also prompted a U.S.-backed initiative for the International Ice Patrol, a fleet of ships that has since monitored the treacherous northern sea lanes.

On September 1, 1985, the world got its first photographic view of the *Titanic* in more than seven decades, when an expedition led by Dr. Robert Ballard located the ill-fated ship on the ocean bed, some 13,000 feet deep.

—Colin Evans

Suggestions for Further Reading

Davie, Michael. *Titanic: The Death and Life of a Legend.* New York: Alfred A. Knopf, 1986.

Lord, Walter. *A Night to Remember.* New York: Holt, Rinehart & Winston, 1955.

Marcus, Geoffrey. *The Maiden Voyage.* New York: Viking Press, 1969.

Reade, Leslie. *The Ship That Stood Still.* New York: W. W. Norton, 1993.

Henriette Caillaux Trial: 1914

Defendant: Henriette Caillaux **Crime Charged:** Murder
Chief Defense Lawyer: Fernand Labori **Chief Prosecutor:** Charles Chenu
Judge: Louis Albanel **Place:** Paris, France
Dates of Trial: July 20–28, 1914 **Verdict:** Not guilty

SIGNIFICANCE

The trial of Madame Caillaux provides insight into *la Belle Epoque*, the era in France between the final years of the 19th century and the start of World War I. Well-to-do women of the period enjoyed social position and extravagance but had to endure the extramarital *liaisons élégantes* of straying husbands and were not expected to assert independence in the male-dominated society. The verdict reflected the last gasp of such traditional 19th-century values.

Henriette Rainouard Claretie had been unhappily married for 13 years to a man 12 years her senior and was ready for divorce even before she met Joseph Caillaux in 1907. Caillaux was the leader of the Radical Party, former minister of finance and former prime minister of France. They immediately fell in love and began an intense affair. Within a year, her husband agreed to a divorce. Caillaux's wife, however, refused to divorce him until October 1911, after which Henriette and Joseph married.

Henriette found, she later said, "the most complete happiness" with Joseph. They enjoyed great wealth—some 1.5 million francs' worth of investments and inherited property. But Joseph had political enemies. Not only the gutter (tabloid) press but also such influential journals as *Le Figaro* had reported that Caillaux, while in high office, had permitted France to cede the Congo—the nation's prized colony—to Germany in a transaction that had brought him advantageous financial information he used to make a fortune on the Berlin stock exchange.

Le Figaro's three-month campaign of character assassination—including 110 cartoons, anecdotes, and articles—reached a climax on March 13, 1914. On that day, its editor, Gaston Calmette, broke an unwritten rule that the private correspondence of a politician was sacrosanct. He published a facsimile of a letter written by Caillaux 13 years earlier to his mistress, who later became his first wife. The letter included information that implicated Caillaux in double-dealing. It was signed *Ton Jo*, or "Your Joey"—to any Frenchman, an impassioned signature. The publication of the letter, obtained from Joseph's first wife, humiliated him and Henriette.

"Je Suis une Dame"

At 6 P.M. on March 16, Madame Caillaux called at *Le Figaro* and asked to see editor Calmette. Although the visitor was the wife of his enemy, the editor said, in the spirit of *la Belle Epoque,* "I cannot refuse to receive a woman."

Henriette Caillaux testifies during her 1914 murder trial.

Madame Caillaux wore an expensive fur coat, a formal gown, an unpretentious hat. Her hands were hidden in a large fur muff. "You know why I have come?" she asked.

"Not at all, madame."

Wordlessly, Madame Caillaux pulled a small Browning automatic from the muff and rapidly fired six shots. The editor fell to the floor, mortally wounded. His associates rushed in. "Do not touch me," commanded Henriette. *"Je suis une dame."* ("I am a lady.")

When the police arrived, Madame Caillaux informed them that she would go downstairs to her car and her driver would take her to the police station. The police followed agreeably.

As the trial opened on July 20, 1914, Germany had maneuvered Austria into provoking Serbia to the threshold of what would evolve into World War I. France's president, Raymond Poincaré, was in St. Petersburg shoring up the Triple Entente of England, France, and Russia. But Parisians knew little of the international crisis, for every front page was filled with the story of the Caillaux trial.

The drama of the French courtroom, or *Cour d'assises,* vied with that of the theater. Lengthy speeches were permitted not only from the lawyers but from the defendant, judge, and witnesses as well. Evidence was introduced, witnesses were questioned, exhibits not previously revealed to the opposition were shown—all without procedure or limitation. Any trial could easily become a free-for-all.

The unhampered press had published most of the evidence presented at the pretrial investigation, during which the defendant had admitted killing Calmette. All Paris, if not all France, had already formed opinions on whether she should be held responsible for her actions. Jurymen were under no restrictions against discussing the case or reading about it. When, at the outset, Judge

Louis Albanel invited Madame Caillaux to tell "everything that seems useful to you," millions of newspaper readers were eager to devour her story.

"I Was Overwhelmed with Emotion"

Determined to prove extenuating circumstances, Madame Caillaux spoke for several hours. She reviewed the emotional devastation of the long newspaper campaign against her husband and its wide influence in spreading lies about him. As a result, she said, "Everyone greeted me with ironic smiles. I felt that all were making fun of me. I was overwhelmed with emotion." The threat to her standing in society, she testified, had made her miserable. Then had come publication of the letter, raising the prospect that Calmette would soon publish letters Joseph had written to her as well. She lost all self-control. Hers was, she concluded, a crime of passion intended only to frighten the editor, not kill him.

Prosecutor Charles Chenu insisted there were no other letters. The shooting's purpose, he contended, had been to end the political revelations that underlined Caillaux's duplicity.

The next day, Joseph Caillaux took control of the case and made himself the focus of attention. In a three-hour deposition, he defended his politics as well as his wife's act. And for seven days more, he interrupted constantly, delivering another 11 vocal depositions and effectively controlling the tempo of the trial.

Shooting Lessons Three Hours Earlier

The prosecutor introduced witnesses and evidence that Madame Caillaux not only had purchased the Browning but also had taken shooting lessons on the gun dealer's firing range only three hours before the murder. She was not, he insisted, an emotional and vulnerable woman driven to a crime of passion but a calm woman whose determination and capabilities were those of a man. To prove this point, Chenu asked witness Georges Fromentin, the gun shop clerk who had sold her the Browning and taught her how to use it, "During the course of all these operations, did Madame Caillaux remain calm, normal, attracting no attention?"

"Absolutely," answered Fromentin.

Finally, the prosecutor presented evidence that the crime had not been committed to punish the editor for publishing the *Ton Jo* letter but rather to prevent his publishing other self-incriminating letters written by Caillaux.

Now, to prove how fear of the publication of such letters had led to a crime of passion, the defendant allowed her lawyer, Fernand Labori, to read several letters that detailed the adulterous love she and Joseph had shared while married to others. As Labori read the last line of the second letter—"a thousand million kisses all over your adored little body"—Henriette fainted.

Jury deliberations began at 7:55 P.M. on July 28. Fifty-five minutes later, the verdict was "Not guilty." The all-male jury had decided, 11 to 1, that the lady had committed only a crime of passion. Angry cries and ebullient cheers rang out in the crowded courtroom and the throng beyond.

In 1918, convicted of crimes of "intelligence with the enemy" during World War I, Joseph Caillaux was sentenced to two years' imprisonment. Henriette Caillaux earned a diploma from the École du Louvre in 1935. She lived in continuing wealth with her adoring Joseph until he died at age 81 in 1944. Her death, in near-solitude, came a few years later.

—Bernard Ryan, Jr.

Suggestions for Further Reading

Allain, Jean Claude. *Joseph Caillaux*. Paris: Imprimerie Nationale, 1978.

Benton, Ralph. *Defeated Leaders: The Political Fate of Caillaux, Jouvenal, and Tardieu*. New York: Columbia University Press, 1968.

Berenson, Edward. *The Trial of Madame Caillaux*. Berkeley: University of California Press, 1992.

Bredin, Jean-Denis. *Joseph Caillaux*. Paris: Hachette, 1980.

Caillaux, Joseph. *Mes Mémoirse Clairvoyance et force d'âmedans les épreuves 1912–1930*. Paris: Plon, 1947.

Martin, Benjamin F. *The Hypocrisy of Justice in the Belle Epoque*. Baton Rouge: Louisiana State University Press, 1984.

Archduke Franz Ferdinand's Assassins Trial: 1914

Defendants:
Gavrilo Princip, Nedeljko Čabrinović, Trifko Grabež, Danilo Ilič, Vaso Čubrilovič, Cvetko Popovič, Nedjo Kerovič, Mihajlo Jovanovič, Jakov Milovič along with 16 others accused of either helping the conspirators hide or smuggle weapons and/or of failing to report them to the authorities when they heard about the assassination plans

Crimes Charged: High treason, accomplices to high treason

Chief Defense Lawyers:
Dr. Max Feldbauer, Wenzel Malek, Dr. Srecko Perišič, Dr. Konstantin Premužič, Franz Strupl, Dr. Rudolf Zistler

Chief Prosecutors: Dr. Franjo Švara, assisted by Rudolph Sark

Judges:
President of the Court Luigi von Curinaldi, assisted by Bogdan Naumowicz and Dr. Mayer Hoffmann

Place: Sarajevo, Bosnia **Dates:** October 12–28, 1914

Verdicts: Guilty for 16 of the accused, acquittals for 9

Sentences:
Death by hanging for Danilo Ilič, Nedeljko Čubrilovič, Nedjo Kerovič, Mihajlo Jovanovič, Jakov Milovič (on appeal, Kerovič's sentence was commuted to 20 years and Milovič's to life imprisonment). For Princip, Čabrinović, and Grabež, 20 years' hard labor; for Vaso Čubrilovič, 16 years' hard labor; and for Popovič, 13 years—all five to be subjected to solitary confinement in a dark cell on each June 28. The other six received sentences from three years to life.

SIGNIFICANCE
The trial, in which the Austrians sought to prove Serbian government involvement in the assassination, was less significant than the assassination itself, which had given Austria the pretext to declare war on Serbia ten weeks earlier, lighting the fuse for World War I.

I n Sarajevo, Bosnia and Herzegovina, the assassin of Archduke Franz Ferdinand, Gavrilo Princip, is today regarded as a martyr and a national hero. A museum commemorates his life, his grave is a pilgrimage site, a bridge was renamed after him, and his footprints are set in concrete, alongside a wall plaque inscribed *Here in this historical place, Gavrilo Princip was the instigator of liberty, on the day of St. Vitus, the 28th of June, 1914.* At that time, Bosnia and Herzegovina, as well as much of the territory later known as Yugoslavia, belonged to the Austro-Hungarian Empire. How Princip came to be so honored is a tale typical of Sarajevo's tangled history.

The Assassination

In 1913, General Oskar Potiorek, the Austrian governor of Bosnia and Herzegovina, countered widespread Serb nationalist activity by temporarily suspending the provincial parliament, censoring the press, and increasing police activity. He then invited the archduke, heir to the Habsburg throne and inspector general of the Austrian army, to observe military maneuvers during a one-day visit on June 28, 1914, to the Bosnian capital of Sarajevo. The choice of day, St. Vitus' Day, was an especially unfortunate one, as it was on that date in 1389 in the battle of Kosovo, that the Serbs lost their independence for nearly 500 years after being trounced by the Turks.

Because no independent commission was ever appointed to study the archduke's assassination, key questions probably will never be answered. Was the St. Vitus' Day visit intended as a deliberate provocation to the Bosnian Serbs? It was certainly perceived as such by radical activists. What was Potiorek's motivation in issuing the invitation? He had reason to resent the archduke, who twice had denied him promotion. At the very least, Potiorek was criminally negligent in his failure to provide adequate security in such a volatile situation.

A newspaper announcement of the impending visit spurred youthful Bosnian-Serb radical Gavrilo Princip to action. He decided to assassinate the archduke and asked Nedeljko Čabrinovič to join him. At the time, they were in Belgrade, the Serbian capital. Princip and a third conspirator, Trifko Grabež, had gone there to study after being expelled from their Bosnian schools, and Čabrinovič had been banished from Sarajevo for his involvement in a printers' strike. The trio obtained from the Black Hand, the common name of *Ujedinjenje ili Smrt* ("Union or Death"), a secretive Serbian nationalist group, pistols and bombs, training in their use, help in smuggling the arms across the border to Bosnia and back to Sarajevo through intermediaries. This radical Serbian terrorist organization was headed by Colonel Dragutin Dimitrijevič, known to his fellow Serbian conspirators by the code name "Apis," who was then the director of intelligence for the Serbian army. When Princip obtained the weapons, he wrote to Danilo Ilič to find several more conspirators in Sarajevo. Ilič, a radical intellectual with nationalist, Russian revolutionary, and anarchist interests, recruited the second trio of Mehmed Mehmedbašič (a Muslim carpenter previously involved in a plot to murder Potiorek), Vaso Čubrilovič, and Cvetko Popovič, both high school students.

As the time drew close, Ilič, as chief technical organizer, began to have doubts about the assassination and unsuccessfully tried to dissuade Princip and Grabež. Apis also sent an agent to try to stop the plot. In the end, Ilič went ahead and formulated the final plans. A newspaper had reported the archduke's itinerary, so Ilič spaced the conspirators on the riverside street called the Appel Quay, the route along which the imperial motorcade was to pass twice. The first two youths were to strike with their bombs; if they failed, the next two would make their attempt; if they failed, the last two would try. Ilič passed out the pistols and bombs, along with instructions on their use. The conspirators mingled in the waiting crowd, but the first two, Mehmedbašič and Čubrilovič, did nothing as the motorcade passed by, and Popovic, Princip and Grabež also held back. Only Čabrinovič acted, tossing a bomb at the archduke, but it hit the car's folded-back roof and fell under the following car, wounding 12 people. The archduke's car immediately left the scene. Čabrinovič tried unsuccessfully to kill himself by taking a cyanide pellet and jumping into the water, where he was captured. All the other conspirators fled, except Princip, who decided to wait for a second chance.

After visiting the town hall, the archduke and his wife set out to the hospital to see an aide wounded by the bomb. On the way, the driver of the lead car made a wrong turn and slowed down to turn around on the Appel Quay, where Princip was still waiting. This brought the second car to a halt in front of Princip, who raised his pistol and shot the archduke and his wife; both died shortly thereafter. Princip was seized on the spot.

Pictured are the men accused of assassinating Archduke Franz Ferdinand and his wife. Front row (l–r): Grabež, Čabrinovič, Princip, Ilič, Veljko Čubrilovič. Second row: Misko Jovanovič, Jakov Milovič.

The Investigation

The pretrial interrogations of Princip and Čabrinovič, along with extensive police investigations, and the capture of Serbian customs documents by Austrian troops led to the arrests of 23 more suspects. Only Mehmedbašič escaped to Montenegro.

On July 13, Austrian Foreign Minister Count von Berchtold received a secret cable from an aide in Sarajevo, evaluating the information gathered:

> Statements by accused show practically beyond doubt that accused decided to perpetrate the outrage while in Belgrade, and that outrage was prepared ... with help of Serb officials ... who also procured bombs, [pistols], ammunition and cyanide.... Hardly any room for doubt that Princip, Grabež, Čabrinovič smuggled across border with help from Serb customs.... However, no evidence of complicity of Serb government ministers in directly ordering assassination or in supplying weapons....

During August, the major powers of Europe chose sides over this incident and went to war even before the preliminary investigation in Sarejevo ended on September 19. The indictment was handed down on September 28. When Potiorek considered delaying the trial until the end of the war, Berchtold disagreed in a letter dated October 1 in which he laid out the course the judges and prosecutors should follow. The main point was that Austria wanted to assign to Serbia the moral responsibility for starting the world war.

The Trial

The trial of the 25 defendants opened on October 12 in a room of the military prison. With no jury, it was presided over by a panel of three judges. The trial outcome desired by Austria also dictated the nature of the charges. Although murder was a capital offense, accessory to murder was not. Moreover, apart from Ilič, the other five conspirators were "schoolboys" of 19 years of age or younger—and as such, under the Austrian criminal code, could not be executed. The gravity of the crime required more than one execution; hence, the charge was made high treason, since accessories to high treason could be executed.

It was, in effect, a show trial—11 days was far too short a time to thoroughly examine such a complicated affair or permit an adequate defense. Though it was ostensibly a public event, access to the courtroom was limited to a few people by special invitations (and only supporters of Austria merited these). Only six journalists were present—three from Sarajevo, two from Budapest, and one from Vienna; no representatives from the opposition press were allowed. The trial was conducted in Serbo-Croatian.

Until the end of the trial, the defense lawyers virtually kept silent as the prosecutors grilled the accused about the details of the plot and about their upbringing, education, occupation, political opinions and, especially, their membership in secret revolutionary societies. The prosecution focused on *Narodna Odbrana* ("National Defense"), a legitimate "cultural" association that disseminated nationalist propaganda, which the prosecution apparently confused with the role of Serbia's Black Hand, which was not mentioned in the trial. Persistent prosecution attempts to implicate Serbia failed, as it did in this exchange:

Prosecutor: You were an adherent of the idea that Serbia declare war and take Bosnia and Herzegovina from Austria?

Čabrinovič: I would prefer if possible that there not be war, for I am a cosmopolitan and I do not wish to shed blood.

His opinion of Austria was clear:

Prosecutor: In the pre-trial hearing you said that Austria was rotten?

Čabrinovič: An empire which is not national, which suppresses others, cannot be considered a unit; within it there is no cohesion, there is only discipline. There is only the power of the bayonets.

Princip passionately proclaimed his motive for the assassination:

Princip: I am a Yugoslav nationalist and I believe in the unification of all South Slavs in whatever form of state, and that it be free of Austria.

Prosecutor: That was your aspiration. How did you think to realize it?

Princip: By means of terror.

Prosecutor: What does that signify?

Princip: That means in general to destroy from above, to do away with those who obstruct and do evil, who stand in the way of the idea of unification.

The trial was conducted in a haphazard manner. In her book, *Black Lamb and Grey Falcon*, Rebecca West commented on "the shocking muddle of the court procedure. Dates were hardly ever mentioned and topics were brought up as they came into the heads of the lawyers rather than according to any logical programme."

At the conclusion of the trial, the defense lawyers half-heartedly tried to excuse their clients on the grounds of poor upbringing, influence by bad companions, and pro-Serbian propaganda. Only Dr. Rudolf Zistler mounted a spirited defense—he questioned the validity of the high treason charge. The 1908 annexation act stated that absorption into the Austro-Hungarian Empire required the consent of both parts. Hungary still had not given consent. Thus, Bosnia and Herzegovina were separate states, and, hence, high treason was not applicable. The court admonished him for this effrontery and allowed the charge to stand.

On October 28, the court announced its verdict: 16 of the accused were found guilty, the nine others were acquitted for lack of evidence. The guilty were then immediately sentenced: Five of the accused—none of them actually on the assassination squad—were sentenced to hang, although the sentences of two were reduced on appeal.

The Aftermath

Sentenced to 20 years of hard labor, Princip, Čabrinovič, and Grabež were taken to Theresienstadt in Bohemia. All three had died by April 28, 1918, ostensibly of tuberculosis, a disease aggravated by extreme cold, starvation, and inadequate medical attention. It was, in essence, an excruciating form of slow execution. After the war and the collapse of the Austro-Hungarian Empire, the new Czechoslovakia sent back to the new Yugoslavia the remains of its martyrs.

What is usually forgotten is the second act to the Sarajevo drama. It occurred in Salonika, then under control of the Austro-Hungarians, on April 2, 1917, when the trial of Black Hand leader Apis opened. He had been relieved of his official duties and arrested on the orders of Alexander, prince regent of Serbia, who feared that Apis was plotting his assassination. Also arrested was the elusive Mehmedbašič. In a rigged trial, Apis offered a coerced confession of his role in the archduke's assassination, on the understanding that he would go free. Nevertheless, he was found guilty and executed on June 26, 1917, in a form of judicial murder.

In the years that followed, numerous theories were put forth as to who was ultimately responsible for the Sarajevo assassination, but no solid facts support any top-level conspiracy. It still appears that the assassination was the work of a group of idealistic and ardently nationalistic youths operating on their own. They were decidedly amateurish in carrying out the tyrannicide, as they viewed it, and their success was due in large measure to pure blind luck. And this blind luck, in turn, led to a series of historical events that were to cast dark shadows across the rest of the 20th century.

—Eva Weber

Suggestions for Further Reading

Dedijer, Vladimir. *The Road to Sarajevo*. New York: Simon & Schuster, 1966.

Gilfond, Henry. *The Black Hand at Sarajevo*. Indianapolis, Ind.: Bobbs-Merrill, 1975.

Graham, Stephen. *St. Vitus' Day*. New York: D. Appleton and Co., 1931.

Morton, Frederic. *Thunder at Twilight, Vienna 1913/1914*. New York: Charles Scribner's Sons, 1989.

Owings, W. A. Dolph. *The Sarajevo Trial*. Vols. 1 and 2. Translated and edited by W. A. Dolph Owings, Elizabeth Pribic, and Nikola Pribic. Chapel Hill, N.C.: Documentary Publications, 1984.

West, Rebecca. *Black Lamb and Grey Falcon: A Journey through Yugoslavia*. New York: Penguin, 1982.

Edith Cavell Trial: 1915

Defendant: Edith Cavell   **Crime Charged:** Aiding enemy forces
Chief Defense Lawyer: Maitre Sadi Kirschen   **Chief Prosecutor:** Dr. Eduard Stoeber   **Judges:** Five-member German military tribunal; names not recorded   **Place:** Brussels, Belgium   **Dates of Trial:** October 7–8, 1915
Verdict: Guilty   **Sentence:** Death

SIGNIFICANCE

Few incidents have so galvanized a nation as the execution of Nurse Cavell during World War I. But was the wave of moral indignation that swept across Britain really justified?

On August 4, 1914, German army divisions invaded Belgium in the first major military offensive of World War I. For those British soldiers cut off by the irresistible advance, all hope of repatriation rested with the fledgling Belgian resistance. Ironically, the resistance worker whom history recalls best was not a Belgian but a 48-year-old Englishwoman named Edith Cavell. She had spent much of her adult life in Belgium, first as a governess, then as a nurse at the Berkendael Institute, a clinic in Brussels. Wartime brought Red Cross status to the clinic, yet through its doors passed upward of 200 soldiers, all seeking passage back across the Channel to England. Cavell first tended their wounds, then arranged for their safe conduct by the Belgian resistance to the coast, in defiance of the German occupiers.

She oversaw proceedings with an almost saintly detachment and scant regard for security, even to the point of keeping an album of photographs of many of the soldiers. In March 1915, she wrote to her cousin: "Do you think you could find out news of the soldiers on the enclosed list? They are relations of some of the girls here." In truth, the list contained names of dozens of men she had helped to escape.

Such laxity made detection inevitable, and one day the clinic was visited by members of the police. British soldiers, still wearing boots and uniforms, hurriedly jumped into bed and did their best to act like patients. The searchers left empty-handed, but suspicions were aroused.

Soon men began arriving at the clinic from outside the usual channels and requesting assistance to escape. Workers at the institute begged Cavell to be on her guard. Then, on June 30, 1915, a Frenchman named George Gaston Quien arrived, with strident demands that he be allowed to work for the resistance. By this time, even Cavell was aware of the dangers, and she turned him away, certain by now that the clinic was under 24-hour surveillance.

All through July, German counterespionage agents compiled a list of the most prominent resistance members. High on that list was Phillipe Baucq, an architect who, besides drawing sketches of airship bases for English soldiers to take home, published an underground newspaper. On July 31, Baucq was arrested at his house, with an acquaintance of Cavell's, Louise Thuliez. Ominously, just days before, Quien had been observed loitering outside the house. Within days most of the resistance members were behind bars.

Edith Louisa Cavell in her early twenties (circa 1890).

Solitary Confinement

Cavell was arrested on August 5 and taken to Saint Gilles Prison, where she spent nine weeks in solitary confinement. A deeply religious woman with strong moral objections to any form of deceit, she admitted her complicity with a disarming honesty. (Later, her captors would claim that of all those arrested, only Cavell betrayed her colleagues, but this was a gross oversimplification of the facts and must be viewed in light of German attempts to neutralize the furor that had been kindled by their incredibly poor judgment in this affair.) In one area Cavell was sorely handicapped: Although the interviews were conducted in French and Cavell gave her answers in French, the statements she signed were written in German, a language with which she was unfamiliar.

Despite protests from Belgian nurses, the German military commanders were adamant—Edith Cavell would be tried for aiding the enemy. During the pretrial period, the chief prosecutor, Dr. Eduard Stoeber, refused permission for defense lawyers to see or talk to the defendants and even refused to divulge the exact nature of the charges that would be brought.

On October 7, 1915, Cavell was just one of 35 defendants brought before the Tribunal of the Imperial German Council of War. Some were guides who had organized escape routes; others had used chemistry skills to develop passport photographs; a few had tended safe houses along the underground routes. Their defense was handled by a Romanian lawyer, Maitre Sadi Kirschen. He faced a miserable task, hamstrung by the restrictions imposed upon him, having to think on his feet, without any time to prepare a proper case.

After the charges were read, the other prisoners were removed from the court, and Cavell was questioned alone. Her cross-examination could hardly have been more brief:

Stoeber: From November 14 to July 15 you lodged French and English soldiers including a colonel, all in civilian clothes. You ... helped Belgian, French and English of military age, furnishing them the means of going to the front, notably in receiving them at your nursing home and in giving them money.

Cavell: Yes.

Stoeber: With whom were you concerned with in committing these acts?

Cavell: With Monsieur Capiau, Mademoiselle Martin ... [and others]

Stoeber: Who was the head, the originator of the organization?

Cavell: There wasn't a head.

Stoeber: Wasn't it the Prince de Croy?

Cavell: No, the Prince de Croy confined himself to sending men to whom he had given a little money.

Stoeber: Why have you committed these acts?

Cavell: I was sent to begin with, two Englishmen who were in danger of death, one was wounded.

This propaganda postcard, commemorating Edith Cavell's death, was published after the sinking of the *Lusitania*.

Stoeber: Do you realize that in thus recruiting men it would be to the disadvantage of Germany and to the advantage of the enemy?

Cavell: My preoccupation has not been to aid the enemy but to help the men who applied to me to reach the frontier. Once across the frontier they were free.

Stoeber: How many people have you thus sent to the frontier?

Cavell: About two hundred.

Four more questions and it was over. Cross-examination of the other prisoners followed. All were quietly defiant. That afternoon, the prosecution produced its only serious witness. Fourteen-year-old Philippe Bodart was the son of one of the accused and had been threatened with ten years' hard labor unless he told the truth. The evidence he gave was especially damaging to Baucq.

Five to Die

The next day, in a speech lasting several hours, Stoeber demanded the death sentence for nine of the prisoners. At its conclusion, the defendants were led away; they would learn their fate later. After a brief deliberation, the five-man tribunal recorded verdicts of guilty. Stoeber then read out the sentences—five prisoners, including Cavell, were to die; the remainder would serve long periods of hard labor.

The weekend passed. On Monday, Cavell received the news. A fellow prisoner urged her, "Madame, make an appeal for mercy."

"It is useless," she replied. "I am English and they want my life."

Sensitive to the clamor of public opinion, the tribunal sought to keep the sentences secret, but Brussels was soon humming with rumors, prompting a delegation from neutral nations to petition the German political minister, Baron von der Lancken, on Cavell's behalf. Shrewder than most, Von der Lancken realized the harm that Germany's reputation would suffer abroad and promised to do his best. But the matter was out of his hands. It had already been decided that Cavell and Baucq would die at dawn the following day. The Belgian prison chaplain broke the news to Cavell that afternoon. She remained perfectly calm. Asked if she would like the Reverend H. Sterling Gahan, the British chaplain in Brussels, to accompany her at her execution, she replied, "Oh no. Mr. Gahan isn't used to things like that." But she did agree to see him that evening.

The next morning at seven o'clock, Cavell and Baucq faced the firing squad together. Her last words were said to be: "I realize that patriotism is not enough; I must have no hatred or bitterness towards anyone."

News of Nurse Cavell's execution so inflamed international feeling—especially in the United States, where outrage over the sinking of the civilian liner *Lusitania* by a German U-boat was still a fresh memory—that Germany hastily commuted the remaining death sentences to terms of imprisonment. For the British government, Edith Cavell was a propaganda gold mine. Overnight, the number of men enlisting for army duty almost doubled, urged on by the words of Prime Minister Herbert Asquith: "She has taught the bravest man among us the supreme lesson of courage." After the war, Cavell's body was carried back to England on May 14, 1919, and reburied at Norwich, in her home county.

So, was Cavell's execution justified? Although the folly of the decision to shoot her is undeniable, so is the fact that she materially aided the British war effort, thereby rendering herself liable to the supreme penalty if caught. That being said, though Cavell's execution might have been good law, it was terrible politics.

—Colin Evans

Suggestions for Further Reading

Clarke-Kennedy, A. E. *Edith Cavell.* London: Faber, 1965.

Richardson, N. *Edith Cavell.* London: Hamish Hamilton, 1985.

Ryder, Rowland. *Edith Cavell.* New York: Stein and Day, 1975.

Roger Casement Trial: 1916

Defendant: Sir Roger Casement   **Crime Charged:** High treason
Chief Defense Lawyers: Arthur M. Sullivan, K.C.; Thomas Artemus Jones;
John H. Morgan   **Chief Prosecutors:** Sir F. E. Smith, K.C.; Archibald Bodkin;
Travers Humphreys   **Judges:** Lord Chief Justice Reading, Sir Horace Avory,
Sir Thomas Horridge   **Place:** London, England
Dates of Trial: June 26–29, 1916   **Verdict:** Guilty   **Sentence:** Death

SIGNIFICANCE

Traitor or patriot? There is no shortage of subscribers to either view of Sir Roger Casement, but one fact is undeniable—his was the most controversial British treason trial of the 20th century.

At daybreak on April 21, 1916, three men waded ashore on a desolate stretch of coastline in southwest Ireland. All were exhausted. Since putting off from a German submarine under cover of darkness, they had spent hours rowing through the rough seas in a small boat. For the leader of the group, Sir Roger Casement, a 51-year-old former diplomat in the British Consular Service and fervent Irish nationalist, this day marked the culmination of an 18-month campaign. Since shortly after the outbreak of World War I, he had been scouring Germany for captured Irish soldiers prepared to return to Ireland and fight for independence from Britain. Casement's compatriots on this Good Friday morning were fellow nationalist Robert Monteith and Daniel Bailey, a private in the Royal Irish Rifles, who had signed on only to escape detention in a German prisoner of war (POW) camp.

After burying most of their gear in the dunes, the trio headed inland. Despite the early hour—not yet five o'clock—their progress did not pass unnoticed. Strangers in this part of County Kerry were rare, and several watchful eyes followed the three men as they made their way to a ruin known as McKenna's Fort. Here, they split up. Monteith and Bailey pressed on to rendezvous with the Irish Volunteers, while Casement, overcome with fatigue, stayed behind to regain his strength. Before leaving, Monteith handed Casement a communication code from the German General Staff intended for the Republican HQ in Dublin.

Meanwhile, a farmer named John McCarthy had found the boat on the beach, and when, later that morning, his eight-year-old daughter uncovered several revolvers, he contacted the local police. At around 1 P.M., Casement was caught and taken into custody. (Monteith subsequently escaped to America; Bailey was arrested and charged but later acquitted.) Among his possessions were a pair of field glasses, ammunition, and various maps. As if this were not bad enough, a young lad handed over to the police two scraps of paper that Casement had hurriedly ditched by the side of the road at the time of his arrest. When pieced together, they formed the German communication code.

After further questioning, Casement was taken to London and charged with high treason, a capital offense. There, a search of his former lodgings in Belgravia yielded perhaps the most deadly evidence yet.

Diaries Reveal Homosexual Activity

Although never introduced into testimony, there can be no doubt that the Casement diaries colored every minute of testimony. The diaries were packed with graphic accounts of homosexual activity, and to this day, there is argument regarding their authenticity. Casement's defenders have branded them forgeries, fabrications of a vindictive government determined to blacken Casement's name by any means possible. Other, perhaps more impartial, observers have no doubt they are genuine. (The Crown actually offered them to the defense should it wish to advance a plea of insanity, since it was thought that the actions described could only be those of a madman. The offer was refused.)

Some highly dubious newspaper leaks concerning the diaries' contents meant that public feeling ran high against Casement

Irish Nationalist, Roger Casement, in an 1890s portrait. Casement was convicted of high treason in 1916 and condemned to death by hanging.

when it came time for him to face his accusers on June 26, 1916. Opening for the Crown, Attorney General F. E. Smith, K.C., said, "The charge upon which the prisoner is arraigned is a very grave one, the law knows no graver," and concerned Casement's attempts to recruit POWs in Germany for the Irish Brigade. In the event of German naval success, the intent was for Casement to land the brigade in Ireland "to defend the country against the enemy England"; should Germany lose the war, each brigade member would receive a bonus of up to £20 ($80) and free passage to America.

After describing the circumstances of Casement's arrival in Ireland and subsequent arrest, Smith concluded icily: "I have, I hope, outlined these facts without heat and without feeling. Neither in my position would be proper. . . .

Rhetoric would be misplaced, for the proved facts are more eloquent than words. The prisoner, blinded by a hatred to this country, as malignant in quality as it was sudden in origin, had played a desperate hazard. He has played it and he has lost it. Today that forfeit is claimed."

The prosecution led off with testimony from several former POWs at Limburg Lahn camp in Germany. Private John Neill recounted how Casement had stood on a table in the barracks to address those present. "He spoke of how much the Germans liked the Irish, and how much the Irish liked the Germans," a statement that apparently provoked as much mirth in the barracks as it did in court.

Next, it was the turn of a Kerry laborer named Michael Hussey. On the night of April 20, at around 9:30, he had seen some unusual activity about half a mile out to sea. "It was a red light, and it lasted for a few seconds." The next morning, he had gone down to the shoreline to gather seaweed at a spot adjacent to where he had seen the light, and there, among the dunes, he spotted the boat.

Constable Bernard Riley described Casement's arrest at McKenna's Fort. "I told him to stand where he was . . . that my rifle was loaded, and if he moved a foot, I should shoot him. He said that was a nice way to treat an English traveler." It was Riley who had been approached by the young lad Martin Collins with the pieces of paper that Casement had attempted to throw away. They contained details of future arms shipments and how to make contact with foreign agents. Noticing that the figure 7 was written in the Germanic fashion—with a dash across the downstroke—Riley returned to McKenna's Fort and conducted a more thorough search that yielded three overcoats.

In one of the coat pockets, Frederick Britten, an inspector in the Royal Irish Constabulary, found "a first-class sleeping railway ticket from Berlin to Wilhelmshaven, dated 12th April, 1916." This was devastating evidence.

Defiant Speech

Against all these witnesses, defense counsel Arthur Sullivan, K.C., could make little headway. He decided to call no witnesses, instead relying on his own oratorical powers to win the day. But there was one final gambit—a request for his client to read a statement from the dock. Presiding over the three-judge bench, Lord Chief Justice Reading granted Casement this privilege but cautioned the jury to remember that, because the defendant had declined to give evidence, this should not be regarded as sworn testimony.

Casement made little attempt to deny the main body of the charges and concerned himself mainly with rebuffing suggestions that he had accepted any financial inducement from enemy powers. "Money was offered to me in Germany more than once . . . but I rejected every suggestion of the kind, and I left Germany a poorer man than I entered it. . . . I trust, gentlemen of the jury, I have made that statement clearly and emphatically enough for all men, even my most bitter enemies, to comprehend that a man, who in the newspapers is said to be just another Irish traitor, may be a gentleman."

When it came time for Sullivan to take up the cudgels on his client's behalf, he protested that all Casement's activities had been for the furtherance of Ireland and not Germany. "I would most respectfully subscribe to the doctrine that no Irishman has a right to take views or risk his life for any cause that is not in the service of Ireland." Sullivan argued hard and at great personal cost. With the strain etched deep in his face, he began drifting off into uncorroborated areas that had not been entered into testimony, digressions that drew reproach from the bench. Sullivan's incoherence only worsened. As the court began to fidget with embarrassment, he suddenly swayed and whispered, "My Lords, I regret to say I have completely broken down." He then sank back into his seat and buried his head in his hands. Court was immediately adjourned for the day.

The next morning, with Sullivan confined to bed, Thomas Artemus Jones concluded the defense. Smith's response, for the Crown, was simple and deadly: Had Casement wanted to advance the cause of Irish separation, then that was his business, but why go to Germany? "The question . . . has never been answered. Why? . . . You can sweep away all these belated . . . sophistries about old Irish politics and the Volunteers in the North of Ireland. They were never in his mind when he made these speeches. . . . they are afterthoughts when it is necessary to attempt to exhume some defense, however remote, from the facts in which the prisoner finds himself."

The case went to the jury at 2:53 P.M. on the fourth day of the trial. At 3:48, they were back with a guilty verdict. Before a sentence of death was passed, Casement was permitted to address the court. He had clearly expected this outcome and concluded his speech with a direct taunt at Smith, his principal accuser: "I am prouder to stand here today in the traitor's dock to answer this impeachment than to fill the place of my right honorable accusers."

At this, Smith smiled and was heard to murmur, "Change places with him? Nothing doing."

The next day, June 30, it was announced that Casement had been stripped of his knighthood. As agitation for a reprieve gained momentum, so did rumors about the infamous diaries. What part they played in the decision to deny

The Casement funeral procession as it crossed through O'Connell Street by the Dublin General Post Office.

clemency remains a matter of conjecture. For the man in the condemned cell at Pentonville Prison, it mattered not one jot: He could not wait to assume his role as martyr, aware, like other freedom fighters before and since, that, politically, he was of more use dead than alive. He got his wish on the morning of August 3, 1916.

—Colin Evans

Suggestions for Further Reading

Inglis, Brian. *Roger Casement.* New York: Harcourt Brace Jovanovich, 1973.

Montgomery Hyde, H. *Trial of Sir Roger Casement.* London: Hodge, 1960.

Reid, B. L. *Lives of Roger Casement.* New Haven, Conn.: Yale University Press, 1976.

Sawyer, Roger. *Casement: The Flawed Hero.* London: Routledge, 1984.

Mata Hari Trial: 1917

Defendant: Margaretha Geertruida Zelle MacLeod   **Crime Charged:** Spying
Chief Defense Lawyer: Edouard Clunet   **Chief Prosecutor:** Lieutenant
André Mornet   **Military Tribunal Judge:** Lieutenant Colonel Albert E.
Sompron   **Place:** Paris, France   **Dates of Trial:** July 24–25, 1917
Verdict: Guilty   **Sentence:** Death

SIGNIFICANCE
France in 1917 was exhausted by war with Germany. Scapegoats were needed to draw public attention away from the trenches, where the Germans had slaughtered half a million French troops at Verdun-sur-Meuse, and away from the high seas, where German submarines dominated. A successful spy hunt was needed to counteract and explain the bad news. Numerous spies were arrested, tried, and executed, but none gained the enduring fame of Mata Hari.

Since 1917, the name Mata Hari has been a synonym for "spy." The woman who bore that exotic Javanese name was actually Margaretha (M'greet) Geertruida Zelle MacLeod, a Dutch native born in 1876. After her father disappeared and her mother died, a godfather enrolled her at age 13 in a school for kindergarten teachers. There, after the headmaster found the lissome 5-foot 10-inch young beauty irresistible, she was expelled.

M'greet answered a matrimonial advertisement placed by middle-aged John Rudolph Campbell MacLeod, a Dutch Colonial Army captain, and married him at age 18. MacLeod soon revealed the drinking and gambling habits that had landed him in debt. The ravishing M'greet paid off his debts by blackmailing a wealthy admirer.

"The Eye of Dawn"

In 1897, the captain was posted to Java. There, M'greet learned the Malay language and the intricate rhythms of the native ritual dances. The natives called her "Mata Hari" from the Malayian words *mata* (eye) and *hari* (dawn): "the eye of the dawn" (or "the sun").

Rudolph retired, and the MacLeods returned to Holland, where M'greet won a legal separation. Determined to dance, she moved to Paris, a city vibrant with gaiety and excess. Her first private-salon performance produced a newspaper report of a woman from the Far East in whose "veils encircling and discarded there was just a suggestion of naughtiness."

Soon, a wealthy collector of Oriental art sponsored a performance. Mata Hari, the Hindu dancer, was born. All Paris responded to her amber skin and black hair, her somber eyes and tall, slim figure.

The alluring M'greet MacLeod, known as Mata Hari, poses in one of her famous dance costumes. (Archive Photo)

The Courtesan Dancer

Lucrative dance contracts took Mata Hari to Madrid, Monte Carlo, Vienna, Marseilles, Alexandria, Berlin, London, Rome, and Amsterdam. A cigarette was named for her. She shared intimacy with a "who's who" of lovers: the duke of Brunswick, the head of the French secret service, French Minister of War Adolphe Messimy, German Foreign Minister Traugott von Jagow, even the crown prince of Germany. One lover, a wealthy banker, gave her a home in Neuilly.

In the summer of 1914, sensing the waning of her career in Paris, Mata Hari moved to Berlin. When the assassination of Archduke Franz Ferdinand at Sarajevo launched a world war, Mata Hari's German friends enrolled her in an Antwerp school for spies. After training, she arrived in Paris, permitted to enter because she was a citizen of a neutral country (Holland) who owned property in France (the house at Neuilly). Over the next year, she resumed intimate relationships—or launched new ones—with French military and government officials, not realizing that French, Italian, and British secret services were regularly reporting her activities as they sought direct evidence that she was a spy.

"Either I Am Dangerous . . . or . . . Nice"

Among the 40-year-old courtesan's lovers was a 24-year-old Russian aviator, Captain Vadime de Massloff. An earlier lover, Jean Hallaure, knowing that Mata Hari sought a pass to visit a spa at Vittel, near the air base where Massloff was stationed, sent her to the Military Bureau for Foreigners, which was secretly the French Bureau of Counter-Intelligence. Its commandant, Georges Ladoux, asked her if British Intelligence was correct in telling him she was a German spy. "Either I am dangerous," she replied, "and you must expel me from France, or I am just a nice little woman." Ladoux issued the pass.

After visiting her young lover, Mata Hari returned to Ladoux and proposed herself as a secret agent for France. Ladoux warned her that he was certain she was a German spy and that she was gambling her life. "I've already thought about it," she said, unaware that she was falling into a trap devised earlier by Hallaure and Ladoux. So Mata Hari became a double agent.

Arrest and Trial

The French sent her to Spain, where she met frequently with German intelligence agents. Then the Germans ordered her back to Paris. There, on February 13, 1917, she was arrested by the French, who had intercepted a German telegram that ordered her from Madrid to Paris and promised her a check for 15,000 pesetas. The uncashed check was on her person when she was arrested.

Mata Hari lived in this house, the Chateau de la Doree at Esvres-sur-Indre from 1910–11.

Mata Hari's trial began at 1:00 P.M. on July 24 before a jury consisting of the president of the military tribunal, Lieutenant Colonel Albert E. Sompron, and six military men. The chief evidence was a report by Captain Pierre Bouchardon that accused Mata Hari of obtaining information "susceptible to damage the operations of the army or to endanger the safety of places, posts, or other military establishments," including "information dealing with interior politics, the spring offensive, the discovery by the French of the secret of a German invisible ink, and the disclosure of the name of an agent in the service of England." Altogether, the report estimated, the accused was responsible for the deaths of some 50,000 Allied soldiers.

The trial was closed to the public. Prosecutor Lieutenant André Mornet reviewed evidence of Mata Hari's particular interest in men in uniform, her lie that her trip to Vittel was to visit the spa when its true purpose was to see her lover Vadime de Massloff, and the large amounts of money she had received from the consul and other Germans, who were known to pay their mistresses very poorly. Her answer was that, as a woman accustomed to living in villas, chateaus, and first-class hotels all over Europe, such small amounts of money were of no interest to her. In fact, she said, the Germans paid their mistresses out of government funds allocated for paying spies.

But, said Mornet, she had accepted 30,000 francs from the Germans simply as a mistress. Why, then, did she ask the French for a million as a spy? She replied that she was willing to spy for France because she really wanted to help the country.

Try as he could with questions based on Bouchardon's report, Mornet could prove only that she had spoken with certain people but not what she had been paid for. Finally, in an exhaustive summing-up that lasted several hours, Mata Hari's 74-year-old lawyer, Edouard Clunet, pleaded for a not-guilty verdict. Within 45 minutes, the jury affirmed that the accused spy had "maintained intelligence with the enemy in Paris," even though she had not been seen with the enemy and no German agents had been apprehended, produced as witnesses, or brought to trial. The sentence was death.

The Netherlands Foreign Ministry asked the French Council for Revision to reduce the sentence. It refused, as did the Court of Appeals. The French Minister of Foreign Affairs refused to ask the president of France to grant a pardon.

At 6:15 A.M. on October 15, 1917, Mata Hari stood before 12 Zouave soldiers. She wore her best shoes, a pearl gray dress, a straw hat and veil, and gloves. She refused to be tied to the traditional pole or to be blindfolded. Of the 12 bullets, only 3 reached their mark. One pierced the heart. An officer administered the coup de grâce—a pistol shot in the ear.

—Bernard Ryan, Jr.

Suggestions for Further Reading

Knight, David C. *The Spy Who Never Was and Other True Spy Stories.* Garden City, N.Y.: Doubleday, 1978.

Ostrovsky, Erika. *Eye of Dawn: The Rise and Fall of Mata Hari.* Boston: G. K. Hall, 1978.

Waagenaar, Sam. *Mata Hari.* New York: Appleton-Century, 1965.

Rosa Luxemburg's Assassins Trial: 1919

Defendants: Otto Runge, Kurt Vogel   **Crimes Charged:** Attempted manslaughter (Runge); illegal disposition of a corpse (Vogel)
Chief Defense Lawyer: Name not recorded   **Chief Prosecutor:** Paul Jörns
Place: Berlin, Germany   **Dates of Trial:** May 8–14, 1919   **Verdicts:** Guilty
Sentences: Runge—two years' imprisonment, four years' loss of civil rights, dismissal from army; Vogel—28 months' imprisonment

SIGNIFICANCE

The feeble prosecution of Luxemburg's killers created a festering controversy in German politics during the years following World War I.

Marxist theorist Rosa Luxemburg was one of the most hated and admired figures in German politics during her lifetime. After emigrating to Berlin in 1898, the Polish-born Luxemburg earned a reputation as an eloquent debater whose propensity for irking the staid German socialist establishment ensured that her power remained limited.

As World War I approached, Luxemburg sympathized with the working classes, who would fight and suffer most in such a war, regardless of their nationality. When the country entered the war in 1914, the dominant German Socialist Party (SPD) agreed to support the war effort. Disgust with the SPD's decision led Luxemburg, Reichstag representative Dr. Karl Liebknecht, and their allies to form a new radical socialist movement called the Spartacus League.

Luxemburg's and Liebknecht's antiwar agitation meant the end of their relations with the powerful SPD. It also ensured that both spent the war in government prisons. When the war ended and Luxemburg was freed in November 1918, she immediately resumed her revolutionary work.

Isolated from the socialist coalition in control of the postwar government, the Spartacists allied themselves with the German Communist Party (KPD) in December 1918. Yet, despite the apparent success of the Bolsheviks in Russia and her fiery public rhetoric, Luxemburg did not feel that Germany was ready for revolution. She counseled patience, but was outnumbered by radicals who wanted to boycott an impending national election in favor of armed confrontation.

On January 6, 1919, a mass demonstration took place in Berlin to protest the government's dismissal of the chief of police. The protest itself was peaceful, but Communist extremists saw it as a precipitous moment available for exploitation into the long-awaited revolution. The KPD declared the government illegitimate, occupied several public buildings, and waited for the masses to rise.

Polish-born Rosa Luxemburg (pictured here circa 1886) was murdered along with Karl Liebknecht during the 1919 Berlin Revolt.

Luxemburg and Liebknecht Killed

No popular revolution ensued, but the government acted immediately. Volunteer units called Freikorps attacked the revolutionaries, ruthlessly crushing the "revolt" in three days of street fighting. Luxemburg and Liebknecht went into hiding but were betrayed. On January 15, 1919, they were arrested by a volunteer army unit of Horse Guards and taken to the regiment's headquarters in the Hotel Eden.

The international press reported that officials claimed the Spartacist leaders were to be taken from the hotel to ensure their safety. Then came the government's version of the truth: Liebknecht was beaten by an angry mob while being hustled toward a waiting car, which sped away toward Moabit Prison. En route, the car suffered a flat tire. While waiting for a fresh vehicle to arrive, Liebknecht's guards shot their prisoner when he tried to flee into the wooded Tiergarten. Or, so the officials claimed.

Like Liebknecht, the story went, Luxemburg had been beaten by a hostile crowd in the lobby. She, too, had been rushed into a waiting car, which departed but soon returned. Her guards reported that they had been stopped by a mob that demanded to know the identity of their prisoner. When the soldiers admitted that their prisoner was Luxemburg, a man jumped on the running board and shot her in the head. Luxemburg's body was then dragged out of the car and carried off. Theories were that she had either been rescued by Spartacists or thrown into a canal by her enemies.

Liebknecht's body turned up in a morgue, but Luxemburg's body was nowhere to be found. On January 23, it was rumored that her corpse was found in the Landwehr Canal and that her body was being hidden to prevent Spartacist revenge. A week later, Luxemburg was rumored to be alive, awaiting a revolution that would allow her to come out of hiding. The former rumor was prophetic.

Newspaper Exposes Truth

Because Chancellor Friedrich Ebert had requested Freikorps volunteers to crush the Spartacist revolt, suspicion of government complicity increased when the Horse Guards regiment was allowed to investigate the case itself. Two Workers' Council members participated in the inquest but resigned when their recommendations to arrest suspects were ignored.

The truth about the killings was nevertheless exposed in the Spartacist newspaper, *Die Rote Fahne*, by Leo Jogiches, Luxemburg's colleague and former lover. Jogiches—and the public—learned that Luxemburg and Liebknecht had not died at the hands of "the people."

Trooper Otto Runge had been stationed at the Hotel Eden's door, where he had followed orders to club the prisoners with his rifle as they left. The bleeding Liebknecht was driven to the Tiergarten, where his guards asked if he could walk. He staggered a few steps and was shot for "trying to escape." His body was left at the nearest mortuary, identified only as an unknown corpse.

No mob had stopped Luxemburg's car. She was clubbed senseless by Runge and thrown into another car, where Lieutenant Kurt Vogel shot her in the head. Vogel ordered soldiers loitering by the Landwehr Canal to dump the body into the water. Later that night at the hotel, the Horse Guards were photographed celebrating their work. Jogiches obtained the photo and published it.

After Jogiches exposed the killers, he was arrested and murdered by police. By then, however, the real story was publicly known. Runge, Vogel, and six other officers were arrested.

Two enlisted soldiers testified that Lieutenant Vogel had shot Luxemburg while standing on the running board of the car. Vogel had also ordered them to throw her into the canal. Vogel denied both claims. Runge confessed to hitting the prisoners with his rifle. Other witnesses implied that hush money had changed hands. Yet the implications of the evidence were blunted by state prosecutor Paul Jörns, whose sympathy for the accused was reflected by his praise of their war service and acceptance of their animosity toward the victims.

Court Gives Killers Token Jail Terms

On May 14, the court declared that it could not determine who had performed the killings. Five officers were acquitted of complicity in the murders, including Captain Horst von Pflugk-Harttung, whom the press had identified as Liebknecht's killer. Lieutenant Rudolf Liepmann, one of Liebknecht's guards, was sentenced to six weeks of barracks confinement for giving Runge false identity papers.

Only Vogel and Runge were convicted of serious charges. Vogel was acquitted on charges of murder, allowing his subordinates to act improperly, and neglecting his duty. He was convicted of improperly disposing of a corpse and submitting a false report on the incident.

Vogel, who had been furnished with a false passport before the trial, was sentenced to two years and four months' imprisonment. Three days later, he escaped to Holland. When the German government filed an extradition request in December 1920, the Dutch government replied that Vogel had fled to South America. Vogel was amnestied before the month ended.

Rosa Luxemburg's murderers celebrate by toasting to her death at the Eden Hotel January 16, 1919. Runge, Luxemburg's killer, is seated at the table, third from the left.

Runge was sentenced to two years' imprisonment for attempted manslaughter, assault, misuse of his weapon, and using false documents. He was also dismissed from the army. The court closed its decision by declaring that Runge had acted freely, without coercion.

On May 31, a little more than two weeks after the sentencing, Luxemburg's corpse was found at a Landwehr Canal lock. The body was hidden at an army base, but the discovery did not remain a secret. Luxemburg was publicly buried on June 13.

Like Vogel, Runge was furnished with false identity papers, but he remained in prison. Angry at his superiors for reneging on their promises to protect him, he told his story to the press in 1921. Runge called his trial "a comedy," during which the accused officers lived in unlocked cells, enjoying wine, music, and women. Runge accused prosecutor Jörns of persuading him to confess and accept a minimal four-month sentence in exchange for future assistance. Runge said he was threatened with death if he did not learn his confession properly.

As a 10-year statute of limitations ticked away, the radical press harried those responsible for the murder and its whitewash. In 1928, the *Daily Tagebuch* accused Jörns of helping the killers rather than dutifully prosecuting them. Jörns twice sued editor Josef Bornstein for libel, losing both times. On February 14, 1930, the Berlin Court of Assizes found that Bornstein had sufficiently proved Jörns's lax attitude toward the murderers. Jörns later continued his career as a prosecutor during the Nazi regime.

Rosa Luxemburg's desire to destroy the capitalism by which Europe's imperial governments flourished made her a martyr to some leftists, but her criticism of Lenin's use of terror earned her the posthumous hatred of doctrinaire Communists. Surprisingly, disagreement over Luxemburg's role in political history was nearly outlasted by debate over her murder.

In 1962, the German press interviewed Waldemar Pabst, a captain who had interrogated Luxemburg and Liebknecht after their capture. Pabst claimed that the murders were carried out with the full support of Gustav Noske, the government's chief military commissioner. When the West German government information bureau agreed with Pabst's contention that the killings were state-sanctioned executions, memories of the two slain revolutionaries were stirred by a fresh controversy.

—Tom Smith

Suggestions for Further Reading

Ettinger, Elzbieta. *Rosa Luxemburg: A Life*. Boston: Beacon Press, 1986.

Hannover-Drück, Elisabeth, and Heinrich Hannover. *Der Mord an Rosa Luxemburg und Karl Liebknecht*. Frankfurt: Suhrkamp Verlag, 1967.

"Liebknecht Cool in Facing Death." *New York Times*, January 19, 1919.

Lutz, Ralph. "The Spartacan Uprising in Germany." *Current History Magazine*, April 1921, 78.

Nettl, J. P. *Rosa Luxemburg*. New York: Schocken Books, 1969.

Waite, Robert G. *Vanguard of Nazism: The Free Corps Movement in Postwar Germany 1918–1923*. New York: W. W. Norton, 1969.

Mohandas Gandhi Trial: 1922

Defendant: Mohandas Gandhi **Crime Charged:** Sedition
Chief Defense Lawyer: Mohandas Gandhi **Chief Prosecutor:** Sir J. T. Strangman **Judge:** C. N. Broomsfield **Place:** Ahmadabad, India
Date of Trial: March 18, 1922 **Verdict:** Guilty
Sentence: Six years' imprisonment

SIGNIFICANCE

Remembered in India 75 years later as "the Great Trial," the 1922 trial of Gandhi stands as a milestone in the history of liberation. It marked a turning point in India's long struggle for divorce from the British Empire, as veteran British officials in the civil service began to realize that a fearless India was using its own standards of ethical behavior to defeat British colonialism.

Mohandas Karamchand Gandhi was born in 1869 in western India. His father was of the Vaisya, or merchant, caste and served as prime minister of the state of Porbandar. At 19, Gandhi entered University College in London, England, and was called to the bar at Inner Temple. Returning to India, he practiced law in the Bombay High Court, then moved in 1893 to South Africa, where he conducted a lucrative law practice.

In the Boer War (1899–1902), Gandhi organized an Indian ambulance corps that served British troops. He repeated the service in 1906 when the British fought the Zulus. Meantime, he had been stirred by restrictions imposed on Indian immigrants in South Africa. In 1908, determined to lead the Indian struggle for social and political equality, he quit his law practice.

In 1914, Gandhi succeeded in obtaining an agreement from General Jan C. Smuts, a founder of the Union of South Africa and later its prime minister, that removed many restrictions on the Indian community. But Gandhi paid a price: three separate prison terms for organizing campaigns of civil disobedience.

Truth Seeking and Home Rule

Soon after World War I began in 1914, Gandhi returned to India and established *Satyagraha*, or "truth seeking," a movement that combined politics and religion. By now, he was a fervent supporter of Indian home rule. When in

1920 the British passed the Rowlatt Act, which harshly punished sedition, Gandhi led the opposition, promoting noncooperation with the government while staunchly supporting nonviolence.

Gandhi had earned a worldwide reputation. To Indians, he was the beloved Mahatma—the "great-souled" one. He dominated the political party called the Indian National Congress as it led a boycott of all government services, including the legislatures and the courts. Students walked out of colleges. Leading lawyers refused to practice in British courts.

Rebellion and rioting broke out across India. Determined to make his country worthy of independence from Great Britain, which by the admission of its own leaders had conquered the Asian country as an outlet for its goods, Gandhi opened shops that sold handwoven khaddar cloth. He supervised street bonfires in which foreign-made clothing was burned. On March 10, 1922, Gandhi—by now clad daily in a simple loincloth to symbolize simplicity of life, promote handmade Indian textiles, and identify himself with the impoverished Indian—was arrested. He was charged with sedition.

"The Great Trial" Begins

"The Great Trial" was held on a hot day, March 18, 1922. Sir J. T. Strangman, British advocate general, presented the prosecution charge: "bringing, or attempting to bring, into hatred or contempt, or exciting, or attempting to excite, disaffection toward His Majesty's government, established by law in British India." The evidence of Gandhi's guilt, the prosecutor told District and Sessions Judge C. N. Broomsfield, could be found in three articles he had written and published in his magazine, *Young India*. It could be proved, he added, if such proof were needed, that Gandhi had long preached disaffection.

Mohandas Karamchand Gandhi, known also as the Mahatma ("Great Teacher"), served as a barrister-at-law in South Africa in 1904.

Gandhi interrupted: "I plead guilty to all the charges."

The prosecutor continued. He acknowledged that Gandhi's educational background was of high quality and that his writings reflected his position as an established leader. Gandhi, the prosecutor charged, had instigated a campaign whose goal was to spread disaffection systematically and openly. The accused's published articles, he went on, prescribed nonviolence, yet events he had promoted in recent months had brought the destruction of private property and a large number of murders: In Bombay, after Gandhi had urged the masses to boycott a celebration for the visiting Prince of Wales (later King Edward VIII), a large number of people were wounded and killed when the mob attacked those Indians—mostly Parsis—who insisted on attending the event; and in the village of Chauri Chaura, 22 policemen had lost their lives when a mob drove the police into their own building, set it on fire, and beat to death all who tried to escape.

In sentencing the accused, the prosecutor concluded, the court would have to consider not only Gandhi's writings but these events. He recommended severe sentencing.

"If I Was Set Free I Would Do the Same"

The judge asked Gandhi whether he wished to make a statement. Gandhi spoke at length, including these comments [condensed here]:

> I entirely endorse the learned advocate-general's remarks. He was entirely fair to me. I have no desire to conceal the fact that to preach disaffection toward the existing government has become almost a passion with me.
>
> It is impossible to dissociate myself from the diabolical crimes of Chauri Chaura or the mad outrages of Bombay. I should have known the consequences of my acts. I knew that I was playing with fire, I ran the risk, and if I was set free I would do the same.
>
> Non-violence is the first article of my creed. But I had either to submit to a system which I considered has done an irreparable harm to my country, or incur the risk of the mad fury of my people bursting forth when they understood the truth. I do not ask for mercy. I do not plead any extenuating act. I am here to invite and cheerfully submit to the highest penalty that can be inflicted for what in law is a deliberate crime and what appears to me to be the highest duty.

Gandhi then read a long statement on how, over three decades, "from a staunch loyalist and co-operator" he had become "an uncompromising disaffectionist and non-co-operator." He reviewed his experiences in South Africa and his shock at the Rowlatt Act, "a law designed to rob the people of all real freedom," and his conclusion was that "the British connection made India more helpless than she was before, politically and economically."

"The greatest misfortune," added Gandhi, "is that Englishmen and their Indian associates do not know that they are engaged in the crime I have attempted to describe. They do not know that a subtle but effective system of terrorism and an organized display of force on the one hand, and the deprivation of all powers of retaliation or self-defense on the other, have emasculated the people."

The judge, obviously moved, replied: "The law is no respecter of persons. Nevertheless, it will be impossible to ignore the fact that you are in a different category from any person I have ever tried or am likely to try. It would be impossible to ignore the fact that in the eyes of millions of your countrymen you are a great patriot and a great leader. It is my duty to judge you as a man subject to the law. I do not forget that you have continually preached against violence. But having regard to the nature of your political teaching, how you could have continued to believe that violence would not be the inevitable consequence of it passes my capacity to understand."

The judge then said he proposed to follow the precedent set in a similar case—that of Bal Gangadhar Tilak, a Hindu who had preceded Gandhi as Indian nationalist leader. Tilak's sentence, 12 years earlier, had been 6 years' imprisonment. In setting the sentence, the judge said, "If the course of events in India makes it possible for the government to reduce the period and release you no one will be better pleased than I."

Gandhi, smiling, said he considered it an honor to be associated with Tilak's name. The judge and the prisoner bowed soberly to each other, and Gandhi was taken to the Yeravda Prison. Released after two years, he worked daily at a spinning wheel—it became the symbol of India's goal of political and economic independence—to encourage Indians to spin and weave their own cotton cloth. By 1925, Gandhi was concentrating on bettering the status of the Harijans, or untouchables, whom he called "the Children of God," and in 1930 he was again imprisoned, this time for a year, for campaigning against salt taxes.

The Architect of India's Freedom

For nearly two more decades, Gandhi urged civil disobedience, was imprisoned frequently, and fasted "unto death" to make his points. In 1942, after demanding immediate British withdrawal from India in the midst of World War II and declaring, "either we get freedom or we die," he served 21 months behind bars.

On August 15, 1947, as Great Britain transferred governmental authority to Pakistan and the Dominion of India, Viscount Mountbatten, formerly viceroy of the Indian Empire, declared Gandhi "the architect of India's freedom through non-violence."

On January 30, 1948, as Gandhi walked toward a New Delhi pergola where he delivered his daily prayer message, he was assassinated by the editor of a small newspaper who was a member of an extreme Hindu faction that opposed the partition of India.

—*Bernard Ryan, Jr.*

Suggestions for Further Reading

Brown, Judith M. *Gandhi: Prisoner of Hope.* New Haven: Yale University Press, 1989.

Erikson, Erik H. *Gandhi's Truth.* New York: W. W. Norton, 1969.

Gandhi, Mohandas K. *An Autobiography, Or The Story of My Experiments with Truth.* Translated from the Gujarati by Mahadev Desai. Ahmadabad, India: Navajivan, 1927.

Green, Martin, ed. *Gandhi in India in His Own Words.* Hanover, N.H.: University Press of New England, 1987.

Shirer, William L. *Gandhi: A Memoir.* New York: Simon & Schuster, 1979.

Woodcock, George. *Mohandas Gandhi.* New York: Viking, 1971.

Herbert Armstrong Trial: 1922

Defendant: Herbert Rouse Armstrong   **Crime Charged:** Murder
Chief Defense Lawyers: Sir Henry Curtis Bennett, K.C.; Samuel Bosanquet,
K.C.; Edwin Godson   **Chief Prosecutors:** Sir Ernest Pollock, K.C.; Charles
Vachell, K.C.; St. John Micklethwait   **Judge:** Justice Charles Darling
Place: Hereford, England   **Dates of Trial:** April 3–13, 1922
Verdict: Guilty   **Sentence:** Death

SIGNIFICANCE
Among the most famous of all English murder trials, this case is unique in its
outcome.

On the Wales-England border lies the market town of Hay-on-Wye, and it was here that Herbert Armstrong practiced law as a solicitor. Middle-aged, meek-mannered, and diminutive, he had the misfortune to marry a domineering hypochondriac who made his life a misery. Outside the house, Armstrong strutted his army rank of major; at home, he was little more than a tight-lipped lackey.

In July 1920, Katherine Armstrong, a compulsive imbiber of proprietary medicines, became so disturbed that the family physician certified her as insane. After several months in an asylum—which saw her health improve markedly—she returned home in late January 1921. Exactly one month later she succumbed to an agonizing illness. Armstrong recorded the event laconically in his diary: "February 22—K died." Cause of death was given as gastritis, with related ailments. Reveling in his newfound freedom, Armstrong soon acquired considerable local notoriety as a philanderer.

Armstrong's business interests, too, became erratic. In August of that same year he found himself in dispute with Hay's only other solicitor, Oswald Martin, over a collapsed real estate deal. Martin became angry when Armstrong seemed unwilling to return a deposit of £500 ($2,000) that had been entrusted to him. Late in October, in an attempt to assuage Martin's concern, Armstrong invited his rival for afternoon tea, during which he handed him a single scone with the apology, "Excuse fingers." On returning home Martin became violently ill with vomiting and diarrhea. His father-in-law, the town pharmacist, aware that Armstrong had recently purchased large amounts of arsenic—ostensibly to kill weeds in his garden—asked a doctor to analyze a sample of Martin's urine. It tested positive for arsenic.

Because of Armstrong's position, the police moved cautiously. Oblivious to the official interest being shown in him, Armstrong bombarded Martin with further invitations to tea. In between conjuring up excuses not to attend, Martin suddenly recalled a box of chocolates that had arrived anonymously at his home through the mail in September. A guest had eaten one chocolate and had suffered severe gastric pains. The remaining chocolates were sent for analysis and found to be laced with arsenic. On New Year's Eve, 1921—much to Martin's relief—Armstrong was finally charged with attempted murder. This was later amended to murder after Home Office pathologist Dr. Bernard Spilsbury exhumed Katherine's body and found massive amounts of arsenic.

There was snow in the air on April 3, 1922, when Armstrong went on trial for his life at Herefordshire Assizes. Attorney General Sir Ernest Pollock, K.C. (King's Counsel), for the Crown, attributed the symptoms of Katherine's final illness to systematic poisoning over the last weeks of her life, culminating in a final dose administered within 24 hours of her death when she was lying comatose in her bed, unable to move her limbs or to feed herself. "Who poisoned her?" Pollock asked rhetorically, "I am going to submit to you that the evidence points conclusively to the fact that she was poisoned by her husband."

A crucial point in the trial came early on when Pollock sought to introduce into evidence details of the attempt on Martin's life. Armstrong's chief counsel, Sir Henry Curtis Bennett, K.C., one of the cagiest performers at the bar, was on his feet immediately, demanding to know how any symptoms of arsenic poisoning suffered by Martin could possibly shed light on whether Mrs. Armstrong had been murdered by her husband.

Major Herbert Armstrong arriving at the courthouse on the day of his trial.

Defense Setback

After considering both sides of the argument—and not for the last time in this trial—Justice Charles Darling sided with the prosecution, which cleared the way for Martin's testimony. Martin recounted the series of events leading up to the invitation to tea at Armstrong's house and how, in the dimly lit room, he had been deliberately handed a single scone. In his cross-examination, Bennett tried to demonstrate that Martin was resentful toward the defendant. "Am I right in saying that from time to time you had received acts of kindness from Major Armstrong?"

"That is quite true, yes, but that would have been a matter of form in any case."

"That is the way you look at it, do you?"

"That is the way I look at it . . . there [was] no need to be rude."

"Let's have it out—did you dislike Major Armstrong before October 1921?"

"No, I did not dislike him."

"What did you mean, then, by disinclination to be rude?"

"My feelings were neutral as far as he was concerned. I never liked nor disliked him." The manner in which Martin equivocated under questioning created an unfavorable impression among observers. By the time he left the stand, there were few who felt that his testimony had been fueled by other than personal rancor.

When called to testify, Dr. Thomas Hincks, who had committed Katherine to the asylum and had attended her in her final illness, gave his opinion that the delusions he had misinterpreted as madness had actually resulted from long-term arsenic poisoning. In anticipation of Spilsbury's evidence, which would show that Katherine had ingested a large dose of arsenic within 24 hours of her death, Pollock asked Hincks, "Supposing this lady had within her reach . . . a number of bottles containing anything, do you think in her condition it would be possible for her to have administered them to herself during the last three or four days of her life?"

Hincks had no doubt. "Absolutely impossible!" he exclaimed, thus under-lining a nurse's earlier testimony that Katherine's feebleness made unaided movement all but impossible.

Call Dr. Spilsbury

With the first week of the trial drawing to a close, the Crown called its premier "expert" witness. By this stage of his career Dr. Bernard Spilsbury's exploits as Home Office pathologist had made him a national celebrity. Judges and juries had listened in awe to his accounts of pioneering medical detection that seemed to defy belief; and defendants by the dozen had heard their lives sworn away by his lucid testimony. After Armstrong's trial, doubts would surface about Spilsbury's seeming infallibility, but at the time of the trial his word was sacrosanct. He began with his customary assurance:

> It is clear that a large dose of poison must have been taken certainly within twenty-four hours of death, and from the amount of arsenic which was found in the liver . . . the poison must have been given in a number of doses extending over a period, certainly of some days, possibly not less than a week.

An excellent showman, Spilsbury used colored charts to show the jury from where in the body he had taken his samples.

Curtis Bennett's line of cross-examination was soon apparent: "Am I right in saying that in very extreme cases . . . a person may live up to fourteen days after a fatal dose of arsenic?"

"It is conceivable, and I daresay cases have been recorded," Spilsbury replied coolly. He discounted the defense's contention that Katherine had deliberately taken arsenic as an act of suicide, because she had continued vomiting right up until her death; had she received arsenic 14 days earlier, Spilsbury said, its purgative effects would have abated. A long and tense battle of wits over the deceased's last few days came to a dramatic conclusion when Curtis Bennett asked incredulously, "You are putting it now that the whole of the symptoms are due to arsenic?"

Spilsbury snapped back angrily, "Yes, of course I am!"

John Webster, senior Home Office analyst, whose career dated back to the turn of the century, described the 208 milligrams of arsenic he found in Katherine's organs as "the largest amount of arsenic I have found in any case of arsenical poisoning."

Spilsbury's fellow pathologist Sir William Willcox was equally adamant that "there must have been a good deal of arsenic absorbed during the last few days of life." The last question put to Willcox came from Justice Darling. Referring to the defense's theory of suicide, he asked, "Is that hypothesis, in your opinion, a possible one?"

"Quite impossible," Willcox replied.

When Curtis Bennett rose to begin the defense, he told the jury, "I am going to suggest to you . . . that . . . the case that Mrs. Armstrong took this poison herself is an infinitely stronger one than the case which is made against Major Armstrong." The accused was then called to give evidence. He was led through his story by junior defense counsel Samuel Bosanquet. As a practicing solicitor, Armstrong had done a thorough job of preparing his answers, but the sympathetic prompting of one's own counsel is light-years removed from the rigors of cross-examination, as he soon discovered.

Pollock was eager to get to Armstrong's purchases of arsenic, obtained, so he claimed, to kill dandelions. The defendant admitted buying four ounces of arsenic, then dividing half into 20 portions. Nineteen were allegedly used for the task at hand; the 20th was found in a paper sachet in Armstrong's pocket when he was arrested, which left two ounces unaccounted for. Someone else very keen to get to the bottom of Armstrong's poison use was Justice Darling, who virtually assumed the role of secondary prosecutor.

Judge Intervenes

"When . . . you realized that you had got white arsenic in your pocket, did you realize that it was just a fatal dose of arsenic, not for dandelions only, but for human beings?"

"No, I did not realize that at all," Armstrong retorted.

"If you were simply dosing dandelions, why did you make . . . twenty little packets such as that found in your pocket?"

"Because of the convenience of putting it in the ground."

"But you did it all in one day?"

"I dosed them."

"All at the same time?"

"Yes."

"Why make up twenty little packets, each a fatal dose for a human being, and put [them] into your pocket?"

"At the time it seemed to me the most convenient way of doing it. I cannot give any other explanation," Armstrong replied lamely. The image Darling had created of the little major marching around town with handy lethal-sized portions of arsenic in his pocket was devastating.

These were clearly the most important few questions in the trial. What followed was rather anticlimactic, as two doctors, Frederick Toogood and William Ainslie, testified that the defense theory regarding arsenic ingestion was not wholly implausible; but neither physician could match the impact made by Spilsbury.

The final nail in Armstrong's coffin was hammered in by Justice Darling. Only on rare occasions did his summing-up achieve the impartiality that such a situation demanded—throughout, his antipathy toward the accused had been palpable—so it was somewhat surprising to learn that among experienced court watchers the odds were heavily in favor of acquittal. The Crown, they felt, had fallen short of proving its case beyond a reasonable doubt. Sadly for Armstrong, these doubts were not shared by the jury. The jury found him guilty, and, on April 13, 1922, he was sentenced to death.

On May 31, 1922, Armstrong made a dubious form of history by becoming the only British solicitor to be hanged for murder. Coincidentally, 18 months earlier, yet another Welsh solicitor, Harold Greenwood, had been accused of poisoning *his* wife with arsenic. Greenwood's acquittal had made headline news, and among the keenest followers of his trial was Herbert Rowse Armstrong. Interestingly, it was shortly after this that Armstrong's interest in weed killer began to blossom.

—Colin Evans

Suggestions for Further Reading

Mortimer, John, ed. *Famous Trials*. London: Penguin, 1984.

Odell, Robin. *Exhumation of a Murder*. New York: St. Martin's Press, 1988.

Rowland, John. *Murder Revisited*. London: John Long, 1961.

Young, Filson. *Trial of Herbert Rouse Armstrong*. London: William Hodge, 1927.

Hitler's "Beer Hall" Putsch Trial: 1924

Defendants: Adolf Hitler, General Erich Ludendorff, Ernst Roehm, seven others **Crimes Charged:** High treason **Chief Defense Lawyer:** None **Chief Prosecutor:** District Attorney Ludwig Stenglein assisted by Hans Erhard **Judge:** Chief Justice Georg Neithardt and a panel of judges **Place:** Munich, Germany **Dates of Trial:** February 26–April 1, 1924 **Verdicts:** Ludendorff—acquitted; Hitler and others—guilty **Sentences:** Hitler and three others, five years of fortress arrest with possibility of parole after six months; Roehm and four others, lesser sentences

SIGNIFICANCE
This trial gave Adolf Hitler a national audience, and his boldness and rhetoric established him as a contender for the hearts and minds of the German people.

Near the end of World War I, the political party that would eventually become known by the name Nazi (which was based on the pronunciation of the first two syllables of the German word for national) had attracted the attention of Adolf Hitler, a young Austrian who had served as a lance corporal in the German army during the war. Hitler had grown up in the Austro-Hungarian Empire, but he detested what he regarded as the "mongrel-like" quality of that realm; he identified himself much more strongly with the Germany of Kaiser Wilhelm II. Hitler was, therefore, crushed to learn in November 1918—while in a hospital recovering from temporary blindness caused by mustard gas—that the kaiser had abdicated, and Germany had surrendered to the Allied powers. For the rest of his life, Hitler remained convinced that Germany had not really been defeated in that war—rather, that a sinister combination of Jews, liberals, and Marxists had stabbed the country in the back and brought about the surrender that so crippled Germany. Hitler joined the German Workers' Party in 1919; by 1920, he had become the chief spokesman of what was renamed the National Socialist German Workers' Party.

In the summer and autumn of 1923, Germany was rife with social and political unrest. The country was in a state of crisis, having suffered military defeat in World War I, the humiliating terms of the Versailles Treaty, and the painful task of having to pay reparations for the damage caused by the war to

Allied countries. Into this matrix of loss, pain, and despair stepped group—the National Socialist German Workers' Party—and its chief spokesman, Adolf Hitler.

The Attempted Putsch

In the fall of 1923, Hitler organized his Nazi party into a paramilitary organization, with Ernst Roehm as the leader of its so-called storm troopers, little more than an army of thugs. He then forged an unlikely alliance with General Erich Ludendorff, the former quartermaster general of the German army and an important hero of World War I. Feeling the strength of his party and the weakness of the Bavarian state government, Hitler determined to carry out a *putsch*, or coup, against that government in early November 1923. Originally planned for the weekend of November 10–11 (to avenge the signing of the armistice), the putsch was moved up to the night of November 8 because the Bavarian leader. Gustav von Kahr was to make a speech in the Buergerbraeu, a popular beer hall, that evening.

Hitler and his storm troopers invaded the beer hall at 8:30 P.M. Hitler proceeded to inspire the crowd with a speech and then sought to intimidate the three leading members of the Bavarian government present—von Kahr, General Otto Hermann von Lossow, and Colonel Hans von Seisser—to join him in his coup attempt. The men withheld their decision until Ludendorff arrived; they then agreed to join with Hitler and the famous general. By 11:00 that evening, Hitler seemed to have succeeded, but his plan began to unravel when it became apparent that the German regular army, the Reichswar, remained loyal to Berlin. The three Bavarian leaders renounced their word to Hitler and Ludendorff early the next morning, and by daybreak of November 9, Hitler's putsch was in serious trouble.

Attempting to break the stalemate, Ludendorff agreed to march with Hitler and his Nazi followers through the center of Munich, the capital of Bavaria. They anticipated that this would spark such a popular uprising that they could seize control without firing a shot. The march began at noon, and throngs of bystanders began to join the 2,000-plus Nazis. At 12:20, however, Bavarian state police opened fire on the column. Hitler threw himself to the ground and suffered a separated shoulder; Ludendorff marched stiffly past the police and was taken into custody. The Nazis had 16 men killed, and the state police lost three. Hitler was soon captured, and Bavarian authorities were able to report to Berlin that the revolt had been crushed. Hitler was taken to the fortress prison of Landsberg, outside Munich, where he conducted a brief hunger strike and sought to use the newspapers to bring further attention to his cause.

The Trial

The trial began on February 26, 1924, in a large brick lecture hall on the campus of the Infantry School in Munich. Charged with high treason, Hitler,

Ludendorff, Ernst Roehm, and seven Nazi followers were brought before the People's Court of Bavaria. Under the court system of the time, there was no jury; the decision would rest with two professional judges and three lay judges. It would soon emerge that the presiding judge, Georg Neithardt of Nuremberg, was completely sympathetic to Ludendorff and unable or unwilling to curb Hitler and his fellow defendants. The three lay judges were clearly in favor of the defendants from the start.

What should have been a cut-and-dried trial of high treason soon became a sensational "reverse" trial, whereby the defendants were able, symbolically, to put the government in Berlin on trial for its poor performance on behalf of the German people. The chief prosecutor, Ludwig Stenglein, made only halfhearted efforts to demonstrate the guilt of the defendants, leaving his assistant, Hans Erhard, to present most of the evidence.

All of Germany followed the trial—by radio, newspaper, and word of mouth—during the 25 days it went on. Newspaper reporters from around the world were present to hear from the 368 witnesses expected to be called by the prosecution and defense. In reality, far fewer should have been needed; it was clear that Hitler, Ludendorff, and their associates had intended to overthrow the legal government of Bavaria and Germany. However, those who might have expected the trial to proceed smoothly or in a predictable manner had not reckoned on the demagogic talent of the then relatively obscure Adolf Hitler.

From the first day, Hitler dominated the proceedings. In his opening speech, he denounced the German government and linked its leaders with the surrender of 1918. "How can I be considered guilty of high treason," he brazenly asked, "when there is no such crime as an act of treason against the traitors of November 1918?" By contrast, Hitler's co-conspirator General Ludendorff made a poor showing. Vaguely suggesting that he was a victim of events, Ludendorff neither stood by Hitler nor denounced him. Although Ludendorff had been brave on the streets of Munich on November 9, 1923, he proved to be stolid and uninspired in the courtroom. The crowd that attended the trial thus swung its sympathy from the general to Hitler, who was ready to make the most of the situation.

The former lance corporal was strong, uncompromising, and defiant. Again and again, he deflected the questions and launched into diatribes on the state of affairs in Germany and the need for a new and effective leader. During the weeks of the trial, a good many Germans came to see that Hitler viewed himself as that new leader. Knowing that the crowd was swinging to his side, Hitler continued to repeat his basic argument: "I cannot declare myself guilty. True, I confess to the deed, but I do not confess to the crime of high treason. There can be no question of treason in an action which aims to undo the betrayal of this country in 1918." With few exceptions, Chief Justice Neithardt allowed Hitler to ramble, ruminate, and digress during his responses to questions from the prosecution; on one occasion, Hitler's response ran to four hours. Confronted with this fact, Neithardt commented only that it was impossible to stop the putsch leader from talking. (As a people, Germans would discover this after 1933.)

By the time closing arguments were heard on March 27, Hitler had gained the sympathy of millions of Germans. Although the prosecution had no difficulty in establishing the facts of the case, it was Hitler who captured the sentiment of the audience, both in person and through the newspapers. He concluded his defense by stating: "Gentlemen, judgment will not be passed on us by you; judgment will be passed on us by the Eternal Court of History. . . . You may say 'Guilty' a thousand times, but the Goddess who presides over the Eternal Court of History will, with a smile, tear up the indictment of the public prosecutor and the verdict of this court, for she acquits us." Hitler's closing statement struck a deep chord within many Germans who felt that they had played—and suffered—by the rules long enough. Beyond that, Hitler had given the world a glimpse of the consummate actor and propagandist who would eventually lead the German people with such disastrous consequences.

The Verdicts and the Aftermath

The verdicts were handed down on April 1, 1924. Chief Justice Neithardt read the results, which had been reached by a vote by the judges of four to one. Ludendorff's acquittal surprised no one; the former general was too potent a symbol of Germany's past to discard. All the other nine defendants were found guilty. Hitler and three others were found guilty of high treason but were given the minimum sentence: five years of fortress confinement, with the possibility of parole after six months. Five others, including Roehm, were found guilty of a lesser charge, aiding and abetting high treason.

Taken to Landsberg Prison, Hitler made excellent use of his time. While indulging in chocolates sent to him by admirers—many of them female—he composed the first volume of what was published as *Mein Kampf* ("My Struggle"). Although the book received only modest attention in the 1920s, it showed that Hitler's theories of racial supremacy and his belief in a new and victorious Third Reich were already fully articulated in his mind. When he was paroled for good behavior on December 20, 1924 (having served less than nine months of his sentence), Hitler walked out of the prison doors a stronger, more confident, and indeed more popular man than he had been prior to the trial. The Munich trial had brought him publicity and sympathy; many Germans now regarded him as a heroic, although perhaps misguided, nationalistic figure.

In recognition of the Nazi belief that "November 9, 1923 gave birth to January 30, 1933" (the day that Hitler became chancellor of Germany), the former prison inmate returned time and again to commemorate the events of November 8–9, 1923. Every November 9, Hitler restaged the attempted coup, marching through the center of Munich behind a swastika flag stained with blood. The fearless leader of Germany gave no indication that he had dropped to the pavement when the first shots had been fired in 1923. If this meant that his pageant was based on something less than the facts, it shows again Hitler's

Adolf Hitler upon his release from prison on December 20, 1924. (Prints & Photographs Division, Library of Congress)

ability to make a situation other than it truly was, a skill that he had employed with great effect during the Munich trial of 1924.

—*Samuel Willard Crompton*

Suggestions for Further Reading

Bullock, Alan. *Hitler: A Study in Tyranny*. New York: Harper & Row, 1962.

Dornberg, John. *Munich, 1932: The Story of Hitler's First Grab for Power*. New York: Harper & Row, 1982.

Flood, Charles Bracelen. *Hitler: The Path to Power*. Boston: Houghton Mifflin, 1989.

Gordon, Harold, Jr. *Hitler and the Beer Hall Putsch*. Princeton: Princeton University Press, 1972.

Hanser, Richard. *Putsch! How Hitler Made Revolution*. New York: Peter H. Weyden, 1970.

Tscuppik, Karl. *Ludendorff: The Tragedy of a Military Mind*. Translated by H. W. Johnston. Westport, Conn.: Greenwood Press, 1975.

Tsuyoshi Inukai's Assassins Trial: 1933

Defendants: Eitan Goto, Kameshiro Ito, Choko Kawasaki, Seishi Koga, Taku Mikami, Shumei Okawa, Ichinosuke Shinohara, Kosaburo Tachibana, Idezo Toyama, Horishi Yamagishi, 37 others   **Crimes Charged:** Murder, attempted murder, violation of regulations on explosives, preparation of mutiny
Chief Defense Lawyers: Naoyoshi Tsukasaki, Itauro Hayashi
Chief Prosecutor: Procurator Yamamoto (no record of first name)
Judges: Captain Shirotakasu, four naval officers   **Place:** Tokyo, Japan
Dates of Trial: July 24–November 30, 1933   **Verdict:** Guilty
Sentences: Tachibana—life imprisonment; Okawa, Koga, Mikami, and two others—15 years; ten others—10 to 15 years; three others—10 years; Toyama—8 years; 11 cadets—4 years; three others—2 years; one other—1 year

SIGNIFICANCE

The assassination of Tsuyoshi Inukai marked the end of political party participation in the government of Japan and the beginning of the dominance of the military in the period leading to World War II.

At noon on Sunday, May 15, 1932, the premier of Japan, 77-year-old Tsuyoshi Inukai, was in his official residence chatting with a visitor when several young men in naval uniforms and with guns in hand rushed into the room. The premier leaped up, shouting, "Don't shoot; I will listen to your demands!"

One of the men shouted, "Shoot him!" Two held the premier's shoulders. Another fired. The premier died in a hospital within hours. His visitor, wounded, recovered.

Simultaneously, a bomb exploded at the home of Count Nobuaki Makino, who, as lord keeper of the privy seal, was one of the emperor's closest advisers. The count was unharmed, but the house was severely damaged. Bombs also hit the Bank of Japan, the Mitsubishi Bank, the metropolitan police station, and other buildings.

Young Men in Uniform Surrender

That afternoon, 17 men in uniform surrendered at the headquarters of the military police. Five were naval sublieutenants, and the others were army cadets at the military academy. Observers noted that the voluntary surrender was in the Japanese tradition of registering a protest against intolerable conditions at the cost of one's life.

Next came the voluntary surrender of a 38-year-old civilian named Kosaburo Tachibana. An admirer of Count Leo Tolstoy's philosophy of the importance of farm life, Tachibana had developed the Native Land Loving School. Its 25 students were committed to the reconstruction of Japan through a working life on a farm.

Tachibana had preached the defeat of the United States and the League of Nations. "If the villages were released from the burden of sustaining the cities," he had said, "the national power of Japan would increase. At a stroke, we could exclude the influence of America from the Pacific, liberate China from the yoke of the war lords, set India free, and enable Germany to rise again."

Young military minds had bought the Tachibana gospel that their nation of farmers was being destroyed by capitalism. Premier Inukai, only a year earlier, had taken Japan off the gold standard, producing a boom in exports so strong that Japan had become the first nation to recover from the impact of the Great Depression. He was a likely target for a terrorist coup by young militarists influenced by Tachibana.

47 Indicted

Tsuyoshi Inukai in 1930 (National Archives, Washington, DC)

A year after the assassination, the procurator's report brought the indictment of 47 persons for murder, attempted murder, violation of regulations on explosives, and preparation of mutiny. It cited 16 naval officers, 11 army cadets, and 20 civilians—all in their 20s—for executing a conspiracy directed by patriots in their mature years.

Opening on July 24, 1933, the trial began with the court-martial of 10 naval officers, including 28-year-old Lieutenant Taku Mikami, who had pulled the trigger to kill the premier. The defendants had acted, said justice department procurator Yamamoto, after sharing the navy's disappointment with the recent international London Naval Conference and resulting treaty, which had created a crisis in politics, economics, and disarmament. The cause? Disregard of national interests and graft on the part of politicians, financiers, and the ruling classes. Believing their country was headed for ruin, he concluded, they had embarked on desperate projects to arouse the nation.

Let Down by Failure in London

Sublieutenant Seishi Koga testified that he and his patriotic fellows had been "let down" by Japan's "failure" at the London conference—a failure he attributed to a government dominated by business interests. Describing how the army and navy officers and their civilian compatriots planned the coup, Koga disclosed that the assassination and bombings had been expected to result in a declaration of martial law, thus creating a military government.

Army cadet Eitan Goto boldly read a statement: "My determination to reform Japan remains unchanged. I am prepared to die seven times, but I will bomb seven times, if necessary, until the country is fortified. I ask to be punished according to law."

Cadet Ichinosuke Shinohara recited a long list of grievances, including the London Naval Treaty, the Russian foreign policy and superiority over Japan in the air, China's anti-Japanese policy, and the "predominance" of Anglo-Saxon interests in Asia.

Lieutenant Horishi Yamagishi, who had given the command to shoot the premier, told the judges that he and his codefendants had feared that the United States might try "further domination of Japan and the Orient" at a planned naval conference in 1936. The Japanese leaders who accepted the naval treaties, he and his companions insisted, had betrayed the nation and deserved assassination.

"Destruction Is Construction"

Sublieutenant Kameshiro Ito, who was charged with the preparation of a mutiny, said, "We seek to bring about a new government based on unity of the Emperor and the people. We will not stop at murder or robbery. Destruction is construction. The present system must be destroyed." He described one of the civilian leaders, Dr. Shumei Okawa, as "trying, in collaboration with the German-minded military leaders, to overthrow Japan's great financial families and set up a militarist government."

On August 19, the little fingers of nine civilians, severed and preserved in a bottle of alcohol as evidence of public sympathy for the defendants, were brought to the courtroom. The procurator, admitting that patriotic motives had been established, insisted that the serious offense against military discipline must be punished.

Lieutenant Horishi Yamagishi contended that Japanese naval leaders had the right to all the strength they deemed necessary for the security of the empire. Civilian authorities, he argued, should have no part in making such decisions.

Three Elements of Mutiny

Closing his case, the procurator pointed out that the defendants' activities had included three major elements of mutiny: They had formed groups, had taken up arms, and had participated in an uprising. For the defense, attorney Naoyoshi Tsukasaki closed with Shakespeare, reciting passages from *Julius Caesar* to compare Inukai's assassination with that of the Roman emperor. "The accused had as their purpose the establishment of a better, purer state," he said. "Their aims were entirely unselfish. Their heroic decision should make even the devils weep."

The trial produced strong public sentiment for the defendants. On September 16, six court attendants staggered to the judges' bench carrying boxes of letters and petitions—estimated at more than a million—received on behalf of the prisoners. Among them, 1,022 letters were signed in blood. On October 10, the police banned use of the incidents of May 15, 1932, as subject matter for the stage, film, and popular song.

Accepting guilty pleas, the court-martial sentenced Lieutenant Koga, as bomber of Count Makino's home and chief organizer of the coup, to 15 years' imprisonment. Lieutenant Mikami, who had shot the premier, also received 15 years' imprisonment. Three others each received 10 years' imprisonment, three received 2 years, and one received 1 year.

Of the civilians, Tachibana was sentenced to life imprisonment. Okawa and two others received 15 years' imprisonment. Idezo Toyama, who was accused of providing pistols to the terrorists, was sentenced to 8 years.

—Bernard Ryan, Jr.

Suggestions for Further Reading

Beasley, W. G. *The Rise of Modern Japan*. New York: St. Martin's Press, 1990.

Behr, Edward. *Hirohito: Behind the Myth*. New York: Villard, 1989.

Borton, Hugh. *Japan's Modern Century*. New York: Ronald Press, 1955.

Mason, R. H. P. and J. G. Caiger. *A History of Japan*. New York: The Free Press (Macmillan), 1972.

Storry, Richard. *The Double Patriots: A Study in Japanese Nationalism*. Boston: Houghton Mifflin, 1957.

The Reichstag Fire Trial: 1933

Defendants: Marinus van der Lubbe, Ernst Torgler, Georgi Dimitrov, Blagoi Popov, Wassil Tanev   **Crimes Charged:** High treason; arson, by setting fire to the Reichstag (the German parliament building)
Chief Defense Lawyers: Philipp Seuffert, Alfons Sack, Paul Teichert
Chief Prosecutor: Karl Werner   **Judge:** Wilhelm Buenger   **Place:** Leipzig, Germany   **Dates of Trial:** September 21–December 23, 1933
Verdict: Van der Lubbe—guilty, all others—acquitted
Sentence: Execution by beheading

SIGNIFICANCE
Although the evidence and the trial in general were far from conclusive, by using this show trial to allege a conspiracy by the international Communist movement to threaten German institutions, Hitler and his National Socialists provided themselves with the excuse to justify seizing and holding absolute power.

In the years following his release from prison after his failed putsch in Munich in 1923, Adolf Hitler had led his National Socialist German Workers' Party to become a major force in German politics. Exploiting the continuing resentment of the Germans over their "hard times" since the Armistice of 1919—a resentment aggravated by the very real economic depression that was spreading throughout the world in the early 1930s—he had managed to advance the Nazi Party so that by the election of November 1932, it held the largest number of seats in the German Reichstag, or parliament. Although the leader of a minority party, Hitler so manipulated affairs that on January 30, 1933, the president of Germany, war hero Paul von Hindenburg, now exhibiting some signs of senility, chose Hitler as chancellor.

For Hitler, this was not the climax of his ambitions; this was simply the beginning of his scheme to take total control of Germany. Now he needed elections that would give his Nazi Party a full majority—and then he would begin to show the world what a true Führer could do. The problem was that there were so many parties vying for votes, among them the Communist Party—holder of the third-largest bloc of seats in the Reichstag. With the Communists already in control of the Soviet Union, many Europeans were in fact fearful that this movement might seize power in their own countries. Hitler and his Nazis saw themselves as offering not just an alternative to Communism but also its total eradication. As Joseph Goebbels, one of Hitler's most trusted assistants, wrote in his diary the very day after Hitler was appointed chancellor: "In a conference with the Führer, we lay down the line for the fight against the Red terror. For the moment we shall abstain from direct countermeasures. The Bolshevik attempt at revolution must first burst into flame. At the proper moment we shall strike."

The Reichstag Fire

At about 9 P.M. of February 27, with the election campaign well under way, a flame burst out—literally. A policeman stationed outside the Reichstag, the monumental 50-year-old stone building where the German legislature sat, was alerted to the sound of breaking glass. Peering into the ground floor of the Reichstag, he saw some flames and a shadowy figure who seemed to be rushing through the building, setting fires. More police were called, and alarms summoned the fire department. By about 9:20, the first fire ladders were being raised. At about the same time, the police and others who had by then gained entry were finding that even the huge glass-domed chamber of the deputies was burning; within 10 minutes, the glass dome shattered from the explosion of the gases in the chamber.

Also at about 9:30, a search party inside the Reichstag came across a man crouching in a small side room. Stripped to the waist, begrimed, sweating, and breathing heavily, he looked almost like a hunted animal. He gave himself up at once; a pass to a local relief shelter identified him as Marinus van der Lubbe, a Dutchman. Hustled off to the police station, he was almost immediately labeled a Communist. In fact, he had for some years been vaguely involved with the Dutch Communists, but he was far from being an ideologue or a revolutionary. He was really a rather confused, unbalanced individual, somewhere between a vagabond and a sociopath. The 24-year-old van der Lubbe, a poorly educated laborer, had lost much of his sight in an industrial accident. With his allowance from the Dutch government, he had set off in 1931 to travel around Europe. By 1933, he had shown up in Berlin, where he drifted about, attended at least one Nazi rally, and had evidently tried to set fire to two other buildings out of some need to call attention to himself.

The Charges Fly

But the Nazi leaders did not wait to learn all this. Indeed, even before they knew much of anything about van der Lubbe, they were calling the Reichstag fire a Communist plot. Hermann Goering was the first Nazi leader on the scene, and even as the fire was raging, he blamed it on the Communists. Adolf Hitler showed up a few minutes later and proclaimed, "A sign from heaven!" He then ordered mass arrests of Communists. Within 24 hours, some 4,000 Communists, Socialists, pacifists, and others were rounded up and detained. While this was going on during the day of February 28, Hitler persuaded President Hindenburg to sign an act suspending all guarantees of civil liberties as a "defensive measure against Communist acts of violence endangering the state." In effect, Hitler and his Nazis now had license to do as they pleased.

To strengthen the impression that only the Nazis stood between the German people and a Communist conspiracy, Hitler decided to make a major production of the Reichstag fire investigation and trial. It would not be enough to have only the pathetic van der Lubbe to blame. During the night of the fire, various individuals reported that Ernst Torgler, a Communist parliamentary leader, had been seen in the Reichstag as late as 8:15 that evening. When he read in the morning papers that he was considered a suspect, Torgler turned himself in to show that he had nothing to hide. He, too, would be brought to trial. Meanwhile, a waiter in a Berlin restaurant claimed to have seen van der Lubbe dining with some foreigners the afternoon before the fire. When they were eventually apprehended, they turned out to be three Bulgarian Communists. One of them was none other than Georgi Dimitrov, a member of the executive committee of the Communist International. He and the two others, Blagoi Popov and Wassil Tanev, were also to be brought to trial.

On March 5, national elections were held, and again, although they won the largest bloc of seats in the parliament, the Nazis did not have an outright majority. But because all the Communist delegates were either under arrest or in hiding, the Nazis could in practice command a majority in any voting. The National Socialists proceeded in the ensuing weeks to pass legislation that enabled Hitler to rule by decree.

Meanwhile, as Hitler's government proceeded to organize the case against the Communists who had set fire to the Reichstag, the world at large was taking notice. The international Communist network instantly launched a campaign to blame the Nazis and so discredit the forthcoming trial. In August, the Paris Communist secretariat issued an impressive "documented" study, *The Brown Book of the Hitler Terror and Burning of the Reichstag*. Along with attacking the Nazi regime in general, this book charged that the fire was a plot by Goebbels and Goering, with van der Lubbe merely a tool. *The Brown Book* even printed what it claimed was an authentic memo by a Nazi deputy, Dr. Ernst Oberfohren, who set forth the details of the plan by the Nazis. (Historians now agree that the memo was fabricated.)

The Communists also organized a committee of distinguished international lawyers and legislators who held a "countertrial" in London in September. As a result of these hearings, the committee announced on September 20, one day before the trial in Germany began, that only van der Lubbe could possibly be guilty, but that there was indeed some suspicion that the Nazis might be implicated.

The Trial

The trial commenced in a courtroom in Leipzig on September 21, 1933. The presiding judge of the state supreme court was Dr. Wilhelm Buenger.

Rather than by jury, the decision was to be made by Buenger and a panel of four other judges. When the five accused were brought into the courtroom, everyone noticed how terrible they looked after having been held in irons for months. But van der Lubbe looked more than weak and spiritless—he seemed positively devastated. His eyes appeared drowsy, mucus dripped from his nose and saliva from his mouth, his head drooped, and his arms hung lifeless at his sides. (Throughout the trial, his lawyer would occasionally mop his face.) Not unnaturally, many people concluded that he had been drugged by his captors.

Ernst Torgler, the Communist deputy, had cleverly hired a respectable trial lawyer, Alfons Sack, who also happened to be a National Socialist. From the beginning, they made sure that Torgler's defense was totally divorced from the others' defense. Avoiding the ideological implications of the case, Torgler simply fought back on the basis of lack of real evidence. The Bulgarians were assigned a lawyer, Paul Teichert, but because German law allowed defendants to cross-examine witnesses, it was Georgi Dimitrov who effectively conducted their defense in the ensuing weeks. This brilliant, bold, clever man employed both soaring eloquence and ingenious tactics to outsmart the prosecutors. Time after time, he exposed the shallowness of their case and the depth of their prejudices.

The only real case, of course, was that against van der Lubbe, and his demeanor in court undercut the prosecution's charge that he had set the fire, even after the court called a psychiatrist who pronounced him able to stand trial. Van der Lubbe seemed barely able to speak German, and when he did, it was often to give contradictory answers. At times, he appeared to be completely out of touch with the proceedings, giving the trial the air of an absurdist drama, as in this typical exchange:

> Buenger: Stand up, van der Lubbe! Why are you suddenly laughing . . . instead of being serious? . . . Does it have to do with these proceedings or is it something entirely different?
> Van der Lubbe: (Says nothing.)
> Buenger: Speak up! Do you think what is going on here is amusing?
> Van der Lubbe: No.
> Buenger: Do you understand the trial?
> Van der Lubbe: No.
> Buenger: Then it is not these proceedings, or what we have just been talking about that made you laugh? What is it, then? . . . Tell me!
> Van der Lubbe: About the trial.
> Buenger: Something seems amusing to you?
> Van der Lubbe: No.
> Buenger: If something isn't amusing, one doesn't laugh.

Quite apart from van der Lubbe's bizarre behavior, the whole trial had an unreal quality. Van der Lubbe himself continually insisted that he had fired the Reichstag and that he had done so all by himself: He claimed that he had used fire starters and then his own clothing as torches as he rushed about lighting any inflammable materials, such as curtains. There were inconsistencies in the testimony of experts, and there were several unanswered questions: How could an individual have set so many fires in so little time? (Not to mention that van der Lubbe was half blind, not especially bright, and had never been in the place before.) How did whoever set the fire gain entrance to the Reichstag? (An underground tunnel from the residence of the president of the Reichstag—none other than Goering—was said to have been the route.) But little was done to follow through on these issues. Instead, the government continued to hammer away on the charge that it was part of a broad Communist plot. This was, of course, the weakest part of the case, and Dimitrov continually exploited this weakness. Ironically, Dimitrov achieved just what Hitler had during his Beer Hall Putsch Trial in 1924; he turned the trial into a forum for embarrassing the government and advancing his own cause.

In a typical exchange with Dimitrov, Goering—war hero, Nazi bigwig, president of the Reichstag—was goaded into a petulant explosion: "I'll tell you what the German people know. They know you are behaving disgracefully here, that you are a Communist scoundrel who came to Germany to burn down the Reichstag. In my eyes, you are a crook who belongs on the gallows!"

The judge then observed, "The witness's outburst is quite natural."

Dimitrov smoothly replied, "I am quite content with the Minister's answer."

This further provoked Goering to shout, "Get out you scoundrel, get out!"

Dimitrov again got in a dig, "Are you afraid of my questions, Herr Goering?"

"Get out of here, you crook!" shouted Goering.

Marinus van der Lubbe after he was found guilty on charges of high treason and arson on December 23, 1933. He was beheaded by guillotine on January 9, 1934. (Hulton-Deutsch Collection)

The whole world followed these proceedings as they moved from Leipzig to Berlin, where van der Lubbe reenacted his version of what he had done, then back to the courtroom in Leipzig. The longer the trial dragged on, the less convincing the government's case appeared, even after it had called in some 250 witnesses, made some 7,000 gramophone recordings of testimony, and filled more than fifty 10,000-page volumes of evidence and documentation. In the end, the chief prosecutor himself recommended that the three Bulgarians be acquitted—and they were. He asked that Torgler be found guilty of implication "in some manner or another," but he was also acquitted. Only van der Lubbe was found guilty, but it was not clear whether anyone believed he had done it on his own, with the aid of Communists, or with the aid of Nazis.

Aftermath

On January 9, 1934, Marinus van der Lubbe was beheaded by guillotine. Torgler was held in "protective custody" until November 1936. (Because he had not taken the Communist line in his defense, he was never again really accepted by the Communists.) The three Bulgarians were deported to Moscow in February 1934; Dimitrov headed the Comintern (1935–43) and emerged after World War II as the leader of Bulgaria.

The question of who set the Reichstag fire has never been totally resolved to everyone's satisfaction. There are two extreme schools of thought: One believes it was altogether a plot by the Nazis and that van der Lubbe was totally innocent; the other believes that van der Lubbe carried it out as part of some Communist conspiracy. In between these two extremes are several theories, the most plausible being that it was done by both the Nazis *and* van der Lubbe. Douglas Reed was a British journalist who was as close as anyone to the whole episode, first covering the fire on the night itself and then covering the trial. Reed was convinced that the fire was the work of the Nazis, who tricked van der Lubbe into setting some fires while they set the most serious ones. During van der Lubbe's imprisonment and the trial, Reed believes, the defendant was drugged. But Fritz Tobias, a German civil servant, spent years researching the event and in 1962 published his conclusions that van der Lubbe had in fact done it just as he said: entirely on his own.

Whoever set the fire, Hitler turned the burning of the Reichstag into a conflagration of Europe and a holocaust for many of its people.

—*John S. Bowman*

Suggestions for Further Reading

Bullock, Alan. *Hitler: A Study in Tyranny.* Rev. ed. New York: Harper & Row, 1962.

Reed, Douglas. *The Burning of the Reichstag.* London: Victor Gollancz, 1934.

———. *Fire and Bomb.* London: Jonathan Cape, 1940.

Shirer, William. *The Rise and Fall of the Third Reich.* New York: Simon & Schuster, 1960.

Tobias, Fritz. *The Reichstag Fire.* Translated by Arnold Pomerans. New York: Putnam, 1964.

The Moscow Purge Trials: 1936 and 1937–38

Defendants: Three groups of approximately 70 "Old Bolsheviks," former political opponents of Joseph Stalin **Crimes Charged:** Murder, terrorism, espionage, political deviation **Chief Defense Lawyers:** In most cases, none **Chief Prosecutor:** Andrey Vyshinsky **Judge:** Vasily Ulrikh **Place:** Moscow, Soviet Union **Dates of Trials:** August 1936; January 1937; March 1938 **Verdicts:** Guilty, in every case **Sentences:** Death, in all but a few cases

SIGNIFICANCE

These proceedings perfected the confessional trial, in which a despotic leader's critics publicly recant. The Moscow trials grew out of "the Great Terror" of the 1930s, which established Stalin as the unchallenged authority in the USSR. The purge left a legacy of state-sponsored terror in the Soviet Union as well as a permanent system of labor camps—the Gulag—to which dissidents of all types could be banished.

By 1934, Stalin had won out over his rival claimants for supreme power in the Soviet Union. One after another, the challengers fell into line. After the upheaval of collectivization, a comparative calm had settled over the country. For many ordinary people, material conditions were finally beginning to improve. Soviet frontiers were secure. Despite all this, or perhaps because of it, Stalin set in motion a campaign of unexampled savagery against his political opponents, real or imagined, and against hundreds of thousands of ordinary Soviet citizens.

The murder of Sergei Kirov on December 1, 1934, touched off "the Great Terror." Stalin may have arranged the killing himself, as a means of resolving a political dispute. At any rate, he used it as a pretext for repression on an unprecedented, heretofore inconceivable scale. Over the next four years, thousands of Communist Party officials were framed. Stalin's invented conspiracy spread outward from the Kirov murder to plots to assassinate senior party leaders, sabotage, wrecking, espionage. Ultimately, millions were arrested— more than 5 million from 1936 to 1938 alone. In 1937 and the three years that followed, the purge destroyed some 70 percent of the officer corps of the Red Army.

A nationwide network of informers ensured a ceaseless supply of victims. Children denounced parents; colleagues denounced colleagues; friends denounced friends. According to one authority, one of every five persons in a given office or factory doubled as a spy for the NKVD (the Soviet secret police agency). Stalin's functionaries carried out mass executions and filled the Arctic labor camps with political prisoners.

The actual number of killings will probably never be known; several hundred thousand during the purge years is a conservative figure. The historian Robert Conquest puts at 3 million the number who were executed or died in the camps during the height of the terror, 1936–38. Estimates of the total number of Stalin's victims—by execution, by illness and overwork in prison camps, by starvation as a result of failed economic policies—have ranged upward to 20 million.

The three Moscow show trials of 1936–38 were the public expression of the Great Terror. The proceedings explained and justified the leader's measures to preserve the Soviet state. Fewer than 70 "conspirators" were involved in the public trials, most of them "Old Bolsheviks," some with distinguished revolutionary résumés dating to czarist times. These men, so the prosecutors alleged, had made it possible for such an astonishing number of terrorists, spies, and other enemies of the people to remain at large. Stalin blamed them for the massive crop failures that led to famine and for the industrial miscalculations and blunders that created shortages of nearly every kind of product and service.

All three trials had this in common: the "confessions" of the accused, obtained through blackmail, torture, threats to wives and children, false promises, and, not least, an appeal to the perverse, all-purpose logic that held the party's interests to be paramount. As Conquest has written, "Stalin required not only submission but complicity." As a last service to the party, many of the defendants agreed to abase themselves, to confess abjectly to imaginary crimes. At no time during any of the show trials did the state scruple to present evidence, documentary or material, linking the accused to their alleged crimes.

The First Trial

A wave of arrests followed the Kirov killing, the first phase of the Great Terror. The NKVD hauled in the assassin, Leonid Nikolayev, at once and liquidated him (the phrase of the day) before year's end. Within a few months, 30,000 to 40,000 people in Leningrad alone were arrested and deported, charged with complicity in Kirov's murder. One woman's fate illustrates the method. She once worked at a Young Communist library that Nikolayev frequented. On the basis of this tenuous connection, she was arrested. So were her sister, her sister's husband, and the secretary of her party cell.

Stalin's real targets were the Old Bolsheviks Lev Kamenev and Grigori Zinoviev. In mid-January 1935, they were brought to trial in secret in Leningrad. The two were persuaded to admit moral responsibility for the killing, though they denied any actual involvement. According to the authorities, Zinoviev conceded that Stalin's challengers had misled the conspirators who had moved against Kirov. Said Zinoviev: "The former activity of the former opposition could not, by the force of objective circumstances, but stimulate the degeneration of those criminals."

The terror intensified during 1935 as Stalin continued to replace moderates in key positions with people absolutely loyal to him. Stalin arranged the first show trial, in August 1936, to demonstrate the necessity for the purges. Zinoviev and Kamenev were to be tried again; they were joined by another Old Bolshevik, Ivan Smirnov, and 13 other defendants.

The trial opened shortly after noon on August 19 in the October Hall of the Trade Union House in Moscow—a large, bright, gaudily decorated former ballroom of what had been, before the revolution, the Nobles' Club. Nearly everything had been arranged beforehand. To encourage the confessional mood, the accused had been beaten and denied sleep. One by one, the defendants agreed to admit their guilt in open court in return for Stalin's guarantee that their lives and those of their families would be spared.

The "conspirators" faced charges of plotting to kill Stalin, Andrei Zhdanov, the Leningrad party boss, and other leaders. Vasily Ulrikh presided; Andrey Vyshinsky presented the state's case. Most of the 200 or so spectators were carefully selected NKVD agents. Some 30 diplomats and foreign journalists were allowed in, too, to carry the report of the conspiracy to the world.

Ulrikh initiated the proceedings by asking whether any of the accused wanted a lawyer. All agreed to forgo legal services. The court clerk read out the indictment: direct involvement in the Kirov assassination, plots to murder the chief party leaders, links to the exiled anathema Leon Trotsky. The accused pleaded guilty on all counts, except for the stubborn old revolutionary Smirnov and one other defendant. Zinoviev, Stalin's chief target, confirmed he had acted under Trotsky's instructions. He and the others provided evidence against Smirnov, who continued to accept general responsibility while denying the specific charges.

"There could be no acting on one's own, no orchestra without a conductor among us," E. A. Dreitzer testified. "I am surprised at the assertions of Smirnov, who, according to his words, both knew and did not know, spoke and did not speak, acted and did not act. This is not true!"

The next day, August 20, Kamenev confessed. As for Smirnov's position, he said, "It is ridiculous wriggling, which only creates a comical impression." Zinoviev, a famous orator, could barely speak. Nevertheless, he managed to croak out a response to Smirnov's accusation that he had lied.

"Yes, I often told untruths," Zinoviev admitted. "I started doing that from the moment I began fighting the Bolshevik Party. In so far as Smirnov took the road of fighting the Party, he too is telling untruths. But it seems the difference between him and myself is that I have decided firmly and irrevocably to tell at this last moment the truth, whereas he, it seems, has adopted a different decision."

On August 21, several defendants attempted to explain why, with such vast conspiracies, so little had been accomplished. In fact, only the Kirov assassination plot had been successful. One plotter said he had been unable to obtain a ticket for a Comintern meeting, making it impossible to carry out Trotsky's order to shoot Stalin there. Another had intended to gun down Zhdanov at a May Day parade in Leningrad. "We marched by too far away," he said, accounting for the failure.

Vyshinsky presented his final arguments on August 22. They were hardly subtle. "I demand that these dogs gone mad should be shot—every one of them," he said in conclusion. On August 23, the accused made their final pleas. Kamenev addressed his remarks to his two children. "No matter what my sentence will be, I consider it just," he said. "Don't look back. Go forward. Together with the Soviet people, follow Stalin."

The court reassembled at 2:30 in the morning of August 24 to deliver the verdict: All were guilty; all were to be shot. Smirnov remained defiant to the last. "We deserve this for our unworthy attitude at the trial," he said. The others went meekly, perhaps in the expectation that Stalin would fulfill his pledge to spare their lives. But there were no pardons or stays. Zinoviev, Kamenev, Smirnov, and the others were taken to the execution cellars and shot, each with a bullet to the back of the head, probably within a week of the end of the proceedings.

A few days later, Stalin ordered the NKVD head, Genrikh Yagoda, to execute 5,000 political prisoners in the labor camps. But Stalin, for some reason, soon found Yagoda wanting. He replaced him in September 1936 with a rising party functionary named Nikolai Yezhov. Under Yezhov, the terror intensified. He gave his name to its most ferocious phase—*Yezhovshchina*.

The Second Trial

The second show trial opened on the numbingly cold January 23, 1937, again in the October Hall, again with Ulrikh presiding and Vyshinsky conducting the prosecution. The 17 accused were mostly veteran Bolsheviks, once prominent and respected party members, now dubbed "The Anti-Soviet Trotskyite Center."

The four chief targets, Grigori Pyatakov, Grigori Sokolnikov, Leonid Serebryakov, and Karl Radek, were accused of plotting to destroy the Soviet economic system and of spying for Germany and Japan. Trotsky, the state alleged, ordered and directed the plotters' entire program from exile.

The defendants admitted to responsibility for poor planning in industry and agriculture and to having organized terrorist acts: factory explosions, mine pit fires, train wrecks. I. A. Knyazev admitted arranging 13 to 15 railway smashups. One method, he explained, involved slack supervision of locomotive maintenance and repair. "Almost all the water gauges were reduced to a ruinous condition. As a result of this neglect, a boiler burst in January 1936 on the Rosa-

Vargashi stretch," Knyazev said. Another official confessed to supplying poor-quality coal to a power station. And so it went.

"This is the diabolical infinitude of crime!" Vyshinsky declared in his summing-up on January 28. He airily dismissed the absence of any evidence other than the defendants' confessions: "A conspiracy, you say, but where are the documents? I am bold enough to assert, in keeping with the fundamental requirements of criminal procedure, that in cases of conspiracy such demands cannot be put." Some of the junior defendants had state-appointed counsel. The defense lawyers agreed with Vyshinsky: Evidence, or rather the lack of it, had no bearing on the case.

The accused offered their pleas, one after another. Said Pyatakov, a recovered oppositionist, the mastermind of Soviet industrialization, and absolutely loyal to Stalin since his recantation of Trotskyism in 1928: "In a few hours, you will pass your sentence. And here I stand before you in filth, crushed by my own crimes, bereft of everything through my own fault, a man who has lost his party, who has no friends, who has lost his very self."

At 3 A.M. on January 30, the court returned with the verdict: guilty, with sentences of death for everyone except Sokolnikov, Radek (who would later die in the Arctic camps), and two of the small fry. Stalin again had allowed Western journalists into the courtroom. It seems hard to credit now, but some of the journalists actually believed the affairs to be legitimate, the charges real, the admissions genuine. "It is unthinkable that Stalin ... and the court-martial could have sentenced their friends to death unless the proofs of guilt were overwhelming," wrote Walter Duranty of *The New York Times*.

The Third Trial

The terror had taken on a life of its own. Nobody could feel safe. Across the hall, on the floor below, in the building opposite, the NKVD men would come in the middle of the night, knocking on the door. People were compelled to denounce someone before they were denounced themselves. By March 1938, Stalin could not possibly have believed the few surviving Old Bolsheviks were a credible threat. "The third trial," notes Conquest, "was in this sense little more than a victory parade." Even so, it provided a grand finale, tying together every sort of opposition into one great conspiracy: wreckers, deviationists, right and left oppositionists, Trotskyites, spies.

The chief defendants were Nikolai Bukharin, Alexei Rykov, and Nikolai Krestinsky. All had been members of Lenin's Politburo. Bukharin was editor in chief of *Isvestia;* Krestinsky, a prominent diplomat; Rykov, a former premier. Also accused was Yagoda, the former NKVD commissar and organizer of the first phase of the terror. The charges were familiar enough: spying for Germany and Japan, wrecking, plotting the return of capitalism, conspiring to assassinate Stalin. Bukharin individually was charged with scheming to seize power in 1918 and kill Lenin. For the finale, Nikolai Yezhov, Yagoda's successor, had added a novel element: accusations of medical murder against a number of Kremlin physicians.

The puppet masters of the earlier trials, Ulrikh and Vyshinsky, reassembled in October Hall for the Great Trial, which opened on March 2, 1938. Only three of the accused, all doctors, had legal counsel. All 22 defendants pleaded guilty, except for Krestinsky. He withdrew his "confession" without warning.

As in the earlier trials, the accused accepted responsibility for the general failures of Soviet industry and agriculture. A former leading finance ministry official admitted trying to "dislocate the economy and thus rouse among the population discontent with the financial policy of the Soviet power." A former commissar of agriculture accepted blame for crop failure and the widespread destruction of livestock, including an anthrax outbreak in eastern Siberia.

On the evening of the second day, Krestinsky rose to speak. Dull and diminished, he looked "more than ever like a small bedraggled sparrow," one observer thought. He had probably been tortured in the Lubyanka prison during the night. "Yesterday," Krestinsky said, "under the influence of a momentary keen feeling of shame, evoked by the atmosphere of the dock and the painful impression created by the public reading of the indictment, I could not bring myself to tell the truth, I could not bring myself to say that I was guilty." He felt no such squeamishness now. He admitted everything.

Bukharin had been arrested more than a year earlier. He had not been beaten, though an intensive three-month interrogation surely qualified as a form of torture. Threats to his young wife and child led him to make a full confession. But when he saw it written out, especially the accusation of plotting Lenin's death, he disavowed it. Bukharin agreed, finally, to accept general responsibility but no direct involvement in the crimes alleged.

In fact, on the stand, he talked at such great length in abstractions that Ulrikh found it necessary to admonish him. "So far you are still beating about the bush, you are saying nothing about your crimes," the judge told him. Yagoda showed some fight, too, at least in the early phase. A pharmacist before he became a secret policeman, and known as a "poison man," Yagoda admitted ordering the medical murder of the author Maksim Gorky, who supposedly had died of natural causes. But he denied other charges. "You can drive me, but not too far," he said. "I'll say what I want to say but . . . do not drive me too far." Later, though, Yagoda came around. Possibly he, too, had been tortured. At any rate, he confessed to everything.

Vyshinsky presented his final arguments the morning of March 11. He asked for the death penalty for all but two of the accused. "Our people are demanding one thing: crush the accursed reptile," he told the court. The defendants' last pleas followed. One, Christian Rakvosky, offered a double-edged admission.

"I confess to all my crimes," he said. "What would it matter for the substance of the case if I should attempt to establish here before you the fact that I had learned of many of the crimes, and of the most appalling crimes of the 'bloc of Rights and Trotskyites,' here in court, and that it was here that I first met some of the participants?''

The court retired at 9:25 P.M. March 12. At four o'clock the following morning, the judges reconvened in the October Hall. True to Stalin's form, all were guilty on all counts; 19 of the 22 defendants received death sentences. Bukharin, Rykov, and some of the others were executed promptly, probably the night of March 15. Bukharin had not broken. In his final plea, he denied having spied for the Germans; he denied having masterminded the assassination plots. He and Rykov, it was said, remained defiant to the end, which came suddenly and painlessly with the sharp crack of a pistol in the Lubyanka cellars.

—Michael Golay

Suggestions for Further Reading

Conquest, Robert. *The Great Terror: Stalin's Purge of the Thirties*. New York: Macmillan, 1968.

Ginzburg, Evgeniia. *Into the Whirlwind*. Translated by Paul Stevenson and Manya Harari. London: Collins, Harvill, 1967.

Koestler, Arthur. *Darkness at Noon*. Translated by Daphne Hardy. New York: Macmillan, 1941.

Medvedev, Roy. *Let History Judge: The Origins and Consequences of Stalinism*. Translated by George Shriver. New York: Columbia University Press, 1989.

Ulam, Adam. *The Bolsheviks*. New York: Macmillan, 1965.

Leon Trotsky's Assassin Trial: 1940–43

Defendant: Ramon Mercader (aliases Frank Jacson, Jacques Mornard)
Crime Charged: Murder   **Chief Defense Lawyer:** Octavio Medellin Ostos
Chief Prosecutor: Ligorio Espinosa y Elenes   **Judge:** Manuel Riviera
Vazquez (presiding over a three-judge panel)   **Place:** Mexico City, Mexico
Dates of Trial: August 22, 1940–April 16, 1943   **Verdict:** Guilty
Sentence: Nineteen years six months for murder; six months for
illegal possession of firearms

SIGNIFICANCE

Then the president of Mexico, Lazaro Cardenas perhaps put it best when he said: "[This] recent crime ... will be censured throughout all time by history as dishonorable for those who inspired it and foul for those who actually perpetrated it." But even he could not know at the time that the eventual significance would stem from the revelations of just who inspired it—namely, Joseph Stalin—and the true identity of the perpetrator—a Communist nonentity.

Leon Trotsky, the coleader with Lenin of the revolution that overthrew czarist Russia in 1917 and established the Communist Soviet Union, had been living under a death sentence for many years. The sentence had been passed by Joseph Stalin who, at Lenin's death in 1924, had swiftly taken control of the Communist Party, expelled Trotsky from the party in 1927, and deported him from the Soviet Union in 1929. During the 1930s, Stalin staged a series of trials in which most defendants implicated Trotsky in attempts to subvert the Communist Party or overthrow the government; in every case, the defendants were found guilty and imprisoned or shot. Not content with eliminating all opposition within the Soviet Union, Stalin had his secret police force, the GPU, carry out assassinations in any part of the world where his perceived enemies could be found. Most of Trotsky's associates, many friends, and even his son had been killed. Trotsky himself, having been originally deported to Turkey, had fled to France and then to Norway before finally taking refuge in Mexico in 1937.

The Assassination

At first, Trotsky lived in the home of the famous artists Diego Rivera and his wife, Frida Kahlo. Then, in 1939, Trotsky moved to a nearby walled and guarded villa in Coyoacán, on the edge of Mexico City; with him were his wife, Natalya, his grandson, Seva, and his friends the Rosmers, a French Communist couple. Although he had been expunged from Soviet history by Stalin, Trotsky remained a prominent figure in the international Communist movement and so was visited frequently by various political figures, writers, and intellectuals from many parts of the world. At all times, though, Trotsky's villa remained well guarded against possible intruders and only those well known to or vouched for by Trotsky's inner circle were allowed access.

Among the tight-knit inner circle at the villa was a New York–born Communist, Sylvie Agelof, who in 1939 had become one of several secretaries and couriers Trotsky used. She was often driven to and from the villa by her boyfriend, a young man who went by the name of Frank Jacson. Sylvie had met Jacson at a Communist conference in France in 1938 and believed his real name to be Jacques Mornard; he explained his need for dual identity by telling her he was a citizen of Belgium in possession of a Canadian passport to avoid being drafted by the Belgium army. For some months, Jacson was not granted access to Trotsky, but he seemed content to do small favors for the villa's residents.

On May 24, during the night, a group of Mexican Stalinists attacked the villa with machine guns but somehow failed to kill Trotsky or any of the others living in the villa. (One of the guards was taken away and killed later.) Four days later, by coincidence, Jacson met Trotsky in the villa garden, and gradually Jacson's presence was accepted inside the compound. By August 18, Jacson had convinced Trotsky that he was working on a serious article in support of Trotsky's version of Communism, and Trotsky agreed to look it over; Trotsky's wife would later reveal that he was already beginning to have his suspicions about Jacson.

On August 20, Jacson took Trotsky a copy of this article, and the two went into Trotsky's study. As the old revolutionary bent over the paper at his desk, Jacson brought out from under his overcoat a small ice ax used in mountain climbing and bashed Trotsky in the head. Instead of falling forward, Trotsky lunged screaming at his attacker and bit his hand. His screams brought the guards, who were installing a siren on the roof of the villa, and his wife, Natalya.

The guards caught and beat Jacson but heeded Trotsky's plea spare him so he could be made to talk. Shortly after the attack, Trotsky was taken to a hospital, where he lapsed into a coma after surgery and died the next day. Jacson was also hospitalized, under police guard. His girlfriend, Sylvie Agelof, was arrested and held under suspicion of being an accomplice; she was soon released and was never implicated in the assassination plot. On August 26, Jacson was moved to a cell in a police station.

The Investigation

At the time of Jacson's arrest, police found a three-page letter on his person signed "Jac" with the demand that it be published should anything happen to the author. The rambling letter stated that he came from an established Belgian family, that he had been a journalist in Paris, and that he had joined the Trotskyite organization out of a passion for justice. The letter stated that he had grown disillusioned with Trotsky, "chilled by his skill in sowing discord" in the party. Jacson also made other attacks on Trotsky's integrity as a party leader. It was obvious that this letter had been carefully composed to reflect the standard Stalinist line about Trotsky.

Colonel Leandro A. Sanchez Salazar, chief of the Mexican secret service, took charge of the investigation. Under interrogation, Jacson amplified what he had written in the letter, claiming to be Jacques Mornard Vandendreschd and spinning a story of an idealistic young man who had become an active follower of Trotsky. He said the Trotskyites had selected him for important missions, including being sent to the Soviet Union to assassinate Stalin, but he had become disillusioned. The Mexican authorities soon punctured this story in several areas, in particular his claims about the details of his family and former life. Jacson was visited by a diplomat from Belgium, for instance, who ascertained by questioning him on points raised in his letter of confession that he was not Belgian. Yet throughout the entire investigation and his trial, Jacson maintained his identity to be that of Mornard. He was never shaken or tricked into revealing anything about his true identity.

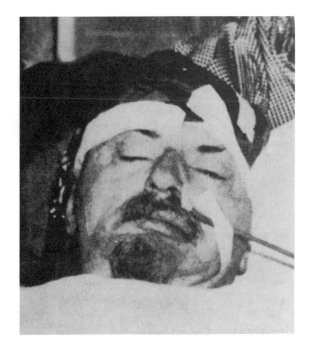

Leon Trotsky in his death bed, on September 2, 1940, soon after Ramon Mercader tried to assassinate him. (Hulton-Deutsch Collection)

In September 1940, the examining magistrate, Raoul Carranca y Trujillo, appointed two psychologists to examine the prisoner. Drs. José Gomez Robleda and Alfonso Quiroz Cuaron functioned as officers of the court and spent the next six months and a total of 972 hours examining the prisoner. Their report, *Organic-Functional and Social Study of the Assassin of Leon Trotsky*, was 1,359 pages long. Its findings included a complete physical description of the prisoner; his various abilities, mental and physical; and an assessment of his state of mind. The report did not find in Jacson any hint of remorse for his crime.

The Trial

Under Mexican law at that time, the trial had technically begun 48 hours after the arrest of Jacson-Mornard: In effect, the questioning and investigation that commenced shortly after his arrest were considered part of the trial. The trial was conducted by three judges, often sitting alone, and because there was no jury, there was no need to rush the proceedings. Simultaneous with the psychologists' examination of Jacson, all the relevant witnesses and principals were questioned by one or another judge and various lawyers. Trotsky's widow, Natalya, took a major role in pursuing the case.

Since there was no question of Jacson-Mornard's guilt, the main issues to be determined were just who Jacson-Mornard was and who was behind his actions. The prosecution would maintain throughout the trial that Jacson was acting as a Soviet agent in killing Trotsky but the defense responded that the prosecution was unable to prove its contention. Prospective witnesses from the United States who might have testified to support the prosection's allegation never appeared in court.

The world's media paid little attention to the trial, primarily because World War II was raging at the time and this seemed like such a minor event. Moreover, Stalin was by then regarded as at least a necessary ally by many in the West, and there was probably a reluctance to report on anything that might embarrass him. The only American periodical to cover the trial in any detail was the New York City–based Trotskyite newspaper *The Militant*.

The trial dragged on for months, and near the end was further delayed when Jacson's lawyer tried to get the presiding judge declared biased. This was set aside by an appeals court. Finally, in February 1943, the two sides presented their closing arguments to the panel of three judges. Near the end of his trial, Jacson had changed his story from one of murder by a disillusioned Trotskyite to one of self-defense. Through his defense attorney, he claimed that Trotsky had called him "nothing but a military idiot" and then had physically attacked him; Jacson had thus struck out only in self-defense. As for the confession Jacson had given to the police, he maintained that it had been taken from him when he was in no condition to know what he was doing. During the final reading of his testimony, in fact, Jacson sent notes to reporters saying, "the statements being read had been extorted from me by policemen while I was wounded and semi-conscious in the police jail."

The prosecution, it is true, never could prove that the defendant was acting on behalf of any Soviet or other organization. But there was no question that Jacson had killed Trotsky, and so the prosecutor asked the presiding judge to find Jacson guilty of homicide and of the illegal bearing of arms. Mexico did not have the death penalty, so the prosecutor asked for a sentence of 23 years. On April 16, 1943, the court sentenced Jacson to 20 years in prison—a total of 19 years and 6 months for premeditated murder and 6 months for the illegal bearing of weapons. In reading its 118-page verdict, the court found that Jacson's attitude was one of "falseness and artifice," and that, whoever he was, he had come to Mexico "with the sole object of killing Trotsky." During the reading, which was being broadcast, Jacson threw his hat over the microphone to disrupt the transmission. His sentence was upheld despite an appeal.

Imprisonment

In prison, Jacson proved to be a model inmate; he was apparently treated well, given comfortable quarters, and allowed frequent visits from a girlfriend. (The Mexican penal system permitted regular conjugal visits between prisoners and their wives or girlfriends.) He taught inmates how to read and began an apprentice system for the radio and television repair shop in the prison. This blossomed into a program to teach electrical engineering to inmates. In time, he was put in charge of maintaining the prison's entire electrical system, and since prisoners were paid for their labors, he reportedly became relatively prosperous. (It is also assumed that the Communist Party gave him any money he needed, as when he bought a car for his girlfriend to drive on her visits.)

Under Mexican law, when an inmate completed two-thirds of his sentence, he was entitled to parole. Before this time had elapsed, on August 20, 1953, Jacson was shocked by the news that his identity had been uncovered. The prison warden announced that official records from Spain, including fingerprints, collected by Dr. Alfonso Quiroz Cuaron, one of the original investigating psychologists, established that Jacson, alias Mornard, was really Jaime Ramon Mercader del Rio Hernandez, a Spanish Communist. In 1954, Jacson hired a lawyer to wage a fight for his parole. In a report on the parole petition, Dr. Quiroz wrote: "Our subject . . . believes he achieved a high purpose by murdering; he believes that he remained a moral man after having assassinated." A second psychologist favored parole because he found the problem a political, not a psychiatric, one. In 1956, Jacson was denied parole again on the grounds that he expressed "no moral regrets." To the end of his sentence, Jacson never acknowledged who he was nor did he give any factual information about himself. He was released on May 6, 1960, and met by two guards from the Czechoslovak embassy in Mexico City. He was flown to Moscow via Havana and Prague. The name on his diplomatic passport was Jacques Vandendreschd.

Epilogue

By this time, much of the story of Jacson's life had been uncovered. He had been born in Spain in 1913 to a Spanish father and a Cuban mother. He had joined the Stalinist Communist Party under the influence of his mother, Caridad Mercader, a flamboyant, even unstable, woman who joined the party in France at the time of the Spanish Civil War. In 1935, he had been arrested in Barcelona, photographed, fingerprinted, and tried on charges of organizing an underground Communist cell. Released during a political amnesty, he continued his work in the Communist Party and was recruited into Soviet intelligence. He was trained by the GPU in Moscow and sent to Mexico by Stalin for the express purpose of assassinating Trotsky. Because Ramon Mercader, alias Frank Jacson, had succeeded where so many others had failed, Stalin awarded his mother the Order of

Lenin, and Ramon the Order of Hero of the Soviet Union, a medal that his mother held for him through his years in prison. Evidently, he spent his years after release working as an electrical technician in Prague and made no attempt to capitalize on his notoriety. On October 18, 1978, Ramon Mercader died in Havana, where he had gone for treatment of cancer. He was buried in Moscow with a grave epitaph that reads "Hero of the Soviet Union."

—Janet Bond Wood

Suggestions for Further Reading

Deutscher, Isaac. *The Prophet Outcast: Trotsky: 1929–1940*. London: Oxford University Press, 1963.

Glotzer, Albert. *Trotsky: Memoir & Critique*. Buffalo, N.Y.: Prometheus Books, 1989.

Levine, Isaac Don. *The Mind of an Assassin*. New York: Farrar, Straus and Cudahy, 1959.

Life, September 2, 1940, 17–21.

The Militant, (New York City), September 7, 1940; September 14, 1940; September 21, 1940; October 11, 1942; February 13, 1943; April 24, 1943.

Newsweek, September 2, 1940, 23.

The New York Times, February 5, 1943; February 10, 1943; April 17, 1943; August 23, 1953; November 6, 1978.

Payne, Robert. *The Life and Death of Trotsky*. New York: McGraw Hill, 1977.

Wyndham, Francis, and David King. *Trotsky: A Documentary*. New York: Praeger, 1972.

Anti-Hitler Conspirators Trial: 1944

Defendants:
Field Marshall Erwin von Witzleben; General Erich Hoepner; Major General Helmuth Stieff; Lieutenant Albrecht von Hagen; General Paul von Hase; Lieutenant Colonel Robert Bernardis; Captain Friedrich Klausing; Lieutenant Peter, Count Yorck von Wartenburg

Crimes Charged:
High treason and sedition, for participation in a conspiracy in the summer of 1944 by "a small clique of disaffected officers" to assassinate Hitler, thereby to eradicate the Nazi regime; conspiracy to seize power over the armed forces and the state; conspiracy to end the war by means of "disgraceful" pacts with the enemy

Chief Defense Lawyers:
Dr. Weissmann, Dr. L. Schwarz, Dr. Neubert, Dr. Gustav Schwarz, Dr. Kunz, Dr. Falck, Dr. Boden, Hugo Bergmann

Chief Prosecutors: Dr. Lautz, Dr. Görisch

Judges:
Roland Freisler; a panel of government officials consisting of General Hermann Reinecke, Counselor Lemmle, Dr. Köhler, Senate President Günther Nebelung; a panel of "the People," represented by Hans Kaiser, gardener; Georg Seuberth, businessman; Kurt Wernicke, engineer; Emil Winter, baker

Place: Berlin, Germany **Dates of Trial:** August 7–8, 1944 **Verdict:** Guilty

Sentence: Death, loss of civil rights

SIGNIFICANCE
Since the Nazis showed themselves quite capable of executing anyone they chose to without judicial proceedings, the intent of the tribunal was humiliation, vengeance, and Nazi propaganda. By means of his bombastic courtroom antics, Chief Justice Roland Freisler sought here, and in the many trials that followed of other anti-Hitler conspirators, to portray the defendants as fools as well as traitors.

"**S**ince the generals have achieved nothing so far, it is now for the colonels to take over." With these words Colonel Claus, Count Schenk von Stauffenberg, signaled his intent to assassinate Adolf Hitler. Opposition to Hitler and his Nazi regime had existed among some in the military, the aristocracy, the church, and among intellectuals, Communists, socialists, and other segments of German society since Hitler's 1933 seizure of power. From 1937 to 1944, Hitler survived some 10 known plots against his life—3 made by military officers. Stauffenberg's unsuccessful attempt of July 20, 1944, was the last and most dramatic such attempt, before Hitler ended his own life on April 30, 1945, in the final days of the Third Reich.

German resistance to the Nazis took many forms: from helping fugitives, printing and distributing clandestine pamphlets and newspapers, and rare instances of strikes, sabotage and partisan activity, to relatively minor acts such as failing to use the "Heil Hitler" greeting and tuning into British Broadcasting Corporation (BBC) radio broadcasts ("black listening")—all punishable crimes. The most intensive resistance activity centered in four areas—the Kreisau Circle, the Foreign Office, the military intelligence service (the Abwehr), and the army—in which key individuals operated independently and in small groups, having limited contact with each other.

The Kreisau Circle, an informal association of intellectuals, political figures, and others, focused on discussions and drawing up plans for a post-Hitler Germany, going so far as to propose a shadow government. Foreign Office resisters actively tried to help Germany's opponents through diplomatic missions warning of Hitler's plans for attack; they also assembled a dossier of Nazi crimes. Those in the Abwehr provided the enemy with military and technical secrets, supplied disinformation to Hitler, and forged documents helping Jews to escape. The widespread army network, led by retired officers, had begun planning a putsch, or seizure of military and political power, in Germany before the outbreak of World War II. They had been appalled at Hitler's tricky maneuvers to make himself commander in chief, his ineptitude at carrying out this office, the atrocities committed against civilians and prisoners of war in Poland and Russia, and the inevitability that Hitler would bring total ruin upon the nation. The assassination of Hitler became part of the plan only later. At first they felt constrained by their loyalty oath to Hitler personally, by a wish to hold on to some of his territorial gains, and by a fear that ensuing instability might open the door to communism.

The Plot: Operation Valkyrie

Time was running out when Stauffenberg made his attempt, as the Allies already had landed on the Normandy beaches. After recovering from serious wounds from the North Africa campaign—he had lost an eye, his right hand, and two fingers of his left hand—Stauffenberg became chief of staff to the head of the reserve army in Berlin. Working secretly with other officers there, he helped to formulate Operation Valkyrie, a detailed plan to seize power that involved the assassination of Hitler.

On July 20 at Hitler's East Prussia stronghold, Stauffenberg left a bomb in a briefcase under the table at a staff meeting and slipped away. He witnessed the explosion from afar and rushed off to fly back to Berlin. Miraculously, Hitler escaped with only slight injury, and the confusion over whether he had died or survived threw the attempted putsch into disarray. Upon his arrival at headquarters in Bendlerstrasse, Stauffenberg took charge and tried to rally the plotters back into action. But in the end, he and others were overpowered by forces led by General Friedrich Fromm, Stauffenberg's superior, who had seemed to be supportive of the plot. Within hours, Fromm announced the verdict of a sum-

Adolf Hitler shakes hands with General Fromm at the Wolfsschanze on July 15, 1944, only five days before high ranking military officers tried to assassinate him. To the left of Fromm is Graf Stauffenberg, one of the key conspirators. German field marshall Wilhelm Keitel is standing next to Hitler. (Still Picture Branch, National Archives, Washington, DC)

mary court-martial (though there is no evidence one had taken place) and ordered the immediate execution by firing squad of Stauffenberg and three others.

The First Trial

The Nazis prevented further executions that night, deciding to submit other conspirators to a show trial before the People's Court, the Nazi puppet court for trying enemies, both real and perceived, of the fascist state. To make those accused eligible for judgment in this civilian venue, they first were expelled from the army by a military "court of honor." The accused neither appeared nor were allowed to offer a defense; their dismissal was based solely on a "mere excerpt" from the investigators' files and took only a few minutes. The August 4 session of this body expelled 22 officers, some of them posthumously; in all, 55 officers were ousted by this means.

Presiding over the People's Court was the notorious Roland Freisler, a sadist, who was judge, prosecutor, inquisitor, avenger, censor, and jury all rolled into one. Intent on humiliating the defendants in every way possible, he had them appear in ill-fitting clothes, without belts or suspenders, and without false teeth. (The August 7–8 trial of Field Marshall Erwin von Witzleben and the others was filmed for propaganda purposes, as was their execution, a sentence that was a foregone conclusion. Hitler was said to have enjoyed viewing the film.) Freisler carried on his questioning with sarcastic remarks, screamed insults, and long tirades, all generally met with stoic dignity on the part of the accused. An exchange between Freisler and Major General Helmuth Stieff is illustrative:

> Freisler: Is it true that . . . murderous lout Count von Stauffenberg urged you to join him, and that you did not refuse?
> Stieff: He did come to see me, and I did not refuse.
> Freisler: Is it true that you didn't refuse because you wanted to shove your fingers in that pie?
> Stieff: Yes.
> Freisler: That's what you told the police, and you damn well did shove your fingers in it, not to mention your head. And your honor, which is gone now forever. Do you realize that?
> Stieff: I refer to the statement explaining my motives.
> Freisler: Did you take in what I said?
> Stieff: Yes, but I wish to refer to my statement.
> Freisler: You can refer to it until you're blue in the face. What matters is that you have broken faith, broken the oath of loyalty of a National Socialist—
> Stieff: I owe my loyalty to the German nation.

To maintain the guise of legality, Freisler asked the defense counsel, all of whom he had appointed to speak. Witzleben's representative, Dr. Weissmann answered his own question "Why conduct a defense at all?" with the words "It is part of the defense's task to help the court find a verdict. Undoubtedly . . . it will prove impossible for even the best counsel to find anything to say . . . in mitigation of the accused." The other counsel all complained of their "thankless task." When allowed to speak near the end of the trial, most of the defendants asked for an honorable death by firing squad rather than by hanging. This request was denied them, and later the same day they died from slow strangulation by suspension from meat hooks.

More Trials, Other Verdicts

This trial was the first of many. By the time it was all over, more than 200 were dead as a result of the July 20 plot. Of them, 22 were generals (of whom 13 committed suicide) and 50 bore aristocratic titles. Thousands more were arrested, including the families of the accused, along with anyone the regime might have reason to fear in the future, and many were sent to concentration camps. Near the end, many were executed without a trial. Freisler himself died from injuries suffered in an Allied air raid that interrupted yet another trial in the People's Court.

After the war, the German Federal Court of Justice reexamined the actions of the military conspirators in light of the then valid penal code; it came to the conclusion that they, indeed, had had both the right and the duty to resist Hitler. The justifying circumstances included "the crimes of the [Nazi] regime, which went so far as . . . to annul the basis of justice; the tyranny imposed by the terroristic rulers on their own people; and the preparation for and waging of a criminal war of aggression." This opinion concluded, "It is clear that the right of resistance exercised in a state of emergency must be exercised uncompromisingly." Thus, the traitors officially were reclassified as the patriotic and self-sacrificing martyrs that they in fact had been.

—Eva Weber

Suggestions for Further Reading

Balfour, Michael. *Withstanding Hitler in Germany 1933–45*. London: Routledge, 1988.

Gill, Anton. *An Honorable Defeat: A History of German Resistance to Hitler, 1933–1945*. New York: Henry Holt, 1994.

International Military Tribunal. Document 3881-PS: "Stenographic Report of the Trial Before the German People's Court on 7 and 8 August 1944: Proceedings Against General Field Marshall von Witzleben and Seven Other Officers for the Attempt on Hitler's Life on 20 July 1944" (Exhibit GB-527; in German), vol. 33, 299–530; Testimony of Hans Bernd Gisevius, Vol. 12, 240–287, 298–305. In *Trial of the Major War Criminals Before the International Military Tribunal*, 42 vols. Nuremberg, Germany: International Military Tribunal, 1949.

Manvell, Roger, and Heinrich Fraenkel. *The Men Who Tried to Kill Hitler*. New York: Coward-McCann, 1964.

Zeller, Eberhard. *The Flame of Freedom: The German Struggle Against Hitler*. Translated by R. P. Heller and D. R. Masters. Coral Gables, Fla.: University of Miami Press, 1969.

Zimmerman, Erich, and Hans-Adolf Jacobsen. *Germans Against Hitler: July 20, 1944.* 3rd ed. Translated by Allan and Lieselotte Yahraes. Bonn, West Germany: Press and Information Office of the Federal German Government, 1960.

Henri Philippe Pétain and Pierre Laval Trials: 1945

Defendants: Henri Philippe Pétain, Pierre Laval   **Crimes Charged:** Treason (Pétain), plotting against the state, intelligence with the enemy (Laval)
Defense Lawyers: Fernand Payen, Jean Lemaire, Jacques Isorni (Pétain); Pierre Laval, Albert Naud, Jacques Baraduc (Laval)   **Chief Prosecutor:** André Mornet   **Judge:** Paul Mongibeaux   **Place:** Paris, France
Dates of Trials: July 23–August 13, 1945 (Pétain); October 4–8, 1945 (Laval)   **Verdicts:** Guilty   **Sentences:** Execution (Pétain's sentence commuted to life imprisonment)

SIGNIFICANCE

The trials of Pétain and Laval gave the French people, and the world, their first deep insight into the extent of the treachery of France's Vichy government during World War II.

In August 1945, Henri Philippe Pétain was 89 years old. France had known him as a leader since he was made a brigadier general at the outbreak of World War I in 1910. In 1916, his brilliant victory in driving the Germans back through four miles of valuable gun positions at Verdun-sur-Meuse had made him a national hero, and in 1918 he had capped that achievement by masterminding the offensives that pushed the enemy back to the Ardennes forests. Following World War I, he had served as France's minister of war and as its ambassador to Spain. In World War II, as Paris fell to the invading Germans and the French government fled to Bordeaux, Pétain became premier, on June 17, 1940.

He then sought an armistice with Reichsführer Adolf Hitler and, on July 11, assumed dictatorial powers over the French state, establishing headquarters at Vichy, a health resort in central France.

Pierre Laval was 62 in 1945. A Socialist politician since 1914, he had been elected senator in the French parliament and had served as undersecretary of state, as minister of justice and minister of labor, and, by 1931, as premier for one year. Premier again in 1935, he had negotiated a treaty with Italian dictator Benito Mussolini that helped Italy to invade and conquer Ethiopia. In 1940, Laval joined Pétain's Vichy government as vice premier.

As the war raged for five years, the Allies—led by U.S. president Franklin D. Roosevelt, British prime minister Winston Churchill, Soviet dictator Joseph Stalin, and General Charles de Gaulle, head of the Free French forces, which had fled to London—knew that Pétain's Vichy government was cooperating with the Germans but did not know the extent of the collaboration. The French people knew even less until Pétain and Laval were brought to trial soon after the German surrender in the spring of 1945. They knew so little because as France fell in 1940, the widespread confusion had generated little accurate news (newspaper staffs had joined the millions who fled south from Paris) and Pétain had been so beloved that he could seize power at Vichy without challenge.

Five Judges, Two Juries

The Pétain trial opened on Thursday, July 23, in a cramped, hot, and shabby courtroom in the Palais de Justice in Paris. In bright red robes sat five judges, with Paul Mongibeaux presiding, and two 12-man juries heard the evidence. One jury was chosen from members of the French Resistance (those who had fought underground against the Nazi occupation); the other, from "the Bordeaux parliament" (those who had maintained the semblance of a French government in the south and who had voted against putting the autocratic Pétain in charge of the wartime administration). They beheld an elderly defendant, ashen-faced but still handsome in his marshall's uniform and wearing his medals, settled in a tattered leather armchair.

Prosecutor of the Republic, André Mornet, opened by reciting from memory the details of the June 22, 1940, armistice, signed by Pétain at Wiesbaden, which permitted the Nazis to occupy two-thirds of French soil.

Pétain jumped from his seat. "That's unfair!" he cried. "You've no right to begin with the worst part."

"I have a right," replied the prosecutor, "to begin where I choose and where my good memory dictates."

"I sacrificed my prestige for the French people," responded Pétain. "If I treated with the enemy, it was to spare France. I prepared the road to liberation." The overcrowded courtroom erupted with catcalls. To quiet the tumult, the judge threatened to arrest every rowdy spectator.

After that moment, Pétain sat silent, refusing to speak but flapping his gloves to fan his face, as, for five days, witnesses droned on by the hour. The presiding judge, with clear bias, wittily castigated the defendant. A deputy juror interrupted the testimony of former premier Paul Reynaud with comments. Two Resistance jurors leaped to their feet, protesting Pétain's insults to their cause. The judge permitted such prominent witnesses as former premiers Reynaud and Edouard Daladier and former president Albert Lebrun to quote hearsay evidence—what a third person said to yet another person.

Extent of Collaboration Revealed

On the sixth day, the facts began to come out. General Paul Doyen, who had served as French president of the Wiesbaden Armistice Commission, revealed how Germany had annexed Alsace-Lorraine illegally in August 1940—a fact unknown beyond that region until his testimony. He told how the Vichy government had complied with Nazi requests for occupation of airfields in the Middle East and of the port of Bizerte in Tunisia, as well as met demands for war matériel, food, and trucks to be shipped to German general Erwin Rommel's forces in North Africa.

Other witnesses testified to dictator Pétain's abolishing parliamentary functions and trying French politicians who had refused to collaborate with the Nazi "new order." They described how Pétain's military courts had imposed death sentences on those working in the underground movement—Vichy had condemned some 15,000 resistance fighters as traitors. Witnesses reported Pétain's drafting French labor for work in Germany and his severing of diplomatic relations with the United States after it had participated in the Anglo-American invasion of North Africa in November 1942. They testified that when Germany invaded the unoccupied section of France on November 11, 1942, Pétain's Vichy government had not resisted. And final figures on German brutality in the last days of the occupation revealed that some 60,000 French men and women had been executed, and 150,000 had died in German concentration camps or as a result of forced labor—all with the compliance of Vichy.

At last, former French President Léon Blum, who had been a Nazi captive in Buchenwald, took the witness stand. Judge Mongibeaux asked if Pétain had committed treason. "There is a Pétain mystery," said Blum. "An absence of moral confidence was the base of the Vichy government, and that is treason. Treason is the act of selling out."

Sentenced to life imprisonment for treason, Henri Philippe Pétain listens solemnly to testimony at his 1945 trial. (Hulton-Deutsch Collection)

"I Thank You for Having Cleansed French Soil"

Now the judge read aloud Pétain's own words from a radio broadcast in the early days of Vichy:

> The responsibility for our defeat lies with the democratic political regime of France, which fell more under the weight of its own errors than under the blows of the enemy.

In a letter to Hitler, after meeting with him to offer collaboration, Pétain wrote "France preserves the memory of your noble gesture." From another letter to Hitler, after the Nazis repulsed the British commando raid at Dieppe, Judge Mongibeaux read: "I thank you for having cleansed French soil." Finally, the judge revealed, Vichy cooperation with anti-Jewish laws had brought the deportation to Germany of 120,000 Jews, of whom 1,500 lived to return.

On August 13, after the judges, in response to the prosecution's summation, reduced the charge from treason to intelligence with the enemy, the juries found Pétain guilty. They recommended clemency, but he was condemned to death. Two days later, General de Gaulle, president of the provisional government of France, commuted the sentence to life imprisonment.

Trial of Laval

Pierre Laval came to trial on October 4, 1945, as the most despised man in France. The crowd in the same courtroom as Pétain's trial shouted angrily at him, and he screamed back. The French knew that in December 1942 he had released a press statement from Vichy that said, "Germany's victory will prevent our civilization from foundering in the communistic chaos," and "an American victory would bring in its train the triumph of Jews and Communists." And they knew that in June 1943 he had announced over Paris radio that 200,000 Frenchmen were ordered to work in Germany.

Laval appeared dressed in an ill-fitting, wrinkled, gray-striped suit. He spoke through dark, stained teeth under a mustache colored by tobacco juice. As a witness in the Pétain trial, he had indignantly refused to be seated in the witness stand's cane-seated parlor chair, tossing his hat and briefcase onto it while he stood to testify. Now, opening his own defense in the absence of his lawyers, Albert Naud and Jacques Baraduc—who were boycotting the opening in protest against the conduct of the preliminary investigation—he spoke so vehemently for three hours that the judge ordered him removed from the courtroom. Readmitted and more temperate, he held the audience spellbound for another three hours.

For three days, Laval dominated the courtroom, a prisoner set on proving that he knew the law better than the judge. Laval remembered his policies verbatim while the judge, groping for references, shuffled papers. A newspaper cartoon that depicted two lawyers chatting was captioned, "'Do you think he will be able to pull himself out of all this?' 'Who?' 'Mongibeaux, the judge.'"

"Twelve Balls in the Skin"

Laval proved himself the least inept individual in the courtroom. Jurors arrived late for duty. When the judge thoughtlessly answered his own questions as he asked them, the defendant responded, "As the victim of a judiciary crime, I do not aspire to be also the accomplice." On the third day, several parliamentary jurors called Laval foul names and pledged him "twelve balls in the skin"—that is, the firing squad. He responded with an outburst so violent that Judge Mongibeaux again ejected him. This time, Laval retaliated by sending a formal written statement from his cell to the judge to say that he refused to return to the courtroom. Confounded, the judges and juries dragged the trial on for two days without the defendant present. In the process, they produced such circus-like events as the judge's ordering the sheriff to bring in more witnesses and the sheriff's replying, "There aren't any witnesses anywhere. Perhaps we forgot to order any."

The jury returned its verdict—guilty, with sentence of execution and confiscation of all Laval's properties—on October 8. Laval demanded a retrial, citing the courtroom hysteria he had endured. De Gaulle, as head of state, denied the plea. On October 14, just before his execution, Laval swallowed a cyanide pill. The poison did not work. He was rushed to a hospital. His stomach was pumped. He was hurried back, retching and in pain, to the yard of Fresnes Prison. The police chief asked de Gaulle whether to proceed. "Pierre Laval no longer belongs to us," said de Gaulle. "The officer commanding the firing squad must do his duty." Laval shouted, "Vive la France!" and was executed.

Pétain died at age 96, in a fortress prison on the Island of Yeu, on July 23, 1951.

—Bernard Ryan, Jr.

Suggestions for Further Reading

Aron, Robert. *The Vichy Regime, 1940–44*. London: Macmillan, 1958.

Chapman, Guy. *Why France Fell*. New York: Holt, Rinehart and Winston, 1968.

Flanner, Janet (Genet). *Paris Journal 1944–1965*. New York: Atheneum, 1965.

Ouston, Philip. *France in the Twentieth Century*. New York: Praeger, 1972.

Shirer, William L. *The Collapse of the Third Republic*. New York: Simon & Schuster, 1969.

Tournoux, J. R. *Pétain et de Gaulle*. Paris: Plon, 1964. London: Heinemann, 1966.

Werth, Alexander. *France 1940–1955*. London: Robert Hale, 1956.

Williams, Charles. *The Last Great Frenchman: A Life of General de Gaulle*. New York: Wiley, 1995.

Vidkun Quisling Trial: 1945

Defendant: Vidkun Abraham Lauritz Jonsson Quisling
Crimes Charged: High treason, persecution of Jews, execution of Norwegian citizens, plotting to bring about invasion of Norway by Germany
Chief Defense Lawyer: Henrik Bergh   **Chief Prosecutor:** Annaeus Schjodt
Judge: Erik Solem   **Place:** Oslo, Norway   **Dates of Trial:** August 20–
September 10, 1945   **Verdict:** Guilty   **Sentence:** Execution

SIGNIFICANCE

Soon after Germany invaded Norway early in World War II—on April 9, 1940—the word *quisling* became another word for *traitor*. The trial of Norway's former premier in 1945 permanently confirmed *quisling* as a synonym for traitor in any language.

Vidkun Quisling was born to a family respected in Norway for more than 600 years. Young Quisling was a bright student who read widely, showed an unusual (some said genius) aptitude for mathematics, and seemed born to the outdoor Norwegian life of hiking miles at a time and bear hunting.

Reaching manhood, Quisling stood well above the average Nordic male, and his tough, robust physique pointed him toward a military career. He entered Krigskola, the West Point of Norway, in 1905. He graduated with the highest average grade ever achieved in the more than 100-year history of the military academy.

Captain Quisling was appointed military attaché to Petrograd just after the Russian revolution in November 1917. There, he became an expert on Russia, learning its language and every aspect of its capability for war, as he witnessed firsthand the vast changes wrought by the Communist regime. In 1918, he saw his country's Labour Party, which was strongly sympathetic to the Communists, proclaim revolution as its official policy, advocating the dictatorship of peasants and proletariat and approving the use of force when needed.

Back in Norway in 1931, Quisling was appointed minister of defense, then resigned the post in 1933 to found the Nasjonal Samling (National Unity Party). Its goals were the suppression of Communism and unionism. Meantime, the

Labour Party, to which Quisling was bitterly opposed, gained control of the government.

Proposals to England and Germany

In October 1939, Quisling proposed to British Prime Minister Neville Chamberlain that a commonwealth of European nations be organized. He was politely thanked for his suggestion. A few days later, he sent German authorities a proposal for disarmament, federalization of Europe, cooperation on currencies and foreign exchange, freedom of the seas, and other international arrangements. It was too late. Within weeks, the Red Army marched into Finland. Quisling then obtained an appointment with Adolf Hitler and visited him in December 1939.

On April 8, 1940, British destroyers laid minefields in Norway's West Fjord. The British minister warned the Norwegian government not to remove the mines. Norway demanded that Britain remove them or face war. Germany demanded that Norway remove them or face war. The next morning, Norway's military chief of staff proposed mobilization. The defense minister did nothing. By afternoon on April 9, German ships were landing troops in Norway. The entire government and general military staff, 146 of the 150 members of parliament, and the king and royal family fled to Sweden.

The invaders took charge. In September, they appointed Quisling as sole political leader of Norway, heading a council of 13 Nazi-controlled commissioners. On February 1, 1942, he was made minister-president, a position he held until the Germans were ousted in May 1945. Quisling's countrymen then arrested him.

Treason and Other Charges

An angry investigation of Quisling and the Nasjonal Samling activities during the five war years began. Many questioned whether the government-in-exile, which was now returning from England to Norway, had constitutional authority. No one knew what to charge Quisling with. But charges were hastily assembled. Included were treasonable activities on April 9, 1940; treason in declaring a government on February 1, 1942; persecution of Jews; execution of Norwegian citizens; and plotting to precipitate the invasion by discussing "with the German authorities the question of German occupation of Norway."

World attention focused on Oslo on August 20, 1945, for the trial of a man whose name had already become synonymous with traitor. The presiding judge was Erik Solem, who had spent several years in a concentration camp. With him sat two assistant judges and four assessors. Defense counsel, appointed by the court, was Henrik Bergh, who had long supported the government-in-exile. Bergh made the uniqueness of the circumstances clear with his opening remarks:

The indictment is based upon sections of the penal code, and the case is to that extent a criminal case. The background, however, and the counts of the indictment, show that the case concerns the political viewpoint of the defendant. In this assembly, no one belongs to the political movement of which he was the leader. Neither in the court nor at the bar is there anyone who shares his views, not even his own counsel, for all lawyers of his party are barred from pleading if they are not, as most of them already are, in prison.

Norwegian politician, Vidkum Quisling, at his trial in Oslo. He was arrested, convicted of treason, and executed by the Norwegians in 1945. (Hulton-Deutsch Collection)

Prosecutor Annaeus Schjodt produced evidence that Quisling's government had introduced, in October 1942, a law confiscating Jewish property and had acted in 125 cases. Witnesses testified to Quisling's November 1942 decree that all Jews be registered within two weeks—a span that allowed some 500 to escape to Sweden before the Gestapo threw 782 into a concentration camp. A written appeal by five bishops and two dozen church organizations that condemned the confiscations and arrests was presented, with testimony that Quisling had never submitted it to the German authorities.

Other testimony indicated that Quisling had put the state police under military law and that when the Germans condemned a state policeman to death for failing to make a routine arrest they had ordered, he had neglected to exercise his right to reprieve the man.

Among other evidence was a letter from Quisling to Hitler's head of chancellery proposing that Norwegian volunteers be recruited to fight alongside German forces. The defense tried to make the point that Quisling had wanted

Norwegians to fight the Bolsheviks, for he knew that the Third Reich was about to turn against its Soviet ally, but had not intended them to fight the British.

The Hitler Visit

In his defense, Quisling explained that he had gone to see Hitler in December 1939 because he knew that Germany would soon occupy Denmark and Norway to block Soviet expansion in Scandinavia. He told Hitler the Nasjonal Samling movement was not strong enough to take over the government. Hitler, according to Quisling, said that he hoped Norway would remain neutral but that he would invade it if Great Britain tried to establish itself there. When he went home, said the defendant, he did not report on his meeting with the Führer because he knew the Labour Party distrusted him and thought he exaggerated the threat of German aggression. Quisling insisted he had had no further dealings with Hitler.

It was a matter of record, however, that Quisling had met as early as 1934 with Alfred Rosenberg, head of the Nazi Party's Office for Foreign Affairs and a devout racist, with whom the Norwegian discussed the supremacy of Nordic and Germanic strains. Quisling's defense held that he had realized Germany was destined to spread war across Europe and he had intended to influence the Nazis in favor of Norway. He also maintained that during the occupation, his goal was to preserve Norway's independence within the greater Germanic community rather than see his country become a German protectorate like Poland.

The Rosenberg Memo

The prosecution's most damaging evidence was a lengthy memo by Rosenberg, dated June 15, 1940, and discovered just as the trial opened. It told how Quisling "pointed out Norway's geopolitical significance" and said Quisling "requested, anticipating the intentions of greater Germany, backing for his party and press in Norway. . . . Quisling saw it as his duty," said the memo, "to bind Norway's fate with that of Germany."

The defense tried to bolster its case with character witnesses. General Otto Ruge, longtime general staff officer with Quisling, said he had never seen the defendant disrespectful of other persons, nor cruel or brutal, and described him as "a man who is convinced about his own greatness and ability and who sought the chance to use his capacities." A major general said he saw "no resemblance to the Quisling depicted in court by the prosecution."

As the trial ended, an exhausted Quisling spoke for eight hours without notes, justifying his wartime actions and detailing his political career. He denied any act of treason and suggested that others should be tried in his place and that he should be honored for his patriotism.

On Monday, September 10, the court found Vidkun Quisling guilty of all charges. The sentence was execution. Defense counsel Bergh immediately appealed to the supreme court of Norway, where five judges dismissed the case.

At 2 A.M. on October 24, after waiting in the cold for nearly an hour while Judge Solem and other spectators assembled, Quisling was blindfolded against his wishes. His request to shake hands with the 10-man firing squad was granted. Then six or seven of their bullets hit his heart.

Quisling's body was displayed in a garage. Norwegian citizens, offering sarcastic and ribald remarks, prodded it to be sure that he was dead.

—Bernard Ryan, Jr.

Suggestions for Further Reading

Hayes, Paul M. *Quisling.* Bloomington: Indiana University Press, 1972.

Hewins, Ralph. *Quisling: Prophet Without Honor.* New York: John Day, 1966.

Unstad, L. I. *Vidkun Quisling: The Norwegian Enigma.* Selinsgrove, Pa.: Susquehanna University Press, 1964.

William Joyce Trial: 1945

Defendant: William Joyce   **Crime Charged:** Treason
Chief Defense Lawyers: Gerald Slade, K.C.; Derek Curtis-Bennett, K.C.;
James Burge   **Chief Prosecutor:** Sir Hartley Shawcross, K.C.
Judge: Justice Francis Tucker   **Place:** London, England
Dates of Trial: September 17–19, 1945   **Verdict:** Guilty
Sentence: Death by hanging

SIGNIFICANCE

No one disputed that William Joyce broadcast enemy propaganda, but far less certain was Great Britain's legal authority to try him for treason.

On September 18, 1939, with World War II just 15 days old, a British passport holder named William Joyce joined the German Broadcasting Service and began targeting Britain with propaganda from radio stations in Zeesen, Hamburg, and Bremen. Delivered with a nasal, sneering drawl and affected upper-class accent, his catchphrase, "This is Jairmany calling, Jairmany calling," became a much-mimicked feature of British life. Any threat that Joyce might have posed to national morale dissipated when a journalist dubbed him "Lord Haw-Haw." Thenceforth, the loathsome propagandist became an object of ridicule.

Although assumed to be British, Joyce was actually born in Brooklyn, New York, on April 24, 1906. Twelve years earlier, his British-born parents had become U.S. citizens. In 1909, the family returned to Ireland. When the family moved to England in 1922, they were assumed to be British subjects, a misapprehension that Michael Joyce did nothing to correct in a letter written to accompany his son's application to join the University of London Officer Training Corps. "With regard to my son, William. He was born in America. I was born in Ireland. His mother was born in England. We are all British and not American citizens." Clearly, this was a lie.

At college, Joyce combined academic achievement with an appetite for extremist politics. Pathologically anti-Semitic, he became a mouthpiece for the British Union of Fascists (BUF). Many of the meetings he addressed broke up in brawls; one such street battle resulted in his receiving the razor slash across his right cheek that would scar him for life.

On July 4, 1933, Joyce applied for the first of what would be several passports, misrepresenting himself as a British subject "having been born at Rutledge Terrace, Galway, Ireland." The five-year passport was renewed first in September 1938, then again on August 24, 1939. It was the second renewal that would cause him so much trouble.

William Joyce, pictured here far left, acquired the title "Lord Haw Haw" because of his heavy aristocratic accent in the radio broadcasts he made from Berlin, Germany to Britain during World War II. (Hulton-Deutsch Collection)

One week before the commencement of World War II hostilities, Joyce fled to Germany, arriving in Berlin on August 27, 1939. His Nazi masters—more impressed with Joyce than were his audience—granted him German nationality on September 26, 1940, and six months later, he was given a German military passport. In November 1944, he acquired yet another German passport, this time in the name of Wilhelm Hansen. He was carrying both documents when arrested after the war by British officers in the German coastal town of Flensburg, near the Danish border.

Triple Treason

On September 17, 1945, the clerk of the court at London's Old Bailey read out three separate charges of treason and asked Joyce how he wished to plead. His distinctively drawled reply of "Not guilty" would be the only words he would utter during the trial. In his opening address, Attorney General Sir Hartley Shawcross, K.C. (King's Counsel), reminded the jury that it was for the defense to prove that Joyce was born in the United States, of American parents.

"If that is true . . . it would mean that at all times prior to this case the prisoner was an American citizen, owing no natural allegiance to the British Crown, but still capable as an alien of placing himself under the protection of the Crown."

The Crown's case was complex and twofold, predicated on the primary assertion that any alien who lived in the United Kingdom was subject to its laws and owed allegiance to the protecting monarch. Should that argument fail, there was the secondary contention that, despite being an American citizen, Joyce, as the holder of a British passport, enjoyed British protection even after leaving England and owed Britain allegiance until his passport expired on July 2, 1940.

Although various witnesses confirmed Joyce's residence in Britain and his passport applications, it soon became clear that the entire prosecution case hinged on the testimony of one man—Inspector Albert Hunt of Scotland Yard's Special Branch. In the fall of 1939, Hunt had been stationed at Folkestone, on the English south coast, with orders to vet potential spies entering the country from neutral Belgium and Holland. While at Folkestone, he had tuned in a radio broadcast in which the speaker claimed that Luftwaffe bombers had destroyed Dover and Folkestone. Hunt had only to look out the window to realize that this was manifest nonsense. (In fact, since the declaration of war a month earlier, not a single bomb had been dropped on Britain by German planes.) Hunt recognized the broadcaster's voice as that of William Joyce, whom Hunt had monitored in Joyce's prewar rabble-rousing days with the BUF. It was a peculiarity of this case that, although the entire nation knew Joyce had broadcast for Germany, hopes for a conviction rested on this single transmission, since the British Broadcasting Corporation (BBC) had not identified Joyce's voice until August 1940, by which time his passport had expired.

A few months earlier, Hunt's uncorroborated testimony would have been inadmissible without a second witness to provide substantiation, but the very day before Joyce was flown back to Britain, a new Treason Act (1945) had received royal assent. Whereas the previous act (1695) had required at least two witnesses to verify an act of treason, or in the case of more than one act of treason, a separate witness to verify each act, the new statute required that only one witness be present to substantiate a single act of treason.

The statute made Hunt's identification of Joyce absolutely vital if the prosecution was to succeed. Alarmingly vague about the actual date of the broadcast—it was during September or early October, he wasn't sure which—Hunt was also unable to identify the broadcasting station. "I was just tuning in my receiver round the wavelengths when I heard the voice," he said. After drawing from Hunt the admission that the broadcast might not have emanated from the German Ministry of Propaganda at all, chief defense counsel Gerald Slade, K.C., began to lay out his own case. At its heart was one incontrovertible fact—despite having lived in the United Kingdom for 30 years, Joyce had never been a British citizen. To Slade's way of thinking, if anyone had the right to try Joyce, it was the United States; but even here the issue was far from clear-cut, since Joyce had become a German citizen on September 26, 1940, and at that time the United States had still not entered the war. "I submit to your lordship as a matter of law," said Slade, brandishing Joyce's birth certificate, "that there is no case to go to the jury."

But Justice Francis Tucker wanted confirmation that Joyce was the same person shown on the birth certificate. This came from Frank Holland, who had known Joyce's mother in her native Lancashire and later when she had emigrated to New York, where she married Michael Joyce. Holland testified that the person in the dock and the person on the birth certificate were undoubtedly one and the same.

No Room for Doubt

Official corroboration came from Henry Stebbings, first secretary at the American embassy in London. When Michael Joyce swore the oath in October 1894,

> he thereupon, by American law, became an American citizen. . . . If the Michael Joyce referred to in this document married in New York and a son was born to him after he had become an American citizen, the nationality of that son would be American by birth. . . . If at some subsequent time, the father lost the American nationality he had acquired in 1894, according to American law there would be no effect on the status of the son who was born in America.

Justice Tucker was quick to concede the point. "I think everybody must agree that the evidence which has been tendered is really overwhelming. That leaves us with count three as the only effective matter which we have to deal with." This charged that, as an American citizen fraudulently in possession of a British passport, Joyce committed treason while enjoying British protection in Germany until July 2, 1940. Reliance on this single count led the prosecution into some very muddy legal waters. Shawcross himself questioned the lawfulness of hanging someone for treason against Britain who had been an American at the time of the offenses and who had committed them in Germany.

Assistance came from a surprising quarter. What if, suggested Justice Tucker, Joyce had intended to leave the country only temporarily in August 1939 and to return after a little while? It would be absurd to say that he ceased to be resident in England merely because he took a short vacation abroad? Shawcross grasped the argument with both hands, declaring it unthinkable that a man who had been domiciled in England, who professed himself to be British, and who held a passport should not owe allegiance to the Crown while in Germany. With impeccable logic, Slade counterargued that an alien owed allegiance to the Crown only so long as he was resident in British territory: All precedent supported that. Justice Tucker promised to consider the matter over lunch.

At 2 P.M. on September 19, Tucker announced his decision. "I shall direct the jury on count three that on August 24, 1939, when the passport was applied for, the prisoner beyond the shadow of a doubt owed allegiance to the Crown of this country. On the evidence given, if they accept it, nothing happened at the material time thereafter to put an end to the allegiance that he then owed."

These few words consigned William Joyce to the gallows. Confirmation came when the jury returned its inevitable verdict of guilty. Joyce smiled briefly and disappeared from public view. By British standards, his appeal process was protracted and contentious, but the outcome was never in doubt. On January 3, 1946, William Joyce was hanged.

Any objective consideration of this trial is bound to leave a sense of unease: At times it appears as though the law was being manufactured on the spot to suit the circumstances. The content of Joyce's broadcasts reveals what kind of creature he was; the content of his trial proves similarly illuminating about the British government's determination to kill him.

—Colin Evans

Suggestions for Further Reading

Hall, J. W. *Trial of William Joyce.* London: William Hodge, 1946.

Mortimer, John, ed. *Famous Trials.* London: Penguin, 1984.

Selwyn, Francis. *Hitler's Englishman.* London: Penguin, 1993.

Shawcross, Sir Hartley. *Life Sentence.* London: Constable, 1995.

The Nuremberg Trial: 1945–46

Defendants: Twenty-two leading Nazis   **Crimes Charged:** Conspiracy, crimes against peace, war crimes, crimes against humanity
Chief Defense Lawyers: Otto Stahmer, Fritz Sauter, Alfred Seitel, others
Chief Prosecutors: Representatives of the United States, Great Britain, the Soviet Union, France   **Judges:** Chief Judge Geoffrey Lawrence of Great Britain, seven associates   **Place:** Nuremberg, Germany
Dates of Trial: November 20, 1945–September 30, 1946
Verdicts: Nineteen of the 22, guilty on one or more counts   **Sentences:** 12, death by hanging; the others, prison terms

SIGNIFICANCE

The Nuremberg Trial documented Nazi Germany's appalling crimes and punished some of the chief architects of Nazi evil. The proceedings established the principle that wartime leaders are accountable under international law for illegal and immoral actions—that individuals are responsible for the wars they start.

In Sir Winston Churchill's view, summary justice would be justice done. Drumhead courts-martial and firing squads, the British war leader suggested, were sufficient to deal with the leading Nazis. The Americans and the Soviets insisted on full-scale prosecution of the makers of World War II. The three major Allies, along with the French, agreed early in 1945 to establish an international tribunal to try Germany's leaders for complicity in the deaths of at least 12 million men, women, and children.

Joseph Stalin doubtless had a show trial in mind. "In the Soviet Union, we never execute anyone without a trial," he told Churchill primly. The Americans argued for a fair, impartial prosecution. "If we want to shoot Germans as a matter of policy, let it be done as such," said Robert Jackson, the U.S. chief prosecutor-designate. "But don't hide the deed behind a court. The world yields no respect to courts that are merely organized to convict." The American view prevailed. The forms of due process were to be strictly observed.

All the same, the Allies from the start ruled out the most obvious defense strategy. The accused would not be permitted a defense of *tu quoque*—the "you did it too" argument. Allied saturation bombing of German cities, for example, could not be offered in extenuation of Nazi crimes.

The Tribunal

The International Military Tribunal assembled in the Palace of Justice in Nuremberg in October 1945. Nuremberg's Zeppelin Field had been the site of the great Nazi Party annual rallies of the 1930s. The anti-Semitic Nuremberg Laws had been proclaimed in the city. A Nazi judge had tried conspirators in the July 20, 1944, bomb plot against Hitler in the Palace of Justice. The victors regarded the bomb-devastated Franconian city as the symbolic capital of Nazidom.

Hitler, the Allies argued, had come to power, started a war, and murdered millions of innocents through a conspiracy of military leaders, diplomats, industrialists, and Nazi Party functionaries. In a conspiracy, the leaders could be punished even though, in many cases, they had no actual blood on their hands. In addition, key Nazi organizations were to be tried as criminal. Soldiers, police officers, concentration camp administrators and guards could be arrested and punished simply for belonging to the proscribed groups.

The tribunal indicted 23 principal Nazis on four counts: conspiracy, crimes against peace, war crimes, and crimes against humanity. Among the accused were Hermann Goering, builder of the Luftwaffe and Hitler's chief deputy; the foreign minister, Joachim von Ribbentrop; Generals Wilhelm Keitel and Alfred Jodl; armaments minister Albert Speer; Hjalmar Schacht, minister of the economy; Hans Frank, the governor of Nazi-occupied Poland; and Reichsbank head Walther Funk. One of the defendants, Robert Ley, committed suicide in prison before the trial began. Another, Martin Bormann, had vanished and was tried in absentia.

The Allies in concert dealt only with the leading conspirators. National courts would handle the thousands of lesser cases. "Nuremberg was only a small part of the whole," wrote Telford Taylor, one of the American prosecutors. "The Nuremberg Tribunal's functions were to pronounce on only the most notorious of the accused under the law ... and thereby set a precedent and guidelines for trials and treaties in the years to come." Only a few days before the Nuremberg Trial opened, a U.S. military court hanged five German civilians convicted of killing the crew of a downed B-17 bomber. Other war crimes trials were conducted parallel to the Nuremberg trial.

Critics claimed the Allies were creating ex post facto law at Nuremberg. No machinery had existed to punish the guilty in previous major wars. No laws had decreed the Nazi Party or the Gestapo criminal organizations. Goering alluded to this in a note he scribbled on his copy of the indictment: "The victor will always be the judge and the vanquished the accused." Robert Jackson worked out an effective rationale. The Nazis, after all, had committed acts of unexampled barbarity on an unprecedented scale.

"Let's not be derailed by legal hair-splitters," Jackson argued. "Aren't murder, torture, and enslavement crimes recognized by all civilized people? What we propose is to punish acts which have been regarded as criminal since the time of Cain and have been so written in every civilized code."

267

Jackson chose to build the prosecution case on documentary evidence— "self-proving briefs" he called the trove of orders, reports, manifests, logs, letters, and diary entries that demonstrated Nazi guilt beyond question. The Germans had recorded everything in obsessive detail. Hermann Graebe, a civilian contractor working for the German army, left a matter-of-fact account of an incident near Dubno in the Ukraine on October 5, 1942. Out of curiosity, Graebe had followed an SS (elite guard) detachment and several thousand Jewish men, women, and children to a high earthen embankment looming above a newly dug pit on the outskirts of town.

The Palace of Justice in Nuremberg, Germany, where ex-Nazi leaders went on trial in front of an International Military Tribunal on November 17, 1945. (Still Picture Branch, National Archives, Washington, DC)

"Without screaming or weeping," Graebe wrote, "these people undressed, stood around in family groups, kissed each other, said farewells. . . . I well remember a girl, slim, with black hair, who, as she passed close to me pointed to herself and said, 'twenty-three years old.'" SS executioners turned automatic weapons on some 5,000 people that afternoon. The victims were buried in the pit behind the embankment.

The Prosecution

The tribunal president, Lord Justice Geoffrey Lawrence of Great Britain, opened the trial in Courtroom 600 of the Palace of Justice on November 20, 1945. The two American and two British judges wore black robes. The two French judges were resplendent in sable robes with white bibs and ruffles at the cuffs. The two Soviets wore brown military uniforms with green trim. At 10 o'clock, the first group of defendants—Goering, Ribbentrop, and Rudolf Hess—entered from a sliding door that opened onto the dock. The reading of the indictment took all of the first day and part of the second. One after another, the accused entered pleas of not guilty. Then Jackson launched into his opening statement.

"The wrongs which we seek to condemn and punish have been so calculated, so malignant, and so devastating that civilization cannot tolerate their being ignored, because it cannot tolerate their being repeated," he began.

"The real complaining party at your bar is civilization," Jackson went on, addressing the issue of the tribunal's jurisdiction. "Civilization asks whether the law is so laggard as to be utterly helpless to deal with crimes of this magnitude by criminals of this order of importance."

Over the next several days, the American prosecutors introduced masses of documents into evidence. The blizzard of paper overwhelmed the judges, the translators, the defense, even the British, French, and Soviet legal teams. After a while, too, the documents began to blunt the horrific edge of the case. It had become, thought William J. Donovan, one of the senior prosecutors, "confused and flat from so much paper evidence."

Donovan, the legendary head of the Office of Strategic Services during World War II, argued hard for living witnesses to add drama and pathos to the trial. On November 29, Jackson relented a bit, introducing a motion picture titled *Nazi Concentration Camps*. The film depicted conditions in the Dachau, Buchenwald, and Bergen-Belsen death camps. One scene showed bulldozers pushing mounds of stacked corpses into open graves. Another, spliced in from confiscated German film, showed SS troops leading a group of prisoners into a barn, then dousing the building with gasoline and setting it afire.

The images seemed to stun the defendants. Recalled Taylor: "Schacht turned his back to the screen to show that he had had no connection with such bestiality; Goering tried to brazen it out; the weaker ones like Ribbentrop, Frank, and Funk appeared shattered."

Until then, the proceedings had amused Goering, especially the prosecution's depiction of him as the mastermind of the Nazi annexation of Austria in 1938. "They were reading my telephone conversations on the Austrian affair, and everybody was laughing with me," he said later. "And then they showed that awful film, and it spoiled everything."

The prosecution accused Speer and Ernst Sauckel of primary responsibility for Germany's system of forced labor. Sauckel rounded up slave laborers from all over occupied Europe, some 5 million altogether; Speer, the armaments chief, assigned workers as needed to keep Hitler's war plants running at maximum output.

The laborers were half-starved and often worked to death, particularly the Soviets and other Slavs. Soviet workers were given three-quarters of a cup of tea at the 4 A.M. start of the workday. At quitting time 14 hours later, they were fed a quart of watery soup and two slices of bread.

Sauckel disclaimed all responsibility for conditions in the barracks and factories. "I was like a seaman's agency," explained Sauckel, a former merchant sailor. "If I supply hands for a ship, I am not responsible for any cruelty they may experience on board." Speer, he said, had actually put the hands to work.

Head Nazis stand trial in Nuremberg, Germany, on November 22, 1945. Hermann Wilhelm Goering, on the left side in the box, writes down notes while Rudolf Hess, seated next to him, solemnly watches. Former foreign minister Joachim von Ribbentrop sits to his left. In the back row (l–r) are Admirals Karl Doenitz and Erich Raeder. (Still Picture Branch, National Archives, Washington, DC)

The numbers were staggering and difficult to comprehend, even after six years of the most destructive war in history. Of 5.7 million Soviet troops taken prisoner, 3.7 million died in captivity. Four million Jews died in the extermination camps; the SS and other agencies murdered an additional 2 million Jews elsewhere.

Once again, the weight of the documents tended to obscure the human dimension of the outrage. Some of the evidence turned out, frankly, to be boring. The dead were men, women, and children, not aggregate statistics or words on paper. At one point, an assistant U.S. prosecutor departed briefly from Jackson's strategy. Thomas Dodd displayed the shrunken head of an executed Pole that Ilsa Koch, the wife of the commandant of the Buchenwald concentration camp, had used for a paperweight. At another point, a French woman who had survived Auschwitz took the stand. "One night, we were awakened by terrible cries," she testified. "The next day we learned that the Nazis had run out of gas and the children had been hurled into the furnaces alive."

Beginning January 8, 1946, the prosecution laid out its case against the individual defendants. Admiral Karl Doenitz, commander-in-chief of Hitler's navy (1943–45) had issued orders that German U-boats were not to pick up survivors of ships they had sunk; he had used slave labor in his naval shipyards. Goering had validated the anti-Jewish Nuremberg Laws as president of the Reichstag in 1935. He had contributed materially to the destruction of the Jews. He bore responsibility for the execution of escaped prisoners of war.

Wilhelm Frick had drawn up the legal code that had denied Jews the most basic protections of the law. Julius Streicher had carried on a hate campaign of unspeakable vileness in the pages of his newspaper, *Der Sturmer.* Alfred Rosenberg, the "philosopher" of Nazism in the 1930s, later had been minister of the Occupied Eastern Territories, where millions were murdered. Keitel had unquestioningly carried out orders from Hitler that had turned all of Europe into a killing field.

On March 6, 1946, the prosecution rested.

The Defense

The accused were held in isolation cells, under 24-hour guard, in the prison wing of the Palace of Justice. They had been among the most powerful men in the world, able to decree life or death at whim. Now, in their frayed and ill-fitting secondhand suits, they were diminished, ordinary looking. "Who'd have thought that we were fighting this war against a bunch of jerks?" John Kenneth Galbraith remarked the first time he saw all the defendants together.

Of all the Nazis, Goering, defiant from first to last, showed the most animation and attentiveness. He was "a brain without a conscience," *New Yorker* correspondent Janet Flanner thought. Hess and Streicher both looked as though they had long since passed the outer boundaries of sanity. (Streicher continually shot lecherous looks at the women court functionaries. The writer Rebecca West described him as "a dirty old man of the sort that gives trouble in parks.") Frank wore sunglasses for most of the trial. Keitel and Jodl, the former generals, sat stiffly at attention throughout.

The defense case opened on March 8. Goering's testimony began five days later. Generally, he did not evade the issues. He admitted, for example, to entering the Nuremberg Laws into the books. He admitted setting up Germany's system of concentration camps. But he denied he had issued orders to implement "The Final Solution"—the extermination of the Jews.

Ribbentrop took the stand April 1. Asked on cross-examination about the death camps, he said, "I knew nothing about that."

The prosecution had characterized Keitel as Hitler's lackey, executing the dictator's criminal designs without comment or question. Still, he summoned up a certain dignity on the witness stand. Referring to orders issued over his name to shoot allied commandos and to carry out savage reprisals for guerrilla attacks, Keitel's lawyer asked:

"What can you say in your defense?"

"I bear the responsibility for whatever resulted from those orders," Keitel responded. "Furthermore, I bear the moral as well as the legal responsibility."

Ernst Kaltenbrunner, head of the Reich Central Security Office (RHSA), had affixed his signature to orders sending hundreds of thousands of people to extermination camps. Because the signatures were always typewritten, or facsimiles, he claimed, he could be judged guilty only in a formal sense.

"I never saw a gas chamber," Kaltenbrunner swore.

Frank, Doenitz, Nazi youth leader Baldur von Shirach, Sauckel, Jodl, and Arthur Seyss-Inquart followed Kaltenbrunner to the stand. During his term as governor of Holland, Seyss-Inquart presided over the execution of 41,000 Dutch men and women. Another 50,000 died of starvation. More than half of Holland's Jewish population perished.

Franz von Papen, Hitler's predecessor as chancellor, followed Seyss-Inquart. Speer, brilliant, cosmopolitan, a case study in ambiguity, testified on June 21. He had balanced the German war industry on the backs of half-starved Soviets. Speer claimed he had tried to thwart Hitler at the end, even to kill him. Still, he accepted a limited culpability. "I, as an important member of the leadership of the Reich, share the total responsibility," he said. Hans Fritzsche, a second-level propagandist, one-time head of Hitler's radio service, testified at the end of June, completing the defense case.

The summations occupied more than a month. The defense of the seven indicted Nazi organizations consumed another month. On August 31, the accused were each given 15 minutes for a final statement. Goering again derided "victor's justice." Hess rambled. Keitel was contrite. "I did not see that there is a limit set even for a soldier's performance of his duty. That is my fate," he said.

Speer warned of the dangers ahead. He had done much to develop rocket and other technology that would make a future world war the final one. "A new large-scale war will end with the destruction of human culture and civilization," he warned. "That is why this trial must contribute to the prevention of such wars in the future." But Speer said little of his own role or of his guilt.

The Judgment

The judges returned to the courtroom on September 30 to deliver their verdicts. They declared the Nazi party hierarchy, the SS, the Gestapo, and the SD illegal organizations. On October 1, the tribunal announced the individual verdicts. Declared guilty on all four counts and sentenced to hang were Goering, Ribbentrop, Keitel, Rosenberg, and Jodl. Kaltenbrunner, Frank, Frick, Streicher, Sauckel, and Seyss-Inquart were all found guilty of crimes against humanity and, in some cases, of additional crimes. They were sentenced to hang. Had Bormann survived the devastation of Hitler's Germany? In the event he had, the judges sentenced him to death in absentia.

Hess, Funk, and Doenitz's predecessor as Navy commander, Erich Raeder, each guilty on two or more counts, received life sentences. The court found the elusive Speer guilty of war crimes and crimes against humanity. Though his crimes seemed indistinguishable from the plebeian Sauckel's, he received a 20-year prison term. Baldur von Shirach received 20 years for crimes against humanity. Konstantin von Neurath, guilty on all four counts, drew a 15-year sentence. Doenitz had obtained an affidavit from American Admiral Chester Nimitz saying the United States and Germany had waged submarine warfare on identical principles. Even so, the tribunal found Doenitz guilty of crimes against peace and war crimes and gave him 10 years.

Schacht, Papen, and Fritzsche were acquitted on all four counts.

In early October, the Allied Control Council denied all pleas for clemency and rejected the appeals of Goering, Keitel, and Jodl to be shot rather than hanged. Three gallows, painted black, eight feet high, were put up in the prison gym at the Palace of Justice. A few hours before the executions, Goering escaped the noose by biting into a glass vial of cyanide he had kept hidden in his cell. He died within a few minutes.

The U.S. Army hangman attended to a black-hooded Ribbentrop first, at a little after one o'clock in the morning of October 16, 1946. Keitel followed, then Kaltenbrunner, then the others at intervals of a few minutes. They were clumsy hangings: Keitel, for instance, lingered on for nearly half an hour. Seyss-Inquart, Hitler's governor of the Netherlands, who had sent tens of thousands of Hollanders to their deaths, was the last to swing, at 2:45 A.M. A few hours later, the 10 bodies were taken to a crematorium near Munich and burned.

—Michael Golay

Suggestions for Further Reading

Conot, Robert E. *Justice at Nuremberg.* New York: Harper & Row, 1983.

Gilbert, Gustav M. *Nuremberg Diary.* New York: Farrar, Strauss, 1947.

Maser, Werner. *Nuremberg: A Nation on Trial.* Translated by Richard Barry. New York: Charles Scribner's Sons, 1979.

Persico, Joseph. *Nuremberg: Infamy on Trial.* New York: Viking, 1994.

Smith, Bradley F. *Reaching Judgment at Nuremberg.* New York: Basic Books, 1977.

Taylor, Telford. *The Anatomy of the Nuremberg Trials.* New York: Alfred A. Knopf, 1992.

Tokyo War Crimes Trial: 1946–48

Defendants:
Sadao Araki, Kenji Doihara, Kingoro Hashimoto, Shunroku Hata, Kitchiro Hiranuma, Koki Hirota, Naoki Hoshino, Seishiro Itagaki, Okinori Kaya, Koichi Kido, Heitaro Kimura, Kuniaki Koiso, Iwane Matsui, Yosuke Matsuoka, Jiro Minami, Akira Muto, Osami Nagano, Takasumi Oka, Shumei Okawa, Hiroshi Oshima, Kenryo Sato, Mamoru Shigemitsu, Shigetaro Shimada, Toshio Shiratori, Teiichi Susuki, Shigenori Togo, Hideki Tojo, Yoshijiro Umezu

Crimes Charged:
Conspiracy to wage aggressive war against China, the United States, the British Commonwealth, the Netherlands, France, and the USSR; ordering, authorizing, or permitting atrocities; disregard of duty to secure observance of and prevent breaches of laws of war; total number of counts—55

Chief Defense Lawyers:
Somei Uzawa, Norris N. Allen, Ben Bruce Blakeney, George Francis Blewett, John Brannon, Alfred W. Brooks, Beverly Coleman, Owen Cunningham, Valentine Deale, George Furness, John Guider, Joseph Howard, Tadashi Hanai, Joseph F. Hynes, Ichiro Kiyose, Aristides Lazarus, Michael Levin, William Logan, Jr., Floyd Mattice, Lawrence McManus, David F. Smith, Kenzo Takayanagi, Franklin E. N. Warren, Carrington Williams, George Yamaoka, Charles T. Young

Chief Prosecutors:
Joseph Berry Keenan (U.S.A.), W. G. Frederick Borgerhoff-Mulder (the Netherlands), Arthur S. Comyns-Carr (Britain), John A. Darsey, Jr. (U.S.A.), Robert Donihi (U.S.A.), S. A. Golunsky (USSR), Che-chun Hsiang (China), Pedro Lopez (the Philippines), Alan Mansfield (Australia), Henry Nolan (Canada), Robert L. Oneto (France), Ronald Quilliam (New Zealand), and A. N. Vasiliev (USSR)

Judges:
Sir William Webb (Australia); Henri Bernard (France); John P. Higgins, succeeded by Myron C. Cramer (U.S.A.); Delfin Jaranilla (the Philippines); Edward Stuart McDougall (Canada); Ju-ao Mei (China); Harvey Northcroft (New Zealand); Radhabinod Pal (India); Lord Patrick (Britain); H.V.A. Roling (the Netherlands); I. M. Zarayanov (USSR)

Place: Tokyo, Japan   **Dates of Trial:** May 3, 1946–April 16, 1948   **Verdicts:** Guilty

Sentences:
Doihara, Hirota, Itagaki, Kimura, Matsui, Muto, Tojo—execution by hanging; Araki, Hashimoto, Hata, Hiranuma, Hoshino, Kaya, Kido, Koiso, Minami, Oka, Oshima, Sato, Shimada, Shiratori, Susuki, Umezu—life imprisonment; Togo—20 years' imprisonment; Shigemitsu—7 years' imprisonment; (Matsuoka and Nagano—died during trial; Okawa—committed to psychiatric ward, later released)

SIGNIFICANCE
One of the most complex trials in history followed the indictment of 28 men who had led Japanese aggression in World War II. Whereas the Nuremberg trial had charged war crimes against 17 civilians and 5 military leaders in Germany, at Tokyo only 9 of the 28 were civilians. In Germany, the government had controlled the military; in Japan, the military had co-opted the government. Like the trial at Nuremberg, the trial in Tokyo had no precedent in international law. Rather, it was based on concepts of conspiracy that were common among the world's major legal systems.

The Tokyo War Crimes Trial followed a formal declaration by American five-star general Douglas MacArthur, supreme commander of the Allied Powers in the Pacific, after the Japanese surrender that ended World War II. Dated January 16, 1946, the declaration said:

> In order to implement the Terms of Surrender which requires [sic] the meting out of stern justice to war criminals . . . there shall be established an International Military Tribunal for the Far East (IMTFE) for the trial of those persons charged individually, or as members of organizations, or in both capacities, with offenses which include crimes against peace.

The charter was modeled on the earlier Big Four agreement that initiated the Nuremberg trial of Nazi war criminals. Among its 17 articles, the charter called for conviction and sentencing to be by majority vote of the judges, and it carefully defined crimes against peace as "the planning, preparation, initiation, or waging of a declared or undeclared war of aggression or a war in violation of international treaties," thus ensuring that no Japanese could be indicted for only fighting in the war. Violations of the customs of war and crimes against humanity—that is, inhumane acts against "any civilian population, before or during the war"—were included.

"Class A" Responsibility

Japanese suspected of war crimes dating back to 1931 had been arrested and held in Sugamo Prison. Of several hundred, more than 80 were considered "Class A"—responsible for planning, initiating, or waging war "in violation of international treaties." As prosecutors gathered evidence in the spring of 1946, they narrowed the Class A group down to 28 for indictment. This group included former generals (six), premiers (four), war ministers (four), foreign ministers (three), economic and financial leaders (three), navy ministers (two), ambassadors (two), and an admiral, a colonel, a radical theorist, and a nobleman who had been an imperial adviser. Emperor Hirohito was neither indicted nor called as a witness, for MacArthur had cabled Washington that "his indictment will unquestionably cause a tremendous convulsion among the Japanese people, the repercussions of which cannot be overestimated."

The trial opened on May 3, 1946, in the former War Ministry building in Tokyo. The 1,000-seat courtroom (including 660 spectator seats in the balcony), was heavily guarded. It had been wired so that English, Japanese, or Russian translations reached every seat, and was brightly, and warmly, klieg-lighted for news cameras. The courtroom swarmed with military police in white gloves and helmets, who daily checked every chair for weapons, messages, or contraband.

Clogs and Tailcoats

The defendants filed in to their assigned seats—some in rumpled dress uniforms from which all medals and emblems of rank had been torn, one clomping in wooden clogs, another in tropical open-throated jungle jacket, yet another in traditional striped trousers and tailcoat. All eyes sought the notorious

General Hideki Tojo, once Japan's top militarist, who a few months earlier had shot himself in a suicide attempt and now appeared well and dapper in his khaki bush jacket.

Setting the tone, presiding judge Sir William Webb noted that "the onus will be on the prosecution to establish guilt beyond a reasonable doubt." The court clerk then read the indictment. As he reached count 22, which charged several defendants with initiating a war of aggression on December 7, 1941, (date of the Japanese attack on the U.S. military base at Pearl Harbor, Hawaii), defendant Shumei Okawa, sitting directly behind Tojo, slapped the general hard on top of his head, repeated the attack, and was seized by the military police. The court ordered Okawa transferred from the dock to a psychiatric ward, where he was found to be hallucinating and incapable of testifying in his own defense; his ill health was induced by syphilis and drug abuse.

The accused all pleaded not guilty. The courtroom then rang for several days with debate over the court's jurisdiction. Crimes against the peace and against humanity did not exist in international law, argued the defense, because "war is not a crime." Therefore, the court was imposing ex post facto law on those accused. Furthermore, argued four defendants, the court was infringing on their rights as prisoners of war. On May 17, the court dismissed the defense motions.

"Declared War Upon Civilization"

Prosecutor Joseph B. Keenan opened by reminding the court that Japan had been one of the Allies who, at the end of World War I, agreed at Versailles that "a war of aggression constitutes an international crime." Japan had earlier signed the Hague Conventions of 1907 that instructed states not to start war "without previous and explicit warning." The Japanese had also signed the Kellogg-Briand Pact of 1920, renouncing war "as an instrument of national policy." Yet, said Keenan as he pointed to the defendants, "they declared war upon civilization."

Keenan set out to establish that the most important issue in the trial was an individual's liability for committing crimes in the name of the state. His strategy was three-pronged: (1) The defendants had risen through Japan's unique police-state milieu of the 1930s, in which thought control, counterespionage, and terrorism were standard operating procedures; (2) the militarists had fabricated "incidents" to consolidate their authority; and (3) the numbers of fanatics, both civilian and military, had encouraged aggressive wars driven by expansionist policies.

A dozen witnesses testified to the prewar power of the Kempeitai, military police much like Hitler's Gestapo, who were encouraged to "decide whether or not a person is suspicious from his external appearance, such as his features." Other witnesses showed how the empire was governed by the army: All war ministers were army generals, and the army could head off the formation of a government by not appointing a war minister or could bring down a government by forcing the war minister to resign. Incidents as far back as the 1929 resignation of Japanese Premier Giichi Tanaka and his cabinet—after corrupt Japanese officers murdered a Chinese warlord in Manchuria—were cited. Young Japanese spectators gasped when one witness described the army's invasion of Manchuria "without the imperial sanction."

As the days of testimony on such distant events as those in Manchuria in the early 1930s lengthened, the objections, challenges, and legal scuffling steadily increased. Realizing that the defense attorneys' attention to legal technicalities was combining with the need for translations—questions from English to Japanese, answers from Japanese to English—to consume days and then weeks, the prosecution moved for the court's permission to offer affidavits by witnesses. Assured that court time would be cut by one-third, the bench approved, finding that the Nuremberg trials had established a precedent. Ultimately, the prosecution presented affidavits from 1,200 witnesses in addition to courtroom testimony of 102 witnesses.

The Puppet Emperor

A key witness on the conquest of Manchuria, begun in 1931, was Henry P'u Yi, who had been appointed emperor when the Japanese militarists set up the puppet state of Manchukuo. On the stand for 11 hot and humid August days—longer than any other witness—he described the brutalization of Manchuria, where 25 million Chinese, under the thought control of their Japanese invaders, were kept docile. "Political parties and political bodies," said a directive introduced as evidence, "shall not be permitted to exist." Altogether, 24 of the 28 defendants were shown to have been associated with the emperor's puppet government.

Witnesses testified on several "incidents" created by the Japanese in China, from the 1931 Mukden incident that gave the Japanese an excuse to invade Manchuria to the Marco Polo Bridge incident of 1937, which resulted in 124,130 Chinese solders killed, 242,232 wounded, and left vast numbers of civilian casualties uncounted in the first year of slaughter. The six-week rape of Nanjing in 1937, with 20,000 women literally raped and the Chinese Red Cross left to bury 43,000 mutilated and rotting corpses, was described through the vivid recollections of eyewitnesses.

The prosecution turned to narcotics. Although pretending to control the use of opium, witnesses testified, Japan had established monopolies over the sale of opium, heroin, and morphine to the Chinese, bringing in massive revenue while weakening the Chinese will to oppose the military occupation.

Prosecution witnesses also described how the Berlin-Tokyo Axis was established and how the sneak attack on the U.S. base at Pearl Harbor was planned. They testified on atrocities committed on prisoners of war, ranging from experimental surgery performed without anesthesia to the seven-day Bataan Death March that killed more than 10,000 of 70,000 American and Filipino troops. Witnesses described the beheading of POWs in jungles and on prison ships. The numbers became overwhelming: 18,000 Filipinos murdered in the village of Lipa; 450 French and Vietnamese machine-gunned, then bayoneted at Langson, Vietnam; dozens of young Manila women gang-raped by hundreds of Japanese; 30,000 Burmese slave laborers forced to build the Siam-Burma railroad (and were fed only a bowl of rice daily) while thousands ill with cholera were simply abandoned in the jungle.

Hideki Tojo listens as Chief Justice Sir William Webb reads the Court's judgment against him. Found guilty of war crimes, he was sentenced to death by hanging. (Still Picture Branch, National Archives, Washington, DC)

Concluding the prosecution case, Keenan turned to the defense claim that Japan had waged war in self-defense. "It is significant," he said, "that no one has claimed a threat from any power to attack or invade the Empire of Japan. . . . We reject the contention that it is self-defense for a nation to attack another because the latter refuses to supply materials of war to be used against it and its allies."

The Defense Opens

The defense opened its case on February 4, 1947. "The punishment of crimes against peace in violation of treaties," argued counsel Kenzo Takayanagi, "has never been known to the laws of nations." War was not illegal, according to the argument presented over several weeks, and the idea that those who had plotted and waged war, despite international law, were criminally responsible was "a perfectly revolutionary doctrine."

The defense tried to establish its position that Japan's motive in the war had been self-defense. The United States, it held, had been the aggressor by fortifying Pearl Harbor, sending matériel to China, and demanding that Japan withdraw from Manchuria. All of Japan's economic and military development before December 1941 had been defensive, according to defense counsel Ichiro Kiyose, who represented the notorious Prime Minister General Hideki Tojo.

Tojo, cross-examined by the prosecution, accepted responsibility for his country's actions, saying the 1941 economic blockade by the Allies had forced Japan to start the war in order to preserve its "national existence."

Indeed, argued the defense, the Allies had repeatedly violated the Kellogg-Briand Pact and other treaties, making the agreements "worthless." The idea that a criminal conspiracy had stretched from 1928 to 1941 was absurd, for 15 Japanese cabinets had resigned in that period and countless individuals, with many different agendas, had served. How could they, asked the defense, have had an "organized plan"?

Obedience: Not a Crime

The concept of superior orders was argued. Obedience to lawful orders in military matters was not a crime, claimed defense counsel Kenzo Takayanagi, and if Japan's leaders had committed criminal offenses, then so had Soviet, British, and American leaders. The defendants, he said, "must be declared innocent unless it is proved beyond a reasonable doubt that they committed some criminal offense known to the established law of nations."

The defense rested on April 16, 1948. By then, the trial transcript had reached 48,412 pages, and 419 witnesses and 779 affidavits had been presented in 818 court sessions over two and a half years.

The 11 judges spent seven months reviewing the evidence. On November 12, ending a week-long presentation of their 1,218-page opinion, they found 25 defendants guilty. (Of the original 28, two had died of natural causes during the trial and one had been declared mentally unfit to be tried.) Seven were condemned to death, including Tojo. Sixteen were sentenced to life imprisonment, one to 20 years' imprisonment, and another to 7 years' imprisonment.

The executions, by hanging, occurred shortly after midnight on December 23, 1948. MacArthur permitted no Japanese witnesses and no photographers to be present.

—Bernard Ryan, Jr.

Suggestions for Further Reading

Brackman, Arnold C. *The Other Nuremberg.* New York: William Morrow, 1987.

Brines, Russell. *MacArthur's Japan.* Philadelphia: Lippincott, 1948.

Hanayama, Shinso. *The Way of Deliverance: Three Years with the Condemned Japanese War Criminals.* Translated by Hideo Susuki. New York: Scribner's, 1950.

Minear, Richard H. *Victors' Justice: The Tokyo War Crimes Trial.* Princeton, N.J.: Princeton University Press, 1971.

Mosley, Leonard. *Hirohito, Emperor of Japan.* Englewood Cliffs, N.J.: Prentice-Hall, 1966.

Piccigallo, Philip R. *The Japanese on Trial.* Austin: University of Texas Press, 1979.

Sebald, William, with Russell Brines. *With MacArthur in Japan.* New York: Norton, 1965.

Shigemitsu, Mamoru X. *Japan and Her Destiny.* Translated by Oswald White. Edited by F. S. Piggot. New York: Dutton, 1958.

Ward, Robert E., and Frank Joseph Shulman. *The Allied Occupation of Japan, 1945–1952.* Chicago: American Library Association, 1972.

Mohandas Gandhi's Assassins Trial: 1948

Defendants:
Nathuram Godse, Narayan Apte, Vishnu Karkare, Madanlal Pahwa, Shankar Kistayya, Gopal Godse, Vinayak Savarkar, Dattatraya Parchure

Crimes Charged:
Conspiracy to murder Mahatma Gandhi; attempt to murder Gandhi (Pahwa), murder of Gandhi (N. Godse), aiding and abetting of these actions, unlawful possession of arms and ammunition (all except Savarkar and Parchure), abetting the carrying of arms and ammunition (Parchure), illegal possession of explosives (Pahwa)

Chief Defense Lawyers:
L. P. Bhoptkar and B. Banerji, K. L. Bhoptkar, N. D. Dange, P. L. Inamdar, P. R. Das, Hansraj Mehta, P. H. Mengale, V. V. Oke, Ganpat Rai

Chief Prosecutors:
C. K. Daphtary, advocate general of Bombay; Raibahadur Jwalaprasad; J. C. Shah; Sri Vyvaharkar

Judge: Atma Charan   **Place:** New Delhi, India

Dates of Trial: May 27–December 30, 1948

Verdict: Seven guilty; Savarkar acquitted for lack of evidence

Sentences:
N. Godse and Apte, death by hanging, along with three, five, and seven years' rigorous imprisonment, to run concurrently; Karkare, Kistayya, and G. Godse, transportation for life, along with three, five, and seven years' rigorous imprisonment, to run concurrently; Pahwa, transportation for life, with three, five, seven, and ten years' rigorous imprisonment, to run concurrently; Parchure, transportation for life. On appeal, Parchure and Kistayya acquitted

SIGNIFICANCE
Although the trial and appeals process apparently resulted in the correct verdicts, questions of lax security and of a wider conspiracy remained unanswered. The 1965–69 Kanpur commission revealed the degree of police incompetence and of official negligence, some of it perhaps deliberate, which allowed the plot to move forward. It was, in effect, a "permissive assassination."

It is one of the more blatant ironies of history that Mohandas (Mahatma) Gandhi, who dedicated his life to nonviolent action, was felled by the violence of an assassin's bullets only months after he had helped to bring about independence for India from British rule. Armed only with his moral authority and his unswerving conviction of what was right, Gandhi had tried for nearly five decades to transform India—a cauldron bubbling with religious, ethnic, caste, and communal discord—into a kinder, more humane society.

Gandhi Opposes Hindu Extremists

Independence on August 15, 1947, along with partitioning off the Muslim region, which became the nation of Pakistan, led to widespread riots, massacres, revenge killings, and desperate refugees streaming across the new borders. By the time it was all over, some 12 million people had been uprooted and around 200,000 were dead. In an attempt to ease this chaotic transition, on January 13, 1948, Gandhi announced a "fast unto the death" to force the Indian government to honor its obligation to pay to Pakistan 550 million rupees it had been withholding. At the time, Gandhi was staying at the New Delhi house of his patron and supporter, millionaire G. D. Birla. Three days later, the government agreed to pay, but Gandhi vowed to continue his fast to force communal peace and a reconciliation of Hindus and Muslims. Satisfied with progress toward this goal, he ended his fast on January 18, 1948.

Meanwhile, the January 13 report of Gandhi's fast had galvanized the conspirators to action. According to Nathuram Godse, Gandhi's fate had been sealed as early as August 15, 1947, the day of independence as well as of partition—a geographic solution that Godse and other Hindu nationalists saw as a catastrophe. In a November 1, 1947, speech, Godse held Gandhi responsible: "Gandhi said India would be divided over his dead body. India is divided, but Gandhi lives. Gandhi's nonviolence has left the Hindus defenseless before their enemies. Now, while Hindu refugees are starving, Gandhi defends their Muslim oppressors. Hindu women are throwing themselves into wells to save themselves from being raped, and Gandhi tells them 'Victory is in the victim.'"

Godse was editor of the Poona newspaper *Hindu Rashtra*, and his chief accomplice, Narayan Apte, was managing editor. Both were members of the Hindu Mahasabha (Great Hindu Society), a right-wing political party. They both revered Vinayak Savarkar, 65, its former president, a one-time terrorist linked to several assassinations and founder of the Hindu Rashtra Dal, the party's militaristic arm, whose members, all Brahmans, had sworn allegiance to him.

Hindu Militants Plot Gandhi's Murder

Active preparation for the assassination began in November 1947 as Godse and Apte sought arms and more participants. The original plan was the 19th-century Russian terrorist strategy of backing frontline units with reserves who would act if the first assassins failed: They planned an attack from all sides, using pistols and hand grenades. The plotters turned to Digambar Badge, a bookseller and dealer in contraband weapons, who, along with his servant Shankar Kistayya, assisted them by locating weapons and ammunition. Meanwhile, they were joined by Vishnu Karkare, a restaurateur, former actor, and Hindu Mahasabha member, and Madanlal Pahwa, Karkare's employee and a Hindu refugee who had seen his father and aunt massacred by Muslims. Godse's younger brother, Gopal Godse, a storekeeper at an army depot, rounded out the cabal.

By January 10, 1948, Badge had found hand grenades and guncotton but still lacked pistols. On January 14, the conspirators conferred in Bombay at the Hindu Mahasabha office, planning their trip to New Delhi. Following the meeting, Nathuram Godse and Apte paid a short visit to Savarkar, the "spiritual leader" of their planned action. By January 19, all had arrived in New Delhi. Badge had purchased a pistol, and Gopal Godse had brought his old service revolver. On the morning of January 20, four of them boldly took a taxi to Birla House and checked out the layout of the pavilion where Gandhi held his prayer meetings at the rear of the estate. That afternoon's assassination attempt, in which Badge was to do the shooting, turned out to be a fiasco. Pahwa's diversionary guncotton explosion failed to panic the crowd. He was captured, and four plotters fled in a taxi; the other two slipped away in the crowd.

In police hands, Pahwa soon betrayed the names of his co-conspirators. Newspaper reports of his arrest reached Bombay university professor Dr. Jagdish C. Jain, to whom Pahwa had described the plot on January 13. Jain, who initially disbelieved the youth, now urgently informed officials of his knowledge. Unaccountably, the police and authorities did little to find the other plotters during the ten days before their second, successful, attempt on January 30.

Meanwhile, the others had returned to Bombay, and a disgusted Badge, together with his servant, Kistayya, refused to have anything more to do with them. Undiscouraged, the remaining four—the Godse brothers, Apte, and Karkare—planned a second try. Gopal Godse was to remain behind. Nathuram Godse, who now decided to do the deed alone, still needed a gun, because the first two they had obtained proved unreliable. On January 27, Nathuram Godse and Apte flew back to New Delhi and took a train 200 miles south to Gwalior to try to get a gun from Dattatraya Parchure, a well-off medical practitioner and important Hindu Mahasabha figure. They were able to purchase a pistol from one of his acquaintances and promptly returned to New Delhi.

On the morning of January 30, rejoined by Karkare, they tested the pistol in some woods and in the afternoon traveled by horse cab to Birla House, where they mingled among the waiting devotees. When Gandhi arrived shortly after 5 P.M., Godse rushed up and fired off three fatal shots before he was wrestled to the ground. To the world at large, another lone gunman had succeeded in killing a great leader; the Indian authorities would soon prove otherwise.

Trial Points to Wide Conspiracy

The trial opened on May 27, 1948, in New Delhi's Moghul stronghold, the Red Fort. By order of the government, the specifically constituted court, presided over by a specially appointed judge, was empowered to exercise a unique right—that of giving a full pardon to an accused in a murder case. Badge, the bookseller who had dropped out from the second attempt, was granted a free pardon before the hearing of evidence started on June 22. He turned state's evidence and testified against the others.

With no jury, Judge Atma Charan presided alone. The trial dragged on for months, largely because all questions and answers from the 149 witnesses had to be translated from English (still the common language of India) by Hindustani, Marathi, and Telugu interpreters. Open to the press, the trial was extensively reported in newspapers worldwide. The sweltering courtroom was open to the public, a limited number of whom were admitted with one-day passes. Strict security was imposed, and all were searched at the entry gate.

Aided by Badge's damning testimony, the prosecution built up an impressive circumstantial case centering around Nathuram Godse, Apte, and Savarkar. The others were seen as having played relatively minor roles. The examination of witnesses and the recording of evidence lasted until November 6, 1948, and revealed how carelessly and amateurishly the accused had carried out their plot. By January 17, it became clear that some 50 people had known of their plans.

The defendants all had entered not guilty pleas to the conspiracy charge, although Nathuram Godse admitted the murder. Summed up, the defense maintained there had been no conspiracy, that the attacks of January 20 and 30 were unrelated and committed by individuals acting alone. The defense elected to call no witnesses and essentially dismissed the prosecution's version on the principle that "a bad case needs no rebuttal." Specifically, Apte and Karkare denied returning to New Delhi on January 30; Kistayya submitted that, as a servant, he had obeyed his master's orders. Gopal Godse denied all, even his presence in New Delhi on January 18–20. Parchure insisted that Apte and Nathuram Godse had approached him only for volunteers for a peaceful demonstration and that he had given no help with the pistol. Pahwa said his explosion, carefully detonated far away from anyone, was an expression of resentment against the treatment of refugees.

The other two defendants were another matter. The sinister Savarkar, who had studied law in London, was well versed in courtroom procedure and was able to impress the judge with his closely reasoned, legalistic analysis of the circumstantial evidence, read from a 52-page manuscript. Despite Savarkar's successful denial of any complicity and his expressed admiration for Gandhi, he was seen by many as morally responsible, at least, for the assassination. He had encouraged young Hindu militants to oppose Gandhi and the Congress Party with all means possible.

Nathuram Godse took the opposite tack. He tried to assume total responsibility for Gandhi's murder by denying the existence of a conspiracy. He, too, was allowed to enter a lengthy statement into the record on November 8. Reading from a 96-page manuscript in English, he explained his reasons: "I declare here before man and God that in putting an end to Gandhi's life I have removed one who was a curse to India, a force for evil, and who . . . brought nothing but misery and unhappiness, not merely to the Hindus . . . but to the Muslims." Citing

Hindu mythology, Godse predicted: "I warn my country against the pest of Gandhism. It will mean not only Muslim rule over the entire country but the extinction of Hinduism itself. There are pessimists who say that the great Hindu nation, after tens of thousands of years, is doomed to extinction."

What came after was anticlimactic, as were the verdicts. Pronouncing sentence, the judge added that had "the slightest keenness been shown by [the police] in the investigation of the case at that stage [following the bomb incident on January 20], the tragedy probably could have been averted."

The Aftermath

Before the appeals court, the defense again tried to break down the links between the plotters. Although they acquitted Parchure and Kistayya, the judges found ample evidence to uphold the verdicts and sentences against the others. Nathuram Godse and Apte were hanged on November 15, 1949. But the saga did not end there. After serving some 15 years, Gopal Godse, Karkare, and Pahwa were released on October 12, 1964. A November 12 reception celebrated their freedom and glorified Nathuram Godse as a patriot; at this event an Indian newspaper editor spoke of his prior knowledge of the plot. The affair was widely reported in the newspapers and led to heated parliamentary debates. The result was the creation on March 25, 1965, of a special Commission of Inquiry to investigate the assassination again.

By January 24, 1969, the commission had methodically questioned 101 witnesses and examined 407 documents. Its conclusions were clear: Many people knew of the plot in advance, the police were negligent in pursuing the conspirators after January 20, security for Gandhi was woefully inadequate, and various officials failed to respond to the developing situation with the necessary urgency.

Yet, the assassination had another ironic twist. Many had come to view Gandhi as irrelevant or as a nuisance. He might have died from ill health or old age. Godse's bullets provided him with a glorious martyr's death—what the *Hindustani Times* called "the second crucifixion"—and ensured his reputation as one of the great leaders of history.

—Eva Weber

Suggestions for Further Reading

Collins, Larry, and Dominique LaPierre. *Freedom at Midnight.* New York: Simon & Schuster, 1975.

Inamdar, P. L. *The Story of the Red Fort Trial.* Bombay: Popular, 1979.

Kapur, J. L. *Report of Commission of Inquiry into Conspiracy to Murder Mahatma Gandhi.* New Delhi: Government of India Press, 1970.

Khosla, G. D. *The Murder of the Mahatma, and Other Cases from a Judge's Notebook.* London: Chatto & Windus, 1963.

Malgonkar, Mahonar. *The Men Who Killed Gandhi.* New Delhi: Macmillan, 1978.

Payne, Robert. *The Life and Death of Mahatma Gandhi.* New York: E. P. Dutton, 1969.

Victor Kravchenko Trial: 1949

Defendants: *Les Lettres Françaises*, Claude Morgan, and Andre Wurmser
Plaintiff: Victor A. Kravchenko   **Plaintiff's Claim:** Libel
Chief Defense Lawyer: Joe Nordmann   **Plaintiff's Lawyer:** Georges Izard
Judge: Henri Durkheim   **Place:** Paris, France   **Dates of Trial:** January 24–
April 4, 1949   **Verdict:** Against Defendants. Damages—150,000 francs
(about $500); fine—15,000 francs (about $50); court costs—estimated
1,000,000 to 6,000,000 francs ($3,000 to $18,000)

SIGNIFICANCE

Early in the Cold War, this trial spotlighted the truth about the Communist purges
and reign of terror in Russia in the 1930s. In the trial's hysterical debate over the
defects and merits of both its plaintiff and the Communist system, it was unique.

Victor A. Kravchenko was a member of the Soviet Purchasing Commission stationed in Washington by the USSR during World War II. As the war ended in 1945, he defected. In 1946, the book *I Chose Freedom*, with the subtitle *The Personal and Political Life of a Soviet Official*, was published in the United States with his name on the title page as author. The book described the life of terror and oppression endured not only by those who rose through the Communist bureaucracy but by most Russians.

"Morally Insane" and "Illiterate"

In November 1947, a newspaper in Paris, France, began serializing the book. Immediately, a Paris weekly, *Les Lettres Françaises*, published by the Communist Party, attacked Kravchenko. It declared him a "morally insane" traitor "so illiterate as to be incapable of writing a book," and asserted that he had once embezzled from a Soviet factory. The article attributed its information to an interview with "a former official of the American wartime secret services, the OSS." Quoting that unidentified official, it said of Kravchenko:

> Often he remained in night clubs, drinking until morning.... On such occasions he was not averse to playing the perfect "stool pigeon." It was necessary to induce him to break with the Russians, and then to keep him as a hostage.

The "escape" of which he writes was a mere pleasure ride. . . . Over several months he wrote some sixty pages which were practically illegible. Without even paying any attention to this, the book of over a thousand pages had already been drafted by our friends.

On January 20, 1948, the U.S. House of Representatives voted Kravchenko permanent residence in the United States, directing the Justice Department to waive immigration laws barring residence to anyone known to have advocated the overthrow of the U.S. Government.

Kravchenko sued *Les Lettres Françaises*, its editor, Claude Morgan, and its writer, Andre Wurmser, for libel, asking 1,000,000 francs (about $3,000) in damages. The paper, however, continued to repeat its charges.

In French jurisprudence, a defendant is considered guilty until he proves his innocence. *Les Lettres*, said Kravchenko in bringing his suit, would have to disprove his position that the OSS "never had anything to do with the fact that I decided to leave the Soviet Purchasing Commission in Washington." The defendants, he added, would have to prove that the Politburo was not the sole master of Soviet foreign policy and that the USSR was not a police state.

January 1949 found the Palais de Justice throbbing with the greatest excitement since the 1945 trial of Marshall Henri-Philippe Pétain for high treason. In the specially renovated courtroom, 200 gilt chairs were moved in for important personages. Press passes were limited to every other day for each of the several hundred reporters from near and far.

The Trial Opens

On the opening day, January 24, the defense lawyer, Joe Nordmann, introduced a number of leading French Communists. One was atomic physicist Frederic Joliot-Curie, whose testimony was deemed valuable despite his recent statement that he would not turn over atomic energy secrets to the Soviets.

The *Lettres* editors repeated their charges. Kravchenko challenged their definition of *traitor*, reminding them that Maurice Thores, head of the French Communist Party, had "left France in 1939 in the face of the enemy, but now he is called a hero." The defense attorney explained that the party had ordered Thores from France as a patriotic act "to keep him out of the hands of the fifth column," and that "any Communist is automatically a patriot." The courtroom burst with laughter.

The next day, defense witness Pierre Courtade, a writer known as an official chronicler of the Communist line, said that the present anti-Soviet policy of the United States had begun with the publication of *I Chose Freedom*. The book, he said, was nothing more than "Fascist" propaganda from Washington.

Confusion multiplied. Defense witnesses contradicted defense positions. One witness, a wartime collaborator of Charles de Gaulle who had since turned to the left, agreed that Kravchenko had not written the book but surprised the packed courtroom by declaring it had been concocted by a writer paid by "a large New York bank, the Fulton Trust Company."

Kravchenko witnesses appeared. Three were Russians from displaced persons camps. They gave agonizing descriptions of life in the Soviet Union: One woman's newborn child had died in the cold after she was thrown out of her house; one man had seen a workman punished with 30 days hard labor for arriving on the job 20 minutes late; another's "confession" had been coerced by keeping him awake while strapped to a stool for six days, after which he was sentenced to 18 years in a concentration camp from which he escaped. Four former Russian citizens swore that, as one said, "Kravchenko's book exactly reflects life in Soviet Russia," where communism ruled "by hunger, agitation, and terror."

"Not a Bolshevik Invention"

Next, defense witness Konni Zilliacus, a left-wing Labour Party member of the British Parliament, testified that the book was full of "inexactitudes, inaccuracies, and obvious lies." Although Kravchenko described Russian industrial inefficiency, he said, the Red Army "got only 10 percent of its tanks and planes from lend-lease" yet "accounted for 80 percent of all the Germans killed in the war." But the witness embarrassed the defense, which kept insisting that purges and terror had not taken place in Russia, by adding, "That sort of cruelty is not necessarily a Bolshevik invention."

Defense witness Albert Kahn, American author of *The Great Conspiracy Against Russia*, confounded the defense by testifying that the theory of OSS authorship of the Kravchenko book was improbable but that it had been written at the behest of "the enormous Ukrainian group in the United States." He could prove this, he said, with letters from the U.S. Justice Department and Army and Navy Intelligence.

The counterarguments, the bickering, the shouting grew so wild that, to prevent violence, Judge Henri Durkheim ordered a police guard to be positioned between Kravchenko and the defendants and their lawyer. Undeterred, the defense introduced the plaintiff's former wife, Zinalda Gorlova, who said marrying him had been "the biggest mistake of my life—he beat me, he broke dishes, he even tried to shoot me." On his orders, she said, she had had an abortion.

"I'd Tear Your Head Off!"

Defense witness Nicolai Kolikalov, a former member of the Soviet Purchasing Commission, testified that Kravchenko had once embezzled 60,000 rubles (about $15,000), had been sentenced to two years in prison (later reduced to one year of labor), and, during a medical examination, had been found mentally deficient. Upon hearing this, Kravchenko leaped to his feet. "We are not in Moscow!" he screamed. "If you weren't a witness, I'd tear your head off."

Plaintiff attorney Georges Izard countered. Taking the defense by surprise, he produced a speech made in 1938 by Vyacheslav M. Molotov, then

Soviet premier as well as foreign minister, that was extremely complimentary to Kravchenko in naming him as head of a giant new plant designed to produce 160,000 tons of industrial tubing a year—the largest factory of its kind in all Europe.

The defense had promised to bring 17 witnesses from the Soviet Union. Four appeared: the former Mrs. Kravchenko and three engineers. One accused Kravchenko of desertion from the Red Army. The plaintiff countered that he had been an engineer, not an officer. Another, the general who had been chief of the Soviet Purchasing Commission, spoke of Russia's deep and mature affection for France and deposed that the plaintiff was a traitor and a criminal. Kravchenko asked him how the Soviets could be friends of France when in 1939 and 1940 they had helped Germany, the enemy of France. Furious, the general picked up his cap and stormed from the courtroom.

When the parade of witnesses ended, Judge Durkheim pondered the heaps of testimony recorded over 25 trial days. On April 4, he announced his verdict: Victor Kravchenko had been libeled. He was "a cultured man" who had been "grossly insulted . . . more out of desire to harm than out of a desire to report the truth."

The Communists lost on all points. But because the defendants' records showed them to be "patriots," the judge ruled, he would impose only nominal amounts: 150,000 francs (about $500) damages, a fine of 15,000 francs (about $50), and court costs that were estimated between 1,000,000 and 6,000,000 francs ($3,000 and $18,000).

The defendants, editor Claude Morgan and writer Andre Wurmser, were not present to hear the judge. They were busy touring Belgium, lecturing on the trial.

On February 25, 1966, in New York City, Victor Kravchenko died of a self-inflicted gunshot wound.

—Bernard Ryan, Jr.

Suggestions for Further Reading

Kravchenko, Victor. *I Chose Freedom: The Personal and Political Life of a Soviet Official*. New York: Scribner's, 1946.

Sayers, Michael, and Albert E. Kahn. *The Great Conspiracy Against Russia*. Boston: Little, Brown, 1946.

József Cardinal Mindszenty Trial: 1949

Defendant: József Mindszenty   **Crime Charged:** Conspiracy to overthrow the Hungarian government   **Chief Defense Lawyer:** Koloman Kiczkó   **Chief Prosecutor:** Julius Alapi   **Judge:** William Olti   **Place:** Budapest, Hungary   **Dates of Trial:** February 3–8, 1949   **Verdict:** Guilty   **Sentence:** Life imprisonment

SIGNIFICANCE

The Prince Primate of Hungary became one of the world's best known victims of the Soviet Union's post–World War II domination of Eastern Europe, a symbol of resistance to oppression and a Cold War cause célèbre.

The political cardinal already knew the look and feel of the inside of a prison. In 1919, Hungarian Communist revolutionaries had locked up József Mindszenty, then a 27-year-old teaching priest with a taste for right-wing journalism, for two months. And late in 1944, Hungary's fascist dictatorship had jailed Mindszenty, bishop of Veszprém, for seeking a separate peace before the Soviets could arrive to destroy the country.

The 1919 revolution failed, and Hungary's Nazi German allies lost World War II. In each case Mindszenty went free—and prospered. In October 1945, in fact, Pope Pius XII appointed him archbishop of Esztergom, Prince Primate of Hungary. The Communist rise to power in 1947 proved, however, to be enduring, the new leaders a single-mindedly ruthless set of cutthroats to rival any Hungary had yet endured.

Mindszenty may not have recognized at first that the authority of the Roman Catholic Church and its head in Hungary had been disempowered. Pursuing his own conservative political course, defending the traditional prerogatives of the Church, not doubting he would continue to operate as a quasi-independent power, Mindszenty challenged the new rulers. He protested state interference with the Church, confiscation of Church property, and persecution of parish priests. He asked the Americans and the British to protest Communist excesses. He met with the last empress of the Hapsburgs and her pretender son.

Shortly after taking power, the Hungarian Communists, following the Stalin pattern and with assistance from Moscow, embarked on a program of state terror against their political opponents. They had little fear of going after the cardinal. Long identified with the old social and economic order, he lacked a large popular following. Still, the Communists doubtless would have moved to silence him even if he had been the idol of ordinary Catholics. In any case, in late 1948 a group of senior officials, including the foreign minister and the war minister, decided to "liquidate the Mindszenty problem."

Interrogation and Torture

The political police waited until after sunset on Sunday, December 26, 1948, to arrest Mindszenty at the archiepiscopal palace in Esztergom. In a nationwide sweep, the police also pulled in hundreds of priests, opposition politicians, and others for "complicity" with the cardinal's schemes—more than 3,300 were detained by the end of January.

The arresting officers brought Mindszenty at once to the interrogation rooms at police headquarters in Budapest, where he was charged with conspiracy against the Hungarian people's republic, espionage, and abuses of the foreign currency regulations. They took away his priest's cassock. Using rubber truncheons, they beat him unconscious. When he came to, the questioning began. On December 28, the police released a statement: "Mindszenty, under the weight of the evidence produced against him, has made a confession. His arrested accomplices also have admitted the charges against him."

On December 29, Wednesday, the interrogators pressed the cardinal for details that would convince Hungarian Catholics that he really had attempted to betray the country. While he stood with his arms raised above his head, they shot question after question at him, hour after hour. The work exhausted even experienced secret policemen, so they worked in relays, a few hours on, a few off.

"A priest does not lie," one interrogator said to the cardinal in a sort of singsong voice. "A priest tells the truth; a priest confesses; a priest cannot receive absolution for his sin of lying."

Through it all the cardinal stood. "End it all," he said finally, after 66 hours on his feet, without sleep and without food. "It is useless. Kill me. I am ready to die." There have been suggestions the police used drugs, including mescaline, to keep Mindszenty going so far beyond a middle-aged man's usual limits. After 84 hours, he signed the confession, admitting he had been part of a royalist plot to overthrow the people's republic with American and British aid. That was not all. The police gave him a few days to recover, then demanded he write out the confession in his own hand, to give it the stamp of authenticity.

Convicted at Show Trial

The arrest and jailing converted the cardinal into a martyr overnight. The Pope issued an edict excommunicating all who knew themselves, in their consciences, to be guilty of persecuting Mindszenty. Hungarian churches were crowded not only with the observant but with the politically active too. The authorities allowed the churches to remain open, though their police spies watched Mass-goers and sermons were censored. With the groundswell of support for the cardinal, the Communists regarded as essential that the trial destroy or at least damage his aura.

The proceedings opened at 9 in the morning of February 3, 1949. The cardinal wore a plain black suit with a clerical collar. He kept his eyes downcast as the court president, William Olti, a former Nazi turned Communist, read out the indictment. Mindszenty had met in the United States with Zita, the widow of the Emperor Charles, the last reigning Hapsburg, and with their son, Otto von Hapsburg, to plot the return of royal rule. He had asked United States officials, including successive American ministers to Hungary, to use force to expel the Communists. He had appealed directly to President Truman for assistance.

The court asked: "Do you plead guilty?"

"I feel guilty," Mindszenty said. "What I have done, I do not wish to place in a favorable light. This does not mean that I accept the conclusions of the indictment. I do not subscribe to the conclusion that I have been planning the overthrow of the democratic republic, even less, as the indictment states, that I might have played the leading role."

All the same, the cardinal admitted that he had agreed, should something happen to overthrow the Communists—such as an American offensive through Hungary or the outbreak of a third world war—to serve as head of a provisional government, pending the coronation of Otto von Hapsburg. And he acknowledged his contacts with the Americans.

"Every state, every people, may shape its life and the form of its government according to its desires and needs," the prosecutor, a functionary named Julius Alapi, admonished.

"That is so," Mindszenty answered. "Unfortunately, I overlooked these principles, and that is why I asked for this intervention."

In December 1946, in response to a plea from Mindszenty, the U.S. minister in Budapest had written to say it was against his government's policy to interfere in the internal affairs of independent countries. After reading aloud the envoy's reply, the prosecutor asked: "Wasn't it unpleasant for you that the American minister gave you such a lesson?"

"It was," the cardinal admitted.

"Now, you were thinking of a third world war," Alapi went on. "That they would establish a system of government here which would suit you, instead of concentrating all your strength here and abroad to prevent the outbreak of such a third world war."

"I beg your pardon," Mindszenty interjected excitedly. "I was not working for a third world war."

Testimony continued until nearly midnight and resumed the next day, and then the next. The cases of several codefendants, among them Mindszenty's secretary, were presented. The court heard the summations at the end of the third day.

On September 30, 1971, after nearly 23 years of confinement, Cardinal Mindszenty (left) joins Pope Paul and the presidents of the third synod of bishops for mass in the Sistine Chapel. (Hulton-Deutsch Collection)

"Is there anyone who, seeing the defendants, would dare maintain that they were intimidated, harassed or influenced in any way?" Alapi asked. He rejected any suggestion that the defense of religion had been the cardinal's motivation: "There is no need for defending religion in the Hungarian people's democracy for the simple reason that nobody wants to harm it."

Mindszenty's counsel, Koloman Kiczkó, conceded the evidence had been irrefutable; besides, his client had confessed. "My defendant, in his dignity as a primate, lived, one might say, in an ivory tower and he was not aware of the inevitable path of history," Kiczkó offered lamely. And he went on to plead for "an adequately lenient judgment."

As for Mindszenty, prison, interrogation, and torture had made him docile. "I never meant to violate the laws of the country," he told the court. "If, for reasons of environment or for reasons beyond me, this occurred on one or two occasions, I confess to it here without embellishing the facts. I regretted and I still regret it, and I think that I might take a different stand in certain matters if I were again in a similar situation."

The court reconvened on Tuesday, February 8, for the reading of the sentences—penal servitude for life for Cardinal Mindszenty.

Cold War Cause Célèbre

The arrest, show trial, and imprisonment of the prince primate became a Cold War cause célèbre in the West, cited as reason for the delay of Hungary's admission to the United Nations. During the anti-Communist uprising in October 1956, insurgent soldiers freed Mindszenty; a squadron of tanks escorted him to his residence in Budapest. Thereupon, the tottering Communist government declared he had been unjustly prosecuted and belatedly ordered his release.

During the first days of November 1956, Soviet forces moved into position to crush the insurgency. On November 3, Mindszenty went on the radio to plead for independence from the Soviets, asking that Hungary be allowed to live in peace in the shadow of "the Russian Empire." He called, too, for fair elections, the restoration of private property, and an end to Communist oppression of the Catholic Church.

At daybreak on November 4, Soviet tanks rolled into Budapest. Within a few days, all resistance had been crushed. Mindszenty disappeared into the U.S. Legation in the Hungarian capital. There he remained for 15 years, a martyr and potent symbol of the irreconcilable differences between communism and Catholicism. Several times the embarrassed Hungarian regime offered Mindszenty safe passage out of the country, but he refused, in part out of fear of treachery but, perhaps more important, because he believed his presence in Budapest gave hope to Catholic anti-Communists. Finally, in September 1971, Pope Paul VI persuaded Mindszenty to come to Rome in an attempt to improve Church-state relations in Hungary. Mindszenty died in 1995 in Vienna.

—Michael Golay

Suggestions for Further Reading

Lomax, Bill. *Hungary 1956*. New York: St. Martin's Press, 1976.

Mindszenty, József Cardinal. *Memoirs*. New York: Macmillan Publishing Co., 1974.

Swift, Stephen K. *The Cardinal's Story: The Life and Work of Joseph Cardinal Mindszenty*. New York: The Macmillan Co., 1949.

Jomo Kenyatta Trial: 1952–53

Defendants: Jomo Kenyatta, Fred Kubai, Richard Achieng Oneko, Bildad Kaggia, Paul Ngei, Kungu Karumba, all executives of the Kenya African Union
Charges: Membership in the Mau Mau, managing that "unlawful society" declared "dangerous to the good government of the Colony"
Chief Defense Lawyers: D. N. Pritt, A. R. Kapila, Chaman Lall, D. W. Thompson, H. O. Davis, Peter Evans, Fitzwell de Souza, and Jaswart Singh
Chief Prosecutor: Anthony Somerhough   **Judge:** Ransley S. Thacker
Place: Kapenguria, Kenya   **Dates of Trial:** November 24, 1952–April 8, 1953   **Verdict:** Guilty   **Sentence:** All defendants—seven years' hard labor for managing the Mau Mau, three years' hard labor for membership in the Mau Mau, the sentences to run concurrently; Kenyatta also given "indefinite restriction" in a remote village

SIGNIFICANCE

Under pressure from European settlers terrorized by Mau Mau killings, the colonial Kenya government arrested, convicted, and imprisoned legitimate African nationalist leaders, including Kenyatta, by means of a rigged trial. This tactic backfired—just over a decade later Kenya became independent, with Kenyatta as its first African president. Many historians believe the trial may well have hastened the arrival of independence.

As with many political trials, the verdict in this case was determined well before the trial ever started. Although the British judicial system possessed a reputation for fairness, the colonial courts were apt to stray from the ideal when attempting to thwart independence.

The trial was immediately preceded on October 20, 1952, by a declaration of a state of emergency (equivalent to martial law) by the Kenya government in response to the armed resistance and brutal slayings of colonists and Africans by Mau Mau guerrillas. The Mau Mau's stated goal was to drive all whites, some 35,000 in number, from Kenya. During the night of October 20, police and army units rounded up hundreds of suspects, including Kenyatta, a prominent nationalist and leader of the Kenya African Union, which counted some 100,000 dues-paying members.

Kamau Kenyatta was born in the 1890s to Kikuyu parents in a tribal homestead. The young boy was educated by Scottish missionaries. After he went to London in 1929 to lobby for Kikuyu land rights and to study, he changed his name to Jomo ("Burning Spear") Kenyatta. His classic anthropological study of Kikuyu society, *Facing Mount Kenya*, written under the tutelage of Bronislaw Malinowski, earned him an advanced degree from the London School of Economics. During the same period, he helped organize the Pan-African Federation. While abroad, his ventures included marriage to an Englishwoman (the second of his four wives), work as an extra on the film *Sanders of the River*, friendship with Paul Robeson, and study in Moscow.

In 1946, Kenyatta returned to Kenya, where he developed a Kikuyu cultural association into a national political party, the Kenya African Union (KAU), while working as the principal of a teachers college, where he prepared instructors for independent African schools. For these activities, Kenyatta became a prominent target for Kenya's colonial government.

The round-up of suspects at Thompson Falls, during the Mau-Mau revolt, in Kenya (1953). (Hulton-Deutsch Collection)

The Trial

After their arrests, Kenyatta and his codefendants—Fred Kubai, Richard Achieng Oneko, Bildad Kaggia, Paul Ngei, and Kungu Karumba—initially were denied access to legal counsel and were deported on November 18 to the remote settlement of Kapenguria in the scorching heat of the Rift Valley. There, Kenyatta and the others were "released" and then immediately rearrested. This was a ploy to create jurisdiction to hold the trial in Kapenguria, a "restricted area" that no one could enter without a permit. The government hoped the venue would enable it to avoid publicity, prevent Kenyatta's supporters from attending the trial, and appoint a handpicked judge, as the region had none.

Kenyatta was able to get out a message requesting defense lawyers to represent him and the others. Money was raised, and an impressive multiracial and multinational team was assembled. A large number of lawyers was necessary, not only to conduct the defense in court but also to search out witnesses across Kenya, interview them, protect them from police interference, bring them to Kapenguria to give evidence, and procure the necessary travel permits. Because government agents might intercept and read defense letters and telegrams or eavesdrop on telephone calls, members of the defense team drove long distances over hazardous roads to attend secret meetings or hand-deliver sensitive documents.

When D. N. Pritt, a former socialist member of the British Parliament, agreed to become part of the defense team, Kenyatta obtained the services of one of the most accomplished advocates at the English bar. Experienced in political persecution trials, Pritt had defended anticolonial leaders from Africa to India and the Far East. Perhaps even more valuable than Pritt's legal skill was his ability to attract publicity for his clients.

To try the case without assessors (a jury), the government appointed as resident magistrate Ransley Thacker, a retired judge of the Kenya Supreme Court well known as a strong supporter of the colonialist point of view. Taking charge of the case on November 24, Thacker refused a defense request to order Deputy Public Prosecutor Anthony Somerhough, previously a judge advocate at the Nuremberg trials, to release particulars of the charges, which had been stated in such vague terms that it was nearly impossible to develop a defense to refute them. Thacker adjourned the trial until December 3, when Pritt would be ready to lead the defense.

An initial defense motion to transfer the trial to another court and another magistrate was rejected by the Kenya Supreme Court on December 1. Pritt repeated the arguments of this motion in a telegram to British members of Parliament who had requested information from him about the trial facilities in Kapenguria's agricultural school, which was surrounded by barbed wire and guarded by armored cars on the ground and helicopters overhead. Pritt's telegram read in part:

> Am protesting continuously firstly against inconveniences hearing in remote region where must send 280 miles to Nairobi to look up authorities on the frequently arising points [of] law or to get documents or witnesses and there are no facilities for research or study nearer than Nairobi and no means even of eating nearer than Kitale 24 miles secondly against trial in closed district virtually constituting exclusion public from court thirdly against inexcusable exclusion some counsel from colony and others from district of trial although accused have asked for them stop All this makes proper preparation defense case almost impossible greatly increases expense and wastes time stop Amounts in all to denial [of] justice. . . .

Parts of the telegram were reprinted in English and African newspapers, causing a sensation and resulting in an adjournment of the trial to serve a motion of contempt of court on Pritt. On December 31, the Kenya Supreme Court dismissed the charge against Pritt, and the trial continued on January 2.

Problems with translation led to further adjournments. The trial had opened with Dr. Louis Leakey as interpreter. Leakey who would later become a world-famous anthropologist but then was curator of Nairobi's natural history museum. The defendants had objected to Leakey all along, and Pritt finally complained to the magistrate, "Here we have an interpreter who is biased and has written a book against my clients. . . . He puts things in and he puts things out. He is a partial interpreter." Offended, Leakey walked out when the trial reopened on January 2. Further delays were caused by an attempt to find an acceptable replacement translator.

The prosecution case was a weak one. On the night of Kenyatta's arrest, the police had carried away a ton and a half of papers, documents, and books from his house. These they proceeded to examine but were unable to find anything connecting Kenyatta to the Mau Mau. Prosecutor Somerhough tacitly admitted this in his December 3 opening statement:

> The Crown cannot bind themselves to any particular place in the colony where this society was managed. The Society is Mau Mau. It is a Society which has no records. It appears to have no official list of members. . . . Some details of its meetings and its rites, the instruments of which are got from the local bush, will be heard later in the proceedings. Arches of banana leaves, the African fruit known as the Apple of Sodom, eyes of sheep, blood and earth—these are all gathered together when ceremonies take place.

The prosecution thus was forced to base its case on the testimony of African witnesses, who in return were promised substantial payments for protection and relocation. Somerhough led off with Rawson Macharia, his most important and best-educated witness. During the Mau Mau initiation ceremony Macharia reported that Kenyatta had said:

> If you see any African killing anyone, you must not disclose it. . . If you shall see an African stealing you must help him. You must pay sixty-two shillings and fifty cents to this society. . . . And that is Mau Mau, and you must not ask how this money is used, and if you shall be asked whether you are a member of this society you must say your are a member of KAU.

In response to these words during the ceremony, Macharia said he had to pass through the arch and eat some meat. Then he had to swear seven times and to repeat Kenyatta's words.

That Macharia's story was refuted by nine defense witnesses and by Kenyatta himself had little effect on the judge, who summed up, "Although my finding of fact means that I disbelieve ten witnesses for the defense and believe one for the prosecution, I have no hesitation in doing so. Rawson Macharia gave his evidence well."

Accounts by other witnesses connecting Kenyatta to the Mau Mau were even more inconsistent and confused. The seven-day cross-examination of Kenyatta provided the prosecution with its best case as it made Kenyatta seem evasive by a series of badgering questions. Despite defense protests, the judge allowed numerous questions that should have been inadmissible under Kenya and English law. The judge also accepted the prosecution view that Kenyatta had failed to denounce the Mau Mau at public KAU meetings, although the defense provided newspaper evidence to the contrary. When the defense tried to subpoena government tape recordings to prove its point, the judge ruled such evidence inadmissible.

In his summation, Pritt stated that this was "the most childishly weak case ever brought against any man in the history of the British Empire." The judge, however, found the defendants guilty, imposed maximum sentences, and was flown out of Kenya immediately afterward. The appeals process took more than a year. The initial appeal cited lack of jurisdiction, inadmissible evidence, and bias of the judge in accepting all prosecution submissions while rejecting nearly all defense submissions, and in believing all prosecution witnesses while disbelieving nearly all defense witnesses. The Kenya Supreme Court found for the defense on a technicality in the matter of jurisdiction—the government had mistakenly appointed the judge to Northern Province rather than to Rift Valley Province—and ordered a retrial. When the East African Court of Appeal reversed this decision, the defense moved on to the highest forum, the English Privy Council sitting in London, which refused to hear the case. Pritt commented, "I fear that I was wrong in thinking that when it came to politics the Privy Council would behave any better than anyone else!"

The Aftermath

The defendants served the first part of their sentences at Lokitaung, a northern frontier desert station, doing hard labor: They were made to break rocks and dig holes and refill them. Because of his age, Kenyatta was assigned the duties of cook.

In late 1958, chief prosecution witness Rawson Macharia admitted his perjury in the Kenyatta trial, saying government agents had bribed and coached him and other witnesses. He was charged with swearing a false affidavit in 1958, rather than for perjury in 1952. In this, often called the second Kenyatta trial, Macharia was defended by Pritt, who had the pleasure of grilling prosecutor Somerhough on the witness stand. Although Macharia was found guilty, Pritt said the case had "done infinite political good, both directly and indirectly."

Kenyatta served out his sentence plus two years in a remote village. Later, as president, he would demonstrate the statesmanlike qualities suggested by his trial testimony. When questioned about the aims of the Kenya African Union, he had replied:

> We do not believe in violence at all: We believe in negotiation, that is, we ask for our rights through constitutional means—through discussion and representation. We feel that the racial barrier is one of the most diabolical things that we have in this Colony, because we see no reason why all races in this country cannot work harmoniously together without any discrimina-

tion. . . . And we believe that if people of goodwill can work together they can eliminate that evil.

—Eva Weber

Suggestions for Further Reading

Howarth, Anthony. *Kenyatta, A Photographic Biography.* Nairobi: East African Publishing House, 1967.

Iguh, Thomas. *The Struggles and Trial of Jomo Kenyatta.* Omitsha, Nigeria: Appolos Brothers, c. 1959.

Kenyatta, Jomo. *Facing Mount Kenya, the Tribal Life of the Gikuyu.* London: Secker & Warburg, 1938, 1956.

———. *Suffering Without Bitterness, the Founding of the Kenya Nation.* Nairobi: East African Publishing House, 1968.

Lynch, Hollis, ed. *Black Africa: The Great Contemporary Issues.* Compiled from *New York Times* articles, 1929–73. New York: Arno Press, 1973.

Macharia, Rawson. *The Truth About the Trial of Jomo Kenyatta.* Nairobi: Longman Kenya, 1991.

Murray-Brown, Jeremy. *Kenyatta.* London, Boston: Allen & Unwin, 1979.

Pritt, D. N. "The Defense Accuses." Part 3 of *The Autobiography of D. N. Pritt..* London: Lawrence & Wishart, 1966.

Slater, Montagu. *The Trial of Jomo Kenyatta.* London: Mercury Books, 1956, 1965.

Fidel Castro Trial: 1953

Defendants: Fidel Castro, approximately 120 rebels and opposition leaders
Crime Charged: Attempt to overthrow the government
Chief Defense Lawyers: Twenty-two lawyers, Fidel Castro
Chief Prosecutor: Francisco Mendieta Hechavarria
Judges: Chief Judge Adolfo Nieto Pineito-Osorio, Juan Francisco Mejias
Valdivieso, Ricardo Diaz Olivera **Place:** Santiago de Cuba, Cuba
Dates of Trial: September 21–October 5, 1953; October 16, 1953
Verdicts: Castro and all rebels found guilty; opposition leaders acquitted
Sentences: Seven months to 13 years in prison

SIGNIFICANCE

Fidel Castro was known in only limited political circles in Cuba when Fulgencio Batista seized control of Cuba in March 1952. It was not until the attack on the Moncada army barracks and, more important, the trial following, that Castro gained national recognition as a leader in the movement to unseat the Batista dictatorship. Castro's willingness to accept the charges and then use the trial as a pulpit from which to denounce the abuses of the Batista government earned him the respect of the many Cubans dissatisfied with Batista. Without the limelight placed on him during the Moncada trial, Castro might never have emerged as the revolution's leader.

In March 1952, Fulgencio Batista aborted Cuba's elections and seized control of the government in a military coup. The establishment of the Batista dictatorship in Cuba came at the precise moment that a young lawyer and radical activist, Fidel Castro, entered the political arena as a congressional candidate. Only 25 years old in 1952, Castro had already devoted several years to political activism, struggling against government corruption as a student, lawyer, and colleague of a prominent opposition party politician. The success of Batista's coup led Castro to believe that Cuba's only chance of liberation from the corruption of its government and military was an armed insurrection.

Attack on Moncada

With the elections canceled, Castro and a small group of revolutionaries began to prepare for the overthrow of the Batista regime, training for combat at the University of Havana and in the neighborhoods of the movement's disciples. Fidel quickly emerged as one of the movement's leaders, the most charismatic and forceful personality among them. Then, in early 1953, Castro developed a plan to seize the Moncada army barracks in Santiago de Cuba, hoping to take possession of the weapons stored there and thus arm his movement and give it a stronghold from which to rally all those opposed to the Batista regime. Castro also knew that there were at least two other revolutionary groups discussing the possibility of an armed uprising. Castro may have rushed his attack on Moncada in order to be the first and thus the principal leader of a revolution.

On July 26, 1953, Castro led approximately 125 young rebels (including two women) in an attack on the Moncada barracks and two other nearby buildings, the Palace of Justice and the Civil Hospital. (Another 22 rebels launched a simultaneous attack on the army barracks at Bayamo in Oriente province.) His plan called for a surprise attack on the barracks in the early morning aftermath of carnival festivities in Santiago. Several accidents (including a flat tire), poor timing, and Castro's underestimation of the difficulties of entering the Moncada fort all contributed to the lack of surprise and the total failure of the attack. After barely an hour of fighting at the main fort—during which Castro displayed amazing courage—Castro and his force had to flee (although some of his people held on for a while at the other two buildings). The exact number of casualties in the actual firefight has never been established, but numbers ranged from 2 to 8 of Castro's rebels and 19 to 22 soldiers. (In an equally disastrous failure at Bayamo, 6 to 12 of the rebels were killed.)

Immediately following the attack, dozens of captured rebels were brutally tortured and killed by the army; during the next four days, many other rebels and opposition leaders were killed wherever they were found by the army and police. Castro and a handful of rebels were able to escape into the mountains of Oriente province. On August 1, Castro and the rebels who remained with him were captured and taken to the city jail in Santiago to join their surviving comrades.

The First Phase of the Trial

The trial began on September 21, 1953, before the Urgency Court of Santiago de Cuba in the Palace of Justice. The case was heard by the three-judge Provisional Tribunal of Santiago, whose verdict could not be appealed. The chief judge was Adolfo Nieto Pineito-Osorio, and the prosecutor was Francisco Mendieta Hechavarria. Fidel Castro was charged along with more than 100 other defendants; they were represented by 22 lawyers. Many of the defendants were political leaders—Communists and others—who had been arrested after the attack and had little or no connection to Castro's movement. Batista could not believe that the attack on Moncada did not have sponsorship from more prominent opposition parties in Cuba, including supporters of the ousted former president Carlos Pria.

All the defendants were charged under Article 148 of the Social Defense Code, which allowed for a prison sentence of between 5 and 20 years for any "leader of an attempt at organizing an uprising of armed persons against Constitutional Powers of the State." Castro's strategy was to identify the true leaders of the movement, who he felt could not avoid conviction and sentencing, and ask them to confess. The remaining defendants, he believed, should plead innocent because it would be difficult to prove them leaders under Article 148.

From the first day of the trial, Castro made a strong impression on the court. Even before taking his seat in the courtroom, he held up his manacled hands and shouted, "Mr. President . . . I want to call your attention to this incredible fact. . . . Not even the worst criminals are held this way in a hall that calls itself a hall of justice." The handcuffs were immediately removed from all the prisoners.

Castro admitted his role in the attack from the outset and treated the courtroom as an audience for his version of history. Asked about his fellow defendants, he declared, "These young people, like me, love the freedom of their country." He argued against the government's charge that the attack was connected with former president Pria, asserting that "the only intellectual author of the attack on the Moncada is Jose Marti, the apostle of our independence." By the end of the first day in court, Castro had requested and received permission to serve as his own lawyer. Throughout the trial he would don the robe of a Cuban lawyer whenever he was acting in that capacity. (Castro has always appreciated the value of a bit of theater in making a revolution.)

Castro used his role as lawyer in the courtroom to charge the Batista regime with gross injustice, cruelty, and criminal disregard for the national constitution. By cross-examining the prosecutor's witnesses, Castro was able to elicit gruesome testimony on the atrocities committed against the rebels following the attack. With the aid of journalists, particularly Marta Rojas from the magazine *Bohemia*, Castro's version of events and his indictment of the Batista regime was widely reported in Cuba.

On September 26, the trial's third session, Castro was not present in court. A report from Colonel Chaviano, commander of the Moncada unit, stated that Castro was ill. In reality, Castro had suspected that a plan to assassinate him was afoot and on the previous evening had slipped a note to one of his codefendants, Melba Hernandez. She now produced this note, from out of her hair, in which Castro stated he was in perfect health. The three judges—who were proving to be independent of and even unsympathetic to Batista—were soon satisfied that Fidel was not suffering from any illness, but pressure from the military forced them to continue the trial without Castro's presence. It was clear that Castro's popularity in the courtroom and his indictments of Batista had finally become threatening to Batista.

By October 5, on the 10th session of the trial, only the 29 actual participants of the Moncada and Bayamo attacks were found guilty and sentenced, receiving a range of sentences from 7 months to 13 years. The remaining defendants were acquitted.

The Second Phase

Eleven days later, on October 16, 1953, the trial of Castro was reconvened (along with that of a rebel who had been seriously injured in the attack and thus unable to attend the first stage). This time the trial was held in the nurses' lounge of the Santiago Civil Hospital, in an attempt to isolate the proceedings from the public. Marta Rojas from *Bohemia*, however, managed to be present.

In a speech now known as "History Will Absolve Me" (from his closing phrase), Castro spoke for two hours in his own defense. He said little about the attack on Moncada but spoke eloquently about the injustice and suffering endured by Cubans, and, in classic Castro form, he argued for the necessity of revolutionary change. Marta Rojas later reported: "There was something very unusual in 'History Will Absolve Me.' I was simply carried by his words. . . . It was the first time I was listening to such things. I had heard nothing similar to that before. The same was true with the guards. I was watching the guards standing with their weapons loose . . . listening, carried away by Fidel. . . . They were simply absorbed and engrossed by his words. When Fidel was through with his speech, there was silence, and he had to slap on the table and say something like, 'Well, I finished. This is all.'"

Castro's speech astounded everyone in the room. He was very quickly declared guilty, however, and sentenced to 13 years in prison. On his way out of the courtroom, Castro confirmed that Marta Rojas had taken notes on his famous speech, although it was his own reconstruction from memory that would become the manifesto for the Cuban revolution.

Aftermath

Castro and his comrades were imprisoned at the Presidio Modelo on the Isle of Pines, some 60 miles off the southwest coast of Cuba. There, Fidel enjoyed relative freedom and began schooling his young fellow revolutionaries in history, political theory, literature, mathematics, and geography. Fidel also used prison as a place to further educate himself: in letters he wrote from the Presido Modelo, he described reading lists that included everything from Shakespeare, Victor Hugo, and Karl Marx to William Thackeray and A. J. Cronin.

On February 12, 1954, Batista made a visit to the prison. After organizing a protest among the prisoners against this visit, Castro and several others were placed in solitary confinement. Castro's cell in solitary was in a building for the mentally ill, and today in the Museo de la Revolución in Havana, there are photos and a replica of this cell. Even in solitary, Castro managed to order the distribution of 10,000 copies of his speech "History Will Absolve Me" all over Cuba.

In 1954, Batista called for national elections; the elections were rigged, however, and in the end Batista's only challenger withdrew. Elated by his reinauguration in February 1955, and in an attempt to gain some legitimacy for his regime, Batista was persuaded to release all political prisoners. On May 7, 1955, Batista granted amnesty to all political prisoners, and Castro and his followers were set free on May 15, 1955. On July 7, 1955, fearing for his life, Castro flew to Mexico, where in exile he began planning for the revolution that would climax with his triumphant return to Havana in January 1959.

—*Michela Bowman*

Suggestions for Further Reading

Bourne, Peter G. *Fidel: A Biography of Fidel Castro.* New York: Dodd, Mead, 1986.

Castro, Fidel. *History Will Absolve Me.* English translation unattributed. Secaucus, N.J.: Lyle Stuart, 1961.

McManus, Jane, ed. *From the Palm Tree: Voices of the Cuban Revolution.* Secaucus, N.J.: Lyle Stuart, 1973.

Mencia, Mario. *El Grito del Moncada.* Havana: Editora Politica, 1985.

———. *Time Was on Our Side.* Havana: Editora Politica, 1982.

Merle, Robert. *Moncada: Premier Combat de Fidel Castro.* Paris: Robert Laffont, 1965.

Szalc, Tad. *Fidel: A Critical Portrait.* New York: William Morrow, 1986.

Taber, Robert. *M-26-7: Biography of a Revolution.* Secaucus, N.J.: Lyle Stuart, 1961.

Milovan Djilas Trial: 1956

Defendant: Milovan Djilas   **Crime Charged:** Slandering Yugoslavia
Chief Defense Lawyers: Veljko Kovacevic   **Chief Prosecutor:** Aleksandar
Atanackovic   **Judges:** Five-judge panel presided over by Vojislav Jankovic
Place: Belgrade, Yugoslavia   **Date of Trial:** December 12, 1956 (first trial);
May 14, 1962 (second trial)   **Verdict:** Guilty   **Sentence:** Three years'
imprisonment plus one year from a formerly suspended sentence (first trial);
five years' imprisonment (second trial)

SIGNIFICANCE

Milovan Djilas's 1956 slander trial resulted in the first of his imprisonments by
Yugoslavia's Communist government, in which he had once played a major role.

When Milovan Djilas was imprisoned in 1933 to serve three years for political activities prohibited by the royal Yugoslav government, the young law student was a committed Communist. He never anticipated becoming the leading voice of dissent against a Yugoslav Communist regime he helped to create.

Djilas rose quickly in the banned party after his release from prison. In 1937, he met Josip Broz, better known by his underground name, Tito. After Tito assumed control of the Yugoslav Communist Party two years later, Djilas became a member of the Politburo, the illegal party's highest council.

The Communist struggle against Yugoslavia's royalty was eclipsed in 1941, when Hitler's invading armies defeated the royal forces and plunged the country into a nightmare of guerrilla warfare and savage retribution. Yugoslav Communism assumed a strongly nationalist aspect during four years of struggle against the occupying Nazis and their collaborators. When the war ended in 1945, Tito wasted no time in consolidating his power and transforming Yugoslavia into an autonomous Communist state. By not aligning Yugoslavia's economy more closely with that of the Soviet Union and its satellite countries, Tito angered Soviet dictator Joseph Stalin. Yugoslavia and the Soviet Union severed relations in 1948.

Djilas had proved himself an able leader in the partisan resistance army and was one of Tito's closest aides in the postwar years, serving as vice president of Yugoslavia. Over the next two decades, however, Djilas began a slow philosophic evolution toward humanism, which took him steadily further from his earlier Marxist beliefs.

Djilas Challenges Party Elite

In late 1953, Djilas wrote a series of articles for the Sunday edition of the official Communist Party newspaper. He objected to the antidemocratic tightening of party discipline. He also criticized the party leadership for acting like a privileged elite class. Djilas believed that his critiques had Tito's support, but the party hierarchy Djilas criticized was outraged. In January 1954, Djilas was expelled from the Yugoslav Communist Party for calling for democratic reforms.

In December 1954, an interview in which Djilas appealed for a two-party system in Yugoslavia appeared in the *New York Times*. Djilas was arrested for this "hostile propaganda." Tito's official biographer, Vladimir Dedijer, spoke in Djilas's defense and was also arrested for confirming to the Western press that he had been questioned about Djilas's case. Both were charged under Article 118 of Yugoslavia's criminal code, a broad statute under which antigovernment sentiments or actions could result in indictment. After a secret trial from which all foreign reporters were barred, Djilas and Dedijer received suspended sentences of 18 months and 6 months, respectively.

Djilas was politically ostracized, but he continued to write. His continuing troubles did not result solely from the antagonism of Yugoslavia's Communist ruling class. Relations with the Soviet leadership had begun to improve after Stalin's death in 1953. This fact directly affected Djilas's future collisions with Article 118.

Jail Sentence Follows Secret Trial

When the Soviets crushed the Hungarian uprising in November 1956, Djilas criticized Yugoslavia's abstention from United Nations Security Council debate on the issue. He saw Tito's tacit support of the Soviet invasion as a retreat from Yugoslavia's previous policy of nonalignment.

Alluding to the Soviet Union, Djilas wrote:

The Yugoslav people cannot remain indifferent to intervention in the affairs of a neighboring country by the same imperialist power that recently openly threatened and still secretly threatens Yugoslavia's independence.

Djilas's statement was printed in France, but not in Yugoslavia. The interview, along with a Djilas article published by an American anti-Communist magazine, convinced the Yugoslav government of his "criminal intent." He was arrested on November 19, 1956, and charged under Article 118 for "slandering Yugoslavia by twisting facts with the intention of harming this country, of misleading public opinion about Yugoslav policy, and of seeking to provoke interference by foreign powers in Yugoslav affairs."

Seeking to keep the proceedings secret, prosecutor Aleksandar Atanackovic motioned that the trial be closed on grounds that Yugoslavia's foreign policy might be harmed by courtroom testimony. Djilas and his attorney, Veljko Kovacevic, with whom he had shared a prison cell 22 years earlier, protested. Djilas said his statements were the opinions of a private citizen, but the court ruled in favor of the prosecution argument that state secrets might be exposed during testimony.

The December 12, 1956, trial lasted for 12 hours. Five judges hearing the case convicted Djilas after less than 10 minutes of deliberation. He was sentenced to three years' imprisonment—two years for the slander charge, plus one year added from his suspended 1955 sentence.

While he was serving his sentence, Western publishers received manuscripts of three new Djilas books. Among them was *The New Class*, a critique accusing Communist leaders of becoming a privileged elite whose hunger for power made them resemble the bourgeoisie they had replaced. The book was banned in Yugoslavia, but publication of *The New Class* in the United States resulted in a new Article 118 indictment against the imprisoned Djilas. He was tried in a local courthouse near the Sremska Mitrovica prison on October 4, 1957.

As soon as the indictment was read aloud, the international press was ordered to leave the courtroom. Djilas protested the trial's secrecy by refusing to answer any questions from the prosecutor or the judge. After one day of testimony, seven years were added to Djilas's sentence and he was returned to prison. He continued to protest by refusing to appeal.

Djilas was paroled in January 1961. The prolific writer quickly finished three more books, including *Conversations With Stalin*. As Tito's deputy, Djilas had met the Soviet dictator in four important meetings, including the fateful 1948 conference preceding the severance of Soviet-Yugoslav relations. Djilas's unflattering memoir of the Soviet leadership—with which Tito was now on friendly terms—was scheduled for publication in the West in the spring of 1962.

Jailed Again for Revelations on Talks with Stalin

Djilas was arrested on April 7, 1962, just weeks after a new statute was added to Yugoslavia's laws. Article 320 forbade government officials from making available to unauthorized persons any confidential information obtained while serving in an official capacity. When Djilas was brought to trial on May 14, he was accused of revealing information he had learned during the diplomatic missions described in *Conversations With Stalin*. Djilas replied that everything in the book had been previously published without official reaction. The court, however, accepted the prosecution's argument that the book contained confidential information.

The prosecution again asked that the trial be held in secret. This time, Djilas angrily demanded a public trial and refused to hire an attorney. After six and a half hours of secret testimony, Djilas was convicted and sentenced to five years' imprisonment. The three years and eight months remaining on his previous sentence at the time of his 1961 parole were added to the term. Djilas later reflected that this imprisonment was a diplomatic sop designed to improve

Yugoslavia's relations with the Soviet Union and meant as a warning to socialist reform movements throughout Eastern Europe.

After Djilas was released in 1966, he continued to write of his life and his relationship with Tito, who died in 1980. Djilas's writings also detailed his philosophical evolution from a committed Marxist to a defender of the freedom of individual thought. He died in Belgrade on April 20, 1995.

—Tom Smith

Suggestions for Further Reading

Abel, Elie. "A Defiant Djilas Is Tried In Secret." *The New York Times*, October 5, 1957.

Djilas, Milovan. *Tito: The Story from Inside*. New York: Harcourt Brace Jovanovich, 1980.

———. *Of Prisons And Ideas*. New York: Harcourt Brace Jovanovich, 1986.

Underwood, Paul. "Djilas Is Convicted Over Book. *The New York Times*, May 15, 1962.

Cuban Revolutionary Tribunals: 1959

Defendants: Jesús Sosa Blanco, Ricardo Luis Grau, Pedro Morejon (first trial); 44 members of Cuban air force (second trial)
Crimes Charged: Murder, arson, looting, theft (first trial); genocide (second trial) **Chief Defense Lawyer:** Aristedes de Acosta (both trials), accompanied in second trial by five additional attorneys **Chief Prosecutors:** Jorge Zerquera, Mario Colon Davila (first trial); Antonio Cejas, Augusto Martínez Sánchez (second trial) **Judges:** Humberto Sorí Morín, Universo Sánchez, Raúl Chibás (first trial); Presiding judge Félix Lugerio Peña, replaced by Manuel Piñeiro Losada (second trial) **Places:** Havana, Cuba (first trial); Santiago de Cuba, Cuba (second trial) **Dates of Trials:** January 22, 1959, retrial on February 16, 1959 (first trial); February 14–March 2, 1959 (second trial) **Verdicts:** Guilty (first trial); not guilty (second trial) **Sentences:** Death (first trial); none, although lengthy prison sentences resulted from subsequent retrials (second trial)

SIGNIFICANCE

The controversial methods of Fidel Castro's 26th of July Movement war crime tribunals replaced Cuba's traditional legal system and shook the faith of many of his foreign supporters, who had believed he was a liberal reformer.

After dictator Fulgencio Batista fled Cuba on January 1, 1959, the world waited to see if rebel leader Fidel Castro could maintain law and order while trying to organize a new government. Observers also wondered how Castro's guerrillas would treat the forces they had vanquished in their hard-won revolution.

Most of Batista's armed forces returned home unmolested when the fighting ended, but many informers, police officers, and soldiers accused of atrocities were arrested by the new regime. Before Castro's uprising, the death penalty had been abolished by Cuban civil courts. Yet justice was now administered by temporary "revolutionary courts," operating under the Code of the Sierra Maestra. This criminal code, formulated by Castro's 26th of July Movement during the revolution, decreed that torture, murder, extortion, treason, espionage, rape, and other serious offenses were capital crimes. The death penalty was reinstated for anyone convicted of crimes listed in the Sierra Maestra directive.

Nature of "Revolutionary Justice"

Castro's critics in the United States, already suspicious of his postponement of free elections, viewed the substitution of revolutionary tribunals for civil courts as proof that the new government was reneging on promises to reform Cuba's system of justice. Americans, comfortable with the legal mandate of "innocent until proven guilty," were appalled by the summary nature of the trials, unaware that Cuban justice was based on the Napoleonic Code, under which defendants face the burden of proving their innocence. As the number of executions climbed toward 300 and Judge Advocate Dr. Humberto Sorí Morín announced that 1,000 more "war criminals" would be prosecuted under the Code of the Sierra Maestra, scrutiny and criticism of the summary nature of "revolutionary justice" intensified.

Castro responded with a mass demonstration in Havana. Addressing hundreds of thousands of Cubans, Castro wondered aloud how the United States could criticize death sentences handed down by revolutionary courts, since the Americans had never criticized atrocities committed by U.S.-supported dictators in Nicaragua, the Dominican Republic, and Cuba. Castro asked the crowd if it wanted war criminals prosecuted. The answer was a long, enthusiastic ovation.

The provisional Cuban government was nevertheless eager to win international support and convince the world of the justice of verdicts rendered by revolutionary courts. Castro announced that a public trial of three accused war criminals would be held in Havana's huge sports stadium. Three prominent revolutionary officers would act as both judges and jury. Four hundred Cuban and international journalists were guaranteed seats to cover the trial. The new government intended the trial to be a worldwide public relations coup called Operation Truth.

Operation Truth's Show Trial

When the trial began on January 22, 1959, it immediately turned into a chaotic spectacle, as 18,000 Cubans filled the stands.

The first defendant was Major Jesús Sosa Blanco, an army officer accused of committing 108 crimes, including murder and arson, in rural Oriente province. The first witness was a young woman who accused Sosa Blanco of killing all nine members of one family. The elderly widow of a peasant swore that Sosa Blanco had shot her husband despite her pleas. One man said that he had watched Sosa Blanco shoot 19 people. Another said he had seen him give the command to burn 200 houses. Other witnesses stumbled in their testimonies, leading to suspicions that they had been crudely coached by the prosecution.

Sosa Blanco maintained that if he had killed anyone or burned any homes, he had done so only in the commission of his wartime duty.

"Assassin!" roared the crowd. "Thug!"

"This is not a traffic offense," protested Lieutenant Aristedes de Acosta, the appointed defense attorney. He was answered with jeers from the crowd and threats from the prosecution.

Judge Humberto Sorí Morín repeatedly ordered the spectators to be quiet, without much success.

"This reminds me of the Coliseum in Rome," scoffed Sosa Blanco. "This is not a court of justice, it is a court of murder. You will one day be judged as you are judging me now."

A group of rebel soldiers soon after they were court-martialed by military judges in Cuba. (Hulton-Deutsch Collection)

Lieutenant de Acosta argued that most of the prosecution testimony was hearsay (evidence obtained secondhand, not by personal knowledge). He also held that his client could not be held responsible for alleged capital crimes that occurred before the death penalty was legally reinstated by the provisional constitution, which was only one year old.

The court replied that Sosa Blanco was being tried not under constitutional law but under the Code of the Sierra Maestra, signed on February 1958, before Sosa Blanco committed his crimes. De Acosta persisted, saying that the dates of the crimes had not been conclusively proved.

Thousands left the stadium as the trial dragged on through the night. Just after 6 A.M., after 13 hours of proceedings, Sosa Blanco was found guilty and sentenced to death.

Operation Truth was meant to give the world a positive image of how the revolutionary tribunals provided justice. Instead, massive television and press coverage produced almost unanimous agreement abroad that the tumultuous proceedings had been a farce.

To avoid repeating the public relations disaster, Pedro Morejon and Ricardo Luis Grau were tried with less fanfare. The press, attorneys, and civic groups attended, but the public was not invited. Morejon was found guilty of murder, robbery, and burning homes. He was shot by a firing squad hours after his appeal was rejected on January 31. Grau was found guilty of murdering 53 people and was also executed.

Sosa Blanco was automatically entitled to an appeal. On February 14, the day Castro officially became prime minister, Sosa Blanco's retrial began before the same judges. He was found guilty again and was promptly executed.

Criticism of the prosecution of Sosa Blanco stemmed less from questions about his guilt than from the atmosphere at the show trial. Within weeks, however, the provisional government's judicial image suffered an even more dramatic blow.

Trial of the Airmen

On February 14, 44 pilots, gunners, and mechanics of Batista's air force were tried for "genocide." Resentment against the air force was rife. In Batista's efforts to terrorize the populace into withholding support for Castro's rebels, the air force had bombed many innocent civilians. Castro publicly counted the 44 airmen facing trial in Santiago de Cuba among the worst of the accused war criminals.

Yet the provisional government's case ran into trouble immediately. Prosecutor Antonio Cejas, judge advocate of the Revolutionary Air Force, wanted the pilots and gunners executed for bombing and strafing attacks that had killed 8 farmers and wounded 13. Cejas demanded ten years' imprisonment for each of the mechanics who had serviced the warplanes.

Defense counsel de Acosta, who had also been Sosa Blanco's counsel, replied that 20 airmen actually responsible for the attacks had already fled Cuba. One of the villages cited in the indictment was found never to have been bombed at all. It had been burned by Batista's army. De Acosta also noted that the headline-grabbing charge of genocide was not among the crimes listed in the Code of the Sierra Maestra. Despite heckling from spectators and an attempt by the prosecutor to bully the judges behind closed doors, all 44 airmen were acquitted for lack of evidence.

They were not released, however. Castro announced on television in Havana that the acquittal had been "a grave error" and that a "review" of the trial would take place. Members of Santiago de Cuba's bar association and international critics protested that a second trial would violate the basic principle of double jeopardy, which holds that a defendant cannot be tried twice for the same offense. Nevertheless, Castro selected a second, more dependable tribunal to retry the airmen. Judge Peña was replaced with Santiago's military commander, Major Manuel Piñeiro Losada. Cuba's new minister of defense, Augusto Martínez Sánchez, replaced the prosecutor.

Politics Replace Rule of Law

No new evidence was introduced by either side at the retrial, although two of the mechanics were released. Insults aimed at the defense counsels by the prosecutor and spectators continued without interference by the new presiding judge. Suspicion that the outcome was a foregone conclusion was bolstered late in the trial when a leak revealed that the court had already agreed upon a death sentence for eight of the defendants. The resulting embarrassment stopped the court from announcing its verdict until days after the hearings had ended. Eventually, the court found the accused airmen guilty and sentenced them to terms of imprisonment ranging from 2 to 30 years.

Castro was satisfied with the verdict of the second court. "Revolutionary justice is based not on legal precepts, but on moral conviction," he replied to critics disturbed by the retrial of the acquitted men. "Since the airmen belonged to the air force of the former president . . . Batista . . . they are criminals and must be punished."

The Revolutionary Air Force's appointed representative on the defense team found Castro's moral certitude of the defendants' guilt ironic. In a deposition later given to the International Commission of Jurists, the counsel recalled that Castro himself had absolved the same 44 airmen of any crimes shortly after Batista's defeat, but had used them as scapegoats to satisfy public demand for retribution against guilty air force officers who had escaped into exile.

The airmen were not the only ones punished. Lieutenant de Acosta and the defense lawyers were dismissed from service and publicly harassed. The judge in the first court, Major Peña, was found in his car, shot dead.

The fate of the airmen seemed to erase any hope that the new regime would fulfill its promise to reform the existing justice system. The temporary tribunals were convened to prosecute war crimes, but their methods increasingly became a fact of Cuban life. By the time of the Bay of Pigs invasion in 1961, trained attorneys and judges working within the revolutionary courts were completely replaced by militia members, cementing the politicization of justice in Castro's Cuba.

—Tom Smith

Suggestions for Further Reading

Brennan, Ray. *Castro, Cuba and Justice*. Garden City, N.Y.: Doubleday, 1959.

Cuba and the Rule of Law. Geneva: International Commission of Jurists, 1962.

Szulc, Tad. *Fidel: A Critical Portrait*. New York: William Morrow, 1986.

Thomas, Hugh. *Cuba: The Pursuit of Freedom*. New York: Harper & Row, 1971.

Steven Truscott Trial: 1959

Defendant: Steven Murray Truscott **Crime Charged:** Murder
Chief Defense Lawyers: Frank Donnelly, John O'Driscoll, G. Arthur Martin,
E. B. Jolliffe **Chief Prosecutors:** H. Glenn Hays, Donald H. Scott, William
Bowman **Judge:** Robert Irving Ferguson **Place:** Goderich, Ontario, Canada
Dates of Trial: September 21–30, 1959 **Verdict:** Guilty
Sentence: Execution

SIGNIFICANCE

No case in the history of Canadian jurisprudence has produced more debate than
this conviction of a 14-year-old boy for murder. It brought into question the full
scope of Canada's handling of juvenile offenders and resulted in a change in the
dominion's criminal code to provide that no one under 18 may be sentenced to
death for murder. The case also resulted, some eight years after the conviction, in
a most uncommon step: intervention by the federal cabinet of Canada with an
order to the supreme court of Canada.

After supper on June 9, 1959, 12-year-old Lynne Harper, who lived with her
family on the Royal Canadian Air Force base in Clinton, Ontario, walked
toward her nearby schoolyard. She did not come home that night.

The next morning, Lynne's father searched the neighborhood. At one
home, 14-year-old Steven Truscott told Lynne's father that he had ridden his
bicycle to the schoolyard at about seven o'clock. There, he said, Lynne, who was
a schoolmate, told him she had just finished dinner and wanted to go see a man
who lived in a white house over on Highway 8 who kept ponies. Steve said she
asked him to give her a ride down County Road to Highway 8.

Steve pushed his bike, he said, as they walked over to County Road.
There, Lynne hopped onto the bike's crossbar, and Steve pedaled toward
Highway 8. They crossed a small bridge over the Bayfield River. Several youngsters, cooling off in the stifling-hot early-summer evening by swimming in the
river, waved to them. At a stop sign where County Road met Highway 8, Lynne
got off Steve's bike. He watched her start walking down the highway shoulder.
Then he saw a car, coming along Highway 8 from Clinton on the left, headed
toward Seaforth. It stopped. Lynne got in. The car was a gray 1959 Chevrolet
with a yellow license plate.

The Police Visit School

The police went to the school that morning and asked Lynne's schoolmates if they had seen her. Steve told them he had given her a lift to Highway 8 on his bike. The next day, the officers returned. Again they asked Steve about the bike ride. On the third day, they questioned him again. Each time, Steve consistently repeated the timetable of his activities on the evening of June 9.

Meanwhile, a search party of airmen fanned out through the farms around the base. Near a tractor trail on the Lawson family's farm, they found the body of Lynne Harper; she had been strangled with her own blouse. The coroner's examination revealed that she also had been raped.

That evening, a provincial police officer ordered Steve Truscott into his car and took him to the guardhouse at the RCAF station. There he was grilled through the evening by Inspector Harold Graham of the Ontario Provincial Police Headquarters in Toronto. No charge had yet been filed, nor had Steve been advised of his rights. No lawyer was present, nor had Steve been told that he had a right to call a lawyer.

Finally, Steve's father arrived. Then a doctor examined the boy. Next, Inspector Graham announced, "You will be taken to Goderich. There, you will be charged with the murder of Lynne Harper." At 2 A.M., a Goderich justice of the peace signed the indictment.

In juvenile court, Steve Truscott's name was not revealed because he was under age 16. Because of the seriousness of the charge, however, Justice Dudley Holmes remanded the case to the adult court. At once, all of Huron County, most of Ontario, and much of the rest of Canada found the name Steve Truscott in its headlines and on the lips of its residents. The preliminary hearing brought the press in droves, with all the emphasis on the lurid and sensational that arises when murder, rape, and children are combined in a single news story. Only when the trial itself began, with the court's rule that any trial of a child under 16 be held "without publicity," did the titillating headlines cease.

Steven Truscott prior to his murder trial in 1959. (The London Free Press Collection, D.B. Weldon Library, University of Western Ontario; London, Ontario)

The grand jury returned a true bill on September 16. The trial immediately got under way in the supreme court of Ontario at Goderich.

The Prosecution's Cornerstone

Leading for the Crown, prosecutor Donald Scott established a simple cornerstone for his case: Two boys testified that they had seen Steve riding down County Road with Lynne on his cross bar, headed toward the woodlot where her body was found. They had seen him ride home alone soon afterward.

Pathologist John L. Penistan, basing his testimony on the girl's stomach contents and the time of her disappearance, estimated the time of her death at between 7:15 and 7:45 P.M. on June 9. He said his estimate assumed digestion to have been normal.

The doctor who had examined Steve at the RCAF guardhouse testified that he had found a scratch on the boy's arm, a bruise on his knee, and a lesion of some sort on his penis. Establishing a major point for the Crown's case, he said the latter could be consistent with intercourse or attempted intercourse with a young girl. A second doctor, who had examined the boy after his arrest, agreed.

The prosecution introduced more young witnesses who had played in the schoolyard or had been swimming in the river that hot June evening. Others said they had seen Steve ride across the bridge with Lynne in one direction and return alone. Some said they had seen Steve and Lynne ride across the bridge in *both* directions.

14-Year-Old Defendant Does Not Testify

Steve's lawyers did not ask him to testify in his own defense. They did produce witnesses who testified that Steve's appearance and behavior had been entirely normal when he returned to the schoolyard from his bike ride. Their forensic experts testified that the victim's body showed no trace of Steve's hair. Their medical experts offered "uncontradicted evidence" that intercourse with a young girl would not have produced lesions on the youth's penis and added that the sores had been caused by a skin disease.

When the defense rested on September 30, some 70 witnesses had testified either for or against Steve Truscott. Referring to his own notes rather than to the transcript of testimony, the judge vigorously charged the jury on its obligation to heed the strong web of circumstantial evidence against the young defendant. The jury deliberated for three and a half hours and found Truscott guilty. The law mandated the death penalty. The jury recommended mercy.

"Hanged by the Neck Until You Are Dead"

Mr. Justice Robert Ferguson spoke the Crown's traditional closing words:

Steven Murray Truscott, I have no alternative but to pass the following sentence upon you. The jury has found you guilty after a fair trial. The sentence of this court upon you is that you be taken from here to the place from whence you came and there be kept in close confinement until Tuesday, the eighth of December, 1959, and upon that day and date you be taken to the place of execution and that you there be hanged by the neck until you are dead, and may the Lord have mercy on your soul.

Steve Truscott became the youngest person sentenced to death in Canada since 1875.

Pending an appeal, the execution date was postponed until February 18. On January 22, the day after the Ontario Court of Appeal confirmed the sentence, Canada's Justice Minister E. Davis Fulton commuted the sentence to life imprisonment. Steven was sent to the Ontario Reformatory at Guelph.

The supreme court of Canada refused to consider an appeal and later declared it would not permit a new trial even if any or all new evidence were presented.

Within two years, the Parliament of Canada changed the nation's criminal code, making it unlawful to sentence any person under 18 to death for murder.

In 1966, Isabel LeBourdais's book *The Trial of Steven Truscott*, which presented a strong argument for Steve's innocence, induced the federal cabinet in Ottawa to order the supreme court of Canada to review the case. Truscott then testified that in 1959 he "had been too embarrassed" to tell his father or the doctors of the sores on his penis, which had appeared several weeks before the murder of Lynne Harper. Forensic experts testified that the time of the girl's death, based on the stomach contents, might have been as much as two hours later than that established by the 1959 testimony. Eight of the nine judges agreed that Truscott had received a fair trial. The ninth said the police had violated the boy's rights and recommended a new trial.

After serving ten years, Steve Truscott was paroled. He married a woman who had long worked for his release, changed his name, and moved to a distant part of Ontario. There he has worked steadily for the same employer, and he and his wife have raised three children.

—Bernard Ryan, Jr.

Suggestions for Further Reading

Erickson, Donald L. *The Silent Courtroom*. Seagrave, Ontario: D. L. Erickson, 1988.

Jonas, George. *The Scales of Justice*. Vol. 2. Toronto: Lester & Orpen Dennys/CBC Enterprises, 1986.

LeBourdais, Isabel. *The Trial of Steven Truscott*. Toronto: McClelland and Stewart, 1966.

Trent, Bill. *Who Killed Lynne Harper?* Montreal: Optimum, 1979.

———. *The Steven Truscott Story*. Richmond Hill, Ontario: Simon & Schuster of Canada, 1979.

Truscott, Mary R. *Brats*. New York: Dutton, 1989.

Francis Gary Powers Trial: 1960

Defendant: Francis Gary Powers **Crime Charged:** Espionage
Chief Defense Lawyer: Mikhail I. Griniev **Chief Prosecutor:** Roman A.
Rudenko **Judges:** Lieutenant General Viktor V. Borisoglebsky, Major General
Dmitry Z. Vorobyev, Major General Alexander I. Zakharov **Place:** Moscow,
USSR **Dates of Trial:** August 17–19, 1960 **Verdict:** Guilty
Sentence: Ten years' confinement, first three to be served in prison

SIGNIFICANCE
A single event in the 45-year Cold War, this case provides insight into the behavior
of chiefs of state and the CIA, a look at Soviet jurisprudence during that long reign
of suspicion, and of technological progress in the sinister art of espionage.

Francis Gary Powers, the son of a coal miner, enlisted in the United States Air
Force after graduating from Tennessee's Milligan College in 1950. He
quickly earned his wings, was commissioned a second lieutenant, and qualified
as a jet pilot. In January 1956, Powers was stationed at Turner Air Force Base at
Albany, Georgia, when he was tapped by representatives of the Lockheed
Aircraft Company and the Central Intelligence Agency (CIA). Would he like to
fly a new reconnaissance jet that could cruise at the unbelievable altitude of
70,000 feet? Would he like to triple his Air Force pay?

Powers was a born flier who had been hooked on aviation since boyhood.
He was also a newlywed who was finding it hard to support his wife on military
pay. He signed a document, cosigned by Donald A. Quarles, then secretary of
the Air Force, that promised that upon completion of CIA service, Powers could
return to the Air Force with no loss of time in grade or toward retirement, and
with rank corresponding to that of his contemporaries. Under CIA policy, the
agency kept the only signed copy.

Photographing Golf Balls from 50,000 Feet

At Burbank, California, Powers was introduced to a strange jet-powered
tube with an 80-foot wingspan—almost twice the length of its fuselage. Called
the U-2, it could fly some 8,000 miles at altitudes well above the range of any
known aircraft—or antiaircraft missile. The U-2 was loaded with sophisticated

electronic gear, including cameras, radar, tape recorders, and radios. Its photographs could reveal a golf ball on the green from 50,000 feet. In April 1956, while Powers was in training in California, the U-2 began flying over the Soviet Union from the Middle East, photographing Soviet air force bases.

By the spring of 1960, Powers had logged 500 hours in the U-2 and had completed 27 missions from the Incirlik Air Base in Turkey as a member of a top-secret detachment known to the U.S. military as "10-10," and to the outside world as the Second Weather Observational Squadron (Provisional). In late April, he left his wife at their Incirlik home and flew by transport to Peshawar, Pakistan. There he was briefed for three hours on a U-2 reconnaissance flight to Bodo, Norway, 2,919 miles across the Soviet Union. His objective was to photograph a site where American intelligence suspected the Soviets were building their first intercontinental ballistic missile base. He took off at 6:36 A.M. local time on Sunday, May 1.

Thirty miles south of Sverdlovsk, Powers was about halfway through his trip, in clear weather with excellent visibility. He had just banked into a 90-degree left turn—the sharpest on his plotted course. As he recorded altitude and engine readings in his log book, he felt and heard an explosion. In seconds, he knew the tail section of his plane had been blown off. His body was sucked partway from the cockpit. He tried to activate destruct switches that would explode the plane 70 seconds later. He could not reach them. Then he was in the air, floating under his parachute, although he had not pulled the rip cord.

Spy Mission Revealed

On Monday, a stringer for an Istanbul paper reported that "an American plane of the U-2 meteorological reconnaissance type" was missing. On Wednesday, May 4, President Dwight D. Eisenhower's press secretary, James C. Hagerty, learned—as reporters demanded explanations—that the "weather" plane presumed missing on Turkish soil was a U.S. spy plane on a mission over the Soviet Union.

The next day, Soviet Premier Nikita S. Khrushchev announced that the U-2 had been shot down, its pilot captured, the wreckage and its incriminating equipment recovered. The United States, he declared, was trying to "torpedo" a long-planned summit meeting of the Big Four—the Soviet Union, France, England, and the United States—scheduled to open on May 16 in Paris.

On Saturday, May 7, after 48 hours of frantic discussion among the U.S. State Department, the CIA, and the White House, the U.S. government admitted publicly that it had lied about the weather missions, practiced espionage, and violated Soviet territory. On Monday, President Eisenhower took personal responsibility, saying the spying overflights had been carried out for years and might continue "as safeguards against surprise attack and aggression."

A Summit Doomed

Eisenhower went to Paris for the summit meeting. Before it opened, British Prime Minister Harold Macmillan pressured him to halt the flights, and Khrushchev demanded that French President Charles de Gaulle persuade Eisenhower to stop them. At the opening meeting, Khrushchev seized the floor and announced that the U.S. espionage policy "dooms the summit conference to complete failure in advance."

Eisenhower backed off. "In point of fact," he told the conference, "these flights were suspended after the recent incident and are not to be resumed."

Khrushchev, who continued to insist that Eisenhower apologize, huffily canceled plans for Eisenhower to visit Moscow later that summer. At 2:06 P.M., the 1960 summit conference ended on its opening day.

The Powers trial opened on Wednesday, August 17, 1960, in the great white Hall of Columns within the House of Trade Unions in Moscow—the site of the Stalinist purge trials in the 1930s. The crowd of nearly 1,000, including the defendant's wife, mother, and father, was jammed into a hot, unventilated building thronged with vendors selling publications about the U-2, salami sandwiches, sweet rolls, coffee, tea, and soda.

Lieutenant General Viktor V. Borisoglebsky, presiding judge of the Military Collegium, read the indictment, then demanded, "Accused Powers, do you plead guilty of the charge?"

"Yes. I plead guilty."

Prosecutor Roman A. Rudenko quizzed Powers about the flight, explosion, destruction buttons, parachute descent, and a poison needle found among his possessions. Powers said the needle was "in case I was captured, tortured, and couldn't stand the torture and would rather be dead."

"Were you tortured?"

"No. I have been treated very nice."

"I Am Sincerely Sorry"

Mikhail I. Griniev, Powers's court-appointed attorney, questioned him on his working-class background, his pilot training, and his taking the CIA job to improve his financial position.

"Are you sorry about the flight?"

"Well," said Powers, "the situation I am now in is not too good. I understand that as a direct result of my flight the summit conference did not take place and President Eisenhower's visit was called off. There was, I suppose, a great increase in tension in the world, and I am sincerely sorry I had anything to do with this."

The next day, Rudenko carefully questioned Powers about the 68,000-foot altitude of the plane over Sverdlovsk. He then introduced as evidence a report of the commander of the rocket battery that shot down the U-2. It set the altitude at "over 20,000 meters [65,600 feet]." The prosecutor did not try to elicit any more specific information on the U-2's performance.

The presiding judge probed whether Powers felt he had done "a good or a bad service" for his country.

"I would say a very bad service."

"Did it occur to you that you might torpedo the summit conference?"

"I did not think of it."

"Did it occur to you," continued the judge, "that a flight might provoke military conflict?"

"The people who sent me," said Powers, "should have thought of these things."

"Do you regret making this flight?"

"Yes, very much."

A Ten-Year Sentence

Friday brought lengthy closing arguments. The prosecutor did not insist on the death penalty but asked for 15 years' imprisonment. The defense pleaded: "The appearance of Powers over the Soviet Union was not a manifestation of his own will, but was predetermined by the will of the aggressive circles behind him. . . . The witness was frank and truthful."

Powers was allowed to make a last plea. He read a prepared statement, ending with, "I plead to the court to judge me not as an enemy but as a human being who is not a personal enemy of the Russian people, who has never had any charges brought against him in any court, and who is deeply repentant and profoundly sorry for what he has done. Thanks."

The infamous U-2 spy plane that Gary Powers flew to obtain vital intelligence data on Russia's missile and space programs and military installations. (Lockheed Corporation)

The judges retired. Four hours and 40 minutes later they returned. Judge Borisoglebsky again reviewed the evidence at length, ending with the finding that Powers had committed "a grave crime" but that the court was impressed by his "sincere confession of his guilt and his sincere repentance." With "socialist humaneness," he announced, the sentence was limited to "ten years of confinement with the first three years to be served in prison." The prisoner was permitted a one-hour visit with his family, then sent to Vladimir Prison, where he was put to work weaving rugs.

On February 9, 1962, Powers was flown to East Berlin, some 1,200 miles away. The next morning, he was escorted by three Soviet officials to the center of the Glienicker Bridge. It spanned the Havel River, which divided East and West Berlin. At a white line at midspan, a thin, balding man waited with three American officials. At a signal, Powers and the thin man each walked forward, crossing to the other side. Powers was free. He had been exchanged for Rudolf Ivanovich Abel, the Soviet master spy convicted in the United States and, until then, serving a 30-year sentence. The trade had been arranged by James Donovan, a New York attorney who was formerly counsel to the Office of Strategic Services, forerunner of the CIA.

Powers went home. The U.S. Air Force said he could reenlist at comparable rank (that is, as a major) to his contemporaries, as his contract had specified, but refused to credit his six and one-half years of CIA service—including 21 months in Soviet prisons—toward his retirement. He joined Lockheed as an engineering test pilot, checking out U-2 planes as they came in for maintenance or when new or modified equipment was installed. The planes performed significant service in the Cuban missile crisis and in the Vietnam War. Powers flew for Lockheed until 1970, when he was told his services were no longer required.

—*Bernard Ryan, Jr.*

Suggestions for Further Reading

Dulles, Allan. *The Craft of Intelligence.* New York: Harper & Row, 1963.

Kirkpatrick, Lyman B. *The Real CIA.* New York: Macmillan, 1968.

Knight, David C. *The Spy Who Never Was and Other True Spy Stories.* Garden City, New York: Doubleday, 1978.

Powers, Francis Gary, with Curt Gentry. *Operation Overflight.* New York: Holt, Rinehart and Winston, 1970.

Seth, Ronald. *The Anatomy of Espionage.* New York: E. P. Dutton, 1963.

Wise, David, and Thomas B. Ross. *The U-2 Affair.* New York: Random House, 1962.

Portland Naval Spy Ring Trial: 1961

Defendants: Gordon Lonsdale, Peter Kroger, Helen Kroger, Ethel Gee, Harry Houghton   **Crime Charged:** Espionage   **Chief Defense Lawyers:** Victor Durand, Q.C; Robin Simpson; James N. Dunlop; Henry Palmer; William M. F. Hudson; John Maddocks   **Chief Prosecutors:** Sir Reginald Manningham-Buller, Q.C.; Alastair Morton; Mervyn Griffiths-Jones   **Judge:** Lord Chief Justice Hubert Parker   **Place:** London, England   **Dates of Trial:** March 13–22, 1961   **Verdict:** Guilty   **Sentence:** Lonsdale—25 years; Krogers—20 years; Gee and Houghton—15 years

SIGNIFICANCE

The major British Cold War spy trial.

In 1958, a high-ranking Polish intelligence officer, Michael Goloniewski, began passing information to the West about the activities of Soviet-bloc agents in the United States and in Europe. Among this information was reference to an English spy named something like "Huton," who worked for the navy and had been recruited in Warsaw. By a process of elimination, counterespionage agents from MI5, a branch of British military intelligence, zeroed in on Harry Houghton, a 55-year-old clerk in the Underwater Weapons Establishment at Portland, Dorset. Houghton, and his mistress, Ethel Gee, a filing clerk, had access to top secret information on antisubmarine warfare and nuclear submarines, and both seemed to enjoy a lifestyle beyond their modest salaries.

Each month, the couple traveled to London, where Houghton would meet a Canadian businessman named Gordon Lonsdale, whose company leased jukeboxes to cafés. During these meetings, MI5 agents watched from a distance as various documents were exchanged. Lonsdale, in turn, was trailed to a house in Ruislip, West London, the home of Helen and Peter Kroger, ostensibly antiquarian book dealers. Long-term surveillance convinced MI5 that Lonsdale was running a Soviet spy ring, a suspicion confirmed when agents covertly opened Lonsdale's bank safe deposit box to find miniature cameras and one-time cipher pads, essential tools in the world of espionage. Fearful that Lonsdale might realize his cover had been blown and vanish behind the Iron Curtain, detectives swooped down on a London street in January 1961 and arrested him, together with Houghton and Gee. That night, the Krogers were detained at their home.

By their very nature, British trials involving the Official Secrets Act (1911) tend to be murky affairs, so when Sir Reginald Manningham-Buller, Q.C. (Queen's Counsel), opened for the Crown on March 13, 1961, he did so in the most guarded of terms. Understandably reticent about background details to the case, he outlined Houghton's and Gee's classified work at Portland and the manner of their London assignations with Lonsdale. The first meeting had occurred on July 9, 1960, when Houghton was seen passing Lonsdale a carrier bag. In return, the naval clerk received a white envelope—payment, so the prosecution maintained, for secrets. It was Manningham-Buller's contention that Houghton and Gee had been solely motivated by money; the remaining defendants, he said, were committed Communists. He described how Lonsdale, Houghton, and Gee had been arrested on January 7, 1961. In Gee's shopping basket was a parcel containing four Admiralty test pamphlets and several rolls of undeveloped film, later found to be photographs of *Particulars of War Vessels*, a top secret naval book.

More detailed information regarding the surveillance campaign came from a succession of witnesses—all MI5 agents—who were referred to in court only by letters of the alphabet. Mr. D described following Lonsdale and Houghton to a restaurant on August 6, 1960. Sitting at an adjacent table, he overheard Lonsdale say, "You seem to have plenty in your attaché case." Houghton had replied, "Yes, I have more than my sleeping and shaving kit." They had then discussed arrangements for future meetings. "These will be the first Saturday in every month," Lonsdale had said.

Although defense counsel Henry Palmer, for Houghton, and William Hudson, for Lonsdale, did what they could to undermine D's testimony— claiming that ambient noise in the restaurant made it impossible to overhear anything—neither managed to make any headway.

Radio Under Floor

The evidence snowballed. Chief Inspector Ferguson Smith told how, after a lengthy search of the Krogers' house, he had found a trap-door in the kitchen floor. The space below was occupied by a high-speed transmitter powerful enough to reach Moscow; a shortwave radio for receiving messages; one-time cipher pads hidden in flashlights and in a cigarette lighter; a microdot reader concealed in a box of face powder; equipment for microdot construction; thousands of pounds, dollars, and travelers checks; and seven passports.

Gee's treachery, too, was manifest. Apart from the contents of her shopping basket, officers from the Underwater Weapons Establishment confirmed that other documents found at her home were also classified. Junior prosecution counsel Mervyn Griffiths-Jones asked Commander Stewart Irskine Crew-Read about Gee: "Hers was a responsible job, given only to people thought to be responsible and honest?"

"Yes," Crew-Read answered.

When Gee took the stand, her counsel, James Dunlop, struggled to downplay her involvement. "When was the first time you heard the name Lonsdale?"

"In Bow Street Court," she replied, a reference to earlier committal proceedings.

"Had you heard the name Gordon before?"

"No," she said, insisting that Lonsdale was known to her as Alec Johnson.

Her lover's testimony was more colorful and inventive. Houghton blamed everything on a mysterious Polish secret service agent who had threatened the very worst kind of physical harm unless he handed over state secrets. "I told him that things like that could not happen in this country." One day, Houghton continued, two thugs showed up to administer what he called "the biggest hammering I ever had in my life."

Palmer: "Did you tell anyone about this?"

Houghton: "No, I couldn't tell the doctor because I would have had to tell him how I got it. I was not prepared to go to the police. I did not think they could do anything about it." In an attempt to mitigate his own treachery, he claimed that he had deliberately blurred the photographs of the top secret naval book so they would be of limited use. This determination to save his own skin had been evidenced earlier when one of the arresting officers, Detective Superintendent George Smith, testified that Houghton "wanted to strike a bargain with me not to appear here, but to turn Queen's evidence. I told him I could not have that."

In this photo released by Scotland Yard, John Kroger's radiogram is clearly seen, along with the headphones and tape recorder used during Kroger's surveillance. (Hulton-Deutsch Collection)

If honor is lacking among thieves, it soon became clear that KGB agents more than made up for the deficit. Although he declined to testify, Lonsdale did make a statement from the dock, maintaining that the Krogers knew nothing of the transmitter and other equipment he had stashed at their house. "I realize it is too late to make amends now, but I feel the least I can do in the circumstances is to accept full responsibility for my actions, irrespective of the consequences to me personally. I am making this statement because I am anxious that Mr. and Mrs. Kroger should not suffer for what I have done by putting my property in their own house." Lonsdale assumed responsibility for everything at the house, including the passports. "I knew if the contents of the hiding place were discovered it would land Mr. and Mrs. Kroger in very serious trouble. I decided to obtain false passports which could be used by the Krogers if such an event took place."

Counsel for the Krogers, Victor Durand, Q.C., announced that, though he did not intend to bring any witnesses, Peter Kroger wished to make a statement. Describing Lonsdale as a "businessman," Kroger said that they had met through their mutual interest in books. Kroger said Lonsdale would often drop by their house during the week for meals and to help Helen Kroger with her photography.

Closing arguments for the defendants were unsurprisingly brief. James Dunlop said, "The case, quite shortly, for Miss Gee is that she was wholly deceived and duped," and Henry Palmer insisted that Houghton had acted "as a result of pressure . . . imposed by fear."

Bizarre Transmission

Only William Hudson, on behalf of Lonsdale, tried a different tack. Noting that, several hours after news had broken of Lonsdale's arrest, Moscow was still beaming messages to the Kroger household, he said, "If this man was a Russian spy, whoever was responsible for his activities would know within a matter of moments that he had been arrested. In spite of that, these signals were sent. The evidence gives rise to the gravest doubt that the signals were meant for the defendant Lonsdale." It was a curiosity, nothing more; no one could seriously doubt his client's guilt.

On March 22, 1961, all five defendants were convicted. Lonsdale received 25 years; the Krogers, 20 each; Houghton and Gee, 15 each. In passing sentence, Lord Chief Justice Hubert Parker singled out Lonsdale: "You are clearly a professional spy. It is a dangerous career and one in which you must be prepared, as you no doubt are, to suffer if and when you are caught."

Lonsdale knew the risks; espionage had been his life. His real name was Konon Trofimovich Molody, and he was born in Moscow in 1922, the son of a prominent Russian scientist. At age seven, he was sent to live with an aunt in Berkeley, California, where he went to school. In 1938, he returned to the Soviet Union and joined the NKVD, forerunner of the KGB. Trained as an "illegal," Molody entered Canada in 1954 on a forged passport and obtained the birth certificate of a deceased Finnish Canadian, Gordon Arnold Lonsdale, whose identity he adopted. In 1955, under his new Canadian identity, he traveled to London, enrolled in a Chinese course at the School of Oriental and African Studies, and set himself up as a businessman. Over the next six years, he ran one of the most effective spy networks ever. His main allies, the Krogers, were equally committed. In the early 1950s, under their real names of Morris and Lona Cohen, they had fled the United States to escape arrest when their involvement with American Communist spies Julius and Ethel Rosenberg became known. Later, as the Krogers, they resurfaced in London.

Agents of this caliber were too important for the KGB to let languish in jail. On April 22, 1964, Molody was exchanged for convicted British spy Greville

Wynne. Six years later, the Krogers were similarly repatriated. Molody returned to the Soviet Union as a hero. Some idea of his worth can be gauged from the fact that when he died in 1970, his body lay in state at the KGB officers' club. Among the chief mourners was Yuri Andropov, subsequent leader of the Soviet Union.

—Colin Evans

Suggestions for Further Reading

Andrew, Christopher, and Oleg Gordievsky. *KGB: The Inside Story.* London: Hodder & Stoughton, 1990.

Houghton, Harry. *Operation Portland.* London: Rupert Hart-Davis, 1972.

Knightley, Phillip. *The Second Oldest Profession.* London: André Deutsch.

Pincher, Chapman, *Their Trade Is Treachery.* London: Sidgwick & Jackson, 1981.

Adolf Eichmann Trial: 1961

Defendant: Adolf Eichmann   **Crimes Charged:** Crimes against Jews with intent to destroy the people, crimes against humanity, and membership in criminal organizations   **Chief Defense Lawyers:** Robert Servatius, Dieter Wechtenbruch   **Chief Prosecutors:** Gideon Hausner, Jacob Baror, Gabriel Bach, Jacob Robinson   **Judges:** Moshe Landau, Benjamin Halevy, Yitzhak Raveh   **Place:** Jerusalem, Israel   **Dates of Trial:** April 11–August 14, 1961   **Verdict:** Guilty   **Sentence:** Execution

SIGNIFICANCE

The trial and conviction of Adolf Eichmann, the most despicable (except for Adolf Hitler himself) of all Nazi officials in the German high command before and during World War II, stands as a testament to persistence. Ignored by the vast postwar body of knowledge and presumed dead, Eichmann was brought to justice 15 years after the Nuremberg trials. Furthermore, the trial was held under the jurisdiction of Israel, a country that had not existed when the crimes were committed.

On August 8, 1945, soon after Germany's unconditional surrender ended combat in Europe in World War II, the United States, Great Britain, France, and the Soviet Union signed the London Agreement. It established the International Military Tribunal, chartered "to try and punish persons who, acting in the interests of the European Axis countries, whether as individuals or as members of organizations," committed war crimes and crimes against peace. Among the descriptions of such crimes, the charter stated:

> Crimes against humanity: Namely, murder, extermination, enslavement, deportation, and other inhumane acts committed against any civilian population, before or during the war, or persecutions on political, racial, or religious grounds in execution of or in connection with any crime within the jurisdiction of the Tribunal. . . .

> At the trial of any individual member of any group or organization the Tribunal may declare (in connection with any act of which the individual may be convicted) that the group or organization of which the individual was a member was a criminal organization. . . .

In October 1945, the Tribunal opened the trial of 24 Nazi leaders at Nuremberg. More than 10 months later, the four judges found three defendants not guilty on any of the counts. Seven defendants were sentenced to prison terms. The other twelve were sentenced to execution and were hanged, with the exception of Hermann Goering, who committed suicide, and Martin Bormann, who was tried in absentia.

The tribunal also found that three organizations were criminal: the SS (Hitler's special guards), along with its subsidiary, the SD (security service); the Gestapo, or secret state police; and the leadership corps of the Nazi Party.

Not Even His Photograph

Prosecutors at Nuremberg noticed that several defendants, when questioned about the Nazi program to kill off the Jews, brought up the name Adolf Eichmann. But when asked about Eichmann's whereabouts, each surmised that he had died or been killed. Not even his photograph appeared at Nuremberg. In its final summation of the genocide procedure, the tribunal commented, "Adolf Eichmann, who had been put in charge of this program by Hitler, has estimated that the policy pursued resulted in the killing of 6,000,000 Jews, of which 4,000,000 were killed in the extermination institutions."

As the Nuremberg trial marched into history, the name Adolf Eichmann was all but forgotten.

Seized in Buenos Aires

Nearly 15 years later, early in the evening of May 11, 1960, seven men in two cars stopped before a house on Garibaldi Street in Buenos Aires, Argentina. Five of them then hovered around one car with its hood up. As a man known as Ricardo Klement came home, they grabbed him. They sped him to a safe house, where he admitted he was Adolf Eichmann. Within days, the prime minister of Israel, David Ben-Gurion, announced to the Israeli Knesset, or parliament, that after searching the world for several years, the Mossad, the Israeli secret service, had seized Eichmann in Argentina and flown him to Israel.

In the United Nations, Argentina filed a formal complaint against Israel for violating Argentina's sovereignty by abducting Eichmann. Israel apologized but kept Eichmann. The UN Security Council resolved that Eichmann "should be brought to appropriate justice for the crimes of which he is accused."

On April 11, 1961, the trial of Eichmann, on the charges of crimes against Jews, crimes against humanity, and membership in criminal organizations, opened in the district court of Jerusalem. A bulletproof glass cage large enough for Eichmann and two guards had been installed in the courtroom of the newly built Beth Ha'am, or House of the People. The building was specially fenced. Heavily armed guards were stationed on the rooftop, patrolled the basement, and carefully frisked all who entered the building.

"Looking Like a Bank Clerk"

The three judges sat high atop a plain dais. Directly below them were translators ready to render all questions and testimony in English, French, German, and Hebrew. Glaring lights and white walls emphasized the parched yellow skin of the defendant, whose appearance was so ordinary that the press described him as "looking like a bank clerk."

Nazi war criminal Adolf Eichmann sits in the bullet proof box during his trial on April 24, 1961. (Hulton-Deutsch Collection)

Gideon Hausner, attorney general of Israel, opened for the prosecution: "With me stand six million accusers. But they cannot point an accusing finger toward the man who sits in the glass dock and cry: 'I accuse.' For their ashes were piled up in the hills of Auschwitz and in the fields of Treblinka, or washed away by the rivers of Poland, their graves are scattered over the length and breadth of Europe. Their blood cries out, but their voices are not heard."

Over eight hours, Hausner reviewed the rise of anti-Semitism and racism and the Nazi "Final Solution" program of annihilation. Next, a six-volume transcript of 76 tapes recorded by Eichmann was placed into evidence. Some were played. The court heard Eichmann claim he was "only a minor transport officer." They heard him offer to hang himself in public "for expiation."

A long parade of witnesses took the court on a chilling tour of Eichmann's Europe. They recounted how he had bragged to six leaders of Viennese Jewry, early in Nazi rule, that he would clear all Austria of Jews "in the shortest possible way." They also described the flight of Czech Jews from Prague after Eichmann took charge there in 1939; the forced march of Polish Jews to the Soviet border and their inevitable mass extermination; the 1942 liquidation of the Warsaw ghetto which left 60,000 survivors from half a million Jews; the "children's operation" in Lithuania, which tore youngsters from their mothers; the vast scourge of Jews across France, Holland, Norway, Denmark, and other areas. All these horrors, as witnesses testified, took place under the direction of Eichmann.

"In What Order, in What Countries"

A key witness was an American judge, Michael A. Musmanno. A naval officer in 1945, he had questioned the Nuremberg defendants. He testified that Hermann Goering "made it very clear that Eichmann was the man to determine in what order, in what countries, the Jews were to die." Judge Musmanno also said Nuremberg had produced evidence that any Nazi who was unwilling to participate in the extermination procedures was free to volunteer to serve at the front.

Eichmann's power over the concentration camps was shown by testimony on Strasbourg University's Institute of Ancestral Heredity, which requested Jewish skeletons for its studies. On Eichmann's direct order, an anthropologist had selected 115 men and women at Auschwitz and had them gassed to provide "fresh" skeletons.

One witness, Dean Grueber, summed up the defendant's Nazi persona: "Eichmann was what we called in German a *Landsknecht,* by which we meant a man who, when he puts on his uniform, leaves his conscience and his reason in the wardrobe."

Other witnesses spoke of the slaughter of Jews in Hungary and of Eichmann's cooperation with Arab and Iraqi leaders to prevent Jewish children from moving to Palestine. The grisly procedures of the death camps were detailed: the endless trains bringing the victims, the shooting of the naked prisoners at the edges of mass graves, the piles of bodies.

Opening Eichmann's defense, Dr. Robert Servatius explained why he had not cross-examined the prosecution witnesses: Eichmann did not dispute the facts of the Jewish annihilation or his participation in it. Rather, he had simply followed orders. He had shown no initiative. He was merely a "transmitter" with no power of his own. "I never took any decision by myself," he said; ". . . I never did anything, great or small, without obtaining in advance express instructions from my superiors." Even in Hungary in the last days of the war, he claimed, "I had only railway timetables to take care of, and even this only marginally. . . . Everything was done by my superiors."

"I Will Leap Into My Grave Laughing"

Cross-examining, prosecutor Hausner asked Eichmann, "Do you consider yourself guilty of participation in the murder of millions of Jews?"

"Legally not, but in the human sense—yes, for I am guilty of having deported them."

Hausner produced a 1945 boast by Eichmann: "I will leap into my grave laughing because the feeling that I have 5 million human beings on my conscience is for me a source of extraordinary satisfaction."

Eichmann said he was then referring only to "enemies of the Reich." Judge Yitzhak Raveh questioned him. He admitted he had spoken of 5 million Jews.

"The only front on which you were active all the years from 1937 on," asked the prosecutor, "was the fight against the Jews?"

Eichmann looked at the floor. "Yes, that is true."

"The Nature of a Subaltern"

Defense witnesses, all former high-ranking Nazis, were promised safe conduct from their German and Austrian homes to testify in Jerusalem. All refused, but sent depositions. None strengthened Eichmann's "only obeying orders" defense. In fact, most incriminated him. Typical was the comment from Otto Winkelmann, former senior SS and police leader in Budapest, who said, "He had the nature of a subaltern, which means a fellow who uses his power recklessly, without moral restraints. He would certainly overstep his authority if he thought he was acting in the spirit of his commander."

An even more damaging deposition came from Alfred Six, former brigadier general in the SD (security service) Head Office, who said,

> Eichmann was an absolute and unconditional believer in National Socialism. It was his world. In case of doubt he would invariably act according to the most extreme interpretation of the party doctrine. Eichmann had much greater powers than other department chiefs.

Six also verified that Eichmann could have obtained a transfer from the Reich Security Head Office (RSHA) to the front if he had so desired. "There were cases," he said, "of SD leaders who were transferred elsewhere from RSHA at their own request." He himself had succeeded in getting transferred from the murderous duty, and "all I suffered was minor discomfort in my career."

After 14 weeks, more than 1,500 documents, 100 prosecution witnesses (90 of whom had survived Nazi captivity), and dozens of defense depositions delivered by diplomatic couriers from 16 countries, the Eichmann trial ended on August 14, 1961. The three judges deliberated for four months. On December 11, they announced their verdict. Under "crimes against Jews with intent to destroy the people," Eichmann was convicted on the first four counts: (1) by "causing the killing of millions of Jews," (2) by placing "millions of Jews under conditions which were likely to lead to their physical destruction," (3) by "causing serious bodily and mental harm" to Jews, and (4) by "directing that births be banned and pregnancies interrupted among Jewish women." On the charge of "crimes against humanity," he was convicted on counts 5 through 12, including persecution of Jews on racial, religious, and political grounds; the plunder of property of Jews; and crimes against non-Jews—including the expulsion of thousands of Poles and Slovenes from their homes, the deportation of gypsies from the Reich to Auschwitz, and the deportation of children from Lidice, Czechoslovakia. On the final three counts of "membership in the three organizations judged 'criminal' at Nuremberg"—the SS, along with its subsidiary the SD (security service); the Gestapo, or secret state police and the Nazi

Party's leadership corps—he was also found guilty. The first 12 convictions carried the death penalty.

Eichmann appealed. On May 29, 1962, Israel's Court of Appeal confirmed and revised the lower court's judgment, finding that Eichmann "had received no 'superior orders' at all. He was his own superior, and he gave all orders in matters that concerned Jewish affairs . . . the idea of the Final Solution would never have assumed the infernal forms of the flayed skin and tortured flesh of millions of Jews without the fanatical zeal and the unquenchable blood thirst of the appellant and his accomplices."

On May 31, Israeli president Itzhak Ben-Zvi turned down Eichmann's petition for mercy. Just before midnight, after refusing to don the traditional black hood, Eichmann was hanged. His body was cremated. Early the next morning on the Mediterranean, a police boat carried his ashes beyond the Israeli three-mile limit. They were scattered in international waters.

—Bernard Ryan, Jr.

Suggestions for Further Reading

Arendt, Hannah. *Eichmann in Jerusalem*. New York: Viking, 1963.

Averbach, Albert, and Charles Price, eds. *The Verdicts Were Just*. New York: David McKay, 1966.

Harel, Isser. *The House on Garibaldi Street*. New York: Viking, 1975.

Hausner, Gideon. *Justice in Jerusalem*. New York: Harper & Row, 1966.

Malin, Peter Z., and Harry Stein. *Eichmann in My Hands*. New York: Warner, 1990.

Papadatos, Peter. *The Eichmann Trial*. London: Stevens, 1964.

Pearlman, Maurice. *The Capture and Trial of Adolf Eichmann*. New York: Simon & Schuster, 1963.

Reynolds, Quentin. *Minister of Death*. New York: Viking, 1960.

Robinson, Jacob. *And the Crooked Shall Be Made Straight*. New York: Macmillan, 1965.

Russell, Lord Edward Frederick Langley. *The Trial of Adolf Eichmann*. London: W. Heinemann, 1962.

Obafemi Awolowo Trial: 1962

Defendant: Obafemi Awolowo   **Crimes Charged:** Treasonable felony, conspiracy, illegal importation of firearms   **Chief Defense Lawyers:** Fifty attorneys for Chief Awolowo and his 24 codefendants
Chief Prosecutor: B. A. Adepipe   **Judge:** George S. Sowemimo
Place: Lagos, Nigeria   **Dates of Trial:** November 2, 1962—September 11, 1963   **Verdict:** Guilty   **Sentence:** Ten years' imprisonment

SIGNIFICANCE
The trial of Chief Awolowo destroyed the Action Group political party, upsetting the balance of power in Nigeria's fragile democracy and setting the stage for years of open political violence.

"Nigeria is not a nation," Chief Obafemi Awolowo wrote in his 1947 book *Path To Nigerian Freedom*. "It is a mere geographical expression." Although Awolowo dedicated his political life to the concept of a unified Nigeria, he was often an unwilling participant in the regional strife that plagued his African nation.

Resentment between ethnic factions has been the central fact of Nigeria's political life throughout its short history. The nation itself is the historical creation of British commercial interests, which determined that more than 250 ethnic groups within Nigeria's borders should become a single cohesive colony. After more than a century of control, the departing British sought to bind this cultural patchwork together as a federal constitutional democracy, containing three regions—the Northern, the Eastern, and the Western. Nigeria was granted independence within the British Commonwealth on October 1, 1960.

Nigeria's first political parties quickly fell into place along regional lines, with the country's major ethnic groups vying for national political and economic dominance. The predominantly Hausa-Fulani Muslim Northern Region was controlled by the Northern People's Congress (NPC), and in the Eastern Region, the Ibo tribe dominated the National Council of Nigerian Citizens (NCNC). The Yoruba tribe of Nigeria's Western Region was represented by a third major party, the Action Group, which became the official opposition to the ruling NPC-NCNC coalition government.

Action Group founder Chief Awolowo was already a powerful leader in the Yoruba community by the time independence arrived. A lawyer by profession, he had helped draft the country's first constitution. He had served as a trade union organizer, Yoruba cultural leader, and premier of the Western Region during the late 1950s. Politically, Awolowo felt that the best path for Nigeria's future lay in a form of African socialism similar to that espoused by Ghanaian leader Kwame Nkrumah.

Although the Action Group's roots lay within Yoruba society, Awolowo hoped to make it a national party by attracting young, educated, reform-minded voters across Nigeria. This tack placed him in direct confrontation with another Action Group leader, Western Region prime minister S. L. Akintola, who favored cooperation with the ruling coalition. When Awolowo's supporters engineered Akintola's expulsion from the party in May 1962, tensions were so high that riot police fired tear gas into the chambers of the provincial parliament to subdue brawling between the two factions.

The chaos presented a tempting political opportunity for the Action Group's foes in the ruling coalition. Nigeria's federal government declared a state of emergency in the Western Region, suspended the constitution, and restricted the movement of Awolowo and 60 other Action Group officials. The Western Region was placed under the control of a federal administrator, who immediately announced an investigation of corruption within the Action Party.

Corruption Charges Fly

Two hundred witnesses, including Chief Awolowo, were summoned to Lagos in July 1962. The government charged the Action Party with diverting more than $168 million in public development funds into Action Group accounts during Chief Awolowo's tenure as Western Region president in the 1950s. That graft existed in the government was no surprise to Nigerians, but many were surprised at the depth to which Action Party leaders were accused of complicity. To its detractors, the investigation looked like a flagrant attempt by the ruling NPC-NCNC coalition to dismantle its only real opposition.

The corruption inquiry was only a prelude to the prosecution of Chief Awolowo. On September 22, the government placed him under house arrest without publicly declaring the reason. On November 2, he was formally charged with treason. The indictment accused Awolowo and 26 others, including many Action Group leaders, of conspiring to overthrow the government.

Among those indicted was Action Group Vice President Anthony Enahoro, who fled to England when he heard of the impending charges. The Nigerian government's attempts to extradite Enahoro became an ugly and embarrassing issue for British politicians. Using the arcane Fugitive Offenders Act of 1881, the British Conservative government argued that Nigeria's status as a Commonwealth nation required that Enahoro be extradited. Despite the Labour Party's efforts to grant Enahoro the political asylum he requested, Conservative politicians narrowly prevailed after a six-month debate. Enahoro was returned to

Lagos under guard on May 16, 1963, and the case against the Action Group proceeded in earnest.

Treason Trial Staged

Federal prosecutor B. A. Adepipe charged Awolowo with masterminding a plot to depose Prime Minister Abubakar Tafawa Balewa during a state visit by Indian Prime Minister Jawaharlal Nehru on September 23, 1962. Large quantities of arms were said to have been smuggled into the country by Action Group supporters. Coup plans allegedly included blowing up the Lagos power station and simultaneously kidnapping the nation's leader, allowing Chief Awolowo to step forward as prime minister.

Chief Awolowo, the prime minister of the Western Region of Nigeria, at a speaking engagement. (Hulton-Deutsch Collection)

The list of defendants immediately shortened as the government called one of the indicted men as the first prosecution witness. Dr. Oladipo Maja testified that he had been recruited to act as a liaison between the plotters and Ghanaian arms suppliers, to whom 200 men were to be sent for training. The government produced 52 other witnesses who echoed the details of the "arms plot" scenario.

Yet all the defendants maintained their innocence. Some observers doubted the prosecution's contention that a powerful figure like Awolowo would have risked his future in a haphazard coup plot. Awolowo, who had campaigned for democratic policies for years, saw no mystery about the prosecution's motives. He denounced the proceedings as a "political trial" and commented on the irony of having to argue for his freedom in a Nigerian court after having spent three terms in British prisons during the struggle for independence.

The court was ultimately overwhelmed by the parade of prosecution witnesses. Enahoro was convicted and sentenced to 15 years' imprisonment for treasonable felony, conspiracy, and illegal importation of firearms. (An appeal shortened his sentence to 7 years.) On September 11, 1963, Awolowo was found guilty of identical charges and sentenced to 10 years' imprisonment. Three other defendants were acquitted, but the rest received jail terms of varied duration.

The Army Takes Over

With its leadership imprisoned, the Action Group faded from the national political scene. Yet friction within the NPC-NCNC coalition caused the ruling alliance to fray as the first federal parliamentary election since independence neared in December 1964. Unconcealed election fraud in the November 1965 legislative elections provoked deadly riots and rumors of a coup by the Nigerian army to restore order.

On January 15, 1966, a small group of Ibo army officers moved with deadly precision against federal leaders. Prime Minister Balewa and Chief Akintola were assassinated, as were many prominent politicians and senior army officers sympathetic to the ruling regime. Coup leaders declared that they would restore peace and plot a progressive course for Nigeria, including new elections. Within days, however, the coup collapsed and the Nigerian military assumed control.

The new leader, Major General Johnson Aguiye Ironsi, declared that only a unitary government could eliminate the factional strife rampant under the federal system. Yet the appearance of favoritism toward his Ibo tribe left Ironsi open to suspicions that a new unitary government would be Ibo-dominated. When Ironsi moved to abolish Nigeria's federal system and eliminate the powerful regional governments, more riots resulted. Ironsi was killed in a second coup on July 29, 1966. He was replaced by a young army officer, Major Yakabu Gowan, who immediately withdrew Ironsi's decrees, reinstating Nigeria's federalism. Gowan also released Awolowo and Enahoro from prison on August 3, hoping to consolidate power with their help.

Aftermath

One result of the Action Party "arms plot" trial was felt in England after leadership of the government passed into Labour Party hands. Largely as a result of the Enahoro debacle, the British government announced on May 24, 1966, that its custom of honoring requests for political asylum would be extended to Commonwealth nations.

Peace continued to elude Nigeria. In 1967, the country slipped into a civil war between the Ibo and other tribes. The carnage lasted for two and a half years and claimed as many as 3 million lives. Chief Awolowo, who opposed the Biafran secession, served as finance minister during the war. He resumed his private law practice in 1971, quitting government over the military's refusal to return the country to civilian rule. When free elections were finally held in 1979 and 1983, Awolowo was a presidential candidate on the United Party of Nigeria slate. He lost to Shehu Shagari both times.

Chief Awolowo's vision of a democratic and tranquil Nigeria was not realized during his lifetime. He was forced to surrender his passport during yet another military takeover in December 1983. He died in his hometown of Ikenne on May 9, 1987.

—Tom Smith

Suggestions for Further Reading

Lewis, Anthony. "Britain To Widen Right of Asylum." *The New York Times*, May 25, 1966.

Meredith, Martin. *The First Dance of Freedom: Black Africa in the Post-war Era*. New York: Harper & Row, 1984.

Metz, Helen Chapin, ed. *Nigeria: A Country Study*. Washington, D.C.: Library of Congress Federal Research Division, 1992.

"Verdict in Lagos." *Time*, September 20, 1963, 39.

De Gaulle Assassination Conspirators Trial: 1963

Defendants: Lieutenant Colonel Jean-Marie Bastien-Thiry, Serge Bernier, Pascal Bertan, Lieutenant Alain Bourgenet de la Tocnaye, Louis de Conde, Alphonse Constantin, Etienne Ducasse, Gerard Duisines, Pierre Magade, Lajos Marton, Jean-Pierre Naudin, Jacques Prevost, Lazlo Varga, Georges Watin
Crime Charged: Conspiracy to assassinate Charles de Gaulle
Chief Defense Lawyers: Jacques Isorni, Jean-Louis Tixier-Vignancour
Chief Prosecutors: Brigadier General Charles Gerthoffer, Brigadier General Claude Sudaka **Judges:** Lieutenant General Roger Gardet, Colonel Andre Reboul, three other officers **Place:** Vincennes, France
Dates of Trial: January 28–March 4, 1963 **Verdict:** Guilty
Sentences: Bastien-Thiry, Bernier, Bourgenet de la Tocnaye, Marton, Prevost, Watin—death; de Conde, Duisines, Naudin—life imprisonment; Magade, Bertan—15 years; Varga—10 years; Constantin—7 years; Ducasse—3 years

SIGNIFICANCE

The attempted assassination and resulting trial underlined President Charles de Gaulle's long struggle with France's extreme right wing over his liberal policy on independence for Algeria. Of at least nine attempts on de Gaulle's life by *Algerie française* extremists, the August 1962 ambush was one of two that very nearly succeeded.

O n August 22, 1962, French President Charles de Gaulle, his wife, and their son-in-law, Alain de Boissieu, were being driven through the Paris suburb of Petit-Clamart on their way to Villacoublay Airport. Suddenly their car was ambushed by two other cars, guns blazing. Chauffeur Francis Marroux sped up. They seemed to escape. De Boissieu, seeing two more cars, shouted to de Gaulle, who ducked, pulling his wife down with him. The car was hit by 14 of some 150 machine gun bullets. No one was harmed.

Five months later, on January 28, 1963, fourteen alleged conspirators were brought to trial before the five-man Military Court of Justice in a barrackslike building within the ancient Fort of Vincennes, on the outskirts of Paris. Only nine were present, however. Five were to be tried in absentia, for they had not been caught.

Before any witness was called, defense attorney Jacques Isorni, a prominent right-wing lawyer who had defended Marshal Henri Pétain in his trial for treason in 1945, accused France's finance minister, Valery Giscard d'Estaing, of having befriended and given information to the Secret Army Organization, a right-wing terrorist group opposed to the French government over the issue of independence for Algeria.

Two Weeks of Wrangling

The defense also disputed the jurisdiction of the court, arguing that the entire procedure was illegal because an ordinance setting up the special tribunal had been invalidated the preceding October by the Council of State. On January 15, the parliament had passed a bill setting up the new Court for the Security of the State and, at the same time, validating the past decisions of the old court. The next day, de Gaulle had signed a decree handing over the nine defendants to the Military Court of Justice. That decree, contended the defense, was illegal.

The following day, the defense lawyers harangued the court at length on its legality and its competence to judge the case. Before the charges were even put into the record or testimony was begun, it was clear that the defense would try to stretch the trial beyond February 25, when the court was scheduled to go out of existence, replaced by the new court. As all concerned knew, the decisions of the new Court for the Security of the State could be appealed, whereas those of the Military Court of Justice would be final.

As the defense wrangled over procedures, two weeks went by. On February 5, after defense counsel Isorni contemptuously questioned the impartiality of one of the judges, he was disbarred by the Military Court for three years. Isorni stalked from the courtroom, singing the French version of "Auld Lang Syne"—*ce n'est qu'un au revoir, mes frères*, meaning "it's not good-bye forever, my brothers."

In the meantime, the French cabinet, in hopes of stopping the "parody of justice" that it said the defense lawyers' "obstructionist tactics" were creating, sent to parliament a bill that, if passed, would extend the life of the Military Court of Justice for the duration of the trial.

The Defense: Kidnap, Not Kill

At last, the defense stated its position. Air Force Lieutenant Colonel Jean-Marie Bastien-Thiry testified that his commando team's goal had not been to kill de Gaulle but to kidnap him. As part of Georges Bidault's National Council of the Resistance, successor to the Secret Army Organization (which had decided to give up the struggle shortly before France's July 1, 1962, referendum voted overwhelmingly for Algeria's freedom), his group, said Bastien-Thiry, still sought to fight Algerian independence. The group's military tribunal had condemned de Gaulle to death, but, insisted the defendant, he could be executed only after he was brought to trial and found guilty.

Bastien-Thiry said the plan had been to stop the president's car by puncturing its tires, capture de Gaulle, and take him to Versailles for trial. He named several cabinet ministers he claimed were in on the plot, including d'Estaing. The finance minister immediately declared the accusation absurd and said he had never heard of the colonel before this case.

One prosecution witness, police inspector Maurice Bovier, who had headed the investigation that led to the arrest of the defendants, testified that during police interrogations none of them had spoken of seizing the president or of holding him for trial.

On February 19, the National Assembly, overruling the senate, adopted a bill prolonging the life of the Military Court.

A Broken Promise

As the defense summarized its case, a main argument was that de Gaulle had reneged on promises to keep Algeria French. He had gained power, defense attorneys claimed, after the Fourth Republic (in power from 1946 to 1958) had failed to stop the rebellion in Algeria and an uprising of citizens and army officers had demanded that he take charge. As he formed his Fifth Republic government, they had a right to expect him to carry out their policies.

Summing up for the prosecution, Brigadier General Charles Gerthoffer asked for a death sentence for seven of the nine defendants. He ridiculed the defense position that the purpose of the ambush had been to "arrest" de Gaulle and hold him for a "trial." The machine gunners' aim, he noted, had been directly at the president, not at the tires of his car.

"First Act" of a Civil War?

The prosecutor also reminded the judges of the testimony of defendant Lieutenant Alain Bourgenet de la Tocnaye on the planned arrest. "Can you see General de Gaulle," he said mockingly, "saying, 'Here are my suspenders and my glasses. I will follow you.'" Rather, alleged Gerthoffer, the assassination was planned as "the first act" of a civil war as part of terrorist action in Algeria and in France by the extremists. The Algerian struggle for independence, he added, typified the worldwide movement of colonial peoples for political freedom, and France could have remained in Algeria only by using force. De Gaulle's position, he concluded, was that of the popular will.

The Military Court deliberated for three hours and found all guilty. On March 4, it sentenced three men to death: Bastien-Thiry, who had organized the plot; Bourgenet de la Tocnaye, who had been Bastien-Thiry's deputy; and Jacques Prevost, who had directed the machine-gun fire. In absentia, Serge Bernier, Lajos Marton, and Georges Watin were sentenced to death. Gerard

Duisines, one of those who had fired on de Gaulle's car, received life imprisonment. Pierre Magade, an air force deserter, and Pascal Bertan, a young student, were sentenced to 15 years each; and Lazlo Varga, a refugee from the 1956 Hungarian uprising, received 10 years. One plotter, Alphonse Constantin, who had not joined the attack because he had lost his nerve, nevertheless was sentenced to 7 years. Etienne Ducasse, who had sheltered the conspirators in his apartment, was given 3 years.

Louis de Conde and Jean-Pierre Naudin were sentenced to life imprisonment in absentia. The judges noted that those convicted in absentia would have to be retried if they were caught. Finally, the judges reminded the defendants that their only appeal was directly to the president for commutation of sentence.

Death for One, Clemency for Others

From death cells at Fresnes Prison outside Paris, where the guard was heavily reinforced, the three condemned men appealed to de Gaulle for clemency. He spared Bourgenet de la Tocnaye and Prevost, commuting their sentences to life imprisonment.

With clemency denied and his execution scheduled for the next morning, Bastien-Thiry asked for paper and pen. He then wrote a letter to de Gaulle in which he demanded a stay of execution because, as he had just learned, Georges Bidault, former premier and head of the National Council of the Resistance, who was a fugitive from French justice, had been detained the day before in West Germany. It was expected that Bavarian state authorities would grant Bidault asylum in West Germany.

His plea refused, Bastien-Thiry asked, "Am I the only one to be executed?" Told that he was, he took communion in the prison chapel, put on his air force cap—stripped of the braid that denoted his rank—refused to be blindfolded, and faced the firing squad with a rosary in his hand. He was executed at 6:40 A.M. in the gray dawn of March 11, 1963.

—Bernard Ryan, Jr.

Suggestions for Further Reading

Alexandre, Philippe. *The Duel: de Gaulle & Pompidou*. Boston: Houghton Mifflin, 1972.

Cook, Don. *Charles de Gaulle: A Biography*. New York: Putnam's, 1983.

De Gaulle, Charles. *Memoirs of Hope: Renewal and Endeavor*. Translated by Terence Kilmartin. New York: Simon & Schuster, 1971.

Kersaudy, Francois. *Churchill and de Gaulle*. New York: Atheneum, 1982.

Lacouture, Jean. *De Gaulle: The Ruler 1945–1970*. Translated by Patrick O'Brian. New York: W. W. Norton, 1991.

Ledwidge, Bernard. *De Gaulle*. New York: St. Martin's, 1982.

Williams, Charles. *The Last Great Frenchman: A Life of General de Gaulle*. New York: Wiley, 1993.

Nelson Mandela Trial: 1963–64

Defendants:
Nelson Mandela, Walter Sisulu, Dennis Goldberg, Govan Mbeki, Raymond Mhlaba, Elias Motsoaledi, Andrew Mlangeni, Ahmed Kathrada, Lionel Bernstein

Crimes Charged:
(1) The commission of acts of sabotage together with the Communist Party; (2) conspiracy to aid or procure wrongful acts concerning the recruitment of persons for training in the preparation and use of explosives for committing acts of violence, conspiracy to commit acts of guerrilla warfare, acts of assistance to military units of foreign countries invading South Africa, and acts of participation in violent revolution; (3) the execution of the common purpose of committing the acts set out above; (4) soliciting money in South Africa and abroad, and disbursing those funds in the interests of their campaign

Chief Defense Lawyers:
Bram Fischer, Senior Counsel; Arthur Chaskalson; Joel Joffe; Vernon Berrangé; George Bizos

Chief Prosecutors:
Percy Yutar, deputy attorney general of the Transvaal, assisted by A. B. Krog and others

Judge: Quartus de Wet, judge-president of the Transvaal

Place:
Supreme Court of South Africa (Transvaal Provincial Division), Palace of Justice, Pretoria

Dates of Trial: October 9, 1963–June 12, 1964

Verdict:
Mandela, Sisulu, Goldberg, Mbeki, Mhlaba, Motsoaledi, Mlangeni—guilty on all four counts; Kathrada—guilty on one count; Bernstein—acquitted

Sentence: Life imprisonment for the eight found guilty

SIGNIFICANCE
In the Rivonia trial, South Africa sought to end antigovernment activity by discrediting and condemning the leaders of the African National Congress by any means possible. For Mandela, the trial provided a forum in which to present his powerful and eloquent case against the racist policy of apartheid before the court of world opinion. As a result, international pressure began to mount and eventually helped to end the brutal regime.

O n May 10, 1994, when he was sworn in as South Africa's first black African president, Nelson Mandela looked back to the old South Africa as a "valley of darkness." Rich with natural resources, including gold and diamonds, the country was first colonized by the Dutch and then by the English. Becoming independent in 1910, South Africa continued to be ruled by the white minority, which in 1948 made official the policy of apartheid. Apartheid segregated the races, denied blacks the vote, and severely limited their economic and educational opportunities and their basic human rights. All this was enforced by repressive police-state tactics.

Mandela's Activities

A stint as a gold mine policeman opened Mandela's eyes to the dire conditions under which South African blacks subsisted. Previously, he had been groomed as a future tribal chief, had been expelled from college for political activity, and had escaped to Johannesburg to avoid an arranged marriage. With Walter Sisulu's help, Mandela was able to complete his legal studies, and together with Oliver Tambo he opened the nation's first black law firm in 1952.

At the same time, Mandela and Tambo, led by Sisulu, became active in the African National Congress (ANC), a nationalist political organization dedicated to seeking justice and full citizenship rights, including the vote, for South African blacks. Joining the ANC national executive board in 1949, Mandela, who long had endorsed African autonomy, now proposed a united effort, together with Indians and supportive whites, against racist laws. In 1952, he directed the ANC's Defiance Campaign, a strategy based on mass acts of civil disobedience and Gandhian passive resistance, using boycotts, noncooperation, and work stoppages to overwhelm the justice system with mass arrests. The government reacted with increasing violence to such actions, culminating in the 1960 Sharpeville massacre. Some 180 people were injured, and 69 were killed when the police opened fire on a crowd.

South African organizer of the African National Congress (ANC), Nelson Mandela in 1961. (Hulton-Deutsch Collection)

Following this, the government declared an emergency, banned the ANC, and arrested thousands. In 1961, because of the banning of the ANC and because nonviolent action had provoked increasingly violent reaction from the authorities, Mandela and others organized Umkhonto we Sizwe (MK), or "Spear of the Nation." Although the ANC remained committed to nonviolence, the MK was to force change by means of acts of sabotage against installations but not human beings. Lilliesleaf, a small farm in Rivonia on the outskirts of Johannesburg, was rented as MK headquarters. Pursued by the police, Mandela went underground as "the Black Pimpernel" and traveled in disguise to start up regional commands of the MK. On his return from a 1962 trip to other African nations and to England to raise funds and arrange for military training, he was arrested. He was tried and found guilty of incitement to strike and of leaving the country without a passport; he was sentenced on November 7, 1962, to five years' imprisonment on Robben Island.

Acts of sabotage continued, and the government arrested hundreds under the new 90-day detention law, passed May 1, 1963, whereby the police could hold anyone without a trial, often incommunicado, in solitary confinement for up to 90 days, a period that could be extended again and again until the police had finished their interrogation, often using physical torture. Tipped off by an informant probably thus interrogated, the police swooped down on the Rivonia farm on July 12, 1963, capturing Sisulu and seven others. They all vanished into 90-day detention, and Mandela was transferred to the Pretoria prison.

The Rivonia Trial

The Rivonia trial opened on October 9, 1963, with prosecutor Percy Yutar leading the state case before the scarlet-robed Justice Quartus de Wet, presiding alone in a courtroom packed with security police and the press, and with diplomats and other important visitors sitting in the empty jury box. The trial had been moved to Pretoria from Johannesburg for security reasons. The defendants' families had hired Bram Fischer to lead a group of lawyers experienced in political trials. Despite repeated requests, it was not until the trial opened that the defense received a copy of the indictment, which appeared on the streets that day in a special edition of a newspaper. Fischer immediately asked for a six-week adjournment so that the defense could prepare its case; he also complained of the severe imprisonment conditions. The judge granted a three-week adjournment, until October 29.

At that point, the government's attempt to stage a show trial began to backfire. Fischer delivered a devastating two-day attack on the indictment as a legal document: The prosecution had failed to provide particulars of what acts of sabotage had been carried out by whom and where, of how the conspiracy had been formed, of how the ANC and the Communist Party had conspired together, and so forth. The dates and places mentioned in the preamble did not match the information in the actual charges. The defense moved for dismissal of the indictment on the grounds that it did "not conform with the law and inform the accused adequately and with reasonable clarity of the precise charge or allegation they had to meet." The judge agreed, and the long buildup in publicity climaxed in an embarrassing defeat for the prosecution. In answer to Prosecutor Yutar's protests, the judge admonished him: "The whole basis of your argument . . . is that you are satisfied that the accused are guilty. . . . All preliminary matters like this must be approached on the assumption that the accused are not guilty. . . . That is the correct approach."

The reason for quashing the indictment was shoddy legal work by the prosecution, a motif that was to run throughout the trial. Time after time, Yutar ignored legal formalities and legal arguments and analyses, instead basing his tactics on the free use of sarcasm, innuendos, gossip, hearsay, publicity stunts, fishing expeditions, coerced testimony, and inadmissible and concocted evidence. With the indictment declared invalid, the defendants technically were free, but they were immediately rearrested in the courtroom and returned to their cells.

The trial formally resumed on December 3 with an amended indictment. In the interim, the defense had found some 40 major errors in the reworked indictment, but this time the judge ignored them and moved forward. Yutar opposed a defense request for postponement with a schedule itemizing how many hours the defense lawyers had spent in consultation with their clients in the Pretoria jail. Yutar had been spying, in effect, on the defense team and had instructed prison staff to record the defense team's movements. The police had also harassed the defense in their meetings with the accused in numerous petty ways and had bugged those sessions.

On December 3, the accused entered their formal pleas. Mandela led off with, "My lord, the Government, not I, should be in the dock. I plead not guilty to all charges." The other defendants responded similarly. As Yutar rose for his opening statement, Fischer objected to the presence of a South African state radio microphone, which had appeared overnight on Yutar's desk in an era when broadcasting of any part of a trial was unheard of in South Africa. The judge ordered the microphone removed. Yutar went on with his address, which was to prove his best piece of work in the entire proceedings. He explained what the prosecution intended to prove: a conspiracy, centered on the Rivonia farm, to commit sabotage as a prelude to guerrilla warfare, armed invasion, and the violent overthrow of the government in a war of liberation, all planned for 1963.

Finally, the direction and goal of the trial had been revealed. Because the verdict was almost certainly going to be guilty for most of the defendants, the job of the defense would be, primarily, to prevent the death sentence and, secondarily, to expose evidence the defendants maintained was incorrect or manufactured. The defendants insisted to their counsel that although guerrilla warfare had been considered, it had not been decided upon; there had been no plan to invite foreign military forces to join them. The struggle for liberation had been envisioned as a lengthy ongoing process, rather than as an event planned for 1963.

The prosecution's case depended to a great extent on witnesses, some 173 in all. Of these, 23 were being held under the 90-day law and thus were themselves victims of the system. First came domestic workers and then farm laborers (one of whom dared to complain to the judge of police torture), along with other miscellaneous witnesses, including attendees at ANC meetings. They were followed by various taxi drivers, some of them "traveling witnesses" who had appeared on behalf of the government at numerous trials. The testimony mixed fact with fiction, including scraps of gossip, hearsay, irrelevancies, "induced memories," and blatant lies, often coerced or coached by the police. The police themselves were questioned, and the quality of much of their testimony was open to question as well. A revealing admission on their interrogation methods came from one Sergeant Card: "We tell them what we want to know, and wait until [they confirm] it!"

The stars of the prosecution witness parade were the dramatically anonymous trio X, Y, and Z. X was a former MK member who offered the most damaging testimony about acts of sabotage and the MK membership; Y testified only about defendant Dennis Goldberg; Z, another MK activist, offered perjured testimony against Elias Motsoaledi in order to save his own skin. A number of the hundreds of documents seized from Rivonia were read sporadically into the record by Yutar. He neither provided advance copies to the defense nor followed proper procedure in "proving" them. Hilda Bernstein, wife of defendant Lionel Bernstein, reported:

> We are witnessing the trappings of a trial, and through this trial we are also witnesses to the last stages in the destruction of South Africa's legal tradition, the abandonment of codes of legal behavior and standards of justice for the sole purpose of hounding and exterminating those considered to be enemies of the State. The State is revealing for the first time the extent to which it will go, that it will stop at nothing, neither in forcing testimony from witnesses under duress, in the suborning of false evidence, nor in the coaching of witnesses. All involved in the court procedures ... become participants in this tragedy which will be compounded again and again through hundreds of trials in the future.

The defense case opened on April 14, 1964, after five weeks in which the defense examined and analyzed the masses of documents, statements, and evidence. In summary, the defense denied the major charges: that Goldberg, Kathrada, Bernstein, and Mhlaba were members of the MK, much less of its high command; that the MK was a section of the ANC—the two organizations were distinctly and deliberately separate; that the ANC was a tool of the Communist Party; that the MK had a plan known as Operation Mayibuye, allegedly the blueprint for a guerrilla war.

The highlight of the defense case came on April 23 when Mandela, from the dock, gave a five-hour address in which he spoke of his own life and of the history of the ANC, the MK, and the Communist Party. He movingly ended his speech with these words:

> During my lifetime I have dedicated myself to this struggle of the African people. I have fought against white domination and I have fought against black domination. I have cherished the ideal of a democratic and free society in which all persons live together in harmony and with equal opportunities. It is an ideal which I hope to live for and achieve. But, if need be, it is an ideal for which I am prepared to die.

Censorship regulations had been lifted in this trial, so Mandela's talk received wide publicity. Sisulu also offered an account of his personal odyssey and emphasized that the ANC and the MK were distinct entities and that they had never committed to the path of guerrilla warfare. Under cross-examination, the accused consistently maintained the principles they had set: They would state the facts as fully as possible to explain and justify their political stance but would not reveal information that could place others at hazard or endanger their organizations. This was a unique development. As Hilda Bernstein put it: "There had been a series of trials ... in which many of the accused had tried to exonerate themselves by naming and implicating dozens of others, so spreading the prosecution even wider. The refusal of the Rivonia accused broke new ground. . . . [T]he example they set became a precedent and many unwilling witnesses would also refuse to testify and face the prospect of twelve months' imprisonment for this refusal."

Long-Term Justice

For the defense, the trial was a victory, at least in relative terms. The judge accepted that the defendants had not made any decision about undertaking guerrilla war, and he sentenced seven of the defendants to prison rather than to death (Kathrada was given a short sentence; Lionel Bernstein was acquitted). Mandela, who had decided not to appeal, was returned, with Sisulu, Mbeki, Mhlaba, Motsoaledi, Mlangeni, and Kathrada, to serve his term under harsh conditions on Robben Island; because prisoners were segregated by race, Goldberg was sent to a different prison. It would be a quarter of a century before all of them would be freed.

All the while, Mandela's wife, Winnie Mandela, who was both his loyal supporter and respected representative on the outside, spent the decades protesting and periodically being tried, imprisoned, and banned for her political activity. Just as Mandela and the others were released, her reputation began to disintegrate. Implicated variously in misappropriation of funds, kidnapping, deaths, and cover-ups, she was brought to trial on February 4, 1991. After she was found guilty as an accessory after the fact in kidnapping and assault, she was released pending appeal. (In 1993, the appeals court upheld the conviction but gave her a suspended sentence and fined her.) Her headstrong attitude and behavior continued to embarrass Mandela, and the marriage eventually ended.

Winnie Mandela's legal problems, though, failed to diminish the towering importance of the Rivonia trial. Following the sentencing of Mandela and his codefendants, the *Rand Daily Mail* had summed up: "The case has captured the imagination because it seems to tell a classic, ancient story of the struggle of men for freedom and dignity, with overtones of Grecian tragedy in their failure. . . . Rivonia is a name to remember." But neither that writer nor anyone who observed the trial could have imagined that four years after Mandela finally gained freedom in 1990, he would be elected president of South Africa.

—*Eva Weber*

Suggestions for Further Reading

Benson, Mary. *Nelson Mandela: The Man and The Movement*. New York: W. W. Norton, 1986.

Bernstein, Hilda. *The World That Was Ours: The Story of the Rivonia Trial*. London: SAWriters, 1989.

Gilbey, Emma. *The Lady: The Life and Times of Winnie Mandela*. London: Vintage, Random House, 1994.

Mandela, Nelson. *Long Walk to Freedom: The Autobiography of Nelson Mandela*. Boston: Little, Brown, 1994.

———. *The Struggle Is My Life: His Speeches and Writings* . . . 3d ed. New York: Pathfinder, 1990.

Mandela, Winnie. *Part of My Soul Went with Him.* New York: W. W. Norton, 1985.

Meer, Fatima. *Higher Than Hope: The Authorized Biography of Nelson Mandela.* New York: HarperCollins, 1990.

Regis Debray Trial: 1967

Defendant: Regis Debray   **Crimes Charged:** Entering Bolivia to participate in an armed insurrection   **Chief Defense Lawyer:** Captain Raul Novillo Villarroel   **Chief Prosecutor:** Colonel Remberto Iriarte Paz   **Judge:** Colonel Efrain Guachalla   **Place:** Camiri, Bolivia   **Dates of Trial:** September 26–October 31, 1967   **Verdict:** Guilty   **Sentence:** Thirty years' imprisonment

SIGNIFICANCE
At the height of Cuban efforts to export communism to Latin American nations, Debray's status as a political prisoner became a cause célèbre with leftist European and American intellectuals, many of whom admired Communist ideology and supported Debray's unrepentant stance.

The path that led French intellectual Jules Regis Debray to stand before a military tribunal in a fly-specked Bolivian village was a circuitous one. Debray was born in 1941 to a privileged and conservative family—his father was a lawyer and his mother was a fighter for the French resistance in World War II and was later a Paris councilwoman. Debray studied at the elite École Normale Supérieure, where he came under the influence of Professor Louis Althusser, a Marxist philosopher. In 1957, the Algerian war for independence from France had a formative impact on the 16-year-old youth, effectively politicizing him.

Four years later, the transformation was completed when he discovered Fidel Castro, the Cuban revolutionary leader. During a 1961 vacation in the United States, Debray hitchhiked from New York to Miami, eventually ending up in Cuba, where he taught in rural schools and became an intimate of Castro's—Castro had taken control of Cuba in 1959—spending long hours in discussion with him. Debray became convinced of the righteousness of the Communist cause, and back in Paris, he began to construct a Marxist theory for interpreting Latin American history and politics.

In July 1962, he traveled to Venezuela to direct a French documentary film on guerrilla activities there and afterward journeyed throughout the rest of the continent. Following his return to France, he wrote various articles on the subject and taught philosophy for a while. In 1965, through a French exchange program with Cuba, Debray returned as a teacher to Havana, where he renewed his close friendship with Castro. In 1966, he went to Bolivia to lecture at several universities and to study the nation's political situation. After a return to Cuba in early 1967, he quietly reentered Bolivia by way of Chile, disappearing until his capture on April 20 near a deserted guerrilla camp in southeastern Bolivia.

The Bolivian military accused him of active involvement in guerrilla activity, a position undoubtedly reinforced by the publication of Debray's book *Révolution dans la Révolution?* In this volume, Debray advocated Castro's theory of revolution and called for insurrection in every Latin American country. Regarding Bolivia, he specifically discussed strategy that might have succeeded during the violent riots of 1965.

Debray was held prisoner by the army for more than five months before the trial started. During this time he was interrogated, tortured, and initially kept incommunicado. He was neither formally charged before a magistrate nor permitted a lawyer. Among his interrogators were two Cuban exile agents of the CIA, Eduardo Gonzalez and Felix Ramos, who had arrived by plane from the Panama antiguerrilla training center soon after Debray's capture. Debray later said that he had refused their offer of freedom in exchange for collaboration. Regardless, the CIA's insistence on a thorough interrogation, along with international pressure for a proper trial, probably saved Debray from summary execution.

On May 19, a La Paz lawyer and deputy dean of the Faculty of Law, Walter Flores Torrico, applied for a writ of habeas corpus and was criticized by Bolivian commander in chief General Ovando, who insisted, "a Bolivian ought not to do that." After much trouble, Flores discovered that Debray was being held in Camiri and finally, on June 28, with a group of journalists, went to interview him there. In a series of conflicting accounts of his actions, Debray denied being a Communist, taking up arms against the Bolivian army, and knowing the whereabouts of Ernesto "Che" Guevara, the Argentine-born revolutionary and guerrilla leader who had helped Castro seize power and who had not been seen for some two years. Rumors had placed Guevara at the heart of the Bolivian insurrection.

Bolivian President Rene Barrientos called Debray a "Castro agent" and described him as "an adventurer who has come to Bolivia to bring sorrow to Bolivian families," referring to a March 23 ambush in which 18 soldiers had died. In an August press interview, Debray continued to maintain his innocence while conceding his Marxism, "I am still a Marxist—perhaps a stronger one than ever—and as a reporter I still do not believe in objective reporting. I have written a book, no more. And for that I am being persecuted." He clarified, "I am an intellectual revolutionary.... All aspiring intellectuals, however, should be revolutionaries and vice versa. Any revolutionary should be willing to change the world on an intellectual basis." He insisted he was in Bolivia solely as a journalist working for Mexico's *Sucesos para todos*. In differing statements, Debray both denied and confirmed Guevara's presence in Bolivia.

Finally obtaining permission to see him, Debray's parents and his childhood nanny arrived and soon caused more confusion. Firing his Bolivian lawyer and persuading Debray to lead his own defense, the elder Debray compared his son's case to those of Joan of Arc and of Alfred Dreyfus, a French Jewish army officer wrongly convicted of treason. In La Paz to appeal to the Bolivian president, Mme. Debray tactlessly asserted, "A secret dossier from the CIA was on President Barrientos' desk within 48 hours of my son's arrest. They forced the Bolivian government to hold him, and as a result everything about his imprisonment has been illegal from the beginning." She also infuriated the Bolivian people by defending the guerrillas before an audience that included family of the soldiers killed by the guerrillas. Meanwhile, posters portraying Debray as an assassin and threatening, "He who kills with steel will die by steel" appeared on walls everywhere.

International support for Debray, however, remained strong. Petitions and letters poured in from governments, politicians, and writers, including French President Charles de Gaulle, Bertrand Russell, Robert Kennedy, Mary Mc-Carthy, Robert Lowell, the Vatican, André Malraux, and Jean-Paul Sartre. Press scrutiny remained intense as well.

The Trial

The trial opened on September 26. Charged with Debray were Ciro Roberto Bustos, an Argentine painter; three miners who had joined the guerrillas; a peasant who had supplied them; and Jorge Vazquez Viana, a guerrilla and the son of a noted historian. Vazquez, who had been captured with serious wounds and lay recuperating in a weakened postoperative state, had mysteriously disappeared from his hospital bed. The army claimed he had escaped to Argentina but set an empty chair for him in the courtroom as a "witness for the prosecution." By this time, Debray had a new defense lawyer, Captain Raul Novillo Villarroel.

The prosecution made a central issue of Debray's book, which it described as "a guerrilla handbook that is causing terror and death in the country." Captain Novillo answered the charges by asserting that Debray had entered Bolivia openly under his own name and carrying a valid passport; that his attested credentials proved him to be an accredited journalist seeking information on guerrilla activities; that Debray was led by underground contacts to the hidden camp at Nancahuazu, where he interviewed Che Guevara, and then openly returned to army territory; and that, although sympathetic to the guerrilla cause, he had used a rifle only for hunting and had not helped the guerrillas in any way or participated in ambushes. The journalists present who examined the photograph supposedly showing Debray with a rifle, determined that though he was shown with guerrillas, the image was not clear and did not show him with a rifle.

During a break in the trial on October 2, Debray said to a Bolivian student, "For me it is an honor and a glory at this time to be a guerrilla, and much more to be a leader of a liberation movement. Why should I take that honor away from myself when I am going to be condemned anyway? I would prefer to be sentenced to 30 years . . . as a guerrilla, rather than to be martyred as a journalist. I am in agreement with the guerrillas, but I have not been a member of the Bolivian National Liberation Army."

Nearly two weeks into the trial, the unexpected occurred. On October 7, 75 miles north of Camiri, the Bolivian army captured a wounded Che Guevara and executed him the next day. In his backpack soldiers found a personal diary, along with decoded messages. These items, when presented as evidence at the trial, proved that Debray, under the code name "Danton," was in reality a courier between Che Guevara and Fidel Castro, who had been providing arms, money, medical supplies and other support to the guerrillas. Debray had arrived at Guevara's camp on March 19. In a diary entry on March 21, Guevara had written: "The Frenchman wants to join us. I asked him to go organize a network of support in France, where he would return after passing through Havana." On March 25, Guevara had reported: "Long oral report on the situation to the Frenchman. We decided to call the movement the National Liberation Front of Bolivia."

Despite this evidence, in his concluding statement Captain Novillo insisted that no proof existed that proved Debray had committed the crimes of murder, robbery, and rebellion and urged the tribunal to absolve him of all guilt. Furthermore, Novillo argued, Debray had not organized or helped to organize the guerrillas, nor had he participated in any ambushes. Prevented by an uproar in the courtroom from making a full statement in his own defense, Debray, though still shaken by Guevara's death, did manage to make some telling points at the trial's end. He compared Guevara's attempt to liberate Latin America from the United States to Simón Bolívar's liberation of the continent from the Spanish. He again denied being the guerrillas' political commissar, said that his book was only one of many read by the revolutionaries. He insisted he had not taken part in any military actions, and held that his statements of moral and political sympathy with the cause had been wrongly presented as proof of his responsibility for guerrilla military activities. He concluded, "I want to make clear that this mission of mine to tell people abroad of the aims of the guerrillas is an integral part of revolutionary work. In this sense, I not only affirm but demand that the tribunal consider me morally and politically co-responsible for the acts of my guerrilla comrades." He and Bustos each received a sentence of 30 years in prison, with permission denied for any appeals.

Aftermath

The trial turned out to be an embarrassment in many ways to the Bolivian government. To placate the army, President Barrientos had ordered that it be a military tribunal, which was not carried out with much appearance of fairness or justice. Debray somehow was allowed, at least in part, to make his powerful statement at the end. The officers in charge were inadequate in answering the criticisms of the international press corps present. And the tribunal members all were promoted to generals after the trial. Perhaps most devastating were the revelations about the degree of involvement in Bolivian counterinsurgency operations by the CIA.

In a jailhouse interview on November 24, an unfazed Debray vehemently called for "armed rebellion in Latin America against U.S. colonialism." Over the next several years, the government repeatedly refused to pardon or amnesty Debray, despite endless pleas for his freedom. Debray married Elisabeth Burgos in February 1968, and she was permitted to visit him for ten days every three months. In May 1969, a Red Cross delegate found him in good health and reading and writing a lot, although his mail was censored. Suddenly, on December 23, 1970, Debray and Bustos were secretly released and flown to Chile. In 1981, Debray was appointed a specialist adviser to French President François Mitterrand on Third World affairs.

—Eva Weber

Suggestions for Further Reading

Debray, Regis. *The Chilean Revolution: Conversations with Allende.* New York: Pantheon Books, 1972.

———. *Critique of Political Reason.* Translated by David Macey. London: NLB, 1983.

———. *Prison Writings.* Translated by Rosemary Sheed. New York: Random House, 1973.

———. *Revolution in the Revolution? Armed Struggle and Political Struggle in Latin America.* Translated by Bobbye Ortiz. New York: Monthly Review Press, 1967.

———. *Strategy for Revolution.* New York: Monthly Review Press, 1970.

Guevara, Ernesto. *The Complete Bolivian Diaries of Che Guevara, and Other Captured Documents.* New York: Stein & Day, 1968.

Huberman, Leo. *Regis Debray and the Latin American Revolution: A Collection of Essays.* New York: Monthly Review Press, 1981.

Baader-Meinhof Trial: 1975–77

Defendants: Andreas Baader, Ulrike Meinhof, Gudrun Ensslin, Jan-Carl Raspe
Crimes Charged: Murder, attempted murder, robbery, and the forming of a criminal association **Chief Defense Lawyers:** Marie-Luise Becker, Peter Grigat, Hans Heinz Heldmann, Dieter Konig, Manfred Kunzel, Karl-Heinz Linke, Arndt Muller, Rupert von Plottnitz, Helmut Riedel, Otto Schily, Dieter Schnabel, Eberhard Schwarz, Gerd Temming **Chief Prosecutors:** Siegfried Buback, Werner Widera, Heinrich Wunder, Peter Zeis **Judges:** Theodor Prinzing, Eberhard Foth **Place:** Stammheim, West Germany **Dates of Trial:** May 21, 1975–April 21, 1977 **Verdict:** Guilty **Sentence:** Life imprisonment

SIGNIFICANCE

This extended trial, lasting nearly two years, underscored the fact that the notorious Baader-Meinhof gang—which had terrorized much of Europe for several years—severely injured, rather than advanced, the cause of radical politics. During the trial, the defendants' disruptive behavior caused a change in the Code of Criminal Procedure to permit a trial without the defendants present. The trial also prompted the Bundestag to pass a law permitting the justice minister to prohibit communication between unruly prisoners and their lawyers, other prisoners, or the outside world. Finally, the trial provoked the assassination of West Germany's federal prosecutor general.

The Baader-Meinhof gang originated in West Germany among student idealists who believed that capitalist society was unjust. Its young people, whose backgrounds were almost entirely middle class, drew inspiration from such left-wing publications as *konkret*, edited by Ulrike Meinhof, whose radical writings were known throughout Europe.

Andreas Baader and his lover, Gudrun Ensslin, were convicted in 1968 of firebombing two Frankfurt department stores but were later released pending appeals. Their appeals rejected, they went underground to avoid imprisonment. In February 1970, they met Ulrike Meinhof. Their mutual interests in left-wing causes and such drugs as LSD soon banded them together.

Guerrilla Training in Jordan

Baader and Ensslin established a Berlin headquarters for their followers. The group robbed banks, stole cars, and hid in the apartments of sympathizers. Members of the group traveled to Jordan for intensive training in guerrilla warfare and terrorist tactics. Back in Germany, they put together an organization known as the Red Army Faction, or RAF.

Courthouse guards stand watch outside while accused group leaders from the Baader-Meinhof gang begin their first day of trial on May 21, 1975. (Hulton-Deutsch Collection)

Authorities soon realized that the RAF had taken the law into its own hands. It was heavily armed and did not stop at arson and bombing. After American military forces mined harbors in North Vietnam in May 1972, terrorist bombings began in Germany. At the Fifth U.S. Army Corps officers' mess in Frankfurt, one person was killed and 13 were injured. The RAF declared responsibility, saying, "West Germany will no longer be a safe hinterland for the strategists of extermination in Vietnam." Also in May, a pipe bomb injured 5 policemen in Augsburg, 60 cars were blown up in Munich, the wife of a federal judge was severely injured in Karlsruhe, 17 people were injured in Hamburg, and 5 GIs were injured and 3 killed in the mess of the U.S. Army in Heidelberg.

Leaders Seized

On June 1, 1972, the West German Federal Border Police laid siege to a garage in Frankfurt, where they found large amounts of explosives. Amid tear gas and gunfire, the police seized Andreas Baader, Jan-Carl Raspe, and Holger Meins. Baader was wounded in the thigh by a police sharpshooter.

A week later, Gudrun Ensslin was arrested in a Hamburg dress shop after a salesclerk noticed a pistol in her jacket. Next, acting on a tip, police found Ulrike Meinhof in an apartment in Hannover.

Imprisoned for nearly three years awaiting trial, the terrorists undertook a hunger strike, insisting they would eat only if released from isolation. Holger Meins died of starvation.

The trial opened on May 21, 1975, in a fortresslike building constructed for the event. Outside its barbed-wire perimeter, mounted police patrolled. Steel netting covered the roof to catch any dropped explosives, but aircraft were banned from the airspace over the building.

"Shut up, Linke!"

From the outset, some 200 spectators witnessed chaos and confusion. The defendants protested the use of courtroom microphones, interrupted incessantly, and refused to sit down. Baader almost constantly told his court-appointed counsel, "Shut up, Linke!" Ensslin ordered defense counsel Manfred Kunzel not to speak for her. The clamorous wrangling soon included shouts from the audience. The judges frequently ordered the four defendants removed. Contending that their clients were physically unfit to stand trial—all suffered from such low blood pressure and loss of weight that their powers of concentration (so court-appointed doctors reported) were reduced, and Baader's pulse was unusually weak—counsel Otto Schily led the defense lawyers in walking out. The next day, Baader and Raspe in turn told the court they considered their attorneys "arseholes." The four were again expelled. Brought back one by one (Meinhof was carried in, her hands and feet held by four officers), they repeated their foul language, modifying "arsehole" with the adjective "Fascist" and adding "old swine" to epithets addressed to the presiding judge.

At last, after 26 courtroom days, Federal Prosecutor General Siegfried Buback was able to present the charge against Baader, Ensslin, Meinhof, and Raspe:

> . . . that maliciously and by methods constituting danger to the public they did on two occasions murder in all four persons, and on other occasions attempted to murder at least fifty-four other persons;

> . . . that they did employ explosive materials . . . endangering life and limb and causing danger to other objects of particular value . . . and they did form an association with the object of committing criminal offenses.

The defendants were not present. They were held in their cells, which were described by guards as masses of cluttered, rotting food, cigarette butts, ashes, books, files, and newspaper clippings.

In the Absence of Defendants

On the trial's 40th day, the Code of Criminal Procedure was changed to permit a trial to continue despite the absence of defendants if the judge ruled that they were themselves responsible for their unfitness. Noting that the prosecution had promised to present 997 witnesses, including 80 experts, Judge Theodor Prinzing ordered the proceedings to continue. In the meantime, several of the prisoners' guards requested transfers, and one suffered a nervous breakdown.

The defense lawyers charged bias. Ulrike Meinhof pleaded, "The prisoner kept in isolation has only one possible way of showing that his conduct has changed, and that's betrayal. When you're in isolation, either you silence a prisoner, by which I mean he dies, or you get him to talk. And that means confession and betrayal."

On January 13, 1976, the defendants conceded membership in a guerrilla group and claimed "political responsibility" for the bombings but did not admit criminal responsibility. In February, March, and April, with the defendants usually absent, witnesses presented evidence on the bombings in Heidelberg, Augsburg, Munich, and Hamburg.

Prison guards reported bitter conflicts between Meinhof and the others, especially Ensslin. Meanwhile, defense lawyers moved to call several prominent witnesses, including former U.S. president Richard M. Nixon, former U.S. secretary of defense Melvin Laird, and former German chancellor Willy Brandt, to determine whether "the use of force against certain military establishments of the U.S.A. on West German territory [was] . . . justified." The motion was denied.

"The Last Act of Rebellion"

On May 9, guards found Ulrike Meinhof hanging from the grating of the window of her cell. She had made a rope by tearing prison towels into strips and tying them together. She left no note. But months earlier she had written, "Suicide is the last act of rebellion."

The suicide brought a defense motion to adjourn the trial. It was denied amid spectators' cries of "Prinzing, murderer!" and "The suicide's a lie!"

The defense proposed calling five American witnesses to testify that the I. G. Farben building in Frankfurt had been a center of U.S. operations during the Vietnam War. "The Vietnam War is not the subject of this trial," ruled Judge Prinzing in refusing to admit the witnesses.

Witness Gerhard Muller described how Meins, Raspe, and Baader had carefully planned the execution of gang member Ingeborg Barz because she had wanted to drop out, with Baader firing a shot through Barz's neck. Defense witnesses—gang members arrested since the trial began—testified to seeing Barz alive after the day Muller said she died.

Witness Klaus Junschke, another gang member, calling Judge Prinzing "you Fascist," leaped from the witness box and grappled with the jurist. Both fell to the floor as Junschke shouted, "For Ulrike, you swine!"

Raspe, ordered to leave the courtroom after continued disruptions, had to be forcibly expelled. Baader and prison guards exchanged blows. Ensslin, when not screaming abusively at her guards, was permitted to play her violin in her cell.

On December 8, 1976, the presiding judge ordered defense counsel thenceforward to remove their shoes and open their trousers at the checkpoint before the courtroom, for a search of the prisoners' cells had revealed the presence of hashish as well as a toaster and a camera. Three weeks later, the defense brought its 85th challenge of bias against Judge Prinzing. This time it was upheld by the judge's colleagues. He was replaced by Judge Eberhard Foth.

Prosecutor Assassinated

Three court-appointed lawyers, demanding suspension of the trial as they protested that conversations with their clients were bugged, walked out. And on the morning of April 7, 1977, Federal Prosecutor General Siegfried Buback and his driver were assassinated en route to court. A letter to the German Press Agency said "the Ulrike Meinhof Commando" took responsibility.

The trial ended on April 21, 1977. One week later, Judge Foth rendered the verdict, finding Baader, Ensslin, and Raspe each guilty of three murders in conjunction with six attempted murders, one further murder in conjunction with one attempted murder, and 27 other attempted murders in connection with bomb attacks. They were also found guilty of having formed a criminal association. All were sentenced to life imprisonment.

A high-security block was constructed on Stammheim prison's seventh floor by prisoner laborers. There, 10 additional gang members, awaiting trial or already convicted of RAF terrorism, joined their leaders in "the safest prison in the world."

September 5, 1977, brought the kidnapping of Hanns Martin Schleyer, the president of the Employers' Association. His driver and three policemen were killed. A ransom note demanded the release of Baader, Ensslin, Raspe, and other gang members, with their free passage to "a country of their choice," in exchange for Schleyer's life. A Europe-wide manhunt for kidnappers and victim began. Over 44 days, more ransom notes arrived, audiotapes and letters from Schleyer reported on his health and mental condition, and high German authorities debated how to negotiate with the kidnappers. On September 20, the Bundestag passed a special law that permitted the justice ministers to cut off all contact among the prisoners and with their lawyers and the outside world. Baader, Ensslin, and Raspe threatened suicide.

Jet Hijacked

A Lufthansa jet, bound from Palma de Mallorca to Frankfurt with 86 passengers, was hijacked to Rome on October 13. There, the hijackers' leader announced that Schleyer's life depended upon the release of the RAF prisoners as well as that of two Palestinians imprisoned in Turkey; the leader also asked for $15 million in ransom. The plane's passengers were held as hostages. Refueled, the plane was flown to Bahrain in the Persian Gulf, then to Dubai, United Arab Emirates.

In the meantime, German authorities worked to arrange delivery of the ransom money, and Baader, Raspe, and Ensslin filled out written questionnaires on the destinations they preferred if they were freed. In a radio interview, the Dubai defense minister praised the Lufthansa captain for giving coded information on the number of hijackers aboard. The hijackers heard the broadcast, executed the pilot, and ordered the copilot to take off for Aden, Yemen. Refueled there, the plane was flown on to the Mogadishu airport in Somalia. There, German commandos who had followed the hijacked plane's zigzag course stormed aboard, killing three of the four hijackers and wounding one. All hostages were rescued.

That night in Stammheim prison, Baader and Raspe each committed suicide with pistols, and Ensslin hanged herself. Searches of the cells revealed that hiding places for guns, radios, and other contraband had been built into the walls when the prisoner-laborers constructed them.

Two days later, the body of Schleyer was found with three bullets in the head. His six kidnappers were ultimately caught. They received life sentences.

—Bernard Ryan, Jr.

Suggestions for Further Reading

Aust, Stefan. *The Baader-Meinhof Group: The Inside Story of a Phenomenon.* Translated by Anthea Bell. London: The Bodley Head, 1985.

Becker, Jillian. *Hitler's Children: The Story of the Baader-Meinhof Terrorist Gang.* Philadelphia and New York: Lippincott, 1977.

Carr, Gordon. *The Angry Brigade.* London: Victor Gollancz, 1975.

Fromm, Erich. *The Anatomy of Human Destructiveness.* New York: Holt, Rinehart and Winston, 1973.

Grosser, Alfred. *Germany in Our Time.* London: Pelican, 1974.

Haberman, Jurgen. *Toward a Rational Society.* Boston: Beacon, 1971.

Hunt, Sir David. *On the Spot.* London: Peter Davis, 1975.

Guildford Four Trial: 1975

Defendants: Patrick Armstrong, Gerard Conlon, Paul Hill, Carole Richardson
Crimes Charged: Murder, conspiracy to cause explosions
Chief Defense Lawyers: John Leonard, Q.C.; Arthur Mildon, Q.C.; Eric Myers, Q.C.; Gordon Ward; Lord Basil Wigoder, Q.C.   **Chief Prosecutors:** Sir Michael Havers, Q.C.; Michael Hill, Q.C.   **Judge:** Sir John Donaldson
Place: London, England   **Dates of Trial:** September 16–October 22, 1975
Verdict: Guilty   **Sentence:** Life imprisonment

SIGNIFICANCE

When the Irish Republican Army bombed three pubs, killing seven people, the British people were outraged. Police investigators were determined to produce quick arrests and convictions that would calm the public and press. This case is a tragic example of how the overzealous investigation of terrorist activities led to a miscarriage of justice.

During 1974, Irish Republican Army (IRA) threats to import terrorism into the British mainland became a brutal reality. The carnage peaked on October 5, when bombs exploded at two pubs popular with servicemen in Guildford, Surrey—the Seven Stars, and the Horse and Groom—killing five people, including four army recruits. A month later, on November 7, a second bomb thrown through the window of the Kings Arms in Woolwich, South London, killed two customers. On each occasion, there was massive, nonlethal injury as well. Before the month was out, Parliament had passed the Prevention of Terrorism Act, the most significant provision of which empowered the police to arrest without warrant anyone they reasonably suspected of being involved in terrorism.

The very first person arrested under this act was Paul Hill, age 20, Belfast-born but living in a derelict house in Kilburn, North London. Officially, Hill's name first came to police attention from an informant's tip, although he was already suspected of involvement in the Belfast abduction and murder of a former soldier, Brian Shaw, an offense for which he was later convicted. However Hill came to be detained, what is certain is that, while in custody, he signed a statement admitting responsibility for the Guildford and Woolwich bombings and naming Gerard Conlon, 20, as a coconspirator. The next day, Conlon was arrested at his home in Belfast. Further details extracted from these suspects under interrogation led to more arrests, among them the arrests of Patrick Armstrong, 24, and his 17-year-old English girlfriend, Carole Richardson.

It appeared to be an open-and-shut case. Certainly the British tabloids thought so; one informed its readers on September 16, 1975, that "Snipers Guard the Old Bailey as Bombers Go On Trial." When asked to plead, each defendant answered "not guilty," except for Hill, who defiantly declared, "I refuse to take part in this. Your justice stinks!" Hill's refusal to plead—a tactic commonly employed by IRA prisoners—dealt untold harm to his codefendants, who desperately needed every scrap of help available; after all, for the men, their sole defense was that the "confessions" had been extracted under duress, either at the point of a gun or in the face of police threats that their immediate family members would be harmed, even killed, if they did not comply.

Strong Alibi

Carole Richardson was on far firmer legal ground. In late December 1974, a friend, Frank Johnson, had gone to police to say that on October 5, he and Richardson had been watching a band together in South London at the time of the Guildford explosion. The band had checked its records and confirmed the date, and there were even photographs of Richardson taken in the band's dressing room to confirm her presence. According to Johnson, such disclosures did not please the police, and he was repeatedly beaten until he retracted his story. But on the witness stand, he stood by his original statement. Eric Myers, Q.C. (Queen's Counsel), for Richardson, told the jury that the police had not "breathed a word" of Johnson's statement to the defense, adding that "this was straight out of the dirty tricks department."

Chief prosecutor Sir Michael Havers, Q.C., chose to ignore the most inconvenient aspect of Johnson's testimony—that he had met Richardson in London at 6.30 P.M.—and concerned himself with showing that Richardson had time to place the bomb in Guildford at 7 P.M. and get to the concert 50 minutes later, triumphantly announcing that a police car had managed this 30-mile trip across congested South London in a quite remarkable 48 minutes.

When Detective Inspector Timothy Blake took the stand, counsel for Conlon, Lord Basil Wigoder, Q.C., raised accusations that he had physically abused Conlon during questioning. Blake retorted that he had not even set eyes on Conlon until committal proceedings, whereupon Wigoder asked Blake to roll up his sleeves. During the course of his beating, Conlon had seen tattoos on Blake's arms and was able to describe them clearly; now the court was able to see just how accurate Conlon's description had been. Asked how Conlon could have come by such personal details, Blake weakly suggested that Conlon might have seen him in his shirtsleeves at the police station.

As one of the main interviewing officers, Detective Sergeant Anthony Jermey stoically denied defense claims that Hill had been threatened by a gun-wielding fellow officer while in custody. He was less convincing, though, when

Wigoder asked about the manner in which the various confessions had been obtained. Jermey had produced 20 pages of confessions, the record of Conlon's interrogation, the questions and answers; all of it was incriminatory and, understandably, made no mention of any police brutality. Wigoder asked Jermey when he had written these notes.

"Seven hours later," said Jermey. When Wigoder complimented him on his powers of recall, the officer explained how a good memory was a prerequisite for good police work, at which point Wigoder inquired, "What was the first question I put to you in the witness box?"

Jermey blustered, his mind a blank. He had just claimed to be able to recall a 13-hour interrogation word for word 7 hours after it had ended, yet he could not repeat a question put to him just minutes earlier!

When it came time to testify, Hill maintained his cocksure attitude, refusing to answer questions or responding sarcastically. For his part, Conlon had to fend off accusations from Havers that he had deliberately peppered his confession with inconsistencies in order to pull the wool over the jury's eyes.

"I have no need to pull the wool over the jury's eyes," Conlon protested. "I am telling the truth."

"Did you enjoy leading the gang which blew up these people in Guildford?"

"I'd never been to Guildford till the police took me there. If they'd told me to put down the Pope's name as one of the bombers, I would have done it. I'd have put down anybody's name to save my Ma! [a reference to threats against family members]."

In summing-up, Justice Donaldson crystallized the trial into a single issue, telling the jury that it had to decide whom to believe—police officers with many years of distinguished service, or the defendants.

On October 22, 1975, the jury made it clear which version they preferred. The verdict was guilty. In passing sentence of life imprisonment on all four defendants, the judge sounded regretful that capital punishment was no longer available to him, but he did recommend that Hill should be released only "on grounds of old age or infirmity," thus making Hill's the longest sentence ever handed down in a British court.

Captured IRA Militants Claim Responsibility

As the case of the Guildford Four faded from the headlines, its place was taken by yet another notorious trial arising from IRA atrocities. On January 24, 1977, four Irishmen arrested after a siege in Balcombe Street, London, stepped into the dock at the Old Bailey. All of the defendants—committed and admitted terrorists—refused to plead because the indictment failed to include those bombings for which the Guildford Four had been convicted. On behalf of his fellow defendants, Joseph O'Connell admitted carrying out both bombings and substantiated his claim by mentioning that he had spoken to a soldier at the

Guildford pub about late-night bus schedules just before the bomb had exploded. This incident, deposed by the soldier at the time of the investigation, had never been made public or admitted into evidence.

In light of these revelations, an appeal was filed on behalf of the Guildford Four. For security reasons, it was held at the Old Bailey instead of at the customary Royal Law Courts, and on October 10, 1977, the hearing began. All the Balcombe Street defendants—Joseph O'Connell, Harry Duggan, Eddie Butler, and Brendan Dowd—gave evidence, freely admitting their terrorist activities and disclaiming all knowledge of Hill and the others. At this appeal, Havers, again leading for the Crown, was forced to admit that O'Connell, Duggan, and Butler had indeed been responsible for the Guildford bombing, yet he remained adamant that Hill had assisted them. Despite this fresh evidence, the court preferred to rely on the alleged confessions. On October 29, in a judgment running to 50 pages, Lord Justice Roskill said, "We are all of the clear opinion that there are no possible grounds for doubting the justice of any of these four convictions or for ordering new trials."

Such seeming perversity had its defenders. A large body of opinion believed—and still believes—that O'Connell, a hardened terrorist destined to spend the rest of his life behind bars, had nothing to lose, and possibly much to gain, by admitting to the Guildford and Woolwich bombings, thereby causing massive embarrassment to the British government and maximizing the IRA's political advantage.

Doubts about Statements

Elsewhere, those with a less Machiavellian turn of mind preferred to debate the justness of the Guildford Four convictions. Nor were those voicing concern the type ordinarily to be found trumpeting the terrorist cause, including, as they did, two men at the peak of the judiciary, Lords Devlin and George Scarman. As far back as the 1950s, Patrick Devlin, a distinguished trial judge, had expressed doubts about the veracity of certain confessions and statements ostensibly dictated to police officers. Years of sitting on the bench, listening to supposedly verbatim accounts, had often revealed to Devlin alarming discrepancies in speech patterns between those of the alleged statement and those of the witnesses who appeared before him.

Such support inevitably kept the Guildford Four case in the public eye and ultimately led to a request for an independent panel of police officers from another force to examine all the evidence to ferret out any hint of irregularity. Exposed at last to a merciless, impartial scrutiny, the Crown's case first sagged, then collapsed, as investigators found draft notes that clearly proved that police officers had lied in saying that statements made by the accused had been contemporaneous. Investigators also found that genuine statements made by the accused had been either deliberately suppressed or doctored.

Once such duplicity became known, the case against the Guildford Four perished. On October 19, 1989, a court under Lord Chief Justice Geoffrey Lane quashed the convictions of all four defendants. Three were released immediately; Hill was released shortly after. The events of this and other related cases have been dramatized in the 1993 movie *In the Name of the Father*.

The latest chapter in this tragedy came on April 20, 1993, when three police officers connected with the investigation, Vernon Attwell, John Donaldson, and Thomas Style, went on trial, charged with conspiring to pervert the course of justice. In effect, their hearing became a retrial of the Guildford Four, as defense counsel advanced the view that, although corners might have been cut in the original bombing inquiry, the right culprits had been convicted. Whatever the ethical merits of this particular ploy, it worked: On May 19, 1993, each officer was acquitted.

Writing in 1961, famed critic Cyril Connolly said, "The test of a country's justice is not the blunders which are sometimes made, but the zeal with which they are put right." Judged by this criterion, it is difficult to avoid the conclusion that when it came to the Guildford Four, certain sectors of the British judicial process were less interested in justice and more concerned with retribution.

—*Colin Evans*

After spending 15 years in prison, the Guildford Four were finally cleared on charges of terrorism. Pictured is Gerard Conlon, 32, clenching his fist in a victory salute. (Hulton-Deutsch Collection)

Suggestions for Further Reading

Bennett, Ronan. *Double Jeopardy*. London: Penguin, 1993.

Conlon, Gerry. *Proved Innocent*. London: Penguin, 1991.

Hill, Paul and Ronan Bennett. *Stolen Years*. London: Doubleday, 1990.

Maguire, Anne. *Miscarriage of Jutsice*. Boulder, Colo.: Roberts Rinehart, 1994.

McKee, Grant and Ros Franey. *Time Bomb*. London: Bloomsbury, 1988.

Woffinden, Bob. *Miscarriages Of Justice*. London: Hodder & Stoughton, 1987.

Václav Havel Trials: 1977–89

Defendant: Václav Havel **Crimes Charged:** Subversive activities, helping foreigners produce antistate propaganda, inciting participation at a demonstration, impeding the execution of safety measures
Chief Defense Lawyer: Dr. Josef Lžičař **Chief Prosecutor:** Karel Florian
Place: Prague, Czechoslovakia **Dates of Trials:** October 18, 1977; October 22, 1979; February 21, 1989 **Verdict:** Guilty **Sentence:** Nine months' imprisonment

SIGNIFICANCE
The last of playwright and human rights activist Václav Havel's trials helped to consolidate public opposition to Czechoslovakia's doomed authoritarian regime.

In late 1976, a network of dissident Czechs drafted a manifesto they hoped might hasten the end of a decade of repressive government. The secretly composed document was called Charter 77. Although its signers were persecuted, the document began Czechoslovakia's fitful return to democracy.

Charter 77 listed a variety of freedoms denied by the Communist regime of President Gustáv Husák. It further asked Husák to guarantee basic human rights specified in Czechoslovakia's constitution, as well as those specified in the United Nations human rights covenants and the 1975 Helsinki Accords, which had been signed by the Czech government.

The 242 Charter 77 signers declared themselves to be "a loose, informal and open association of people of various shades of opinion," not an organized political movement with a fixed agenda for creating political change. The charter designated three official spokesmen: former diplomat Dr. Jiří Hájek, philosopher Jan Patočka, and Václav Havel, an internationally acclaimed playwright whose plays were banned by the Husák government.

Charter 77 organizers planned to mail copies of the manifesto to each signer and to deliver copies to President Husák and the Czech Federal Assembly. On January 6, 1977, however, Havel and several companions were arrested while mailing bundles of addressed charters. The Czech government acted immediately to stop circulation of Charter 77, but it was too late. The text was published in the Western European press and broadcast by Western radio to thousands of Czechs who had been unaware of its existence.

The tone of Charter 77 was plainspoken and community minded, but it challenged the government to live up to its human rights laws and international agreements. To an authoritarian regime, one believing that the rights of individuals are to be dispensed according to the greater interests of the state, the document was a threatening challenge.

Havel was released soon after his arrest but was detained again a week later and charged with subversion. Dr. Hájek and Professor Patočka were not arrested but were questioned repeatedly. The elderly Dr. Hájek died of a brain hemorrhage on March 13 after an interrogation by state police.

Other charter signers were subjected to the kinds of intimidation listed in their manifesto. Workers lost their jobs, their passports were revoked, and educational opportunities were denied to their families. Some, like Havel, were pressured to emigrate.

Charter 77 was not reprinted or broadcast by the state-controlled media, which nonetheless vilified the document and its signatories. While detained, Havel filed an unsuccessful slander suit against a state-employed radio commentator who had accused Havel of being a paid agent of Western intelligence services. Havel also filed an official request for release and carelessly told his jailers that he intended to resign as charter spokesman someday. The state media announced that Havel had turned his back on the charter and had resigned as a spokesman, but he remained unaware of the hoax until his release on May 20, 1977. The chagrined writer threw himself deeper than ever into pro-democracy activities.

Earlier Czech Communist administrations, in keeping with their Stalinist model, might have answered Charter 77 with executions and imprisonments. Yet, by the late 1970s, the Czech judiciary generally pretended to honor rights contained in the Czech constitution, while actually safeguarding government control. Formally charging Charter 77 organizers without disturbing this façade presented a problem for the government, which found no legal grounds for prosecuting the organizers for pro-Charter 77 activities alone. Instead, Havel and three others were brought to trial for smuggling abroad a manuscript for a banned memoir.

On October 18, 1977, the group was tried and convicted of attempting to harm the international interests of the Czech republic. Havel was sentenced to 14 months' imprisonment, with a conditional postponement of three years.

Founding of Committee for the Defense of the Unjustly Persecuted

While living under this suspended sentence, Havel, along with other dissidents, founded the Committee for the Defense of the Unjustly Persecuted, also known by its Czech initials, VONS. The group monitored human rights arrests, filed official complaints, and offered financial assistance to the families of people imprisoned for dissident activities. The group also smuggled critiques of government policy to Czech émigré publications abroad.

The Czech government struck back in May 1979. Havel and five others were accused of attempting to harm the interests of the Czech state with subversive activities. Since the group's statements had been broadcast by Western anti-Communist media, such as the Voice of America and Radio Free Europe, the defendants were also accused of helping foreigners produce antistate propaganda.

The subversion trial began on October 22, 1979. The presiding judge allowed only 12 family members into the tiny courtroom; more than a hundred supporters, foreign diplomats, reporters, and international human rights monitors were denied entry. Many of those who waited outside the court were arrested. Some were beaten by police. When the trial began, defendant Petr Uhl's wife was carried from the courtroom for attempting to take notes.

The defendants and their lawyers pointed out that VONS members had been publicly petitioning the state in human rights cases for over a year before charges were brought. If VONS was dangerous and subversive, asked the defense, why had the state waited so long to file charges? The defendants pointed to the Czech constitution's guarantee of the right to petition as proof of their innocence.

The trial lasted only two days. All six defendants were found guilty and received prison sentences ranging from two to five years. Havel was sentenced to four and a half years. Despite international condemnations from sources as disparate as the French Communist Party and Pope John Paul II, Havel remained in prison until March 1983, when he was released because of illness.

Deep dissatisfaction with the government's economic and repressive social policies remained. On August 21, 1988, the 20th anniversary of the Soviet army's seizure of Czechoslovakia, 10,000 Czechs marched in the streets of Prague. When demonstrations continued after the date had passed, security forces responded with increasing ferocity. By October, thousands of peaceful demonstrators were braving police attacks in the worst public unrest since 1968.

Another politically charged anniversary neared in January 1989. Twenty years had passed since a student named Jan Palach burned himself to death to protest the Soviet occupation. On January 9, Havel received an anonymous letter from a student claiming to represent a group of Charter 77 supporters. The letter's writer declared his intention to follow Palach's example by burning himself to death in Prague's Wenceslas Square on January 15. Havel wrote a reply, urging the student not to kill himself. When Havel's request for help in publicizing his appeal to the student was ignored by the state media, the playwright turned to foreign broadcasters for help. Radio Free Europe and the Voice of America aired Havel's message. In a radio interview, Czech state security thanked Havel for saving the student's life. Before the interview ended, Havel mentioned the date and time of the impending Palach memorial.

Havel went to Wenceslas Square alone on January 16 to watch the memorial. As he left, he was arrested for obstructing the police, who had ordered the crowds to leave. By the time the case reached court on February 21, 1989, he was further charged with incitement to riot by publicizing the Palach memorial—during the same interview in which the government had thanked him for preventing the anonymous student's self-immolation.

The proceedings were as cruelly farcical as Havel's previous trials. One prosecution witness admitted that he had not even attended the demonstration. When he charged police with threatening him into accusing Havel of provoking demonstrators, the witness was ejected from court. With a touch of absurdity befitting one of Havel's plays, a secret-police major produced a pile of photos of Havel standing in Wenceslas Square but steadfastly denied that the writer had been tailed by security forces.

Havel's lawyer, Josef Lžičař, argued that his client was being prosecuted for a lifesaving act, which the state had publicly acknowledged. Havel himself used the trial as an opportunity to repeat his political convictions:

> As a citizen for whom it is important that our country develop peacefully, I firmly believe that in the end, the authorities will learn a lesson from what has happened and establish official dialogue with all sectors of society, a dialogue from which no one will be excluded because they have been designated as "antisocialist." I firmly believe that in the end, the authorities will stop behaving like an ugly girl who breaks a mirror because she believes it to be guilty of what it reflects.

"I do not feel guilty," Havel added, "but if sentenced, I will accept the punishment as a sacrifice for a good cause, which is nothing in the face of the ultimate sacrifice of Jan Palach, which we sought to commemorate."

Prosecutor Karel Florian complimented Havel on his patriotic sentiments but condemned the act of announcing the Palach demonstration over the airwaves. Again, the outcome was a foregone conclusion. Havel was found guilty and sentenced to nine months' imprisonment.

This time the security forces and their allies in the judiciary had overstepped their bounds. The sentence provoked a public campaign for Havel's release. Authorities were presented with 3,800 signatures on a petition demanding Havel's release. The pressure induced his captors to reduce his sentence by one month. He was released for "good behavior" on May 17, after having served less than a third of his sentence.

Czech Democratic Reforms Grow

Increasing political freedom in the Soviet Union left Czech hard-liners further isolated. Unlike their Soviet-backed predecessors, Czechoslovakia's leaders could not count on support from other Eastern bloc countries, most of which were dismantling their repressive regimes by 1989. Public rejection of Communist candidates promising to reform the existing system finally convinced the Czech government that new leaders would have to be freely elected.

Havel pressed the struggle for democratic reforms and religious freedom with a petition titled "Just a Few Sentences." Forty thousand Czechs signed the document. On November 27, 1989, ten days after police had charged violently into a massive demonstration in Prague, millions of Czechs protested with a work stoppage that paralyzed the entire country. A new opposition party called Civic Forum was hastily organized to vie with the Communists for control of the government.

The ruling structure began to collapse quickly. Civic Forum took control of cabinet positions and the parliament, as the public rejected promises of reform by hard-liners and their protégés. Alexander Dubček, who had been removed as president of Czechoslovakia by the invading Soviet army in 1968, was elected chairman of the parliament. To complete the transition of power, the parliament needed only to elect a president. The sole candidate was agreed upon by both Civic Forum and the remaining Communist legislators. After a unanimous parliamentary vote on December 29, 1989, Václav Havel became the first non-Communist president of Czechoslovakia in more than 40 years.

Havel remained president until July 17, 1992, when Slovakian nationalists voted to secede from the Czech Federal Republic. Havel did not want to preside over the dissolution of the country for which he and many others had struggled for so long. When elections took place later that year, however, he won election as president of the new independent Czech Republic created by the territorial division. President Havel was inaugurated on February 2, 1993.

—Tom Smith

Suggestions for Further Reading

Gawdiak, Ihor, ed. *Czechoslovakia: A Country Study*. Washington, D.C.: U.S. Government, 1989.

Havel, Václav. *Disturbing the Peace*. New York: Alfred A. Knopf, 1990.

———. *Open Letters: Selected Writings, 1965–1990*. New York: Alfred A. Knopf, 1991.

Kiriseová, Eda. *Václav Havel: The Authorized Biography*. New York: St. Martin's Press, 1993.

Anatoly Shcharansky and Alexandr Ginzburg Trials: 1978

Defendants: Anatoly Shcharansky, Alexandr Ginzburg
Crimes Charged: Treason, anti-Soviet agitation and propaganda, espionage (Shcharansky); anti-Soviet agitation and propaganda (Ginzburg)
Chief Defense Lawyers: Shcharansky his own lawyer; name of Ginzburg's lawyer not reported   **Chief Prosecutors:** Pavel N. Solonin in the Shcharansky trial; name of prosecutor in Ginzburg's trial not reported
Judges: P. P. Lukanov (Shcharansky trial); name of judge in Ginzburg's trial not reported   **Places:** Moscow, United Soviet Socialist Republic (USSR) (Shcharansky); Kaluga, USSR (Ginzburg)   **Dates of Trials:** July 10–14, 1978 (Shcharansky); July 10–13, 1978 (Ginzburg)   **Verdicts:** Guilty (both trials)
Sentences: Shchransky—three years' imprisonment and ten years in hard-labor camp; Ginzburg—eight years in a hard-labor camp

SIGNIFICANCE

The trials of Shcharansky, Ginzburg, and other activists were intended to intimidate human rights and Jewish emigration movements in the USSR. Instead, international protest helped make them the most important trials since the Stalinist era.

Two notable protest movements emerged in the Soviet Union during the 1970s. Although each group had distinct goals, they sometimes shared members. They also shared prisons for daring to confront the security policies of the Soviet state.

Political dissidents, like Alexandr Ginzburg, were committed to reforming Soviet society. They pressed for freedoms specified in the 1975 Helsinki human rights accord, signed by the Soviets and the Western powers. Religious minorities, including many Jews, had less interest in reforming the USSR than in leaving it entirely.

The latter group became known abroad as "refuseniks" because of the Soviet government's refusal to allow them to emigrate to Israel or the United States. Tens of thousands of Jews were allowed to leave the USSR for the official reason of "family reunification," but the most vociferous refuseniks were persecuted. Application for an exit visa often provoked instant dismissal from one's job, followed by vilification in the press or an order to report for induction into the armed forces. Refusal to respond to a conscription notice invited trial and imprisonment.

Soviets Hound Jewish Activists

Anatoly Shcharansky was a brilliant mathematician whose 1973 application for an exit visa caused his dismissal from the Oil and Gas Research Institute. As other prominent refuseniks were imprisoned, Shcharansky's importance grew. His articulate protests, translation work, and meetings with visiting foreign diplomats shed a widening circle of light upon the official harassment of Soviet Jews. Shcharansky also aided the broader dissident movement. In 1976, he joined the Helsinki Watch Group, which monitored Soviet human rights violations.

The refuseniks' peaceful insistence that Jews should not be persecuted for wanting to emigrate was an increasing embarrassment to the Soviet government. On March 4, 1977, a letter in the official Soviet newspaper, *Izvestia* accused Shcharansky and three other Jewish activists of espionage. To their shock, the letter was signed by Sanya Lipavsky, a Jewish doctor who had participated in refusenik activities for over a year. Lipavsky's betrayal alerted the refuseniks that the government would act soon.

Shcharansky was arrested in Moscow on March 15, 1977. For 16 months, he was interrogated daily by KGB investigators planning to construct a still unspecified indictment against him. On July 7, 1978, it was announced that he would be tried for treason and for participating in anti-Soviet agitation and propaganda. The former charge carried a possible death sentence.

Shcharansky's Trial

When Shcharansky's trial began three days later, the court was packed with KGB officials. The defendant was allowed to have only one spectator in court. Still, Shcharansky had to refuse to participate in the trial before his brother, Leonid, was admitted. The state effectively barred Shcharansky's mother by declaring its intention to call her as a witness. Foreign diplomats, the Western media, and Shcharansky's supporters were also barred. Reports of the proceedings were limited to a twice-daily briefing by Soviet press officers, whose versions of the events differed substantially from the news Leonid Shcharansky brought to supporters waiting outside the building.

Shcharansky was relieved when he was allowed to dismiss his court-appointed lawyer. This removed the possibility of capital punishment, which by Soviet law was not pronounced upon any defendant who conducted his own defense. After listening to the 40-minute-long indictment against him,

Shcharansky replied, "I do not plead guilty. I consider all the charges against me to be absurd."

Shcharansky was denied most of the materials and witnesses he requested for his defense, but his tenacity was not dimmed by months in isolation. Prosecutor Pavel Solonin asked Shcharansky why he had not mentioned negative aspects of American culture, like poverty and prostitution, in a congratulatory telegram to President Gerald Ford during the U.S. Bicentennial. Shcharansky agreed that he had expressed his admiration for the free emigration policy in the United States but noted that the Soviet government's official telegram to Ford had similarly contained no social criticism. When asked why only the Western media attended refusenik press conferences, Shcharansky replied that no Communist reporters had ever accepted their invitations.

The espionage charge was introduced on the second day of the trial. Allegedly to protect state security, the session was barred to spectators. Lipavsky, the KGB mole who had infiltrated the refuseniks, nervously claimed that he had worked for the CIA but as a double agent. He testified that he had witnessed Shcharansky's plotting to hamper trade relations between the United States and the USSR under the guise of human rights activities. A refusenik named Adamsky echoed Lipavsky's accusation that Shcharansky had smuggled lists of dissidents to the West. When Shcharansky pressed Adamsky for details, the witness's memory failed. The judge accepted Adamsky's previous statement to investigators in lieu of court testimony.

Lipavsky and Adamsky fumbled with dates and details, allowing Shcharansky to debunk some of their accusations later in open court. Other witnesses were ill-informed about what they were expected to say in court. One elderly man knew nothing about Shcharansky's case but had once been in prison with Alexandr Ginzburg, who was being tried that day in a town more than 100 miles away. The witness had apparently been brought to the wrong courtroom.

The espionage charge stemmed from Shcharansky's relationship with *Los Angeles Times* correspondent Robert Toth, for whom he had translated interviews. Toth had been expelled from the USSR after Shcharansky's arrest and was accused of collecting sensitive information for the CIA.

Upon his return to the United States, Toth signed affidavits denying any connection with CIA activities. The court rejected Toth's affidavits. One of Shcharansky's neighbors recalled seeing the two men together but denied witnessing any suspicious behavior. The most incriminating testimony she offered the embarrassed prosecutors was an observation that Shcharansky was a slightly messy housekeeper.

Prosecutors next called Shcharansky's mother, Ida Milgrom, to the stand. The order was sent out to the street, where Milgrom stood with supporters. Word swiftly returned that she refused to testify.

The court was shown two documentaries made by Western filmmakers. Both films contained underground interviews with Shcharansky about Soviet emigration policy, which the prosecution offered as evidence of "clandestine slanderous activity."

"All the information I transmitted to the West was exclusively for open use," Shcharansky replied. "The fact that I gave an interview for Western television is the best proof of that. The fact that those who filmed this interview had to conceal it until they brought the film out of the USSR says nothing about the closed nature of our activity, but it says much about the closed nature of Soviet society."

Prosecutor Solonin's summation was a lengthy critique of social ills in the Western world and a condemnation of Zionism. Solonin accused Shcharansky of participating in an international campaign of anti-Soviet propaganda. Yet Solonin repeated almost none of the testimony by prosecution witnesses. He merely reread Shcharansky's indictment and requested a sentence of 3 years' imprisonment to be followed by 12 years of "reeducation" in a hard-labor camp.

Shcharansky's final statement lasted for more than a day. He accused *Izvestia* of pronouncing him guilty even before his arrest and argued that forbidding him to refute the allegations made against him in the closed sessions, prevented him from defending himself. He explained that the Jewish desire to emigrate was a cultural process, not a political rebellion.

"For more than 2,000 years the Jewish people, my people, have been dispersed," Shcharansky concluded. "But wherever they are, wherever Jews are found, each year they repeat, 'Next year in Jerusalem.' Now when I am further than ever from my people, from Avital [his wife], facing many arduous years of imprisonment, I say, turning to my people, my Avital, 'Next year in Jerusalem!' And I turn to you, the court, who were required to confirm a predetermined sentence—to you I have nothing to say."

The court sentenced Shcharansky to 3 years' imprisonment and 10 years in a hard-labor camp. Outrage over the sentence was immediate. President Jimmy Carter denounced the verdict and called the KGB's claim that Shcharansky was an American spy "patently false." The Carter administration pressed hard for Shcharansky's release.

Ginzburg's Trial

The international community was already in an uproar over Soviet action against other dissidents when, on the same day that Shcharansky's trial began, Alexandr Ginzburg went on trial in Kaluga for anti-Soviet agitation and propaganda. The charge grew from Ginzburg's friendship with expelled Soviet writer Aleksandr Solzhenitsyn. In 1974, Solzhenitsyn had organized a financial fund to support the families of political prisoners in the USSR. Ginzburg administered the fund, which was subsidized by publishing royalties from Solzhenitsyn's banned exposé of Stalinist labor camps, *The Gulag Archipelago*. This activity, coupled with Ginzburg's membership in the Helsinki Watch Group, provoked his arrest on February 3, 1977.

Ginzburg had been imprisoned twice before. In 1960, his editorship of an underground literary journal earned him a two-year sentence. In 1968, Ginzburg and three codefendants were convicted of producing and smuggling abroad an account of the trial of Yuli Daniel and Andrei Sinyavsky, two writers accused of "anti-Soviet slander." His conviction for "anti-Soviet agitation" provoked protests but cost Ginzburg five years in a hard-labor camp. When the judge at his 1978 trial asked Ginzburg the nature of his ethnic background, the defendant replied with little irony, "Prisoner."

Anatoly Shcharansky is reunited with his mother, Ida Milgrom, on August 25, 1986, some months after his release from a Soviet prison. (AP/ Wideworld Photos)

Prosecution witness Arkady Gradoboyev accused Ginzburg of giving him banned books deeply critical of the USSR's Stalinist past. Gradoboyev, a convicted forger, pornographer, and thief, also accused Ginzburg's wife, Arina, of threatening him outside the courtroom.

"That's a dirty lie!" shouted Arina Ginzburg. She was thrown out of the court and barred from attending the remainder of the trial.

Ginzburg faced a possible 10 years in prison and 5 years of Siberian exile. On July 13, he was sentenced to 8 years in a hard-labor camp, a punishment that supporters doubted his fragile health would withstand. Yet on April 27, 1979, Ginzburg and four other political prisoners were exchanged for two Soviet spies under indictment in the United States.

Shcharansky Finally Reaches Jewish Homeland

Shcharansky completed his prison term and was transferred to a remote labor camp in April 1980. The battle of wills between Shcharansky and his jailers became an ongoing cycle of withheld privileges and hunger strikes. When authorities offered to release the emaciated Shcharansky if he would sign a request on grounds of ill health, he refused.

Appeals for Shcharansky's release continued until the administration of Soviet General Secretary Mikhail Gorbachev. On February 11, 1986, Shcharansky was taken from prison, stripped of Soviet citizenship, and allowed to walk to freedom across a bridge connecting East and West Berlin.

Within hours, Shcharansky was reunited with his wife in Jerusalem. During the 1990s, he became active in the Movement for Israel and Immigration, a political party dedicated to finding employment opportunities for his nation's growing population of Russian immigrant Jews.

—*Tom Smith*

Suggestions for Further Reading

Gilbert, Martin. *Shcharansky: Hero of Our Time*. New York: Viking, 1986.

Jerusalem Post. Anatoly and Avital Shcharansky: The Journey Home. New York: Harcourt Brace Jovanovich, 1986.

Scammell, Michael. *Solzhenitsyn: A Biography*. New York: W. W. Norton, 1984.

Shcharansky, Natan. *Fear No Evil*. New York: Random House, 1988.

Jiang Qing and the Gang of Four Trial: 1980

Defendants: Jiang Qing, Chen Boda, Huang Yongsheng, Jiang Tengjiao, Li Zuopeng, Qiu Huizuo, Wang Hongwen, Wu Faxian, Yao Wenyuan, Zhang Chunqiao   **Crimes Charged:** Counterrevolutionary acts, including sedition and conspiracy to overthrow the government, persecution of party and state leaders, suppression of the masses, plotting to assassinate Mao and foment a counterrevolutionary armed rebellion   **Chief Defense Lawyers:** Ma Rongiie, Jiang representing herself   **Chief Prosecutors:** Huang Huoqing, 23 special prosecutors   **Judges:** Jiang Hua, a special 35-judge panel   **Place:** Peking, China   **Dates of Trial:** November 20–December 29, 1980   **Verdict:** Guilty   **Sentences:** Jiang Qing, Zhang—execution, commuted to life imprisonment; Wang—life imprisonment; Yao—20 years' imprisonment; Chen, Huang, Li, Jiang Tengjiao, Qiu, Wu—16 to 18 years' imprisonment

SIGNIFICANCE

The trial of the Gang of Four formally ended the radicalism of China's late chairman Mao Zedong and enabled the Communist Party to assess him officially as a brilliant revolutionary who made "grave blunders" in his later years. The ultimate result was not only the downgrading of Mao but also the suicide of his imprisoned widow.

In 1963, Mao Zedong, the 70-year-old chairman of the Chinese Communist Party's Central Committee, launched his Cultural Revolution. Its "revisionist" goal was to destroy the governing class of intelligentsia and bureaucrats that had become powerful within the Communist Party—a class that Mao had created by manipulating the peasants of his country to overthrow and destroy the landlords who had long been the ruling class. After more than a decade of rule, the cadre of Communist officials had translated the "dictatorship of the proletariat" into a growing inflexibility and a cynical intolerance of criticism. In a word, Mao thought the revolution had decayed.

10 Million Red Guards

This time, Mao turned not to the peasants but to young students to lead the revolution. By September 1966, the young people were calling themselves "Red Guards" and marching and demonstrating across China, crying, "Long live the Red terror." They urged destruction of old ideas, old culture, old customs, and old habits. Some 10 million strong, the Red Guards often, during their various attacks on anything identified with the past, destroyed entire museums of valuable artifacts.

By January 1967, Mao was replacing officials nationwide with inexperienced young people. The People's Liberation Army, called to fight the Red Guards, itself split into factions. In the summer of 1968, sensing that civil war threatened, Mao disbanded the Red Guards, believing that he had destroyed his opponents and ensured his command of the party organization. His goal—to rule China single-handedly—seemed won.

Meanwhile, Mao's fourth wife, Jiang Qing, who was 21 years younger than he, had become an astute student of politics. Jiang Qing was a former movie actress with a peasant background. She aspired not only to westernized dress and culture but also to political power. She and Lin Biao, who had commanded the Communists' Fourth Army in the 1930s, decided to work toward seizing power across China. By April 1969, Jiang and Lin were made members of the politburo, and Lin was named Mao's heir apparent.

Attempted Coup d'Etat

In August 1970, the Lin-Jiang group announced at a major party conference that Lin had surpassed Mao as the people's leader. A year later, Lin and Jiang attempted a coup d'état. It failed. Lin and his wife and other supporters fled for the Soviet Union aboard a military aircraft. They were reported shot down over Mongolia. Jiang had succeeded in hiding her participation in the coup.

As Mao lost his influence, the infighting continued, led secretly by Jiang. But in the summer of 1973, she and her followers were recognized as the inside group in the politburo and dubbed "the Gang of Four." All China became aware of them a year later when Mao publicly warned his wife and her three close associates—Wang Hongwen, Yao Wenyuan, and Zhang Chunqiao—not to become "a four-member small clique" and to stop seeking power.

Arrest and Imprisonment

Mao died on September 9, 1976. Within a month, the Gang of Four and a number of supporters were arrested on the orders of politburo chief Hua Guofeng. A barrage of political posters and media cartoons and releases depicted Jiang as a fox (a Chinese metaphor for a floozy), an empress, and a snake.

The Gang of Four languished in prison for several years while Hua and other officials declared the Cultural Revolution a disaster and tried to dispel the "myth" of Mao's successful leadership of China's transition from feudal state to 20th-century power. Construction of memorials to Mao were banned, and his portraits were removed from the Great Hall in Tiananmen Square.

Wang Hongwen, member of the "Gang of Four" and former vice chairman of the Chinese Communist Party, testifies during his trial on November 25, 1980. (AP/Wideworld Photos)

As the ultimate downgrading of Mao, the Gang of Four (totaling 10 individuals) was brought to trial. The 20,000-word, 48-count indictment charged the Gang of Four with "persecuting to death" more than 34,000 people, including six mayors and deputy mayors of Peking and Shanghai, as well as persecuting some 730,000 others who had not been killed. Other charges included plotting to attack Mao's train during a 1971 tour, attempting to seize power in a rebellion in Shanghai just after Mao's death, and training a large militia to oppose the regular army.

Listed as defendants in absentia were six others, all deceased: Lin Biao; his wife, Ye Qun; their son, Lin Liguo; Zhou Yuchi, an air force political officer; and public security chiefs Kang Sheng and Xie Fuzhi.

The start of the trial was delayed in the expectation that Jiang would confess (the Chinese legal tradition emphasizes the value of the accused's confessing guilt as a sign that justice is being done). She refused, insisting that whatever she had done during the Cultural Revolution was done at Mao's request. Zhang Chunqiao also refused. The others confessed.

Trial Begins

The trial opened on November 20, 1980, before 600 representatives of the nation, in an air force auditorium in western Peking. The foreign press were not admitted, but five-minute excerpts from the trial were televised. Jiang Qing was led into the courtroom, her arms held by two matrons who wore pistols.

Among the first to testify, defendants Wang Hongwen and Yao Wenyuan admitted that in 1974 they had tried to persuade Mao not to appoint Deng Xiaoping as his first deputy prime minister. They said they had intimated to Mao that Deng and Prime Minister Zhou Enlai were conspiring against him. Two former generals, Huang Yongsheng and Li Zuopeng, admitted that, by passing information on Mao to Lin Biao, they had participated in Lin's 1971 plot to assassinate Mao. Another general, Jiang Tengjiao, admitted joining in a secret meeting at which he was named head of the conspirators.

Jiang Qing testified for the first time on November 26. Speaking in tones scarcely audible, she denied conspiring with the three other leading defendants to keep Mao from naming Deng Xiaoping as first deputy prime minister in 1974, with the result that Deng was purged. Her testimony was contradicted by two women who had been aides to Mao, Wang Hairong and Tang Wensheng. Tang had been born in the United States and had served as Mao's English interpreter. Until they appeared at the trial, neither woman's whereabouts had been known since Mao's death.

The next day, the prosecutors demanded that Zhang reply to charges of persecuting several of the Chinese leaders. Appearing angry and gaunt, he refused to speak. The chief judge, concerned at the defendant's obstinacy in the face of the Chinese legal tradition, in which confession helps prove that justice is being done, warned him that he could be convicted despite his silence. Zhang and Jiang continued as the only defendants who refused to confess.

The trial's sensationalism heightened as former general Jiang Tengjiao testified. With 40 people masquerading as Red Guards on Jiang Qing's orders, he said, he had carried out raids on the Shanghai homes of actors and writers. Why? He had been searching, he revealed, for love letters incriminating to Jiang Qing that she had written while an actress in the 1930s. His testimony was followed by a dramatic confession by Jiang Qing, as the prosecutors turned to the persecution of former chief of state Liu Shaoqi and his wife during the Cultural Revolution. Liu had been Mao's chief rival, and many believed Mao had launched the Cultural Revolution to get rid of Liu and his pragmatic policies. Liu had died en route to exile in 1969, and his wife, who was Jiang Qing's adversary, had been held in solitary confinement for 10 years. Shown documents and tapes and hearing witnesses, Jiang reversed her plea of innocence and admitted personally directing the special group that had attacked Liu. She claimed, however, that she had acted on orders from Mao.

As many witnesses read from scripts (almost all were lesser-known codefendants or were individuals who had been held in prison for years), the testimony turned to evidence of torture. The prosecutors played tape recordings of the questioning of professor Zhang Zhongyi, who had died of mistreatment in

1967, and of teacher Yang Chengzuo, who had also been tortured to death on Jiang's orders during a search for evidence that Liu's wife was a United States spy.

December 12 brought Jiang's expulsion from the courtroom after she repeatedly interrupted a witness. Jiang was bitterly attacked by the widow of a former movie director who had been tortured to death on Jiang's suspicion that he possessed one of her letters from the 1930s. Another outburst came on December 23 when Jiang, shouting, called the judges fascists and Nationalist Chinese agents. She was charged with contempt of court and warned that her behavior could lead to a heavier sentence.

Taking the stand again on December 25, Jiang declared that she was justified in attacking officials as counterrevolutionaries and that she was innocent of all charges of persecution because she had acted at Mao's behest. Two days later, she announced that it would be "more glorious to have my head chopped off" and dared the court to execute her.

"I Am Prepared to Die!"

Summing up the case, the prosecutor noted that Mao's "great contributions" to China would not be forgotten but that it was clear that Mao was responsible for the people's "plight" during the Cultural Revolution. He then demanded the death sentence for Jiang. Dragged from the courtroom, Jiang shouted, "I am prepared to die!" and upbraided not only the court but also China's leadership, crying, "Making revolution is no crime."

On January 25, 1981, Jiang was sentenced to death but given a two-year suspension. Again she was dragged from the courtroom at her sentencing after she shouted for the overthrow of Deng, who had twice been ousted by her husband but had regained power after Mao's death. Zhang Chunqiao, who had refused to speak throughout the trial and who was reported to be dying of lung cancer, received the same sentence. Wang was sentenced to life imprisonment and Yao to 20 years. The others were given 16 to 18 years behind bars. There was no appeal process.

On January 25, 1983, the sentences of Jiang and Zhang were reduced to life imprisonment. Early in the morning of May 14, 1991, after a total of 17 years' imprisonment before and after the trial, Jiang, 77, committed suicide in prison. On October 5, 1996, Yao was freed. Wang and Zhang remain locked up.

—Bernard Ryan, Jr.

Suggestions for Further Reading

Bloodworth, Dennis. *The Messiah and the Mandarins: Mao Tse-tung and the Ironies of Power*. New York: Atheneum, 1982.

Bonavia, David. *The Chinese*. New York: Lippincott & Crowell, 1980.

Carter, Peter. *Mao.* New York: Viking, 1979.

Chang, Jung. *Wild Swans: Three Daughters of China.* New York: Simon & Schuster, 1991.

Cheng, Nien. *Life and Death in Shanghai.* New York: Grove, 1980.

Clayre, Alasdair. *The Heart of the Dragon.* Boston: Houghton Mifflin, 1985.

Dimond, E. Grey. *Inside China Today: A Western View.* New York: W. W. Norton, 1983.

Hoyt, Edwin P. *The Rise of the Chinese Republic: From the Last Emperor to Deng Xiaoping.* New York: McGraw-Hill, 1989.

Lawson, Don. *The Long March: Red China under Chairman Mao.* New York: Crowell, 1983.

Salisbury, Harrison E. *The New Emperors: China in the Era of Mao and Deng.* Boston: Little, Brown, 1992.

Schwartz, Benjamin Isadore. *Chinese Communism and the Rise of Mao.* Cambridge, Mass.: Harvard University Press, 1979.

Terrill, Ross. *The Future of China After Mao.* New York: Delacorte, 1978.

———. *Mao: A Biography.* New York: Harper & Row, 1980.

Isabel Perón Trial: 1981

Defendant: Isabel Perón   **Crimes Charged:** Fraud, corruption
Chief Defense Lawyer: Julio Isaac Arriola   **Chief Prosecutor:** No
information available   **Judge:** Federal Judge Pedro Carlos Narvaiz
Place: Buenos Aires, Argentina   **Date of Trial:** March 20, 1981
Verdict: Guilty   **Sentence:** Eight years' imprisonment and lifetime prohibition
against holding public or political party office

SIGNIFICANCE
Argentine military leaders used corruption charges against deposed president
Isabel Perón to diminish the political strength of the powerful Perónist Party.

J uan Domingo Perón's supporters expected him to restore order to the
Argentine political scene when he returned from exile in Spain on June 20,
1973. Before he had a chance to implement his program, he died on July 1, 1974.
Leadership of the nation passed to Perón's vice president and third wife, María
Estela, popularly known as Isabel. She was no match for the turbulent world of
Argentine politics.

For decades, government succession in Argentina amounted to a repeating
cycle of civilian rule and military takeovers, such as the coups that first brought
Juan Perón to power in 1943 and forced him out in 1955. Exiled and widowed
after the death of his popular second wife, Evita, Perón met "Isabelita" in a
Panama City nightclub, where she was performing as a dancer. They married in
1961. She shared his exile in Spain until a resurgence of Perónist sentiment
prompted his return to Argentina in 1973.

Economic instability and political violence had begun to shake the country
even before Juan Perón's return to power. Under Isabel's administration, however, the situation worsened dramatically. Inflation soared over 700 percent.
Political murders and bombings occurred daily, with right-wing death squads
and left-wing terrorists attacking each other mercilessly. The new administration was powerless to halt the chaos. Many Argentines expected and even hoped
for a military takeover to restore order.

The coup came on March 24, 1976. After an evening spent negotiating
with military leaders, who were fruitlessly pressuring her to resign, Perón
stepped aboard a helicopter for the flight from the palace to her official resi-

dence. Instead, she was flown out of Buenos Aires to a mansion in a remote province, where she remained under house arrest.

Junta Presses Corruption Charges

The power of the Perón name in Argentina was sufficiently strong for the new military junta to avoid prosecuting the deposed president on overtly political grounds, in spite of her unpopular rule. Perón escaped the fate of thousands of less fortunate Argentines, who were kidnapped, tortured, and murdered in the junta's so-called "dirty war" against rivals and imagined subversives. Yet the junta was determined to damage the Perónist Party beyond repair. To accomplish this, they resurrected the greatest scandal of Isabel Perón's last year in office.

As president, Perón was chairwoman of the Justicialist Crusade for Solidarity, a Perónist-controlled charitable agency that distributed national lottery profits to social welfare projects. On July 26, 1975, the Banco de la Naçion Argentina received a check for nearly $750,000 from the charity, signed by Perón. The check was not to be used to pay for medical equipment or a similarly worthy expenditure, however; it was to be deposited into the late Juan Perón's estate account, of which his widow was executor and sole beneficiary. Bank officials questioned the curious transaction. Within days, the check was withdrawn by Isabel Perón's secretary. The president called the deposit an honest mistake.

Perón's opponents immediately moved to transform the aborted transaction into political capital. Her allies successfully thwarted calls for a congressional investigation, but a government inquiry by federal Judge Alfredo Noscetti Fasolino proceeded to investigate the deposit. On December 31, under alleged political pressure, Judge Fasolino cleared Perón of all criminal liability but issued arrest warrants for several of her assistants, who were by then living in exile.

Such easy absolution was not possible after the junta took power two months later. With the Perónist Party in disarray, Isabel, already under house arrest, was indicted for the charity check scandal. On May 6, 1976, Federal Judge Nino J. García Moritan formally charged her with mishandling public funds for personal gain.

If found guilty, Perón faced a possible ten years in prison. Her monetary assets were already frozen, and she was banned from holding political office under a new law, which also allowed the junta to detain anyone indefinitely without charges. Despite its wish to banish her from Argentine politics, however, the new government seemed uncertain of how to dispose of the former president without mobilizing her supporters. The answer consisted of new fraud indictments. On October 25, Judge Moritan found Perón guilty of embezzling half a million dollars in charity funds. She was detained at a naval base and her personal assets, amounting to $400,000 in cash and real estate, remained frozen by the court.

The Junta's Dilemma

Yet the junta still could not be quietly rid of their troublesome hostage. One week after her conviction, a federal appeals court ruled that Perón should not be liable for the original fraud charge because she had been cleared by Judge Fasolino in December 1975. Federal prosecutors groused that Fasolino's ruling was the real travesty of justice.

Unsure of how to prosecute Perón without making her a martyr, the junta did nothing. She was moved to one of her late husband's country estates. Four years passed with no legal action taken against her. She was not seen in public until early 1981, when her indictments made their way through the courts.

Argentine federal judges were responsible for both determining culpability and dispensing penalties in such cases. On February 4, 1981, Perón was acquitted on one corruption charge. On March 20, she was less lucky. She was acquitted of misusing presidential funds and of accepting a gift of $14,000 worth of jewelry from a bank but was found guilty of diverting $1 million in charity funds for her own use. She was also found to be criminally responsible for the controversial 1975 transfer of charity funds to her husband's estate.

Her two convictions earned Perón a sentence of eight years' imprisonment. The time she had already spent in detention made her eligible for parole within a month. This unsettled Argentina's military rulers, who could not agree among themselves whether their interests would be best served by imprisoning Perón or by letting her leave the country. They decided to use the judiciary to hold her hostage awhile longer by pressing two more charges dating back to her presidency. She was accused of transferring ownership of a government building to the Perónist Party and of using presidential funds to buy personal possessions and make home repairs.

On June 24, Judge Pedro Carlos Narvaiz found insufficient evidence to convict Perón on the latter charges. He found her guilty of the illegal property transfer but ordered that her 18-month sentence run concurrently with the time she was already serving.

Parole and Voluntary Exile

The junta's judicial gambit did not merely fail to add time to Perón's imprisonment. Mounting international pressure for her release and a resurgence of the Perónist Party suggested that her image as a martyr was growing, in spite of the junta's desperate wish to produce exactly the opposite result.

Having already served two-thirds of her sentence, Perón was paroled and released on July 6, 1981. The conditional release barred her from participating in or speaking openly about politics. She was granted permission to visit Spain. Perón settled in Madrid and did not return to Argentina, thus fulfilling the junta's real wish.

Discredited by their abysmal handling of the economy, disgraced by the loss of the 1982 Falkland Islands War, and loathed by much of the populace for the bloody "dirty war," the Argentine military had little choice but to allow free elections in 1983. As a conciliatory gesture on September 9, President Reynaldo Bignone pardoned Perón for her fraud conviction. The exile was now free to run for public office, although Bignone had cleverly waited until the Perónist Party had already nominated Senator Italo Luder as their presidential candidate. (Ironically, Perón had hired Luder as an additional attorney during her last court case.) The Perónists elected Isabel president of their party and immediately set about planning her return from Spain.

A renaissance of the once powerful Perónist dynasty did not occur. Senator Luder lost to Raúl Alfonsín, who became president on December 10, 1983. The Perónist Party eventually regained power in Argentina but without Isabel, who resigned as party leader in February 1985 and resumed her comfortable life in Madrid. "Isabelita" was gone, but Argentine politicians continued to invoke her name whenever they required an image of a heroine or a failed leader to enhance their oratory.

—Tom Smith

Suggestions for Further Reading

Rudolph, James D., ed. *Argentina: A Country Study*. Washington, D.C.: The American University, 1986.

Schumacher, Edward. "Five Years a Captive, Mrs. Perón Is Still a Rallying Point." *The New York Times*, May 12, 1981, 2.

———. "Argentine Government Frees Mrs. Perón After Five Years." *The New York Times*, July 7, 1981, 1.

Simpson, James, and Jana Bennett. *The Disappeared and the Mothers of the Plaza*. New York: St. Martin's Press, 1985.

Paul Wakwaro Ekai Trial: 1981

Defendant: Paul Wakwaro Ekai   **Crimes Charged:** Murder, robbery
Chief Defense Lawyer: Name not reported   **Chief Prosecutor:** Name not reported   **Judge:** Justice Matthew Muli   **Place:** Nyeri, Kenya
Dates of Trial: July 11–October 28, 1981   **Verdict:** Guilty
Sentence: Detention "at the President's pleasure" (indefinite imprisonment)

SIGNIFICANCE
Paul Ekai was convicted of killing famous naturalist Joy Adamson, author of the best-selling book *Born Free.*

Joy Adamson's passion for African wildlife was at first thought to have cost the 69-year-old naturalist her life. The irony was chilling. Word spread around the globe that Adamson had been mauled to death by a lion, one of the big cats to whose survival she had dedicated her life.

At the time of her death, Adamson and her game warden husband, George, had been controversial figures in Kenyan wildlife conservation debates for over two decades. They were also international celebrities, thanks to Joy's 1960 book about Elsa, an orphaned lion cub the Adamsons had raised and reintroduced to the wild. The book, *Born Free*, was an instant worldwide best-seller and inspired an equally popular film.

In 1977, Joy Adamson's efforts focused on raising and studying an orphaned leopard cub. Adamson set off for the rugged northern wildlife reserve of Shaba and established a camp with a small group of hired hands. Although her research was successful, disaster struck in the summer of 1979, when an electrical fire ravaged the site.

The camp was rebuilt, but Adamson's troubles continued. In late November, she broke her leg. A few weeks later, thefts of money and other belongings began to plague the compound. The remote location inevitably suggested that the culprit must have been one of Adamson's employees. Known for her hot temper, Adamson accused a young worker named Paul Ekai of the thefts and fired him. Ekai was given his wages and told to leave immediately.

Police Reject Lion as Cause of Death

On January 3, 1980, Adamson went for her customary evening walk in the bush surrounding the camp. When she failed to return, her worried assistant, Pieter Mawson, went looking for her. He found her corpse lying a few hundred yards away. A wound in Adamson's abdomen suggested that a lion had killed her. Mawson's truck became stuck in the mud at the scene, so he ran back to camp for help. Mawson later returned for his truck, but the battery had mysteriously disappeared.

While the international press was reporting that a lion had killed Adamson, Kenyan police were coming to a different conclusion. The single abdominal puncture wound, lack of claw marks, and the surprisingly small amount of blood on Adamson's body aroused the suspicion of investigators. Human footprints were found leading away from the camp, which had been robbed again while Mawson and the hired hands were recovering Adamson's body. Pathologists determined that Adamson had been killed by a simi, or double-edged Kenyan short sword.

Police focused their attention on Adamson's employees, who frequently bore the brunt of her quarrelsome nature. As camp workers were eliminated as suspects, suspicion fell upon Paul Ekai, the Turkana tribesman Adamson had dismissed in early December. When police went to Ekai's home to question him, villagers told the investigators that Ekai had fled.

A month later, 200 miles away, three men reported to police that they had been robbed by bandits. When the police asked for identification, one of the victims handed them a card identifying himself as Ekai. A policeman recalled the name and had Ekai transported back to Shaba for questioning. After a night in police custody, Ekai confessed to the murder of Adamson and the robberies. He was formally charged on February 5, 1980.

Confession Recanted

After a preliminary hearing began on June 26, Ekai attempted to withdraw his confession. He claimed that Isiola police had driven him to a remote spot in the bush and had severely tortured him until he confessed. Ekai's accusations stopped the case against him dead in its tracks. Months passed before his claims were investigated, and his case formally came to trial on July 11, 1981.

Under oath, Ekai claimed that he had been recuperating from malaria at an aunt's home at the time of the murder. His aunt corroborated the alibi. The judge, however, refused to disallow Ekai's earlier confession.

Ekai's own words were the prosecution's most damaging evidence. In his statement to the Isiola police superintendent, Ekai had said that he had waited outside Adamson's camp to berate her for not paying him all of his wages when she fired him. A furious argument ensued. When Adamson angrily refused to pay Ekai all he felt he was due, he stabbed her with a simi. He threw the weapon into a swamp and went to the camp, robbing it while Adamson's body was being recovered.

Ekai's rejection of his confession might have carried more weight had he not led police to so much physical evidence. The murder weapon had disappeared into the mire of the swamp, but Ekai led police to the battery that had disappeared from Mawson's stranded truck. At his sister's home, Ekai produced a haversack that had been stolen from one of Adamson's assistants. He then led police to the home of a neighbor and handed over Adamson's flashlight. Both items had been missing since the first camp robbery in December 1979. Pathologists testified that bloodstains found on the haversack belonged to Joy Adamson's blood group, suggesting that Ekai had handled the hidden pack after the murder.

In Kenyan courts, at the time, trials for serious crimes like murder were not heard by juries. Instead, defendants faced three-member panels of local citizens who were familiar with area customs and tribal law. These three assessors would deliver a nonbinding advisory verdict, which a presiding judge had the option of using in passing final judgment. Ekai's assessors delivered a split verdict on August 6. Two assessors, both members of Ekai's Turkana tribe, found him innocent. The third assessor, the wife of an American missionary, considered him guilty.

On October 28, 1981, Justice Matthew Muli pronounced Ekai guilty of both murder and robbery. Ekai would have faced a mandatory death penalty had it not been for confusion about his age. He was estimated to be between 17 and 23 years old. Kenyan law established 18 as the minimum age for application of the death penalty. Because Ekai's claim that he was only 17 at the time of the murder could not be disproved, he was sentenced to be detained "at the President's pleasure," a euphemism for indefinite imprisonment.

Aftermath

Ekai's lawyers appealed the verdict on the basis of his confession, which they claimed was untrue and obtained under duress. The attorneys also pointed out that police had not produced a murder weapon. An appeals court, however, found no evidence that the confession had been obtained by torture. Ekai's alibi that he had been stricken at his aunt's home collapsed under the fact that he had led police directly to evidence stolen from Adamson's camp on the night of the murder. The conviction was upheld on December 14, 1981.

Ekai's imprisonment provided some emotional closure for George Adamson, who was irritated by the length of time it took for Ekai to be brought to trial. Adamson was fond of his wife, even though they had lived apart for many of the last years of her life. Ironically, George Adamson himself met a violent end in the bush eight years later. On August 20, 1989, he and two staff members were shot to death while rescuing a guest from Somali bandits. Evidence suggested that the shooting might have been an ambush, plotted by tribesmen angered by Adamson's efforts to bar them from Kenyan wildlife reserves, but no one was convicted of his murder.

—Tom Smith

Suggestions for Further Reading

Adamson, George. *My Pride and Joy.* New York: Simon & Schuster, 1987.

House, Adrian. *The Great Safari: The Lives of George and Joy Adamson.* New York: William Morrow & Co., 1993.

Nelson, Harold, ed. *Kenya: A Country Study.* Washington, D.C.: The American University, 1984.

Mehmet Ali Agca Trials: 1981 and 1985–86

Defendant: Mehmet Ali Agca   **Crimes Charged:** Attempted assassination of a head of state (first trial), complicity in illegally importing a weapon (second trial)   **Chief Defense Lawyers:** Piero d'Ovidio (first trial); Giuseppe Consolo and Adolfo Larussa (second trial)   **Chief Prosecutors:** Achille Gallucci, Italy's attorney general, and Nicoló Amato (first trial); Antonio Marini (second trial)   **Judges:** Severino Santiapichi (both trials), Ilario Martella (examining magistrate for continuing investigation)   **Place:** Rome, Italy   **Dates of Trials:** July 20–22, 1981 (first trial); May 27, 1985–March 29, 1986 (second trial)   **Verdicts:** Guilty (both charges)   **Sentences:** Life imprisonment, with the first year spent in solitary (first trial); one year in prison, with two months in solitary (second trial)

SIGNIFICANCE
There was no question of Agca's having shot the pope. The real question was, Who sponsored the assassination attempt?

P ope John Paul II was just five days away from his 61st birthday on May 13, 1981; his Wednesday afternoons on Saint Peter's Square had become a much-loved tradition. On this sunny late afternoon, standing in his special vehicle, he was riding slowly through an estimated 10,000 pilgrims from all over the world. Suddenly the pope slumped forward—few had heard the sound of gunshots. Before the crowd could understand what was happening, three more shots rang out. Of the four bullets fired, two hit and injured the pope, one in his abdomen, the other in his right arm and left hand; two women in the crowd were also wounded. As the crowd surged toward the pope, a young man holding a 9mm Browning pistol was trapped only a few yards from the Pope's vehicle. The 23-year-old Turk, Mehmet Ali Agca, was easily apprehended by Vatican police.

The First Trial

Italian authorities decided to try Agca strictly on charges that he had
attempted to assassinate an Italian head of state and defer all other matters,

including questions of motive, until later. This would result in a speedy and more secure trial. Authorities had reasons for concern about securing Agca: It was soon discovered that he had escaped from a Turkish military prison in 1979, where he had been jailed for killing a Turkish newspaper editor.

During his interrogation, Agca claimed to be an international terrorist with no particular orientation or loyalty. He was quoted as saying, "I make no distinction between Fascist and Communist terrorists. My terrorism is not red or black; it is red and black." He insisted that he was not a religious fanatic, claiming that he had never intended to kill the pope, just attack him.

As the trial opened, Agca's defense attorney, Piero d'Ovidio, challenged the court's jurisdiction to hear the case since the crime had been committed in the Vatican. The court found, however, that the 1929 Lateran Treaty gave it jurisdiction. D'Ovidio also tried to persuade the court to find Agca a schizophrenic psychopath, which would have opened the door for a reduced sentence of 30 years in prison instead of life. After extensive psychiatric evaluation, however, Agca was found mentally stable. Other than to deny that he had shot the pope, Agca refused to cooperate during the trial because he claimed the court had no jurisdiction. After refusing to answer any and all questions, he was found guilty and sentenced to life in prison, with the first year in solitary confinement.

The Investigation

In September 1981, Judge Severino Santiapichi issued a 50-page "Statement of Motivation," in which he clearly stated the court's belief that Agca was acting as part of a conspiracy. The report stated,

> Everything points to the conclusion that Agca was no more than the emerging point of a deep conspiracy, complex and threatening, orchestrated by secret forces, carefully planned and directed down to the smallest detail.

The official investigation began in November 1981 and, under the Italian legal system, was conducted by an examining magistrate judge, Ilario Martella. Although the investigation would be conducted with secrecy, questions raised in the "Statement of Motivation" provide several clues as to its direction:

- Who helped Agca escape from the Istanbul prison, supplied him with a false passport, money, places to stay?

- Was he part of some Turkish underground movement? Where had he come from?

- What did he do while in Bulgaria (50 days) and while in Rome (34 days)?

- How did he learn to use the Browning 9mm automatic so effectively?

- Why did he shoot the pope?

On February 14, 1982, police in Hamburg, Germany, arrested Omer Ay on a traffic violation; it turned out that he had forged the passport that Agca had been using to travel about Europe. He was extradited to Turkey. Then in September, two reports—one by American freelance journalist Claire Sterling published in the *Reader's Digest* and the second aired on NBC by reporter Marvin

Kalb—raised the possibility of Soviet involvement in the attempted assassination. The connection was made through suspected involvement of the Bulgarian intelligence service with the Turkish underworld, specifically with an organization called Gray Wolves, to which Agca allegedly belonged. At the time, Bulgaria was a faithful satellite of the USSR, so it was assumed that Bulgarian secret police would not do anything without the knowledge and approval of the USSR. Soviet interest in assassinating the pope was linked to the destabilization of Poland, another country in its sphere of influence. The labor union Solidarity was growing in strength—riots, strikes, and demands for economic reform in Poland threatened economic and political havoc elsewhere in Eastern Europe. Poland had become a thorn in the side of the Soviet Union.

Pictured is Mehmet Ali Agca after his 1979 arrest for killing a Turkish journalist in Istanbul. (Hulton-Deutsch Collection)

Pope John Paul II was the former Polish cardinal Karol Wojtyla. Within six months of assuming the papacy, he had paid a visit to Poland (1979); he had even received Solidarity's leader Lech Walesa in Rome. According to NBC reporter Marvin Kalb, the pope had sent a private message to then Soviet President Leonid Brezhnev vowing to "lay down the crown of St. Peter and return to his homeland to stand shoulder to shoulder with his people" if Soviet troops invaded Poland. Said Kalb, "A Soviet connection [with the assassination attempt] is strongly suggested but it cannot be proved."

In the spring of 1982, Agca changed his story. He had not acted on his own, he told the Italian investigators, but had been working with a group of Bulgarians. On November 25, 1982, Italian police arrested the head of the Rome office of the Bulgarian National Airline, Serge Ivanov Antonov, 35, and charged him with complicity in the attempted assassination of Pope John Paul II. The Bulgarian government denounced the arrest. Eventually, two more Bulgarians would be indicted, but they were safe in Bulgaria.

In June 1983, the Agca case took a startling turn. Emanuela Orlandi, the 15-year-old daughter of a Vatican official, was kidnapped. The note claiming responsibility was signed by members of the so-called Anti-Christian Turkish Liberation Army; the ransom demanded was the release of Agca. When Agca was taken to the police station for questioning about the kidnapping, he called for the release of the girl and told members of the press that the KGB and the Bulgarian secret service had helped with the assassination attempt and further implicated the Bulgarian Antonov. Continuing his investigation, examining magistrate Martella went to Sofia, Bulgaria, in July; the Bulgarians refused to extradite the two others charged.

In November 1983, Agca reenacted the assassination attempt for police, a standard procedure in Italian criminal investigations. On December 27, Pope John Paul II met with Agca in his jail cell, where the accused assassin kneeled to the pontiff and kissed his ring.

In May 1984, after three and a half years of investigation, Judge Ilario Martella submitted a 25,000-page report of his investigation to Italian State Prosecutor Antonio Albano for his review and assessment as to whether a trial was warranted. Albano's report requesting specific indictments was filed with the court and, on June 9, 1984, was leaked to journalist Claire Sterling. The report linked the papal assassination attempt to the Soviet Union:

> In some secret place, where every secret is wrapped in another secret, some political figure of great power took note of this most grave situation and, mindful of the vital needs of the Eastern bloc, decided it was necessary to kill Pope John Paul II.

In October, the court formally indicted the three Bulgarians, Agca, and four other Turks in the assassination attempt. Agca, already convicted of the assassination attempt, was now charged with complicity in illegally importing the weapon used. The indictment also alleged that

- the Bulgarians and three of the Turks had direct contact with Agca, guaranteeing him assistance and support in his assassination attempt;
- "more than 3 million deutsche marks ($900,000 in U.S. currency at the 1984 exchange rate) had been paid out to support the attack;
- Agca had been accompanied to the square by one Turk and one Bulgarian;
- "the Turks had brought bombs with them to 'spread panic.'" (The bombs were never exploded.)

The Second Trial

The trial to determine culpability in the plot to assassinate Pope John Paul II opened on May 27, 1985. The Italian press called it "the trial of the century" because of the prosecution's charges of the Soviet Union's involvement in the plot. Agca, whose prison interviews with investigators substantially influenced the investigation and provided the basis for many of the charges, took center stage again by shouting, "I am Jesus Christ. In the name of the omnipotent God, I announce the end of the world." This delighted the Bulgarian defense attorney, who cited the remarks as "proof that he has led Italian Justice around by the nose for three years." Prosecutor Antonio Marini said of Agca, "I do not believe he's crazy. When he begins to talk about the facts, he is extremely reliable." Agca's bizarre behavior was cited by the Soviet news agency Tass, which called the trial a "dragged-out tragicomedy."

On May 28, Agca refused to answer questions about how he got the gun he had used to shoot the pope. He requested a postponement of the trial and used the pope's December 1983 jail visit to substantiate his claims to divinity. Judge Santiapichi called for an adjournment and suggested Agca "go have a coffee." Agca said, "I am going to consult with God."

The trial continued month after month, ultimately requiring 98 sessions and generating 14,000 pages of testimony. On February 28, 1986, Chief Prosecutor Antonio Marini called for acquitting the three Bulgarians because of "lack of proof" and a court debate that "was not sufficient, was not exhaustive." On March 29, 1986, after six days of deliberation, a jury of two judges and six lay jurors announced their verdicts. They acquitted the three Turks and three Bulgarians of conspiring to assassinate Pope John Paul II. The one Turk present at the trial was found guilty of a weapons charge; his three-year prison sentence could not be enforced because his extradition from Sweden had been on a conspiracy charge, of which he had been acquitted.

Agca himself was found guilty of smuggling a gun into Italy. He was sentenced to one year in prison, with two months in solitary confinement. Because of his unpredictable behavior, he had not been present through much of this second trial, but as he was being led away after the sentencing, he called out, "I am not God, I am Jesus Christ the Son of God, I am an angel in human form!"

Living with Loose Ends

The verdicts did not put an end to many of the issues raised by this event. Charges and countercharges had abounded throughout the investigation and trial. The Soviet KGB claimed that the entire story of Eastern bloc involvement had been fabricated by the CIA. According to a Bulgarian who defected to France, the KGB believed that Cardinal Wojtyla's election to the papacy had been orchestrated by United States government officials to encourage the unrest in Poland. The CIA downplayed the idea of official Bulgarian involvement in the case, although the agency did acknowledge that the three Bulgarians arrested and charged in the case were intelligence officers. To this day, the exact role of the various parties has never been absolutely established.

As for Agca himself, it emerged that this young Turk from an impoverished family had lived quite well after his escape from prison in Istanbul. Clearly, he had been supported by someone or some group. It was also speculated that he himself might have been a target of assassination: Two individuals alleged to have accompanied him to Saint Peter's Square were said to have been under orders to shoot him once he had completed his job. If this were so, the plot failed, for Agca lives on in an Italian jail. But perhaps the most tragic "loose end" is the fate of the young Italian girl kidnapped in 1983. Despite various ransom notes and promises, she was never released, and it is assumed she was killed within a short time after being kidnapped.

—*Janet Bond Wood*

Suggestions for Further Reading

Henze, Paul. *The Plot to Kill the Pope.* New York: Charles Scribner's Sons, 1983.

Newsweek Magazine, May 25, 1981, 22.

The New York Times, March 30, 1986, June 10, 1984.

Sterling, Claire. *The Time of the Assassins: Anatomy of an Investigation.* New York: Holt, Rinehart and Winston, 1983.

Red Brigades Trial: 1982–83

Defendants: Mario Moretti, Prospero Gallinari, 61 others
Crimes Charged: The murder of Aldo Moro and his five bodyguards, 11 additional murders, related terrorist crimes
Chief Defense Lawyers: Various   **Chief State Prosecutor:** Nicoló Amato
Judge: Severino Santiapichi   **Place:** Rome, Italy   **Dates of Trial:** April 14, 1982–January 24, 1983   **Verdicts:** 32—life imprisonment; 27—lesser sentences; 4—acquitted.

SIGNIFICANCE

The arrest, imprisonment, trial, and conviction of 63 terrorists effectively broke the power of the Red Brigades, a terrorist organization that nearly paralyzed Italian political life from 1976–80.

Someone asked Mario Moretti, a leader of the Red Brigades, what he expected from his trial on charges of killing the former Italian prime minister Aldo Moro. "The Moro trial has already taken place," Moretti said, turning away from the questioner. "It was held four years ago, by us."

That mock trial ended in the execution of Moro, the leader of Italy's centrist Christian Democratic Party and the moving spirit behind the party's historic 1978 alliance with the Communist Party of Italy. Moro hoped to broaden his party's political base with a tactical alliance with the Communists. In their turn, the Communists, denied a voice in the seemingly endless succession of postwar Italian governments, longed for a share of power.

The alliance drew intense opposition from both political extremes. Rightists viewed any dealings with Communists as consorting with the forces of Satan. Leftists accused the Communist leader Sergio Berlinguer of selling out to bourgeois politicians in the interest of expediency and his own advancement. Nevertheless, Moro and Berlinguer forged ahead. By March 1978, the alliance seemed a certainty.

And, in fact, on March 16, 1978, Moro was en route to a session of parliament in Rome to celebrate the agreement when the Red Brigades struck. A new government, one that contained Communists, was to be sworn in that day. Moro never reached the palace. In a meticulously planned and flawlessly executed ambush on the Via Fani near the Christian Democratic Party's headquarters and Moro's apartment, a commando squad opened fire on Moro's car, killing his five bodyguards, seizing Moro unharmed and whisking him away to a terrorist hideout on the Via Montalcini. There began the 55-day ordeal that Moretti dubbed the "people's court trial" of Aldo Moro.

The Red Brigades had grown out of the radical student movement of the late 1960s. With Karl Marx, Vladimir Lenin, and Mao Tse-Tung as revolutionary mentors, this extreme tip of the left wing had turned increasingly to violence. By the early 1970s, the Red Brigades had evolved into a terrorist organization, calling for "revolutionary violence" against such phantoms as "exploitative CIA-financed managerial imperialism" and "Fascist capitalism." Police officers, magistrates, and businessmen became targets for kneecappings, kidnappings, extortion, and murder by the Red Brigades.

Aldo Moro, his captors charged, had been "for twenty years the supreme manager of power in Italy."

Moro Murdered by Captors

An intense manhunt failed to uncover the hideout of the Red Brigades. There, the movement's political theorists mercilessly harangued the five-time Italian prime minister. Moro appears to have acquitted himself with dignity. Told he was being prosecuted in "the name of the people," Moro responded that the party he headed had polled 12 million votes in the last election. And he issued pleas through his captors to the Italian government and to Pope Paul VI to negotiate in good faith for his release.

The government of Giulio Andreotti, with the support of Berlinguer's Communists, pursued a hard-line policy, categorically refusing to consider exchanging 13 terrorists being held in Italian prisons for Moro. For this, Moro's wife, Eleonora, would later accuse the Italian government and the United States with dual responsibility in his death. In any event, Moro's captors allowed him a last letter home. "A kiss and a caress for everyone," he wrote Eleonora and their children, "face by face, eye by eye, hair by hair." Then the shots rang out. On May 9, 1978, the police found Moro's bullet-riddled corpse in the trunk of a car parked in the Via Fani near the Christian Democratic headquarters.

The authorities launched an intense manhunt. Suspects were hauled in, interrogated, turned loose. Finally, in 1982, the kidnapping of an American general in Italy by the Red Brigades led to the big break in the case. Italian police raided the safe house in which General James Dozier was being held, freed him unharmed, and arrested a number of his kidnappers. Then Mario Moretti's plumbing sprang a leak, the second big break. Tenants on the floor below spotted a water stain on the ceiling and called the fire brigade. One thing led to another, and the police took possession of a cache of evidence and the mastermind of the Moro killing.

Scores Tried and Convicted

The proceedings opened in mid-April 1982 to a burst of gunfire. Terrorists opened up on security guards surrounding the trial venue, the Olympic Sports Center on the Vatican bank of the Tiber River. Three men were wounded; ultimately 1,500 troops and police were assigned to the security detail. Trial sessions took place in a fortified gymnasium in which basketball had once been played. Inside, the 63 defendants—23 charged in connection with Moro's death; the others, with various other murders, kidnappings, and lesser crimes—were held in six white cages. They were not handcuffed; they were allowed cigarettes. They could even chat with journalists and other observers, though some of the defendants threatened those who had written unfavorably of them with violent reprisal. There were far more men than women in the cages. Male or female, most were of a fairly nondescript appearance.

The Red Brigades are crowded into vans by the Italian Army State Police after the first day of their trial. (Hulton-Deutsch Collection)

"The Brigadists are mostly short, compact men," journalist Desmond O'Grady wrote. "They seem competent, specialized workers who one day decided to make a revolution. It requires an effort to bring to mind that this means, for them, the right to hunt people, try them in secret, and butcher them with no recourse against the sentence."

The prosecution presented Moretti, a short, stocky 26-year-old, as the undisputed leader of the Moro operation. Prospero Gallinari, 33 years old, was Moro's jailer and executioner. The government accused Gallinari (and, later, a second man) of killing the captive with a pistol shot, followed by a burst from an automatic weapon. Antonio Savasta and Patrizio Peci—known as the *pentiti*—turned state's evidence and testified against their former comrades. When Peci recanted, members of the Red Brigades still at large kidnapped and killed his apolitical brother in revenge. Savasta stood accused of involvement in a total of 17 killings. Observers saw something repellent in him—he had, an Italian journalist thought, the face of a "hypocritical seminarian." Nor did he seem particularly penitent. Like many of the others, Savasta spoke in an almost impenetrable jargon and in maddening euphemism. He spoke, for example, not of killing people but of "expressing violence."

The judge, Severino Santiapichi, questioned Savasta closely in an attempt to peel off his outer cover of abstraction. Savasta resisted. Impatient and unwilling to abandon his obscure manner of expression, he lost his temper and lashed out at the judge.

"You have to respect my human dignity," Savasta shouted. "You have to understand that inside the Red Brigades there is difficult debate, much indecision. You should show there's not only scorn for us."

"I do my duty by respecting the accused's dignity," Santiapichi answered. "Avoid raising your voice and giving moral judgements. We're trying to ascertain individual responsibility. You have to give us a chance to understand why so many people were killed. Remember that no one can bring them back to life."

The trial plodded on deep into the long Roman autumn: dozens of witnesses, tens of thousands of pages of documents, bursts of jeering from the defendants in their cages. Another five suspects joined the *pentiti*, renouncing terror, though they refused to give evidence against any of the others. Moretti remained defiant. "You are trying to wipe out five years of armed struggle, but you will not succeed," he told the court. Moro's widow and children sat through many of the sessions, as did the families of the five slain bodyguards and the other victims.

Italy's political powers testified toward the end of September. Andreotti, the prime minister, said the government regarded the attack on Moro as the possible opening phase of widespread revolt. For that reason, the authorities decided against any form of compromise. "In the first moments we had no idea whether the Moro kidnapping was an isolated incident or part of a nationwide armed revolution," Andreotti testified on September 27. Handing over 13 experienced revolutionary leaders, he suggested, would thus have been a blockhead piece of policy.

Bettino Craxi, the Socialist leader, took the witness stand on September 28. His party, he testified, established private links to the Red Brigades for the purpose of winning Moro's release. But the Socialists, too, refused to go along with the terrorists' demands for the freedom of the 13 terrorists, and so the Craxi talks broke down.

The Christmas and New Year's holidays came and went. Finally, in early January, Judge Santiapichi sent the case to the jury of 11 men and 1 woman.

After a week's deliberation, the jurors announced their multiple verdicts. Santiapichi handed down the sentences on January 24, 1983.

Altogether, 32 Red Brigades terrorists, among them Moretti and Gallinari, received life imprisonment. (There is no death penalty in Italy.) Other defendants were given sentences ranging from 4 months' to 30 years' imprisonment. Four were acquitted. Four of the defendants, including a senior Red Brigades leader convicted in the Dozier kidnapping, remained at large in 1983. They had been convicted in absentia, as permitted under Italian law.

Some of the defendants looked grim, even stunned; others joked and lit up cigarettes; a few climbed the bars of the white cages to wave at friends or relations in the back of the courtroom.

Moro's Bitter Last Words Discovered

The government hailed the verdicts as a substantial blow to the Red Brigades terror organization, and so they proved to be. "I remember, almost five years ago, a feeling of impotence," Virginio Rognoni, the interior minister, said afterward. "It seemed impossible to think that one day those responsible for the massacre would be in front of the judges."

Red Brigade attacks continued for several years, but the organization's back had indeed been broken. The Moro case lingered on, however. In 1996, the government finally convicted the second of Moro's killers, Germano Maccari. He received a life sentence for the crime. In October 1990, the authorities announced a group of workmen in a former Red Brigades apartment in Milan had found a packet of letters Moro had written during his two months' captivity. In them, Moro had harsh words for Andreotti and other senior government officials; Andreotti, Moro wrote, "moved at ease with his colleagues from the CIA." There were poignant as well as bitter words in the doomed man's last communications.

"Norina," he wrote his wife, "you can imagine the choir of angels that will conduct me from earth to heaven."

And finally: "I have been killed three times—through insufficient protection, through refusal to negotiate, through inconclusive politics."

—*Michael Golay*

Suggestions for Further Reading

Drake, Richard. *The Aldo Moro Murder Case*. Cambridge, Mass.: Harvard University Press, 1996.

Haberman, Clyde. "Italy Sees Hidden Hand Reviving Moro Case,"
The New York Times (October 21, 1990): A6.

Katz, Robert. *Days of Wrath: The Ordeal of Aldo Moro*. Garden City, N.Y.: Doubleday, 1980.

O'Grady, Desmond. "The Trial of the Red Brigades," *Commonweal* (July 16, 1982): 389–91.

Lindy and Michael Chamberlain Trial: 1982

Defendants: Lindy and Michael Chamberlain   **Crimes Charged:** Murder
(Lindy Chamberlain); accessory to murder (Michael Chamberlain)
Chief Defense Lawyers: John Phillips, Q.C.; Andrew Kirkham; Peter Dean
Chief Prosecutors: Ian Barker, Q.C.; Desmond Sturgess, Q.C.; Tom Pauling
Judge: James Muirhead   **Place:** Darwin, Australia
Dates of Trial: September 13–October 29, 1982   **Verdict:** Guilty
Sentences: Life in prison (Lindy Chamberlain); 18 months in prison—later
suspended (Michael Chamberlain)

SIGNIFICANCE
Charges that a young mother had killed her nine-week-old baby and blamed wild
dogs developed into the most notorious and baffling murder trial in Australian
history.

Situated almost at the geographical heart of Australia lies Ayers Rock, an awesome red-stone pile 5 miles in circumference and rising 1,600 feet from the flat, arid outback. Regarded as one of the great wonders of the natural world, Ayers Rock is visited by thousands of sightseers every year, and on August 16, 1980, two such tourists, Lindy and Michael Chamberlain, together with their three children, pitched a tent in its massive shadow. The next day Michael, a pastor in the Seventh-Day Adventist Church and a keen photographer, took the two eldest children to explore the rock, while Lindy stayed with the most recent addition to the family, nine-week-old Azaria.

That night, with Azaria asleep inside the tent, the Chamberlain family prepared a meal at an adjacent barbecue site. At around 8 P.M., Michael heard a short, sharp cry. Lindy immediately went to check on Azaria and saw a dingo—a wild dog—backing out through the flaps of their tent, shaking its head as though carrying something in its mouth. Dingoes were by no means uncommon at Ayers Rock, though usually they skirted the perimeter of the campsite in search of food and rarely troubled the tourists. In horror, Lindy cried, "The dingo has got my baby!"

The dingo disappeared with its prey into the darkness. A police search of the surrounding area found nothing, but other campers did confirm the presence of dingoes by the Chamberlains' tent earlier that evening. Nightmare turned to tragedy eight days later, when a tourist found a small pile of baby clothes next to a large boulder, 2½ miles from Ayers Rock. The bloodstained and torn jumpsuit, singlet, and bootees were identified as those worn by Azaria on the night of her disappearance. The only item of clothing missing was a lemon-edged matinee jacket. So bizarre were the circumstances of Azaria's disappearance that rumors began to circulate that the story of the dingo had been a fabrication and that the Chamberlains had killed their child and disposed of the body.

To investigate these rumors, an inquiry was held, at which the coroner pronounced himself satisfied with the Chamberlains' explanation. Police were discontent with this decision and sent the baby clothing to Professor James Cameron, pathologist at the London Hospital and one of the world's foremost medicolegal experts. He and his colleagues examined the clothing yet could find no evidence of dingo contamination—no saliva, no hairs, nothing that would substantiate Lindy Chamberlain's story. Largely because of these findings, a second inquiry was ordered, and this time Lindy Chamberlain was charged with murder and her husband, with being an accessory after the fact.

Dingo Lie

When the Chamberlains faced trial at the Darwin courthouse on September 13, 1982, prosecutor Ian Barker, Q.C. (Queen's Counsel), told the jury that, although Azaria's body was never found, it was reasonable to assume that the baby was dead. "The Crown says that the dingo story was a fanciful lie, calculated to conceal the truth, which is that the child Azaria died by her mother's hand."

More than most, this trial relied on "expert" witnesses to decide the outcome. Joy Kuhl, a forensic biologist, described finding stains in the Chamberlains' car caused by fetal blood, the kind found in babies up to six months old; and Professor Malcolm Chaikin said that four areas of damage on the jumpsuit appeared to have been caused by sharp scissors, not by a dingo's teeth. Experimenting with a dingo's tooth mounted on a machine, he had thrust the tooth into clothing wrapped around a freshly killed rabbit. At no time did it rupture the material, even when the fabric-covered tooth penetrated the carcass to a depth of 1/3 inch. The inference was clear—a dingo's tooth would penetrate but not cut.

Greatly experienced, Professor Cameron oozed confidence on the stand. His examination of the jumpsuit had revealed the apparent bloody print of a small right hand of an adult. He also felt that bloodstains on the jumpsuit were consistent with having been caused by "a cut-throat type of injury."

John Phillips, Q.C., for the defense, wanted clarification of the alleged handprint. "Would you not agree that blood from an injury, purely by accident, can take up apparent shapes of objects?"

"They must have a contact point," agreed Cameron, "by or against such an object."

"It can occur purely by accident, an apparent pattern of an object?"

Cameron had to concede the possibility. "Yes."

As often happens in matters of forensic science, for every prosecution expert, the defense was able to produce one of its own. Professor Vernon Pleuckhahn took a diametrically opposed view to that of Cameron, saying he had seen several cases of people brought into hospitals with severe head injuries whose patterns of bleeding had produced stains similar to those found on the jumpsuit.

"You don't agree with Professor Cameron, that there is evidence of the impression of a human hand?" asked Phillips.

"With due respect to his eminence . . . I cannot in the wildest imagination . . . see the imprint of a hand. And, as I've said, I've tried to convince myself there could be."

Dr. Dan Cornell was less tactful. As the scientist who had introduced into Australia the blood-screening technique known as crossover electrophoresis, which Joyce Kuhl had used to detect the alleged fetal blood, Cornell was scathing about Kuhl's competence, stating boldly that "she didn't know what she was doing."

After reminding the jury of the conflicting medical testimony, Justice James Muirhead sent the jury out to do its duty. That evening, October 29, 1982, the jury found both defendants guilty. Lindy Chamberlain was sentenced to life in prison, and her husband received a surprisingly lenient 18-month suspended sentence, supported by a good behavior bond of 500 Australian dollars.

When three federal court judges dismissed Lindy Chamberlain's appeal on April 29, 1983, that appeared to be the end of this sensational case. But three years later, there came a stunning revelation.

Amazing Discovery

In February 1986, a searcher looking for a missing tourist at Ayers Rock stumbled across an item of baby clothing. By chance, this same person had taken part in the search for Azaria Chamberlain and recalled the missing matinee jacket. This seemed to be that same jacket—lemon-edged and the size that Lindy Chamberlain had mentioned. When Lindy Chamberlain positively identified the jacket as the one worn by Azaria, the authorities announced on February 7, 1986, that an inquiry was to be held. In the meantime, it was announced that the remainder of Lindy Chamberlain's sentence was being remitted. The edict contained a curious last paragraph: "Although Mrs. Chamberlain's remission is subject to the usual conditions of good behavior, it is not my intention that she be taken back into custody regardless of the outcome of the inquiry."

On May 22, 1988, after a lengthy and rambling judicial review conducted in several cities over several months, Commission Judge Trevor Morling submitted his report to the governor-general of the Northern Territory. Citing slipshod forensic work, he wrote, "I conclude that none of Mrs. Kuhl's tests established that any such blood was Azaria's," adding in reference to evidence given by park rangers and animal experts, "Although a dingo would have had difficulty in removing Azaria's body from her clothing without causing more damage to it, it was possible for it to have done so."

There was one final blast for the expert witnesses: "With the benefit of hindsight it can be seen that some of the experts . . . were over-confident of the ability to form reliable opinions on matters that lay on the outer margins of their fields of expertise. Some of their opinions were based on unreliable or inadequate data. It was not until more research work had been done after the trial that some of these opinions were found to be of doubtful validity or wrong. . . . In my opinion, if the evidence before the Commission had been given at the trial, the trial judge would have been obliged to direct the jury to acquit the Chamberlains on the ground that the evidence could not justify their convictions."

Although accepting the Morling Report, the Northern Territory Legislative Assembly declined to accept it as proof of innocence and merely pardoned the Chamberlains, thus leaving the verdicts, in law, unchanged.

In 1988, *A Cry in the Dark*, a motion picture based on this unique case and starring Meryl Streep, was released.

—Colin Evans

Suggestions for Further Reading

Bryson, J. *Evil Angels*. New York: Summit Books, 1985.

Chamberlain, Lindy. *Through My Eyes*. London: Heinemann, 1991.

Tullet, Tom. *Clues To Murder*. London: The Bodley Head, 1986.

Wilson, Colin and Donald Seaman. *The Encyclopedia of Modern Murder*. New York: Putnam's, 1985.

Argentina's "Dirty War" Trial: 1985

Defendants: Jorge Videla, Emilio Massera, Orlando Agosti, Roberto Viola, Armando Lambruschini, Leopoldo Galtieri, Jorge Anaya, Omar Graffigna, Basilio Lami Dozo **Crimes Charged:** Murder, kidnapping, illegal detention, torture, robbery, use of false identification to conduct illegal searches
Chief Defense Lawyers: Twenty-two defense attorneys
Chief Prosecutors: Julio Strassera, Luis Moreno Ocampo **Judges:** Six-member Federal Court of Appeals, presiding judge León Arslanian
Place: Buenos Aires, Argentina **Dates of Trial:** April 22–December 9, 1985
Verdicts: Videla, Massera, Viola, Agosti, and Lambruschini—guilty; Galtieri, Anaya, Graffigna, and Lami Dozo—not guilty **Sentences:** Videla and Massera—life imprisonment; Viola—17 years' imprisonment; Lambruschini—8 years' imprisonment; Agosti—4½ years' imprisonment

SIGNIFICANCE
The trial of military officers responsible for the "dirty war," in which thousands of innocent civilians perished, was Argentina's first major step in restoring the rule of law after years of dictatorship and political violence. It was also the first civilian trial of military dictators in Latin American history.

When the ineffectual government of Isabel Perón toppled in a military coup on March 24, 1976, many Argentines hoped that a new order would emerge to stabilize the economy and end a chaotic cycle of leftist terrorism and rightist counterinsurgency. Indeed, Argentina's new military junta acted swiftly to crush the most violent leftist groups. Between 1976 and 1979, however, this obsession with order hemorrhaged into a national nightmare.

The junta—army lieutenant general Jorge Videla, navy admiral Emilio Massera, and air force brigadier general Orlando Agosti—disbanded the nation's congress, dismissed elected officials, and banned all political activity. The new government was secretive about their broader agenda. The junta and their allies within the military establishment agreed that Argentina needed fundamental social change if "Western, Christian values" were to survive there. To accomplish this end, all persons engaged in or suspected of "subversive" activity would be exterminated. The official name of this policy was "the Process of

National Reorganization." It soon came to be known by a name coined by the junta itself—"the dirty war."

The terror began quietly. Argentines were slow to recognize an enormous increase in arrests amid the chaos of the government's overt war with Perónist guerrillas. Blue-collar workers and professionals, students, journalists, nuns, teachers, psychiatrists, union members, and thousands of ordinary citizens with no known link to any political activity were abducted, tortured at secret detention centers, and killed. Some were buried in secret mass graves. Many more were thrown out of aircraft over the ocean, often while still alive.

The terror became so pervasive that many Argentines would not openly speak of friends or relatives taken away by soldiers or plainclothes paramilitary squads for fear that they, too, might be taken away. From 1976 to 1979, between 9,000 and 30,000 men, women, and children vanished. Hushed voices called them *los desaparecidos*, or "the disappeared."

Writs of habeas corpus drafted by worried family members demanding that their loved ones either be freed or charged with a crime were rejected by the courts. Authorities reasoned that since the police and security forces had no record of those named in the writs, no charge against them existed, making the writs meaningless. In fact, writs often provoked the disappearance of those who offered them or hastened the death of a prisoner whose release was being sought.

News of the Argentine government's secret war on its own people continued to leak out of the country. Yet despite international condemnation and economic sanctions, the dirty war continued well into 1979.

The juntas that followed Isabel Perón's government were even less successful than their civilian predecessor in restoring economic order. Hoping to divert attention from their mismanagement of the economy, Argentina's military leaders provoked England into a war over the disputed sovereignty of the Falkland Islands in 1982. Argentina quickly lost the war, and the third junta resigned in disgrace, clearing the way for free civilian elections. Before ceding control, the military enacted a retroactive amnesty law, pardoning anyone involved in the dirty war.

Junta Leaders Face Prosecution

Upon taking office on December 10, 1983, President Raúl Alfonsín signed an executive decree ordering the court-martial of the nine junta members who had held power between March 1976 and June 1982, as well as the Buenos Aires police chief, General Ramón Camps. The amnesty the military leaders had awarded themselves was annulled.

In spite of Alfonsín's campaign pledge to investigate the dirty war, prosecutions were slow in coming. The Supreme Council of the Armed Forces, a judicial body composed of retired military officers formed at Alfonsín's request, was originally charged with trying the accused officers. After eight months of hearings, the council announced that it was having difficulty reaching a verdict, stating that the defendants could be held only "indirectly responsible" for the actions of their subordinates.

To allay fears that the military was incapable of policing itself, however, Alfonsín had also appointed the National Commission on Disappeared Persons (CONADEP) to investigate the "disappearances." Its report arrived in September 1984, the same month the military council declined to charge the officers.

CONADEP's 50,000 page report, *Nunca Más* ("Never Again"), was a portrait of efficiently organized, state-sanctioned sadism. Depositions described hundreds of cases of abduction, robbery, rape, murder, and secret burial. The report documented 8,921 disappearances and concluded that thousands more lives had probably been lost in this "national tragedy." The investigation also identified 1,300 military and police personnel involved in the terror, but their names were not made public.

Jurisdiction over the cases was taken away from the uncooperative military council and was assumed by the Federal Court of Appeals. The cases of several hundred accused junior officers remained before the military council, but the architects of the terror would now face a civilian court.

None of the junta commanders was charged with personally kidnapping, torturing, or killing any of "the disappeared." However, the indictments held the military leaders responsible for atrocities committed by their subordinates. Six defendants—Generals Jorge Videla, Roberto Viola, and Leopoldo Galtieri; Admirals Emilio Massera and Armando Lambruschini; and Brigadier General Orlando Agosti—were charged with homicide, illegal detention, torture, robbery, and conducting illegal searches with false identification. Brigadier General Omar Graffigna faced identical charges, except homicide. Admiral Jorge Anaya and Brigadier General Basilio Lami Dozo were charged with illegal detention and using false documents.

Testimony Recounts Horrors

The trial began on April 22, 1985, with hundreds of tense spectators packing the courtroom of the Palace of Justice. Six civilian judges would decide the fate of the accused.

The CONADEP report's litany of horror was repeated in testimony that lasted for four months. Prosecutor Julio Strassera called some 1,000 witnesses. More than 700 individual cases were described as representative of crimes sanctioned by the defendants. One mother who had been arrested for searching for her disappeared child spoke of hearing her daughter's screams through jail walls. Asked if she had anything more to say at the close of her testimony, her reply echoed the heartache of thousands: "I want to know if my daughter is alive or dead."

Final arguments began as bombs exploded in Buenos Aires. President Alfonsín declared a state of siege to thwart right-wing provocateurs bent on prodding the military into a new coup.

Prosecutors argued that as supreme rulers of the country, the nine commanders were not simply following orders by allowing the brutality to take place. Voluminous evidence proved there had been a systematic pattern of crimes against humanity of which the commanders must have been aware.

"A few isolated crimes or facts could be considered excesses," said prosecutor Luis Moreno Ocampo. "But the quantity of crimes proved by the prosecution allows us to say that there was a planned operation dictated by the defendants."

The prosecution's final statement lasted for five days. When prosecutor Julio Strassera ended his final statement, thundering *"¡nunca mas!"*—"never again!"—hundreds of spectators crammed into the court burst into applause.

In contrast to over 1,000 witnesses called by prosecutors, the defense called fewer than 30 witnesses. Argentina's Supreme Court rejected a defense motion to have the trial ruled unconstitutional. A battery of defense lawyers argued that the junta leaders could not be held responsible for any "excesses" committed by junior officers or by the police during an era of civil unrest. The defense also tried to depict the dirty war as a legitimate part of the government's earlier war with leftist guerrillas. Corpses the prosecution claimed were found bound, gagged, and shot were characterized as combat casualties by the defense.

The accused chose not to sit in court during testimony describing the crimes of their regimes. When they appeared during summations, not one was contrite. They considered the proceedings against them to be politically motivated.

"Nobody has to defend himself for winning a just war, and the war against terrorism is a just war," said Admiral Massera.

Too Lenient or Too Harsh?

Although the military rules under which the trial was conducted allowed for capital punishment, prosecutors asked for life sentences for the original junta and the army and navy commanders of the second junta, under whose rule the worst atrocities had occurred. Lengthy prison terms were requested for the remaining defendants.

The verdicts were announced on December 9, 1985. Videla and Massera were found guilty and sentenced to life in prison. Their successors, Viola and Lambruschini, received 17- and 8-year prison terms, respectively. The Argentine air force was found to have been less involved in the terror than were their army and navy counterparts. Instead of life imprisonment, the first junta's air force commander, Agosti, received a sentence of 4½ years. His successors, Graffigna and Lami Dozo, were acquitted. So were Galtieri and Anaya, who had commanded the army and navy, respectively, during the third junta, after the worst violence of the repression was past. All of those convicted were stripped of military rank.

Both prosecutors and defense attorneys were unhappy with some of the verdicts and sentences. Both sides appealed those they objected to, unsuccessfully. Human rights groups condemned the sentences as too lenient. Supporters of the military were equally angered by the convictions. Still other Argentines, however, saw individual assignments of guilt within the verdicts as a hopeful sign that the justice system might finally be free of the government control that had been its curse for too long.

The trial did not end the dirty war controversy. Several more high-ranking officers were convicted in subsequent trials. Like Videla and Massera, they were confined in cozy prison bungalows. President Alfonsín remained under considerable pressure to pardon the men or, at least, to halt the prosecution of hundreds of accused murderers and torturers still serving in Argentina's powerful military. Eager to end the volatile era, Alfonsín agreed to laws that stopped further prosecutions for dirty-war crimes. Alfonsín's successor, Carlos Menem, continued to appease the right wing with pardons for 100 defendants facing prosecution. On December 29, 1990, President Menem pardoned and freed Videla, Massera, and all other convicted officers still in confinement.

Menem stated that the five years he had spent in illegal detention during the dirty war gave him the moral authority to "definitively close a sad and black period of national history." Yet, thousands of Argentines paraded to protest the widely unpopular pardons, proving that the dirty war was an open wound that would not soon heal.

—Tom Smith

Suggestions for Further Reading

Chavez, Lydia. "In Argentine Court, Tales of Horror and Heroism." *The New York Times*, May 28, 1985, p. 2.

Nunca Más: The Report of the Argentine National Commission on the Disappeared. New York: Farrar, Straus & Giroux, 1986.

Rudolph, James D., ed. *Argentina: A Country Study.* Washington, D.C.: The American University Press, 1986.

Simpson, James, and Jana Bennett. *The Disappeared and the Mothers of the Plaza.* New York: St. Martin's Press, 1985.

Timerman, Jacobo. *Prisoner without a Name, Cell without a Number.* New York: Alfred A. Knopf, 1981.

Indira Gandhi's Assassins Trial: 1985–86

Defendants: Satwant Singh, Kehar Singh, Balbir Singh
Crimes Charged: Murder (Satwant Singh); conspiracy (Kehar Singh, Balbir Singh) **Chief Defense Lawyers:** Pran Nath Lekhi, P. P. Grover
Chief Prosecutor: K. L. Arora **Judge:** Mahesh Chandra **Place:** New Delhi, India **Dates of Trial:** May 13, 1985–January 22, 1986 **Verdict:** Guilty; Balbir Singh's conviction overturned by Indian Supreme Court on August 3, 1988 **Sentence:** Death by hanging

SIGNIFICANCE

The killing of Prime Minister Indira Gandhi and the trial of her assassins were among the most dramatic episodes in the struggle between Sikh separatists and the Indian government.

During the early 1980s, Sikh religious fundamentalists began to demand autonomous control of the northern Indian state of the Punjab. Prime Minister Indira Gandhi viewed Sikh separatists with concern. In her eyes, allowing a religious group to secede from India could begin the unraveling of the entire nation.

By late 1983, political murders by Sikh extremists were so common that Mrs. Gandhi declared a state of emergency in the Punjab. As government troops poured into the region, militant Sikhs withdrew into the sanctuary of religious shrines. Sant Jarnail Singh Bhindranwhale, leader of the most violent faction, took shelter in Amritsar within the massive Golden Temple, the holiest of Sikh shrines.

For months, the Indian government resisted the temptation to flush out the terrorists. As murders ordered by Bhindranwhale continued and his arsenal grew inside the Golden Temple, pressure for government action increased.

On June 5, 1984, the Indian army acted on Mrs. Gandhi's orders and stormed the Golden Temple, carrying out "Operation Blue Star." The battle lasted for more than a day and claimed hundreds of lives. Although Bhindranwhale was killed, many of the dead were innocent Sikh religious pilgrims who had become trapped in the shrine when the carnage began.

"What has happened is a tragedy for India," Mrs. Gandhi said. "It should not be celebrated as a victory."

The Indian government helped restore the Golden Temple, but all of the damage caused by Operation Blue Star could not be repaired. Militant and moderate Sikhs alike were outraged by the heavy death toll, as well as the defilement and continued military occupation of the holy site. Mrs. Gandhi was advised to remove Sikhs from her personal staff for security reasons. She refused, explaining that to do so would demonstrate that she was unfaithful to her own government's vision of a united India.

Body Guards Murder Prime Minister

On the morning of October 31, 1984, Mrs. Gandhi was scheduled to be interviewed by actor Peter Ustinov for a television program. The filming would take place on the grounds of her private compound, so Mrs. Gandhi felt safe in leaving her home without the bulletproof vest she wore beneath her sari at public appearances.

As she walked across her garden for the appointment, she encountered Beant Singh, a young Sikh policeman who had served on her personal guard for six years. Singh raised his revolver and shot Mrs. Gandhi three times. A second guard, Satwant Singh, suddenly stepped forward and emptied his automatic rifle into the prime minister. Both guards dropped their weapons and raised their hands.

"We have done what we set out to do," said Beant Singh. "Now you can do whatever you want to do."

While the wounded prime minister was on her way to a hospital, her two assailants were taken to a guardhouse. Minutes later, both were shot. Satwant Singh was seriously wounded. Beant Singh died immediately. Five hours later, Mrs. Gandhi too was dead. Word spread quickly that Sikhs had killed her in revenge for the assault on the Golden Temple.

Mrs. Gandhi's son Rajiv was immediately sworn in as prime minister. The government remained stable, but the worst riots since India's 1947 partition from Pakistan erupted. Mobs of Hindus attacked and killed thousands of innocent Sikhs.

Conspiracy Theories Abound

Rumors circulated that an army general or perhaps the U.S. Central Intelligence Agency might be responsible for the assassination. The guards who had shot Mrs. Gandhi's killers were arrested and held amid worries of a wider conspiracy. The loyal guards were cleared after convincing investigators that the captured men had grabbed for weapons while trying to escape.

Investigators eventually concluded that the assassination was an act of pure vengeance and charged Satwant Singh with murder. Balbir Singh, a former subinspector in the prime minister's security forces, and Kehar Singh, a government clerk and uncle of the slain Beant Singh, were charged with criminal conspiracy. None of the three defendants were related, but shared the name traditionally taken by Sikh men, *Singh*, which means lion.

Their trial began on May 13, 1985, under extraordinary security. Safety concerns were so great that the trial took place in New Delhi's Tihar Central Jail, not in a court building. Judge Mahesh Chandra presided from behind a bulletproof screen. The defendants sat inside a similar enclosure. Newspaper reporters were allowed into the hot, cramped room, but photographers, television cameras, and the general public were barred.

Lingering rumors of conspiracy allowed Pran Nath Lekhi, Satwant Singh's lawyer, to defend his client aggressively. The combative Lekhi was a political enemy of Mrs. Gandhi's and had been imprisoned during her controversial suspension of civil rights in the 1970s. He angrily accused police of torturing Satwant Singh into making a false confession. Lekhi proposed that another assassin might have shot Mrs. Gandhi and then escaped. He noted that forensics tests had been conducted on only two of the numerous bullets lodged in Mrs. Gandhi's body and that no full autopsy had been performed. This left open the possibility that she might have been shot by unknown assailants or poisoned in the hospital. Lekhi wondered why hospital records showed her receiving a blood transfusion 37 minutes after a postmortem report declared her officially dead.

Lekhi's personal animosity toward the Gandhi family flowed freely throughout the trial. Despite warnings to temper his language, Lekhi outraged prosecutors by calling Rajiv Gandhi and his wife potential suspects. Lekhi charged that evidence was being concealed to protect the new prime minister and his political allies. Lekhi attempted to call Rajiv Gandhi and Indian President Zail Singh as witnesses, but Judge Chandra rejected the request.

Attorney P. P. Grover's defense of Balbir Singh and Kehar Singh was less flamboyant, but no less critical of investigators. Grover charged that incriminating documents found in his clients' homes were forgeries.

On January 22, 1986, Judge Chandra found the defendants guilty and sentenced them to death. The judge rejected attorney Lehki's harsh theories about Rajiv Gandhi. "The courtroom is no place to exhibit such flights of imagination, much less to indulge in some political or personal vendetta between some individuals, and least for character assassination," Judge Chandra said in his verdict.

Asked if they had anything to say, the three men simply maintained their innocence. Attorney Lekhi was less reticent. He shouted that the trial was a farce and accused the judge of trying to advance his career.

Appeals and Investigation Drag On

By Indian law, the condemned men were automatically guaranteed appeals. A week after the verdict, the Delhi High Court found several technical errors in Judge Chandra's sentence, including his refusal to allow defense lawyers to argue against the verdict and his failure to specify that the condemned were to be "hanged by the neck until dead." Nevertheless, after four months of hearings, the three-judge panel hearing the appeal declined to reverse or modify the sentence.

The case was next reviewed by the Indian Supreme Court, which overturned Balbir Singh's conviction on August 3, 1988. He was released immediately. Justice G. L. Oza called the evidence against Singh "defective as well as deficient," but the remaining death sentences were upheld in the same decision.

Satwant Singh requested a stay of execution until a pending suit against the guards who had shot him could be settled. Kehar Singh appealed directly to Indian President Ramaswamy Venkataraman for clemency. The petition was denied almost immediately. The swiftness with which the appeal was denied earned Kehar Singh a brief stay of execution, when the Constitutional Bench of the Supreme Court decided that President Venkataraman's hasty decision did not constitute a fair hearing. On January 5, 1989, however, five judges of the Supreme Court upheld the death sentence.

Satwant Singh and Kehar Singh were led to the prison gallows the next day.

"I wish that I am born again and again and each time lay down my life," said Satwant Singh, before the noose was slipped around his neck.

In the years between Mrs. Gandhi's death and the execution of her accused killers, the findings of M. P. Thakkar, the Supreme Court judge specially commissioned to investigate the assassination and review security procedures, remained secret. In March 1989, two months after Satwant Singh and Kehar Singh were hanged, the *Indian Express* newspaper published excerpts from Justice Thakkar's report. It was revealed that Rajendra Kumar Dhawan, a prominent aide to Mrs. Gandhi, had been investigated for his role in rearranging her security detail on the day of her death. Pressured by political foes who hoped to use the report against him, Prime Minister Rajiv Gandhi released the full report. The prime minister said that the report had remained secret at the request of Justice Thakkar, who had wished to avoid influencing the trial of the men in custody.

Yet Justice Thakkar's report was severely critical of security officials and viewed Dhawan's manipulation of Mrs. Gandhi's schedule with extreme suspicion. By the time the report was publicly released on March 27, 1989, Dhawan had been cleared of charges by police and was serving as an adviser to Rajiv Gandhi.

Within days, on April 7, those who assumed that the assassination case was over got another jolt when four more Sikhs were arrested in the plot. Little came of these charges. One of the accused, Simranjit Singh Mann, had already been detained without trial for four years for his alleged complicity. Mann was released in late 1989 after winning a seat in the Indian parliament from prison.

Although thousands of Indians continued to die in sectarian violence, the bloody circumstances were seldom as sensational as those surrounding Indira Gandhi's murder, with one ironic exception. On May 21, 1991, Rajiv Gandhi and

16 other people were killed when a Tamil woman approached him at a campaign rally and detonated a bomb hidden in her belt.

—Tom Smith

Suggestions for Further Reading

Ali, Tariq. *An Indian Dynasty: The Story of the Nehru-Gandhi Family.* New York: G. P. Putnam's Sons, 1985.

Gupte, Pranay. *Vengeance: India After the Assassination of Indira Gandhi.* New York: W. W. Norton, 1985.

———. *Mother India: A Political Biography of Indira Gandhi.* New York: Charles Scribner's Sons, 1992.

Hazarika, Sanjoy. "Protests Follow Hanging of 2 Sikhs." *The New York Times* (January 7, 1989): 3.

———. "New Delhi Trial Starts for 3 in Gandhi Assassination Case." *The New York Times* (May 18, 1985): 5.

Nyrop, Richard F., ed. *India: A Country Study.* Washington D.C.: U.S. Government, 1989.

The Sharpeville Six Trial: 1985

Defendants:
Mojalefa "Ja-Ja" Sefatsa, Reid Mokoena, Oupa Diniso, Theresa Ramashamola, Christiaan Mokubung, Gideon Mokone, Duma Khumalo, Francis Mokhesi

Crimes Charged:
Murder of Jacob Dlamini; a subversion charge of "acting with a common purpose unlawfully . . . [to influence the government . . . and/or to intimidate, demoralize, or persuade members of the public to do or not do something]"; alternative charges of malicious damage to property; arson

Chief Defense Lawyers: Jack Unterhalter, Ismail Hussain, Prakash Diar

Chief Prosecutor: Eben Jordaan

Judges:
Acting Justice Wessel Johannes Human, Assessors Dr. D.W.R. Herzog and I. L. Grindlay-Ferris

Place: Pretoria, South Africa   **Dates of Trial:** September 23–December 13, 1985

Verdicts:
Sefatsa, Mokoena, Diniso, Ramashamola, Khumalo, Mokhesi—guilty of murder; Mokubung, Mokone—guilty of public violence; all—guilty of subversion

Sentences:
Sefatsa, Mokoena, Diniso, Ramashamola, Khumalo, Mokhesi: death by hanging on murder count (death sentences commuted: Sefatsa to 20 years' imprisonment; Mokoena, Diniso, Ramashamola to 18 years' imprisonment; Khumalo, Mokhesi to 25 years' imprisonment); Mokubung, Mokone: five years' imprisonment on count of public violence; all defendants: 8 years' imprisonment on count of subversion

SIGNIFICANCE
Basic human rights were subverted in all phases of the Sharpeville Six case, which was fairly typical of the apartheid era in South Africa. Corrupt police used intimidation and torture to coerce perjured testimony; white judges, acting without juries, implemented a political, rather than a judicial, agenda in judging and sentencing black defendants; appeals courts refused to reconsider judicial errors or to right gross injustices; extreme sentences were handed down for offenses by blacks.

S harpeville, a black township of some 6,000 small brick houses in the Johannesburg region, first attained international notoriety as the site of a 1960 massacre of 69 black South Africans by white policemen. Then on September 3, 1984, widespread protests against service fee increases at Sharpeville left an unpopular black civic leader dead and led to the arrest of eight local blacks. The case of the Sharpeville Six (named after the six of the eight defendants condemned to death) became an international cause célèbre. The defendants had been singled out almost randomly as scapegoats for mob violence and were given capital punishment for an act in which they played either a very minor role or no role at all.

The 1984 Incident and Those Charged

The September 1984 protests in Sharpeville and elsewhere were provoked by the 1982 Black Local Authorities Act, under which the white government shifted responsibility for township governance to elected black councils but denied them adequate funding for such mandated municipal services as road maintenance and construction, trash removal, sewerage, electrification, and basic administrative expenses. To close the financial gap, the councils were forced to raise service fees, on top of the rents already difficult for many to pay. Protests against these increased service fees erupted into violence, often directed at the black officials, many of whom were seen as corrupt, self-serving agents of the white rulers.

In Sharpeville, Jacob Dlamini, a deputy mayor, became the focus of mob antagonism. On the night of September 2, 1984, stones shattered all the windows of his house. The next morning, some several hundred protesters gathered to march to the township administrative offices to picket against service fee increases. They carried placards, sang, shouted slogans and along the way intimidated onlookers into joining them by threatening injury and damage to their houses. As the protesters neared Dlamini's house, which was on the route, they paused to throw stones. Police chased away the crowd with tear gas and rubber bullets and asked Dlamini to leave with them because it was not safe for him to stay. Summoned by emergencies elsewhere, however, the police had to leave Dlamini's house. A mob of some 100 soon reassembled to stone the house once again. Dlamini shot a gun from within and injured at least one person. Enraged, the mob tossed gasoline bombs at the house, setting it on fire. As Dlamini ran out, one or more persons struggled with him and disarmed him. Stones were thrown at him, and he was knocked down. His car was pushed into the street, overturned, and burned. The unconscious Dlamini was also dragged into the street and set on fire. He was dead when the police returned at 9 that morning.

Two months passed before any action was taken. Eight suspects then were arrested. The police first came for "Ja-Ja" Sefatsa, a 29-year-old fruit vendor. Although he insisted that at the time of the murder he had been away at his aunt's house, where he had assisted a black policeman under mob attack, conflicting testimony by Mrs. Dlamini and her neighbor Jantjie Mabuti placed him at the scene. Mabuti also placed five others at the scene. He said that Theresa Ramashamola, a 24-year-old cook, had slapped a woman who had voiced her opposition to the burning of Dlamini. Ramashamola said that she had been forced to join the march, had been hit in the head by a police rubber bullet, had sought treatment, and then had gone home. Both Ramashamola and Sefatsa were tortured by the police during interrogation.

Mabuti also testified that both Christiaan Mokubung and Gideon Mokone were in the mob tossing stones at the house. Mokone, in fact, had been injured by the bullet from Dlamini's gun, had been carried away for treatment, and then had been taken to the hospital. Both had been intimidated into joining the march, and Mokubung had fled when the police dispersed the crowd. Neither was present when the mob regrouped. Mabuti also placed at the scene Duma Khumalo, a 26-year-old teacher-trainee and part-time vendor. Mabuti said Khumalo had handed out gasoline bombs. Khumalo's story was that he had been forced to join the march. He admitted that he had witnessed the stoning of the house (he was, in fact, related to Dlamini and said he had no anger against him) but that he had carried a friend injured by a rubber bullet to a nearby house for treatment and then had taken him home. Therefore, he had not been present when the mob continued its attack.

Mabuti also accused Francis Mokhesi, 28, a professional soccer player, of leading in the making and passing out of gasoline bombs and of helping to push Dlamini's car into the street. Arrested seven months after the murder, Mokhesi had as his alibi a week-long ankle injury that had sidelined him from soccer. Another witness, Joseph Manete, also implicated Khumalo and Mokhesi. (In 1988, Manete would confess in a newspaper interview that he had given false testimony under police coercion.)

Of the remaining two defendants, Reid Mokoena, 21, an unskilled laborer, had been arrested by the police and tortured into signing a false confession that he had thrown a stone at the house. His story was that he had been forced to join the march, had been tear-gassed, and after washing his face at a nearby house, had returned home. He had never reached Dlamini's house. The final defendant, Oupa Diniso, 29, a factory quality control inspector, was arrested on purely circumstantial evidence: possession of what the police claimed was Dlamini's gun. Diniso had spent the day of the riot at a church and at home. The next day, he had come across three young boys arguing over a gun they had found. For reasons of safety, he said, he had confiscated the weapon, taken it home, put it in a toolbox, and forgot about it. The state claimed that he had personally wrested the gun from Dlamini.

The Trial

Arrested and held under Section 29 of the Internal Security Act, seven of the accused were kept in solitary confinement, virtually incommunicado, for more than nine months before the trial. Brought to court for the indictment on April 25, 1985, they finally were made aware of the charges. They were to be held responsible for the actions of the mob. Answering a defense request for further particulars on the subversion, or controversial "common purpose" charge, the state alleged that the defendants' intent had been to make the government abandon the black local authorities' plan, to cause black councilors to resign, and to have service fee increases rescinded. The attorney general intervened to prevent bail. In effect, this had become a political trial that through successful prosecution of the common purpose charge could set a precedent for future trials of rioters.

To obtain the desired outcome, the state brought 72-year-old Wessel Johannes Human out of retirement to preside as judge (even though most of his experience had been as a public prosecutor). The trial opened on September 23, 1985, with autopsy evidence, a recap of the political and economic conditions that had given rise to the protests, and police evidence. The prosecution presented six state eyewitnesses. Of these, three implicated no one; Dlamini's widow implicated Sefatsa; Manete falsely implicated Khumalo and Mokhesi; and Mabuti, the key state witness, implicated all except Mokoena and Diniso. Defense cross-examination revealed numerous serious problems with Mabuti's detailed story. Despite defense witness testimony corroborating the alibis of the accused, the judge refused to accept such testimony and instead chose to accept that of Mabuti.

Nor, at a hearing (October 18–29, 1985) dealing with Mokoena's challenge of the admissibility of his confession, did the judge accept medical testimony pointing to the use of electric shock torture to make Mokoena talk. That the judge had already made up his mind in advance was suggested by his questioning of Mokoena, only the second defendant to give evidence:

Judge: But those people who told you had to walk with them, we know now from all the evidence, which you have also heard, that those people were not on the way to the municipal offices, they were on the way to Dlamini's house in order to burn it down and to burn him to death, these people that you were walking with. Did they not say to you, look, we have to go to Dlamini's house now, and set it on fire and kill him?

Mokoena: No.

The Verdict and Sentences

In his verdict, the judge consistently disallowed the evidence raising reasonable doubt or favoring the accused. Apparently to set a cautionary example for other violent protesters, he disregarded possible extenuating circumstances, such as the effects of mob psychology. Whereas a jury might well have considered the total situation, he simply found the defendants guilty. He condemned six to death and the two others to lengthy prison terms.

While the so-called Sharpeville Six waited on death row and underwent the agony of two stays of execution, the defense, armed with a long list of judicial errors, vigorously but unsuccessfully pursued an appeal. In the end, it was international publicity and pressure that embarrassed the president of South Africa on November 23, 1988, into granting the six a reprieve, commuting their death sentences to 18, 20 and 25 years' imprisonment. This grudging clemency, however, did not wipe out the original injustice of the conviction. The trial was, according to one foreign journalist, an exercise in "judicial terrorism."

At least, though, an attempt was eventually made to right this wrong when the South African government began to reform itself. Christiaan Mokubung and Gideon Mokone—who had been found guilty only of public violence—were released on December 10, 1990. Oupa Diniso and Duma Khumalo were released on July 10, 1991. (They benefited from an amnesty granted to first offenders.) Theresa Ramashamola and Reid Mokoena were released (on parole) on December 13, 1991. Mojalefa Sefatsa and Francis Mokhesi were released (as a result of the Record of Understanding) on September 26, 1992.

—*Eva Weber*

Suggestions for Further Reading

Diar, Prakash. *The Sharpeville Six.* Toronto: McClellan & Stewart, Inc., 1990.

Phillips, Norman. *The Tragedy of Apartheid: A Journalist's Experiences in the South African Riots.* New York: David McKay, 1960.

Reeves, Ambrose. *Shooting at Sharpeville: The Agony of South Africa.* Boston: Houghton Mifflin, 1961.

Smith, William E. "Black Rage, White Fist," *Time,* August 5, 1985, 24–32.

Sicilian Mafiosi Trial: 1986–87

Defendants: 476 alleged members of the Sicilian Mafia
Crimes Charged: Hundreds of crimes, ranging from auto theft to murder
Chief Defense Lawyers: About 200, at various times for the many
defendants **Chief Prosecutors:** Giuseppe Ayala, Giovanni Falcone, Giusto
Sciacchitano **Judges:** Alfonso Giordano, Pietro Grasso **Place:** Palermo,
Italy **Dates of Trial:** February 10, 1986–December 17, 1987
Verdicts: 338 found guilty, 114 acquitted
Sentences: Life sentences for 19, lesser sentences for 219, totaling 2,665
years in prison, $10 million in fines

SIGNIFICANCE

This mass trial altered public perceptions of the Mafia in Italy. Previously regarded
by many Sicilians as relatively small-time criminals who even served some social
use, the Mafia leaders were shown to be brutal organizers of a worldwide trade in
heroin. The trial also cast doubt on the tradition that the Mafia was untouchable in
Sicily, that no court would dare show the will to expose the Mafia's many crimes.

Although many people around the world now associate the Mafia with the
United States—largely because of the influence of American movies and
TV—the Mafia began and remains strongly rooted in Sicily. (*Mafia* is a Sicilian
dialect word that means "boldness," probably based on an Arabic word for
"boasting.") Founded in the 1860s in response to centuries of rule by foreigners
(Greeks, Carthaginians, Arabs, Spaniards, and others), the Sicilian Mafia originally embodied the credo that a Sicilian must find honor, dignity, and retribution
in the world for himself—that no government will ever accomplish that for him.
The Sicilian Mafia, often referred to by insiders as Cosa Nostra ("Our Thing"),
eventually spread its tentacles until they twined around the society and economy of the island, which the Mafia exploited primarily to enrich its leaders.

By the mid-20th century, the Sicilian Mafia had developed extensive
contacts with its offshoots in various countries, particularly in the United States.
But powerful as the Mafia was in the United States, Americans had little concept
of how much more important, more powerful, and more pervasive it had become
in Sicily by the 1970s. There were probably 15,000 formally inducted, or

"made," members of the Sicilian Mafia and thousands of underlings who aspired to enter the ranks of the chosen, the "men of honor."

The Sicilian Mafia faced two important trials during the 1960s. In 1965, 114 Mafiosi were brought to trial in Catanzaro, Calabria, on the mainland of Italy. (It was considered too dangerous to try them on the island itself.) All but 10 of the defendants were acquitted in a trial that exposed the weakness of the Italian government and judiciary when it came to the Cosa Nostra. Four years later, the government tried again. Sixty-four Mafiosi were tried in Bari (again, on the mainland); every single defendant was acquitted in a stunning defeat for the Italian judicial system. The sole success of Italian law enforcement came in 1974 when Don Luciano Leggio, widely regarded as the "chief of chiefs," was seized and imprisoned for life. (He had been sentenced in absentia in 1970.) Even behind bars, Don Leggio proved unstoppable; he not only continued to direct the Mafia but also actually expanded the scope of its operations.

In particular, between 1975 and 1981, the Sicilian Mafia expanded its role in the international heroin trade; by 1980, it was supplying at least half (many have claimed two-thirds) of all the heroin used in the United States alone. Similar connections were made in Brazil and other countries, and by the early 1980s, the Sicilian Mafia was running the heroin trade in numerous countries around the globe.

"Great Mafia War" Rages

The profits were huge. It was estimated that as much as $20 billion was coming into the hands of the leaders of the Sicilian Mafia each year. As their bankrolls expanded, so, too, did their pride and arrogance. Starting in 1981, the "Great Mafia War" raged in Sicily, most particularly in the city of Palermo, long known as the unofficial capital of the mob. Followers of Don Leggio systematically sought to wipe out the members of rival Mafia groups; by 1983, Leggio's group, known as the Corleonesi (for their founding town of Corleone) had gained nearly complete control of the Sicilian Mafia. This huge achievement came at the cost of more than 1,000 lives—most of those killed were members of rival groups, but a number were just innocent bystanders. From his jail cell in Sardinia, Don Leggio directed events and witnessed the destruction of his rivals for power.

Even as they were winning the Mafia war (1981–83), Leggio's henchmen took on a second opponent, one that they deemed worthy of little or no respect: the law and government in Sicily. Starting in 1979 with the murder of the head of the Squadro Mobile in Palermo, the Mafia killed judges, prosecutors, policemen, and law enforcement officials with impunity. In response to the killings, the Italian government dispatched General Carlo Alberto Dalla Chiesa, a tough-minded reformer, to clean up Palermo in 1982. Before he could accomplish much, Dalla Chiesa and his wife were gunned down by Mafiosi on September 3, 1982.

The Mafia had gone too far. Sicilians were outraged; mainland Italians were stunned. The Italian parliament passed a law that made membership in the Mafia a criminal offense and abolished bank secrecy when Mafia accounts were involved. A special team of prosecutors and investigators formed in Palermo and began to piece together the connections of the Sicilian Mafia. (They were aided in this task by United States investigations into the New York City Mafia.) Following the murders of Judge Rocco Chinnici (1983) and Commissario Ninni Cassara (1985), the prosecutors redoubled their efforts. A final element of their case came together when Tommaso Buscetta, who had already testified in trials of Mafia figures in New York, agreed to testify on behalf of the prosecution. He had turned against the Mafia because he had lost two sons and other members of his family during the Mafia war. By early 1986, the prosecution had named 476 defendants, many of whom were already in custody.

"Maxi-Trial"

When what the press dubbed "the Maxi-Trial" opened on February 10, 1986, in Palermo, few observers knew what to expect. Never before had the Italian government taken on so many members of the Mafia, never before had the organization of the Mafia itself been on trial, and never before had the government dared to hold such a trial in Sicily. To house the proceedings, a bunker-courtroom (costing some $19 million) was built adjacent to the L'Ucciardone prison; the defendants were taken to and brought from the courtroom by an underground tunnel. Inside the courtroom, 30 steel cages had been constructed to hold the defendants and witnesses; the witness chair was circled by a booth of bulletproof glass. Tanks guarded the outside, and some 2,000 police and guards were on duty in and around the courtroom. The pale-green octagonal hall only served to heighten the tension and uncertainty.

Seven judges had declined the post of presiding judge before Alfonso Giordano accepted. Two hundred lawyers represented the Mafia defendants, and some 60 lawyers served the interests of the city of Palermo and the families of the murdered people. The 476 defendants were charged with a host of specific crimes, ranging from automobile theft to murder. Don Leggio himself was brought from his prison cell in Sardinia as a defendant; ten days after the trial started, the police captured and brought in one of the major accused, Michele Greco, called "The Pope" because of his prominence in the Sicilian Mafia. A second set of judges and jurors was on the dais to ensure that death— natural or otherwise—would not stop the trial from reaching a conclusion.

Prosecutor Giovanni Falcone and his assistant read the 8,607-page indictment, which was supported by hundreds of thousands of pages of evidence. Aside from the numerous specific crimes that Falcone alleged individuals had committed, he charged the Mafia organization with three crimes: (1) authorizing multiple murders committed between 1975 and 1985, (2) creating and maintaining an international heroin network, and (3) the "oneness" of its organization, which meant that members of the leadership could be charged for murders they had commissioned. Falcone then called his first witness, Tommaso Buscetta, formerly a leading member of the Sicilian Mafia.

Captured by American and Brazilian agents in Brazil in 1983, Buscetta had faced extradition to both the United States and Italy. By offering valuable testimony in New York trials against the Mafia, he was able to enter the U.S. federal witness protection program. Buscetta had no such immunity in his homeland. When he came forward to testify, wearing dark glasses and surrounded by police, observers wondered whether a true Mafia don could ever be expected to provide hard information against other "men of honor." But having lost so many relatives and friends in the Mafia war, Buscetta now turned on the Cosa Nostra. Seeking to draw a distinction between the Mafia he had grown up in during the 1950s and 1960s and the Mafia personified by Don Leggio, Buscetta declared that the original Mafia would never have carried out indiscriminate killings. Buscetta impressed many in the courtroom with his presence and authority. He was unrepentant for being a member of the Mafia; he simply yearned, he said, for the Mafia of his earlier days. After testifying for an entire week, Buscetta came out of the witness chair having done a good deal of harm to the defendants, who called out insults from their cages in the courtroom.

As important as Buscetta was, the second witness to testify exposed even more of the workings of the Cosa Nostra. Salvatore Contorno, a ruffian, extortionist, and kidnapper for the mob since 1975, had been arrested in 1982. He testified at length about a deal made with the Turkish Mafia in 1975 and the huge profits that had been made through the heroin trade. When asked to name names, Contorno stood up and pointed around the courtroom as he called out the names of at least 150 defendants who were mafiosi. When asked specific questions such as, "Is Giuseppe Abate a man of honor?" Contorno answered with simple affirmative declarations. He went even further, discussing the heroin refineries that had been set up in Sicily and naming the owners of the properties, among them Michele Greco. Contorno's testimony was crushing to the defense, who could only shrug in response to many of his specific statements.

The third witness to be called was Luciano Leggio himself. Already in prison for life, the true leader of the Sicilian Mafia responded blandly to the charges brought against him, but no person in the courtroom missed the cynicism and malevolence that he projected. Leggio brushed aside the accusation that he still ran the Mafia from his prison cell: "I was in jail. I'm still in jail. Excuse me, but how could I be running around the country, walk the streets, return to my cell, unless all this was done with permission?"

Following Buscetta, Contorno, and Leggio came 1,337 other witnesses, most of whom testified on smaller matters and to lesser effect. Some witnesses broke down on the stand and refused to continue; others were clearly overwhelmed by the menace visible in the faces of the defendants. However, the body of evidence presented was enormous, and the testimony of several people—notably Buscetta and Contorno—was powerful. (Twelve other former Mafia members testified for the prosecution and became known as *pentiti*, "the repentants.") By the time the court heard the summation of prosecutor

Giuseppe Ayala, the prosecution had done an effective job of presenting its case. One great question remained: Would a six-person Sicilian jury convict members of the Sicilian Mafia in Palermo when juries on the Italian mainland had failed to do so in 1965 and 1969?

The jury began its deliberations on November 11, 1987, having heard testimony and arguments for 21 months. On December 16, 1987, the jury delivered its decision. Three hundred and thirty-eight defendants were found guilty, 19 of whom were sentenced to life imprisonment; 114 defendants were acquitted. (During the trial, the prosecution had dismissed 14 others and 10 of the original accused had died.) Michele Greco was found guilty and received a life sentence, but Don Leggio was acquitted—perhaps because he was already serving a life sentence. The jury's verdicts imposed a collective 2,665 years in prison and $10 million in fines.

The verdicts came as a surprise to many Italians. For the first time, the Italian legal establishment had inflicted a serious defeat upon the Mafia. The mob itself was less surprised than furious, convinced that there had been some secret betrayals (in addition to the 14 *pentiti*). One defendant who had been acquitted was murdered by Mafiosi two hours after he left the courtroom on December 17, 1987.

Aftermath

The victory of the prosecutors turned out to be short-lived. Apparently coincidentally, several rules of the Italian legal system had been changed during the 1980s. A key new provision was that a defendant, and even a convict, could walk free if his case or his appeal was not heard in a speedy fashion. As a result, by January 1, 1989, only 60 of the 338 men who had been sentenced in 1987 were still in custody. During the following six months (January–July 1989) more than 400 people were murdered by Mafiosi in Sicily. It appeared as if the work and sacrifices of men such as Falcone had gone for naught. There were even rumors that Don Leggio himself might eventually be freed.

Although the results of the trial proved disappointing in the long run, the usual assumptions of many mainland Italians and Sicilians about the im-pregnability of the Mafia had been transformed. Before to 1986, no Italian court had dared to confront the leaders of the Mafia. The great courage and tenacity shown by the investigators, prosecutors, judges, and some witnesses at least ensured that after 1987 the Mafia no longer appeared invulnerable.

—*Samuel Willard Crompton*

Suggestions for Further Reading

Arlacchi, Pino. *Men of Dishonor.* New York: William Morrow, 1993.

Catanzaro, Raimondo. *Men of Respect: A Social History of the*

Sicilian Mafia. New York: Free Press, 1992.

"Italy's Ever-Growing Monster." *The Economist,* July 27, 1991, 43–44.

Shawcross, Tim, and Martin Young. *Men of Honor: The Confessions of Tommaso Buscetta.* London: Collins, 1987.

Sterling, Claire. *Octopus: The Long Reach of the International Sicilian Mafia.* New York: W. W. Norton, 1990.

Symonds, William, et al. "The Sicilian Mafia Is Still Going Strong." *Business Week,* April 18, 1988, 48–50.

Peter Wright (Spycatcher) Trials: 1986–88

Defendant: Peter Wright **Crimes Charged:** Breach of confidence, violation of Official Secrets Act **Chief Defense Lawyer:** Michael Turnbull (Australia) **Chief Prosecutor:** Theo Simos (Australia) **Judges:** Justice Phillip Powell (Australia); Justice Michael Kirby (Australian appeal); Lord Bridge (House of Lords, London) **Places:** Sydney, Australia; London, England **Dates of Trials:** November 17–December 10, 1986 (Sydney); July 28–30, 1987 (London); July 27–September 24, 1987 (Sydney) appeal; November 1987–December 1987 (London appeal); February 11, 1988–October 12, 1988 (London appeal) **Verdicts:** Injunction to suppress publication denied (first trial); injunction denied (Australian appeal trial); injunction against quoting from *Spycatcher* lifted October 12, 1988 (House of Lords)

SIGNIFICANCE

The trials brought public attention to the claims by Peter Wright that Roger Hollis, director general of British Security Service (MI-5) from 1956 to 1965, had been a possible Soviet agent and that MI-5 had worked in 1974–76 to oust Prime Minister Harold Wilson because the agency suspected he was a possible Soviet agent of influence. The effort of the British government to suppress publication of a memoir by Wright detailing these charges, *Spycatcher,* resulted in the book's becoming an international best-seller and in discrediting the British effort at censorship.

In September 1980, Chapman Pincher, a British journalist specializing in espionage matters, was called to the home of Lord Victor Rothschild to meet with Peter Wright. Wright, a former official of the British Security Service (MI-5) living in retirement in Australia on a very low pension, suggested to Pincher that they collaborate on a memoir regarding Wright's service. Pincher entered into an agreement in which he interviewed Wright and then, without revealing Wright as a source, published a lengthy exposé of the Security Service, *Their Trade Is Treachery.* Under the agreement, Wright would get half of the book's royalties, after Pincher's expenses.

Pincher did not directly accuse former MI-5 director general Roger Hollis of being the "fifth man" in the ring of Soviet moles that included Kim Philby, Guy Burgess, Donald Maclean, and Anthony Blunt. Pincher did reveal that suspicion had fallen on Hollis and that he had never been fully cleared. If the charges were true, it would mean that the British Security Service had been thoroughly penetrated at the top by the Soviet Union at the height of the Cold War.

Wright had joined MI-5 as the organization's first scientific officer in 1955, specializing in electronic surveillance and countermeasures. He had worked with the U.S. Central Intelligence Agency (CIA), where he was in contact with James J. Angleton, head of CIA counterintelligence. Wright was briefly an assistant director of MI-5 before his retirement in 1976.

In addition to revealing to Pincher MI-5 suspicions about Roger Hollis, Wright indicated that former prime minister Harold Wilson had been the subject of an extensive plot by MI-5 to remove him from power because he was suspected of being a Soviet agent of influence, a view with which Angleton concurred. Wright also revealed in the interviews with Pincher that MI-5 had worked to secure the resignation of several Wilson cabinet members and had bugged a number of conferences and meetings in the effort from 1974 to 1976.

In 1980, Pincher and his publisher, Sidgwick and Jackson, sought the opinion of a well-connected intermediary as to whether *Their Trade Is Treachery* should be published. They did not publicly name the intermediary but referred to him as "the arbiter." The arbiter submitted the manuscript for review to several individuals in both MI-5 and MI-6, the Secret Intelligence Service, which specializes in foreign intelligence. Officials at both agencies at the time decided not to interfere with the publication of, nor seek deletions from, Pincher's book. Pincher believed that the readers in the review process were unaware of how the book manuscript had been routed to them. He later argued that they had hesitated to suppress or censor it because they were under the impression that to do so would blow the cover of a confidential source.

In response to Pincher's book and newspaper serializations of it, Prime Minister Margaret Thatcher admitted in Parliament that Hollis had been investigated but implied that he had been cleared.

British Seek to Block Publication

Five years later, Peter Wright worked with another author, Paul Greengrass, to bring out *Spycatcher: The Candid Autobiography of a Senior Intelligence Officer* (1987), which alluded to the Hollis investigation and the Wilson plot, among other matters. Had Wright been living in Britain, he could have been prosecuted under the Official Secrets Act for having revealed classified information, and the book would have been suppressed. However, violations of the Official Secrets Act are not extraditable offenses in Australia.

The British government sought to suppress the publication of the book in Australia on the grounds that Wright's release of the information represented a breach of confidence. The case was filed in March 1986, going to trial in November 1986. Appeals through 1987 resulted in delayed release of the book in Australia, although Viking Press in the United States brought out an edition in mid-1987.

The appeals by the British government to the New South Wales Appeals Court in Australia and to the House of Lords in Britain to suppress the book and publication of extracts from it failed for several reasons. In the first place, the prior publication of most of Wright's material in Pincher's *Their Trade Is Treachery*, with the implicit consent of the security agencies, suggested that the government was in no position to claim that Wright was violating confidentiality. Second, the book had been published in the United States, and copies and newspaper extracts that were in circulation in Britain and overseas suggested that the government's attempt to suppress the work was futile. Furthermore, several newspapers in Britain that were engaged in publishing extracts or information from Wright's book presented the issue as censorship and an attempt to deny freedom of the press. They claimed that the government sought only to suppress evidence of scandal, rather than to protect national security, a charge that carried considerable weight with British and international public opinion.

In the first trial in Australia, *HM Attorney General v. Heinemann (Australia) and Another* [Peter Wright], Justice Phillip Powell ruled that the British government had "abandoned any claim to confidentiality in respect to" any information contained in Pincher's book and had "acquiesced" in its publication; for these reasons, it could not claim that confidentiality was breached by Wright's later proposed publication with Heinemann in Australia. However, Justice Powell dismissed a claim by Wright's defense attorney, Michael Turnbull, that there had been a conspiracy by MI-5 to publish Pincher's work as a measure of damage control. Powell further offered the opinion that it was to the benefit of Australia that Wright's book be published because it revealed information about Roger Hollis, who had been instrumental in setting up Australia's Security Intelligence Organization.

In writing about the trials in *The Spycatcher Affair* (published in Britain as *A Web of Deception*), Chapman Pincher pointed out that Sir Robert Armstrong, who appeared in the Australian court as the primary witness for the British government, suffered several disadvantages. He was unfamiliar with Australian court practices and had not been fully briefed on the case. Furthermore, he had never been informed of the fact that Pincher's *Their Trade Is Treachery* had been reviewed in MI-5 and MI-6; nor did he realize that those agencies' internal rules of secrecy had prevented a widespread realization that they could have passed back through Pincher's arbiter a request to suppress the book, which would have easily prevented its publication. Pincher argued that it was such practices of confidentiality and secrecy that prevented the British government from presenting its best case before the Australian court. Pincher also pointed out that Armstrong could have emphasized the difference between the credibility of Wright's book, the memoir of a former MI-5 agent, and Pincher's own work, a journalist's report on materials from unnamed sources.

Courts Rebuff All Government Appeals

The British government filed for appeal of the Powell decision in March 1987 in the appeals court of New South Wales. While the appeal was pending, the Viking Press edition of *Spycatcher* was published in the United States, in July 1987. At the same time as the Australian appeal was pending, a high court convened by the British House of Lords took up the British case, July 28–30, 1987. Lords Bridge, Ackner, Brandon, Templeman, and Oliver ruled three to two to continue the ban on publication of the work in Britain, pending a trial involving two newspapers, the *Guardian* and the *Observer*. In February 1988, judges in that newspaper case ruled against the government. After final appeals to the House of Lords, the ban on newspaper coverage of *Spycatcher* revelations was lifted on October 12, 1988.

The New South Wales appeals court, presided over by Justices Sir Laurence Street, Michael Kirby, and Michael McHugh, met in late July 1987. The court did not issue an opinion until September 1987. Kirby, sitting as president of the court, ruled that although the British government sought to bring the case under the principle that publication would represent a breach of confidentiality, the British, in effect, had attempted to use the civil courts of Australia to enforce the British Official Secrets Act, thus using the subterfuge of a civil case to attempt to enforce British penal law in Australia. McHugh concurred, but Street dissented. The case was then appealed to the high court in Canberra (the Australian equivalent of the U.S. Supreme Court), but the Australian ban on publication of the book was lifted in the interim by Judge Sir William Deane on the grounds that continued suppression was unrealistic because so much of the book had already been released. The book was published in Australia by Heinemann in October 1987.

Peter Wright's defense attorney, Michael Turnbull, accused Sir Robert Armstrong of having been sent to Australia to lie for the British government, a charge rejected by Justice Powell. However, Armstrong admitted in court that his position called for him to be "economical with the truth," a remark that earned him considerable public ridicule in the Australian media.

Aftermath

Publicity surrounding the trials and appeals resulted in *Spycatcher* sales of 750,000 to one million copies. Wright, although solving his financial problems, received widespread criticism as a mercenary who had sold his government's secrets. Follow-up works by Pincher, Turnbull, and journalist David Leigh gave further details on the intricate set of revelations, generally concluding that Wright was not always accurate in his memory and tended to sensationalize his own role. However, both Pincher and Leigh reported that the central information regarding the investigations of Roger Hollis and the plot against Harold Wilson had been confirmed by other sources.

Taken together, the revelations in books by Pincher, Wright, and Leigh caused considerable embarrassment to both Conservative and Labour Party politicians in Britain and left the public uneasy about both parties, largely because the books left the fundamental questions unanswered. If the charges against either Hollis or Wilson had any merit, then the Labour Party's leaders were apparently Soviet dupes; if the charges were unfounded, then the Conservatives had revealed their contempt for British democracy by using MI-5 to investigate left-of-center politicians and attempt to drive them from office. In the absence of proof one way or the other, British voters were left only with gnawing uncertainties. One thing was indisputably proved by the "spycatcher affair": Censoring former agents' memoirs, even when such publication violates British law, becomes both pointless and difficult when the publication begins abroad.

—Rodney Carlisle

Suggestions for Further Reading

Leigh, David. *The Wilson Plot.* New York: Pantheon, 1988.

Pincher, Chapman. *The Spycatcher Affair.* New York: St. Martin's Press, 1988.

Wright, Peter. *Spycatcher: The Candid Autobiography of a Senior Intelligence Officer.* New York: Viking, 1987.

Jean-Bédel Bokassa Trial: 1986–87

Defendant: Jean-Bédel Bokassa   **Crimes Charged:** Murder, cannibalism, embezzlement of state funds, illegal use of property, assault and battery
Chief Defense Lawyers: François Gibault, Francis Szpiner
Chief Prosecutor: Gabriel-Faustin M'Boudou   **Judge:** Presiding Judge Edouard Franck   **Place:** Bangui, Central African Republic
Dates of Trial: December 15, 1986–June 12, 1987   **Verdict:** Guilty
Sentence: Death, commuted to life imprisonment

SIGNIFICANCE

The prosecution of Jean-Bédel Bokassa for crimes committed during his notorious reign was the first fair trial by jury of a head of state in the history of postcolonial Africa.

In the two centuries since the French Revolution, many dictators have been brought to justice for mistreating their subjects. In 1986, however, Jean-Bédel Bokassa became the first despot to be prosecuted for eating them.

Army Chief of Staff Bokassa became president of the former French colony known as the Central African Republic in 1966 by deposing his cousin, David Dacko. Later, on December 4, 1976, Bokassa imitated his hero Napoléon Bonaparte by declaring himself Emperor Bokassa I and inaugurated his rule a year later with a lavish coronation that cost $25 million, a withering sum in such a poor country.

The notoriety of Bokassa's coronation was eclipsed by his greed and sadism. He drove the small nation into virtual bankruptcy by helping himself to gems from the Central African Republic's rich diamond mines. Not content to execute known political rivals, he put to death hundreds of imagined enemies. Foreign journalists were beaten and jailed for angering him.

Such treatment was better than the fate reserved for Bokassa's subjects. He celebrated Mother's Day 1971 by hanging all prisoners accused of crimes against women. Crocodiles and lions caged on the palace grounds were rumored to feed on anyone unlucky enough to displease Bokassa. It was whispered that the emperor himself sometimes feasted on the bodies of those he condemned.

Neither the Central African Republic's neighbors nor its former French rulers confronted Bokassa with reports of his butchery, which had been flowing from the country for years. In April 1979, however, Bokassa personally participated in the slaughter of more than 100 schoolchildren. This was too much even for the French government, which had been reluctant to interfere with Bokassa for fear of jeopardizing its access to the Central African Republic's diamond mines. On September 20, 1979, while Bokassa was visiting Libya, French paratroopers landed in Bangui, the capital of the Central African Republic, and restored David Dacko to power.

Bokassa fled into exile, first to Abidjan, the capital of the Ivory Coast, then to Paris, where the French passport he had earned while serving in General Charles de Gaulle's forces during World War II allowed him entry, despite the protests of those who saw him as a criminal. The former despot and his family settled into a seven-year exile that proved embarrassing to those who had supported his rule. Complaining that his French military pension was insufficient, Bokassa wrote his memoirs to supplement his income. But French courts ordered all 8,000 copies of the book destroyed by his publisher because of Bokassa's claim that he had shared women with President Valéry Giscard d'Estaing, who had been a frequent guest in the Central African Republic. Bokassa also claimed to have given Giscard a gift of a quarter of a million dollars' worth of diamonds in 1973 while the French president was serving as finance minister. Giscard's next presidential reelection campaign failed in the wake of the scandal.

Jean-Bédel Bokassa in 1979 during a trip to Paris. In 1987, Bokassa was found guilty of murder and other crimes and sentenced to life imprisonment. (Hulton-Deutsch Collection)

The Emperor Returns to Face Trial

On October 23, 1986, Bokassa flew back to the Central African Republic. Incredibly, he expected his former subjects to welcome his return. Instead, he was arrested as soon as he stepped off the plane. He was indicted on 14 charges, including murder, embezzlement of state funds, and anthropophagy, or procuring human flesh for cannibalism. Bokassa had been convicted and condemned to death in absentia in 1980 on these same charges. Now that he was unexpectedly in the hands of the Central African Republic government, the government was required by law to try him in person, granting him the benefit of defense counsel.

Prosecutors considered trying Bokassa in public in Bangui's sports stadium, the site of his garish coronation almost a decade earlier. Danger of chaos eliminated the idea. "We want an orderly trial with discipline and calm, not a spectacle," explained Justice Minister Bernard Belloum.

The trial began in the humid chambers of the Palais de Justice on December 15, 1986. Bokassa and his two French lawyers, François Gibault and Francis Szpiner, faced a panel composed of six jurors and three judges, presided over by Judge Edouard Franck. A fair jury trial of a head of state was unprecedented in the history of postcolonial Africa, where previously dictators had been executed after show trials or forced into exile. New, too, was public access to the trial, particularly through live broadcasts by Radio Bangui. People all over the country listened to witnesses testify to the brutality they had endured in Bokassa's prisons and about family members they had lost at the hands of his soldiers.

Remembered victims ranged from Bokassa's political enemies to the newborn son of a palace guard commander who had been executed for attempting to kill the emperor. A hospital nurse testified that the officer's pregnant widow told her that Bokassa promised to kill the baby if it was a boy. Bokassa was accused of having the newly delivered child killed with an injection of poison.

Bokassa also faced murder charges for the two incidents that led to his overthrow. In January 1979, he had issued a decree that all students should wear costly uniforms purchased from a factory owned by one of his wives. When a group of schoolchildren rallied in protest, Bokassa had his soldiers fire on the demonstrators, killing several youngsters. When some elementary school students threw rocks at his passing Rolls Royce three months later, Bokassa ordered 180 children arrested and thrown into sweltering cells. That night the emperor went to the prison. Screaming at the youngsters for their insolence, the wrathful Bokassa smashed the skulls of half a dozen children with his ebony walking stick before ordering his soldiers to club the rest to death. Only 27 of the 180 children survived the massacre.

Bokassa denied all the charges against him. He blamed wayward members of his cabinet and army for any misdeeds that might have occurred during his reign. "I'm not a saint," he told the court. "I'm just a man like everybody else."

As the testimony against him mounted, however, he betrayed some of his legendary temper. "The aggravating thing about all this is that it's all Bokassa, Bokassa, Bokassa," he raged at chief prosecutor Gabriel-Faustin M'Boudou. "I have enough crimes leveled against me without you blaming me for all the murders of the last 21 years!"

Cannibalism Described in Lurid Testimony

Cannibalism may have been the most lurid allegation against Bokassa, but the charge was technically superfluous. Statutes forbidding cannibalism in the Central African Republic classified any crime related to the eating of human flesh as a misdemeanor. Upon seizing office from David Dacko in 1981, President André Kolingba had declared an amnesty for all misdemeanors committed during the tenure of his predecessors. Bokassa could not be punished for the crime, even if he was found guilty. The charges against him, however, were drawn from old indictments that resulted in his 1980 conviction in absentia—a year before Kolingba's amnesty—so the anthropophagy charge remained listed among Bokassa's alleged crimes.

Former president Dacko testified that he had seen photographs of butchered bodies hanging in the dank cold-storage rooms at Bokassa's palace immediately after the 1979 coup. Bokassa's chef also testified that he had cooked human flesh stored in the walk-in freezers and served it to Bokassa. The court did not examine rumors that Bokassa had served the flesh of his victims to President Giscard and other visiting dignitaries.

Government prosecutors had hired Bernard Jouanneau, a French lawyer, to recover some of the millions of francs Bokassa had diverted from the national treasury for his own use. Late in the trial, Bokassa's lawyers persuaded the court to bar Jouanneau from taking part in the proceedings. In light of the other heinous crimes Bokassa was charged with, the embezzlement indictment seemed almost insignificant, particularly since Bokassa had clearly already spent most of the money he had stolen.

On June 12, 1987, Bokassa was found guilty. The court acknowledged that many individual allegations of murder had been leveled at Bokassa but found that the evidence was unimpeachable in only about 20 cases. Regardless of the number, the result was the same. Bokassa wept silently as he was sentenced to death. Szpiner and Gibault appealed for a retrial on grounds that the Central African Republic's constitution allowed a former head of state to be charged only with treason. The supreme court rejected the appeal.

On February 29, 1988, President Kolingba demonstrated his opposition to capital punishment by voiding the death penalty in the Central African Republic. Bokassa, who seldom, if ever, had shared such an enlightened concept of mercy during his own rule, was ordered to spend the rest of his life in solitary confinement.

—Tom Smith

Suggestions for Further Reading:

Harmon, Jeff B. "His Former Majesty, Bokassa." *Harper's* (May 1980): 34–39.

Shoumatoff, Robert. *African Madness*. New York: Alfred A. Knopf, 1988.

"Trying the 'Butcher of Bangui.'" *Newsweek* (December 29, 1986): 27.

John Demjanjuk Trial: 1987–88

Defendant: John Demjanjuk   **Crime Charged:** Genocide
Chief Defense Lawyers: Mark O'Connor, Yoram Sheftel, Paul Chumak, John
Gill   **Chief Prosecutors:** Michael Shaked, Yonah Blatman, Dennis Goldman,
Michael Horowitz   **Judges:** Dov Levin, Dalia Dorner, Zvi Tal
Place: Jerusalem, Israel   **Dates of Trial:** February 16, 1987–April 18, 1988
Verdict: Guilty; overturned on appeal   **Sentence:** Death

SIGNIFICANCE

Israel's first televised trial was intended to allay doubts that the nation had "gone
soft" on Nazi war crimes. Instead, it became a debacle when new evidence
emerged that convinced the nation's highest court that the wrong man had been
convicted.

In 1981, a 61-year-old Ukrainian autoworker living in Cleveland, Ohio, was
stripped of his U.S. citizenship when a court found that he had deceived
immigration authorities three decades earlier by concealing his wartime activities. After numerous delays, John Demjanjuk lost his battle against extradition,
and on February 27, 1986, he was escorted onto an El Al 747 jet bound for Tel
Aviv. The choice of destination was significant, for Demjanjuk was en route to
yet another trial, this time to face charges that he was "Ivan the Terrible," a
guard at the Nazi death camp of Treblinka in Poland. The evidence adduced at
his American hearing seemed to leave little doubt that Demjanjuk was the sadist
who, between 1942 and 1943, had personally consigned thousands of Jews to the
Treblinka gas chambers. Several former camp inmates had identified him as
their tormentor, and there was the evidence of a photocopied ID card pur-
portedly issued to one Ivan Demjanjuk at Travniki, a German training camp for
SS guards in Poland. This card had mysteriously surfaced in the Soviet Union
before finding its way to the West. Demjanjuk's unwavering and thin-sounding
defense was that he was a victim of mistaken identity.

Although the original extradition warrant had specified "murder," when
Demjanjuk finally stood trial in a converted Jerusalem theater on February 16,
1987, the charge sheet read "genocide." Such a distinction was critical:
Genocide was punishable by death, whereas murder attracted only life imprisonment; furthermore, there was no extradition treaty between the United States
and Israel for the crime of genocide, clear evidence, according to defense

counsel Yoram Sheftel, that Israel had no jurisdiction in this matter. After brief consideration, the three-member panel appointed to decide this trial—there was no jury—declared that Israel was acting within its rights, and opening arguments began.

Many of the Treblinka survivors who had testified at Demjanjuk's American hearing did so again here; among them was Eliahu Rosenberg, who had cleared dead bodies from the gas chambers. A moment of high drama came when prosecutor Michael Shaked asked Rosenberg to "look at the defendant, if you can; scrutinize him."

Rosenberg responded, "I request that the honorable court order him to take off his glasses."

"His glasses? Why?" intervened Judge Levin.

"I want to see his eyes. May I get a little closer?"

Pandemonium

Over defense protests, Demjanjuk removed his spectacles, and Rosenberg approached to within three feet of the defendant. Suddenly Demjanjuk extended a welcoming hand, which Rosenberg knocked away angrily, crying out, "You murderer! How dare you offer me your hand," then, seconds later, "Beyond a shadow of a doubt, it's Ivan from the Treblinka gas chambers! The man I'm now looking at. I saw the eyes. Those murderous eyes!" Amid pandemonium, Rosenberg resumed his place in the witness-box.

Later, the impact of this identification was compromised when it became known that, in a 1947 statement to an early investigator of the Holocaust, Rosenberg had described seeing Ivan the Terrible being beaten to death during a revolt of Treblinka inmates on August 2, 1943. Under cross-examination from chief defense counsel Mark O'Connor, Rosenberg now claimed that this statement, made in Yiddish, had been mistranslated. What he had meant to imply was that he saw Ivan being dealt some "murderous blows," not that he had actually seen him killed. For the defense, it was a small but significant victory: The first seeds of doubt had been sown.

Further success came with evidence about the manner in which certain Holocaust survivors had identified Demjanjuk from various photographs. Maria Radivker, an investigator of war atrocities, conceded that the eight-man photo spread shown to various Treblinka survivors had been prejudicial to the defendant in that his was the only photograph depicting a bald man, yet she seemed oddly unrepentant about such suggestiveness, saying, "I am not responsible for Demjanjuk's baldness."

Helmut Leonard was supposed to be one of the state's star witnesses: During 1942–44 he had been an SS clerk at Travniki, when the ID card allegedly issued to Demjanjuk was printed. Now, he stunned prosecutors by stating that had Demjanjuk been stationed at Treblinka, this would have been reflected by an assignment number on the card. He further said, "A guard caught at Treblinka with document T/149 [the ID card] would have been arrested, because Treblinka was outside the area permitted him according to what is written on document T/149." Such words confirmed defense claims that the Travniki document, even if not a forgery, could not have belonged to Ivan the Terrible.

Yet another witness who disappointed the prosecution was Otto Horn, an SS sergeant from Treblinka Camp 2. He said that "the photograph only resembles Ivan, and that's what I said before. . . . It could be him." It was hardly the positive identification that the prosecution had expected.

Then it was time for the defense. A chorus of catcalls and hisses rose from the packed courtroom as Demjanjuk gave evidence in his own behalf. Unlike the American judicial system, the Israeli judicial system has no automatic right to silence; a defendant may choose not to testify, but this can be adversely commented upon and often is. Speaking in Ukrainian, Demjanjuk repeated his story that during 1942–43 he had been in two prisoner of war camps, mostly at a camp near Chelm, Poland. But Demjanjuk was a bad witness. His faulty memory—even on points that did not incriminate him—and the halting manner of his replies soon gave rise to the suspicion that he was dissembling, being deliberately evasive.

Worse was to come. Edna Robertson had been brought from the United States to testify as a questioned-documents expert and, from experiments on the Travniki ID card with a video spectrum scanner (VSS), had concluded that two different types of ink had been used in its manufacture, convincing her that it was a forgery. Yet when the prosecution brought a VSS into court and subjected other documents, of impeccable provenance, to the same test, all displayed exactly the same "discrepancy" that Robertson had found so suspicious. Robertson's mistake dealt a dreadful blow to the defense.

A recovery of sorts was staged by Dr. Julius Grant, the London-based questioned-documents examiner who, in 1983, had exposed the notorious "Hitler diaries" as fakes. Comparison of the Demjanjuk signature on the ID card with that of the defendant convinced Grant that the Travniki document could not be an authentic document belonging to Demjanjuk.

Perhaps the most telling defense contribution came from Professor Willem Wagenaar, an internationally recognized psychologist, who described the power of suggestibility in photo-spread layouts and how memory can distort events, especially after an interval of many decades. Avoiding any attempt to blame those who had identified the defendant as Ivan the Terrible, Wagenaar explained how a series of wholly understandable circumstances had conspired to make it "almost certain that every survivor who pointed to one of the pictures would point to Demjanjuk's picture."

Sentenced to Hang

But it was not enough to convince the court. On April 18, 1988, Judge Dov Levin delivered the verdict of the bench: "We determine unequivocally and without the slightest hesitation or doubt that the accused ... is Ivan [the Terrible]." One week later, Demjanjuk was sentenced to be hanged.

Of all the counsel who defended Demjanjuk, none reacted with greater bitterness than Sheftel. A proud Jewish nationalist, he had endured vitriolic abuse at the hands of his countrymen unprepared to accept his defense of a perceived Nazi murderer. Not even having acid thrown in his face could deflect Sheftel from a profoundly held belief that Demjanjuk was not Ivan the Terrible, merely the pawn in a politically motivated show trial. It was a conviction that many in the Israeli legal community were beginning to share.

On May 15, 1990, a lengthy appeal process began, with recently discovered documents strongly suggesting that Ivan the Terrible was not Demjanjuk but another Ukrainian, someone strikingly similar, Ivan Marchenko, who, as early as 1976, had been identified by a Treblinka survivor.

By February 1992, corroborative evidence for this view was multiplying almost exponentially. From Soviet Union archives came 80 statements made by former Treblinka guards—most made in the early 1950s—all naming Marchenko as Ivan the Terrible. In particular, there was a confession from Nikolai Shelaiev, captured by the Soviets and convicted of war crimes. Before his 1952 execution, Shelaiev, who had personally operated the gas chambers at Treblinka, confirmed that he and Marchenko had acted in tandem. Easily the most disturbing aspect of all, though, was a revelation by George Parker, former attorney at the Office of Special Investigation (OSI), a division of the U.S. Department of Justice, who claimed that, as early as 1979, OSI officials knew that the Treblinka gas chambers had been manned by Marchenko and Shelaiev and yet said nothing.

In an attempt to salvage something from the wreckage, Shaked argued that even if Demjanjuk were not Ivan the Terrible, he must have been a guard at some other concentration camp. This shabby maneuver was ill received by the Supreme Court judges, who pointed out to the deflated prosecutors that the U.S. extradition warrant had specifically referred to the camp at Treblinka and nowhere else. When the court heard a deposition from Katarina Kovalenko, the daughter of Marchenko, confirming that in the early 1950s KGB agents had ransacked the family home and removed every photograph of her father, it added to suspicions that the notorious ID card had been a Soviet forgery.

After a year's deliberation, on July 29, 1993, the Supreme Court quashed Demjanjuk's conviction, accepting that he was not Ivan the Terrible. Two months later, he was deported from Israel and returned to the United States to fight the revocation of his citizenship.

Perhaps the best word on this tragic and tortuous trial is left to Israeli Judge Haim Cohen, who wrote later, "It was a spectacle for the people. Any resemblance to justice was purely coincidental."

—*Colin Evans*

Suggestions for Further Reading

Loftus, Elizabeth, and Katherine Ketcham. *Witness for the Defense.* New York: St. Martin's Press, 1991.

Sheftel, Yoram. *The Demjanjuk Affair.* London: Gollancz, 1994.

Teicholz, Tom. *The Trial of Ivan the Terrible.* New York: St. Martin's Press, 1990.

Wagenaar, Willem A. *Identifying Ivan.* Cambridge, Mass.: Harvard University Press, 1988.

Klaus Barbie Trial: 1987

Defendant: Klaus Barbie **Crimes Charged:** War crimes, crimes against humanity **Chief Defense Lawyer:** Jacques Vergès
Chief Prosecutor: Pierre Truche **Judge:** André Cerdini **Place:** Lyons, France **Dates of Trial:** May 11–July 4, 1987 **Verdict:** Guilty
Sentence: Life in prison

SIGNIFICANCE

The trial and conviction of the German SS functionary Klaus Barbie reaffirmed and further refined the principle that there can be no statute of limitations, literal or moral, on crimes against humanity.

Klaus Barbie, a one-time functionary of the German SS, torturer of French resistants, and deporter of Lyons Jews to the Auschwitz death camps, struck most observers as a decrepit old man, with ordinary features and a vacant, even befogged expression on his worn face. "Criminals rarely achieve the dimensions of their crimes," the journalist Jane Kramer wrote, "and Barbie was no exception." One French periodical dissented slightly: Klaus Barbie showed to the world "the emaciated face of a predatory bird," its correspondent thought.

One of his French interrogators asked Barbie what Nazism had meant to him.

"Camaraderie," he replied.

"The Butcher of Lyons"

Barbie served as the head of a section of SS police in Lyons, France, in 1943 and 1944, a minor official in what one of the French prosecutors at the Nuremberg war crimes trials had defined as a "criminal public service." In that job, Barbie tracked down, arrested, and tortured members of the French Resistance to the German occupation. The best known of the Resistance martyrs, Jean Moulin, died at Barbie's hands in Montluc Prison in 1944. Barbie also rounded up 44 Jewish children from their orphan asylum in the village of Izieu near Lyons and sent them on a journey to oblivion. In August 1944, he arranged for the deportation to Auschwitz of 630 Jews and resistants.

Barbie achieved local notoriety as "the Butcher of Lyons." Even so, at war's end, with the assistance of U.S. Army Intelligence, Barbie made good his escape. The Americans evidently prized him for his knowledge of French Communists who were prominent in the Resistance. There is no evidence, however, that the United States knew about his role in the deportation of French Jews—or, for that matter, any evidence that they had looked into any aspect of his past with care. In any case, the Americans helped Barbie leave Genoa, Italy, for South America in 1951. The French tried, convicted, and sentenced him to death in absentia in proceedings in 1952 and 1954.

The former SS torturer established a new life in Bolivia as the German emigrant Klaus Altmann. He hardly bothered to cover his past, and the Nazi hunters Serge and Beate Klarsfeld eventually tracked him down in La Paz, the Bolivian capital, in 1974. In negotiations with Barbie's hosts, the French bought his extradition. The price: $50 million and 3,000 tons of wheat. He was taken to Lyons in 1983. Four years and 23,000 pages of testimony later, Barbie went to trial on charges of war crimes (acts against the resistants) and crimes against humanity (the deportation of Jews).

Nazi SS commander, Klaus Barbie, alias Klaus Altmann, was convicted of war crimes in Lyon, France in 1987. (Hulton-Deutsch Collection)

Double Charges Blur Issues

The double charge created something of a problem. By the 1980s, the statute of limitations for carrying out the death sentence handed down in absentia had expired. Since those first trials, too, capital punishment had been abolished in France. The minister of justice at the time of abolition was Robert Badinter, a Jew whose father had been murdered at Auschwitz. Klaus Barbie had sent him there in 1943. The charge of crimes against humanity had been encoded in French law in a 1960s statute, derived from the Nuremberg trial, that also made possible Barbie's prosecution for crimes against the Resistance.

The problem lay in a blurring of the meaning of Barbie's acts. It is counted a war crime to torture or kill enemy soldiers after they have been taken captive. It is a crime against humanity to arrest, deport, and murder civilian men, women, and children—in this case Jewish men, women, and children—as part of a state policy of extermination. There is a difference, critics of the proceeding argued, between dying for what one did and dying for what one happens to be.

Barbie's Victims Recount His Crime

The trial became something of a media event, partly a consequence of the sensational antics of Barbie's attorney, Jacques Vergès. "The next thing you know," Vergès remarked after a glance at the thick sheaf of the indictment, "they'll say he stole the Eiffel Tower." The son of a French colonial officer who had been forced from the service for marrying a Vietnamese, Vergès hated colonialism. He achieved a certain notoriety in the 1950s and 1960s with his aggressive and unapologetic defense of members of the Algerian independence movement. Vergès argued that the French had no right to try Barbie because they themselves had committed crimes in Algeria and other former colonies and, stretching the analogy taut, because Israel had committed crimes against Palestinians. The prosecutor, Pierre Truche, dubbed this a *défense de dérivation*—the argument that, in an evil world, Barbie's crimes graded no worse than many others.

Media critics claimed that journalists—some 400 were accredited to the trial—showed more interest in Vergès' outrageous defense strategies than in the testimony of survivors of Barbie's torture sessions and of the Auschwitz deportations. Possibly the reporters were bored. To be sure, there was no question, ever, of Barbie's guilt, though he did issue a sort of blanket denial of the worst of the charges:

"I never committed the roundup in Izieu," he said. (His henchmen had.) "I never had the power to decide on deportations." (He had carried them out, though.) "I fought the Resistance, which I respect, with toughness, but that was war and the war is over."

The proceedings opened at a few minutes past 1 o'clock on May 11, 1987, in the Palace of Justice in Lyons. Barbie, 73 years old and unrepentant, signaled at the outset that he did not intend to cooperate; he insisted on his La Paz alias, Altmann. "I can understand why the name of Barbie must be heavy to bear," the presiding judge, André Cerdini, told him. On May 13, Barbie announced he would no longer attend the sessions, claiming he had been extradited illegally. He appeared in court only three more times, twice so victims could identify him, and at the last for the summations, verdict, and sentencing. His absence, of course, deprived his victims of their chance to confront him.

Cerdini questioned one woman about her arrest.

"It was the difference between seeing an accident and being in an accident," she answered.

A man who identified Barbie during one of his brief, forced appearances in court burst out:

"Look at him. He told me, 'You will be N and N [*nacht und nebel*, meaning "night and fog": liquidated]' with the same expression he has now!"

Testifying on June 3, Alice Vansteenberghe reconstructed the day Barbie tortured her and left her a cripple for life, then recounted an incident a few weeks later: August 11, 1944, the day that 331 Jews and 298 others were deported to Germany—the non-Jewish men and women to different concentration camps, the Jews to the Auschwitz death camp.

> That morning I had left my home in the full euphoria of my living body; I never regained that feeling; I have never been able to walk again. We in the Resistance knew the risks we were taking, and I accept everything that I suffered. But in the cell where I was thrown there were other people. I saw a Jewish woman and her child, well-groomed, very blond, with a barrette in her hair. Well, one day Barbie walked in to take this mother from her child. This is not warfare—it's something unspeakable, beyond all bounds.

The train, dodging Allied bombs and detouring around torn-up track and blown bridges, reached Auschwitz after a nightmare trip of 11 days. Twenty-three deportees died en route. On September 7, 1944, 128 out of the surviving 308 Jews were gassed. The others went into the work camp, many of them to endure a long, lingering death.

On July 3, 1987, at 5:38 in the afternoon, the jury of nine women and three men began deliberations. In accord with French legal practice, the three-judge tribunal sat in on the discussions and voted with the jurors. The group reached a verdict a little after midnight on July 4: guilty. Cerdini sentenced Barbie to life in prison.

The French seemed let down by the affair, though perhaps relieved as well: The myth of unbending heroism of the French Resistance remained more or less intact, for Vergès had supplied absolutely no evidence to support his pretrial claim that the Resistance cells were riddled with traitors and that Jean Moulin had died not from the effects of torture but from his own hand, out of despair when he learned his comrades had betrayed him to the SS.

Piece by unsavory piece, the sorry record of the Vichy government's complicity in the destruction of French Jews had come to light in the years before the Barbie trial. Many Frenchmen perhaps hoped the prosecution would clear the record somehow, provide catharsis and a cure. Those who were disappointed in the outcome tended to blame the media for trivializing the issues. Jane Kramer, summing it up for *The New Yorker*, viewed the matter another way:

"The French expected Justice in Lyons. They got justice instead."

—Michael Golay

Suggestions for Further Reading

Finkielkraut, Alain. *Remembering in Vain: The Klaus Barbie Trial and Crimes Against Humanity.* Translated by Roxanne Lapidus. New York: Columbia University Press, 1992.

Kramer, Jane. "Letter from Europe." *The New Yorker* (October 12, 1987): 130–144.

Morgan, Ted. *An Uncertain Hour: The French, the Germans, the Jews, the Klaus Barbie Trial and the City of Lyons, 1940–1945.* New York: William Morrow, 1990.

Beirut Hijacking Trial: 1988–89

Defendant: Mohammed Ali Hamadei **Crimes Charged:** Murder, air piracy, assault, illegal possession of explosives **Chief Defense Lawyer:** Gabriele Steck-Bromme **Chief Prosecutor:** Reiner Hamm **Judge:** Heiner Mückenberger **Place:** Frankfurt, West Germany **Dates of Trial:** July 5, 1988–May 17, 1989 **Verdict:** Guilty **Sentence:** Life imprisonment

SIGNIFICANCE
Although West Germany would not extradite Mohammed Ali Hamadei to the United States to be prosecuted for air piracy and murder, he was tried and convicted of identical charges under the "universal law" principle applicable to serious international crimes.

On the morning of Friday, June 14, 1985, TWA Flight 847 was ascending from Athens airport on its way to Rome when two screaming hijackers bolted for the cockpit with pistols and a live grenade. The commandeered airliner flew to Beirut, where the hijackers read a statement demanding the release of more than 700 Lebanese and Palestinian detainees being held in an Israeli prison.

As soon as the plane was refueled, it took off for Algiers, where the hijackers threatened to kill all the passengers unless their demand was met. Algerian authorities, however, made it clear that the terrorists were no more welcome in Algiers than they had been in Lebanon. After five tense hours, the jet returned to Beirut, where it was allowed to land only after the pilot reported that he was about to run out of fuel.

Some hostages were released during each of the airliner's first stops. Back in Beirut, however, the hijackers decided to increase the pressure by killing an American. Having collected passports from all the passengers, the hijackers selected Robert Dean Stethem, a U.S. Navy diver. Stethem was beaten unconscious before he was shot to death and thrown out of the jet onto the airport tarmac.

Within hours, the jet was headed back to Algeria. The hijackers managed to free a comrade being held in Athens by threatening to kill all the Greek passengers. On Sunday afternoon, however, the plane landed in Beirut a third time. The two hijackers, who were suspected members of the radical Hezbollah, or "Party of God," began negotiating through the Lebanese Amal militia. Amal leader Nabih Berri supervised the transfer of the remaining passengers to secret hiding places in Beirut's war-ravaged suburbs. After 17 days of uncertain negotiations against a backdrop of arriving U.S. warships and Amal demands for an American guarantee against military retaliation, the remaining 39 hostages were driven to Damascus, Syria, and released.

The two men who had commandeered Flight 847 disappeared into the labyrinthine rubble of suburban Beirut, but they were not forgotten in the United States. In November 1985, a grand jury indicted four Lebanese radicals in the case, accusing them of air piracy, assault, and Stethem's murder. If the suspects were captured, the standing 15-count indictment would allow the United States to apply for their extradition immediately.

U.S. Seeks Extradition

On January 13, 1987, a young Lebanese named Mohammed Ali Hamadei was arrested in West Germany while trying to smuggle bottles of liquid explosives through Frankfurt International Airport. A check of his fingerprints revealed that Hamadei was one of the accused TWA Flight 847 hijackers. While Hamadei was being held on a charge of illegally possessing explosives, the U.S. Justice Department declared its desire to extradite Hamadei to the United States. The United States and West Germany immediately encountered the first of several obstacles that would test relations between the two normally friendly governments.

Murder and air piracy were capital crimes under U.S. law. If Hamadei was tried in an American court and convicted, he could face the death penalty. West German law, however, forbade extradition of any defendant to a country where he might face capital punishment. The West German Justice Ministry asked for a written guarantee that Hamadei would not face the death penalty if extradition resulted in his case coming before an American court. Expressing some reluctance, the U.S. government agreed.

At the same time this agreement was being worked out, two West German businessmen were kidnapped in Beirut by Hamadei sympathizers. West German authorities arrested Abbas Ali Hamadei, Mohammed's older brother, charging him with participating in the kidnapping, blackmail, and possessing explosives. Despite the arrest, West German fears for the hostages' safety clouded the issue of Mohammed Hamadei's extradition.

After months of deliberation and fruitless attempts to free its citizens, West German authorities denied the extradition request. Critics charged the Bonn government with surrendering to terrorist blackmail. Rumors circulated that the West Germans might exchange the Hamadeis for the hostages.

The West German government admitted that the safety of its citizens had influenced its decision not to hand Mohammed Hamadei over to the Americans but promised that he would be prosecuted on charges identical to those held against him in the United States. Although Hamadei's alleged crimes had not occurred in West Germany and had not involved West German nationals, West

Germany would try him by the "universal law" principle, under which serious crimes like murder, drug trafficking, and genocide were internationally prosecutable offenses. On July 6, 1987, charges of murder and air piracy were added to Hamadei's indictment for illegally carrying explosives.

First Hamadei Brother Tried and Convicted

On January 5, 1988, Abbas Ali Hamadei went on trial for participating in the kidnapping of the two businessmen whose abduction had influenced the West German government's refusal to extradite his younger brother to the United States. Mohammed Hamadei was summoned as a witness but refused to testify despite the entreaties of his brother's attorney. Although he admitted leading police to explosives, Abbas Ali Hamadei denied any part in the kidnapping and called on radicals in Lebanon to release all remaining hostages. He was nevertheless found guilty and was sentenced to 13 years in prison.

The case against Mohammed Hamadei quickly hit its second major snag. West German authorities concluded that Hamadei had turned 21 years old the day before the hijacking. Although this made him liable for prosecution as an adult, the court decided that, if guilty, Hamadei would have planned the crime before his 21st birthday. Under West German law, the case of a defendant between the ages of 19 and 21 could be referred to either criminal or juvenile court.

Sentences resulting from this preliminary decision could be substantially different. The maximum penalty for juvenile defendants was 10 years' imprisonment; adult defendants stood to spend the rest of their lives in prison. One of the few things Mohammed Hamadei volunteered at his brother's trial was a claim that he was only 16 at the time of the hijacking, not 21.

Younger Brother Tried in $6.7 Million Courtroom

On May 17, it was decided that Hamadei would be tried in juvenile court as an adolescent. Although the court's decision rejected both the defense claim that he was a juvenile and the state's insistence that he be tried as an adult, a guilty verdict would mean that Hamadei could be sentenced under either guideline at the court's discretion. The question of what fate awaited Hamadei if he was convicted would remain in limbo until the end of the trial.

To avoid any risk of terrorist attack, a $6.7 million high-security courtroom was built in Preungesheim Prison, where Hamadei was being held. When his trial began on June 5, Hamadei sat in an enclosure built with two thick panes of bulletproof glass.

For the first two days of the trial, he adamantly refused to answer the court's questions about his age. After a barrage of objections and demands, he fell completely silent. On the third day of the trial, Hamadei began responding to questions. He admitted having carried explosives into the country and hiding them but denied knowing their purpose. He also denied being a member of

Hezbollah, a radical group dedicated to the ideals of Iranian leader Ayatollah Ruholla Khomeini. When the judge asked Hamadei about his political and religious beliefs, he answered, "Religion is politics and politics is religion."

Hamadei stated that he was not sure that hijackings and acts of war were justified, but prosecution witnesses wore away some of his credibility. A co-worker recalled Abbas Hamadei's inebriated boasts that his younger brother had taken part in the TWA hijacking. One of Mohammed Hamadei's fellow employees and his prison cellmate testified that he had proudly told them he was a member of Hezbollah.

On August 9, just over two months into the trial, Hamadei stunned the court by confessing to the second of the three major charges against him. He read a written statement in which he admitted having taken part in the hijacking to free political detainees being held in Israel. He continued to deny that he had killed Stethem. "I pleaded before the hijacking that no blood would be spilled," Hamadei told the court. "I thank God that I've never killed anyone face to face."

As the trial focused on the remaining charge of murder, passengers and crew members of Flight 847 were called to testify about the identity of the man who killed Stethem. Pilot John Testrake admitted confusion over which of the two hijackers was the triggerman but said he felt that Hamadei was the killer. The plane's purser testified that the shooting had taken place behind a drawn curtain but said that both hijackers had beaten Stethem bloody before hauling his senseless body to the door.

Despite Hamadei's claims of reluctance, numerous former hostages remembered the two hijackers as equal partners in beating and robbing the passengers. Yet none could say that they had seen Hamadei pull the trigger and fire the shot that ended Stethem's life.

Guilty Verdict Leads to Life Sentence

It was never conclusively determined whether the killer was Hamadei or the other hijacker, Hassan Izz al Din, who remained at large. On May 17, 1989, the five judges who had weighed the evidence nevertheless found Hamadei guilty as an accomplice in the murder and assaults on passengers. Guilty verdicts were also returned on the air piracy charges and two counts of explosives possession, to which Hamadei had admitted his guilt in court. He was sentenced to life in prison, the maximum penalty.

Speculation lingered that the West German government had proceeded with the trial to mollify the United States before trading Hamadei for the two West Germans held hostage in Lebanon. When Hamadei remained in the West German prison, the suspicion faded. By that time, international airports were operating under stringent new flight security agreements, prompted by the ordeal of Flight 847's passengers.

—Tom Smith

Suggestions for Further Reading

Carson, Kurt. *One American Must Die.* New York: Congdon & Weed, 1986.

Celmer, Marc A. *Terrorism, U.S. Strategy, and Reagan Policies.* Westport, Conn: Greenwood Press, 1987.

Schemann, Serge. "Germans Send Hijacking Suspect to Juvenile Court." *The New York Times*, April 13, 1988.

———. "Sobs in Court over Horror of Hijacking." *The New York Times*, October 13, 1988.

Carl Gustav Christer Pettersson Trial: 1989

Defendant: Carl Gustav Christer Pettersson   **Crime Charged:** Assassination of head of state   **Chief Defense Lawyer:** Arne Liljeros
Chief Prosecutors: Anders Helin, Jorgen Almbladh   **Judges:** Carl-Anton Spak, presiding; Mikael af Geljerstam   **Place:** Stockholm, Sweden
Dates of Trial: June 5–July 10, 1989   **Verdict:** Guilty
Sentence: Life imprisonment

SIGNIFICANCE

A strong conflict can be seen between Sweden's self-image as a country of reason, peace, and decency and the unsolved assassination of the nation's prime minister. The mishandled investigation and trial raised tough questions about its government's competence.

In Stockholm at 11:20 on Friday evening, April 30, 1986, Olof Palme, the 59-year-old prime minister of Sweden, and his wife, Lisbet, strolled along Tunnelgatan Street from a movie theater after seeing the film *The Brothers Mozart*. As they turned the corner onto Sveagaven, a major thoroughfare, Palme dropped to the snow-covered pavement, felled by bullets in his chest and abdomen. Lisbet, immediately bending over him, felt a bullet graze her back. The assassin fled. Taken to Sabbatsberg Hospital, Palme died at 12:06 A.M., May 1.

A popular leader in a country famed for its love of peace, Palme was often seen on Stockholm streets conversing with his constituents. He had dismissed his bodyguards at 11 that morning because he had no official appointments for the rest of the day. The last political assassination in Sweden had been the slaying of King Gustav III during a masked ball in 1792.

Europe's Youngest Premier

Often described as "an aristocrat turned Socialist," Palme had been educated in Sweden's finest private schools, had entered military service as a draftee and risen to cavalry lieutenant, and had then won a scholarship to Kenyon

College in Ohio, where he earned straight A's. He had earned his law degree in 1951 at the University of Stockholm and then followed with activity in the Social Democratic Party and election to Parliament. By 1969, at age 42, he had been elected premier—the youngest in Europe. Fluent in English, French, German, and Spanish, he also spoke some Russian as well as the Scandinavian tongues. Palme became a central figure not only in Swedish politics but on the broader world scene as well. Admirers considered him a man with a "world conscience." He had worked tirelessly, it was noted, for international disarmament and had served as a United Nations mediator in the Iran-Iraq conflict.

Olof Palme, in October 1979, soon after the Swedish Social Democratic party declared solidarity with victims of oppression in Spain. Palme helps by collecting funds for victims and advocating a free and democratic Spain. (Hulton-Deutsch Collection)

The Stockholm police were sharply criticized for the lack of security around the prime minister and for poor performance immediately after the shooting. Roadblocks had not been set up. All officers on duty had not been alerted to the hunt for the assailant. At the crime scene, two days after the shooting, passersby had found what the police had sought in vain: the two copper-dipped .357 magnum bullets that had pierced Palme's body. Stockholm Police Commissioner Hans Holmer said they were bullets of a type not previously seen in Sweden, fired from a powerful Colt or Smith and Wesson revolver. Two days later, he admitted that the bullets could be bought in Stockholm.

A $70,000 Reward

On March 4, the Stockholm police announced a reward—the first ever in a Swedish crime case—of 500,000 Swedish kroners ($70,000) for information leading to an arrest. Theorists offered two conjectures: The shooting might have been the work of the German Red Army Faction known as the Baader-Meinhof gang, who in 1975 had seized the West German embassy in Stockholm in an attempt to free 26 comrades from West German prisons, or it might be attributed to the Kurdish Workers Party, which had recently threatened Palme.

An $8.2 Million Reward

Nearly two years passed. In December 1987, the Swedish National Police Board offered 50 million Swedish kroners (roughly $8.2 million) for information leading to the solution of the crime. Police Chief Holmer resigned, insisting that Kurdish militants had committed the murder. Meanwhile, several suspects had been arrested and released.

Another year went by. On December 14, 1988, press reports disclosed that an unemployed laborer, Carl Gustav Christer Pettersson, 41, had been arrested. Pettersson, an alcoholic and a drug abuser, had previously been convicted of several criminal acts, including a 1970 murder with a bayonet for which he had served three years under psychiatric care. Over the previous two years, police had interrogated him several times, but a neighbor in his apartment building had upheld his alibi that he was at home at the time of the Palme killing. Then the neighbor recanted.

The police had little forensic evidence. They had no murder weapon. They could postulate no motive. Shown a videotaped lineup, Palme's widow picked out Pettersson—a disheveled figure in prison-issued shoes standing amidst 11 clean-cut policemen in civilian clothing—but could say only that she "believed" him to be the man she had seen running from the shooting. Under Swedish law, her testimony had to be considered informal because, having been grazed by a bullet, she herself was considered a victim and thus ineligible to give sworn testimony. But the court would be allowed to hear unsworn testimony, review written statements, and even consider hearsay.

The Trial Opens

The trial opened on June 5, 1989, before judges Carl-Anton Spak and Mikael af Geljerstam and six lay assessors—political appointees who sat as jury members in trials. Observers in the wood-paneled courtroom in downtown Stockholm almost immediately began to see a nation they had not earlier acknowledged: one plagued, despite its reputation for quiet and peace and welfare benefits, with its share of violence, alcohol and drug abuse, and a criminal underclass not unlike that of other nations. Pettersson, on the witness stand on the opening day, said that over the last decade he had spent most of his time "boozing on benches in streets and public squares, and at home, of course."

On the night of the assassination, he testified, he was in one of Stockholm's illegal gambling clubs buying amphetamines and caught an 11:15 train from downtown Stockholm to his housing complex.

Prosecution witness Ulf Spinners accused the police of manipulating him. They had reported to the prosecutors that Spinners had told them he saw Pettersson come home at about 1 A.M. on the night of the murder. That would have given the defendant plenty of time to slay the prime minister and get home. But on the witness stand, Spinners said, "I can't remember the minutes. But I think it was around midnight, but it could have been 9 or 10 minutes after."

The police had said that prosecution witness Harri Miekkalina, who had served time with Pettersson, had told them that the defendant had spoken of his hatred of Swedish society and of the prime minister. But on the witness stand, Miekkalina accused the police of misquoting him. Pettersson, he said, "is neither a left- or a right-wing extremist. And I have never heard him express hatred against Olof Palme."

Testimony without Defendant or Public Present

Even more frustrating to the prosecution was the behavior of Mrs. Palme, who insisted on special treatment. The court acceded to her demands that her testimony be heard without the defendant present and that no tape recordings, broadcasts, or sketches of her court appearances be permitted. But in a letter delivered to the court on June 13, she asked to testify behind closed doors, with the public and the news media kept out. When the court denied her request, she refused to come to the courtroom.

Six days later, the court relented and heard her in the absence of the defendant, the news media, and the public. She said she was sure that Pettersson was the man she had seen standing nearby immediately after her husband was shot. Following her testimony, Pettersson was brought into the courtroom. The premier's widow then made a face-to-face identification.

Toward the close of the trial, prosecutor Anders Helin asked the defendant to take the stand again. He refused. "When, back in December, I laid my hands on your shoulders and said I was innocent," he said, "you replied, 'I hope so.' I see no evidence of your hope and I no longer believe in it. It is therefore meaningless to answer your questions."

The Verdict

The verdict, 17 days after the trial ended, was guilty. "Testimony collectively corroborates Lisbet Palme's identification of Christer Pettersson," said the six lay assessors in a majority opinion, "to such a degree that the District Court finds that he fired both shots beyond any reasonable shadow of doubt."

But the two judges dissented, finding that "the high level of uncertainty presented during the trial makes it impossible to reach a guilty verdict." They noted also that Mrs. Palme had not picked the defendant out of the videotaped lineup until two years after the crime.

Defense attorney Arne Liljeros took the case to the Svea High Court, a regional appeals court that included four professional judges and three lay assessors. There, he produced a surprise witness, a police superintendent, Gosta Soderstrom, who testified that Mrs. Palme, when interviewed minutes after the shooting, "was completely hysterical" and "could not give me any description of the killer."

The court overturned the conviction. Pettersson was freed immediately. Interviewed on television at his home, he said that he would like to meet Mrs. Palme and talk. "She has no reason to be scared," he said.

The case remains unsolved.

— *Bernard Ryan, Jr.*

Suggestions for Further Reading

Hadjor, Kofi Buenor, ed. *New Perspectives in North-South Dialogue: Essays in Honour of Olof Palme.* London: I. B. Tauris, 1988.

"The Swedish Version of 'Who Killed JFK?'" *Newsweek*, 114:32, August 7, 1989.

Nicolae and Elena Ceausescu Trial: 1989

Defendants: Nicolae and Elena Ceausescu   **Crimes Charged:** Genocide, subversion of the state by ordering the massacre of unarmed civilians, destruction of communal property, subversion of the economy, attempting to escape from the country with money in foreign banks
Chief Defense Lawyer: Nicu Theodorescu   **Chief Prosecutor:** Georgica Popa   **Judge:** Georgica Popa   **Place:** Tirgovişte, Romania
Date of Trial: December 25, 1989   **Verdict:** Guilty   **Sentence:** Execution and confiscation of private property

SIGNIFICANCE
Although the demise of Communism in 1989 was relatively peaceful in other countries, it brought two weeks of virtual civil war to Romania, which saw Europe's fiercest street fighting since World War II. The climax came when the country's president and his wife were seized, subjected to a brief, impulsive trial, and immediately executed.

Nicolae Ceausescu was born to a large peasant family in 1918. He joined the Communist Party when he was 15 years old. Before World War II, he was jailed as a political agitator. As Romania was absorbed into the Communist structure behind postwar eastern Europe's "iron curtain," he rapidly gained power. By 1952, he was a full member of the Central Committee. Five years later, he was second only to the Romanian party leader. In 1965, he became the party's first secretary, and three years later, the president and head of state.

A Cult of Personality

Building a cult of personality similar to that of Soviet dictator Joseph Stalin, Ceausescu created a complex web of secret police, informers, personal attendants (including doctors, bodyguards, chefs, and housemaids), party workers, and military officers that both protected and empowered him. He opposed the Kremlin (Russia's seat of government), however, on a number of issues, thus gaining the approval of many in the Western world.

By the 1980s, Romanians were disillusioned. The economy was faltering, but their president continued to rule as a tyrant, naming his relatives to key government and party positions. His wife, Elena, long a politburo member, became first deputy premier. Over eight years, from 1981 to 1989, in an intensive program to reduce Romania's foreign debt, Ceausescu exported food and fuel in wholesale quantities and shifted money away from the maintenance of the nation's superstructure. He paid off some $8.5 billion, but at the cost of the nation's economic development.

In addition, Romania's president implemented his "systemization" program. It forced the country's peasants to evacuate their villages in a planned procedure expected to introduce giant agri-industrial complexes. They never materialized.

Dissidents and Border Barbed Wire

Early in 1989, Ceausescu could read a number of signs that his regime was in trouble. An open letter from several of Romania's retired senior officials accused him of breaching international human rights agreements—in particular, the 1975 Helsinki Final Act—disregarding his people's constitutional rights, mismanaging the country's economy, and alienating its allies. The United Nations Commission on Human Rights, in a resolution cosponsored by Hungary and Western countries, voted to investigate Romania—the first time a Soviet-bloc country had proposed investigating an ally. The British Foreign Office presented Bucharest with a demand for information on 23 dissidents Romania was holding incommunicado. When Spain asked Bucharest for information on 24 dissidents, the European Community froze trade negotiations with Romania. In protest over Romania's poor human rights practices, West Germany recalled its ambassador to Bucharest and canceled a session of the West German–Romanian Joint Economic Commission.

In June 1989, Romania erected a barbed-wire fence along its 180-mile border with Hungary, apparently to prevent Romanians from fleeing across the border. At a Paris meeting of the Conference on Cooperation and Security in Europe, the chief British delegate, Sir Anthony Williams, strongly attacked the fence-building as well as Bucharest's mistreatment of dissidents and its rural-resettlement program. By month's end, Romania was dismantling the fence.

Dissatisfaction boiled into open revolt in December. A month earlier, an ethnic Hungarian who was a popular Protestant minister, the Rev. Laszlo Tokes, had been stabbed by the secret police and, to avoid deportation, took refuge in his church. A crowd of demonstrators protected him from arrest. Dissatisfaction and seething unrest grew on December 16 into large pro-democracy rallies in Timisoara, a city of 350,000 some 300 miles from Bucharest. Ceausescu sent army and Securitate—the president's secret police—tanks and helicopters to quash the demonstrations. An estimated several hundred unarmed men, women, and children were slain on December 17. Some 500 were arrested. Looting was widespread. But the antigovernment demonstrations spread to other cities.

Death in Palace Square

December 20 brought a march of 50,000 people in Timisoara. The next day, from a balcony of the Royal Palace in Bucharest, Ceausescu addressed a government-staged rally of thousands, including many students. When he promised more food and fuel, jeering began. The Securitate moved in. One of its armored cars crushed two youths. The troops opened fire. Forty or more people were killed. The crowd was pushed from Palace Square to nearby University Square.

President Nicolae Ceausescu giving a speech at a crowded civic rally in Sfintu Gheorghe, Romania, shortly before the fall of his regime. (Hulton-Deutsch Collection)

On the night of December 21, 30,000 people fought with the Securitate, whose strength was estimated at 30,000. By morning, the protesters numbered 150,000. They pushed the Securitate back into Palace Square. Army units, which had long resented the Securitate's favored treatment by Ceausescu, shared their automatic weapons with the civilians and fired on the secret police. By day's end, the state TV station, Radio Bucharest, the Communist Party Central Committee Building, and the Royal Palace were all held by the insurgents, and the palace was aflame.

That night a coalition of students, military officers, former Communist officials, and dissidents organized the National Salvation Front as an interim ruling committee. The morning of December 22 revealed that insurgents in Timisoara had found several hundred bodies—those of men, women, and children, mostly naked, many bound by barbed wire and obviously tortured—in shallow mass graves where the Securitate had dumped them.

Mid-morning December 22 brought a Securitate helicopter to the roof of the Central Committee Building. The president and his wife, their bodyguards, and several officials took off toward Tirgovişte, 45 miles away. But, with Ceausescu afraid of being shot down, they landed, commandeered a car, and were captured near Tirgovişte.

55 Minutes in a Schoolroom-Courtroom

For three days, the rebels, dodging the Securitate, drove the Ceausescus around in an army armored car. Then, on December 25, in a tiny schoolroom in Tirgovişte's army barracks, the new National Salvation Front convened an "extraordinary military tribunal." Present were National Salvation Front leader Gelu Voican and General Victor Stanculescu of the Romanian army, who together had organized the trial, and several "observers"—all of whom had flown from Bucharest by helicopter.

Defense lawyer Nicu Theodorescu had already been appointed by Romania's bar association. He urged Ceausescu to plead insanity. "I do not recognize you," said Ceausescu. "I do not recognize this court. I can only be tried before the Great National Assembly and before the representatives of the working class." He did, however, agree to a brief medical examination. It revealed his blood pressure stood at 170/107.

As a major general and head of the military tribunal, Georgica Popa functioned as the judge, but he also served as prosecutor. He wore a crewneck sweater and jeans. He failed to pronounce several unfamiliar words in the brief handed him. He wasted no time, however, for he and the other National Salvation Front leaders, knowing that the Securitate would not quit trying to rescue the president, were anxious to complete the trial and—the foregone conclusion—the execution.

The prosecutor read the charges: Genocide at Timisoara and the massacre of demonstrators led the list. "I will say nothing," said Ceausescu. "I recognize only the Great National Assembly. I refuse to answer those who have fomented this coup d'etat. I am the president of Romania and the commander in chief of the Romanian army. I am the president of the people. I will not speak with you provocateurs anymore, and I will not speak with the organizers of the putsch."

The judge-prosecutor informed Ceausescu that the Great National Assembly had been dissolved. "No one has the right to dissolve it," replied Ceausescu. "That's what the people are fighting for."

On the charge that the president had subverted the economy, Ceausescu did respond: "Speaking as an ordinary citizen I can tell you that for the first time in their lives the workers had 200 kilos of flour a year and many additional benefits. Never in Romania's history has there been such progress."

"What about your $400 million in foreign bank accounts?" demanded the prosecutor.

"Show me proof," said Ceausescu. "It's all lies. There's not a single dollar."

Fifty-five minutes passed. Judge-prosecutor Popa declared a recess for "deliberations" by the trial's organizers and observers. Five minutes later they returned. Popa read the verdict: "On the basis of the actions of the members of the Ceausescu family, we condemn the two of you to death. We confiscate all your property." He asked the couple if they wanted to appeal. Neither Ceausescu replied. Four soldiers stepped forward. They bound the Ceausescus' wrists behind their backs, then led them outdoors and placed them facing the building's wall. As the couple turned from the wall, the soldiers opened fire, hitting each with as many as 30 rounds.

The next day, portions of a videotape of the execution were shown on Romanian television. Ceausescu's body was seen lying in a pool of blood in a courtyard. The full videotape was shown some months later. What became of the two bodies was not disclosed.

By December 30, the nation was controlled by the rebel forces. They revealed that key government and Communist Party buildings were linked to the Royal Palace by a network of tunnels. In the palace, they found rare works of art, including porcelain sculptures and silk tapestries. Solid gold dinnerware, a bathtub with pure gold faucets, a bomb shelter lined with lead, a swimming pool, and tennis courts testified to the lifestyle of the late president and his wife.

In giant warehouses, they found stocks of beef, chocolate, coffee, and oranges intended for export and for the private use of high party and government officials.

On December 28, in the Romanian trade mission in Vienna, Austria, Marin Ceausescu, a brother of Nicolae who had run the mission for 16 years, hanged himself.

On March 2, 1990, Major General Popa committed suicide. In a note, he said he had lived in terror since December 25. "I could not find," he wrote, "any other solution to free myself from the fear and dread that make the rest of my life unbearable."

—Bernard Ryan, Jr.

Suggestions for Further Reading

Bachman, Ronald D., ed., Eugene K. Keefe, coauthor. *Romania: A Country Study*. Washington, D.C.: Library of Congress, Federal Research Division, 1991.

Behr, Edward. *Kiss the Hand You Cannot Bite*. New York: Villard, 1991.

Codrescu, Andrei. *The Hole in the Flag*. New York: William Morrow, 1991.

Fischer, Mary Ellen. *Nicolae Ceausescu: A Study in Political Leadership*. Boulder, Colo.: Lynn Rienner, 1989.

South African Police Death Squads Libel Trial: 1990–91

Plaintiff: Lothar Neethling **Defendants:** *Vrye Weekblad* editor Max Du Preez et al; The *Weekly Mail* **Plaintiff's Claim:** Libel **Judge:** Johan C. Kriegler **Place:** Johannesburg, South Africa **Dates of Trial:** November 1990–January 18, 1991 **Verdict:** Not liable for damages

SIGNIFICANCE

The largest libel suit in South African history forced official recognition of the existence of covert police assassination squads.

In the tense decade before South Africa's white ruling National Party officially abandoned its policy of apartheid, or racial separation, police units waged a secret war against apartheid's foes. Accusing the South African police of covert political murder or sabotage during the 1980s, however, invariably produced prickly denials from government officials.

Former Police Captain Reveals Death Squads

In September 1989, retired security police captain Dirk Coetzee met privately with Jacques Pauw, a reporter for the small Afrikaans-language weekly *Vrye Weekblad*. Coetzee agreed to tell the newspaper everything he knew about police death squads if the paper could assure his safe flight from South Africa. *Vrye Weekblad* secretly contacted the still illegal African National Congress (ANC), which considered giving its former enemy Coetzee safe haven in exchange for information that might profoundly embarrass South Africa's security forces.

On October 19, 1989, a condemned murderer named Butana Almond Nofamela told his lawyer that he had belonged to a secret police "hit squad" and claimed to have participated in eight political murders. Nofamela's attorney quickly obtained a stay of execution so that his client's allegations could be investigated. When the commander of Nofamela's hit squad, Dirk Coetzee, learned that his former subordinate had confessed in a sworn affidavit, Coetzee panicked.

Coetzee feared that his commanders might sacrifice him to contain any damage from Nofamela's claims. He was also afraid of future prosecution if black rule came to South Africa. Coetzee assumed that his life was in danger from both his former friends and his enemies. But Nofamela's affidavit convinced the ANC of Coetzee's credibility. He was slipped to safety in Mauritius, where he began to tell his story to Pauw in the presence of ANC officials.

In 1980, Coetzee claimed, he had been transferred from the South African police's Security Branch to a small farm outside of Pretoria. There, he was ordered to train Section C1, a group of Mozambican guerrillas and captured ANC fighters who had defected to the government. For the next nine years, Coetzee and his secret unit shot, stabbed, bombed, kidnapped, and drugged apartheid opponents, both in South Africa and abroad.

Some killings were disguised as other crimes to avoid attracting attention. Coetzee recalled paying four men to stab human rights lawyer Griffiths Mxenge to death in 1981, instructing them to make the murder look like a robbery. Coetzee admitted his personal complicity in six murders and 23 other serious crimes.

"I decided to confess to cleanse my conscience," Coetzee told the newspaper.

In November and December 1989, *Vrye Weekblad* and *The Weekly Mail* printed Coetzee's story. As if Coetzee's own violent experiences were not sensational enough, the former Security Branch officer claimed that Section C1 was only one of five clandestine death squads working at home and internationally with help from within the South African government.

The uproar over Coetzee's allegations was immediate. Typically, some government officials dismissed the stories as lies spread by the ANC. "They must get the police and the security forces out of the way to make it easier to bring about their aim of creating a Communist state," said Law and Order Minister Adriaan Vlok. South Africans demanding an open investigation were not heartened when President F. W. de Klerk asked minister Vlok to investigate Coetzee's story. In February 1990, Coetzee named Vlok as one of several top officials who were aware of the death squads' existence.

Police Lab Chief Sues for Libel

Among Coetzee's allegations was a claim that Lieutenant General Lothar Neethling, head of the South African police forensic laboratories, had supplied him with poison tablets. The drugs were to be used to murder ANC members.

While government officials fumed over the Coetzee affair, General Neethling struck back directly. He sued the two newspapers that had printed the allegations about him. Neethling sought 1 million rand ($600,000) in damages from *Vrye Weekblad* for defamation of character, and sought another half-million rand from *The Weekly Mail* for carrying the story. If Neethling's claim was upheld, the small *Vrye Weekblad* would be bankrupt. A judgment against the press would also repudiate Coetzee's claims against police, making it easier for government officials to deny any involvement in state-sponsored terrorism.

Momentous changes occurred in South Africa while Neethling awaited his day in court. On February 2, 1990, President F. W. de Klerk removed the ban against liberation organizations like the ANC. Yet after years of resentment, the National Party's opponents were not convinced that its leader intended to move the country toward nonracial democracy. Critics watched closely as de Klerk appointed Justice Louis Harms to head a commission to investigate the Coetzee affair and other charges of state complicity in political crimes.

Justice Harms inspected clearly altered documents and interviewed officials who claimed that requested records could not be found. Undercover policemen wearing elaborate disguises testified that their memory was imperfect regarding alleged misdeeds. Critics noted that Harms was ordered by de Klerk to investigate crimes that had occurred only within South Africa although security forces were accused of carrying out lethal covert operations against antiapartheid activists abroad.

On November 13, 1990, after months of testimony and a trip to London to interview Coetzee, Justice Harms concluded that a South African Defense Force secret unit called the Civilian Cooperation Bureau was implicated in several murders. However, Harms officially announced that he was unconvinced of the existence of the secret police units described by Coetzee, whom the judge described as delusional.

Ironically, the Harms Commission report was released as General Neethling was testifying in Johannesburg's supreme court that he had been libeled. *Vrye Weekblad* and *The Weekly Mail* stood accused, but Dirk Coetzee's veracity was the real issue in the case. Coetzee did not return to South Africa for the trial. He was examined in London, where he had joined the ANC.

Coetzee claimed to have visited Neethling several times to obtain poison and knockout drops to use on ANC prisoners. In one instance, the poison Neethling allegedly provided to kill a secretly held ANC fighter and a C1 guard who had outlived his usefulness failed to work. Coetzee ultimately had both men shot. In another case, drugs provided by Neethling stunned a captured guerrilla suspect prior to his execution.

Coetzee vividly described meeting the general at his laboratory office and at his home. Neethling denied ever having met Coetzee. Defense lawyers, however, were able to produce Coetzee's personal notebook, which contained Neethling's confidential telephone number. Neethling responded to this evidence by stealing it, testing it in his laboratory, and returning it to court with the claim that it was a forgery.

Neethling's attorneys tried to destroy Coetzee's credibility with police statements that the three allegedly poisoned men were not in custody on the dates Coetzee claimed to have participated in their murders. The defense produced documents that proved otherwise. Neethling's lawyers persisted, echoing the Harms Commission's finding that Coetzee's claims were fantasies. In the unlikely event that Neethling had furnished Coetzee with poison, they argued, it was incredible that such a renowned scientist would have produced a substance that did not work.

Judge Rejects Libel Claims

When Judge Johan Kriegler read his decision on January 18, 1991, observers initially believed that Neethling had won his suit. The judge praised Neethling's intelligence and international scientific reputation. Judge Kriegler characterized Coetzee as a clever liar. Nonetheless, the judge decided that the facts substantiated Coetzee's version of the truth. The supporting detail with which Coetzee described his misdeeds and those of his colleagues convinced the court that his disclosures to the press were not mere fantasies. Contrary to the general's claims, Judge Kriegler noted that the minute detail in which Coetzee described Neethling's office and home were overwhelming proof that the two men had met.

In studying the trial transcript, it had become clear to Kriegler that the general had tried to deceive both him and Justice Harms with false and misleading testimony. Unlike Harms, Kriegler criticized the faulty memories of police officers Neethling had called as character witnesses.

Judge Kriegler accepted Coetzee's story of the death squads as being true and found that the newspapers had not acted unlawfully. In fact, the decision found that *Vrye Weekblad* and *The Weekly Mail* had acted in the public interest by exposing abuses of government power. Neethling was ordered to pay legal expenses for *Vrye Weekblad* and *The Weekly Mail*, which rivaled the exorbitant amounts he had sought in damages. Neethling was not the only loser. The decision severely damaged the morale and public image of the South African police. The Harms Commission was discredited. White South Africans who had accepted their government's denials for years were now faced with official recognition that the claims about counterinsurgency death squads were true.

Although General Neethling was not dismissed from his job, his first appeal of the ruling against him was rejected by South Africa's supreme court. On December 4, 1993, however, the appellate division overturned Judge Kriegler's decision, ruling that the press had no legitimate right to publish the allegations against Neethling. The case was returned to the supreme court for consideration of possible damages. Further appeals are prolonging the case indefinitely, amid a political furor over allegations that Neethling is pursuing the case with the help of state funds and legal assistance.

—*Tom Smith*

Suggestions for Further Reading

Ottaway, David. "South African Judge Backs Claims on Death Squads." *Washington Post* (January 21, 1991) p. 18A.

Pauw, Jacques. *In the Heart of the Whore.* Halfway House: Southern Book Publishers, 1991.

Sparks, Allister. *Tomorrow Is Another Country*. New York: Hill & Wang, 1995.

Wren, Christopher. "South African Judge Throws Out Police Suit Against 2 Papers." *The New York Times* (January 19, 1991): 5.

Tiananmen Square Dissidents Trial: 1991

Defendants:
Some 87 students, workers, and intellectuals, including Bao Zunxin, Chen Lai, Chen Xiaoping, Chen Yanlin, Chen Ziming, Guo Haifeng, Kong Xianfeng, Li Chenghuan, Li Shuntang, Li Yuqi, Liu Gang, Liu Xiaobo, Liu Xiaojing, Lu Xiaochun, Ma Shaofang, Pang Zhihong, Ren Wanding, Wang Dan, Wang Haidong, Wang Juntao, Wang Youcai, Xue Jianan, Yang Junzhong, Yao Junling, Yu Yongjie, Zhang Ming, Zhang Qianjin, Zhang Yafei, Zheng Xuguang, Zhou Wanshui

Crimes Charged:
Counterrevolutionary propaganda and incitement, subversion against the People's Government, overthrowing the socialist system, organizing attacks against the army, disrupting public order, conspiring to overthrow the government, arson, looting, larceny, and blocking traffic

Chief Defense Lawyers: Kang Jian for Wang Dan, others undisclosed by Chinese government

Chief Prosecutors: Undisclosed **Judges:** Undisclosed **Place:** Beijing, China

Dates of Trials:
January 5, 1991 (Kong Xianfeng, Li Yuqi, Ma Shaofang, Pang Zhihong, Xue Jianan, Wang Youcai, Zhang Ming, Zhang Qianjin, Zheng Xuguang); January 9 (Chen Lai, Guo Haifeng, Li Chenghuan, Yao Junling); January 15 (Bao Zunxin, Li Shuntang, Liu Xiaojing, Lu Xiaochun, Wang Haidong, Yang Junzhong, Yu Yongjie, Zhou Wanshui); January 16 (Liu Xiaobo); January 23 (Wang Dan); February 4 (Chen Yanlin, Zhang Yafei); February 5 (Chen Xiaoping); February 6 (Liu Gang); February 11 (Chen Ziming); February 12 (Wang Juntao)

Verdicts: Guilty

Sentences:
Imprisonment, including time already served. Chen Ziming, Wang Juntao—thirteen years; Ren Wanding—seven years; Liu Gang—six years; Bao Zunxin—five years; Guo Haifeng, Wang Dan, Wang Youcai—four years; Kong Xianfeng, Ma Shaofang, Zhang Ming—three years; Xue Jianan, Yao Junling, Zhang Qianjin, Zheng Xuguang—two years; Chen Xiaoping, Li Yuqi, Liu Xiaobo, Pang Zhihong, 65 others—no imprisonment beyond time already served

SIGNIFICANCE
The trials of dissidents who survived the bloody military crackdown on demonstrators in Beijing's Tiananmen Square prove, once again, the power of a totalitarian state to subdue, if not entirely prevent, pro-democracy activities. At the same time, the trials provide Western democracies, where one is innocent until proved guilty, with chilling insight into a jurisprudence in which guilt is not only assumed but is also found by the judges in 98 percent of cases.

It all began with the death of Hu Yaobang on April 15, 1989. Hu had become a hero to Chinese liberals two years earlier when he had been compelled to resign as general secretary of the Chinese Communist Party for not stemming student unrest. On April 17, some 500 students marched into Beijing's Tiananmen Square to lay wreaths commemorating Hu's life before the Great Hall of the People, headquarters of the government. The next day, the crowd grew to as many as 10,000 students.

The police tried to disperse the crowd. It swelled. On April 19, the square held some 20,000 to 40,000 students, older intellectuals, and workers. By April 21, the date of the Communist Party's memorial service for Hu, the throng numbered 100,000 people—mostly students—in defiance of a government warning not to assemble.

The assemblage had already become a giant rally for democracy, with the demonstrators demanding such political reforms as freedom of the press, speech, and assembly; greater funding for education; public disclosure of the pay and assets of party leaders; and the formal restoration of Hu's reputation.

"A Grave Political Struggle"

To support the continuing rally in the square, university students in Beijing—by the tens of thousands—began boycotting classes on April 24. The government broadcast strong warnings that "this is a grave political struggle facing the whole party and the people." It outlawed three organizing committees developed by students.

The rally continued through May, becoming one of the largest in Chinese history. Beijing came to a near standstill on May 17, when Soviet leader Mikhail S. Gorbachev joined Chinese Premier Li Peng, China's paramount leader Deng Xiaoping, and Chinese Communist Party head Zhao Ziyang for a summit meeting while more than a million students, workers, intellectuals, and schoolchildren in the square demanded democratic reforms and the resignation of Deng and the other leaders.

On May 20, Premier Li declared martial law. To prevent troops from reaching Tiananmen, students and other citizens established roadblocks of trucks, buses, taxis, and cars. Crowds surrounded stalled military vehicles, begging the soldiers to halt. Three thousand students began hunger strikes in the square, where some 200,000 demonstrators were encamped. With no police evident, the students began directing traffic through the city.

The army held back. The students cheered. But on May 25, the state-run media called on the troops to enforce martial law. Reinforcements arrived, until 200,000 troops surrounded the city. On June 1, the authorities banned press coverage of demonstrations and of troops enforcing the law. June 2 found pop singer Hou Dejian leading a rally as he began a hunger strike. And on the night of June 2–3, tanks and armored personnel carriers led some 10,000 unarmed soldiers in a march toward the square. They were blocked several hundred yards from Tiananmen by the jeering mass of demonstrators. The soldiers retreated, many in tears.

Tear Gas and Cattle Prods

By the next afternoon (June 3), before the Great Hall, police and troops were firing tear gas and beating protesters with electric cattle prods, and demonstrators were throwing bricks and rocks at them. Soon after midnight, armed troops moved in on the square, firing machine guns and automatic rifles directly into the crowds. Many demonstrators fought back with firebombs and pipes and even sticks and stones, destroying 180 army vehicles. By dawn on June 4, the government announced that "the rebellion has been suppressed and the soldiers are now in charge." On June 6, it announced that 300 people (military and civilians, including 23 students) had been killed and 7,000 (including 5,000 soldiers) had been injured.

Arrests of "thugs" and "hooligans" suspected of pro-democracy demonstrations began immediately. By June 21, some 1,500 people were being held. Meanwhile, in protest, the World Bank suspended consideration of $780.2 million in loans to China, and the Bush administration in Washington, D.C., suspended all high-level contacts between U.S. and Chinese officials.

On June 30, China raised the civilian death toll to 300, including 36 students. In August, the United Nations Subcommission on Prevention of Discrimination and Protection of Minorities, a division of the UN Human Rights Commission, censured the Chinese government for the Tiananmen Square incident—the first such censure for abuse of human rights by a UN group against a permanent member of the UN Security Council. At the same time, Amnesty International, a human rights organization based in London, accused China of secretly executing dissidents seized during the June demonstrations. It estimated that at least 1,000 civilians had been killed in the Beijing disturbance and that more than 10,000 had since been arrested and jailed.

A year after Tiananmen, Amnesty International reported that both legs of student leader Wang Dan had been broken and that he had been blinded in one eye while under arrest. By December 1990, U.S. Ambassador to China James R. Lilley observed that China's attitude toward discussing human rights had become more favorable because it wanted to protect trade benefits with the United States that were due for renewal in June 1991.

Trials Begin

The first disclosure that any trials had been held came on January 5, 1991. The official New China News Agency reported the sentencing of nine participants in the Tiananmen demonstrations. Details were scarce, but knowledgeable China hands noted that political trials were among the most murky in the Chinese legal system. The system considers court documents confidential, seldom releasing them to the defendant's counsel—if the defendant is permitted to have counsel. Furthermore, no defendant may hire counsel until the charge has been filed with the court, and the trial usually begins within three days of the filing. In the Municipal Intermediate People's Court, three judges, without juries, decide on guilt or innocence as well as sentencing. One study disclosed that 98 percent of all defendants are found guilty, as the system assumes them to be. An unwritten rule is "leniency to those who confess, severity to those who resist," with longer sentences for those who claim innocence. With the guilty verdict expected, any defendant's counsel strives not to prove innocence but to gain a light sentence by proving remorse.

The News Agency announced that family members and teachers or students of defendants attended the trials. Not all, however, were able to learn when trials were held. Perhaps atypical was the trial of Wang Dan, a Beijing University history student who had headed a police list of 21 most-wanted students. The slight, bespectacled 22-year-old read from a prepared text for nearly 20 minutes during his three-hour trial. He did not admit "counterrevolutionary propaganda and incitement," with which he was charged, but protested that, to aid China's development, his objective had been to produce changes within the Communist Party system. His lawyer, Kang Jian, who had been appointed by the government and who traveled to the trial by police car, said she could defend him only on the presumption that he was guilty. As the trial ended, Wang asked one of the judges, "How was my performance?"

"OK," said the judge. "Not bad." Wang was then sentenced to four years' imprisonment.

"What I Said Before Doesn't Count"

Some of the dissidents faced the death penalty. Thirty-year-old Liu Gang, a physics student, spoke for an hour during his three-and-a-half-hour trial, refusing sarcastically to admit to "conspiring to overthrow the government" and claiming that any errors he confessed to during his prison confinement were invalid because he had been interrogated under threat of death. "What I said before doesn't count," he told the court. "What does count is what I say this morning." He received six years' imprisonment.

Nearly 30 trials were reported held in January and February 1991; observers noted that Chinese authorities were pushing the cases through while world attention was focused on the Persian Gulf War.

The longest sentences were announced on February 12. Wang Juntao, 33, and Chen Ziming, 38, were each sentenced to 13 years, as the judges announced that they had committed "very serious crimes but have shown so far no willingness to repent." Both men had played behind-the-scenes roles at Tiananmen and, paradoxically, had been praised by Communist Party heads after a 1976 Tiananmen protest when they had led support for Deng Xiaoping.

In mid-February, announcements of trials and sentencing ceased. Asia Watch, a human rights organization, listed 960 people still imprisoned. Six months later, Beijing announced that Wang Juntao and Chen Ziming, serving their 13-year terms in solitary confinement in cells smaller than five square yards, had begun hunger strikes. Wang Dan, Ren Wanding, and Bao Zunxin, however, had been released from solitary and mingled with other inmates.

On November 29, 1991, Wang Youcai, serving his four-year sentence, was released because he had shown signs of repentance, and charges were dropped against labor leader Han Dongfang, who had organized laborers to join the student demonstrators in Tiananmen Square. He had been held without trial for nearly two years.

On October 11, 1996, China's Communist Party leaders charged Wang Dan with conspiracy to overthrow the government, a capital crime. They accused him of publishing anti-government articles abroad, accepting a University of California scholarship, and raising funds to support dissidents in need. They also revealed that, after serving his four-year sentence, Wang had been detained for 17 months in a secret police center and was still in custody. Experts considered Wang's conviction a certainty and predicted a 10-year sentence.

—Bernard Ryan, Jr.

Suggestions for Further Reading

Feigon, Lee. *China Rising: The Meaning of Tiananmen*. Chicago: Ivan R. Dee, 1990.

Human Rights in China (with John K. Fairbank, Orville Schell, Jonathan Spence, Andrew J. Nathan, Fang Lizhi). *Children of the Dragon*. New York: Collier Books, Macmillan, 1990.

Lord, Bette Bao. *Legacies: A Chinese Mosaic*. New York: Knopf, 1990.

Ming Pao News photographers and reporters. *June Four: A Chronicle of the Chinese Democratic Uprising*. Fayetteville: University of Arkansas Press, 1989.

Salisbury, Harrison E. *Tiananmen Diary: Thirteen Days in June*. Boston: Little, Brown, 1989.

Schelle, Orville. *Mandate of Heaven*. New York: Simon & Schuster, 1994.

Simmie, Scott, and Bob Nixon. *Tiananmen Square*. Seattle: University of Washington Press, 1989.

Terrill, Ross. *China in Our Time*. New York: Simon & Schuster, 1992.

Yi, Mu, and Mark V. Thompson. *Crisis at Tiananmen*. San Francisco: Chinese Books and Periodicals, 1989.

David Milgaard Hearing: 1992

Defendant: David Milgaard   **Purpose of Hearing:** Review of 1970 conviction for murder   **Chief Defense Lawyers:** Hersh Wolch, Q.C.; David Asper   **Chief Prosecutors:** Murray Brown, S. R. Fainstein, Q.C., for the attorney general of Canada; Eric Neufeld for the Province of Saskatchewan   **Judges:** Antonio Lamer, Peter Cory, Frank Iacobucci, Beverley McLachlin, John Sopinka   **Place:** Ottawa, Ontario, Canada   **Dates of Hearing:** January 21–March 14, 1992   **Decision:** Although David Milgaard's original trial had been fair, continued conviction and imprisonment of the defendant would amount to a miscarriage of justice.

SIGNIFICANCE

Twenty-one years after a 17-year-old's conviction for murder, Canada's justice minister asked the Supreme Court of Canada to review the case under a little-used section of the Criminal Code that allowed its reopening and its reference to any court in the country.

The temperature in Saskatoon was 40 below zero early on January 31, 1969, when children on the way to school found the body of 20-year-old nurse's aide Gail Miller in an alley behind the 200 block of Avenue O South. Beneath the body was the blade of a paring knife. Its handle lay nearby. Items from the victim's purse, apparently strewn by her attacker, were found along the route toward a house at 334 Avenue O South.

An autopsy disclosed that 15 slash wounds and 9 stab wounds had killed Gail Miller and that she had been raped.

"Just Running Around"

In a basement suite at 334 Avenue O South, one block from the murder scene, lived Larry Fisher and his family. Upstairs lived Albert "Shorty" Cadrain. At nine o'clock on the morning of January 31, Cadrain welcomed visitors from Regina: 16-year-old David Milgaard, a runaway whose lifestyle, as Milgaard himself later described it, was "basically kind of just running around, traveling, and hitchhiking." With Milgaard were his sometime girlfriend, Nichol (Nicky) John, and Ron Wilson. They were driving, they said, to Edmonton, Alberta, to buy marijuana and visit Milgaard's former girlfriend, a 16-year-old later identified only as Sharon.

Milgaard had told John and Wilson that he knew Cadrain from a previous trip to Saskatoon. With their resources running low, he had hoped Cadrain could help them out.

Cadrain paid for needed repairs to Wilson's car and joined the trio. The foursome drove to Calgary, bought marijuana, then proceeded to Edmonton. In a motel, Milgaard slept with Sharon; John, who had previously been sleeping with Milgaard, slept (as Milgaard later testified) "with Wilson, or maybe with Albert."

On March 3, 1969, the police found Milgaard in Winnipeg and asked him about the Miller murder. He said he had not heard about it. The police did not arrest him.

Milgaard landed a job that took him to Prince George, British Columbia. He was arrested there in April. Taken back to Saskatoon, he was given a court-appointed attorney.

Stuck in Snow Twice

At the trial in January 1970, Nichol John and Ron Wilson testified as prosecution witnesses that, en route to Saskatoon, the trio had broken into a grain elevator, from which Milgaard had stolen a bone-handled hunting knife. Wilson said that on the morning of the Miller murder they had become stuck in the snow while asking a stranger for directions to Cadrain's house, then had stopped at a motel for directions. Driving on, said Wilson, they again got stuck. Milgaard and Wilson then walked off in opposite directions to look for help. Milgaard was gone, Wilson and John said, for 15 minutes.

In a police statement, Nichol John had said that after Milgaard left the car, she saw him go into an alley with a girl and stab her. "The knife," she had said, "was in his right hand." On the witness stand, however, John said she could not recall having seen the murder or making the statement to the police. Crown prosecutor Bobs Caldwell immediately had her declared a hostile witness so he could ask her leading questions. (The prosecution cannot ask its own witness leading questions unless the witness is declared "hostile" by the judge.) She remained adamant, and Justice A. H. Bence warned the jury that her statement to the police "must be completely disregarded." The jury, however, had heard the statement.

Wilson testified that he returned first to the car. When Milgaard returned after about 15 minutes, said Wilson, he was puffing and saying something like, "I fixed the girl." As they drove on, Wilson testified, John was hysterical.

Bloody Clothes

Cadrain testified that Milgaard's clothes were bloody when he arrived at his house and that Milgaard brought in a bag from the car and changed his pants.

Finally, two witnesses testified that sometime in March, while visiting Milgaard in an Alberta motel to buy drugs, they saw a TV news story about the murder. Milgaard, they both said, acted out the slaying by repeatedly stabbing a pillow while saying, "I killed the bitch."

Cadrain, it was revealed, had earned a $2,000 reward by identifying Milgaard. The knife blade originally reported found under Miller's body and the nearby handle were not entered as evidence. The police said they had been lost.

On advice of counsel, Milgaard did not take the stand at his trial. On January 31, 1970, he was convicted and sentenced to life imprisonment. The Saskatchewan Court of Appeal denied his application for leave to appeal, and in November 1971, the Supreme Court of Canada dismissed his appeal.

Supporters Allege Cover-up by RCMP

In September 1970, Larry Fisher, who lived in the basement of Cadrain's house, was caught in the act of raping an 18-year-old student. In custody, he confessed to four rapes in late 1968 and early 1969, three of them near the January 31, 1969, Miller murder scene. He also admitted he had committed a rape near his home just three weeks after the Milgaard conviction, and another in Winnipeg six months later.

The confession launched Milgaard's supporters on allegations of a cover-up. After a two-year investigation, the Royal Canadian Mounted Police (RCMP) dismissed all allegations.

Convicted, Fisher was sentenced to 13 years, served 9, and was paroled early in 1980. Within weeks, he raped and stabbed a woman, saying, "I've spent 10 years for doing this same thing, only I slit her throat." He received a further 10-year sentence.

Wilson Recants

In 1990, Ron Wilson recanted his trial testimony, telling a private investigator that he had lied in his incrimination of Milgaard. On November 29, 1991, Canada's justice minister, Kim Campbell, citing Wilson's recantation, asked the Supreme Court of Canada to review the Milgaard case. "Compelling" evidence, she added, strongly implicated Larry Fisher, who was then serving his second prison term.

As the review opened on January 21, 1992, in Ottawa, Ontario, Chief Justice Antonio Lamer emphasized that it was a hearing, not a trial or an appeal. Its purpose was to determine whether a miscarriage of justice had occurred.

Questioned by Eric Neufeld, counsel for the Saskatchewan Justice Department, Wilson admitted that he had not seen Milgaard with a knife before the murder. Nichol John had been hysterical after Milgaard returned to the car, he added, only because he was driving too fast, and Milgaard had been away from the car only "a maximum of ten minutes"—not long enough to have committed the murder. Wilson said he had not seen blood on Milgaard's pants.

"Let's Sink Him"

Milgaard's attorney Hersh Wolch cross-examined Wilson. Before the trial, Wolch asked, had he and Nichol John discussed what they were going to say to investigators?

Wilson: All I can remember at this time is, "Let's give them what they want. Let's sink him."

Wolch: Who said that, you or Nicky?

Wilson: I believe I did.

Wolch: And when you said "Let's sink him," what did you mean by that?

Wilson: By giving them what they wanted to get David.

Wolch: Had they convinced you that David was guilty?

Wilson: Yes.

Wolch turned to Wilson's testimony that Milgaard, upon returning to the car, had said he "had hit a girl and grabbed her purse."

Wolch: Has anybody ever questioned you as to the absurdity of that?

Wilson: No, sir.

Wolch: If a man said to you, "I left the car, hit a girl, she was okay, and took her purse" or stole it, you would say, "Idiot, the car is stuck."

Wilson: Yes, sir.

Wolch: Do you follow me how stupid that is? Who leaves a stuck car to purse-snatch? How do you get away?

Wilson: Exactly.

Next, Wolch suggested that Wilson had invented the entire incident about the car being stuck. Wilson agreed, abandoning his recanted position that there had not been time for Milgaard to leave the stuck car and commit the murder. Chief Justice Lamer, suggesting that Wilson had "lied through his teeth" in this hearing, cited him for contempt.

Fair Trial but Miscarriage of Justice

On April 14, the five-judge panel ruled that David Milgaard had had a fair trial and that the Saskatoon police had acted properly. Continued conviction, it said, however, would be a miscarriage of justice because new evidence about Larry Fisher might have affected the original verdict. The case was referred to Saskatchewan for a new trial or a stay of proceedings. The court added that its findings "should not be taken as a finding of guilt against Fisher."

Two days later, Milgaard was freed when Saskatchewan Justice Minister Robert Mitchell said the evidence was too old to hold a new trial.

In 1993, Milgaard filed a lawsuit against two former prosecutors and three police officers for conspiring to withhold information about Larry Fisher that could have helped him overturn his conviction.

In May 1994, having served the remaining four years of his original sentence and the additional ten years, Fisher was released. Ending a two-year investigation, the RCMP's violent crime analysis section concluded in August 1995 that Fisher's "behavior was not consistent with the behavior observed within the murder of Gail Miller."

In 1995, Milgaard sued Justice Minister Mitchell for $1.35 million for libel. The suit is still pending.

In May 1995, while visiting a marijuana crop, Shorty Cadrain was shot dead by a hunter some 80 feet away who later said he mistook Cadrain for a bear.

In January 1996, the Saskatchewan Court of Appeal dismissed an appeal by Milgaard of a lower-court decision that prevented him from separately questioning each of the codefendants in his suit against prosecutors and police. That suit also remains pending.

—Bernard Ryan, Jr.

Suggestions for Further Reading

Karp, Carl, and Cecil Rofner. *When Justice Fails: The David Milgaard Story*. Toronto: McClelland and Stewart, 1991.

Sue Rodriguez Appeal: 1993

Appellant: Sue Rodriguez **Appellant's Request:** A court order invalidating
two sections of Canada's Criminal Code regarding assisted suicide
Appellant's Lawyers: Chris Considine, Shari McGlynn
Opposing Lawyer: Patrick Riley **Judges:** Antonio Lamer, Peter Cory,
Charles Gonthier, Frank Iacobucci, Gerard La Forest, Claire L'Heureux-Dube,
John Major, Beverley McLachlin, John Sopinka **Place:** Ottawa, Ontario,
Canada **Date:** May 20, 1993 **Decision:** Petition denied

SIGNIFICANCE

The petitioner's determination, in the face of her deteriorating health, to be master
of her own fate brought a nation's attention to its law that criminalizes assisted
suicide. The significance of the event is underlined by the fact that the hearing in
Canada's highest court was only the second to be televised nationally.

In 1991, Sue Rodriguez was 40 years old. A Winnipeg native, she had worked as
a freelance photographer in San Diego, California, then married biochemist
Henry Rodriguez and moved to San Francisco, where she worked as a program
assistant at Stanford University. Her son, Cole, was born in 1984, and four years
later the family moved to Victoria, British Columbia.

Lou Gehrig's Disease

In August 1991, after several months of pain, cramps, and weakness in her
left hand, Rodriguez was diagnosed with amyotrophic lateral sclerosis, or ALS—
commonly known as Lou Gehrig's disease. Her doctors told her that, although
her senses and mental capacity would not be affected, she could expect the
disease to attack the motor neurons, or nerves, in her lower brain and spinal cord.
Since the motor neurons transmit electrical impulses to the muscles, thus
generating movement, their failure would mean increasing difficulty in speaking, swallowing, coughing, smiling, and—inevitably—breathing. In 80 percent
of cases, they said frankly, the ALS sufferer dies within three years. In the
meantime, control over all muscles, including those governing digestion and
bodily functions, is rapidly lost.

Rodriguez spent a year on medication and treatment in the hope of slowing the disease. At the same time, she began looking for someone who would help her die when she reached the stage at which, lacking muscle control or strength, she could not single-handedly commit suicide. But, she learned, although there was no law against committing suicide, the Criminal Code of Canada contained a law against assisted suicide.

Rodriguez Goes Public

In August 1992, the director of the Right to Die Society of Canada, John Hofsess, urged Rodriguez to go public with a formal challenge to the law. Hoping her actions would help others in similar suffering, she agreed. On September 18, 1992, a long segment on the CBC evening news made Rodriguez and her right-to-die case a household topic across Canada.

Since Rodriguez was already too afflicted to travel to the Canadian Parliament in Ottawa, the Right to Die Society helped her prepare a videotaped appeal to Parliament to change two sections of the nation's Criminal Code. One section makes it illegal to counsel a person to commit suicide or to help a person to do so. The punishment is a maximum of 14 years' imprisonment, whether or not suicide results. The other section prohibits any person from consenting to have death inflicted on himself or herself. Such consent, says the code, does not provide a defense against criminal responsibility for the person who causes the death.

A parliamentary committee viewed the videotape on Tuesday, November 24, 1992. Speaking with difficulty, Rodriguez said, "I want to ask you, gentlemen, if I cannot give consent to my own death, then whose body is this? Who owns my life? Today I can barely walk. There's much worse to come."

Rodriguez Goes to Court

When Parliament failed to act, Rodriguez, through her lawyer, Chris Considine, presented a petition to the British Columbia Supreme Court, sitting in Victoria. It asked the court to declare the two sections of the Criminal Code to be invalid.

The petition, before Judge Allen Melvin on December 17 and 18, 1992, took the position that both sections are contrary to sections of Canada's Charter of Rights and Freedoms that deal with the right to life, the right not to be subjected to cruel and unusual punishment, and equality before the law. The latter guarantee, it said, entitled Sue Rodriguez to the same opportunity to end her life as that provided to any able-bodied citizen.

The petition included affidavits on the patient's condition and prognosis from her doctor, Donald Lovely. The expectation was that she would soon need a respirator in order to breathe and a gastrostomy to receive food. "I do not wish to face the indignity which will accompany being forced to endure life under such circumstances," Rodriguez testified, "nor do I wish to suffer the discomfort and tremendous mental stress involved in a death by starvation, pneumonia or suffocation."

Judge Melvin turned down the petition, saying that the sanctity of life was the idea on which the Charter of Rights was based and that the ban on aiding suicide protected the young, the innocent, the mentally incompetent, the depressed, and others.

A Higher Court

Attorney Considine immediately went to the British Columbia Court of Appeal, the province's highest court. On March 8, 1993, the three-judge court found against Rodriguez, two to one. Justice Harold Hollinrake said there was a fine line between palliative care (reducing the discomfort of a disease) and doctor-assisted suicide that should not be crossed. Justice Patricia Proudfoot said she would "leave to Parliament the responsibility of taking the pulse of the nation." Dissenting, Chief Justice Allen McEachern said that Rodriguez's rights to liberty and security were violated by the law against assisted suicide. "What is at stake here," he concluded, "is the right of a single person not to have continuing pain and psychological trauma imposed upon her by reason of the state preventing her from obtaining essential medical assistance."

Next, the petition went before the nine justices of the Supreme Court of Canada in Ottawa on May 20, 1993. Unable to travel, Rodriguez watched the daylong TV broadcast—only the second in the court's history—at home. Arguing against the petition were lawyers for British Columbia and for the national government; church groups; and antiabortion groups. Patrick Riley, an attorney representing a group of disabled people, pleaded that the court not make suicide easier or more acceptable in society.

The Supreme Court of Canada Says No

On Thursday, September 30, 1993, the court ruled, five to four, against the Rodriguez appeal of the two lower-court rulings. Justice John Sopinka wrote the majority opinion shared by Justices Charles Gonthier, Frank Iacobucci, Gerard La Forest, and John Major. To legalize assisted suicide, they found, would not guarantee that only those "who are terminally ill and genuinely desire death" were the ones who would die. "I have the deepest sympathy for the appellant and her family," he wrote, "and I am aware that the denial of her application by this court may prevent her from managing the manner of her death. I have, however, concluded that the prohibition . . . is not contrary to the provisions of the Charter."

Dissenting, Justice Beverley McLachlin, joined by Chief Justice Antonio Lamer and Justices Peter Cory and Claire L'Heureux-Dube, found that Sue Rodriguez had the right to seek aid in committing suicide if she became too weak to do it herself. "What is the difference between suicide and assisted suicide," wrote McLachlin, "that justifies making the one lawful and the other a crime, that justifies allowing some this choice while denying it to others? Sue Rodriguez is asked to bear the burden of the chance that other people in other situations may act criminally to kill others or improperly sway them to suicide. She is asked to serve as a scapegoat."

Justice Cory, writing his own dissent, said death is "an integral part of living," and the right to die should be as protected "as is any other aspect of the right to life. State prohibitions that would force a dreadful, painful death on a rational but incapacitated terminally ill patient are an affront to human dignity."

In his own dissenting opinion, Chief Justice Antonio Lamer said he shared "a deep concern" over the pressures that people might have to bear if the law allowed assisted suicide. "Legislation that deprives a disadvantaged group of the right to equality," he wrote, could not be justified "solely on such speculative grounds. The truth is that we simply do not and cannot know the range of implications that allowing some form of assisted suicide will have for persons with physical disabilities. What we do know and cannot ignore is the anguish of those in the positions of Ms. Rodriguez."

At home, in a voice almost inaudible, Sue Rodriguez told a press conference, "It has been worth it, by more than I ever anticipated. I'm pleased that people are looking at this and thinking about the issue. I hope that Parliament will act and allow those who are in my situation to benefit in the future."

On Saturday, February 12, 1994, the morning after a planned farewell dinner with her husband and nine-year-old son, Sue Rodriguez died at home with the assistance of a doctor whose anonymity remains inviolate.

—*Bernard Ryan, Jr.*

Suggestions for Further Reading

Birnie, Lisa Hobbs. *Uncommon Will: The Death and Life of Sue Rodriguez.* Toronto: Macmillan Canada, 1994.

Chisholm, Patricia. "A Wrenching Decision: Canada's Top Court Rejects Assisted Suicide." *Maclean's*, October 11, 1993.

Underwood, Nora. "I am Getting Weaker." *Maclean's*, March 22, 1993.

Karla Homolka and Paul Bernardo Trials: 1993 and 1995

Defendants: Karla Homolka, Paul Bernardo   **Crimes Charged:** Two murders, rape and other sexual assaults   **Chief Defense Lawyers:** George Walker for Homolka (first trial), John Rosen for Bernardo (second trial)
Chief Prosecutors: Murray Segal (first trial), Ray Houlahan (second trial)
Judges: Francis Kovacs (first trial), Patrick LeSage (second trial)
Places: St. Catherines, Ontario (first trial); Toronto, Ontario (second trial)
Dates of Trials: June 28–July 6, 1993; May 18–September 1, 1995
Verdicts: Homolka guilty of manslaughter; Bernardo guilty of murder
Sentences: Two concurrent terms of 12 years for Homolka; life imprisonment for Bernardo

SIGNIFICANCE

The monstrous depravity of the crimes revealed to Canadians a corner of their society that they had not known existed. Beyond that, this case forced Canadians to reexamine the efficacy of their police as well as to reconsider their laws regarding censorship imposed by their legal system.

Canadians have long regarded their society as one relatively free of the violence and bizarre sexual crimes that often seemed so rampant among their neighbors in the United States. Thus, when the story told by Karla Homolka was first published in the early months of 1993, it came as a double shock to Canadians: How could it be that this obviously attractive, seemingly typical—at worst, ordinary; at best, ideal—couple committed such crimes? And how could these crimes have been committed in Canada in the midst of an apparently law-abiding community and under the eyes of the legendarily efficient police? Little did Canadians know at the time that the crimes were far worse than anything revealed in 1993, and that it would be another two and a half years before the full extent of the nightmare would be made public.

The Perfect Couple

Karla Homolka was a 17-year-old high school student when in October 1987 she met Paul Bernardo, a 23-year-old university graduate, just beginning a career as a bookkeeper. Both were attractive middle-class young people from the Toronto area. Paul proceeded to court Karla with lavish gifts and trips to fine restaurants. In the years that followed until their marriage in June 1991, their relationship seemed perfectly normal to their families and friends. The only hint of trouble came on Christmas Eve 1990, when Karla's 14-year-old sister, Tammy, died from choking on her own vomit; it occurred in the basement rec room in the Homolka's home while Karla and Paul were present, but the family and police accepted their story that Tammy had drunk too much liquor.

Although the Homolka family was beginning to have some doubts about Bernardo, the couple married on June 29, 1991. By coincidence, virtually at the same moment they were being married, the Ontario police were pulling the dismembered parts of a young female's body, encased in cement blocks, from Lake Gibson, an isolated fishing pond in nearby St. Catherines, Ontario. No one conceived of ever linking Karla and Paul to this murder as they commenced what seemed to be a typical suburban marriage. She worked as a veterinary assistant, and he continued as a bookkeeper.

The first signs of problems with their marriage came when Homolka's family and coworkers began to notice bruises on her body. She always had excuses—until one day in early January 1993 when she suddenly left Bernardo and moved in with her family. She admitted that her husband had been beating her regularly, most recently with a flashlight; with her family's urging, she went to the police and soon Paul was charged with assault. (Paul Bernardo by this time—undoubtedly knowing that he had much to hide—was in the process of legally changing his surname to Teale, which is how he was—and still is—occasionally identified in some accounts.)

Although at first it seemed that this was yet another case of spousal abuse, as the police pressed their questioning of Homolka, they began to hear even more. Suddenly in February, the police upped the charges against Bernardo to 43 sexual assaults—rape among them—most of them dating back to 1987–90 in the Toronto suburb of Scarborough. Then, in an astonishing turn of events, on May 18, the police filed two counts of manslaughter—against Karla Homolka Bernardo. The next day, Paul Bernardo was charged with two counts of first-degree murder. One of the couple's alleged victims was 15-year-old Kristen French, whose nude body had been found on a remote road on April 29, 1992. The other was 14-year-old Leslie Mahaffy, the girl whose dismembered body had been dredged from a lake on the day of the Bernardos' wedding.

The First Trial

In the weeks that followed these sensational revelations, the Canadian officials released few details about the crimes, but it was soon evident that Homolka was providing information to the police. When the court convened on

June 28, 1993, only Homolka was on trial, and it was clear that she had struck a plea bargain with the prosecution. Meanwhile, the judge had closed his courtroom to the general public and prohibited the publishing or broadcasting of any details about the circumstances of the crimes. This not only aroused considerable protest from residents of the region, who demanded to know just what had been going on, and from the Canadian media, it also consumed most of the time at the ensuing trial. Every day except the last was spent hearing arguments as to whether the ban on publicizing the case should stand. The judge concluded that Paul Bernardo's right to a fair trial would be violated if any details were made public: The public and foreign journalists were banned, and Canadian journalists could not publicize any details about the crimes.

Finally, on July 6, the clerk of court read the charges against Homolka and then the facts agreed upon by the government and her lawyer. Since she had pleaded guilty to the charge of manslaughter, all that remained was for the judge to determine the sentence. Mothers of the two murdered girls were allowed to describe the impact on their families. The judge then gave a 75-minute speech, explaining the factors he had considered, concluding: "No sentence I can impose would adequately reflect the revulsion of the community for the deaths of two innocent young girls." But because he accepted that Homolka was not the worst offender, he gave her two concurrent terms of 12 years.

Restraints and Revelations

Although it was clear that Homolka had struck a plea bargain with the government, Canadian journalists were forbidden to print even this, let alone any details of the crimes that they had learned about in the courtroom. But inevitably details leaked out, and the U.S. media were under no such constraint. U.S. newspapers, magazines, and TV stations (and even the Internet) carried all the bloody details. Although the Canadian authorities managed to keep out individual issues of printed matter and blocked U.S. news reports from cable TV, they could not stop Canadians from obtaining the details over the airwaves or by using satellite dishes.

In December 1993, *The Washington Post* and then the *New York Times* published some truly shocking details of the two murders. Leslie Mahaffy had been sexually abused over a 24-hour period by Homolka as well as by Bernardo before being strangled with an electrical cord; then Bernardo had cut up her body into ten pieces that he put into cement blocks, which he had then dumped into the lake. Kristen French had been held for almost two weeks, during which time she was frequently sexually brutalized by Paul and Karla before she, too, was strangled with an electrical cord and her body then dumped in the countryside. But perhaps the most shocking revelation was that Karla had admitted to the police that she and Paul were also responsible for the death of Karla's young sister, Tammy: They had plied her with liquor and drugs and had sexually abused her before she died choking on her vomit.

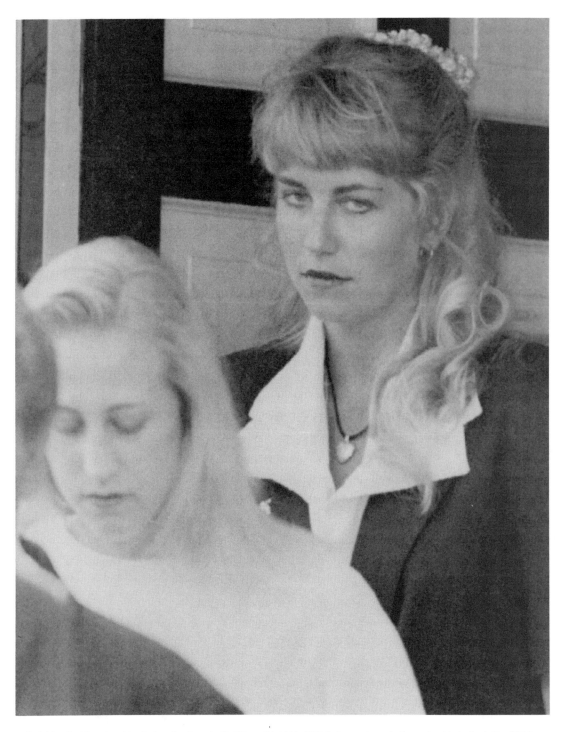

Karla Homolka follows her sister, Lori, as they leave for Paul Bernardo's trial in 1995. Karla was charged with manslaughter in the deaths of Kristen French and Leslie Mahaffy on July 6, 1993. (AP/Wideworld Photos)

The Second Trial

Throughout 1994, occasional details were leaked to the media but nothing that could begin to depict, much less explain, the true horror of the crimes. Finally, in May 1995, the trial of Paul Bernardo opened in Toronto. This time the public was admitted, and the Canadian media were allowed to report details as they came out.

They did not have to wait long for a most astonishing revelation: The Bernardos had made videotapes of their sexual abuse and torture of Tammy Homolka, Leslie Mahaffy, and Kristen French (as well as videotapes of Paul having sex with another drugged teenager who had been allowed to leave). These tapes—three and one-half hours of graphic images and agonizing sounds—would be played frequently for the jury (eight men, four women) during the weeks that followed. But as horrific as the tapes were, they did not actually show Paul killing anyone. And, according to the defense, the tapes revealed that Homolka had been a much more active participant than had been presumed. Bernardo's lawyer soon indicated that he was going to construct a defense that would attempt to shift much of the blame onto Homolka.

On June 19, Karla Homolka Bernardo took the stand as the prosecution's chief witness. In day after day of testimony and then cross-examination, she presented herself as the victim of an abusive husband. She revealed that he had begun to reveal his sexual obsessions and perversities within a few months after she met him, but she claimed she had participated only to please him. She then told in excruciating detail about the death of her sister, about the murders of the two girls, and about various other sexual perversities as well as the physical abuse she herself had experienced at Bernardo's hands. In a final bid to prove that she had been an unwilling participant in her husband's crimes, she told the court, "I have a lot more freedom in prison than I ever had with him."

During the intensive cross-examination that followed, Paul's lawyer managed to raise some doubts about Karla's credibility. For instance, a series of greeting cards and notes from Karla to Paul showed her continually expressing passion for him, despite all his alleged perversions and crimes. The defense also tried to give a different version of the two murders: Paul admitted kidnapping and sexually assaulting the victims, but he claimed they died accidentally—and while left alone with Karla. In the end, though, the defense could not provide any real evidence that absolved Paul of the crimes. After eight hours of deliberation, the jury found Paul Bernardo guilty of all nine charges, including the two first-degree murders. Under Canadian law, this meant an automatic sentence of life imprisonment.

The Aftermath

Homolka had been taken to the Prison for Women in Kingston, Ontario, immediately after her conviction in June 1993; she may be allowed out on parole as early as 1997. Bernardo can apply for parole in 2020, but since the government persuaded the judge to label him a "dangerous offender," he may spend many more years in prison. His lawyer filed an appeal, but it seems unlikely that the sentence will be overturned. Many Canadians were upset that Homolka had been allowed to get off so lightly, but the government defended its plea bargain on the grounds that Bernardo's first lawyer had deliberately withheld the incriminating videotapes until September 1994.

Meanwhile, Bernardo has yet to be tried for the death of Tammy Homolka or for the many charges of sexual assaults he was accused of in Scarborough. There were also several loose ends, most notably the failures in police work that allowed Bernardo to remain at large for several years after there was specific evidence that he was a dangerous sexual predator. He had even been called in as a suspect in the Scarborough sex crimes as early as November 1990, but the police had not bothered to test the blood, saliva, and hair samples they had taken until after he was exposed by Karla Homolka in February 1993.

No legal process or psychological theorizing could ever explain what motivated Paul Bernardo to commit such unspeakable acts. Arguably even more mystifying is why any person would go along with him, whether as a willing accessory or as a victim.

—John S. Bowman

Suggestions for Further Reading

The Boston Globe. (June 4, 1995): 2.

Davey, Frank. *Karla's Web: A Cultural Investigation of the Mahaffy-French Murders.* Toronto: Viking. Special "Blackout" edition, 1994; reissued complete, 1995.

Gould, Allan. *Criminal Acts I: The Canadian True Crime Annual.* Toronto: Macmillan Canada, 1994.

Jenish, D'Arcy. *Maclean's* Magazine. (July 19, 1993): 15–17; (July 1, 1995): 65–66; (July 10, 1995): 12–13; (July 17, 1995): 36–37; (July 24, 1996): 49; (August 14, 1995): 23; (September 4, 1995): 17; (September 11, 1995): 18–23.

Newsweek. (May 29, 1995): 53.

The *New York Times.* (September 2, 1995): 4.

Ottowa Citizen. (November 4, 1995): 4.

Pron, Nick. *Lethal Marriage: The Unspeakable Crimes of Paul Bernardo and Karla Homolka.* New York: Bantam Books, 1995.

Time. (December 13, 1993): 59.

Robert Thompson and Jon Venables
Trial: 1993

Defendants: Robert Thompson, Jon Venables   **Crime Charged:** Murder
Chief Defense Lawyers: David Turner, Q.C.; Brian Walsh, Q.C.
Chief Prosecutor: Richard Henriques, Q.C.   **Judge:** Sir Michael Morland
Place: Preston, England   **Dates of Trial:** November 1–24, 1993
Verdict: Guilty   **Sentence:** To be detained during Her Majesty's pleasure
(with a minimum of 15 years imprisonment)

SIGNIFICANCE

The defendants in this sensational trial were the youngest persons to be tried for murder in Britain in the 20th century. Because of the ages of the victim and his killers, this case made headlines throughout much of the world.

James Bulger was one month short of his third birthday when he vanished from a Liverpool shopping mall on the afternoon of Friday, February 12, 1993. His mother had stopped to buy meat from a butcher's shop in the Strand when little James strayed from her side. In seconds he was gone. Virtually every mother has experienced the anguish felt by Denise Bulger when she realized that her child was no longer with her. Usually, however, a missing toddler is found just yards away or within minutes. But not that day. Bulger ran frantically from store to store, asking strangers along the way if they had seen her little boy. None had. When she contacted the mall's security officers, they scoured every inch of the building, but to no avail.

Later that night, with still no sign of the missing baby, video from a mall security camera was examined for possible clues. What detectives saw first puzzled, then chilled, them. The grainy image showed a toddler—clearly James Bulger—being led out of the mall by an unknown boy, with another lad some yards ahead of them. When computer enhancement of the video revealed that the two abductors were hardly more than infants themselves, it raised hopes that young James would be found unharmed.

As the hours passed, though, hopes dwindled. Total disillusionment came on the Sunday afternoon—Saint Valentine's Day—when the mutilated body of James Bulger was found two miles away from the shopping mall, next to a canal.

He had been battered to death, doused with blue paint, then dumped on some railroad tracks, where a passing train had cut his broken little body in half.

A vast outpouring of grief in the community expressed itself, with people turning out by the hundreds to lay flowers at the spot where James Bulger had met his death. Among those who brought flowers was a chubby-faced 10-year-old with brown hair who lived nearby, Robert Thompson. On the Wednesday evening following a TV broadcast of the security video, a woman contacted Liverpool police to say that one of the boys in the video strongly resembled a neighbor of hers, Jon Venables, age 10. He had come home on the night that James Bulger disappeared with blue paint stains on his clothing. She further recalled that on the day of the crime Jon had been playing hooky from school with another boy—Robert Thompson.

Two days later, after lengthy interviews, Robert and Jon were charged with abduction and murder. Evidence that this was not some spontaneous childish prank came with the revelation that, just before abducting James Bulger, the two boys had attempted to lure another toddler away from the same mall, only to be thwarted when the child's mother chased them off. In light of this, accusations of attempted abduction were added to the charge sheet.

Horrified Nation

News that two 10-year-old boys had been charged with apparent premeditated murder shocked Britain as few crimes have done before or since. As psychologists struggled to provide answers for a stunned nation, detectives set about gathering the evidence to lay before a court. The culmination of their efforts came at Preston Crown Court on the morning of November 1, 1993, under the merciless glare of the world's media.

Given the overwhelming publicity that the case had garnered, it came as no surprise when David Turner, Q.C. (Queen's Counsel), representing Robert Thompson, and Brian Walsh, Q.C., attorney for Jon Venables, submitted that their clients were being denied the right to a fair trial. Although neither defendant's name had been released by the media, details of their alleged crimes were very much in the public domain, and it was for this reason that Justice Michael Morland thought long and hard before deciding that the trial should proceed.

Also at issue was the admissibility of police photographs graphically portraying the horrific nature of James Bulger's injuries. Both defense lawyers argued that such images would merely inflame the jury and were unnecessary, but again the judge ruled against them, and the Crown was ready to present its case.

In simple yet powerful terms, the chief prosecutor, Richard Henriques, Q.C., described how, after abducting James Bulger from the shopping mall, the two defendants:

> walked him some two and a half miles across Liverpool to Walton, a very long and distressing walk for a two-year-old toddler. James was then taken

up on a railway line and subjected to a prolonged and violent attack. Bricks, stones, and a piece of metal appear to have been thrown at James on that railway line. He sustained multiple fractures of the skull. . . . At some point James's lower clothing was removed. His body was placed across a rail on the railway line and some time later his body was run over by a train which cut his body in two. . . . [At the time of the attack, the defendants] were both ten years, six months old. . . . Notwithstanding their ages it is alleged that they both intended to kill James or at the least to cause him really serious injury and they both knew that their behavior was really seriously wrong.

Henriques then began relating the events of that day, how the defendants had played hooky from school, then went to the shopping mall, where they engaged in shoplifting, before luring James Bulger to his death.

Several witnesses testified to having seen young James being led through the streets of Liverpool by two older boys, but perhaps the most poignant was Elizabeth McCarrick, who was with her seven-year-old daughter when she saw the three children near where the body was found. When she had asked the defendants what they were about, they replied that they were taking the toddler to the police station. "I managed to make the chubby one [Robert Thompson] let go of the toddler's hand . . . that little boy did not make a sound . . . his head was down . . . the taller one said, 'It's all right, we'll take him to the station' . . . the chubby one turned around as if he was going to run away. The taller one called the chubby one back and the chubby one grabbed hold of the little boy's hand."

Another witness, known only as Miss H because of her age, and the last witness to see James Bulger alive, had seen him being pushed toward the railroad tracks.

"Could you see what state the little boy was in?" asked Justice Morland.

"I could only hear laughter."

After killing James Bulger, both boys had gone to help out at a nearby video store. Staff members testified that neither seemed discomforted in any way.

Pathologist Dr. Alan Williams described in graphic detail the full extent of James's injuries. "In my opinion the cause of death was the result of multiple head injuries. There are so many injuries to the scalp and skull one cannot single out one particular blow to the head and say that was the one that was fatal. I would estimate there were at least thirty separate blows to the body . . . given the amount of brick dust at the scene I consider bricks to be a likely implement."

DNA Match

Scientist Graham Jackson had found blood on the toe cap of Jon Venables's shoe and through DNA testing matched it to James Bulger's blood. The chances of such a match occurring randomly, he estimated, were one in one billion. His colleague Phillip Rydeard told the court how a patterned injury on

James's right cheek correlated with the distinctive features of the uppers of Robert's right shoe. He produced an overlay picture showing how the raised stitching, the laces, and the D-rings through which they were threaded all matched the marks on James's face.

Yet another forensic expert, Andrew Mulley, gave evidence linking the paint stains on James and on his clothing with similar paint marks found on Jon's jacket.

Placing Jon and Robert at the crime scene had been easy for the prosecution; now came the hard part—demonstrating willful intent, knowing that what they did was wrong. Dr. Eileen Vizard, a child psychologist, though admitting that Robert was suffering from post-traumatic stress, disputed defense claims that the boy had exhibited similar signs of mental disturbance prior to the attack.

Upon reexamination, Henriques cut through much of the arcane psychological terminology with one simple question: "Was there in your assessment any evidence of abnormality of mind at the time of the killing?"

"No," said Dr. Vizard.

Henriques put a similar set of questions to Dr. Susan Bailey, who had examined Jon. She confirmed that he, too, would have known it was wrong to take a child away from his mother and leave him injured on a railway line. According to tests she had carried out, Jon was of average intelligence.

Several days were given over to tape-recorded interviews with the accused. It would be the court's only chance to hear either defendant's side of the argument. In their eerily high-pitched voices, both at first disclaimed all knowledge of the killing; gradually, though, as the facts came out, their stories changed. Each blamed the other. Jon ultimately expressed deep remorse for what had happened. Robert, on the other hand, lied at every turn, showed no contrition whatsoever, and spared no effort in piling all the blame onto his school friend. He had only touched James, he said, to see if he was breathing: "So, I have nothing to bother about. . . . If I wanted to kill a baby I would kill my own—wouldn't I?"

In the absence of any defense witnesses, counsel for the accused could only plead mitigating circumstances. Their arguments were predictable and similarly framed—each blamed the other for the killing. Turner said, "Robert's case is and always has been that the attack on little James was initiated and carried out by Jon Venables."

Walsh was more blunt: "The prosecution say he [Thompson] is a liar, a sophisticated liar who lied from beginning to end, and I regret to say we agree. He lied to put the blame on Jon Venables and shuffle it off himself. He treated the police interview as a debate, a challenge match, a sparring match. He was confident and assertive." Walsh concluded his assessment of Thompson by describing his as "a cool, calm, collected and brazen little rogue." His own client, he suggested to the jury, had been a helpless pawn in Robert's grasp and, at the time of the abduction, had no thoughts of killing the little boy in his mind. For this reason, Walsh argued, Jon should be convicted of manslaughter, nothing more.

Justice Morland dealt with the matter of intent in his summing-up: "The crucial question is not what was their intention when James Bulger was taken from the Strand or during the long walk of over two miles to the railway line, but what was the intention of each defendant on the railway line when the fatal injuries were inflicted."

On November 24, the jury decided that Jon Venables and Robert Thompson *had* intended to murder James Bulger, though they were unable to agree on the charge of attempted abduction. The judge then ordered both boys to be "detained during Her Majesty's pleasure"—a nonspecific sentence customarily passed on minors convicted of murder in Britain. On this occasion, the current home secretary, Michael Howard, decreed that neither boy would be considered for release until each has served a minimum of 15 years.

—Colin Evans

Suggestions for Further Reading

Smith, David James. *Beyond All Reason*. New York: D. I. Fine, 1995.

Thomas, Mark. *Every Mother's Nightmare*. London: Pan, 1993.

Wilson, Patrick. *Children Who Kill*. London: Michael Joseph, 1973.

Rosemary West Trial: 1995

Defendant: Rosemary West   **Crime Charged:** Murder
Chief Defense Lawyer: Richard Ferguson, Q.C.   **Chief Prosecutor:** Brian
Leveson, Q.C.   **Judge:** Sir Charles Mantell   **Place:** Winchester, England
Dates of Trial: October 6–November 22, 1995   **Verdict:** Guilty
Sentence: Life imprisonment

SIGNIFICANCE
The murder trial of Rosemary West, Britain's most notorious female serial killer, produced some of the most chilling and sensational testimony ever heard in a British courtroom.

When she was just 15 years old, Rosemary Letts met and fell in love with a self-employed Gloucestershire builder named Frederick West. Despite the 12-year difference in their ages and the fact that Fred West was already married with two children, the couple became inseparable. In 1971, the abrupt disappearance of Fred's wife, Rena, and one of his children, Charmaine, cleared the way for Fred and Rose to marry in January of the following year. The new Mrs. West was a prolific mother. By 1983, she had given birth eight times, though not all of the children were fathered by her husband. Fred, unconcerned by such technicalities, treated all the children as if they were his own.

Within the walls of 25 Cromwell Street, a small row house in Gloucester, Fred and Rose carved out for themselves and their family a quite extraordinary existence. Into this heavily charged atmosphere meandered a seemingly endless stream of transients, both male and female. Some stayed just hours, others lasted months, some never left. Drugs were commonplace, but the overriding currency at Cromwell Street was sex. It dominated Fred West's life. Rose, too, was obsessed. At Fred's urging, she threw herself into prostitution, sadomasochism, lesbianism, and—according to the Crown Prosecution Service—murder.

The rumors began circulating in late 1993: murmured hints to social workers from the Wests' children about a long-vanished sister buried under the patio. In February 1994, the police, armed with shovels and picks, came to investigate. Sure enough, beneath the patio they found the remains of 16-year-old Heather West—and many more remains. No fewer than nine bodies, all female and between 15 and 22 years old, were recovered from the grounds of 25 Cromwell Street. At a previous home on Midland Road, the body of yet another of Fred West's daughters, Charmaine, age 8, was found. The grim tally reached 12 with the discovery of Rena, West's first wife, and a second woman, both buried in a remote field.

Facing a dozen murder charges, Fred West freely admitted his guilt and insisted he had acted alone. Rose, at first, was held as an accomplice, but she was soon charged with murder. On New Year's Day 1995, Fred West hanged himself in his prison cell, which meant that when Rosemary West faced her accusers on October 6, 1995, she stood alone in the dock, accused of the murders of the 10 women found in the West home.

House of Horror

In his opening address for the Crown, Brian Leveson, Q.C. (Queen's Counsel), said that Cromwell Street revealed discoveries "more terrible than words can express." He also said, "I make it clear from the outset that there is no direct evidence of anyone—Frederick West or Rosemary West—killing any one of these girls . . . the evidence is circumstantial." But was it possible, he asked, for so many murders to have occurred in such confined quarters and for Rosemary West not to have known?

Over strident defense objections, Justice Charles Mantell allowed the prosecution to introduce testimony from Caroline Owens, age 39, who had been hired as a nanny at 25 Cromwell Street in 1972. When, after four weeks, she had attempted to leave, she was attacked, gagged with sticky tape, and sexually assaulted by both Wests. "What was your reaction?" asked Leveson.

"Terror, panic," replied Owens. Afterward, Fred had ordered her not to mention the ordeal or, he said, he would bury her under the paving stones of Gloucester, adding that there were "hundreds of girls there." Instead, Owens had fled to the police, who arrested the Wests. The couple had been charged with indecent assault and fined.

According to Leveson, this incident had formed the blueprint for all the murders to come: Girls and young women were lured to Cromwell Street for sex; those the Wests felt posed no threat were allowed to live; the others were butchered.

A neighbor, Elizabeth Agius, testified that when the Wests moved into Cromwell Street, Fred had given her a guided tour of the house, pausing in the basement to leer, "I would like to make this my torture room." Agius also said that Rose had admitted being a prostitute and that Fred liked to watch her activities through a spy hole in her bedroom door.

Under cross-examination from Richard Ferguson, Q.C., Agius, like a number of the prosecution witnesses, admitted selling her story to the tabloid press and TV, thus fueling the defense's core argument that much of the prosecution testimony was tainted by the lure of money; the more sensational the tale, the greater the reward.

Such accusations could not be leveled at June Gough, mother of Lynda Gough, whose body was found under the bathroom. In heartrending detail,

Gough told how in May 1973 she had called at Cromwell Street, searching for her missing daughter. A woman she later identified as Rose West had answered the door, wearing items of Lynda's clothing, items she claimed that Lynda had left behind after leaving abruptly.

It was Ben Stanniland who had introduced Lynda into the house. Now, 22 years later, he and fellow lodger, David Evans, recalled events at Cromwell Street. According to Evans, Rose said Lynda had been dismissed from the house for mistreating the children. Both men confirmed that Fred had encouraged them to have sex with Rose and that the house was regularly raided by drug officers.

Yet another lodger, Elizabeth Brewer, told how one of the victims found at Cromwell Street, Shirley Robinson, had feared retribution from Rose after becoming pregnant by Fred. In May 1978, when eight months pregnant, Shirley had suddenly vanished, a disappearance that Fred had explained by saying she had "left to visit relatives in Germany."

Erwin Marshall, who had been dating one of the Wests' daughters, described hearing a scream in the night at Cromwell Street at about the time that Heather disappeared in 1987. Rose had attributed the disturbance to Heather's nightmares. Later, she said that Heather had left home. Shortly afterward, Marshall declared, Fred West began building a patio in the backyard.

Some idea of the horror endured by the Wests' children came from Anne Marie Davis, daughter of Fred and his first wife, Rena. At age eight, she had been raped by her father and Rose. The couple, she said, doted on each other. "Rosemary had so much love for my dad, she would have done anything for him. I believe they always told each other what they were doing. They had total trust."

Ferguson sought to soften the impact. "You never knew that your father had killed anyone?"

"I did not know about any of it until recently."

"Did you suspect it?"

"No."

Hideous Mutilation

The excavation of 25 Cromwell Street had been led by Home Office pathologist Professor Bernard Knight, who testified that all the bodies had been dismembered and that in most cases kneecaps and finger and toe bones were missing. He could not tell if dismemberment had taken place before or after death. Because no body tissue remained, it was impossible to determine the cause of death.

A forensic odontologist, Dr. David Whittaker, had used a photograph of eight-year-old Charmaine West, whose skull was found at Midland Road, to compare dental similarities and attempt to fix the date of her death. Charmaine, he said, had lost her two front baby teeth and the permanent adult teeth had still to come through. In a child of Charmaine's age, the growth of teeth was "very rapid," leading him to conclude that Charmaine had died within three months of having the photograph taken. This was crucial, because at this time in 1971 Fred West was in prison, and it was the prosecution's contention that Rose alone had killed Charmaine.

In a strong rebuttal to the jury, Ferguson said, "I want to tell you now, as loudly and clearly as I can, that Rosemary West is not guilty of any of the counts in this indictment. She neither knew of, nor participated in, any of the acts which led to the deaths of ten girls." After again emphasizing that many of the prosecution witnesses had a vested financial interest in exaggerating their testimony, he called Rosemary West.

Under Ferguson's prompting, the defendant recounted a tragic and traumatic life—raped twice before she was 16, abandoned by her mother. Although admitting her promiscuity, she bitterly denied being a killer. She had, she said, "fallen under Fred's spell . . . because I was so young, I fell for his lies." He had instructed her "to go with other men." Until being told by the police, she said, she had no idea that Fred was a murderer. Her reaction was one of abhorrence. "I hated him. I just couldn't believe I could hate anyone so bad."

Leveson ridiculed such protestations, insisting that Rose had been an eager accomplice to her husband's murderous depravity. "No sir," said the defendant, "I couldn't take someone's life, especially my own daughter's." Sobbing, she added, "I didn't think I was that bad a mom." She was, she said, being made a scapegoat. "I'm the one now in the spotlight. Fred West is dead, and I've got to be made responsible for what he has done."

Next, a woman known only as Miss B described being raped by Fred West in 1960, many years before he met Rose. Other women, too, testified to suffering at the hands of Fred West alone, supporting defense contentions that he had been predisposed to violence and murder from an early age.

Voice from the Grave

Then came the most dramatic evidence of all. For the first time in a British courtroom, tapes made by a deceased murder suspect were entered as evidence. In his flat, West Country accent, Fred West told how he, and he alone, had committed the murders. There was no remorse in any of his revelations, merely a seeming desire to set the record straight. All the women had been killed, he said, because they became too fond of him and wished him to leave Rose. When a police officer suggested that some of the victims had "gone through hell," West replied, "Not all went through hell . . . enjoyment turned to disaster." Then, in one tape, West said, "I have not told the whole truth. The main reason for this has been from the first day of this inquiry to protect other person [sic] or persons. There's nothing else I wish to say at this time."

This ambivalence was eagerly seized upon by Leveson in his closing speech for the Crown. "Rosemary West would have you believe that she saw no evil, heard no evil, and spoke no evil. This flies in the face of all common sense."

Rosemary West, he said, was the "strategist" behind the murder and mutilation of ten girls and young women.

For the defense, Ferguson reiterated his argument that there was no evidence against his client, merely suspicion. The jury, he said, had heard the voice of Fred West: "If what he told you was the truth, then the defendant should be acquitted."

On November 21, Rosemary West was convicted of three murders. The next day, the jury pronounced her guilty on the remaining seven counts. Sentencing her to ten life terms, Justice Mantell said, "If attention is paid to what I think, you will never be released."

With these verdicts, Rosemary West officially became Britain's worst ever female serial killer. The scale of her crimes, and those of her husband, is horrifying. For two decades, they murdered young girls for pleasure, family members for convenience. By any standard, they must be considered unique in the annals of crime. On March 19, 1996, Rosemary West was refused leave to appeal against her convictions.

—Colin Evans

Suggestions for Further Reading

The London Times: Oct. 7, 1995, pp. 1, 5; Oct. 10, 1995, p. 6; Oct. 11, 1995, pp. 1, 3; Oct. 12, 1995, p. 3; Oct. 13, 1995, p. 4; Oct. 14, 1995, p. 5; Oct. 17, 1995, p. 3; Oct. 18, 1995, p. 6; Oct. 20, 1995, p. 5; Oct. 21, 1995, p. 4; Oct. 24, 1995, p. 5; Oct. 25, 1995, p. 5; Oct. 26, 1995, p. 4; Oct. 31, 1995, pp. 1, 5; Nov. 1, 1995, pp. 1, 3; Nov. 2, 1995, p. 8; Nov. 3, 1995, p. 5; Nov. 4, 1995, pp. 1,7; Nov. 8, 1995, pp. 1, 5; Nov. 14, 1995, p. 3; Nov. 15, 1995, p. 5; Nov. 16, 1995, p. 5; Nov. 17, 1995, p. 4; Nov. 18, 1995, p. 4; Nov. 22, 1995, pp. 1, 5; Nov. 23, 1995, pp. 1, 5.

West, Anne Marie, and Virginia Hill. *Out of the Shadows.* London: Simon & Schuster, 1995.

West, Mae, and Stephen West. *Inside 25 Cromwell Street.* Monmouth, England: Peter Grose, 1995.

Navy Seaman Marcus D. Gill, Marine Pfc. Roderico Harp, Marine Pfc. Kendrick M. Ledet Trial: 1995–96

Defendants: Navy Seaman Marcus D. Gill, Marine Pfc. Roderico Harp, Marine Pfc. Kendrick M. Ledet   **Crimes Charged:** Abduction, rape
Chief Defense Lawyers: Masonori Higa (Gill), Matsunobu Matsunaga (Harp), Yutaka Arakawa (Ledet), Charles Beach, Michael J. Griffith, Eric V. Ross
Chief Prosecutor: Masayuki Nomura   **Judges:** Shinei Nagamine, Masao Oono, Kenji Ebara   **Place:** Naha, Okinawa, Japan
Dates of Trial: November 7, 1995–March 7, 1996   **Verdict:** Guilty
Sentences: Gill and Harp—seven years' imprisonment; Ledet—six and one-half years' imprisonment

SIGNIFICANCE

This abduction and rape case severely strained relations between Japan and the United States. It aggravated anti-American feelings on Okinawa and forced a reevaluation of military agreements between the two countries.

At about 8 P.M. on Monday, September 4, 1995, a 12-year-old Okinawa girl stepped out of a stationery store where she had bought a notebook for school. A car stopped beside her. Two men got out, leaving the driver at the wheel. One seemed about to ask directions. The other put his arm around the girl's neck from behind. The first hit her in the face. The second shoved her into the car's backseat. The two men taped the girl's eyes and mouth, wrists and ankles, as the car took off down a farm road and into a sugarcane field. There, in the backseat of the car, as the girl resisted, the men beat her in the face and stomach, and two of them raped her. The third was unable to achieve penetration. They then pushed her out of the car and drove away. She later walked to a nearby home and called for help.

One Got Out

1995–96

Navy Seaman

Marcus D. Gill,

Marine Pfc.

Roderico Harp,

Marine Pfc.

Kendrick M. Ledet

Trial

Word spread. A U.S. serviceman told his superiors that he had been one of four servicemen who had rented a car that evening. One, he said, had proposed a rape. When he realized the three were stopping to buy condoms and duct tape, he had departed.

Two days later, Navy Seaman Marcus D. Gill, 22, of Woodville, Texas; Marine Pfc. Roderico Harp, 21, of Griffin, Georgia; and Marine Pfc. Kendrick M. Ledet, 20, of Waycross, Georgia, were in the Camp Hansen brig.

By September 29, when the three were officially charged by Japanese prosecutors, Okinawa was in an uproar. The incident dramatized the island's long-standing opposition to American military bases, which occupied 20 percent of Okinawa's land and represented 75 percent of all U.S. bases in Japan—with Okinawa hosting 29,000 of the 45,000 U.S. troops in that country.

A joint Japan-U.S. committee immediately started reviewing the Status of Forces Agreement, which permits Japanese police to detain and interrogate American servicemen caught committing crimes while off duty but does not give the police custody of those held in military prison, such as the three in this case, until after they have been indicted. In the meantime, the American newspaper *Stars and Stripes* disclosed that although Americans comprised 4.2 percent of the Okinawa population, they committed 11.5 percent of the island's murders, rapes, and robberies.

60,000 Protest, U.S. Apologizes

On Sunday, October 22, an estimated 60,000 Okinawans gathered in Naha, the island's largest city, to protest the presence of American military bases. Later that week, the Status of Forces Agreement was modified so that any U.S. troops accused of murder or rape would be immediately handed over to the Japanese police. Meanwhile, the U.S. ambassador to Japan, Walter F. Mondale, formally apologized to the Japanese people for the behavior of the three American servicemen, and U.S. Defense Secretary William J. Perry made a trip to Japan to add his apologies and to try to smooth the way for President Bill Clinton's planned summit meeting in Tokyo, scheduled to begin on November 17. The summit had been intended to bolster support for the military alliance between the countries in the era following the cold war. A poll showed that 40 percent of Japanese were ready to dump the treaty, up from 20 percent before the Okinawa rape.

The Trial Opens

On the trial's first day, November 7, the defendants entered their pleas before the three judges of the Naha District Court. Seaman Gill admitted guilt on all counts. Pfc. Ledet denied beating and raping the girl. "All three of us did not beat her," he said. "I did not rape her and beat her."

Pfc. Harp also said he had not raped the girl. "I did hit her" in seizing her in the street, he said, "but I didn't hit her in the back of the car."

Prosecutor Masayuki Nomura promised to offer 79 distinct documents in evidence, including many statements by the defendants. He then described the events of September 4, from the rental of the car to the abandoning of the victim on the roadside.

An outraged group from the New Japan Women's Association stages a protest rally on October 4, 1995. The banner reads "Women in anger protest the rape of a young girl by U.S. soldiers in Okinawa." (AP/Wideworld Photos)

On November 17, in an interview broadcast on Japanese television, President Clinton apologized for the rape incident. He had canceled his summit trip in order to deal with an impasse with Congress over the U.S. budget, sending Vice President Al Gore instead.

Anticipating the next trial session, scheduled for December 4 (Japanese trials do not run continuously, the way American trials do, but usually are active for a day now and then until concluded), lawyers Matsunobu Matsunaga and Yutaka Arakawa for Harp and Ledet, respectively, said that neither man went through with the rape after he realized how young the victim was. When the prosecutor said he had Harp's admission that he had achieved penetration, Harp's lawyer countered that he would challenge the statement, because it had been made under extreme pressure to U.S. military authorities.

Commander of Pacific Forces Resigns

Navy Seaman

Marcus D. Gill,

Marine Pfc.

Roderico Harp,

Marine Pfc.

Kendrick M. Ledet

Trial

Within 10 days, the commander of U.S. forces in the Pacific, Admiral Richard C. Macke, was forced to resign after members of Congress and Japanese officials complained that he had told reporters, "For the price they paid to rent the car they could have had a girl." The admiral issued a statement apologizing for the remark and expressing sympathy for the girl.

In Texas and Georgia, church collections and fund-raising dinners grew in support of sending American lawyers to help the three servicemen. Following the Japanese tradition of making financial reparations for a crime, money raised by the defendants' families and friends was also set aside to send to the victim. Attorney Michael J. Griffith, responding to letters from Gill to his wife in the United States saying that his confession had been coerced by Japanese investigators who grilled him through eight-hour days without a lawyer present, departed for Okinawa to help defend the three.

As the trial resumed on December 4, Harp testified that U.S. military investigators had forced his confession by dragging him out of bed before dawn for long periods of interrogation. But the next court session, on December 11, found him tearfully apologizing. "I'm sorry about what I've done," he said. "I'm sorry for the outrage to your country. I'm sorry for the pain I put the little girl through." He continued to insist, however, that although he had taken part in the abduction, he had not raped the girl. He had confessed, he added, because he thought he would get a lighter sentence. (In Japanese courts, confession and remorse, as well as compensation to the victim, are often the keys to a light sentence.) In the meantime, Harp's wife sent her apologies to the parents of the victim.

Testifying on Tuesday, December 26, Pfc. Harp and Pfc. Ledet, both of whom had been too small to qualify for their high-school football teams, said that Seaman Gill had forced them to take part in the abduction by physically threatening them. Gill had played high school football, and he weighed 275 pounds.

The next day, Gill testified that "everything is pinpointed on me. They want to take as little blame as possible and put it all on me." Under the prosecutor's examination, he gave a description of the men's obscene jokes about the bleeding and unconscious victim that was so graphic the court translator broke into tears.

Change of Venue Denied

American attorney Griffith, protesting at the request of the defendants' families that it was impossible for the men to get a fair trial anywhere in Okinawa, moved for a change of venue. A motion for change of venue at the request of Harp's mother was rejected because Harp himself did not support the request. The change-of-venue motion was rebuffed by Japan's highest court.

January 29 found the prosecution closing its case with a demand for 10-year prison terms for all three defendants. By Japanese standards, the requested sentence was considered severe. March 7 brought the verdict: seven years in prison for Seaman Gill and Pfc. Harp and six and one-half years for Pfc. Ledet.

"This case is an especially cruel one compared with similar incidents," said Judge Shinei Nagamine, "and therefore the fury it brought to the local community was quite large." He added that "there is no room for sympathy" because the rape had been premeditated. The judges, he said, had believed Ledet's statement that he had abducted but not raped the girl, but could not believe Harp's testimony denying his confession. They had, however, considered the defendants' statements of remorse and their offers of compensation to the victim.

American attorneys Michael Griffith and Eric Ross said they would appeal the decision and retain new Japanese lawyers. The Japanese defense attorneys who had tried the case advised against an appeal.

The three servicemen were taken to Yokosuka prison in Yokohama to start their sentences. The U.S. military began processing their discharges "for other than honorable reasons," to take effect upon their release from prison.

—Bernard Ryan, Jr.

Suggestions for Further Reading

Bogert, Carroll, with Gregory Vistica and Hideko Takayama. "Outrage on 'The Rock.'" *Newsweek,* October 2, 1995.

Butler, Steven. "An Alliance under Fire." *U.S. News & World Report,* October 2, 1995, 54–56.

Kunii, Irene M. "Rape of an Innocent, Dishonor in the Ranks." *Time,* October 2, 1995, 51–52.

"Wife Apologizes to Japanese Victim's Parents." *Jet,* December 25, 1995–January 1, 1996, 57.

Lori Berenson Trial: 1996

Defendant: Lori Helene Berenson   **Crime Charged:** Treason
Chief Defense Lawyers: Dr. Grimaldo Achahui, Ramsey Clark, Thomas
Nooter   **Chief Prosecutor:** Identity not revealed   **Judges:** Three military
judges in camera (identities not revealed)   **Place:** Lima, Peru
Dates of Trial: January 6–11, 1996   **Verdict:** Guilty
Sentence: Life in prison

SIGNIFICANCE

Lori Berenson, a young American woman from New York, was convicted of
treason in Peru for her association with members of a revolutionary organization
and her implication in a plot to kidnap members of Peru's congress. The
circumstances of her arrest and trial before a military tribunal and her resulting
life sentence engendered protests in the United States among friends, associates,
and members of the U.S. Congress, who believed she was either falsely accused
or unfairly tried or both.

On November 30, 1995, 26-year-old Lori Berenson was arrested aboard a
public bus outside the Peruvian Congress building in Lima, Peru. A few
hours later, a 12-hour gun battle between the military and members of the
Tupac Amaru Revolutionary Movement (MRTA) culminated in the arrest of 22
members of that organization. The president of Peru, Alberto Fujimori, appeared on national television, held up Lori Berenson's passport, and announced
that she had been arrested as a North American terrorist and suspected member
of MRTA.

Berenson was brought to trial on January 6, 1996. At an open meeting on
January 8, she was encouraged to make a statement to the press in her own
defense. Because she had been told there would be no microphones, she spoke
loudly so that all in the room could hear. As a consequence, she later explained
to a visitor from the American Embassy, she appeared to be screaming as she
made her statement to the assembled media.

"I am to be condemned," she said, "for my concern about the conditions
of hunger and misery which exist in this country. . . . If it is a crime to worry
about the subhuman conditions in which the majority of this population lives,
then I will accept my punishment."

Military Court Imposes Stiff Sentence

Berenson's defense attorney, Dr. Grimaldo Achahui, had only a few hours to review the 2,000 pages of accusations and evidence against Berenson. At her trial the next day, Achahui presented several defenses: that the evidence appeared largely circumstantial; that he had had inadequate time to view the documents; that the charge of treason was inappropriate for a noncitizen of the country; and that since a lesser charge would be the appropriate one, the case should be referred to a civilian court. Civilian courts in Peru protected several basic rights not recognized in military courts, such as the right to remain silent, the right to provide counter-evidence, the right to cross-examine witnesses, and the use of a prosecutor independent of the arresting force.

Lori Berenson speaks to reporters at the headquarters for Peru's anti-terrorism police unit, Diconte. Berenson voices her defense for the Tupac Amaru Revolutionary Movement. (AP/Wideworld Photos)

On January 11, the military judges ruled that Lori Berenson was a member of the MRTA and an international subversive involved in arms traffic. She was sentenced to 30 years in prison, in the Yanamayo Prison in Puno, near Lake Titicaca. The location is at 14,000 feet, and the interior of the prison rarely rises above 40 degrees F. Achahui later explained to Berenson that the militant tone of her address to the press had contributed to the severity of her sentence.

Achahui began the process of appeal, appearing first before a different military tribunal on January 26. That court sustained the first verdict, and a second appeal was rejected March 16.

In the United States, Berenson's parents, Mark and Rhoda, worked to organize support groups. Representatives Joseph Kennedy of Massachusetts and Carolyn Maloney of New York worked to support the request to have the case referred to a civilian court. American supporters were hampered, however, by Berenson's request that she not be singled out for special treatment. Under a treaty between the United States and Peru, she could serve her sentence in the United States. That option had not been taken as of May 1996, pending the course of appeals and her request not to be treated differently than others in Peru.

Defense Hampered by Radical Past and Miscalculations

Although the trial was held in camera, many of the accusations made and evidence used in the trial was subsequently leaked by Dincote, the Peruvian security force. Berenson's defense attorney had not received direct access to some of the material and had learned about some of it from the press.

U.S. State Department officials were quoted as saying that a number of miscalculations made Berenson's case more difficult. Her impassioned address to the media had created the impression that she was indeed prorevolutionary and that there was substance to the accusations against her. Dr. Grimaldo Achahui had already defended a number of MRTA members. Ramsey Clark, a former U.S. attorney general who served as part of Berenson's defense team, had earlier written a protest note to President Fujimori criticizing the use of the military justice system in the case of notoriously violent members of the even more radical Shining Path movement. Thus, both these attorneys may have added to the impression of Berenson's radicalism in the eyes of the court.

Moreover, the Peruvian military was in no mood to be lenient with an American who, at the very minimum, consorted with terrorists. During the late 1980s and early 1990s, the Shining Path had waged a campaign of ruthless terrorism, which only a short time before Berenson's arrest had been suppressed by the Fujimori government with the aid and encouragement of the United States. Many military men had lost their lives in terrorist ambushes and assassinations, which had led to the establishment of secrecy-shrouded military courts with anonymous judges.

Partly because of a lack of clarity as to Berenson's activities over the previous years, U.S. human rights groups showed reluctance to join in her defense. Some conservative American editorialists in the United States accepted her guilt as demonstrated. Others, while recognizing her association with radicals, decried the closed nature of the trial and the lack of judicial rights before the military court.

Some of her former friends remembered that as a high school and college student, Berenson had always displayed an intense concern for the poor and for those she perceived as victims of injustice. Berenson's involvement in social concerns in Latin America apparently sprang out of the solidarity movements between American students and Latin American revolutionaries in the 1980s.

Her personal commitment to these issues continued from the 1980s well into the mid-1990s.

Berenson had first visited Latin America in 1988 as a freshman at MIT. With a Quaker group, she visited Guatemala briefly. She later visited El Salvador on a study-abroad trip in 1989. During her stay at the university there, the El Salvador military opposed the size of the university budget, and students and administrators held public demonstrations in defense of the budget. The home of the dean of the university, where Berenson was staying, was bombed (by the military, many suspected), and Berenson then moved in with two students. The next day, one of the students was taken away by national guard soldiers and was later found brutally murdered.

Berenson returned to the United States and left college to volunteer full time with the Student Central America Network and the Committee in Solidarity with the People of El Salvador, the political wing of El Salvador's Popular Forces of Liberation.

In 1990, Berenson moved to Nicaragua. Leaked Dincote reports indicated that while there she worked with Leonel Gonzales, chief of a revolutionary El Salvador group, the FMLN, based in Nicaragua. She reputedly participated in the peace negotiations between the FMLN and the government of El Salvador. She was briefly married to a Guatemalan in 1992.

According to further leaks, Berenson met with accused gunrunner Pacifico Castrellon and traveled with him to Ecuador, where she met with Nestor Cerpa, head of the MRTA, the revolutionary group in Peru. According to the Peruvian military, Berenson then set up a safe house in Lima for the MRTA. While living in Peru, she obtained press credentials for two New York periodicals, and with these papers, was able to interview members of the Peruvian congress. Part of the military's case against her was her alleged possession of a plan of the congressional chamber, which Dincote claimed was to be used in the plot to kidnap members of congress. Although she denied being at the safe house, Dincote sources contended she had been observed there. They also had traced various financial documents linking her to support of the MRTA. According to the leaked evidence, Castrellon and other MRTA members had testified against Berenson. Independent journalists investigating the claims of Berenson's association with the MRTA were unable to confirm or discredit their accuracy.

A combination of Berenson's commitment to equal treatment for herself, the apparent circumstantial evidence linking her to the Peruvian revolutionary movement, and the intransigence of the Peruvian government made it unlikely that the decision of the military tribunal in her case would be overturned.

—Rodney Carlisle

Suggestions for Further Reading

Richardson, John F. "What's a Nice Girl Like This Doing in Peruvian Prison for Life?" *New York Magazine* (February 1996).

"Accomplice to Terror." *Time Magazine* (January 22, 1996).

Yigal Amir Trial: 1996

Defendant: Yigal Amir   **Crime Charged:** Premeditated murder
Chief Defense Lawyers: Gaby Shachar, Shmuel Fleishman, Jonathan Ray
Goldberg, Mordechai Offri   **Chief Prosecutor:** Pnina Guy   **Judges:** Edmond
Levy, three-judge tribunal   **Place:** Tel Aviv, Israel   **Dates of Trial:** January
23–March 27, 1996   **Verdict:** Guilty   **Sentence:** Life imprisonment

SIGNIFICANCE

Despite attempts to defend his actions on religious grounds, Yigal Amir was
convicted of assassinating Israeli Prime Minister Yitzhak Rabin.

Israeli Prime Minister Yitzhak Rabin passionately condemned violence at a
peace rally in Tel Aviv's Kings of Israel Square on November 4, 1995.

"Violence is eroding the foundation of Israeli democracy," the former
general told a crowd of 100,000 supporters. "It must be rejected and condemned, and it must be contained. It is not the way of the State of Israel.
Democracy is our way. There may be differences, but they will be resolved in
democratic elections as they were in 1992, when we were given a mandate to do
what we are doing and what we are continuing to do."

What Rabin and his foreign minister, Shimon Peres, planned to continue
was an extremely controversial series of negotiations with Palestinian leaders.
Just over a month before, on September 28, the Rabin government had signed
the Oslo II accord, in which Israel agreed to withdraw from portions of the West
Bank and Gaza Strip, thereby paving the way for Palestinian elections.

Many Jews hoped that the accords Rabin championed would bring peace
to the troubled region. To some of Israel's orthodox right wing, however,
Rabin's meetings with the Palestine Liberation Organization and the planned
withdrawal from occupied lands were tantamount to treason. In Israel's relatively short history as a secular state, few issues had so severely polarized the
nation.

Rabin Gunned Down at Peace Rally

One Israeli with no doubts of Rabin's treachery was a 25-year-old law and
religion student named Yigal Amir. As the prime minister left the peace rally,

Amir raised a pistol and fired three times, hitting Rabin and one of his bodyguards.

The gravely wounded Rabin was rushed into his limousine, which sped away to a hospital. His guards pounced on Amir, who calmly told police that he had acted to stop Rabin's agreements with the Palestinians.

"I acted on God's orders," Amir said. "I have no regrets."

In less than two hours, Rabin died from his wounds. While the rest of the world wondered if the assassination might destroy the fragile peace initiatives, Israelis were stunned to learn that Rabin had not been slain by an Arab, but by a Jew. The trial of Rabin's killer would force Israeli society to examine the relationship between biblical and secular law.

Amir remained in good spirits. He told investigators that he had stalked Rabin at three previous rallies and claimed that he had acted alone. He implied that foreign minister Peres had also been a target. Standard police procedure in Israel requires defendants who make confessions to reenact their crime for the record. Amir was returned to the parking lot where Rabin had been shot. Wearing a bulletproof vest and ignoring the angry shouts of spectators, Amir demonstrated to police how he had waited for the prime minister and fired the fatal shots.

Amir continued to insist that he had acted alone, but 10 other suspects were detained by police in the weeks after the assassination. Israeli army sergeant Arik Schwartz was charged with smuggling weapons to Amir's brother, Hagai. With their friend Dror Adani, the Amir brothers were found to have amassed an arsenal of guns and explosives, which they had hidden at a nursery school run by their mother. Police charged that the weapons were to be used in plots against Rabin, Peres, and Palestinian Arabs. The conspiracy sketched by investigators was considerably more complex than Hagai Amir's initial statement to investigators. Hagai admitted that he had crafted homemade hollow-point ammunition and had given it to his brother but denied knowing that Yigal intended to use the explosive dum-dum bullets to kill Rabin.

Trial Opens Amid Conspiracy Allegations

When Yigal Amir was formally charged with premeditated murder on December 5, Hagai Amir and Dror Adani were indicted for conspiracy. Prosecutors announced that they would not try the other defendants until Yigal Amir's trial was over.

The presiding judge spoke directly to concerns that Amir had been prematurely convicted in the media. "We have the sensation that the defendant has already been tried," said Judge Edmond Levy, viewing the photographers and reporters noisily jostling for position in the crowded courtroom. "We intend to hold a proper trial and procedure."

"I didn't intend to murder Yitzhak Rabin as a person," Amir told the court when his trial officially began on January 23, 1996. "I intended to murder the prime minister to deflect him from his path. I have nothing personal against him."

Contradicting himself, Amir also claimed that he had intended to only paralyze Rabin.

"My intention was to shoot him in a way that would prevent him from serving as prime minister, either disabling him or, if there was no choice, death," Amir said. "It wasn't premeditated," he added. "Otherwise, I would have aimed at his head."

This was refuted by police inspector Yossi Gershon, who had driven Amir from the shooting scene to jail. En route, Amir had asked Gershon if Rabin was dead. When Gershon told Amir that Rabin was indeed dead, the prisoner seemed pleased.

"Great," Amir said. "I meant to kill him. I'm happy. Whoever is responsible for the death of Jews deserves it."

Defense attorney Mordechai Offri was openly uneasy about the political defense Amir seemed intent upon pursuing. Offri quit the case on January 28. Amir's remaining attorney was Jonathan Ray Goldberg, a transplanted Texas lawyer who was unskilled in the Hebrew language, in which much of the court business was transacted. The disruption did not faze Amir, who seemed happy with the opportunity to represent himself. The court postponed the trial for one month so that Amir's mental health could be evaluated.

State psychologists declared Amir mentally fit to stand trial. Meanwhile, the court appointed two new defense attorneys, Shmuel Fleishman and Gaby Shachar, who argued that enough plausible doubt of Amir's solitary responsibility existed for the charge against him to be reduced to attempted murder or manslaughter.

Defense Undercut by Amir's Own Words

Two weeks after the assassination, Israel's secret security service, Shin Bet, was reeling from accusations of incompetence and suspicion of conspiracy when the press reported that a paid informant had warned the agency of Amir's intentions. The alleged Shin Bet informant was Avishai Raviv, head of a radical right-wing group called Eyal. Raviv maintained that Amir had talked to him about killing the prime minister, but Raviv denied taking Amir seriously. Police detained Raviv on suspicion of participating in a conspiracy and failure to prevent a felony. By the time Amir went to trial, Raviv had been released. Yet, Amir's lawyers produced one of Amir's former roommates, who testified that Raviv had encouraged Amir to shoot the prime minister.

After a videotape of Amir shooting at Rabin was shown in court, Amir's new lawyers proposed that his gun contained blanks and an unknown conspirator fired the deadly shots with a gun equipped with a silencer.

This theory faltered when it was determined that the two bullets removed from Rabin's body had come from Amir's gun. Any defense moves based on suspicions of a wide conspiracy were also diminished by Amir's smiling insistence that he had acted alone. He continued to defend the shooting as a moral attempt to save Jewish settlers who might be displaced by Israel's withdrawal from occupied territories.

After his arrest and throughout his trial, Amir continually invoked an obscure 12th-century Jewish doctrine called *din rodef,* or "the judgment of the pursuer." By this rule, taking a life may be excused if it is done to prevent someone from imminently committing a murder. Amir held that Rabin's policies had placed thousands of Jews in mortal danger.

"According to Jewish law, the minute a Jew gives over his people and his land to the enemy, he must be killed," Amir said. "I have studied the Torah my whole life and I have all the data."

Experts on rabbinic law watching the trial, however, noted that "the judgment of the pursuer" was a rare, strictly defined religious statute applicable only to action taken in a moment of immediate physical danger. Invoking such a law to settle even grave political differences was prohibited. Furthermore, even if the rule was pertinent, Amir was being charged with murder by a secular court, not by a religious court.

Guilty on All Charges

The three-judge panel hearing the case rejected Amir's contention that he had acted on moral grounds. He was found guilty of premeditated murder on March 27. In their decision, the judges rejected each point of Amir's defense. Numerous admissions to police and in court that he had intended to kill the prime minister invalidated Amir's later defense that he had intended only to grievously wound Rabin.

The judges also rejected Amir's claim to having acted according to "the judgment of the pursuer." With democratic political means available to remove the prime minister from office, Rabin's death was not the only option available to Amir in his desire to eliminate a perceived threat to the Jewish people and state.

"Everything I did was for the God of Israel, the Torah of Israel, the people of Israel, and the land of Israel," Amir replied in his final statement. He remained adamant in his belief that the 1993 and 1995 peace accords were a national disaster. "I was compelled to carry out this act even though it contradicts my character and my personal philosophy, because the damage that was going to be caused [by Rabin's policies] would have been irreversible. What was done in the last three years will cause rivers of blood in this country."

Defending the murder on religious grounds was unacceptable to the court. "There is no greater desecration of God's name," said Judge Levy. "The attempt to give the murder of Yitzhak Rabin the seal of approval of Jewish law is out of place, and constitutes cynical and blatant exploitation of religious law to serve ends that are foreign to Judaism."

After considering sentencing arguments by the prosecution and defense, the judges imposed a mandatory life sentence. It was the most serious penalty available under Israeli law, which reserves the death penalty for spies and Nazi war criminals. An additional six years were added to Amir's sentence for wounding Rabin's bodyguard, Yoram Rubin.

Amir, his brother Hagai, and Dror Adani still faced outstanding conspiracy charges after the Rabin assassination trial concluded. On September 11, 1996, all three men were convicted of planning violence against Palestinians and of conspiring to murder Rabin in plots which, unlike Yigal Amir's solitary act, never came to fruition.

—Tom Smith

Suggestions for Further Reading

Greenberg, Joel. "Rabin's Killer Is Given a Life Sentence In Israel." *The New York Times*, March 28, 1996.

Horovitz, David, ed. *Shalom, Friend*. New York: Newmarket Press, 1996.

Kifner, John, et al. "Belief to Blood: The Making of Rabin's Killer." *The New York Times*, November 19, 1996.

Scheindlin, Raymond. "The Assassination in Light of Jewish Religious Law." *Tikkun*, January–February 1996.

INDEX